FSEU Youth Sunday School

SON OF MAN

"Christ has enc
itself, now to
of God FOR US

Debate: Creation vs. Evolution

College Campus: Who is Jesus Christ?

God's will for my life

The Crucifixion & Resurrection

The Incarnation & Deity of Jesus Christ

The Nature & Character of God

The Origin of Man

The Reliability of the Bible

The GOSPEL
(Worldviews, Truth and Evidence)

HEBREWS 11:1
"...Substance of things hoped for.... Evidence of things not seen"

FSE University

# BOOK 1: Worldviews, Truth & Evidence (Student Workbook)

Copyright © 2018 by Edward A. Croteau.
Images used in this book are with lawful excuse under Fair Use Law 17 U.S. Code § 107 for nonprofit classroom educational purposes only. This material is part of the teaching ministry of Missouri non-profit corporation N01345108, 'Faith, Substance and Evidence'.
ISBN 978-0-692-18628-2

Q&A: Why Christianity is Rational

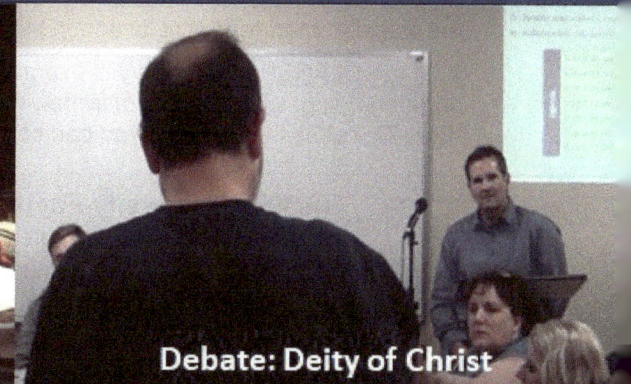

Debate: Deity of Christ

Atheist vs. Christian Volleyball Tournament

FSEU at Public Library

## Book 1: "Worldviews, Truth & Evidence"

### A Biblical & Philosophical Investigation of God as the Source of Truth & Authority for America's Founding

This is Book 1 of 4 in our FSEU (Faith, Substance & Evidence University) series. This book covers Layer 1 of the 7 layers in the FSEU Pyramid.

Book 1 (Layer 1) = Worldviews, Truth and Evidence (answers 2 questions: *'Is what I believe true?'*, *'Who Am I?'*)
Book 2 (Layer 3) = The Origin of Man (answers *'Where did I come from?'*)
Book 3 (Layers 2, 5 & 6) = The Reliability of the Bible & Person of Jesus Christ (answers *'Who am I?'*)
Book 4 (Layers 4 & 7) = God's Will for My Life, The Nature & Character of God (answers *'Why am I here?'*)

### The Foundation of FSE University = Faith, Substance & Evidence University (FSEU) Pyramid

- **The Goal of FSEU:**

Using Hebrews 11:1 as our foundation, we start at the base of the Pyramid (the Gospel), working our way to the top (God's will for my life), building a firm foundation for the Christian worldview layer by layer as we examine the evidence for Jesus Christ as the source of the answers to life's most pressing questions:

1) Is what I believe true?
2) Who am I?
3) Where did I come from?
4) Why am I here?

The <u>substance</u> of our faith is the Person of Jesus Christ. We will examine the <u>evidence</u> for why faith in Christ is the key to finding the answers to these questions.

**The Pyramid (top to bottom):**
God's will for my life
The Crucifixion & Resurrection
The Incarnation & Deity of Jesus Christ
The Nature & Character of God
The Origin of Man
The Reliability of the Bible
The GOSPEL (Worldviews, Truth and Evidence)

# HEBREWS 11:1

*"Faith = **Substance** of things hoped for.... **Evidence** of things not seen"*

- **How to use Book 1:**

1) <u>With WEBSITE LESSONS</u> = Book 1's lessons are accompanied by short videos on the 'Faith, Substance & Evidence' website **www.fse.life**. You can watch the condensed version of the book's lessons on the website, then read that lesson in the book for more in-depth analysis.

2) <u>In the CLASSROOM</u> = we will examine today's culture against biblical truth, then challenge each others' understanding, with the goal of 'renewing our minds' with a biblical worldview. Each of the classes has its own "**Exit Ticket**" with questions you can complete in class individually or as a team.

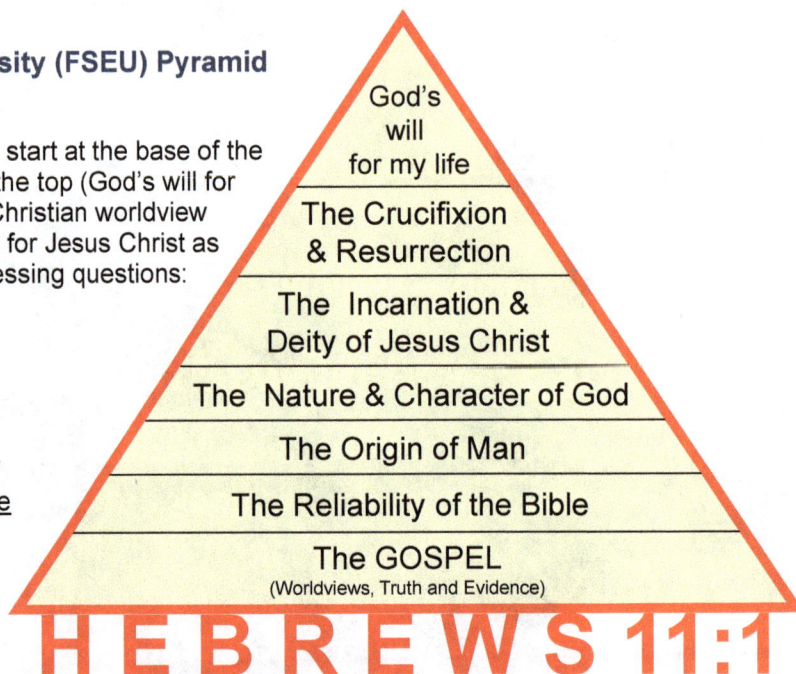

---

### The FSE University Focus: A Challenge to "Know What I Believe and Why"
The following are excerpts from Dinesh D'Souza's book 'What's So Great About Christianity'[13]

"Today's Christians know that they do not, as their ancestors did, live in a society where God's presence was unavoidable. Many of us now reside in secular communities, where arguments drawn from the Bible or Christian revelation carry no weight, and where we hear a different language than in church.

Instead of engaging this secular world, most Christians have retreated into a Christian subculture where they engage Christian concerns. Then they step back into secular society, where their Christianity is kept out of sight until the next church service. Without realizing it, Christians have become postmodernists of a sort: they live by a gospel of the two truths. There is *religious truth*, reserved for Sundays and days of worship, and there is *secular truth*, which applies to the rest of the time... they have sought a workable, comfortable 'modus vivendi' in which they agree to leave the secular world alone if the secular world agrees to leave them alone.

But a group of prominent atheists - many of them evolutionary biologists - has launched a powerful public attack on religion in general and Christianity in particular. The atheists no longer want to be tolerated.

They want to monopolize the public square and to expel Christians from it. They want to control school curricula to promote a secular ideology and undermine Christianity. The atheists have had it too easy. Their arguments have gone largely unanswered. Matthew 5:13-14 calls Christians to be the 'salt of the earth' and the 'light of the world'... That includes confronting the challenge of modern atheism and secularism."

## Welcome to FSE University (FSEU) "Worldviews, Truth & Evidence" Course!

This course is an introductory class in the biblical and philosophical investigation of God as the ultimate Source of Truth and the Authority behind America's founding. We will use logical thinking to develop our worldview, emphasizing how to seek truth and to know what we believe as Christians and why we believe it.

> My most important question: **"Why am I a Christian?"**

This question naturally leads to 4 questions everyone wants to answer, and this Book 1 answers Questions 1 & 2:

1. Do I know what I believe and why I believe it?
2. Who am I?
3. Where did I come from?
4. Why am I here?

As you answer these questions for yourself, you learn how to discover truth through "reasoning with your mind" (reasoning your way through your beliefs)!

> Combine this material with our website **https://fse.life** to apply logic to test the truth of what you believe.

This is a highly interactive class. Your participation is critical for you to get the most from it. Each class has a set of Questions in an "Exit Ticket" to answer, periodic "Jeopardy" competitions and a Finals test, all of which will test your command of what you have learned.

Courtesy of Google Images    Fair Use Law 17 U.S. Code § 107

## How to Use This Book 1

Each class begins with a slide that looks like the picture to the right:

1) an orange background
2) the FSE Pyramid in the middle
3) the class contents on the left side of the Pyramid
4) the videos that accompany the contents on the right side of the Pyramid
5) the online lessons for this class (on FSE University website "fse.life") located underneath the FSE Pyramid

See the next page for the page location of each class within this book.

### Class 15: Who Am I? Part 1

GENESIS 1:26-27 My Original Identity

ROMANS 3:23 My Forfeited Identity

JOHN 1:12, 1JOHN 3:2 My Restored Identity

Comedian Norm McDonald: Why Christianity Makes Sense - Made in God's Image

The Gospel throughout Isaiah - God's 3 Imputations

My Physical Identity: Table of Nations

Was Jesus a good-looking white guy?

God's will for my life
The Crucifixion & Resurrection
The Incarnation & Deity of Jesus Christ
The Nature & Character of God
The Origin of Man
The Reliability of the Bible
The GOSPEL
(Worldviews, Truth and Evidence)

**HEBREWS 11:1**
*"Faith = Substance of things hoped for.... Evidence of things not seen"*

Acts17 Apologetics: 'The Comedian who laughed his way to Jesus' (20:45)

Paul James-Griffiths - 'Tracing your Ancestors through History: Table of Nations in Genesis' (1.01.14)

Matt Chandler- 'Jesus is not a white man - Megan Kelly rebuttal' (2.46)

fse.life Lessons 02 - 08

Each class in this book has a combination of three types of information being shared by the teacher:

1) Powerpoint slides
2) Text that expounds more deeply on information in the slides
3) Selected articles from the "Evidence of Faith's Substance" opinion column in the Lees Summit Tribune newspaper

**Remember Our Goal:** *"Every Christian should know WHAT they believe and WHY they believe it"*

Courtesy of Google Images    Fair Use Law 17 U.S. Code § 107

# CLASSES

# EXIT TICKETS (Homework)

## EXIT TICKETS (Homework)

# Everything You Need to Know... Our In-Person Classes

**KNOW THE RULES**

1) Be on time and ready to go!
2) "Be Here Now" (no distractions - i.e., cell phones)
3) Don't interrupt someone who is talking
4) Think *HARD*
5) Have *FUN* (there will be Competitions ☺ )

**AGENDA**

Kickoff
Teaching
Breakouts
Exit Ticket

**Exit Ticket #1     Class 01: Introduction to FESU**

1) What is the best answer to the question "Why are you a Christian?"

2) What is the difference between "Natural" versus "Revealed" Theology?

3) What is the "Gospel"?

3) Of the 30 Scriptures in this lesson, what top 3 had the most impact in our Introduction to FSEU?

Courtesy of Google Images    Fair Use Law 17 U.S. Code § 107

# ARTICLES, EVIDENCES & SCRIPTURE

# Class 01   Introduction to FSE University

Your Teacher, Class Goals, FSEU Knowledge Base = fse.life

What You'll Learn at FSE University

Why Are You a Christian?

FSEU Pyramid: Growing in Christ in Post-Christian America

FSEU - What is the Christian Gospel?

FSEU - Faith: Why It is Reasonable

Evidences: 16 Reasons Why Christianity is True

Theology's Building Blocks: Natural vs. Revealed

FSEU - Apologetics: Why We Should Care

What is the ONE Essential Ingredient to Sharing the Gospel?

Knowing Jesus Christ = The Word

Christ's 4 Questions to All of Us

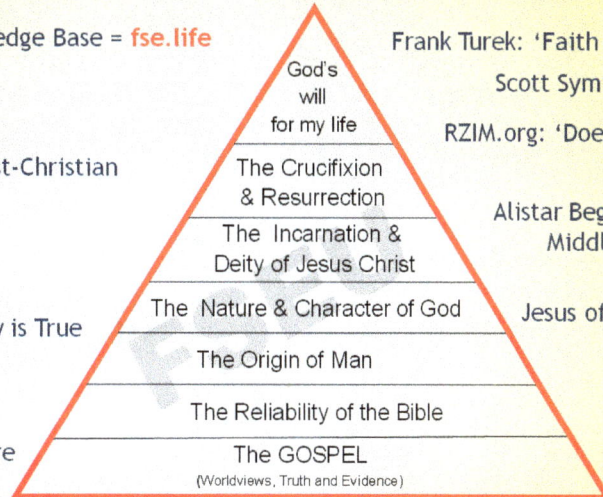

**Pyramid (top to bottom):**
- God's will for my life
- The Crucifixion & Resurrection
- The Incarnation & Deity of Jesus Christ
- The Nature & Character of God
- The Origin of Man
- The Reliability of the Bible
- The GOSPEL (Worldviews, Truth and Evidence)

## HEBREWS 11:1
"Faith = *Substance* of things hoped for .... *Evidence* of things *not seen*"

**fse.life Online Lesson 01**

Frank Turek: 'Faith is not Enough' (4:28)

Scott Symington's Story' (4:00)

RZIM.org: 'Does God Exist Series - Proof' (3:53)

Alistar Begg, 'The Man on the Middle Cross said I could come' (3:52)

Jesus of Nazareth speaking a Parable to Little Children' (3:07)

# About Your Teacher

- **Degreed Engineer, Statistician by Profession**
- **30+ years Business World**
- **Lay Pastor**
- **Founder, "FSE University":**
  - Apologist for Christianity,
  - Focus on getting "outside church" to directly engage the culture
- **Weekly Column in Lees Summit Tribune – "The Evidence of Faith's Substance"**
- **Love young people!**

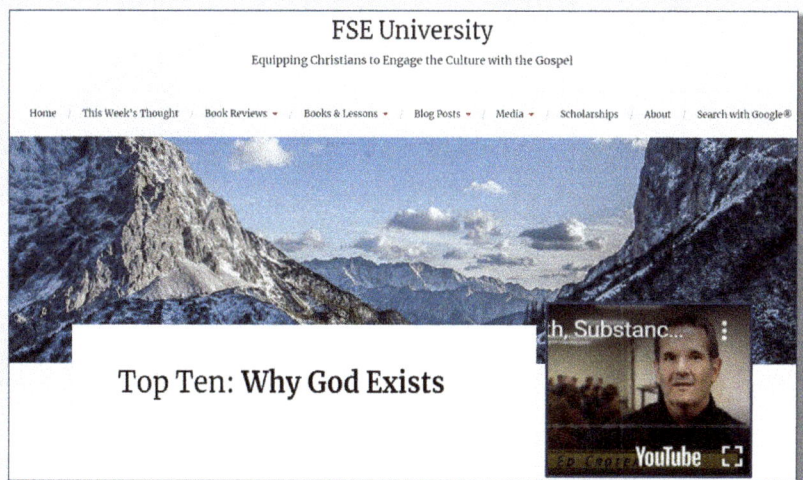

**FSE University**
Equipping Christians to Engage the Culture with the Gospel

Home / This Week's Thought / Book Reviews ▾ / Books & Lessons ▾ / Blog Posts ▾ / Media ▾ / Scholarships / About / Search with Google®

Top Ten: **Why God Exists**

## FSE University Goal:
*"Every Young Person should know WHAT they believe, and WHY they believe it."* (1Peter 3:15)

# Class Goals

1) Grow in our personal relationship with <u>Jesus Christ</u>

2) Learn how to logically present evidence for *YOUR PERSONAL* Christian faith

3) Form logical, biblical arguments for controversial topics in American culture

## Class Questions

1) Am I sure of what I believe and why I believe it?

2) Am I willing to share what I believe?

3) Am I armed to defeat arguments?

4) Am I secure in my relationship with Jesus Christ?

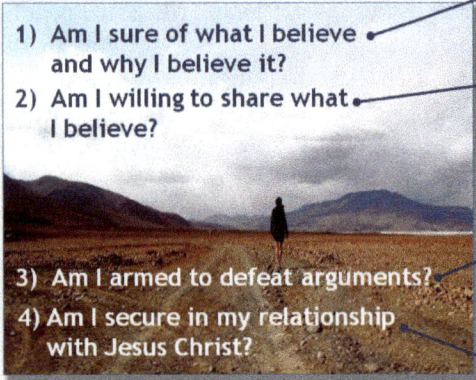

**2Timothy 1:7** *"God has not given us a spirit of fear, but of power and of love and of a sound mind."*

**1Peter 3:15** *"Sanctify the Lord God in your hearts, and always be ready to give a defense to everyone who asks you a reason for the hope in you, with meekness and fear."*

**2Corinthians 10:4-5** *"The weapons of our warfare are not carnal but mighty in God for pulling down strongholds, casting down arguments and every high thing that that exalts itself against the knowledge of God, bringing every thought into captivity to the obedience of Christ."*

**1Corinthians 2:2** *"I determined not to know anything among you except Jesus Christ and Him crucified."*

Courtesy of Google Images    Fair Use Law 17 U.S. Code § 107

# FSE University KNOWLEDGE BASE
## Website fse.life

- Book Reviews

- 216 short lessons
  - Slides with audio

- Weekly Blogs
  - American Culture vs. Biblical Truth

- Media
  - Podcasts, Q&A Forums, Debates

**FSE University**
Equipping Christians to Engage the Culture with the Gospel

Home  /  This Week's Theme  /  Book Reviews ▾  /  Books & Lessons ▾  /  Blog Posts ▾  /  Media ▾  /  Scholarships  /  About  /  Search with Google®

## Top Ten: Why God Exists

**Argument #1 – Origin of the Universe**
Genesis 1:1 "In the beginning, God created the heavens and the earth."

**Argument #2 – Design in the Universe**
Colossians 1:17 "Jesus is before all things, and in Him all things hold together."

**Argument #3 – Fine-Tuning in the Universe**

**Subscribe to our YouTube Channel!**
**Follow us on Instagram!**

**Argument #5 – Information Machines**
Psalm 139:13 "You have formed my inward parts; You have knitted me together in my mother's womb."

THIS WEEK'S THOUGHT

The Wisdom of Comedian Norm McDonald:
Why the Christian Gospel Makes Sense

FOLLOW US

YouTube    Twitter    Facebook
Instagram

Join Us!
FSE University
Classes @ 11:15am every Sunday
Check out our YouTube channel
and subscribe.

*Mind and Cosmos – Why the Materialist Neo-Darwinian Conception of Nature is almost certainly False*

*"My guiding conviction is that mind is not an afterthought or an accident or an add-on, but a basic aspect of nature. The intelligibility of the world is no accident."*
Thomas Nagel Page 16,17

*"A theistic account has the advantage over a reductive naturalistic one in that it admits the reality of more of what is so evidently the case."* (page 25)

# The 5 Main Topics You Will Learn by Taking All 4 Classes for Books 1-4

**TRUTH**
- How to TEST if something is true
- How you DECIDE what is true
- How you are PRESUADED what is true

**THINKING**
- Formal Logic (deduction)
- Informal Logic (induction)
- How to form a Logical Argument

**WORLDVIEWS**
- Religion
- Philosophy
- Culture

**AMERICA**
- Founding
- Today
- The Battle: Christianity vs. Secularism

**THEOLOGY**
- Natural (Science)
- Revealed (Bible & Jesus Christ)
- 16 Arguments: ☑ Why Christianity is True

We'll examine over 800 bible verses in our study!

**What You'll Learn at FSEU**

---

## Why am I a Christian?

**Our Mission**    1Peter 3:15
*"Every Christian should know WHAT they believe, and WHY they believe it."*

**Strategy**    2Timothy 2:24-25
*"Focus on Servant Leadership, training members on how to live out a CHRIST-like witness to a watching world, while speaking the truth in love."*

**Vision**    2Timothy 3:14-15
*"Every Christian should be taught a Bible-based, CHRIST-centered worldview."*

**Structure**    "FSE University"
*"We move up the FSE Pyramid, from a foundation in the Gospel to the capstone of a life that radiates CHRIST's character to those around them."*

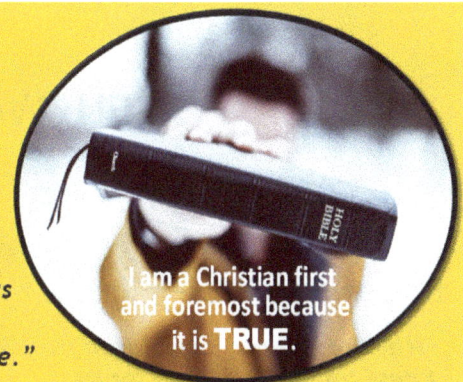

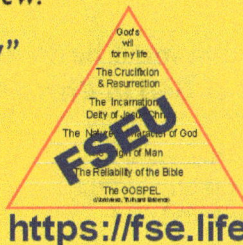

I am a Christian first and foremost because it is **TRUE**.

God's will for my life
The Crucifixion & Resurrection
The Incarnation Deity of Jesus Christ
The Nature & Character of God
The Nature of Man
The Reliability of the Bible
The GOSPEL

**FSE**

https://fse.life

# FSEU Pyramid
## Growing in Christ in    Post-Christian America

**Post-Christian America**            **Christianity**

God's will for my life

The Crucifixion & Resurrection

The Incarnation & Deity of Jesus Christ

The Nature & Character of God

The Origin of Man

The Reliability of the Bible

The GOSPEL
(Worldviews, Truth and Evidence)

- Knowing what is *TRUE* and living by *FAITH* are **opposing** points of view.

- Knowledge can only grow by reasoning through the evidence.

- Faith is a "leap" based on emotions, not reason.

- Knowing what is *TRUE* and living by *FAITH* are **complementary** points of view.

- My faith *grows* with *knowledge*, as I *reason* through the evidence.

- I use my *mind* with my heart to *grow* closer to Jesus Christ and discover His will for my life.

# H E B R E W S 11:1
"Faith = *Substance* of things *hoped for*.... *Evidence* of things *not seen*"

Scott Symington's Story' (4:00)        Courtesy of Google Images   Fair Use Law 17 U.S. Code § 107

---

**FSEU**    God's will for my life / The Crucifixion & Resurrection / The Incarnation & Deity of Jesus Christ / The Nature & Character of God / The Origin of Man / The Reliability of the Bible / The GOSPEL

**https://fse.life**

# FSEU: What is the Christian Gospel?

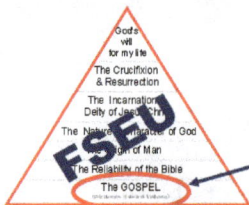

"He (the Father) made Him (the Son) who <u>knew no sin</u> to <u>be sin for us</u> ...

so that we (you and me) might become the righteousness of God (the Father) in Him (the Son)."
**2Corinthians 5:21**

> **Are there *Essentials* a person must believe to become the "Righteousness of God in Christ"?**

The Protestant Reformation – The 5 'Solas':

1) 'Sola Deo Gloria' = To God Alone be the Glory
2) 'Sola Scriptura' = Understood only in God's Word
3) 'Sola Fidei' = Salvation is by faith alone
4) 'Sola Christus' = in Jesus Christ alone
5) 'Sola Gratia' = apart from works, by God's grace alone

**1) Existence of God**
Hebrews 11:6; Psalm 14:1

**2) Deity of Christ**
John 1:1,14; John 8:56-58

**3) Atonement (for Sin)**
John 1:29; Mark 10:45

**4) Repentance**
Luke 13:3,5; Acts 11:18

**5) Resurrection**
1Corinthians 15:1-22

**6) 'Sola Fidei/Christus/Gratia'**
Romans 1:17; John 3:16; Ephesians 2:8

Courtesy of Google Images    Fair Use Law 17 U.S. Code § 107

# FSEU - Faith:   Why It is Reasonable

*"① FAITH is the ②SUBSTANCE of things ③HOPED for, the ④EVIDENCE of things not seen."*

Hebrews 11:1

### ① FAITH = *"pistis"*

Fidelity to a Person (not faith in God's promises, which are opportunities to exercise my faith – it's faith in God Himself)

### ② SUBSTANCE = *"hupostasis"*

"Hupo" (under) + "stasis" (stand upon) = "understanding" (foundation upon which I stand)

### ③ HOPED FOR = *"elpizō"*

What gives me a confident expectation of the future (eternal life)

### ④ EVIDENCE = *"elegehos"*

Convincing proofs that strengthen my faith

Matthew 7:24-27

## Faith  =  Trusting in what I have good *reasons* to believe

Courtesy of Google Images    Fair Use Law 17 U.S. Code § 107

## ☑ 16 Evidences: Why Christianity is True

Origin of the Universe

Design In the Universe

Fine-Tuning In the Universe

Objective Moral Laws & Duties

Evil & Suffering

Contingency Existential Causality

The Human Soul

**Natural Theology**

**God exists based on observed facts in nature**

Anthropic Principle

Resurrection

**Revealed Theology**

**God exists based on supernatural revelation**

Holy Bible Reliability

Information Machines

Biochemical Irreducible Complexity

Design In the Animal Kingdom

Jesus Christ

Israel

Fulfilled Prophecy

**HEBREWS 11:1** *"FAITH is the substance of things hoped for, the EVIDENCE of things unseen."*

RZIM.org "Does God Exist Series - Proof" (3:53)                    Courtesy of Google Images    Fair Use Law 17 U.S. Code § 107

## Hebrews 11:1   Christianity   ⇨ *Substance* with *Evidence*

*"①FAITH is the ②SUBSTANCE of things hoped for, the ③EVIDENCE of things not seen."*

① FAITH = Gr. *"pistis"* = a firm conviction; to "cling" to; the object of faith is a Person (it is not faith in God's promises, which are the occasions to exercise my faith, but rather in God Himself)

② SUBSTANCE = Gr. *"hupostasis"* ⇨ "hupo" = under, "stasis" = stand upon; what I "stand upon, under me" (i.e., "understanding") that defines my future hope and assurance (can be objective by facts or subjective by opinion)

③ EVIDENCE = Gr. *"elegehos"* = convincing proofs that lead to *conviction* (i.e., faith) in or on a matter or subject

### What is Evidence?
Webster's Dictionary = *"that which, when presented clearly, tends to prove or disprove something; an indication or sign; data presented to a court to decide an alleged matter or fact"*

Romans 1:20    *"For since the creation of the world His INVISIBLE ATTRIBUTES ARE CLEARLY SEEN, being understood by the things which are made, even His eternal power and Godhead, so that they are without excuse."*

### What "Evidence" in Hebrews 11:1 is my faith based on?
God provides much empirical evidence for anyone to believe, but my faith does not rest only on the evidence. Its foundation is its *SUBSTANCE*: a *DIVINE ASSURANCE*, which is a *GIFT* from Him (Ephesians 2:8). It's the God-given *conviction* in my *heart* of a future *reality*, made real in history in the Person and work of Jesus Christ.

Acts 3:16 *"And His name, through faith in His name, has made this man strong, whom you see and know. Yes, the faith WHICH COMES THROUGH HIM has given him this perfect soundness in the presence of you all."*

Ephesians 2:8-9 *"...by grace you have been saved through faith, and that NOT OF YOURSELVES; it is the GIFT OF GOD, not of works, lest anyone should boast."*

Romans 8:24-25 *"For WE WERE SAVED IN THIS HOPE, but hope that is seen is not hope; for why does one still hope for what one sees? But if we hope for what we do not see, then we eagerly wait for it with perseverance."*

### Josh McDowell[11]: "The Evidence provides any honest seeker a basis for faith in the Lord Jesus Christ"
*"In my own experience of more than 28 years of sharing the good news of the Savior with the academic world, I personally have never had a single individual – who has honestly considered the evidence – deny that Jesus Christ is the Son of God and the Savior of men. The evidence confirming the deity of the Lord Jesus Christ is overwhelmingly conclusive to any honest, objective seeker after truth… But watch your Attitude: The proper motivation behind the use of this material is to glorify and magnify Jesus Christ – not to win an argument. Evidence is not for proving the Word of God but simply for providing a basis for FAITH."*

### Stephen Meyer (PhD Physics, Geology)[12]: "The Scientific Evidence reminds me my faith is in the Lord"
*"For a 2-year period in my life, I was attracted to Nietzsche's version of existentialism. He asked, 'Why should God rule and I serve?' That resonated within me. Why should a condition of my happiness be submission to the will of God? I sensed I couldn't be happy without Him; I knew my bad lifestyle only brought misery. The intellectual rebellion the apostle Paul talks about is very true in my own life. Even in my Christian thinking today, I find a tendency to slide back into what Paul refers to as the natural mind.*

*And here's what the scientific evidence for God does for me: it realigns me. It helps me recognize that despite my natural tendency toward self-focus and self-absorption, I can't ignore God's accomplishment in this world to let everyone know that He is real, that He is the Creator, and that we need to get right with Him."*

| What is the foundation of my Faith:   God's Sovereignty or Man's Understanding? | |
|---|---|
| **God's Sovereignty** | **Man's Understanding** |
| Daniel 4:35 *"All the inhabitants of the earth are reputed as nothing; HE DOES ACCORDING TO HIS WILL in the army of heaven and among the inhabitants of the earth. No one can restrain His hand or say to Him, 'What have You done?'"* | Bertrand Russell[31](Nobel Prize philosopher, atheist): *"If one day I stand before God and He asks me, 'Why didn't you believe in Me?', I would say, 'Not enough evidence, God! Not enough evidence!'"* |
| Psalm 115:3 *"Our God is in heaven; HE DOES WHATEVER HE PLEASES."* | Francisco Ayala[8]: *"There is no evidence of any vital force directing the evolutionary process toward the production of specified kinds of organisms."* |
| Isaiah 43:13 *"... Indeed before the day was, I am He. And there is no one who can deliver out of My hand; I work, and WHO WILL REVERSE IT?"*<br>1Chronicles 16:31 *"Let the heavens rejoice, and let the earth be glad; and let them say among the nations, 'THE LORD REIGNS'"* | William Provine, Cornell Univ. evolutionist and Historian[8]: *"If Darwinism is true, then there are five inescapable conclusions: 1) there's no evidence for God, 2) there's no life after death, 3) there's no absolute foundation for right and wrong, 4) there's no ultimate meaning for life, 5) people don't really have free will."* |

# Natural Theology: Building Blocks on a SURE FOUNDATION

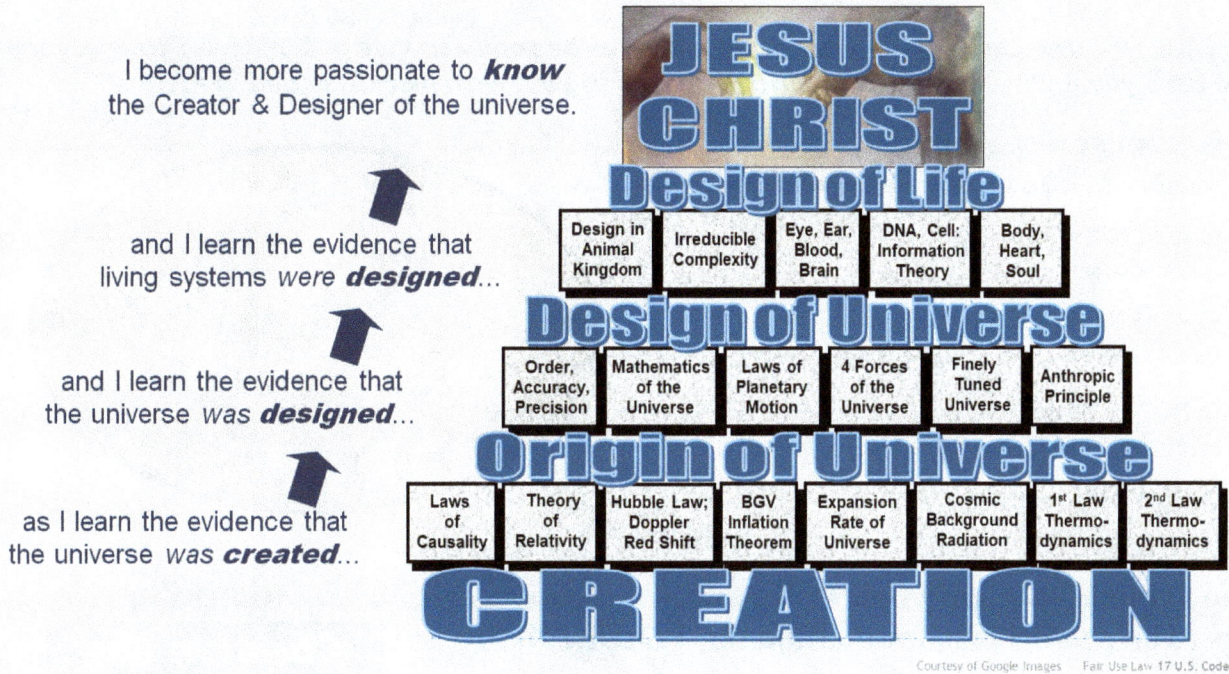

I become more passionate to **know** the Creator & Designer of the universe.

and I learn the evidence that living systems *were* **designed**...

and I learn the evidence that the universe *was* **designed**...

as I learn the evidence that the universe *was* **created**...

## JESUS CHRIST
### Design of Life

| Design in Animal Kingdom | Irreducible Complexity | Eye, Ear, Blood, Brain | DNA, Cell: Information Theory | Body, Heart, Soul |
|---|---|---|---|---|

### Design of Universe

| Order, Accuracy, Precision | Mathematics of the Universe | Laws of Planetary Motion | 4 Forces of the Universe | Finely Tuned Universe | Anthropic Principle |
|---|---|---|---|---|---|

### Origin of Universe

| Laws of Causality | Theory of Relativity | Hubble Law; Doppler Red Shift | BGV Inflation Theorem | Expansion Rate of Universe | Cosmic Background Radiation | 1st Law Thermo-dynamics | 2nd Law Thermo-dynamics |
|---|---|---|---|---|---|---|---|

## CREATION

Courtesy of Google Images      Fair Use Law 17 U.S. Code § 107

# Revealed Theology: Building Blocks on a GOOD FOUNDATION

**1TIMOTHY 6:19** *"Storing up for themselves a GOOD FOUNDATION... that they may lay hold on to eternal life"*

**PERFECTION**:
One day, in heaven, I will be freed from the presence of sin... Until then, does my life *RADIATE* Jesus to those around me?

**PROGRESSION**:
I live freed from the power of sin...

**POSITION**:
I am freed from the penalty of sin...

## HIS GLORIFICATION

| Freed from sin's *presence* | The True Vine | Fruit | Good Works | Reward System |
|---|---|---|---|---|

## MY SANCTICATION

| Freed from sin's *power* | Conformed to Christ's likeness | Filled with the Holy Spirit | God's Character | Morality, Ethics, Character | My Character |
|---|---|---|---|---|---|

## MY JUSTIFICATION

| Freed from sin's *penalty* | God is a Savior | Gospel according to Jesus | God's Way of Salvation | Saving Faith | Repentance | Covenant Consecrated | Eternal Security |
|---|---|---|---|---|---|---|---|

## JESUS CHRIST

I Have A Question

What is this good foundation for these building blocks?

**1Corinthians 3:11** *"No other FOUNDATION can anyone lay than that which is laid, which is JESUS CHRIST"*

Courtesy of Google Images      Fair Use Law 17 U.S. Code § 107

## FSEU - Apologetics: Why We Should Care

"① *SANCTIFY the Lord God in your hearts; always be ready to give a* ②*DEFENSE to everyone who asks you a* ③*REASON for the* ④*HOPE that is in you, with meekness and* ⑤ *FEAR...*"

1Peter 3:15

① SANCTIFY = "*hagiazō*"

to separate, dedicate, consecrate; render sacred

② DEFENSE = "*apologia*"

reasoned argument or answer

③ REASON = "*logos*"

the expression of your mind's thoughts and convictions

④ HOPE = "*elpis*"

confident expectation of the future (eternal life)

⑤ FEAR = "*phobos*"

reverence, with full understanding of God's judgment

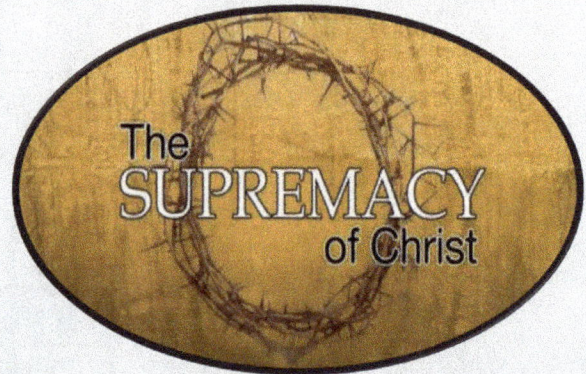

The SUPREMACY of Christ

**The Evidence God provides is not to prove He exists – its to give you a firm foundation for *YOUR FAITH***

**The Key to Apologetics = '*Christ in you*'**

---

## What is the ONE Essential Ingredient to Living the Christian Life?

**DEUTERONOMY 29:29**
(1,450 BC)
"*The secret things belong to the Lord our God, but those things which are REVEALED belong to us and our children forever, that we may do all the words of this law.*"

**COLOSSIANS 1:26**
(60 AD)
"*The mystery (hidden truth) which has been hidden from ages and from generations, but now has been REVEALED to HIS SAINTS.*"

**COLOSSIANS 1:27**
(60 AD)
"*To them God willed to MAKE KNOWN what are the riches of the GLORY of this mystery (hidden truth) among the Gentiles: which is CHRIST IN YOU, the hope of GLORY .*"

**Allowing Jesus Christ to Reign in *ME***

**JOHN 15:5,8** (32 AD)
"*I am the Vine, you are the branches. He who abides in Me, and I in him, bears much fruit; for without Me you can do nothing. By this My Father is GLORIFIED, that you bear much fruit, so you will be My disciples.*"

Alistair Begg, 'The Man on the middle Cross said I could come' (3:52)

Luke 4:16-21

John 9:1-41

John 8:1-11

Mark 10:13-16

Luke 8:22-26

John 4:1-20

Mark 5:25-34

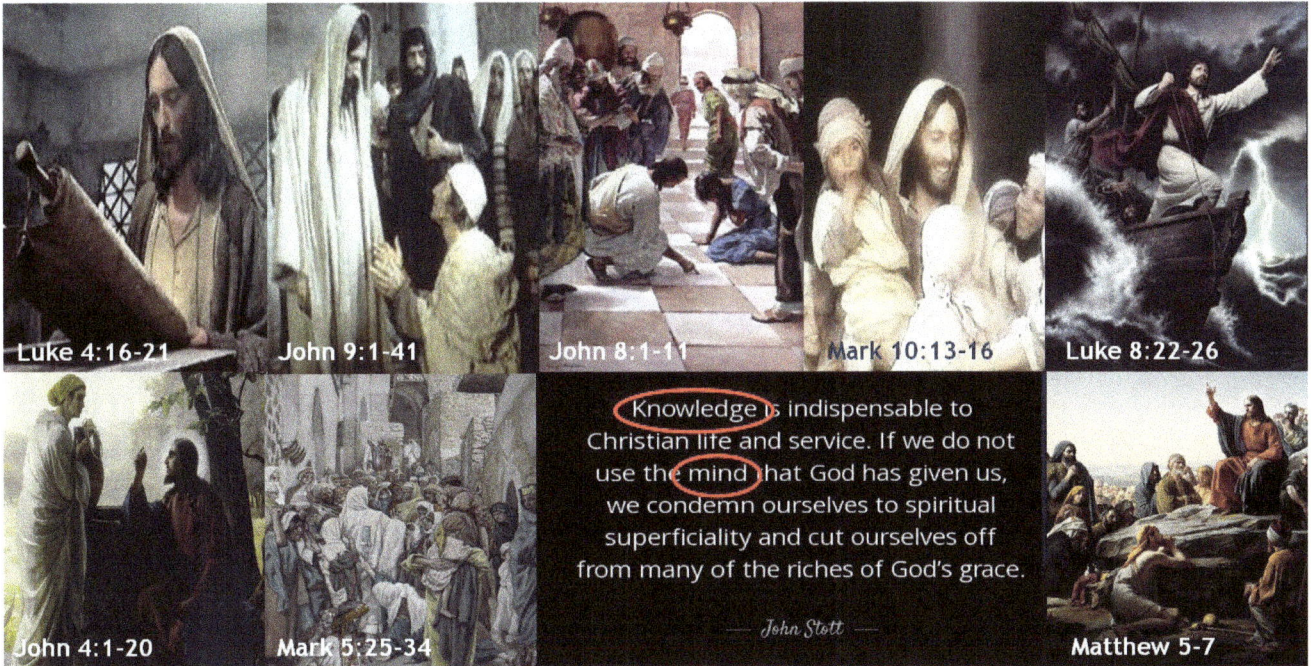

Knowledge is indispensable to Christian life and service. If we do not use the mind that God has given us, we condemn ourselves to spiritual superficiality and cut ourselves off from many of the riches of God's grace.

— *John Stott* —

Matthew 5-7

"The **WORD** became flesh and dwelt among us." John 1:14

"This is eternal life, that they may **KNOW** You, the only true God, and Jesus Christ whom You have sent." John 17:3

# 4 Reasons for How I Choose to Live My Life…
## It's About How You Answer Christ's 4 Questions to *Me*

"Do **YOU** love Me?"
John 21:17

"Will **YOU** lay down **YOUR** life for My sake?"
John 13:38

"Who do **YOU** say that I am?"
Matthew 16:15

"I am the resurrection and the life. He who believes in Me, though He may die, he shall live. And whoever lives and believes in Me shall never die. Do **YOU** believe this?"
John 11:25-26

"No other foundation can anyone lay than that which is laid, which is Jesus Christ" 1 Corinthians 3:11

**Exit Ticket #1**

| | |
|---|---|
| **1) What is the best answer to the question "Why are you a Christian?"** | **2) What is the difference between "Natural" versus "Revealed" Theology?** |
| **3) What is the "Gospel"?** | **4) Of the 30 Scriptures in this lesson, what top 3 had the most impact in our Intro. to FSEU?** |

# Class 02:  Truth

Epistemology: What is *really* the truth?

My Personal Worldview: Have I ever examined it?

My Personal Beliefs: Is My Worldview TRUE ?

Relative vs. Objective Truth

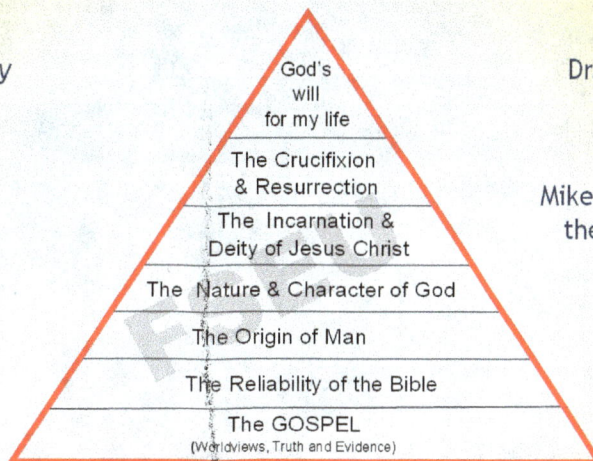

Dr. Frank Turek: "Faith is NOT Enough" (4:28)

Mike Winger: "Essentials of the Christian Faith" (5:07)

God's will for my life

The Crucifixion & Resurrection

The Incarnation & Deity of Jesus Christ

The Nature & Character of God

The Origin of Man

The Reliability of the Bible

The GOSPEL
(Worldviews, Truth and Evidence)

## H E B R E W S 11:1

"Faith = *Substance* of things *hoped for* …. *Evidence* of things *not seen*"

fse.life Lessons 02 - 08

---

## What's *Really* the Truth?

*Epistemology* =

Proverbs 23:23 "Buy the Truth, and don't sell it."

The study of how truth claims are formed.

PART 1:
How people *decide* what is true

1) OPINION (relative / subjective)

2) Justified BELIEF (absolute / objective)

PART 2:
How people *test* for Truth

1) CORRESPONDENCE (fits with reality)

2) COHERENCE (fits the evidence)

## My Personal Worldview: Have I ever examined it?

People often discover, when they really stop and think about WHY they believe a particular view is true, that it's more of an EMOTIONAL reason than an INTELLECTUAL one (it's something they grew up with, that their parents or a close friend taught them, rather than something they've investigated and convinced themselves it's true).

To build a solid foundation for what I believe is true, I must answer these questions:

1) How did I come to believe what I believe? What is my belief based on (what is the *foundation* of my belief)?

2) How certain am I that the particular things I believe are *really* true?

3) Is it OK to be uncertain in areas of my Christian faith (what happens if I admit I'm not sure what I believe)?

4) Are there "essential" beliefs I hold in my Christian faith where I should be absolutely certain that it's really true?

5) Do I have a *standard* to determine my essential Christian beliefs? For example, am I as certain of the doctrine of Creation, or the Trinity, as I am of the Deity of Christ?

> *"The unexamined life is not worth living"* (Socrates)

Courtesy of Google Images    Fair Use Law 17 U.S. Code § 107

## My Personal Beliefs: Is My Worldview *TRUE* ?

I Have A Question

**How does a personal belief become a *TRUTH* ?**

1) Is this belief something I am *consciously aware of*?

2) Does this belief *satisfy* whatever caused me to doubt?

3) Does this belief *motivate* me to form a 'rule of action'?

4) Does this belief *convict* me to live by my 'rule of action'?

Do I take what I believe seriously?

**PROVERBS 23:23**
*"Buy the truth, and don't sell it..."*

Dr. Frank Turek: "Faith is NOT Enough" (4:28)        Courtesy of Google Images    Fair Use Law 17 U.S. Code § 107

## Romans 12:2, John 1:10  "My Personal Worldview = how I see *TRUTH*"

*"…do not be conformed to this ①WORLD, but be transformed by the renewing of your mind…"*
*"He was in the ②WORLD, and all things in the world were made through Him, and the world didn't know Him."*

① WORLD = Greek "*aión*" = age or period in time, marked by its spiritual or moral characteristics

Matthew 13:22  *"…the cares of this WORLD and the deceitfulness of riches choke the word, and he becomes unfruitful."*

Luke 16:8  *"… the sons of this WORLD are more shrewd in their generation than the sons of light."*

Galatians 1:3-4  *"Grace to you and peace from God the Father and our Lord Jesus Christ, who gave Himself for our sins, that He might deliver us from this present evil AGE, according to the will of our God and Father."*

② WORLD = Greek "*kosmos*" = mankind's world system which is alienated from and in opposition to God

John 7:7  *"The WORLD cannot hate you; but it hates Me because I testify of it that its works are evil."*

1John 4:5  *"They are of the WORLD. Therefore they speak as of the world, and the world hears them."*

1Corin. 1:20  *"… Has not God made foolish the wisdom of this WORLD?"*

Coloss. 2:8  *"Beware lest anyone take you captive through philosophy and empty deceit, according to the tradition of men, according to the basic principles of the WORLD, and not according to Christ."*

**What is a "WORLDVIEW"?**[3] "The term means literally 'a view of the world'. It is the window by which a person views the world and decides, often subconsciously, what is real and important, or unreal and unimportant. It may be that a worldview is commonly a collection of prejudices. If so, prejudices are necessary, because we can't start from a blank slate and investigate everything from scratch by ourselves. Understanding worldview is a bit like trying to see the lens of one's own eye. We do not ordinarily see our own worldview, but we see everything else by looking through it."

**What is "TRUTH"?** What corresponds to reality (i.e. "telling it like it is").

Dr. Geisler[12]: Both the Bible and Philosophy are based on the Correspondence view of Truth: *"The Scriptures use the correspondence view of truth quite a bit. The ninth commandment certainly presupposes it. 'You shall not bear false witness against your neighbor' (Exodus 20:16) implies that the truth or falsity of a statement can be tested by whether it checks out with the facts. When Satan said, 'You shall not surely die,' it is called a lie because it does not correspond to what God actually said… Anything that does not correspond to God's Law is considered false (Psalm 119:163). And in the New Testament, Jesus says that His claims can be verified by John the Baptist, saying, 'You have sent to John and he has borne witness to the truth.'*

*Philosophically, lying is impossible without a correspondence to reality. If our words do not need to correspond to the facts, then they can never be factually incorrect. Without a correspondence view of truth, there can be no true or false. There would be no real difference in the accuracy of how a system describes a given fact because we could never appeal to the fact as evidence. There has got to be a real difference between our thoughts about things and the things themselves for us to say whether something is true or false."*

## Epistemology = The Study of "How We Know"  (How People determine what is *TRUE* for them)

People often discover, when they really stop and think about WHY they believe a particular view is true, that it's more of an EMOTIONAL reason than an INTELLECTUAL one (it's something they grew up with, that their parents or a close friend taught them, rather than something they've investigated and convinced themselves it's true).

In order to build a solid foundation for what I believe is true, I first have to honestly answer these questions:

1)  How did I come to believe what I believe? What is my belief based on (what is the *foundation* of my belief)?

2)  How certain am I that the particular things I believe are *really* true?
 - Is it OK to be uncertain in areas of my Christian faith (what happens if I admit I'm not sure what I believe)?
 - Are there "essential" beliefs I hold in my Christian faith where I should be absolutely certain that it's really true?

3)  Do I have a *standard* to determine my essential Christian beliefs? For example, am I as certain of the doctrine of creation, or the Trinity, as I am of the Deity of Christ?

---

**What do I mean when I say I "believe" something is true?**

1)  Does this belief become something that I am *consciously aware of*?

2)  Does this belief *satisfy* the thing that caused me to previously doubt (by whatever means I've chosen)?

3)  Does this belief *motivate* me to start cultivating within me a 'rule of action' based on that belief?

4)  Does this belief *convict* me to maintain the 'rule of action' in spite of times I fail or others' contrary views?

# Relative vs. Objective Truth

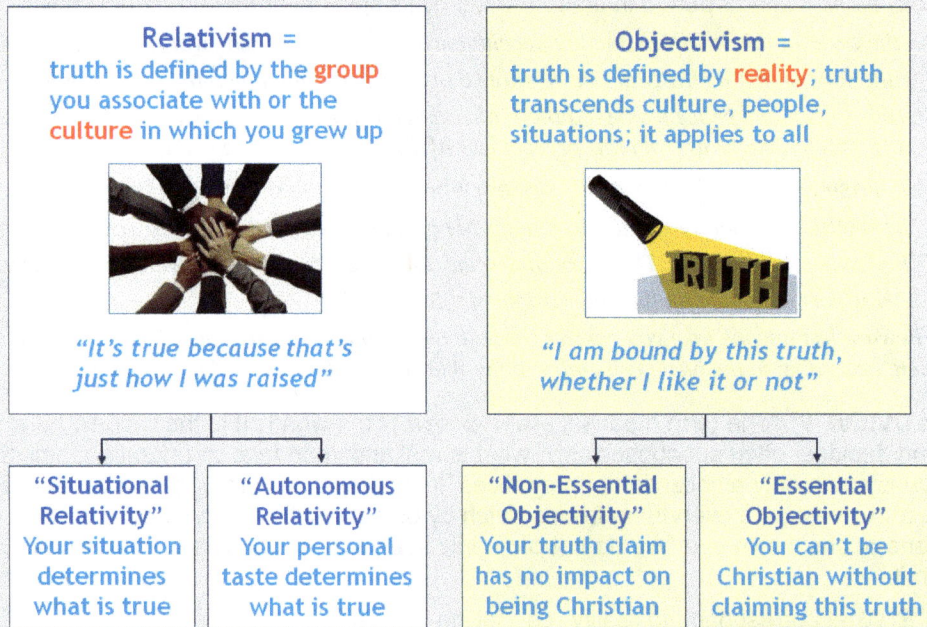

**Relativism =**
truth is defined by the **group** you associate with or the **culture** in which you grew up

*"It's true because that's just how I was raised"*

**Objectivism =**
truth is defined by **reality**; truth transcends culture, people, situations; it applies to all

*"I am bound by this truth, whether I like it or not"*

| **"Situational Relativity"** Your situation determines what is true | **"Autonomous Relativity"** Your personal taste determines what is true | **"Non-Essential Objectivity"** Your truth claim has no impact on being Christian | **"Essential Objectivity"** You can't be Christian without claiming this truth |

Mike Winger: "Essentials of the Christian Faith" (5:07)

Courtesy of Google Images.   Fair Use Law 17 U.S. Code § 107

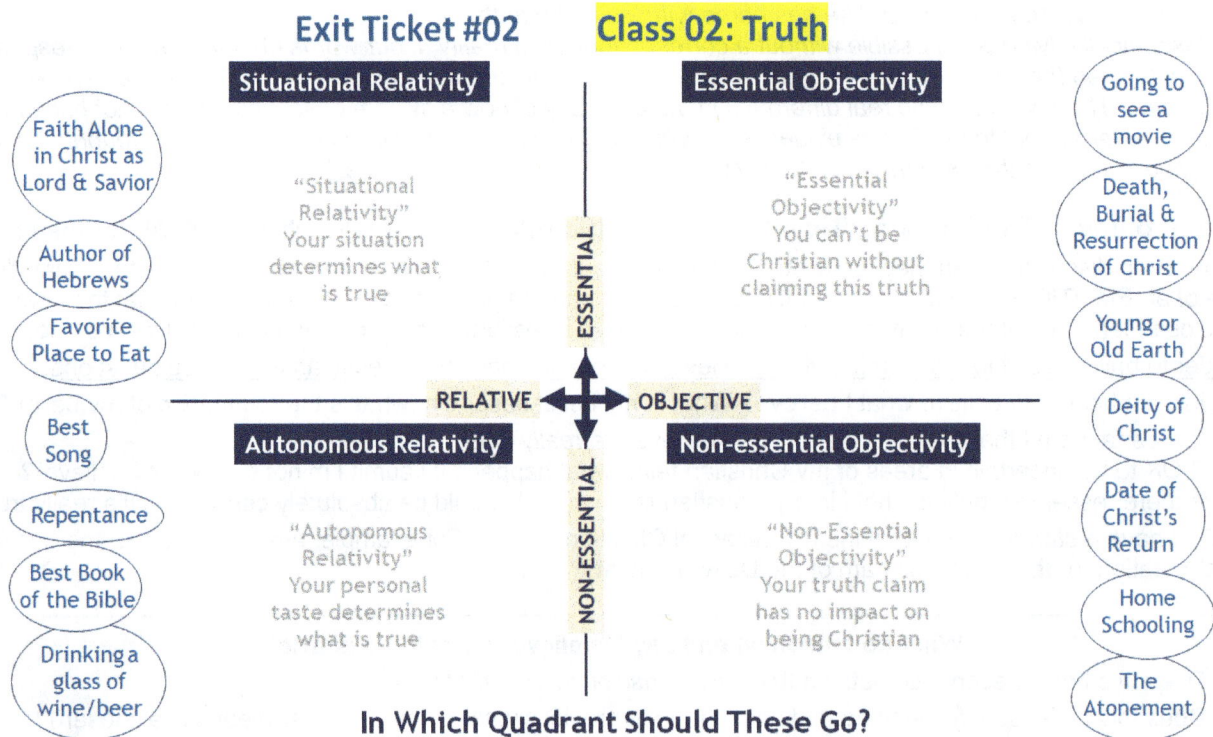

**Exit Ticket #02**     **Class 02: Truth**

**Situational Relativity**

**Essential Objectivity**

Faith Alone in Christ as Lord & Savior

Author of Hebrews

Favorite Place to Eat

Best Song

Repentance

Best Book of the Bible

Drinking a glass of wine/beer

"Situational Relativity" Your situation determines what is true

"Essential Objectivity" You can't be Christian without claiming this truth

ESSENTIAL

**RELATIVE** ⬌ **OBJECTIVE**

NON-ESSENTIAL

**Autonomous Relativity**

**Non-essential Objectivity**

"Autonomous Relativity" Your personal taste determines what is true

"Non-Essential Objectivity" Your truth claim has no impact on being Christian

Going to see a movie

Death, Burial & Resurrection of Christ

Young or Old Earth

Deity of Christ

Date of Christ's Return

Home Schooling

The Atonement

**In Which Quadrant Should These Go?**

**Exit Ticket #2**    Class 02: Truth

| SITUATIONAL RELATIVITY | ESSENTIAL OBJECTIVITY |
|---|---|
|  |  |
| **AUTONOMOUS RELATIVITY** | **NON-ESSENTIAL OBJECTIVITY** |
|  |  |

# Class 03:  Deciding What is True

Epistemology: What is really the truth?

Part 1: How People Decide What is True

Article 398 - In Uncertain & Uncontrollable Times:  Knowing Truth = No Fear

Class Exercise: What Types of Truth Claims are these?

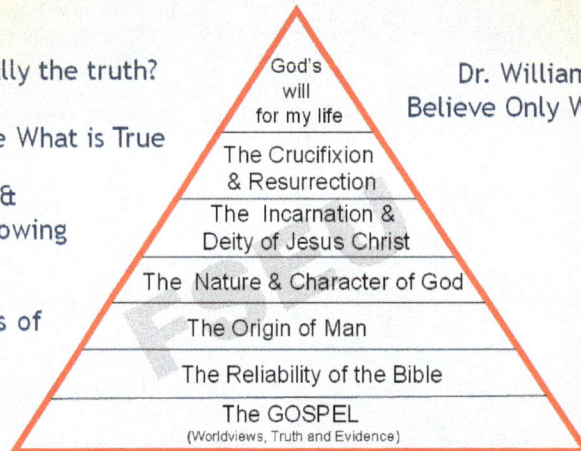

Dr. William Lane Craig: "Should We Believe Only What Can Be Scientifically Proven?" (2:21)

God's will for my life

The Crucifixion & Resurrection

The Incarnation & Deity of Jesus Christ

The Nature & Character of God

The Origin of Man

The Reliability of the Bible

The GOSPEL
(Worldviews, Truth and Evidence)

# HEBREWS 11:1

"Faith = *Substance* of things *hoped for*.... *Evidence* of things *not seen*"

fse.life Lessons 02 - 08

## What's *Really* the Truth?

*Epistemology* = The study of how truth claims are formed.

Proverbs 23:23 "Buy the Truth, and don't sell it."

PART 1:
How people *decide* what is true
1) OPINION (relative / subjective)
2) Justified BELIEF (absolute / objective)

PART 2:
How people *test* for Truth
1) CORRESPONDENCE (fits with reality)
2) COHERENCE (fits the evidence)

# Part 1: How People *Decide* What is True

**Absolute** Truth = true <u>regardless</u> of my CIRCUMSTANCES

**Objective** Truth = true <u>regardless</u> of my OPINION

Can you think of an example where objective and relative truth conflict?

**Absolute vs. Relative:** Are there any circumstances where driving faster than the speed limit is OK?

Ambulance carrying a criticality injured patient to the hospital.

**How about Speeding Tickets?**
There may be circumstances where exceeding the speed limit is OK (ambulance)...

But my *SUBJECTIVE* opinion about how fast I'm driving won't matter when I'm pulled over for exceeding the *OBJECTIVE* speed limit

**Relative** Truth = true <u>depends</u> on my CIRCUMSTANCES

**Subjective** Truth = true <u>depends</u> on my OPINION

## Class Exercise: What Types of Truth Claim are these?

| Truth Claim | Absolute or Relative? | Objective vs. Subjective? |
|---|---|---|
| 1. 2+2=4 | Absolute | Objective |
| 2. A bachelor can never be married | Absolute | Objective |
| 3. Driving over the speed limit is wrong<br>Ambulance rushing someone to hospital | Relative | Subjective |
| 4. Torturing babies for fun is wrong | Absolute | Objective |
| 5. Life couldn't have begun by evolution | Absolute | Subjective |
| 6. People are born with certain rights<br>How does ISIS view womens' rights? | Relative | Subjective |

Absolute = regardless of my circumstances
Relative = depends on my circumstances

Objective = regardless of my opinion
Subjective = depends on my opinion

## Article 398 - In Uncertain & Uncontrollable Times:  Knowing Truth = No Fear

Psalm 23:4 "Though I walk through the valley of the shadow of death, I will fear no evil, for You are with me."

In the recent Atlantic article 'The Unthinkable: Who Survives When Disaster Strikes - and Why', an internal medicine doctor described how 40% of her patients had strange rashes on their face, eyes and throat: "They thought they had contracted a novel form of coronavirus. After talking with all of them, I found one thing in common. They'd been overusing bleach in their homes in response to the coronavirus threat. Some were cleaning 3-4 times a day. They were trying to find ways to handle a threat that's invisible.

They were making things worse in the process. There's so much we can't control, so there's a sense of, 'If we clean enough, the virus will go away.'" COVID-19 is teaching us that control is an illusion. Many are discovering what fear looks like – being at the mercy of an enemy we cannot see. This fear can cripple many of us who, living in the "Land of Plenty", no longer think of thriving but instead just surviving.

Can the Bible give us a different perspective on fear? Is there a type of fear that promotes not only good health but an abundant life? Meet King Solomon and the Old Testament book of Proverbs. Written around 900 BC, he details one theme, found in 13 verses I list in numeric order, that are the "how to" practical guide for a wide range of benefits, each of which is defined below in each verse, that promote an abundant life in the midst of even a pandemic.

This theme is "fearing the Lord". The word for "fear" means "being morally reverent of who the Lord is (not what He does), to the point of being shaken by His holiness and His promise to judge the evilness of sin.

Benefit #1. How to gain knowledge = *"The fear of the Lord is the beginning of knowledge, but fools despise wisdom and instruction"* (Proverbs 1:7).

Benefit #2. How to avoid evil = *"The fear of the Lord is to hate evil; pride, arrogance and the evil way and the perverse mouth I hate"* (Proverbs 8:13).

Benefit #3. How to gain wisdom = *"The fear of the Lord is the beginning of wisdom, and the knowledge of the Holy One is understanding"* (Proverbs 9:10).

Benefit #4. How to have a long life = *"The fear of the Lord prolongs days, but the years of the wicked will be shortened"* (Proverbs 10:27).

Benefit #5. How to be rewarded = *"He who despises the word will be destroyed, but he who fears the commandment will be rewarded"* (Proverbs 13:13).

Benefit #6. How to avoid the second death = *"The fear of the Lord is a fountain of life, to avoid the snares of death"* (Proverbs 14:27).

Benefit #7. How to avoid life's troubles = *"Better is a little with the fear of the Lord, than great treasure with trouble"* (Proverbs 15:16).

Benefit #8. How to be an honorable person = *"The fear of the Lord is the instruction of wisdom, and before honor is humility"* (Proverbs 15:33).

Benefit #9. How to keep away from committing evil = *"In mercy and truth atonement is provided for iniquity; and by the fear of the Lord one departs from evil"* (Proverbs 16:6).\

Benefit #10. How to live a joyous life, free from evil = *"The fear of the Lord leads to life, and he who has it will abide in satisfaction; he will not be visited with evil"* (Proverbs 19:23).

Benefit #11. How to live blessed by God = *"By humility and fear of the Lord are riches and honor and life"* (Proverbs 22:4).

Benefit #12. How to live with real hope beyond this world = *"Do not let your heart envy sinners, but in the fear of the Lord continue all day long; for surely there is a hereafter, and your hope will not be cut off"* (Proverbs 23:17-1).

Benefit #13. How to live a happy, joyful life = *"Happy is the man who is always reverent, but he who hardens his heart will fall into calamity"* (Proverbs 28:14).

But, as in our verse for this week, the Lord reminds us that even when we are walking in the "valley of the shadow of death", which this virus certainly is, we should not be like those scrubbing their homes 3-4 times a day with bleach. We should fear no evil because, as King David says, Jesus Christ is with us.

The prophet Isaiah gave us this same truth: *"Fear not, for I am with you. Be not dismayed, for I am your God. I will strengthen you. I will help you. I will uphold you with My righteous right hand."* (Isaiah 41:10).

As Acts 4:13 confirms, there is a reason why Christians should "not fear", even in the face of these uncertain and uncontrollable times. It is because we cling to the One who holds our lives in His hands: *"When they saw the boldness of Peter and John… they realized that they had been with Jesus."*

**Exit Ticket #3**    Class 03: Deciding What is True

| TRUTH CLAIM | Absolute or Relative? | Why? | Objective vs. Subjective? | Why? |
|---|---|---|---|---|
| People are valuable just because | | | | |
| Killing someone can be ok | | | | |
| The Universe began out of nothing | | | | |
| God exists | | | | |
| Jesus Christ is the only Way to heaven | | | | |

Absolute = regardless of my circumstances
Relative = depends on my circumstances

Objective = regardless of my opinion
Subjective = depends on my opinion

# Class 04:  Testing What is True

Epistemology: What is really the truth?

Aren't These Historical Events Just Legends?

Part 2: How People Test for Truth

Defending Truth - What is a Woman? Testing for Truth

Testing for Truth:  Observable Science, Historical Science

Testing for Truth: The Origin of the Universe; The Resurrection

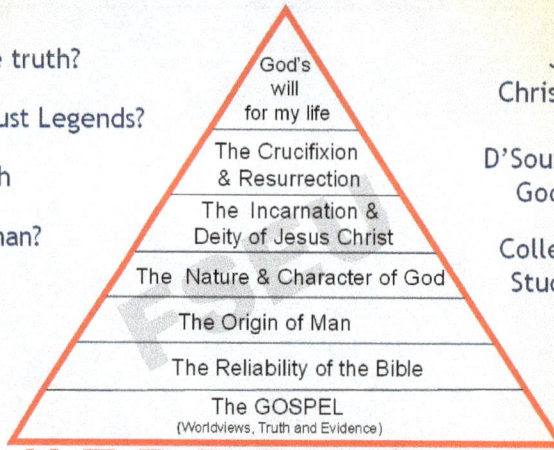

**Pyramid (top to bottom):**
- God's will for my life
- The Crucifixion & Resurrection
- The Incarnation & Deity of Jesus Christ
- The Nature & Character of God
- The Origin of Man
- The Reliability of the Bible
- The GOSPEL (Worldviews, Truth and Evidence)

Jim Warner Wallace: "Is Christianity Rational?" (3:40)

D'Souza vs. Shermer: "Thank God for Christianity" (3:13)

College Professor of Gender Studies gets triggered over the word 'Truth'" (5:18)

Matt Walsh asks Maasai Tribe: "What is a Woman" (1:59)

# HEBREWS 11:1
"Faith = *Substance* of things hoped for.... *Evidence* of things *not seen*"

fse.life Lessons 02 - 08

---

## What's *Really* the Truth?

*Epistemology* =

Proverbs 23:23 "*Buy the Truth, and don't sell it.*"

The study of how truth claims are formed.

PART 1:
How people *decide* what is true

1) OPINION (relative / subjective)

2) Justified BELIEF (absolute / objective)

PART 2:
How people *test* for Truth

1) CORRESPONDENCE (fits with reality)

2) COHERENCE (fits the evidence)

Jim Warner Wallace: "Is Christianity Rational?" (3:40)

# Aren't These Historical Events Just Legends?

**9/11**
Sept 11,
2001

**Battle of
Gettysburg**
July 1,
1863

**Battle of
Arbela**
Oct. 1,
331BC

**Resurrection
of Jesus
Christ**
April,
32AD

How would you
answer this question?

Courtesy of Google Images    Fair Use Law 17 U.S. Code § 107

# Part 2: How People *Test* for Truth

## Correspondence Test

Does the claim accurately describe (i.e.,
correspond to) the way things actually *are*
(reality) - the **FACTS**?

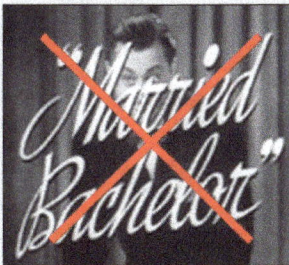

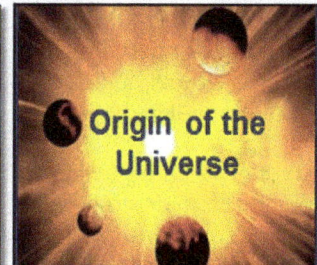

"Married Bachelor"

Apple Computer
"Pregnant Man" Emoji

## Coherence Test

Truth is rational or logical within some set of
propositions or beliefs.

Allows the **EVIDENCE** for competing claims to
be weighed against each other.

Jurors in a Trial

Origin of the
Universe

> **For my BELIEF to be TRUE... measure it against both tests:**
>
> Correspondency:  the truth claim must conform to objective features of the world (i.e. reality, or facts).
>
> Coherency:  the truth claim must make sense when measured against competing claims on the
> same belief or topic.

## Truth Test #1 = The Correspondence Test.

Truth about reality is what corresponds to the way things really are. Truth is "telling it like it is." There is a reality, and truth accurately expresses it. Falsehood tells or claims things like they are not, misrepresenting the facts or the way things are. So if someone makes a truth claim that does not correspond to reality and the facts, their claim is false.

This way of testing whether someone's claim is true or false is how most people live their lives everyday and matches up with what the Bible has to say as well. According to the Bible, a claim is true only if it accords with factual reality. There are numerous passages that contrast truth claims with lies. For example, Deuteronomy 18:22 warns against false prophets whose words do not correspond to reality: *"If what a prophet proclaims in the name of the Lord does not take place or come true, that is a message the Lord has not spoken"*. The 9th Commandment specifically warns against bearing false testimony. For example, in John 14:6, when Jesus says *"I am the way, the truth, and the life,"* there is a correspondence to reality. Since He is the full revelation of God, Jesus is showing us who God is in actual reality.

### How People *Test* for Truth

**Correspondence Test**

Does the claim accurately describe (i.e., correspond to) the way things actually *are* (reality)- the FACTS?

**Coherence Test**

Truth is rational or logical within some set of propositions or beliefs.

Allows for the *evidence* for different perspectives to be weighed against each other.

**For my BELIEF to be TRUE… It must satisfy both tests:**

Correspondency:　the truth claim must conform to objective features of the world (i.e. reality, or facts).

Coherency:　the truth claim must make sense when measured against competing claims on the same belief or topic.

**Truth Test #2 = The Coherence Test.** Truth is what is self-consistent. But by itself it is inadequate for testing truth. For example, to say "All bachelors are unmarried men" is by itself consistent, but it doesn't tell us anything about reality. The statement would be true, even if there were no bachelors. It really means, "If there is a bachelor, he must be single." But it does not inform us if bachelors exist in reality. At best, coherence is a negative test of truth. Statements are wrong if they are inconsistent, but not necessarily true if they are.

## Truth Decision #1 = Objective versus Subjective.

By "objective truth" we mean "independent of people's (including my own) opinion." The opposite of "objective" is "subjective", which means "it's just a matter of personal opinion." For example, if objective moral values and obligations do exist, then everyone would be obligated or forbidden from doing certain actions, regardless of what we think.

## Truth Decision #2 = Absolute versus Relative.

By "absolute truth" we mean "independent of people's circumstances or situation." The opposite of "absolute" is "relative", which means something can be true depending on my

### How People *Decide* What is True

**Absolute**
Truth =
true regardless of my circumstances

**Objective**
Truth =
true regardless of my opinion

**Relative**
Truth =
true depending on my circumstances

**Subjective**
Truth =
true depending on my opinion

Just because my definition of truth is *RELATIVE* to the circumstances I'm in doesn't mean that my truth for that circumstance is *SUBJECTIVE* (that there isn't an *OBECTIVE* truth I should or do live by)

circumstances or the situation I'm in. For example, killing another person may be justifiably true depending on the circumstance, such as if an intruder breaks into my home and physically threatens my family.

# Testing for Truth: What is a Woman?

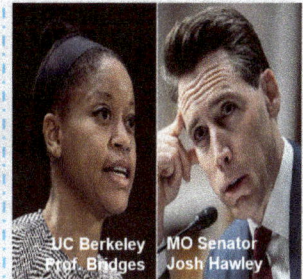

**Genesis 1:27**

"God created man in His own image, in the image of God He created him; MALE and FEMALE He created them."

<u>Postmodern Thinking #1</u> = Where Christianity is about objectivity (singular truth), postmodernism is about subjectivity (multiplicity of truths).

<u>Postmodern Thinking #2</u> = Skeptical of claims to be valid for all groups, cultures, traditions, or races; focus is on the *relative truths of each person.*

<u>Postmodern Thinking #3</u> = Interpretation is everything; reality only exists through our interpretations of what the world means to each of us individually.

Matt Walsh | Univ TN Prof. Pat Grzanka

UC Berkeley Prof. Bridges | MO Senator Josh Hawley

**Walsh:** *'Why is truth uncomfortable?'*

**Grzanka:** *"It sounds deeply transphobic to me. You keep invoking the word 'Truth', which is condescending and rude."*

**Bridges:** *"Do you believe that men can get pregnant?"*

**Hawley:** *"No, I don't think men can get pregnant."*

**Bridges:** *"So, you are denying that trans people exist. Thank you."*

College Professor of Gender Studies gets triggered over the word 'Truth'" (5:18)   Matt Walsh asks Measai Tribe: "What is a Woman" (1:59)   Courtesy of Google Images   Fair Use Law 17 U.S. Code § 107

# Testing for Truth:  Observable Science, Historical Science

| 'Observable Science' | 'Historical Science' |
|---|---|
| 1. Studies how <u>present</u> events happen | 1. Studies how <u>past</u> events happened |
| 2. Studies testable, repeatable, <u>observable</u> events | 2. Studies untestable, non-repeatable, <u>unobservable</u> events |
| 3. Data collected *during* the event, so *direct* evidence | 3. Data collected *after* the event, so *circumstantial* evidence |
| 4. Can recreate and retest events, so conclusions **CAN** be proven false | 4. Can't recreate events, so conclusions **CANNOT** be proven false (only <u>inferences</u> to most likely cause) |

**COLD-CASE CHRISTIANITY**

A HOMICIDE DETECTIVE INVESTIGATES THE GOSPELS

I Have A Question

Is 'Historical Science' used very often to discover truth?

CSI (Crime Scene Investigation)
Legal System (Jury Duty)
Business (Analytics)
Sports (Moneyball)
Stock Market

Origin of Universe
Origin of Life
Reliability of the Bible
Existence of God
The Resurrection

Courtesy of Google Images    Fair Use Law 17 U.S. Code § 107

# Article 511 - Defending Truth Part 3 – What is a Woman? Testing for Truth

Genesis 1:27 *"God created man in His own image… male and female He created them."*

*"'I would like to just start by getting to the truth'. 'I am really uncomfortable with that language – "getting to the truth". 'Why is that uncomfortable?' 'It sounds deeply transphobic to me. And if you keep probing, we are going to stop the interview.' 'If I probe about what the truth is?' 'You keep invoking the word "Truth", which is condescending and rude.' 'How is the word "Truth" condescending and rude?' 'Why don't you tell me what your truth is? And you are walking on 30 seconds more of this interview before I get up.'"*

This is the exchange between Matt Walsh and Dr. Patrick Grzanka, Professor of Women, Gender, and Sexuality Studies at the Univ. of Tennessee, in Matt Walsh's movie 'What is a Woman?'. Grzanka was asked if a person with male physical characteristics who identifies as a woman as in fact male due to his biology. The above exchange then begins, as Walsh appeals to lets "get to the truth" by "telling it like it is".

Grzanka tells Walsh that the word 'truth' is condescending, rude and "deeply transphobic". This occurs throughout the movie. Walsh's interviewees want to distinguish between "my truth" versus "Walsh's truth", but never agree there is actually "the truth". This is the Postmodern worldview in full view in our educational institutions. Everyone is entitled to their own view of truth. Nothing, like a woman, has objective meaning.

Fortunately, we have a simple test that is taught in many schools today - the "Correspondence Test", where truth is based on what corresponds to reality – the facts. Falsehood misrepresents the facts. So, if someone makes a truth claim that does not correspond to reality and the facts, their claim is false.

In another interview in the movie, Walsh asks Maasai tribesmen *"Can a man become a woman?"*. Their answer: *"No."* He then asks, *"What about transgender?"* Their answer: *"If you want to become a lady but you are a man, you have something wrong."*

His next question: *"What about someone who thinks they are neither a man nor a woman (non-binary)?"* Their answer: *"A man has a penis. A woman has a vagina."* His final question: *"What if it is a woman with a penis?"* They all start laughing at the question.

Walsh asks a rhetorical question: *"Everyone is laughing – is that a dumb question?"* Only in America's institutions of higher learning could we teach that a man is no longer defined as an adult boy who produces sperm, and a woman is no longer defined as an adult girl who produces eggs. Yet, in Africa the Maasai tribe understands truth (what corresponds to reality) better than our Postmodern intellectual elites.

In a recent Judiciary Committee hearing, MO Senator Josh Hawley asked UC Berkeley Law Professor Khiara Bridges *"You've referred to 'people with a capacity for pregnancy.' Would that be women?"* Her answer: *"Many women, cis women, have the capacity for pregnancy; many cis women do not have the capacity for pregnancy. There are also trans men who are capable of pregnancy as well as nonbinary people who are capable of pregnancy."* Professor Bridges believes men can get pregnant.

Bridges continued: *"Your line of questioning is transphobic, and it opens up trans people to violence by not recognizing them."* Hawley: *"You're saying that I'm opening up people to violence by asking whether or not women can have pregnancies?"* Bridges: *"1 out of 5 transgender persons have attempted suicide."*

Hawley: *"Because of my line of questioning?"* Bridges: *"Because denying that trans people exist and pretending not to know that they exist."* Hawley: *"I'm denying that trans people exist by asking you if you're talking about women having pregnancies?"* Bridges: *"Do you believe that men can get pregnant?"* Hawley: *"No, I don't think men can get pregnant."* Bridges: *"So, you are denying that trans people exist. Thank you."*

As with Grzanka's exchange with Walsh, the problem is Postmodernist insistence that truth is not tied to reality.

Both Grzanka (Univ. of TN) and Bridges (UC Berkeley) are unwilling to say what the Maasai tribesmen know: only biological women could get pregnant. Instead, both accused their interrogators as using their knowledge as a weapon against trans people. They are not asking others to tolerate and get along with their belief. They are insisting people **compromise** their beliefs and **forfeit** their notion of objective truth.

The Bible begins with God's instruction on the sexes: *"God created man in his own image, in the image of God he created him; male and female he created them"* (Genesis 1:27). There are only two, male and female.

The Bible never says men can become women, or women men. The Maasai, like all of us, know this. It's the supposedly brightest intellectuals who reject what is so obviously true. That's Postmodernism.

# Testing for Truth: The Origin of the Universe; The Resurrection

**Origin of the Universe**

**Resurrection**

**Correspondence Test**

Do things pop into existence from nothing?

Was anyone there to see what happened?

Do people rise from the dead?

Was anyone there to see what happened?

**Coherence Test**

**Any evidence for?**
1) Laws of Cause & Effect
2) 1st & 2nd Laws of Thermodynamics
3) Hubble Law, Doppler Effect
4) General Theory of Relativity
5) Expansion Rate of the Universe
6) Cosmic Background Radiation

**Any evidence against?**
1) Multiverse

**Any evidence for?**
1) Jesus's Death & Burial
2) Empty Tomb
3) Post-Mortem Appearances
4) Disciples' Testimony
5) Explosion of Christianity

**Any evidence against?**
1) Swoon Theory
2) Theft Theory
3) "Unknown Tomb" Theory
4) Impersonation Theory

Correspondence Test = meet the facts/ conform to reality?

Coherence Test = is there evidence to weigh competing views?

Courtesy of Google Images.   Fair Use Law 17 U.S. Code § 107

## Article 507 - To Defend Truth, Speak Up in the Name of the One who is Truth – Jesus Christ

*Isaiah 59:14-15 "Truth is fallen in the street; Truth fails; he who departs from evil makes himself a prey."*

A new video entitled 'She Nails It' has 2.5 million views and growing. A woman gives multiple examples of how we have changed from knowing what is true to accepting obvious lies. She ends with a message: *"Wake up America – like the Titanic, we have hit the iceberg and are taking on water fast. Speak up."* See the list in the table below. Can you see how off course we have allowed America to get?

There is a great source for us to study for this same problem in another country, and how it was solved. The source is the Bible, the country is Israel, the solution is Jesus Christ. Let's read and see.

Isaiah 59:9-11 ➔ The Situation: *"Justice is far from us, nor does righteousness overtake us; we look for light, but there is darkness! For brightness, but we walk in blackness! We grope for the wall like the blind; we grope as if we had no eyes; we are as dead men in desolate places. We all growl like bears, and moan sadly like doves; we look for justice, but there is none; for salvation, but it is far from us."*

Isaiah 59:12- ➔ The Cause: *"Our transgressions are multiplied before You, and our sins testify against us; in lying against the Lord, and departing from our God, speaking oppression, conceiving and uttering from the heart words of falsehood. Justice is turned back, and righteousness stands afar off; for truth has fallen in the street, and integrity cannot enter. So, truth fails, and he who departs from evil makes himself a prey."*

Isaiah 59:12- ➔ The Solution: *"Then the Lord saw it, and it displeased Him that there was no justice. He saw that there was no man, and wondered that there was no intercessor; therefore **His own ARM brought salvation for Him**; His own righteousness, it sustained Him. For HE put on righteousness as a breastplate, and a helmet of salvation on HIS head; HE put on the garments of vengeance for clothing and was clad with zeal as a cloak."*

Who is this "Arm of the Lord" who brought salvation to Israel in God's name?

*"Take up the whole armor of God… gird your waist with truth, put on the breastplate of righteousness, take the helmet of salvation"* (Ephesians 6:13-17). Isn't this the same armor in Isaiah 59? Wait - It gets better.

*"Put on the Lord Jesus Christ, and make no provision for the flesh, to fulfill its lusts"* (Romans 13:14).

So, we put on God's armor, but we also put on Christ? Sounds like God's "armor" is Jesus Christ Himself! If you want to defend truth, speak up in the name of the One who claimed to be truth.

| # | Yesterday:  What was True | Today:  What's the New Truth |
|---|---|---|
| **Gender** | Biology and physiology distinguish men from women | If a guy pretends to be a woman, you are required to pretend with him |
| | Science tells us there are 2 sexes/genders: male and female | People who say there is no such thing as gender… are demanding a female president |
| | Men and womens' physiology are why we have men and women sports | Men pretending to be women can compete in women's sports |
| **Immigartion** | Irish doctors and German engineers who want to immigrate to the US must go through a rigorous vetting process | Any illiterate gang banger who jumps the Southern border fence are welcome |
| | US Immigration screens for highly infectious diseases entering the US | Immigrants with tuberculosis and polio are welcome… but you better prove your dog is vaccinated |
| | If you cheat to get into college you go to prison | if you cheat to get into America you go to college for free |
| | $5 billion for border security is too expensive | $1.5 trillion for free health care is not |
| | Russians influencing our election are bad | Illegal immigrants voting in our elections are good |
| **Human Rights** | Stopping criminals from hurting people is fundamental to human rights | Criminals are caught and released to hurt more people, but stopping them violates their human rights |
| | The NBA and NFL stand up for human rights in America | The NBA and NFL look the other way with China, the world leader in human rights violations |
| | Abolishing slavery was one of America's great human rights victories | People who never owned slaves should pay slavery reparations to people who have never been slaves |
| | Crimes, such as murder, carry the death penalty | Killing murderers is wrong, but killing the unborn is OK |
| **Racism** | People have died from a Chinese virus | Its racist to call it Chinese even though it began in China |
| | If someone breaks in your home, you call the Police to rescue you | City governments demand defunding and abolishing our racist police force |
| | Census Bureau was created to collect data on the American population | Its un-American and racist for the census to count how many Americans are in America |
| **Youth** | 20 is too young to drink a beer | 18 is old enough to vote |
| | You are responsible to pay off your own college loan | People who never went to college should pay the debt of those who did |
| **Policy** | Producing our own oil makes us energy independent from our enemies | We shut down American oil production and buy oil from our enemies |
| | Its OK for Biden to blackmail Ukraine's President | Its an impeachable offense if Trump inquires about it |
| | When a gunman murders 20 children in school, we pray to God | We ban prayer in schools because we want to remove God from education |

## Are Christianity's Truth Claims Believable?  Using EVIDENCE to Test My Beliefs

**HEBREWS 11:1** *"FAITH is the substance of things hoped for, the EVIDENCE of things unseen."*

RZIM.org: 'Does God Exist Series - Proof' (3:53)          Courtesy of Google Images     Fair Use Law 17 U.S. Code § 107

# Is EVIDENCE Necessary for Belief in God?

**Beliefs from Preceding Beliefs =** these must be validated to be true (religious experiences, your belief on abortion).

**Properly Basic Beliefs =** reasonable beliefs that don't need an argument to be true (experience of sadness or joy).

**Beliefs fall into 2 categories\***

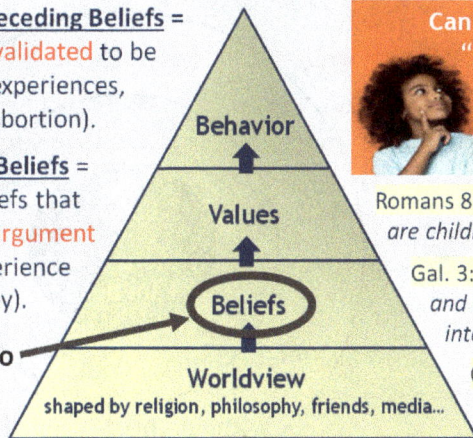

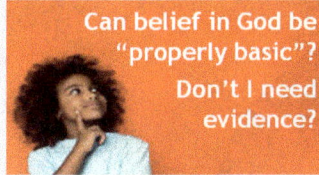

**Behavior**

**Values**

**Beliefs**

**Worldview**
shaped by religion, philosophy, friends, media...

Can belief in God be "properly basic"? Don't I need evidence?

Through the **internal witness of the Holy Spirit**, Christians have an *objective knowledge* of Jesus Christ as their personal Lord & Savior (John 3:3).

Romans 8:16 *"The Spirit Himself bears witness with our spirit that we are children of God."*

Gal. 3:26, 4:6 *"You are all sons of God through faith in Christ Jesus; and because you are sons, God has sent forth the Spirit of His Son into your hearts, crying 'Abba, Father!'"*

Col. 2:2 *"...riches of the full assurance of understanding, to the knowledge of the mystery of God, of the Father and of Christ."*

**The witness of the Holy Spirit is not a premise in a deductive argument for God's existence.**

While you would be wrong to argue God exists because you've had a religious experience (example: Mormons argue God exists because of the "warming of the bosom"), it is **PROPERLY BASIC**.

1Corin. 2:14 *"The natural man doesn't receive the things of the Spirit of God... Nor can he know them, for they are spiritually discerned."*

**Gr. "plerophoria" =** complete confidence through KNOWLEDGE ("assurance of your salvation")

Is Belief in God a Properly Basic Belief? (2:55)   WL Craig: 'Properly Basic Beliefs & Other Religions' (3:01)        Courtesy of Google Images    Fair Use Law 17 U.S. Code § 107

# Properly Basic Belief = "Walking by Faith"
# The Inner Witness of the Holy Spirit

**Watchman Nee "The Normal Christian Life"**

**Romans 8:26**
*"The Spirit helps in my weakness. I do not know what I should pray for, but the Spirit Himself makes intercession for me with groanings which cannot be uttered.*

| | | | | |
|---|---|---|---|---|
| **'Know'** | | An act of my **SPIRIT** ("Inner man": Holy Spirit knowledge) | There are certain things I must know. If I am ignorant of God's Word, I cannot expect the power of God. | Romans 6:6-7 |
| **'Reckon'** | | An act of my **SOUL** (my will: head and heart acknowledge) | I must reckon on the facts I find in God's Word. There must be a decision I make to walk daily by faith. | Romans 6:11 |
| **'Present'** | | An act of my **BODY** (by my reckoning, my resulting actions) | I must present my body daily as a living sacrifice. | Romans 6:19 |

WL Craig: 'Handling Doubt' (5:38)        Courtesy of Google Images    Fair Use Law 17 U.S. Code § 107

## Studying Romans 8:9-10   How Christ **in me** gives me Victory

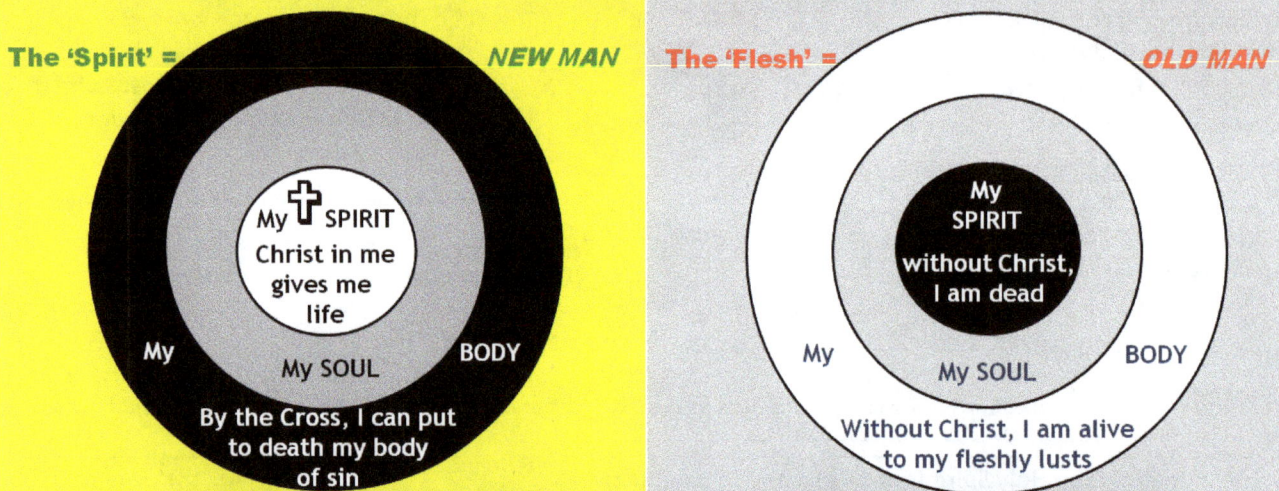

The 'Spirit' =                                            *NEW MAN*

My ✝ SPIRIT
Christ in me
gives me
life

My        My SOUL        BODY

By the Cross, I can put
to death my body
of sin

The 'Flesh' =                                            *OLD MAN*

My
SPIRIT
without Christ,
I am dead

My        My SOUL        BODY

Without Christ, I am alive
to my fleshly lusts

**ROMANS 8:9-10**
*"You are not in the flesh but in the Spirit, if indeed the Spirit of God dwells in you...*
*Now if Christ is in you, the body is dead because of sin (Romans 6:1-7),*
*but the Spirit is life because of righteousness (Romans 6:8-14)."*

Courtesy of Google Images     Fair Use Law 17 U.S. Code § 107

## Do Arguments from Evidence negate the work of the Holy Spirit?

Evangelism is impossible without the Holy Spirit's power, but reasoned evangelism doesn't replace His working. Paul's evangelistic approach: to rely on the Holy Spirit but used doctrine, evidence and arguments to appeal to his audience's minds (Acts 17:16-17), then to argue with their mind, plead with their heart, to move their will, trusting in the Holy Spirit (2Cor. 5:17-21).

John Gresham Machen, former Professor of New Testament at Princeton Theological Seminary, explains the importance of arguments from the evidence and it's alignment with the working of the Holy Spirit: *"There must be the mysterious work of the Spirit of God in the new birth. Without that, all our arguments are useless. But because argument is insufficient, it does not follow that it is unnecessary. What the Holy Spirit does in the new birth is not to make a man a Christian regardless of the evidence, but on the contrary to clear away the mists from his eyes and enable him to attend to the evidence."*

---

### 813 Times:  God says He wants people to KNOW Him and His great truths

To the atheist, agnostic, 'religious': you are ignorant because you won't respond to knowledge He gives.
To the Christian: I recall the great truths about myself. I meditate on them until they grip my mind and mold my character. God's way is to remind me who I truly am because He made me that way in Christ.

The Old and New Testament's constant urging to us: "Don't be ignorant (don't 'not know')"

**"ignorant"** = Hebr. "lô' lô' lôh yâdá" = not knowing; not understanding nor recognizing

Isaiah 56:10  *"His watchmen are blind, they are all ignorant; they are all dumb dogs, they cannot bark."*

**"ignorant"** or **"not know"** = Gr. "agnoeô" = not understanding due to lack of information or intelligence

1Corinthians 12:1-2  *"...concerning spiritual gifts, brethren, I do not want you to be ignorant: you know that you were Gentiles, carried away to these dumb idols, however you were led."*

The Old and New Testament's constant urging to us: "Know with full understanding"

**"know"** = Hebr. "yâdá" =  to know by recognizing; to be sure; to have understanding
**"understand"** =  Hebr. "bîyn" =   to separate out mentally; to regard and discern wisely

Exodus 7:5  *"...the Egyptians shall know that I am the Lord, when I stretch out My hand on Egypt and bring out the children of  Israel from among them."*

Isaiah 43:10  *"You are My witnesses and My servant whom I have chosen, that you may know and believe and understand that I am He. Before Me there was no God formed, nor shall there be after Me.'"*

**"know"** = Gr. "ginóskó" = to know absolutely; to be mentally sure in understanding

John 8:32  *"...you shall know the truth, and the truth shall make you free."*

John 17:3  *"...this is eternal life, that they may know You, the only true God, and Jesus Christ whom You have sent."*

**"know"** = Gr. "eidó" = to know as in seeing; to be sure of

1John 5:13  *"These things I have written to you who believe in the name of the Son of God, that you may know that you have eternal life, and that you may continue to believe in the name of the Son of God."*

**"understand"** = Gr. "noieõ" = to exercise the mind; to think upon and understand

Hebrews 11:3  *"By faith we understand that the worlds were framed by the word of God, so that the things which are seen were not made of things which are visible."*

John 12:39-40  *"...Isaiah said, 'He has blinded their eyes and hardened their heart, lest they should see with their eyes and understand with their heart, lest they should turn, so I should heal them.'"*

**"understand"** = Gr. "suniémi" = to put together mentally; to consider to level of mentally grasping

Matthew 15:10  *"...He called the multitude and said to them, "Hear and understand.."*

Luke 8:9-10  *"...His disciples asked Him, saying, 'What does this parable mean?' And He said, 'To you it has been given to know the mysteries of the kingdom of God, but to the rest it is given in parables, that "Seeing they may not see, and hearing they may not understand."'"*

**God regards knowledge, understanding and wisdom as foundations of my faith (Psalm 11:3)**

Luke 4:16-21     John 9:1-41     John 8:1-11     Mark 10:13-16     Luke 8:22-26

Knowledge is indispensable to Christian life and service. If we do not use the mind that God has given us, we condemn ourselves to spiritual superficiality and cut ourselves off from many of the riches of God's grace.
— *John Stott* —

John 4:1-20     Mark 5:25-34     Jesus Christ:  Think to Access God's Grace     Matthew 5-7

*"The* **WORD** *became flesh and dwelt among us."* John 1:14          *"This is eternal life, that they may* **KNOW** *You, the only true God, and Jesus Christ whom You have sent."* John 17:3

**Exit Ticket #4**          <mark>**Class 04: Testing What is True**</mark>

| | |
|---|---|
| **1) What is the "Correspondence Test"?** | **2) What is the "Coherence Test"?** |
| **3) How do Observable vs. Historical Science connect with Correspondence vs. Coherence Test?** | **4) Write down a truth claim, then back it up by either applying the Correspondence Test, Coherence Test or both?** |

# Class 05:  Rhetoric

What is "Rhetoric"?

How People Can Be Persuaded

'Logos'

'Ethos'

'Pathos'

God's will for my life

The Crucifixion & Resurrection

The Incarnation & Deity of Jesus Christ

The Nature & Character of God

The Origin of Man

The Reliability of the Bible

The GOSPEL
(Worldviews, Truth and Evidence)

## HEBREWS 11:1

"Faith = *Substance* of things *hoped for*.... *Evidence* of things *not seen*"

fse.life Lessons 02 - 08

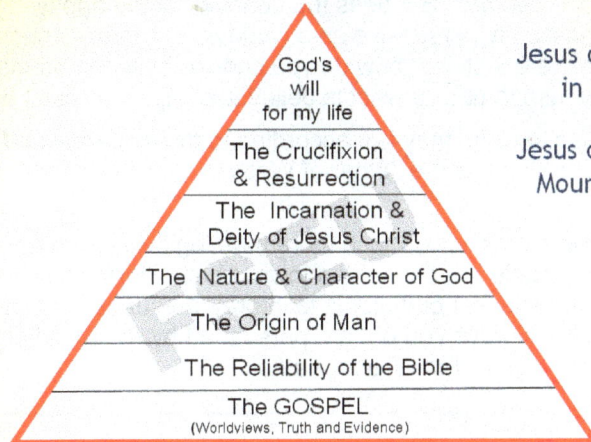

Jesus of Nazareth: 'Woman Caught in Adultery – John 8:1-11' (3:03)

Jesus of Nazareth: 'Sermon on the Mount – Matthew 5: ch 5-7' (3:20)

# How to *Persuade* People what is True

John Dickson: PhD in history from Macquarie University, Honorary Fellow of Dept. of Ancient History (Macquarie); Prof. Univ. of Sydney (Dept of Hebrew, Biblical & Jewish Studies): the Historical Jesus; Founding director of CPA (Center for Public Christianity).

**What is 'Rhetoric'?**    Art form of argument used to persuade an audience.

**Aristotle: 'On Rhetoric'**    A person's worldview is shaped by more than the evidence.

Aristotle

## 3 Techniques People Use to Persuade You to Adopt Their Worldview:

RESEARCH

**More Doctors Smoke CAMELS than any other cigarette!**

Meet Otis.

**'Logos'**
Evidence-based
(Correspondence, Coherence)

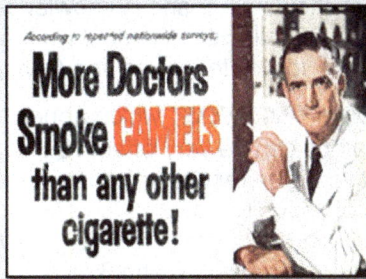

**'Ethos'**
Expert's knowledge
Speaker's charisma

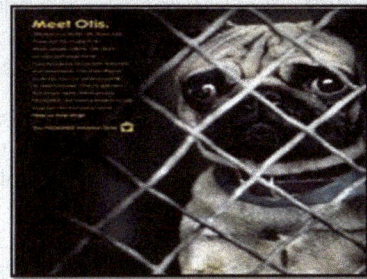

**'Pathos'**
Emotion-based
(my feelings)

## Aristotle's 'On Rhetoric':     How we can be persuaded to adopt our worldview

American has gone through a major cultural shift. We have moved from a world of absolutes and objectivity to one of relativism, subjectivism, and tolerance. The greatest commandment in our society today is '*thou shalt tolerate one another'*. But does the behavior of the apostle Paul in Acts 19:8 still hold true today – is Christianity persuasive as a worldview in today's supposed 'enlightened' America? That raises more questions: how do you choose between so many different beliefs? What criteria do you use to decide what is believable? They all can't be right.

While many of my skeptical friends like to claim they live according to the evidence and form their worldview based on reasoning alone, Aristotle, credited as the 'father of Western civilization' and 'the originator of today's scientific method', would disagree.

He believed that a person's worldview is shaped by much more than logical reasoning. In his famous treatise called 'On Rhetoric', he explains how people are persuaded toward belief. First of all, let's define 'rhetoric'. It's really an art form, where the goal of the speaker or writer is to inform, persuade, or motivate their audience in specific topics. Aristotle explains the three ways you or I are persuaded by rhetorical arguments towards believing something. He calls these three ways '*Logos*', '*Ethos*' and '*Pathos*.'

**'LOGOS'**
Evidence-based
(Correspondence, Coherence)

**'ETHOS'**
Expert's knowledge or
character

**'PATHOS'**
Emotion-based
(my feelings)

The first, '***LOGOS'***, is where we get today's word 'logic'. This form of persuasion is evidence-based, where the depth of the facts presented gives strong reasons for believing. This is Luke's appeal in Acts 1:3 when he writes *"to whom He (Jesus) presented Himself alive after His suffering by many unmistakable proofs…"*. Christianity, unlike other world religions, opens itself up to scrutiny by the skeptic and invites anyone to test its claims.

The second form of persuasion is '***ETHOS'***, where the speaker's personal character or their depth of knowledge on the subject persuades us that he or she is credible. 'Ethos' can be achieved in many ways. One could be a noted expert in the field, like a college professor or a company executive. Or the speaker may have a vested interest in the subject, like a couple who has been married fifty years and is a source of wisdom on marriage. Or the speaker could use impressive 'Logos' that shows he or she is knowledgeable on the topic. Jesus Christ often employed 'Ethos' persuasion, as Matthew 7:28-29 tells us: *"And so it was, when Jesus had ended these sayings, that the people were astonished at His teaching, for He taught as one having authority, and not as the scribes."*

And finally, Aristotle's third form of persuasion is '***PATHOS'***, which appeals to the audience's emotions. We get the words '*pathetic'* and '*empathy'* from it. Pathos can be very effective when it appeals to audience's hopes - where the speaker paints a scenario of positive future results of following the course of action proposed. This is the distinguishing element of the good news of Jesus Christ, and the essence of the most beloved verse in the Bible, spoken by Jesus Himself: *"For God so loved the world, that He gave His only begotten Son, that whosoever believes in Him should not perish but have everlasting life."* (John 3:16).

Now you can understand why Paul, in Acts 19:8, was so bold to proclaim publically the gospel of Jesus Christ. It meets Aristotle's criteria for the three elements of persuasion. Are Christians in America like Paul, boldly sharing the exclusive claims of Jesus Christ? Or is it that we as Christians have not put in the time and effort to examine our beliefs and discuss them in open with others. We cave into our culture, which tells us to keep our Christianity at home or on Sundays in church. Our faith resides in our private world, safe from the critique of those around us.

There is no good reason a Christian can give for why their faith in Jesus Christ should blend into American culture as just one of the many beliefs to be tolerated. Based on Aristotle's dictums, Christianity stands alone. And more importantly, based on the historical reality of the Person of Jesus Christ, it is true. Share it.

# 'LOGOS'

Where we get today's word 'logic'.

Evidence-based:

the depth of the facts gives strong reasons for believing.

Luke's appeal in Acts 1:3

*"many unmistakable proofs..."*

> "Faith is the substance of things hoped for, the EVIDENCE of things not seen."
> Hebrews 11:1

Courtesy of Google Images     Fair Use Law 17 U.S. Code § 107

# 'ETHOS'

Personal Credibility/Charisma:

Speaker's character, charisma, or depth of knowledge persuades others to believe.

How "Ethos" can be achieved:

1) A noted expert in the field (college professor, company exec., professional athlete).

2) One with vast experience on the subject (couple married 50 years - wisdom on marriage).

3) One uses impressive "logos" to show they know their subject matter.

> "When Jesus had ended these sayings, the people were astonished at His teaching, for He taught as one having authority, and not as the scribes."
> Matthew 7:28-29... the closing of the Sermon on the Mount

Woman Caught in Adultery (3:03)                    Courtesy of Google Images     Fair Use Law 17 U.S. Code § 107

## 'PATHOS'

Speaker appeals to the audience's *HOPES* and emotions.

Where we get our words "pathetic" and "empathy".

How speakers achieve "Pathos": They paint a scenario of positive future results from following the course of action they propose.

"Seeing the multitudes, He went up on a mountain. And when He was seated His disciples came to Him. Then He opened His mouth and taught them..." Matthew 5:1-2... the opening of the Sermon on the Mount

Sermon on the Mount (3:20)     Does God Exist: Frank Turek vs. Christopher Hitchens (2:11:51)          Courtesy of Google Images     Fair Use Law 17 U.S. Code § 107

**Exit Ticket #5**        <mark>**Class 05: Rhetoric**</mark>

| | |
|---|---|
| **1) What are the 3 forms of rhetorical persuasion that build your Worldview?** | **2) In the "Sermon on the Mount", which form of rhetoric does Jesus use?** |
| **3) Of 3 forms of persuasion, which is most important in building your personal worldview, and why?** | **4) Of 4 Scriptures in this lesson, which most resonates with you and why?** |

# Class 06:  The Logic of Christianity Part 1

What is Logic?     Why Use It?

Discovering Truth = Learning How to Think

Why Faith is Logical

Our Class Journey to Discover Truth

What is "Formal" Logic?

Evaluating a Deductive Argument

Formal Logic: Let's Try Some More

Article 28 - The Romans Ladder of Character: Using Logic to Present Myself to Jesus Christ

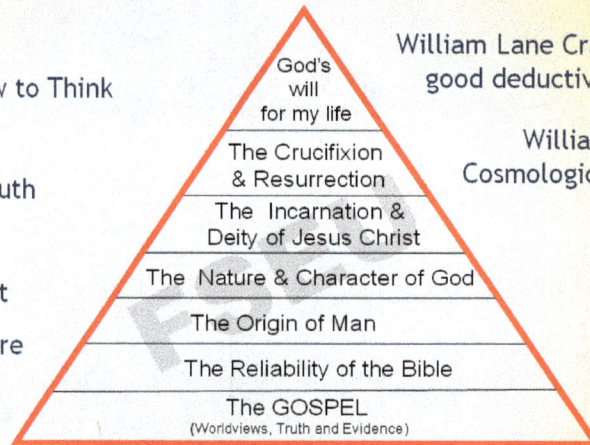

William Lane Craig: "What makes a good deductive argument?" (1:21)

William Lane Craig: "The Cosmological Argument" (4:12)

**Pyramid (top to bottom):**
- God's will for my life
- The Crucifixion & Resurrection
- The Incarnation & Deity of Jesus Christ
- The Nature & Character of God
- The Origin of Man
- The Reliability of the Bible
- The GOSPEL (Worldviews, Truth and Evidence)

# HEBREWS 11:1

"Faith = *Substance* of things *hoped for*.... *Evidence* of things *not seen*"

**fse.life Lessons 02 - 08**

# What is "Logic"?

The art and science of *reasoning* to discover truth.

Method of *reasoning* involving thinking through what we hear/observe to then reach conclusions.

*"'Come now, and let us <u>reason</u> together, says the Lord."* Isaiah 1:18

*"Present your bodies a living sacrifice... which is your <u>reasonable</u> service."* Romans 12:1

# Why Use Logic?    We Should Care about *TRUTH*

"① *SANCTIFY* the Lord God in your hearts; always be ready to give a ②*DEFENSE* to everyone who asks you a ③*REASON* for the ④*HOPE* that is in you, with meekness and ⑤ *FEAR*…"

**1Peter 3:15**

① SANCTIFY = *"hagiazō"*
to separate, dedicate, consecrate; render-sacred

② DEFENSE = *"apologia"*
reasoned argument or answer

③ REASON = *"logos"*
the expression of your mind's thoughts and convictions

④ HOPE = *"elpis"*
confident expectation of the future (eternal life)

⑤ FEAR = *"phobos"*
reverence, with full understanding of God's judgment

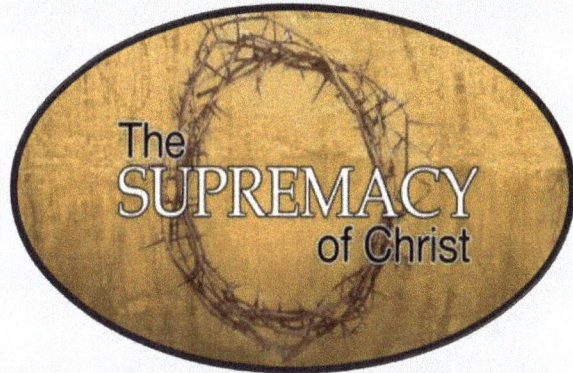

The **SUPREMACY** of Christ

**The Evidence God provides is not to prove He exists – its to give you a firm foundation for *YOUR FAITH***

**The Key to Logic = *'Christ in you'***

Courtesy of Google Images   Fair Use Law 17 U.S. Code § 107

# Discovering Truth = Learning How to Think

## How can I *know* what is *true*?

**What's Better?**

1) Being taught *what* to think…

2) Being taught *how* to think

" The important thing is to never stop questioning. "

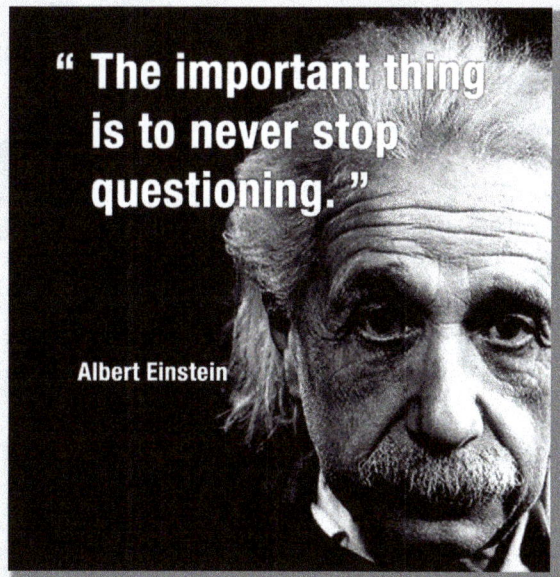

**Albert Einstein**

Courtesy of Google Images    Fair Use Law 17 U.S. Code § 107

# Why FAITH is Logical

"① *FAITH* is the ② *SUBSTANCE* of things ③ *HOPED* for, the ④ *EVIDENCE* of things not seen."

Hebrews 11:1

**① FAITH = "*pistis*"**

Fidelity to a Person (not faith in God's promises, which are opportunities to exercise my faith - it's faith in God Himself)

**② SUBSTANCE = "*hupostasis*"**

"Hupo" (under) + "stasis" (stand upon) = "understanding" (foundation upon which I stand)

**③ HOPED FOR = "*elpizō*"**

What gives me a confident expectation of the future (eternal life)

**④ EVIDENCE = "*elegehos*"**

Convincing proofs that strengthen my faith

Matthew 7:24-27

**Faith = Trusting in what I have good *reasons* to believe**

# FSEU Journey to Live Out Truth

**Does my Christianity pass the tests for truth?**
1) Correspondence Test
2) Coherence Test

**Once I know my worldview is true – am I living the Gospel of Jesus Christ?**

"God has not given us a spirit of fear... but of power and of love and of a sound mind." 2Timothy 1:7

**Am I sharing the Truth?**

As I apply the **rules of logic** to my Christian worldview against the other religious/philosophical/cultural worldviews...

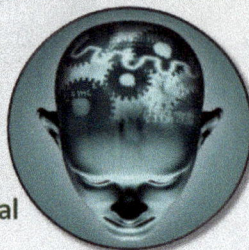

# What is "Formal" Logic?

- Also known as <u>Deductive</u> Logic.

- Evaluate an argument's <u>structure</u>, presented in a set of <u>premises</u>, that lead to a conclusion.

- <u>Premise</u> = statement or proposition that can be demonstrated to be TRUE.

- Each premise must stand on its own (i.e., be *true*) in a logical *sequence* of premises in order to move from "truth-to-truth" towards the conclusion.

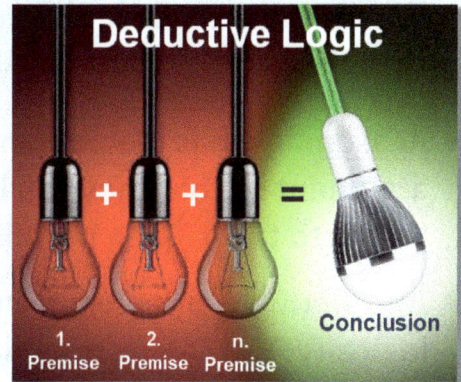

**Deductive Logic**

1. Premise  2. Premise  n. Premise  Conclusion

The Conclusion always follows with <u>CERTAINTY</u> from the Premises!

**The Conclusion in a Deductive Argument MUST be true IF...
The *Premises* supporting the Conclusion are true!**

William Lane Craig: "What is Logic?" (1:30)    Courtesy of Google Images    Fair Use Law 17 U.S. Code § 107

# "Formal" Logic: The Deductive Argument

Socrates

The Universe

Premise 1 = All men are mortal.

Premise 2 = Socrates is a man.

<u>Conclusion</u> = ☑ Socrates is mortal.

Premise 1 = Whatever begins to exist has a cause.

Premise 2 = The universe began to exist.

<u>Conclusion</u> = ☑ the universe has a cause.

**We use the process of DEDUCTION to discover new truths (conclusions) based accepted truths (premises)!**

Dr. William Lane Craig: "What Makes a Good Deductive Argument?" (1:21)    Dr. William Lane Craig: "The Kalaam Cosmological Argument" (4:12)    Courtesy of Google Images    Fair Use Law 17 U.S. Code § 107

# Evaluating a Deductive Argument

- We evaluate someone's deductive argument by determining if their REASONING is correct.

- Reasoning = has the person structured their argument so that they can logically move from "truth to truth" (i.e., premise-to-premise).

- Another way of saying it: Does their conclusion logically FOLLOW from their premises?

- We use the process of deduction to discover new truths (conclusions) based on accepted truths (premises).

**Deductive Arguments are the simplest form of logic because people use SIMPLE TRUTHS they already believe to arrive at NEW TRUTHS**

Courtesy of Google Images    Fair Use Law 17 U.S. Code § 107

# "Formal" Logic: Let's Try Some More Examples

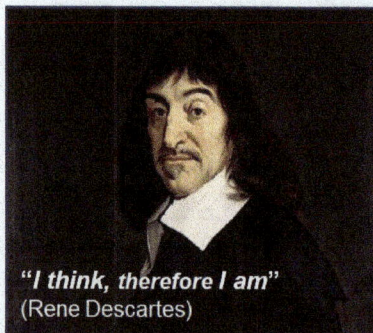

*"I think, therefore I am"*
(Rene Descartes)

Premise 1 = All beings that think exist.

Premise 2 = I think.

Conclusion = ☑ I exist.

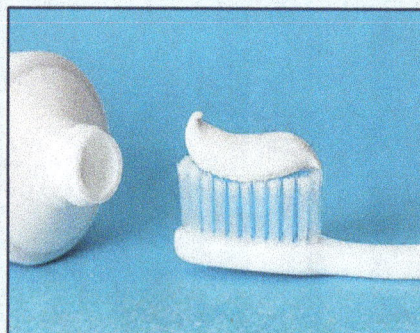

Premise 1 = People wanting whiter teeth use this toothpaste.

Premise 2 = I want whiter teeth.

Conclusion = ☑ I will use this toothpaste.

Premise 1 = Getting good grades requires studying.

Premise 2 = I want good grades.

Conclusion = ☑ I will study.

**"The heart of the righteous STUDIES how to answer"** Proverbs 15:28

Courtesy of Google Images    Fair Use Law 17 U.S. Code § 107

## Article 28 - The Romans Ladder of Character: Using Logic to Present Myself to Jesus Christ

Romans 6:19 *"Just as you presented your members as slaves of uncleanness, and of lawlessness leading to more lawlessness, so now present your members as slaves of righteousness for holiness."*

In his exposition of Romans, Watchman Nee now takes me to the third step and last step in what he has been detailing in the past two articles as the "Normal Christian Life": PRESENTING myself as God's SLAVE to a new lifestyle of HOLINESS. We'll examine all three: presenting, slave, and holiness.

Two weeks ago, we examined what it means to 'know' your old nature has been put to death at the cross by Christ, and then last week it was about 'reckoning' that God has pronounced you dead to sin by Christ's once-and-for-all accomplishment at the cross.

Now, by embracing these truths, Paul says it is only logical that you would see and understand how God has poured out His mercy on you, so you would desire to present yourself to Him as His slave, to live your life by His will and not your own. Nee says it this way: *"God requires of me that I now regard all my members, all my faculties, as belonging wholly to Him. It is a great thing when I discover I am no longer my own but His. Real Christian life begins with knowing this."*

God, through Paul, commands you to 'present' your members as slaves to do what is right in God's sight, as is fitting for holiness (i.e., separation) to Him. This Greek word for 'present' is 'paristemi', which does not mean to passively surrender or "give up". It means 'to actively yield, as a PRISONER'. Think of a criminal, who has broken the law and knows it.

God isn't saying to stop "running from the law" and finally give up. God means you must turn yourself in. You come to God and present yourself as His prisoner, extending your arms, saying "here I am, put the cuffs on me, I'm your prisoner - do whatever You want with me.

This is a theme throughout the New Testament. In Romans 12:1, Paul exhorts you to be a living sacrifice, wholly available to Christ, to be used for His good purpose: *"I beseech you therefore brethren, by the mercies of God, that you PRESENT your bodies a living sacrifice, holy, acceptable to God, which is your reasonable service."*

By the way, Paul doesn't treat this total surrender to the Lord as something noble or spectacular, that somehow marks you as super-spiritual. He says this is your 'reasonable service'.

Paul gives the same message to the early Colossian church: *"…you, who once were alienated and enemies in your mind by wicked works, yet now He has reconciled in the body of His flesh through death, to PRESENT you holy, blameless, and irreproachable in His sight… Him we preach, warning every man and teaching every man in all wisdom, that we may PRESENT every man perfect in Christ Jesus."* (Colossians 1:21-22, 28).

Notice how God shows you here in verses 21 and 22 how He is the One responsible for taking you from His enemy, who was once completely alienated or shut off from a relationship with Him, to His perfect  man or woman, now with complete access to Him as your heavenly Father. How? He says by the accomplishment of Christ on the cross, who has reconciled you back to a relationship with Him by the payment of your sins through Christ's substitutionary death, on your behalf.

But what's this idea of being God's SLAVE to righteousness? The Greek word Paul uses here is "dulos", which means bondservant. Nee describes Paul's point here this way: "What's the difference between a servant and a bondservant, or slave? A servant may serve another, but the ownership does not pass to that other. If he likes his master he can serve him, but if he does not like him he can give in his notice and seek another master.

Not so is it with the slave. He is not only the servant of another but he is the possession of another. How did I become the slave of the Lord? On His part He bought me, and on my part I PRESENTED myself to Him. By right of redemption I am God's property, but if I would be His slave I must willingly give myself to Him, for He will never compel me to do so."

God's command for you is to be His willing slave to life of "holiness". This means you willingly separate yourself from your former life of sinfulness, and now separate yourself to Him, for Him.

In the Old Testament, God commanded each Jew to separate themselves to Him, as holy: *"I am the Lord your God. You shall therefore SANCTIFY yourselves and you shall be HOLY; for I am holy."* (Leviticus 11:44).

But now, with the historical reality of Jesus Christ's death and resurrection, God has extended this same free offer to you and I, and every other non-Jew: *"As He who called you is holy, you also be holy in all your conduct, as it is written, 'be holy, for I am holy."* (1Peter 1:15-16). It is totally your choice.

## Exit Ticket #6     Class 06: The Logic of Christianity Part 1

| | |
|---|---|
| **1) What is the definition of Logic?** | **2) What is "Deductive Logic"?** |
| **3) If the Premises in a deductive argument are true, what does that mean about the Conclusion?** | **4) Of the 7 Scriptures in this lesson, which 1-2 most resonate with you and why?** |

# Class 07: The Logic of Christianity Part 2

What is "Informal" Logic?

Informal Logic: Types of Inductive Arguments

Evaluating Deductive vs. Inductive Arguments

Case Studies: Combining Deductive & Inductive Arguments for Why God Exists

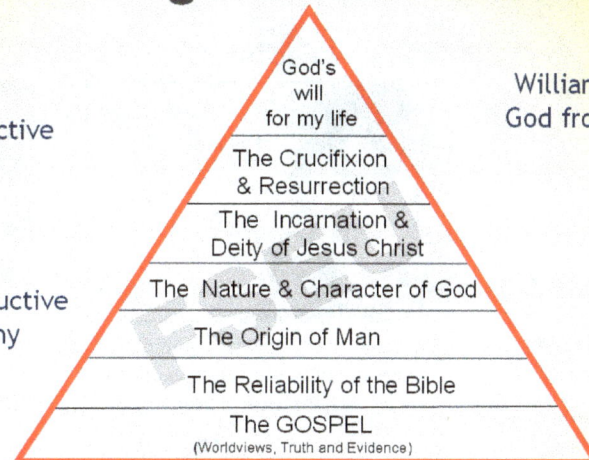

William Lane Craig: "Arguing God from a First Cause" (3:39)

**Pyramid (top to bottom):**
- God's will for my life
- The Crucifixion & Resurrection
- The Incarnation & Deity of Jesus Christ
- The Nature & Character of God
- The Origin of Man
- The Reliability of the Bible
- The GOSPEL (Worldviews, Truth and Evidence)

# HEBREWS 11:1

"Faith = *Substance* of things *hoped for*.... *Evidence* of things *not seen*"

**fse.life Lessons 02 - 08**

# What is "Informal" Logic?

- Also known as <u>Inductive</u> Logic.

- Evaluate an argument's <u>content</u>, presented in a group of evidences, to support a conclusion.

- <u>Evidence</u> = available information or facts to help determine if the conclusion is TRUE.

- The conclusion is probable, but not certain.

- We evaluate the weight and relevance of the evidence presented to reach a conclusion.

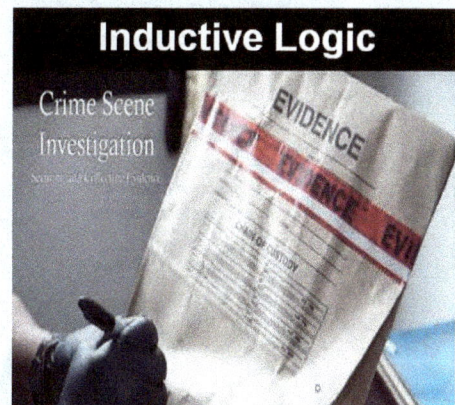

### Inductive Logic

Crime Scene Investigation

EVIDENCE

The Conclusion does not follow with certainty (as in deductive arguments) but rather PROBABILITY!

## While Deductive Logic argues from STRUCTURE... Inductive Logic argues from EVIDENCE!

# "Informal" Logic: Types of Inductive Arguments

### Statistics

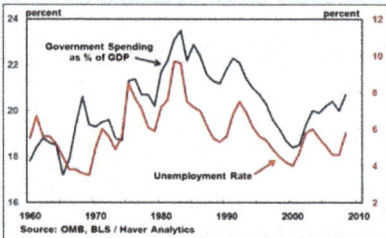

My conclusion is based on a data sample that represents the overall population

1) We surveyed 1,000 people who overwhelmingly said vanilla is the best ice cream

2) Therefore, vanilla is the best ice cream

### Anecdotes

"it worked for me" ✓

My conclusion is based on opinion, not actual data (it can't be reduced to a mathematical expression)

1) So far this year, the Chiefs have won 1 out of 3 games

2) Therefore, the Chiefs will win 33% of their games this year

### Inferences

My conclusion is based on data collected that relates to a specific past event.

*"It was a 16-ft great white shark that fatally attacked a man"*

1) Teeth pattern on surf board

2) Injuries on victim's body

3) Great whites known to frequent the area where attack occurred

## We use the process of INDUCTION to provide a general conclusion: It lacks certainty but can give the best (most reasonable) explanation!

Courtesy of Google Images    Fair Use Law 17 U.S. Code § 107

# Summarizing: Evaluating Deductive vs. Inductive Arguments

### Deductive Logic

Invalid ✗        Valid ✓

Does My Conclusion follow from my premises?

### Inductive Logic

CRIME SCENE RECONSTRUCTION

CRIME SCENE — DO NOT CROSS — CRIME SCENE — DO NOT C

**Stages**

Weak ✗        Strong ✓

- Data collection
- Hypothesis formation
- Examination, testing and analysis
- Determination of the significance of the evidence
- Theory formulation

## Deductive Arguments claim CERTAINTY... They are either VALID or INVALID

## Inductive Arguments claim PROBABILITY... They are either STRONG or WEAK

Courtesy of Google Images    Fair Use Law 17 U.S. Code § 107

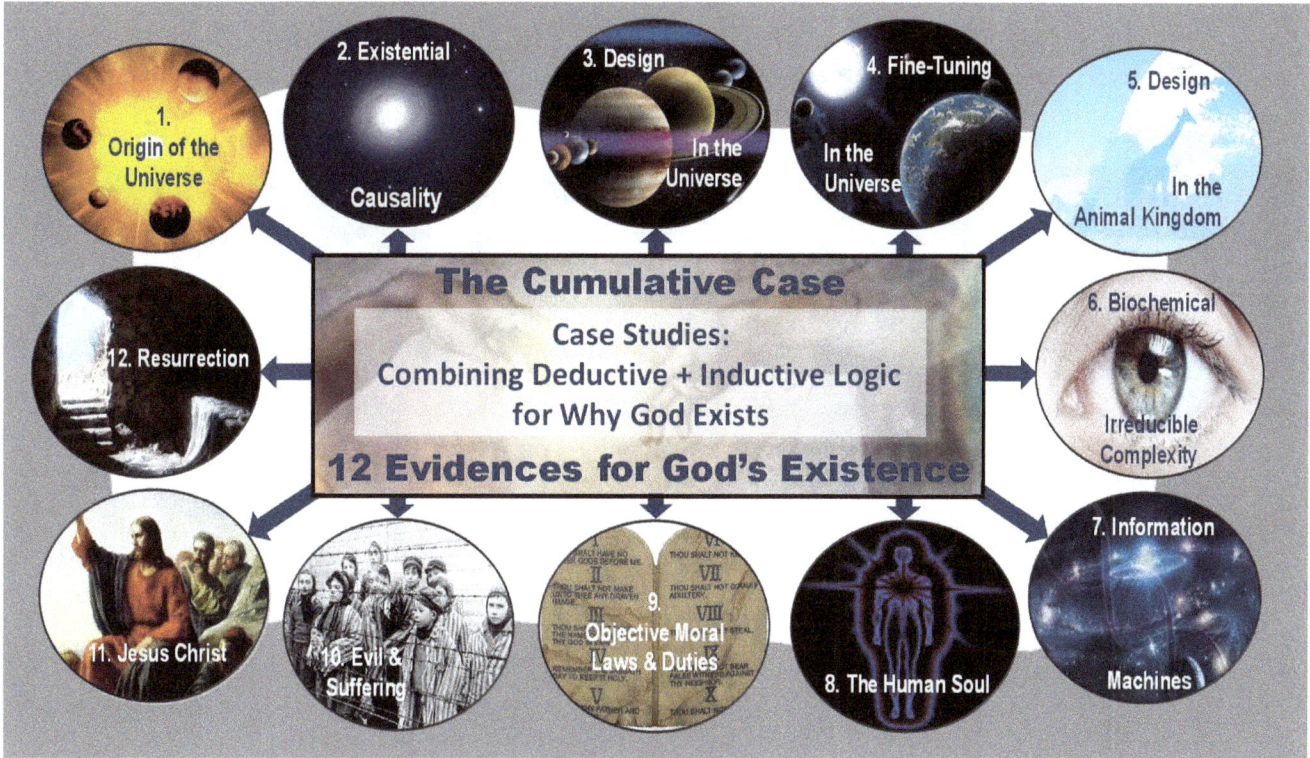

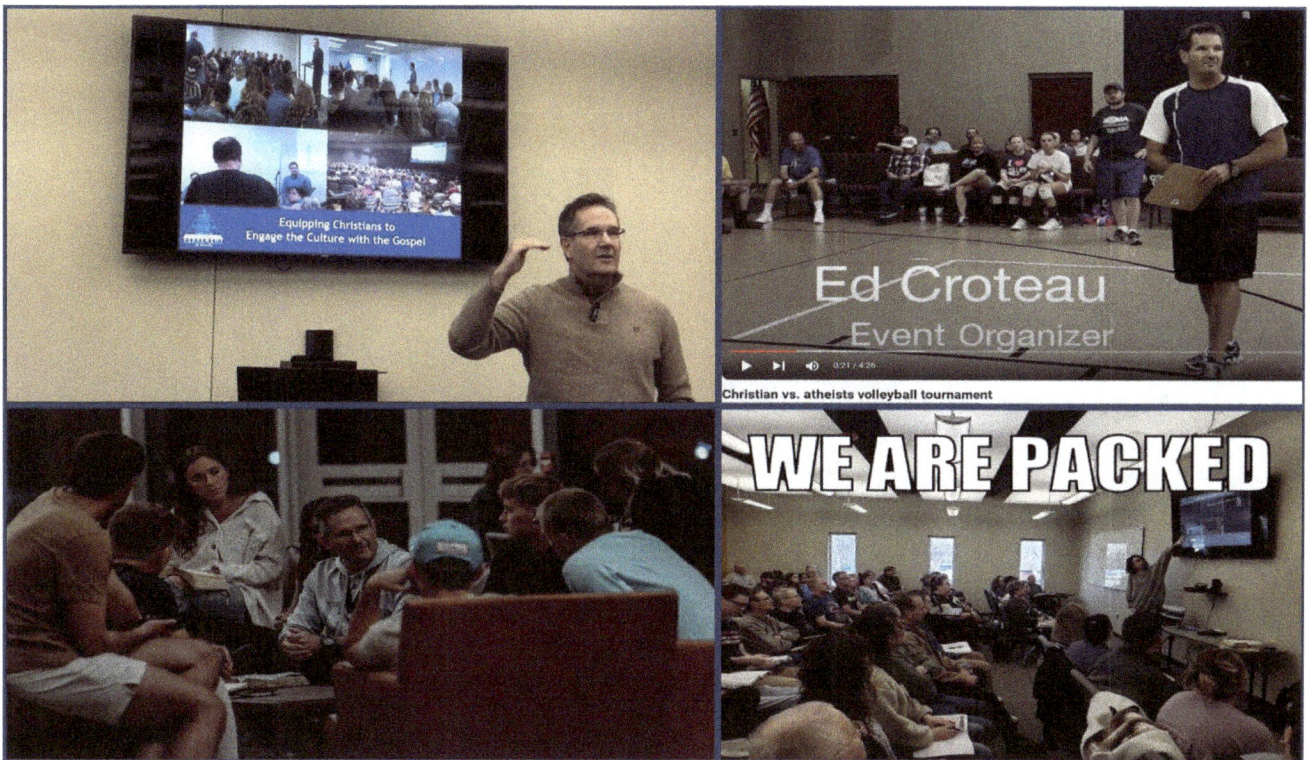

# Formal (Deductive) Arguments for God's Existence –
## Our Universe: Created, Designed, Finely Tuned

### Origin of the Universe

Premise 1 = Whatever begins to exist has a cause.

Premise 2 = The universe began to exist.

Conclusion = ☑ The universe has a cause.

### Design of the Universe

Premise 1 = All designs infer a designer.

Premise 2 = There is great design in the universe.

Conclusion = ☑ There is a Great Designer of the universe.

### Fine Tuning of the Universe

Premise 1 = Fine Tuning infers an intelligent designer.

Premise 2 = There is great fine tuning in the universe.

Conclusion = ☑ There is an Intelligent Designer of the universe

Closer to Truth – Dr. William Lane Craig: "Arguing God from a First Cause"     Courtesy of Google Images     Fair Use Law 17 U.S. Code § 107

# Formal (Deductive) Arguments for God's Existence –
## Our Biochemistry: Irreducibly Complex, Information Machinery

### Irreducible Complexity

Premise 1 = Irreducibly complex systems infer an intelligent design.

Premise 2 = There is irreducible complexity in the biochemical makeup of living organisms.

Conclusion = ☑ There is an Intelligent Designer of life.

### Information Machines

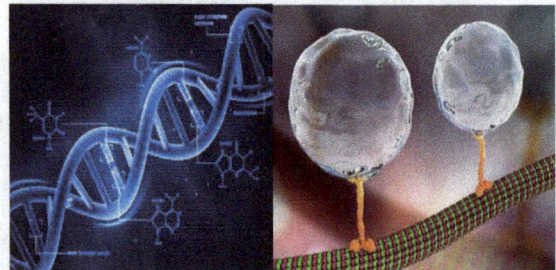

Premise 1 = Specified information infers an intelligent design.

Premise 2 = There is specified information in the DNA and Cells of living organisms.

Conclusion = ☑ There is an Intelligent Designer of life.

Courtesy of Google Images     Fair Use Law 17 U.S. Code § 107

# Formal (Deductive) Arguments for God's Existence –
## <u>Our Humanity</u>: Human Soul, Objective Morality

### The Human Soul

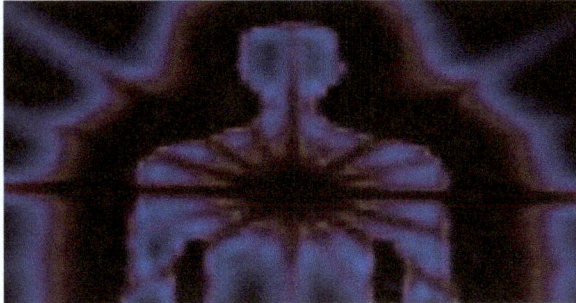

Premise 1 = Freedom to make moral choices can't be explained by physical laws.

Premise 2 = People make moral choices.

Conclusion = ☑ The source of people's moral choices is nonphysical, which the Bible calls the "soul".

### Objective Morality

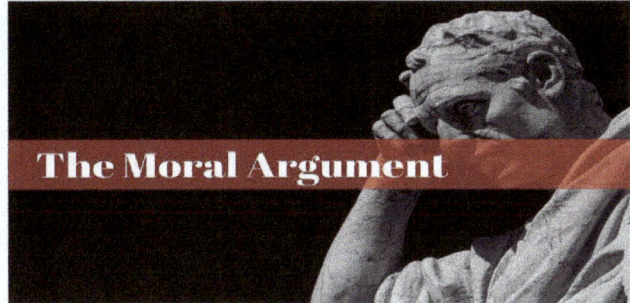

The Moral Argument

Premise 1 = If God does not exist, objective moral values and duties do not exist.

Premise 2 = Objective moral values and duties do exist.

Conclusion = ☑ God Exists.

# Formal (Deductive) Arguments for God's Existence –
## <u>Jesus Christ</u>: His Deity, His Resurrection

### The Deity of Jesus Christ

<u>Premise #1</u> = If a personal God exists, He would want us to know He exists.

<u>Premise 2</u> = Jesus Christ claimed God sent Him to make Himself known to us.

<u>Premise 3</u> = Jesus claimed to be God the Son, equal to the Father.

<u>Premise 4</u> = Jesus Christ said and did things that no man could say or do.

<u>Premise 5</u> = Jesus Christ fulfilled prophecies that no man could fulfill.

Conclusion = ☑ God exists, and made Himself known to all mankind in the Son, Jesus Christ.

### The Resurrection of Jesus Christ

<u>Premise #1</u> = There are 4 established facts concerning the fate of Jesus of Nazareth:
1) His honorable burial by Joseph of Arimathea,
2) the discovery of his empty tomb,
3) His post-mortem appearances, and
4) the origin of his disciples' belief in the resurrection.

<u>Premise 2</u> = The hypothesis "God raised Jesus from the dead" is the best explanation of these facts.

<u>Premise 3</u> = The hypothesis "God raised Jesus from the dead" entails that God exists.

Conclusion = ☑ God exists, and made Himself known to all mankind in the Son, Jesus Christ.

**Exit Ticket #7**          <mark>**Class 07: The Logic of Christianity  Part 2**</mark>

| | |
|---|---|
| **1) What is "Informal Logic"?** | **2) What is the difference in how to evaluate Deductive versus Inductive Arguments?** |
| **3) For the Argument from Design, why would most people say Premise 1 is true?** | **4) Of the 8 Scriptures in this lesson supporting the Deity of Christ, which 1-2 resonate the most and why?** |

# Class 08:  Worldviews

What is My "Worldview"?

Article 400 - Awakening to a Biblical Worldview – Be Intentional in Bible Study with Jesus Christ

5 Major Religious Worldviews

There is a God – How the World's Most Notorious Atheist Changed His Mind

3 Cultural Worldviews in American Society

10 Philosophies Behind Cultural Worldviews

The 10 Philosophies Defined

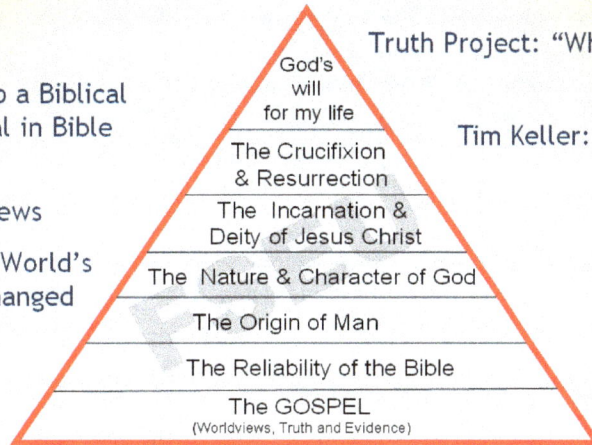

Truth Project: "What is a Worldview?" (2:38)

Tim Keller: "Are All Religions Equally Wrong?" (5:45)

**Pyramid (top to bottom):**
- God's will for my life
- The Crucifixion & Resurrection
- The Incarnation & Deity of Jesus Christ
- The Nature & Character of God
- The Origin of Man
- The Reliability of the Bible
- The GOSPEL (Worldviews, Truth and Evidence)

# HEBREWS 11:1

"Faith = *Substance* of things *hoped for…. Evidence* of things *not seen*"

**fse.life Lessons 02 - 08**

# What is My "Worldview"?

## Worldview ("Weltanschauung")

The window through which I view the world and decide…

what is real, *TRUE* and important, or…

What is unreal, false and not important.

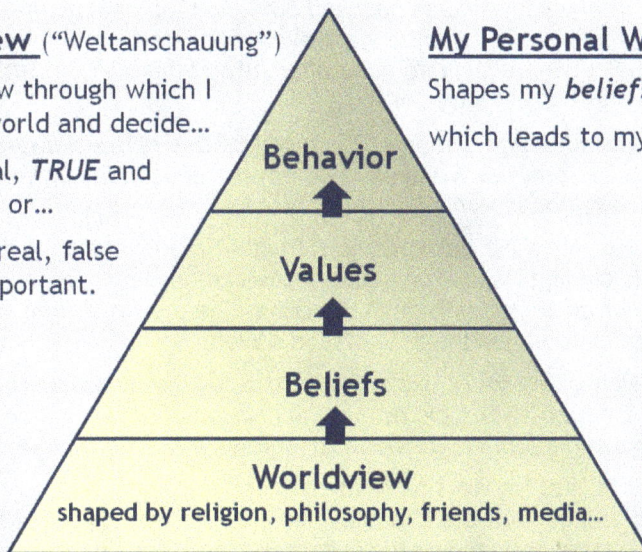

## My Personal Worldview

Shapes my *beliefs*…  and forms my *values*…

which leads to my *behavior*… which shapes a CULTURE*

**Pyramid (top to bottom):**
- Behavior
- Values
- Beliefs
- Worldview
  shaped by religion, philosophy, friends, media…

I often don't see my worldview

But I see          everything else by looking through it.

**PROVERBS 23:7** *"As a man thinks in his HEART, so is he."*

*Culture = collective manifestations of human intellect (arts, customs, social institutions) of a social group (nation, people, etc.)

The Truth Project: 'What is a Worldview?' (2:38)

## Article 400 - Awakening to a Biblical Worldview – Be Intentional in Bible Study with Jesus Christ

Galatians 1:18 "After three years I went up to Jerusalem to see Peter, remaining with him fifteen days."

We are first introduced to the apostle Paul in the New Testament book of Acts. We know that he is one of if not the greatest apostle of the Christian faith, responsible for authoring 14 of the 27 books in our New Testament, including the epistle to the Galatians from which our verse for this week is taken.

His teaching style is unlike the other apostles. Paul is very logic-oriented, often posing questions to get us to think through what we believe and why we believe it. For example, in this same epistle to the Galatian church, Paul asks this question: "Having begun in the Spirit, are you now being made perfect by the flesh?" (Gal. 3:3).

In other words, if the Spirit of God brought you into a saving relationship with Him, do you now become perfected in God's sight though your own works of the flesh? This is Paul in full flight.

So how did Paul, who was once zealous for God as an expert practitioner of the Mosaic law, become not only the author of more than half of the doctrinal teachings of a radical new religious movement, but also a central figure in changing the culture of his world? The answer to this question is in our verse this week.

Very early in Paul's conversion to Christianity, not only did he surrender his life to the Lordship of Jesus Christ, but he then retreated to a 3-year period of study with Christ Himself as His teacher. It was only afterwards that he joined the original apostles to begin the work of the ministry. Here's his explanation in Galatians 1:15-18:

*"When it pleased God, who … called me by his grace, to reveal his Son in me, that I might preach Him among the Gentiles, I did not immediately confer with flesh and blood, nor did I go up to Jerusalem to those who were apostles before me; but I went to Arabia, and returned again to Damascus. Then after 3 years I went up to Jerusalem to see Peter, and remained with him 15 days."*

Does this 3-year period of teaching time with Jesus sound familiar? This was Paul's 3 years with the Lord, just as the first apostles had spent 3 years with Christ while He was here on earth. Few of us realize that Paul's preparation to preach the gospel required a 3-year personal study time with Jesus Christ.

How does this apply to us today? Pastor Randy Frazee, from Westside Family Church, preached at my church this past Sunday to share with the congregation George Barna's analysis of where American Christianity is today: *"7 of 10 Americans claim to be Christians, but only 6% possess a biblical worldview."*

What do we mean by "worldview"? It literally means 'a view of the world'. It is the window by which you view the world and decide, often subconsciously, what is real and important, or unreal and unimportant. Understanding worldview is a bit like trying to see the lens of your own eye. We do not ordinarily see our own worldview, but we see everything else by looking through it. Pastor Frazee continued:

*"The number of American adults holding a biblical worldview has declined 50% over the past quarter century (since 1995). Regarding the youngest adult generation, the numbers are even more startling. A mere 2% of those 18-29 years old possess a biblical worldview. So, we are just one generation away from biblical Christianity going extinct."* What solution was offered to reverse this biblical "free-fall"?

His message: *"The solution has to go beyond one hour on Sunday. This might be one of the blessings of COVID-19. We are spending more time at home, with our families. We need to be having focused family time in teaching the gospel of Jesus Christ to our children, to develop in them a biblical worldview."*

For our youth, and their parents, to be equipped with a biblical worldview, Pastor Frazee is offering the same solution that was used by the early apostles (including Paul). To be an effective ambassador for Jesus Christ, we must first and foremost study and know Him, which we learn through His Bible. There is no greater weapon against the onslaught of secularized American culture than the truth of God's Word.

Paul calls the Bible the "sword of the Spirit" (Ephesians 6:17), explaining how it transforms lives: *"The word of God is living and powerful, sharper than any 2-edged sword, piercing to the division of soul and spirit, and of joints and marrow, and is a discerner of the thoughts and intents of the heart"* (Hebrews 4:12-13).

Our ministry here at FSE University (our website is at fse.life) has as its header "Equipping Young Adults (and Their Parents) to Defend their Faith." Parents and their children can develop a biblical worldview by studying the Bible and then be equipped to share their faith by understanding the culture we live in today.

| DOES GOD EXIST? The 5 Religious Worldviews | | Dr. Geisler ('Christian Apologetics')[29] |
|---|---|---|
| **Worldview** | **Where it contributes...** | **Where it fails as a Worldview...** |
| **DEISM**<br><br>• God created the natural world but is beyond the world, never operating in it in miraculous ways;<br>• The world operates by natural and self-sustaining laws of the Creator.<br>• Deny the Trinity, Deity of Christ, Virgin Birth.<br>• Deny miracles<br><br>Forms of Naturalism | 1) God reveals something personal about Himself through His creation;<br>2) emphasizes using reason in religious matters, to separate truth from falsehood<br>3) use reason to evaluate miracles (don't use miracles as answer for anything you don't understand)<br>4) historical attacks on Christianity gave rise to scholarly defenses of orthodox Christianity | 1) it is self-defeating to admit the miracle of creation but deny other lesser miracles (like the Virgin Birth, walking on water) are possible.<br>2) It is inconsistent to disallow personal communication from the supernatural to the natural realm once admitting God is personal.<br>3) A God concerned enough and strong enough to create man should be concerned and strong enough to help. So, God's nature is compatible with miraculous intervention in the natural world when He deems it.<br>4) Deist arguments to eliminate belief in supernatural revelation also apply to eliminate belief in creation.<br>5) Deism has failed to cast sufficient doubt on the supernatural either in principle or in fact (Deist criticism of trustworthiness of biblical documents and writers is definitely lacking): (a) archaeological confirmation of Scripture is overwhelming (> 25,000 finds confirm biblical world), (b) integrity of eyewitnesses has been sufficiently established, (c) Bible's alleged contradictions have been answered, (d) no scientific errors have been proven in the Bible |
| **PANTHEISM**<br><br>• Polar opposite of Deism<br>• God is the world, and the world is God.<br>• God does not transcend reality but is imminent in reality (all reality is in God). Beyond God is only illusion.<br>• Creation from nothing is meaningless since creation flows from God.<br>• God is an It, not a He (impersonal, beyond rational knowledge).<br>• God is beyond good or evil, and just is. Evil is an illusion.<br>• God is understood not by observation nor by rational inference but by intuition that is beyond the law of noncontradiction (opposing statements on God can both be true).<br><br>Hinduism, Taoism, Native American Religion, Gnosticism | 1) It is both metaphysical and comprehensive (not a piecemeal philosophy) = this is essential in any worldview.<br>2) emphasizes unity (since there is a uni-verse, there must be a basis in reality for uni-ty).<br>3) emphasizes that God is really in the world, at least within the depths of the human soul.<br>4) emphasizes that only one God is absolute and necessary – none of creation is independent or ontologically detached – all is completely dependent on God who is All in all.<br>5) emphasizes the direct and unmediated intimacy with God, the object of knowledge.<br>6) often expresses God in terms of what he is not – 'via negativa' – God can't be expressed in positive terms with limited meaning, since he is infinite and transcendent (all limitations must be negated from terms applied to him). | 1) It is unaffirmable by man, since no finite reality exists that is different from God (the pantheist must affirm, 'God is but I am not', which is self-defeating, since one must exist in order to affirm he doesn't).<br>2) to avoid the above self-defeating argument, pantheists allow some reality to finite man, as only a *self*-conscious mode or aspect of God. But if this is true, why aren't people conscious of this? If I am unconscious of my own existence, how does a pantheist know he is not being deceived when he claims to be conscious of reality as an aspect of God?<br>3) Fellowship and worship is impossible since finite man is not real but only a mode or aspect of God, who is ultimate reality.<br>4) If evil is not real, why is it so persistent and seem so real? Making evil a part of God does not explain evil – it puts God beyond the laws of logic, with no distinction between good and evil.<br>5) God is not personal, but an impersonal force driven by metaphysical necessity and not by volitional and loving choice.<br>6) Since God is 'All' with the universe (the Whole is a collection of all its finite parts or aspects), pantheism is metaphysically the same as atheism ('the universe is all there is, all there was, and all there will ever be'). The only difference is pantheism attributes religious significance to the All, and atheism doesn't.<br>7) To say 'God is All', including things that are opposite, violates the Law of Noncontradiction and says nothing meaningful about him.<br>8) Claiming only what God is not tells one nothing about Him and is meaningless. Pantheist writings contain no information, so why write? It is self-defeating to communicate a view on God only to inform the audience that he has not done so. |

| DOES GOD EXIST? | The 5 Religious Worldviews | Dr. Geisler ('Christian Apologetics')[29] |
|---|---|---|
| **Worldview** | **Where it contributes…** | **Where it fails as a Worldview…** |
| **ATHEISM**<br><br>There is no God, either in or beyond the world.<br><br>Secular Humanism, Buddhism | 1) The principle of Sufficient Reason (that everything needs a cause or explanation) leads to an infinite regress and not to God.<br>2) God cannot have the cause of himself within himself (a self-caused Being is impossible).<br>3) If a moral law exists, it either results from God's will or it doesn't. If by his will, it's arbitrary since he can call anything good. If not from his will, he is subject to it and not God.<br>4) An all-powerful God could destroy evil; an all-good God would destroy evil. But evil exists, so God is either: (a) impotent and can't destroy evil, (b) malevolent and won't destroy evil, (c) both a and b, (d) doesn't exist.<br>5) An all-wise, all-powerful, all-good God would not allow any unjust suffering. One injustice in the world argues against God being all-just.<br>6) It is possible the world happened by blind chance. The universe may be just a 'happy accident'.<br>7) I am free to determine myself, and be accountable to my own actions, so there is no God. | 1) The principle of Causality does not demand that everything needs a cause, but only finite, changing, dependent beings need a cause.<br>2) The principle of causality leads to an infinite, necessary and uncaused Being, which is not contradictory as self-caused.<br>3) Moral law doesn't flow from God's arbitrary will – it is rooted in His unchanging good and loving nature. He is bound by who He is, the very essence of His Person.<br>4) Just because evil is not yet defeated in time by an all-loving, all-powerful God, doesn't mean He never will. And God has done something to this point to defeat evil. Christians believe evil was defeated by Christ on the Cross, and evil will be destroyed when Christ returns. In fact, I can trust in His guarantee that He will one day do just that. A finite God cannot offer such hope. Rather than evil eliminating the logical possibility of God, only God can guarantee the elimination of evil.<br>5) If atheism claims there is unjust suffering in the world, there must be a standard of justice beyond this world, otherwise how can anyone judge what is unjust? But this brings us back to God, the ultimate standard for justice. So atheism's claim there exists a just standard is self-defeating since it points to God.<br>6) The odds against a chance explanation of such an immense universe are great, while the evidences for a designed universe exist.<br>7) Knowing what men will do with their freedom isn't the same as ordaining what men must do against their freedom. Love is persuasive, but never coercive, making God responsible for the fact of freedom but not responsible for the acts of freedom, thus allowing men to determine their own destiny. |
| **PANEN-THEISM**<br><br>• God is *in* the world (Pantheism says God *is* the world).<br>• The world is the 'body' of God. God is to the world as the mind is to the body.<br>• God is finite and limited, in a continual process of change.<br>• God isn't the Creator, but a Cosmic Director. | 1) argue metaphysics that allow classical truth testing (ontology, teleology, morality).<br>2) God transcends the world, so they avoid the self-defeating identification of God and the real world (i.e., Pantheism).<br>3) stresses God's personal interaction with the real world.<br>4) God's being in the world is what saves it from chaos (without Him the world would not exist).<br>5) points to the need to explain the God of Scripture as a personal God of ceaseless creative activity (He actively sustains the creative world process, and is active in history and manifest in nature).<br><br>Hinduism, Ba'Hai Faith, Sikhism, | 1) the bipolar concept of God as eternal potential seeking temporal actualization is self-defeating (no potential can actualize itself - it must be activated by something outside itself, which would lead to a theistic God of pure act in order to account for a panentheistic god).<br>2) A finite, changing god must have an infinite and unchanging basis for its change. Change makes no sense unless there is an unchanging basis by which change is measured (the relative presupposes the absolute).<br>3) A finite god cannot guarantee the defeat of evil, and holds out little prospect for a better world: (a) how does a finite, limited god who cannot triumph over evil assure us there is any real growth in value in the universe? (b) does the supposed increase in value justify the countless numbers of evils suffered to gain it? What significance is there in suffering for the individual?<br>4) the concept of god is based on what he does, not what he is (the error of man creating god in his own image) – there is activity but no Actor, movement but no Mover, creation but no Creator. This god is impotent in being limited in power and always changing. |

| DOES GOD EXIST?     The 5 Religious Worldviews     Dr. Geisler ('Christian Apologetics')[29] | | |
|---|---|---|
| **Worldview** | **Where it contributes…** | **Where it fails as a Worldview…** |
| **THEISM**<br><br>• God is both beyond and within the world, a Creator and Sustainer who sovereignly controls the world and supernaturally intervenes in it.<br><br>*3 Important Points*:<br>*1) Reality must be viewed in terms of the possible, the impossible, or the necessary – there are no other logical possibilities (and logic can be applied to reality).*<br>*2) The world and God are either caused, self-caused or uncaused - there are no other logical possibilities.*<br>*3) Based on 1) and 2) above, forming a metaphysical world-view that includes all the possibilities about reality and to eliminate some as actually impossible, and to establish the remaining one as actually necessary, is not an arbitrary position but a logical one.*<br><br>Monotheism = Christianity, Judaism, Islam, Zoroastrianism<br>Polytheism = Hinduism, Egyptian & Greek Religions | **1) Every finite effect has a cause; the world is a finite effect; therefore, the world has a cause** (whatever exists that has the potential to not exist, i.e., might not exist, is an 'effect' caused to exist by another, i.e., is contingent on another causing it to exist).<br>**2) The world is a whole, not just its parts, needs a cause** (the very nature of the caused parts demands that the whole group of them taken together must be caused – for example, by the very nature of a wooden table, if each part is made of wood, then the whole table must be wooden).<br>**3) An Infinite Regress of causes is impossible** (in an infinite series every cause is being caused by another – if there were one cause that was causing but not being caused it would be the uncaused cause which the infinite series seeks to avoid. So, this one (or more) cause that is doing the causing of every other cause must be causing itself, since it too is being caused by the causality in the series. But the only causality in the series is being given to the series by that cause itself. So, this one cause would be causing itself - it would be a self-caused being, which is impossible.<br>**4) The terms 'Necessary Being' and 'Uncaused Cause' are meaningful** (God is not a logically necessary Being; i.e., we're not making an A Priori argument, but the statement 'God exists' is a logically necessary statement, based on #1 above). An actual effect demands an actual cause, and a contingent being demands a necessary Being to ground it. So, it follows that the actual contingent world demands an actually necessary Being as its cause. | 1) *A Priori Arguments Alone* for God are logically invalid – no reality, including God, can be established by logical necessity (you can't argue for God's existence based on the *concept* of an absolutely perfect or necessary Being (even if it is logically necessary to *conceive* of a necessary Being as necessarily existing, it does not follow that It necessarily exists).<br>2) *A Posteriori Arguments Alone* for God are also logically invalid (experience is never logically necessary – the existence of God cannot be proven without appealing to some principle that is independent of experience). If it is logically possible that *something(s)* can exist without a cause, then any theistic argument based on this principle fail.<br><br>↑<br><br>• *Most criticisms of theism miss the significance of the argument based on existential causality and are directed toward invalid A Priori arguments, such as the ontological argument, or toward insufficient A Posteriori arguments that either assume an unjustified causal premise (as the teleological and moral arguments), or else are based on a rationally unjustified form of the principle of sufficient reason. In this sense neither A Priori nor A Posteriori proofs for God's existence are rationally inescapable.*<br><br>• *There is however a valid argument that COMBINES both the A Priori self-evident principle of existential causality and the undeniable A Posteriori fact that something exists (e.g., I exist). The criticisms of this argument are insufficient.*<br><br>• ***Theism has found a firm ground in existence for the conclusion that God exists. This is a theistic universe."*** |

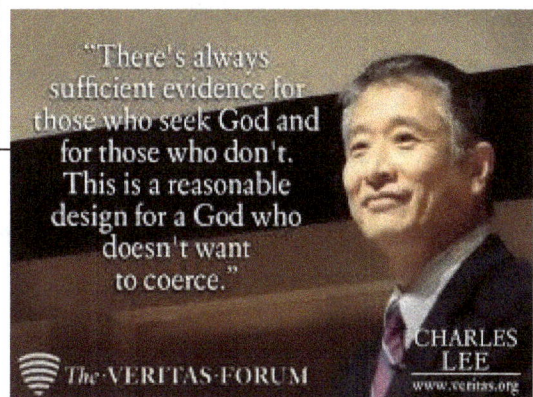

## "There is A God"
## by Dr. Antony Flew[5]

Dr. Antony Flew was the author of over 30 professional philosophical works that helped set the agenda for atheism for over half a century. His 'Theology and Falsification', presented first to the Oxford University Socratic Club (chaired by C.S. Lewis) in 1950, became the most widely printed philosophical publication of the last century. As Ravi Zacharias once said, Flew was the standard for studying atheistic philosophy in his university education.

Dr. Flew wrote for over 50 years on anti-theology with an admired approach that was systematic, comprehensive, original and extremely influential. Why?

### There is a God – How the World's Most Notorious Atheist Changed His Mind

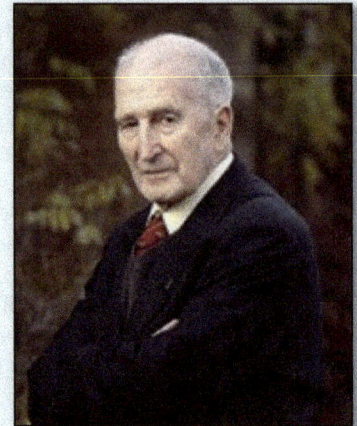

*"My discovery of the Divine has been a pilgrimage of reason and not faith."*

**Antony Flew**
**Page 93**

*"It speaks very well of Professor Flew's honesty. After all these years of opposing the idea of a Creator, he reverses his position on the basis of the evidence."*
Alvin Plantinga

Because unlike so many others such as Dr. Bertrand Russell, Flew's writings didn't originate from a disdain for organized religion. Rather, his focus was on, as he claimed from the very beginning, developing arguments to support HIS position, grounded in the Socratic Method: "We must follow the argument wherever it leads."

Dr. Flew makes two straight-forward confessions in this book that not only prompted many Christian apologists and theologians to praise his openness and courage, but also raised the hostility of atheist leaders to denounce him as "old and senile". On page 12, he says this: *"I have said in some of my later atheist writings that I reached the conclusion about the nonexistence of God much too quickly, much too easily, and for what later seemed to me the wrong reasons"*. Ouch. Then, on pages 29 and 32: *"No one is as surprised as I am that my exploration of the Divine has after all these years turned from denial to discovery… it took years for my philosophical views to mature and solidify. By the time they did so, I had arrived at the guiding principles that would not only govern my lifetime of writing and reasoning, but also eventually dictate a dramatic turn FROM ATHEISM TO THEISM."*

So what exactly prompted Dr. Flew to become a theist? On page 88, Dr. Flew explains: *"It's time for me to lay my cards on the table, to set my own views and the reasons that support them. I now believe that the universe was brought into existence by an Infinite Intelligence. I believe that this universe's intricate laws manifest what scientists have called the Mind of God. I believe that life and reproduction originate in a divine Source. Why do I believe this, given that I expounded and defended atheism for more than half a century (about 60 years)? The short answer is this: this is the world picture, as I see it, that has emerged from modern science… and a renewed study of the classical philosophical arguments."*

Dr. Flew's book was published around the same time many of the New Atheists were gaining in popularity and the phenomenon on college campuses of the Veritas Forum was taking center stage, as a more collegial debate structure also gained popularity in pitting the best Christian apologists against the New Atheism spokesmen.

But Dr. Flew's arguments against atheism, and for theism, have gone largely unnoticed in this age of internet instant information and rhetorical arguments supplanting good old "butt in the seat" diligent study. On page 89, Dr. Flew himself explains what actually led him away from atheism and to theism: *"My departure from atheism was not occasioned by any new phenomenon or argument. Over the past two decades, my whole framework of thought has been in a state of migration. This was my consequence of MY CONTINUING ASSESSMENT OF THE EVIDENCE OF NATURE.*

*When I finally came to recognize the existence of a God, it was not a paradigm shift, because my paradigm remains, as Plato in his 'Republic' scripted Socrates to insist: 'WE MUST FOLLOW THE ARGUMENT WHEREVER IT LEADS."*

In his book, Dr. Flew asks 32 questions to his fellow atheists. These questions are not new – but they are coming from one of the greatest, if not the greatest, atheist philosophical minds in history – and they are meant to be a challenge to atheists to really examine the evidence, because it will lead any open-minded seeker away from atheism and to theism.

# Does God Exist?   5 Major Religious Worldviews

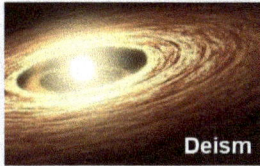

### Deism
**Forms of Naturalism**
1. God created the world but never operates in it
2. The world operates by self-sustaining laws
3. No miracles, no Trinity, no Deity of Christ

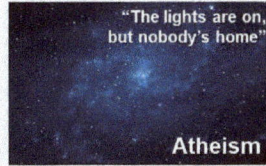

### Atheism
"The lights are on, but nobody's home"
- Secular Humanism
- Buddhism
1. Who created God?
2. Evil & Suffering prove God doesn't exist
3. Universe and life are happy accidents

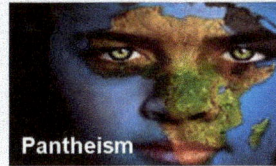

### Pantheism
- Hinduism   • Taoism
- Gnosticism
1. God is the world, the world is God
2. God is impersonal (beyond knowledge)
3. Evil is an illusion

### Panentheism
- Hinduism   • Ba'Hai Faith
- Sikhism
1. God is *IN* the world (the world is God's 'body')
2. God is finite and limited
3. God is Cosmic Director (not the Creator)

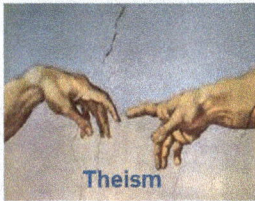

### Theism
**Monotheism**
- Christianity
- Judaism
- Islam

**Polytheism**
- Greek & Egyptian Religions
- Hinduism

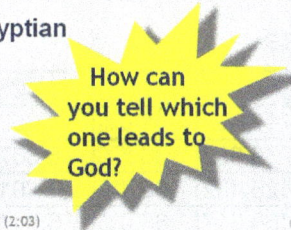

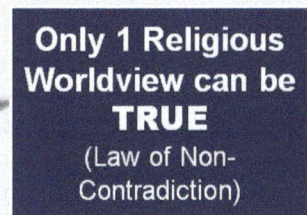

1. God is both beyond (Creator) and in the world (Sustainer)
2. God is personal (can be known)

*How can you tell which one leads to God?*

**Only 1 Religious Worldview can be TRUE**
(Law of Non-Contradiction)

Tim Keller, Veritas Forum - 'Are All Religions Equally Wrong?' (5:45)   Tim Hawkins, 'Atheist Kids' Songs' (2:03)     Courtesy of Google Images     Fair Use Law 17 U.S. Code § 107

# What the World Believes:
## Understanding the Three Major Global Religions outside Christianity

**ISLAM** (Ergun and Emir Caner, "Unveiling Islam"[32]) – Middle East, Africa

Allah: the "Distant One"
The Allah we worshipped as Muslims was a remote judge.
When Christians speak of the intimacy and grace of God, it confuses a Muslim.
In all the terms and titles of Allah, one does not encounter terms of intimacy.
Even the most faithful and devout Muslim refers to Allah only as a servant to master; Allah is a distant sovereign.

Allah: the "Cold Judge"
Islam looks to a god of the scales, as opposed to the atoning Son of God.
Allah forgives only at the repentance of the Muslim, and all consequences for sin and the debt of guilt fall on the Muslim, who comes to Allah in terror, hoping for commutation of his sentence.
One sees a judge, as opposed to a God of Love.

Allah: the "Hater"
Allah's heart is set against the infidel.
He has no love for the unbeliever, nor is a Muslim to "evangelize" the unbelieving world.
Allah is to be worshipped, period.
The theme is conquest, not conversion, of the unbelieving world.

## Middle East

| Country | Population | Muslim | | Christian | |
|---|---|---|---|---|---|
| Pakistan | 156,483,155 | 150,349,015 | 96.1% | 3,614,761 | 2.3% |
| Iran | 67,702,199 | 67,038,717 | 99.0% | 223,417 | 0.3% |
| Turkey | 66,590,940 | 66,351,213 | 99.6% | 213,091 | 0.3% |
| Uzbekistan | 24,317,851 | 20,305,406 | 83.5% | 316,132 | 1.3% |
| Iraq | 23,114,884 | 22,386,765 | 96.9% | 358,281 | 1.6% |
| Afghanistan | 22,720,000 | 22,240,608 | 97.9% | 4,544 | 0.0% |
| Saudi Arabia | 21,606,691 | 20,057,491 | 92.8% | 980,944 | 4.5% |
| Yemen | 18,112,066 | 18,101,199 | 99.9% | 9,056 | 0.1% |
| Syria | 16,124,618 | 14,560,530 | 90.3% | 822,356 | 5.1% |
| Turkmenistan | 4,459,293 | 4,095,415 | 91.8% | 120,401 | 2.7% |
| Oman | 2,541,739 | 2,355,175 | 92.7% | 64,560 | 2.5% |
| United Arab Emirates | 2,441,436 | 1,623,555 | 66.5% | 227,054 | 9.3% |
| Kuwait | 1,971,634 | 1,723,800 | 87.4% | 161,082 | 8.2% |
| | 428,186,506 | 411,188,889 | 96.0% | 7,115,678 | 1.7% |

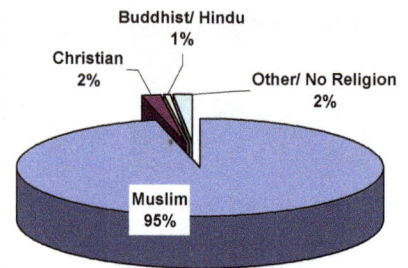

Buddhist/ Hindu 1% — Christian 2% — Other/ No Religion 2% — Muslim 95%

## Africa

| Country | Population | Muslim | | Christian | |
|---|---|---|---|---|---|
| Nigeria | 111,506,095 | 45,717,499 | 41.0% | 58,652,206 | 52.6% |
| Egypt | 68,469,695 | 59,239,980 | 86.5% | 8,887,366 | 13.0% |
| Algeria | 31,471,278 | 30,426,432 | 96.7% | 91,267 | 0.3% |
| Sudan | 29,489,719 | 19,168,317 | 65.0% | 6,841,615 | 23.2% |
| Morocco | 28,220,843 | 28,178,512 | 99.9% | 14,110 | 0.1% |
| Somalia | 10,097,177 | 10,092,128 | 100.0% | 5,049 | 0.1% |
| Tunisia | 9,585,611 | 9,553,020 | 99.7% | 21,088 | 0.2% |
| Libya | 5,604,722 | 5,408,557 | 96.5% | 168,142 | 3.0% |
| Mauritania | 2,669,547 | 2,665,276 | 99.8% | 4,271 | 0.2% |
| | 297,114,687 | 210,449,721 | 70.8% | 74,685,114 | 25.1% |

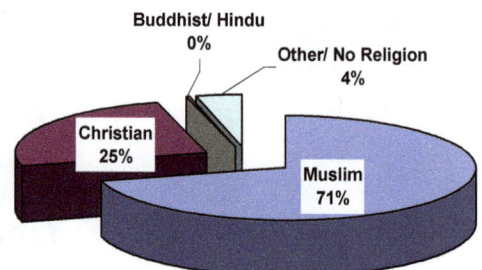

Buddhist/ Hindu 0% — Other/ No Religion 4% — Christian 25% — Muslim 71%

## BUDDHISM (Lit-Sen-Chang, "Zen-Existentialism: The Spiritual Decline of the West") – Far East

Zen Buddhism is a subtle form of Atheism: it is the love of self first, last and always.

It denies the infinity and transcendence of a living, personal God.

It denies the need of a Savior, thus denying the true God and the gift of His grace, by exalting and deifying man.

Salvation can be secured by man's own power and wisdom.

In Zen Buddhism, there is no supernatural intervention. We bear the whole responsibility for our actions and no Sage whosoever he be has the right to encroach on our free will.

## HINDUISM (Walter Martin, "The Kingdom of the Cults"[33]) – Far East

There is no single Hindu idea of God.

He can be pantheist (all existence), animist (all nonhuman objects such as rocks, trees, animals, etc.), polytheist (many gods to worship), henotheist (many gods, but only one worshipped), monotheist (only one god).

Hinduism believes that all souls are eternal and accountable for their actions throughout time.

There is no need for a personal relationship to a Savior, who by grace takes the punishment for their sins.

Rather, it is through "karma" (wheel of suffering) and "reincarnation" (soul inhabits successive human bodies) their bad actions are atoned for as they strive to achieve self-realization ("nirvana") through ritualistic sacrifice and discipline.

## Far East

| Country | Population | Other or No Religion | | Buddhist/ Hindu | | Muslim | | Christian | |
|---|---|---|---|---|---|---|---|---|---|
| China | 1,262,556,787 | 1039968025 | 82.4% | 105,802,259 | 8.4% | 25,251,136 | 2.0% | 91,535,367 | 7.3% |
| India | 1,013,661,777 | 45614780 | 4.5% | 817,011,392 | 80.6% | 126,707,722 | 12.5% | 24,327,883 | 2.4% |
| Indonesia | 212,991,926 | 3194879 | 1.5% | 4,685,822 | 2.2% | 171,032,517 | 80.3% | 34,078,708 | 16.0% |
| Bangladesh | 129,155,152 | 839508 | 0.7% | 16,790,170 | 13.0% | 110,595,557 | 85.6% | 929,917 | 0.7% |
| Vietnam | 79,831,650 | 29649475 | 37.1% | 43,109,091 | 54.0% | 558,822 | 0.7% | 6,514,263 | 8.2% |
| Burma | 45,611,177 | 1870058 | 4.1% | 38,039,722 | 83.4% | 1,733,225 | 3.8% | 3,968,172 | 8.7% |
| North Korea | 24,039,193 | 22551167 | 93.8% | 1,081,764 | 4.5% | 0 | 0.0% | 406,262 | 1.7% |
| Nepal | 23,930,490 | 552794 | 2.3% | 21,728,885 | 90.8% | 1,196,525 | 5.0% | 452,286 | 1.9% |
| Malaysia | 22,244,062 | 1379132 | 6.2% | 5,916,920 | 26.6% | 12,901,556 | 58.0% | 2,046,454 | 9.2% |
| Sri Lanka | 18,827,054 | 84722 | 0.4% | 15,801,546 | 83.9% | 1,506,164 | 8.0% | 1,434,622 | 7.6% |
| Tajikistan | 6,188,201 | 564364 | 9.1% | 0 | 0.0% | 5,538,440 | 89.5% | 85,397 | 1.4% |
| Laos | 5,433,036 | 1953176 | 36.0% | 3,319,585 | 61.1% | 59,763 | 1.1% | 100,511 | 1.9% |
| Tibet | 2,500,000 | 490000 | 19.6% | 2,000,000 | 80.0% | 5,000 | 0.2% | 5,000 | 0.2% |
| | 2,846,970,505 | 1,148,712,081 | 40.3% | 1,075,287,156 | 37.8% | 457,086,425 | 16.1% | 165,884,842 | 5.8% |

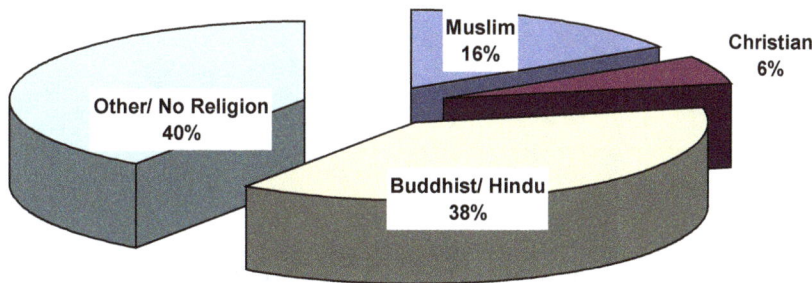

# 3 *Cultural* Worldviews in American Society

| Modern | Postmodern | Christian |
|---|---|---|
|  |  |  |
| • truth can be known, but it is based on what I can see, or reason out | • absolute truth doesn't exist, OR…. it may exist, but it cannot be known | • truth can be known - it is based on the reality as defined by God Himself |
| • places value on man's ability to **reason** (Rene Descarte: "I think, therefore I am") | • places value on **authenticity** above reason ("I am skeptical of your claim to certainty - how can you be so sure?") | • places value on man's capacity to **reason** (God has created man with the capacity to think) |
| • The Enlightenment & Scientific Revolution (late 1600's up to WWII) - truth requires empirical certainty | • Post-World War II until today: mans' scientific & technological advances have turned out to fail us: they are not the answers to our society's problems | • The Bible: God **transcends** our physical world. He has communicated objective truths to us in a language (God's word) that we can understand |

## The 10 *Philosophies* Behind Our Cultural Worldviews:
## Can Truth be Known?

**Modernist**
- Rationalist
- Realist
- Subjectivist

**Postmodernist**
- Pragmatist
- Fideist
- Relativist
- Perspectivist
- Skeptic
- Agnostic

**Christian**
- Objectivist  Absolutist

**Objectivist** = regardless of my opinion
Subjectivist = depends on my opinion

**Absolutist** = regardless of my circumstances
Relativist = depends on my circumstances

Charlie Kirk vs. Narcissist College Student (16:20)          Courtesy of Google Images   Fair Use Law 17 U.S. Code § 107

| Ten Epistemologies People use to Build Their Worldview | | | | |
|---|---|---|---|---|
| **Epistemology** | **What it is** | **What it sounds like** | **Example** | **Worldview** |
| Relativism | truth is defined on the group or the culture in which I grew up | "My beliefs are based on how I was raised" | growing up in India | Postmodernism |
| Subjectivism | truth is defined based on what you personally believe is true | "that's my belief (don't try to change me)" | personal preference | Postmodernism |
| Perspectivism | truth is synthesized with others' views (take into account the other person's perspective) | "my spouse's view weighs in on any decision I make" | marriage | Postmodernism |
| Pragmaticism | truth is defined based on what works for that person | "I'm not happy, so my situation must change" | divorce | Postmodernism |
| Skepticism | truth requires verification (the skeptic *doubts* that anything can be known) | "why should I believe that?" | TV commercials | Postmodernism |
| Agnosticism | means 'no knowledge'; we know reality is true, but we *can't know* what it is | "if God created man, who created God?" | belief in the supernatural is illogical | Postmodernism, Modernism |
| Rationalism | Truth is defined by what is knowable by human reasoning (evidence is not necessary) | "The cosmos is all there is, was, and ever will be" | mathematical equations | Modernism |
| Realism | Some truth can be known when supporting evidence resolves any reasonable doubts | "innocent until proven guilty beyond reasonable doubt" | America's Legal System | Postmodern, Christian |
| Fideism | Truth is personal (subjective), so I just believe it without having to prove it | "the Bible is true because I have faith" | emotional commitment | Christian |
| Objectivism | Truth is defined by reality; truth transcends culture, people, situations; it applies to all | "I'm bound by it, whether I like it or not" | Law of Gravity | Christian |

**Exit Ticket #8**    <mark>**Class 08: Worldviews**</mark>

| | |
|---|---|
| **1) How would you define "Worldview"?** | **2) How does someone's worldview shape their behavior?** |
| **3) Name 3 Cultural Worldviews in America; give 1 trait of each one?** | **4) Explain how Proverbs 23:7 applies to a person's worldview?** |

# Class 09:  Modernism

3 Cultural Worldviews in America Today

Modernism: Trying to Understand It

Modernism's Emergence Today:
Secular Humanism

Where Modernism Has It's
Greatest Impact:  Education

What do Government
Lobbyists promote?

Dr. William Lane Craig: "What Good is
Apologetics in a Postmodern Culture?" (4:55)

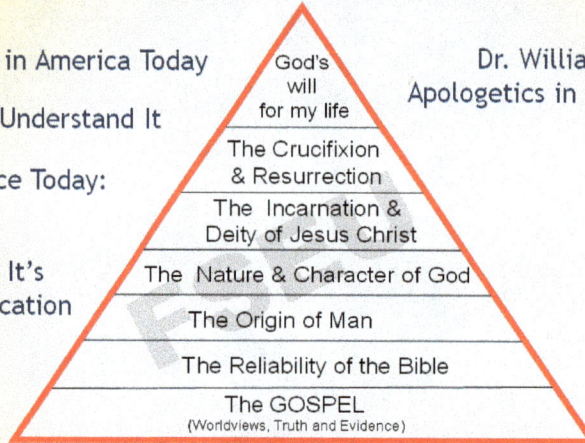

God's
will
for my life

The Crucifixion
& Resurrection

The Incarnation &
Deity of Jesus Christ

The  Nature & Character of God

The Origin of Man

The Reliability of the Bible

The GOSPEL
(Worldviews, Truth and Evidence)

# H E B R E W S 11:1

"Faith = *Substance* of things *hoped for*.... *Evidence* of things *not seen*"

**fse.life Lessons 02 - 08**

## 3 *Cultural* Worldviews in American Society

| Modern | Postmodern | Christian |
|---|---|---|
| • truth can be known, but it is based on what I can see, or reason out | • absolute truth doesn't exist, OR.... it may exist, but it cannot be known | • truth can be known - it is based on the reality as defined by God Himself |
| • places value on man's ability to **reason** (Rene Descarte: "I think, therefore I am") | • places value on **authenticity** above reason ("I am skeptical of your claim to certainty - how can you be so sure?") | • places value on man's capacity to **reason** (God has created man with the capacity to think) |
| • The Enlightenment & Scientific Revolution (late 1600's up to WWII) - truth requires empirical certainty | • Post-World War II until today: mans' scientific & technological advances have turned out to fail us: they are not the answers to our society's problems | • The Bible: God **transcends** our physical world. He has communicated objective truths to us in a language (God's word) that we can understand |

## Worldview #1 in America:      *MODERNISM (SECULAR HUMANISM)*

Stephen Gould ("Ever Since Darwin"): *"Before Darwin, we thought that a benevolent God had created us. No intervening spirit watches lovingly over the affairs of nature. No vital forces propel evolutionary change. And whatever we think of God, his existence is not manifest in the products of nature."*

Richard Dawkins ("The Blind Watchmaker"): *"Darwin made it possible to be an intellectually fulfilled atheist."*

Isaac Asimov (Pres., American Humanist Assoc.): *"Humanism is a NON-THEISTIC RELIGION. Emotionally, I am an atheist. I don't have the evidence to prove that God doesn't exist, but I so strongly suspect that he doesn't that I don't want to waste my time."*

### The Humanist Manifesto (1933):

1) "The universe is self-existing and not created;

2) "Man is a part of nature and has emerged as a result of a continuous process;

3) "The universe, by *modern science*, makes unacceptable any supernatural guarantees of human values;

4) "Realization of human personality is the end of man's life; the goal is its development and fulfillment in the here and now;

5) "*Man is the result of a blind and random process that does not necessitate any kind of meaning*;

6) "*Humanism is fostered by the teaching of EVOLUTION*."

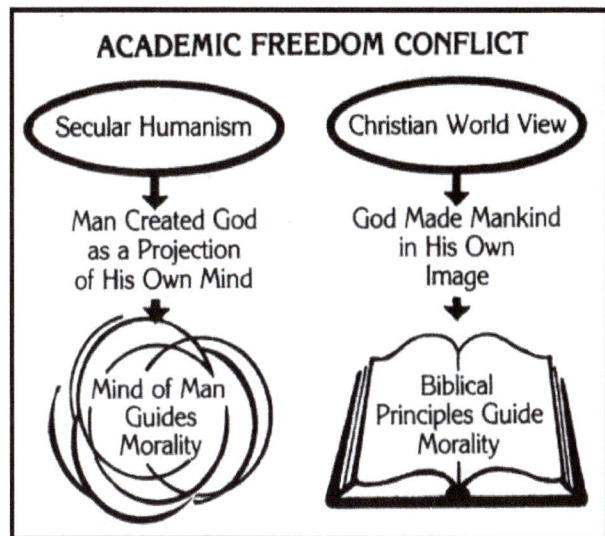

ACADEMIC FREEDOM CONFLICT

Secular Humanism → Man Created God as a Projection of His Own Mind → Mind of Man Guides Morality

Christian World View → God Made Mankind in His Own Image → Biblical Principles Guide Morality

### Isaiah 44:9-10, 13-20 "Idol Worship of 'self': Secular Humanism"

*"Those who make a graven image, all of them are useless, and their precious things shall not profit; they are their own witnesses; they neither see nor know, that they may be ashamed. Who would form a god or cast a graven image that profits him nothing? The craftsman stretches out his rule, he marks one out with chalk; he fashions it with a plane, he marks it out with the compass, and MAKES IT LIKE THE FIGURE OF A MAN. According to the beauty of a man, that it may remain in the house. He hews down cedars for himself, and takes the cypress and the oak; he secures it FOR HIMSELF among the trees of the forest. He plants a pine, and the rain nourishes it.*

*Then it shall be for a man to burn, for he will take some of it and warm himself; yes, he kindles it and bakes bread; indeed he MAKES A GOD and WORSHIPS IT; he makes a carved image, and falls down to it. He burns half of it in the fire; with this half he eats meat; he roasts a roast, and is satisfied. He even warms himself and says, 'Ah! I am warm, I have seen the fire.' And the rest of it he makes into a god, his carved image. He falls down before it and worships it, prays to it and says, 'Deliver me, for you are my god.'*

*They do not know nor understand; for He has shut their eyes, so that they cannot see, and their hearts, so that they cannot understand. And no one considers in his heart, nor is there knowledge nor understanding to say, 'I have burned half of it in the fire, yes, I have also baked bread on its coals; I have roasted meat and eaten it; and shall I make the rest of it an abomination? Shall I fall down before a BLOCK OF WOOD?' He feeds on ashes; a DECEIVED HEART has turned him aside; and he cannot deliver his soul, nor say, 'IS THERE NOT A LIE IN MY RIGHT HAND?'"*

> John MacArthur (commentary on Isaiah ):    *"Like eating ashes, which provide no nourishment, idolatry is a deception, from which the sinner gets nothing but judgment."*

### What's an *IDOL*, anyway?

1) Greek *"eidōlon"* = an image or IDEA made to represent a false god, that is worshipped (1Corin. 8:4-6).

2) Hebrew *"ĕlyil"* = "vanity", or "thing of naught" (Leviticus 19:4) – this is what Paul meant in Acts 14:15-17 when he said what represented a deity to Gentiles was a "vain thing".

3) Romans 1:22-25 = God traces idolatry (sin of the mind against God) and immorality (sins of the flesh) to a lack of acknowledging Him and showing Him gratitude.

4) An idolater = slave to the depraved ideas his idols represent (Galatians 4:8-9).

### N. Pearcey[3]: "Its not *if* I worship…. It's the *object* of my worship that determines my destiny"

*"Humans are inherently religious beings, created to be in relationship with God - and if they reject God, they don't stop being religious; they simply find some other ultimate principle upon which to base their lives. Often that idol is something concrete, like financial security or professional success; in other cases, it may be an ideology or set of beliefs that substitutes for religion. They are far from religiously neutral."*

# Modernism:   Trying to Understand It

1) A trend of thought that affirms the **power of human beings** to create, improve, and reshape their environment.

2) A focus on science and technology to explain nearly all aspects of life.

3) Modern (quantum and relativistic) physics, modern (analytical and political) philosophy and modern number theory in mathematics date from this period.

4) Modernism encompasses the works of thinkers who **rebelled** against 19th century "traditional" forms of art, architecture, literature and religious faith, claiming they are outdated for today's sophisticated "free thinker".

## Modernism

- **Modernistic literature** is the expression of the modern era (1901-45). It tends to revolve around themes of individuality, the randomness of life, mistrust of government and religion and the disbelief in absolute truth.

**Modernism's Failure:**

Science and materialism can't answer the key questions

Who am I?   Why Am I Here?
Where Did I Come From?

# Modernism's Emergence Today:   Secular Humanism

**The Humanist Manifesto (1933):**

1) The universe is self-existing and not created.

2) Man is a part of nature and has emerged as a result of a continuous process.

3) The universe, by *modern science*, makes unacceptable any supernatural guarantees of human values.

4) Realization of human personality is the end of man's life; the goal is its development and fulfillment in the present.

5) Man is the result of a blind and random process that does not necessitate any kind of meaning.

6) Humanism is fostered by the teaching of *EVOLUTION*.

**ACADEMIC FREEDOM CONFLICT**

Secular Humanism

Man Created God as a Projection of His Own Mind

Mind of Man Guides Morality

Christian World View

God Made Mankind in His Own Image

Biblical Principles Guide Morality

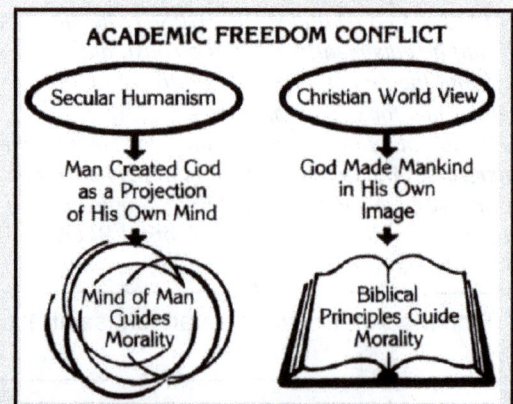

**ISAIAH 44:9-20** Idol Worship of Self:  Secular Humanism

*"Shall I fall down before a BLOCK OF WOOD?'
A DECEIVED HEART has turned him aside; and he cannot deliver his soul,
nor say, 'IS THERE NOT A LIE IN MY RIGHT HAND?'"*

## John 18:37-38    Which Worldview is *TRUE?*

*"'Everyone who is of the truth hears My voice.'    Pilate said to Him, 'What is Truth?'"*

| | Secular Humanism   Worldview | Christian Worldview |
|---|---|---|
| **Ultimate Reality** | Ultimate reality is impersonal matter; no God exists. <br> Carl Sagan[8]: *"The cosmos is all that is, or ever was, or ever will be"…. "We live on a hunk of rock and metal that circles a humdrum star that is one of 400 billion other stars that make up the Milky Way Galaxy, which is one of billions of other galaxies, which make up a universe, which may be one of a very large number – perhaps an infinite number – of other universes. That is a perspective on human life and our culture that is well worth pondering."* | Ultimate reality is an infinite, personal, loving God. <br> Isaiah 42:8 *"I am the Lord, that is My name; and My glory I will not give to another."* <br> Psalm 100:3 *"Know that the Lord, He is God; it is He who made us, and not we ourselves; we are His people, and the sheep of His pasture."* <br> Psalm 14:1 *"The fool says in his heart, 'There is no God.'"* |
| **Universe** | The universe was created by chance, accidental events without ultimate purpose. <br> C.S. Lewis[8]: *"If the solar system was brought about by an accidental collision, then the appearance of life was also an accident, and the whole evolution of man was an accident too. If so, then all our present thoughts are accidents – the accidental by-product of the movement of atoms. And this holds for the thoughts of the materialists and astronomers as well as for anyone else's. But if their thoughts are merely accidental by-products, why should we believe them to be true? I see no reason for believing that one  accident should be able to give me a correct account of all the other accidents."* | The universe was created by God for a purpose. <br> Isaiah 45:12 *"I have made the earth, and created man on it. It was I – My hands stretched out the heavens, and all their host I commanded."* <br> Isaiah 45:18 "*For thus says the Lord, who created the heavens, who is God, who formed the earth and made it, who has established it, who did not create it in vain, who formed it to be inhabited."* <br> Psalm 19:1-3 *"The heavens declare the glory of God; the firmament shows His handwork. Day unto day utters speech and night unto night reveals knowledge. There is no speech nor language where their voice is not heard."* |
| **Man** | Man is the product of the evolutionary process (time plus chance plus matter). Man's value, dignity or meaning is subjectively derived. <br> Donald Kalish (UCLA Prof.)[8]: *"There are no ethical truths. You are mistaken to think that anyone ever had the answers. There are none. Be brave and face up to it."* <br> J.W. Burrow (evolutionist)[8]: *"Nature, according to Darwin, was the product of blind chance and a blind struggle, and man is a lonely, intelligent mutation, scrambling with the brutes for his sustenance."* | Man was created by God in His image and is loved by Him. All men have eternal value and dignity. Their value is not derived from them, but from God. <br> Genesis 1:26 *"Let Us make man in Our image, according to Our likeness."* <br> Jeremiah 29:11-13 *" I know the thoughts that I think toward you, says the Lord, thoughts of peace and not of evil, to give you a future and a hope... you will seek Me and find Me, when you search for Me with all your heart."* |
| **Morality** | Morality is defined by each person by his views and interests. Every person is the final authority. <br> Nietzsche[8]: *"Everything lacks meaning. The advantage of our times is that nothing is true, everything is permitted."* <br> Jeremiah18:12 *"And they said, 'That is hopeless! So we will walk according to our own plans, and we will every one do the imagination of his evil heart."* | Morality is defined by God and immutable because it is based on God's unchanging character. <br> Proverbs 21:30 *"There is no wisdom or understanding or counsel against the Lord."* <br> Micah 6:8 *"He has shown you, O man, what is good; and what does the Lord require of you but to do justly, to love mercy, and to walk humbly with your God?"* |
| **Afterlife** | The afterlife = eternal annihilation (personal extinction) for everyone. <br> William Provine, Cornell Univ. Evolutionary Biologist and Historian[8]: *"If Darwinism is true, then there are five inescapable conclusions: 1) there's no evidence for God, 2) there's no life after death, 3) there's no absolute foundation for right and wrong, 4) there's no ultimate meaning for life, 5) people don't really have free will."* | The afterlife: either eternal life with God (personal immortality) or eternal separation from Him (personal judgment). <br> Prov. 23:17-18 *"Do not let your heart envy sinners, but in the fear of the Lord continue all day long; for surely there is a hereafter, and your hope will not be cut off."* <br> Matthew 25:46 *"...these will go away into everlasting punishment, but the righteous into eternal life."* |

## Why Christianity is on the rise:  The Empty Message in Secular Humanism
The following are excerpts from Dinesh D'Souza's book 'What's So Great About Christianity'[13]

- *"The traditional churches, not the liberal churches, are growing in America. In 1960, for example, the churches affiliated with the Southern Baptist Convention had 8.7 million members. Now (2007) they have 16.4 million… If secularization were proceeding inexorably, then religious people should be getting less religious, and so conservative churches should be shrinking and liberal churches growing. In fact, the opposite is the case.*

- *This is the way of secularization: the idea that as an inevitable result of science, reason, progress, and modernization, the West will continue to grow more secular, followed by the rest of the world. The secularization thesis was based on the presumption that science and modernity would satisfy the impulses and needs once met by religion. But a rebellion against secularization suggests that perhaps important needs are still unmet, and so people are seeking a revival of religion – perhaps in a new form – to address their specific concerns within a secular society.*

- *Biologists like Dawkins and Wilson say there simply must be some natural and evolutionary explanation for the universality and persistence of religious belief, and they are right. There is such an explanation, and I am pleased to provide one in this chapter. The Reverend Randy Alcorn, founder of Eternal Perspective Ministries in Oregon, sometimes presents his audiences with two creation stories (Secular 'Tribe', or worldview vs. Christian 'Tribe', or worldview, parenthesis added) and asks them whether it matters which one is true:*

| Christian 'Tribe' | Secular 'Tribe' |
|---|---|
| *'You are a special creation of a good and all-powerful God. You are created in His image, with capacities to think, feel, and worship that set you above all other life forms. You differ from the animals not simply in degree but in kind. Not only is your kind unique, but you are unique among your kind. Your Creator loves you so much and so intensely desires your companionship and affection that He has a perfect plan for your life. In addition, God gave the life of His only Son that you might spend eternity with Him. If you are willing to accept the gift of salvation, you can become a child of God.'* | *'You are the descendant of a tiny cell of primordial protoplasm washed up on an empty beach three and a half billion years ago. You are the blind and arbitrary product of time, chance, and natural forces. You are a mere grab bag of atomic particles, a conglomeration of genetic substance. You exist on a tiny planet in a minute solar system in an empty corner of a meaningless universe. You are a purely biological entity, different only in degree but not in kind from a microbe, virus, or amoeba. You have no essence beyond your body, and at death you will cease to exist. In short, you came from nothing and are going nowhere.'* |
| *Which of the two tribes is more likely to survive, prosper, and multiply?* ||
| *The religious tribe is made up of people who have an animating sense of purpose.* | *The secular tribe is made up of people who are not sure why they exist at all.* |
| *The religious tribe is composed of individuals who view their every thought and action as consequential.* | *The secular tribe is made up of matter that cannot explain why it is able to think at all.* |
| *Should evolutionists like Dennett, Dawkins, Pinker, and Wilson be surprised, then, to see that religious tribes are flourishing? Throughout the world, religious groups attract astounding numbers of followers and religious people are showing their confidence in their way of life and in the future by having more children. By contrast, atheist conventions draw only a handful of embittered souls. The important point is not just that atheism is unable to compete with religion in attracting followers, but also that the lifestyle of practical atheism seems to produce listless tribes that cannot even reproduce themselves. "* ||

- *…Modernization helps people triumph over necessity but it also produces a profound crisis of purpose in modern life. The greater the effects of modernization, the stronger the social anxiety and the striving for 'something more'. As Wolfhart Pannenberg puts it, 'Secular culture itself produces a deep need for meaning in life and therefore also for religion.'… GK Chesterton calls this the '**REVOLT INTO ORTHODOXY**.' Like Chesterton, I find myself rebelling against extreme secularism and finding in Christianity some remarkable answers to both intellectual and practical concerns… Christianity is winning, and secularism is losing. The future is always unpredictable, but one thing seems clear. God is in the future, and atheism is on its way out.*

- *…it is not religion but atheism that requires a Darwinian explanation. Atheism is a bit like homosexuality: one is not sure where it fits into a doctrine of natural selection. Why would nature select people who mate with others of the same sex, a process with no reproductive advantage at all? It seems equally perplexing why nature would breed a group of people who see no brighter purpose to life or the universe. Here is where the biological expertise of Dawkins, Pinker or Wilson could prove illuminating. Maybe they can turn their Darwinian lens on themselves and help us understand how atheism, like the human tailbone and the panda's thumb, somehow survived as an evolutionary leftover of our primitive past."*

In his book 'What's So Great About Christianity'[13], Dinesh D'Souza explains how the combination of science and education have become the atheist's greatest tools for de-Christianizing the American culture:

## SCIENCE = The *Method* to spread Secular Humanism and minimize Christianity

• *"Alarmed by the rising power of religion around the world, atheists in the west today have grown more outspoken and militant. What we are witnessing in America is 'atheist backlash.' The atheists thought they were winning, but now they realize that, far from dying quietly, religion is on the global upswing. So the atheists are striking back, using all the resources they can command.*

• *Statistics suggest that in America the number of atheists is growing. The Pluralism Project at Harvard reports that people with no religious affiliation now number nearly forty million. That's almost 15 percent of the population, up from less than 10 percent in 1990, and so a virtual doubling of the atheist ranks in a single decade. In this book I use the term 'atheist' in its broad sense to refer to those who deny God and live as if He did not exist.*

• *The distinguishing element of modern atheism is its intellectual militancy and moral self-confidence. Yes, there is a bit of arrogance here, but in the view of the atheists it is justified. What gives the atheists such confidence? The answer, in a word, is* **SCIENCE**. *Many atheists believe that modern science – the best known way to accumulate knowledge, the proven technique for giving us airplanes and computers and drugs that kill bacteria – has vindicated the nonbeliever's position.*

• *While science relies on the principle that 'nothing is more sacred than the facts', Sam Harris charges that 'theology is now little more than a branch of human ignorance. Indeed it is ignorance with wings.'*

## EDUCATION = The *Means* to spread Secular Humanism and minimize Christianity

• *"How then should religion be eliminated? Our atheist educators have a short answer: through the power of science. One way in which science can undermine the plausibility of religion, according to biologist E.O. Wilson, is by showing that the mind is the product of* **EVOLUTION** *and that free moral choice is an illusion. 'If religion... can be systematically analyzed and explained as a product of the brain's evolution, its power as an external source of morality will be gone forever.' The objective of science education, according to biologist Richard Lewontin, 'is not to provide the public with knowledge of how far it is to the nearest star and what genes are made of.' Rather, 'the problem is to get them to reject irrational and supernatural explanations of the world, the demons that exist only in their imaginations, and to accept a social and intellectual apparatus, science, as the only begetter of truth.'*

• *How is all this to be achieved?... through* **INDOCTRINATION IN THE SCHOOLS**. *Some educators argue that children should be taught to have reverence for science, which can replace religion as the object of human veneration. 'We should let the success of the religious formula guide us', urged Carolyn Porco, a research scientist at the Space Science Institute in Colorado, at a 2006 conference on science and religion. 'Let's teach our children from a very young age about the story of the universe and its incredible richness and beauty. It is already so much more glorious and awesome and even comforting than anything offered by any scripture or God concept I know.'*

• *Philosopher Richard Rorty argued that secular professors in universities ought to 'arrange things so that students who enter as bigoted, homophobic religious fundamentalists will leave college with views more like their own.'... Indeed, parents who send their children to colleges should recognize that as professors 'we are going to go right on trying to discredit you in the eyes of your children, trying to strip your fundamentalist religious community of dignity, trying to make your views seem silly rather than discussable.'*

• *Biologist Kenneth Miller, who has testified in favor of evolution in court trials, admits that 'a presumption of atheism or agnosticism is universal in academic life... the conventions of academic life, almost universally, revolve around the assumption that religious belief is something that people grow out of as they become educated.'*

• *Children spend the majority of their waking hours in school. Parents invest a good portion of their life savings in college education to entrust their offspring to people who are supposed to educate them. Isn't it wonderful that educators have figured out a way to make parents the instruments of their own undoing? Isn't it brilliant that they have persuaded Christian moms and dads to finance the destruction of their own beliefs and values? Who said atheists weren't clever?*

# Where Modernism Has It's Greatest Impact:  Education

If I'm not sure *why* I believe what I have been taught is true...

And there are lots of people who want to *tell me* what is true...

It won't be long before I no longer believe what I *thought* was true.

Dr. William Lane Craig: "What Good is Apologetics in a Postmodern Culture?" (4:55)

Courtesy of Google Images   Fair Use Law 17 U.S. Code § 107

---

### Are Our Kids ready for College?  Do they know what they believe, and why they believe it?

*"Every child in America entering school at the age of 5 is insane because he comes to school with certain allegiances toward our founding fathers, toward his parents, toward a belief in a supernatural being, toward the sovereignty of this nation as a separate entity… its up to you TEACHERS to make all of these sick children well by creating the international children of the future."* - Chester M. Pierce , Professor of Education and Psychiatry, Harvard University , Address to the Association for Childhood Education International, April 1972.

*"And in fact, if Jesus did come back, the most likely people to put him back on the cross would be the Christians, and the most likely people to nail him to the cross would be the fundamentalist Christians. They would be the ones who would be nailing that !$%@# back to the cross, because he'd be the one who'd be refuting what they believe, and they wouldn't want that. Fair enough? So the most likely guys to be hammering in the nails, they are the guys who elected George Bush, and believe in the literal truth of the Bible, and don't believe in evolution, because they don't want to use reason, and they don't want to think, they'd rather stick to their illusions that hopefully may convince them that they don't have to be afraid at night when they are all alone, and the devil may whisper in their ears."* - Dr. Lee Carter, Arizona State University, Sept. 2007 during classroom lecture.

*"The battle for humankind's future must be waged and won in the PUBLIC SCHOOL CLASSROOM by teachers who correctly perceive their role as the proselytizers of a new faith: a religion of humanity - utilizing a classroom instead of a pulpit to carry humanist values into whatever they teach. The classroom must and will become an arena of conflict between the old and the new - the rotting corpse of Christianity, together with its adjacent evils and misery, and the new faith of humanism."* - John J. Dunphy, The Humanist, 1983

*"I think the most important factor leading us to a secular society has been the EDUCATIONAL FACTOR. Our schools may not teach Johnny to read properly, but the fact that Johnny is in school until he is 16 tends to lead toward the elimination of religious superstition. The average child now acquires a high school education, and this militates against Adam and Eve and all other myths of alleged history."* - Paul Blanchard.  '3 Cheers for our Secular  Sate' (The Humanist, April 1976).

## "The Declaration in Defense of Science and Secularism"
published Nov., 2006 at the press conference for the opening of The Center for Inquiry, in Washington, D.C.

*"We are deeply concerned about the ability of the United States to confront the many challenges it faces, both at home and abroad. Our concern has been compounded by the failure exhibited by far too many Americans, including influential decision-makers, to understand the nature of scientific inquiry and the integrity of empirical research. This disdain for science is aggravated by the excessive influence of religious doctrine on our public policies.*

*We are concerned with the resurgence of fundamentalist religions across the nation, and their alliance with political-ideological movements to block science. We are troubled by the persistence of paranormal and occult beliefs, and by the denial of the findings of scientific research. This retreat into mysticism is reinforced by the emergence in universities of "post-modernism," which undermines the objectivity of science.*

*These disturbing trends can be illustrated by the push for intelligent design (a new name for creationism) and the insistence that it be taught along with evolution. Some 37 states have considered legislation to mandate this. This is both troubling and puzzling since the hypotheses and theories of evolution are central to modern science. Moreover, the resilience of anti-evolution movements is supported not only by religious dogmatism but also by the abysmal public ignorance of basic scientific principles. Consider these facts:*

- *A recent poll by the Pew Research Center revealed that 64% of Americans are open to the idea of teaching intelligent design or creationism in public schools.*
- *Some 42% totally reject evolution or believe that present forms of life existed since the beginning of time. 38% would teach only creationism instead of evolutionary theory.*
- *Only 26% agree with the predominant scientific view that life evolved by processes of natural selection without the need for divine intervention.*
- *The percentage of individuals who accept the theory of evolution is lower in the United States than in any other developed country, with the exception of Turkey.*

*We think that these dismal facts portend a clear and present danger to the role of science in the U.S. In our view it is not enough to teach specific technical subjects—important as that is—but to convey to the public a general understanding of how science works. This requires both some comprehension of the methods of scientific inquiry and an understanding of the scientific outlook. The cultivation of critical thinking is essential not only for science but also for an educated citizenry—especially if democracy is to flourish. Unfortunately, not only do too many well-meaning people base their conceptions of the universe on ancient books—such as the Bible and the Koran—rather than scientific inquiry, but politicians of all parties encourage and abet this scientific ignorance.*

*It is vital that the public be exposed to the scientific perspective, and this presupposes the separation of church and state and public policies that are based on secular principles, not religious doctrine... Science transcends borders and provides the most reliable basis for finding solutions to our problems. We maintain that secular, not religious, principles must govern our public policy. This is not an anti-religious viewpoint; it is a scientific viewpoint.*

*To find common ground, we must reason together, and we can do so only if we are willing to put personal religious beliefs aside when we craft public policy. For these reasons, we call upon political leaders of all parties:*
*1) to protect and promote scientific inquiry,*
*2) to base public policy insofar as possible on empirical evidence instead of religious faith,*
*3) to provide an impartial and reliable source of scientific analysis to assist Congress, for example, by reviving the Congressional Office of Technology Assessment, and*
*4) to maintain a strict separation between church and state and, in particular, not to permit legislation or executive action to be influenced by religious beliefs.*

*Science and secularism are inextricably linked and both are indispensable if we are to have sound public policies that will promote the common good, not only of Americans but of the global community."*

### So what would the founder of Evolutionary Theory think of this "*Declaration*"?
### Charles Darwin: Letter to Asa Gray (22 May 1860):

*"I cannot anyhow be content to view this wonderful universe, and especially the nature of man, and to conclude that everything is the result of brute force. I am inclined to look at everything as resulting from designed laws, with the details, whether good or bad, left to the working out of what we call chance.*

*Not that this notion at all satisfies me. I feel most deeply that the whole subject is too profound for the human intellect. A dog might as well speculate on the mind of Newton. Let each man hope and believe what he can."*

**Just Thinking:**
**The Atheist Science Professor and the Christian Student debate FAITH**

Professor: "You are a Christian, aren't you, son?"

Student: "Yes, sir."

Professor: "So, you believe in God?"

Student: "Absolutely, sir."

Professor: "Is God good?"

Student: "Sure."

Professor: "Is God all powerful?"

Student: "Yes."

Professor: "My brother died of cancer even though he prayed to God to heal him. Most of us would attempt to help others who are ill. But God didn't. How is this God good then, hmm?"

(Student was silent).

Professor: "You can't answer, can you? Let's start again, young fella. Is God good?"

Student: "Yes".

Professor: "Is Satan good?"

Student: "No."

Professor: "Where does Satan come from?"

Student: "From God."

Professor: "That's right. Tell me, son, is there evil in this world?"

Student: "Yes."

Professor: "Evil is everywhere, isn't it?" And God did make everything. Correct?"

Student: "Yes."

Professor: "So who created evil?"

(Student didn't answer).

Professor: "Is there sickness? Immorality? Hatred? Ugliness? All these terrible things exist in the world, don't they?"

Student: "Yes, sir."

Professor: "So, who created them?"

(Student didn't answer).

Professor: "Science says you have 5 senses you use to identify and observe the world around you. Tell me, son, have you ever seen God?"

Student: "No, sir."

Professor: "Tell us if you have ever heard your God?"

Student: "No, sir."

Professor: "Have you ever felt your God, tasted your God, smelt your God? Have you ever had any sensory perception of God for that matter?"

Student: "No sir, I'm afraid I haven't."

Professor: "Yet you still believe in Him?"

Student: "Yes."

Professor: "According to empirical, testable, demonstrable protocol, Science says your God doesn't exist. What do you say to that, son?"

Student: "Nothing. I only have my FAITH."

Professor: "Yes, *FAITH*. And that is the problem Science has."

Student: "Professor, is there such a thing as heat?"

Professor: "Yes."

Student: "And is there such a thing as cold?"

Professor: "Yes."

**CHRISTIANITY:**

The belief that some cosmic Jewish Zombie can make you live forever if you symbolically eat his flesh and telepathically tell him that you accept him as your master, so he can remove an evil force from your soul that is present in humanity because a rib-woman was convinced by a talking snake to eat from a magical tree.

Makes perfect sense.

Student: "No, sir. There isn't."

(The Lecture Hall became very quiet with this turn of events).

Student: "Sir, you can have lots of heat, even more heat, superheat, mega heat, white heat, a little heat or no heat. But we don't have anything called cold. We can hit 458 degrees below zero which is no heat, but we can't go any further after that. There is no such thing as cold. Cold is only a word we use to describe the absence of heat. We cannot measure cold. Heat is energy. Cold is not the opposite of heat, sir, just the absence of it."

(There was pin-drop silence in the Lecture Hall).

Student: "What about darkness, Professor? Is there such a thing as darkness?"

Professor: "Yes. What is night if there isn't darkness?"

Student: "You're wrong again, sir. Darkness is the absence of something. You can have low light, normal light, bright light, flashing light. But if you have no light constantly, you have nothing and it's called darkness, isn't it? In reality, darkness isn't. If it is, well you would be able to make darkness darker, wouldn't you?"

Professor: "So what is the point you are making, young man?"

Student: "Sir, my point is your philosophical premise is flawed."

Professor: "Flawed? Can you explain how?"

Student: "Sir, you are working on the *premise of duality*. You argue that there is life and then there is death, a good God and a bad God. You are viewing the concept of God as something finite, something we can measure. Sir, Science can't even explain a thought. It uses electricity and magneticism, but has never seen, much less fully understood, either one. To view death as the opposite of life is to be ignorant of the fact that death cannot exist as a substantive thing. *Death is not the opposite of life, just the absence of it*. Now tell me Professor, do you teach your students that they evolved from a monkey?"

Professor: "If you are referring to the natural evolutionary process, yes, of course I do."

Student: "Have you ever observed evolution with your own eyes, sir?"

(The Professor shook his head with a smile, beginning to realize where the argument was going).

Student: "Since no one has ever observed the process of evolution at work and cannot even prove that this process is an on-going endeavor, are you teaching your opinion, sir? Are you not a scientist but a preacher?"

(The class was in an uproar).

Student: "Is there anyone in the class who has ever seen the Professor's brain?"

(The class broke out in laughter).

Student: "Is there anyone here who has ever heard the Professor's brain, felt it, touched or smelt it? No one appears to have done so. So, according to the established rules of empirical, stable, demonstrable protocol, Science says that you have no brain, sir. With all due respect, sir, how do we then trust your lectures, sir?"

(The room was silent. The Professor stared at the student, his face unfathomable).

Professor: "I guess you'll have to take them on FAITH, son."

Student: "That is it sir… exactly! The link between man and God is *FAITH*. That is all that keeps things alive and moving."

# Atheism

The belief that there was nothing and nothing happened to nothing and then nothing magically exploded for no reason, creating everything and then a bunch of everything magically rearranged itself for no reason what so ever into self-replicating bits which then turned into dinosaurs.

Makes perfect sense.

---

**Hebrews 11:1** *"FAITH is the substance of things hoped for, the EVIDENCE of things not seen."*

**Hebrews 11:3** *"By FAITH we UNDERSTAND that the worlds were framed by the word of God, so that the things which are seen were not made of things which are visible."*

**2Corin. 5:7** *"We WALK by FAITH, not by SIGHT."*

**Romans 1:17** *"…the JUST shall LIVE by FAITH."*

**Romans 4:5** *"…to him who does not work but BELIEVES on Him who justifies the ungodly, his FAITH is accounted for righteousness."*

**Romans 11:20** *"….because of unbelief they were broken off, and you STAND by FAITH."*

**Everyone has faith…  It's where you place your faith that counts**

# What do Government Lobbyists promote?

*"We are deeply concerned with too many Americans' disdain for science, aggravated by the influence of religious doctrine on our public policies.*

*We are troubled by the persistence of paranormal and occult beliefs, and by the denial of the findings of scientific research.*

*These disturbing trends are seen by the push for intelligent design (a new name for creationism) and the insistence that it be taught along with evolution. 37 states considered legislation to mandate this.*

*Consider these facts from a recent Pew Research Poll:*

*We call upon political leaders of all parties to base public policy on empirical evidence instead of religious faith…. and not to permit legislation or executive action to be influenced by religious beliefs.*

> **Science and secularism are indispensable if we are to have sound public policies that will promote the common good, not only of Americans but of the global community."**

- *64% of Americans are open to teaching intelligent design or creationism in public schools.*
- *42% reject evolution or believe that present forms of life existed since the beginning of time.*
- *38% would teach creationism over evolutionary theory.*
- *Only 26% agree with the predominant scientific view that life evolved by processes of natural selection without the need for divine intervention.*
- *The percentage of individuals who accept the theory of evolution is lower in the United States than in any other developed country except Turkey.*

## Exit Ticket #9    <mark>Class 09: Modernism</mark>

| | |
|---|---|
| **1) On what does Modernism place its value?** | **2) Why does Modernism fail?** |
| **3) How is Modernism emerging in American culture today?** | **4) How does Isaiah 44:9-20 apply to Modernism?** |

# Class 10: Postmodernism

3 Cultural Worldviews in America Today

Postmodernism: Trying to Understand It

Remember the 10 Philosophical Worldviews - which ones are Postmodern?

The Resurgence of Postmodernism: Abandoning Truth

Consequences #1-#3 of Church's Retreat to "Upper Story"

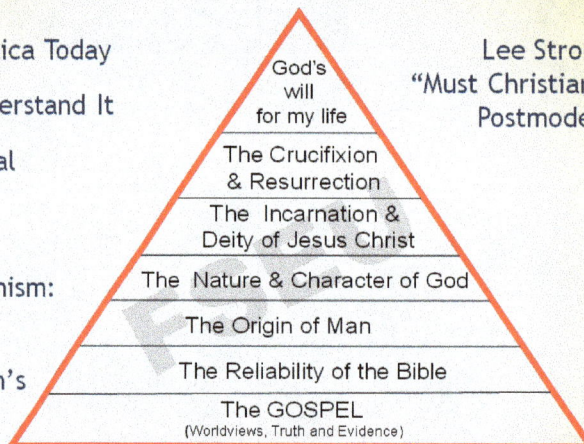

Lee Strobel, Faith under Fire: "Must Christianity Change, or Die? - Postmodernism in the church" (17:00)

God's will for my life

The Crucifixion & Resurrection

The Incarnation & Deity of Jesus Christ

The Nature & Character of God

The Origin of Man

The Reliability of the Bible

The GOSPEL
(Worldviews, Truth and Evidence)

## HEBREWS 11:1

"Faith = *Substance* of things hoped for,.... *Evidence* of things *not seen*"

**fse.life Lessons 02 - 08**

# 3 *Cultural* Worldviews in American Society

## Modern

- truth can be known, but it is based on what I can see, or reason out

- places value on man's ability to **reason** (Rene Descarte: "I think, therefore I am")

- The Enlightenment & Scientific Revolution (late 1600's up to WWII) - truth requires empirical certainty

## Postmodern

- absolute truth doesn't exist, OR.... it may exist, but it cannot be known

- places value on **authenticity** above reason ("I am skeptical of your claim to certainty - how can you be so sure?")

- Post-World War II until today: mans' scientific & technological advances have turned out to fail us: they are not the answers to our society's problems

## Christian

- truth can be known - it is based on the reality as defined by God Himself

- places value on man's capacity to **reason** (God has created man with the capacity to think)

- The Bible: God **transcends** our physical world. He has communicated objective truths to us in a language (God's word) that we can understand

# Worldview #2 in America: *POSTMODERNISM*

Michael Patton[17]: sections from his article 'How to Represent Christ in a *POSTMODERN* World'

"Our world is going through a major cultural shift. We have moved from a world of absolutes and objectivity, to one of **relativism, subjectivism**, and **tolerance**. The greatest commandment in this postmodern society is this, *thou shalt tolerate one another*. As one writer has put it, "Tolerance has become so important that no exception is tolerated. A person may have his or her religion, and may believe it, but he or she has no right to try to persuade another of his or her belief. Why? Because what you are saying is that your belief is superior to their belief. This is the supreme act of intolerance, the primary postmodern taboo.

## RELATIVISM = the heart of the Postmodern.

Because postmoderns are skeptical that there can be absolute truths, relativism is their creed. It is the idea that truth is contained in the eye of the beholder. It is not uncommon to hear, "Christ is *my* way to God, but I don't push *my* beliefs on others." Or, "It doesn't matter what you believe as long as you are sincere."

To the relative postmodern, all truth is contingent upon the situation, culture, or language of the person. With relativism, a moral truth can be true and binding for one person, while for another it is not. Having an abortion may be wrong for one person and right for another.

## OBJECTIVISM = ABSOLUTE TRUTHS do exist in and of themselves (the opposite of relative truths).

They *do not* depend upon the situation, culture, language, or any other variable. They are true even if nobody believes them to be true. An example of an objective truth is that the sun shines. These are truths that exist independently. They do not need anything to affirm them in order for them to be true.

The existence of objective truths is one of the bedrocks of Christianity. It is because of the objective truth of the atonement that you and I can have access to God. It is because of the objective truth that God created us that we exist. There is no room for relativity in these matters. We defend many of these objective truths at all costs.

### What is Christian Tolerance towards non-Christians?

The only truth that the postmodern believes is that there is no truth, or at least no objective access to that truth. Whatever our conclusions are, they are merely our opinions, and our opinions are no better than those of another. To the postmodern, all of us are imprisoned behind the unbreakable walls of this subjective reality, and therefore we must all *"tolerate"* each other. It is not uncommon to hear statements like this: "If you believe that the Bible is God's Word, that is fine and good, but you must also tolerate the person who believes in the Quran or any other religious literature they may choose."

What do the postmoderns mean by "tolerate"? Do they mean the same as the *American Heritage Dictionary's* definition of what it means to tolerate: "To allow without prohibiting or opposing; permit"? Do they simply mean that if I have a neighbor who adheres to a belief system other than mine, that I am supposed to live at peace with him, not prohibiting or oppressing him? If this is the case, I agree.

But this is not what typical postmoderns mean when they cry for "tolerance." They are not asking people to simply tolerate and get along with the opposing belief. The fact is that they are asking people to **compromise** their beliefs. They are asking me to concede that my neighbor's beliefs are just as true as mine, to forfeit my notion of objectivity, and to surrender my view of **exclusivism**.

The result would accomplish nothing less than to render a death blow to my belief in the Scriptures. What they are implying when they push their definition of "tolerance" is that people should never stand up for their beliefs, if standing up for them means stating that their beliefs are the only true beliefs—that they are exclusive. They are not asking people to tolerate the homosexual, but to *change their belief* that homosexuality is wrong *for everyone*.

By tolerance, the postmodern means that we compromise the **objectivity** of God's Word. By tolerance, the postmodern cries for us to stop reaching out to others with the Gospel. By tolerance, the postmodern demands that we approve of their lifestyles. By tolerance, the postmodern is essentially asking us to give up our faith. This we cannot do.

---

**Dr. Norman Geisler ('When Skeptics Ask')[12]:**
**"Dealing with the Postmodern - Skeptics and Agnostics"**

"One great philosopher had an effective way to deal with skepticism. When encountered by people who claimed to doubt everything, he would ask, 'Do you doubt your own existence?' If they answered yes, then he would point out that they must exist in order to doubt and that certainty should remove their doubts. If they answered no, then he could show them that there are at least some things which are beyond doubt.

To counter this assault on their doctrines, the skeptics decided to simply remain silent. Then they would not be caught in this trap. The philosopher was not shaken though. At that point, he said, 'I guess there is nobody here after all. I may as well go talk to somebody else who exists.' And he walked away."

# Postmodernism:   Trying to Understand It

1) A reaction to the assumed certainty of scientific, or objective, efforts to explain reality.

2) Skeptical of explanations which claim to be valid for all groups, cultures, traditions, or races; focus is on the *relative truths of each person*.

3) Interpretation is everything; reality only exists through our interpretations of what the world means to us individually.

4) "Post" = it denies any ultimate principles, and it lacks the optimism of there being a scientific, philosophical, or religious truth which will explain everything for everybody - a characteristic of the so-called "modern" mind.

> Postmodernism was a reaction to modernism. Where modernism was about objectivity, postmodernism was about subjectivity. Where modernism sought a singular truth, postmodernism sought the multiplicity of truths.

**Postmodernism's Failure:**
It's very truth claim, that there are no objective truths, is self-contradictory.

Courtesy of Google Images     Fair Use Law 17 U.S. Code 6 107

# The Resurgence of Postmodernism: Abandoning Truth

1) Churches *withdrew* from intellectually confronting the secular world, limiting their attention to the realm of practical Christian living.

↓

2) Churches *gave up* the truth of Christianity as the objective framework to interpret all of life (Christianity became trapped in the 'Upper Story').

↓

3) Christianity *gave in* to the demand that academics be separated from religion (but it was a cover to introduce philosophies like secular humanism and naturalism).

**Nancy Pearcey ('Total Truth'[3]): How American Churches abandoned Truth**

**Upper Story: CHURCH**
- Values & Meaning
- Personal Preferences
- Private Truth
- Sacred Realm
- Spiritual
- "Heart"

**Lower Story: CULTURE**
- Science & Reason
- Binding on Everyone
- Public Truth
- Secular Realm
- Material
- "Brain"

Lee Strobel, Faith under Fire: "Must Christianity Change, or Die? - Postmodernism in the church"  (17:00)     Courtesy of Google Images     Fair Use Law 17 U.S. Code § 107

---

### Dr. Norman Geisler[12]: "The Impossibility of Denying Absolutes"

*"… there is a fundamental inconsistency to a denial of absolutes: in order to deny absolutes, one must imply that there are absolutes in the process of the denial. To deny absolutes, you have to make an absolute denial. It's just like saying, 'Never say never.' You just did. Or, 'It's always wrong to say always.' You have to say it to say it. How can you be absolutely sure that there are no absolutes?*

*Besides, if relativity were true, then there must be something to which all things are relative, but which is not relative itself. In other words, something has to be absolute before we can see that everything else is relative to it. This is the nature of relations: they exist between two or more things. Nothing can be relative by itself, and if everything else is relative, then no other relations are real. There has to be something which does not change by which we can measure the change in everything else. Even Einstein recognized this and posited absolute Spirit as something to which all else is related (see Book 3 on 'Einstein and Theory of Relativity')."*

---

## RELEVANCE = how to evangelize in the world today

Can we tolerate the postmodern? What are the issues which we are to tolerate? We do not panic when someone says that truth is relative, we explain that they are right, but only *some* truth is relative. When they cry for tolerance, we cry with them, and explain to them the difference between tolerance and compromise.

How do we represent CHRIST to the postmodern? We approach them like we do any other unbeliever of any time, or culture, or language — we hand them the crucified and risen Savior. We bring them what is *RELEVANT*.

### "American Christianity's Abandonment of Truth (*we've lost our minds*)"[3]

1)   Churches *withdrew* from intellectually confronting the secular world, limiting their attention to the realm of practical Christian living.

2)   Churches *gave up* the truth of Christianity as the framework to interpret all of life (Christianity became trapped in the 'upper story').

3)   Christianity *gave in* to the demand that the academic disciplines must be separated from religion, not realizing that it was a cover to introduce new philosophies like secular humanism and naturalism."

**OK…. so what now?** The first step in reclaiming a Christian worldview is to overcome this divide between "heart" and "brain". We have to reject the division of life into a sacred realm, limited to things like worship and personal morality, against a secular realm that includes science, politics, economics, and the rest of the public arena. This dichotomy in our own minds is the greatest barrier to liberating the power of the gospel in our culture today.

**What has never changed**: while our culture is changing at an incredible speed, God's definition of TRUTH has remained steadfast. Jesus still asks me the same FOUR QUESTIONS. How I answer them they will determine where I spend eternity – regardless of what the world defines as their truth.

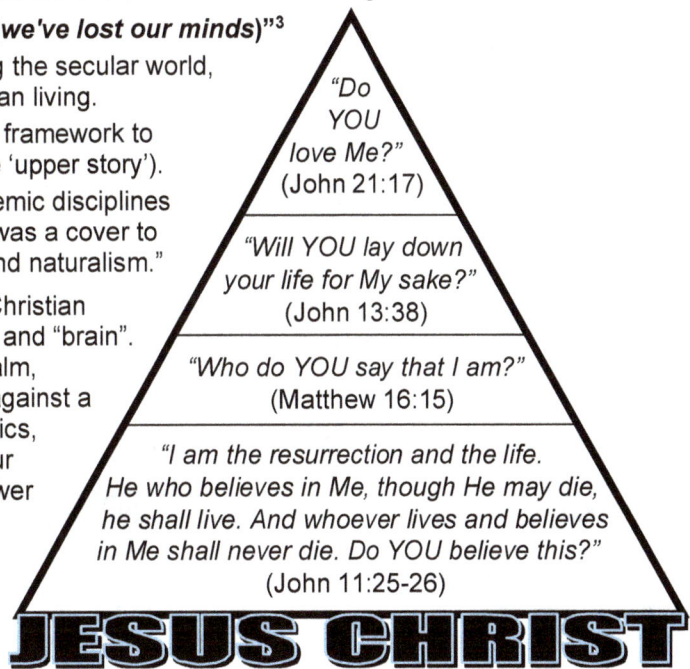

*"Do YOU love Me?"* (John 21:17)

*"Will YOU lay down your life for My sake?"* (John 13:38)

*"Who do YOU say that I am?"* (Matthew 16:15)

*"I am the resurrection and the life. He who believes in Me, though He may die, he shall live. And whoever lives and believes in Me shall never die. Do YOU believe this?"* (John 11:25-26)

**JESUS CHRIST**

1Corin. 3:11  *"No other foundation can anyone lay than that which is laid, which is Jesus Christ"*

---

### Dr. Norman Geisler[12]: "You Christians Are So *Close-Minded*"

*"Open-mindedness has become a self-evident virtue in our society and a closed mind, a sign of ignorance and depravity. However, this thinking is based on HALF-TRUTHS. Surely, it is good to admit the possibility that one might be wrong and never good to maintain a position no matter what the evidence against it. Also, one should never make a firm decision without examining all the evidence without prejudice.*

*That is the half-truth that ropes us into this view, but a half-truth is a whole lie. Are we still to remain open-minded when all reason says that there can be only one conclusion? That is the same as the error of the closed mind. In fact, **openness is the most closed-minded position of all** because it eliminates any absolute view from consideration.*

*What if the absolute view is true? Isn't openness taken to be absolute? In the long run, openness cannot really be true unless it is open to some real absolutes that cannot be denied. Open-mindedness should not be confused with empty-mindedness. One should never remain open to a second alternative when only one can be true."*

DON'T BE SO OPEN-MINDED YOUR BRAINS FALL OUT

## Nancy Pearcey[3]: 'History's Path to a Postmodern America'

"Francis Schaeffer depicted Greek philosophy's classical thought of truth and reality as a 2-Story Building because it drew a stark dichotomy between matter and spirit, treating the material realm as though it were less valuable than the spiritual realm (and sometimes outright evil). Salvation was defined in terms of ascetic exercises aimed at liberating the spirit from the material world so that it could ascend to God.

This concept of what is TRUE and REAL is divided by this "building": In the Lower Story are science and reason, which are considered Public Truth, binding on everyone. Over against it is an Upper Story of noncognitive experience, which is the center of personal meaning. This is the realm of Private Truth, where we hear people say, 'That may be true for you but it's not true for me.'

**Upper Story**
• Values & Meaning
• Personal Preferences
• Private Truth
• Sacred Realm
• Spiritual
• "Heart"

**Lower Story**
• Science & Reason
• Binding on Everyone
• Public Truth
• Secular Realm
• Material
• "Brain"

The first step in forming a Christian worldview is to overcome the sharp divide between 'heart' and 'brain'. We must reject the division of life into a sacred realm, limited to things like worship and personal morality, versus a secular realm that includes science, politics, economics, and the rest of the public arena. This dichotomy in our own minds is the greatest barrier to liberating the power of the gospel across our culture today."

## How 'Upper and Lower Story' Philosophy infiltrated the Early Church

### Plato (350 BC)
**Form (spiritual)**
• eternal reason and rationality
• order and harmony
• spirit = goodness, truth, beauty

**Matter (material)**
• eternally formless and irrational
• disorderly, irrational
• evil, chaotic

Earliest believers: surrounded by a culture steeped in Greek paganism.
Plato: material world is inferior to eternal spiritual ideals of truth and beauty.

The Problem: Plato identified the source of chaos and evil with matter (part of God's creation). Creation was divided into 2 parts: spiritual (good) vs. material (evil).
This opposes a biblical worldview, where God created matter and has absolute control over it, and humanity's problem is MORAL.

### Augustine (430 AD)
**Spiritual**
• eternal reason and rationality
• order and harmony
• spirit = goodness, truth, beauty

**Material**
✓ creation is from God and good
• physical world and bodily functions inferior and causes sin

Reaching higher levels of spiritual life meant avoiding, suppressing and escaping material aspects of life.
• Manual labor - less valuable than prayer and meditation.
• Marriage and sexuality - rejected in favor of celibacy.
• Ordinary social life - on a lower plane than life in a monastery.

The Problem: Augustine kept part of Plato's philosophy (inferiority of the material) in the church, which fostered the concept of spiritual elitism over living a normal life.

### Aquinas (1270 AD)
**Grace**
• supernatural "add-on" to nature
• gift from God, nature, allowing man to have a relationship with Him.

**Nature**
✓ creation (physical world) is good since it's by a good Creator
• "nature", or the "purpose" of things (its goal to which it strives), can be found within the world

He recovered a more biblical view of creation: God and His physical creation are both good; the goodness of the Creation are evidence of the goodness of God.

The Problem: Aquinas allowed the "nature" or purpose of things to be found within the world, so the world didn't need God but was capable of reaching their full potential by its own resources. The problem for people: Don't I have a higher purpose? Don't I need to be in relationship to God to be fulfilled?

# N. Pearcey[3]: "From the Reformers (Luther) to Today: The 2-Story Framework is alive and well"

In her book "Total Truth"[3], Nancy Pearcey gives us a history lesson of how Schaeffer's "2-Story View of Truth & Reality" has so infiltrated our culture that, as she says, "the very concept of being 'professional' has come to have connotations of being secular. Faith is often reduced to a separate 'add-on' for personal and private life - on the order of a private indulgence, like a weakness for chocolates - and not an appropriate topic in the public arena."

Picking up from Aquinas, the Reformers flatly rejected this 2-Story framework of Truth but were unable to extinguish it. The "2 Stories" permeate our culture today, many times subconsciously, leading Christians to feel their spiritual life should be kept in isolation for Sunday mornings, separate from their careers and other areas of their life (Christianity is held captive in the "Upper Story" of "subjective, private truth").

Pearcey explains that "by understanding how these secular dualisms ("Upper-vs-Lower Story') developed throughout history, we can strike them right at the root with an effective strategy that has the potential to: 1) bring Christian truth back into the public sphere, 2) evangelize our world in this post-modern age."

## Luther & Calvin (1500-1600's)

### Reformation

- rejected spiritual elitism (monks, priests) and emphasized priesthood of all believers (1Peter 2:9)
- medieval scholarship accommodated pagan philosophy (like Aristotle)
- reason and truth don't exist apart from God's word

They preached that the Christian life is not a summons to a life *separate* from family and work, but is *embedded within* it. Running a business or a household was as important as being a priest or a nun, because all were ways of participating in God's work in maintaining and caring for His creation.

The Problem: They didn't give their followers any tools to defend their new insights against philosophical attack. Their successors went right back to teaching Greek philosophy's dualistic approach to Christian living ("separate from the world").

## Descartes (1700's)

### Romanticism

- religion and humanities
- MIND (spirit, thought, emotion, will)
- proof of human spirit: *"I think, therefore I am"*

### Enlightenment

- science and reason
- MATTER (mechanical, deterministic machine)
- natural laws with fixed patterns

The Secularization Process: Romanticism conceded the study of nature to the Enlightenment, wanting only their own parallel arena for the arts and humanities. Enlightenment: successes of the scientific revolution led to science enthroned as the path to knowledge and truth. Romanticism: rejected science for religion, philosophy, humanities & the arts (beauty and creativity).

The Problem: Descartes' intention to elevate the mind failed: it was cast into the Upper Story, irrelevant to scientific materialism.

## Kant (1700-1800's)

### Freedom

- autonomy = individual is subject only to laws imposed on oneself by oneself (personal morality)
- socially constructed *values* (what I can't *help* believing to be true)

### Nature

- Newtonian Physics (not Aquinas' purpose/ goal')
- *"everything taking place is infallibly determined by the laws of nature"*
- publicly verifiable *facts* (what I *know* to be true)

Kant knew that a 'machine' image of the universe would be rejected by artists, writers and religious thinkers as an enemy to human values.

The Problems:
1) Kant arrogated God's role of creating moral law to each individual's rational will.
2) Kant's 2 Stories were *contradictory* (if nature is the deterministic machine of Newtonian physics, how can I ever have real freedom?)

## Darwin (1800-1900's)

### Value

- social values that give personal meaning
- Kant's *freedom*

### Fact

- public truth verified by science (naturalistic mechanism for life's origin)
- naturalism became a comprehensive philosophy

R. Dawkins: *"Darwin made it possible to be an intellectually fulfilled atheist."*
The "Lower Story" became self-contained (God not needed for life itself, nevermind moral laws).

The Problems:
1) "Upper Story" cut off from history, science, reason (if evolutionary forces produced the mind, then religion and morality aren't truths but only ideas; I create my own morality and meaning through my choices).
2) This opposes a biblical worldview, where God as Creator is sovereign over everything, including me.

## Today (1900's on)

### Postmodernism

- morality = values
- personal preference
- subjective (private) truth in ethics and morality
- people have moral freedom and dignity

### Scientific Naturalism

- evolutionary science = facts
- binding on everyone
- objective (public) truth in science & history
- people are data-processing machines

The Postmodern Contradiction = science says the human mind is just a complex data-processing machine, while the possibility of morality depends on the idea that we are more than machines, capable of making free choices (S. Pinker: *"a human being is a machine and a sentient free agent, depending on whether we're playing the science game or the ethics game"*).

The Problem: real people don't act like machines; what matters most (purpose, free will, meaning) is reduced to nothing more than useful fiction.

## Consequence #1 of Church's Retreat to "Upper Story" = Withdrawing from American Culture led to Losing Today's Young Adults

| Generation "Z" (ages 18-23) | Millennials (ages 24-38) | What are the Challenges to Reach Them? |
|---|---|---|
| • Internet experts<br>• Online all the time<br>• Can find answers at warp speed<br>• Prefer digital conversations over face-to-face<br>• Entrepreneurial (want their hobbies to turn into their careers)<br>• Very Stressed Out | • Technologically Advanced<br>• Value Friendship Networks<br>• High Levels of Activism<br>• Massive Financial Debt<br>• Idealistic ("anything is possible")<br>• Feel Entitled<br>• As get Older: Idealism is crumbling (things get beyond their reach)<br>• Increasing Sense of Disillusionment | 1) The church is almost NOWHERE on their radar<br><br>2) 45% of ages 11-18 do not know a practicing Christian<br><br>3) Questions/doubts are rarely if ever addressed in Church |

Amy Orr Ewing

Courtesy of Google Images    Fair Use Law 17 U.S. Code § 107

## What Happened in the 2022 Midterms? Generation Z and Millennials

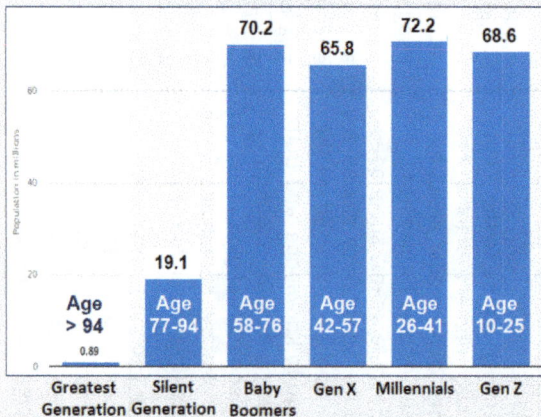

Bar chart — Population in millions:

| Group | Value |
|---|---|
| Greatest Generation (Age > 94) | 0.89 |
| Silent Generation (Age 77-94) | 19.1 |
| Baby Boomers (Age 58-76) | 70.2 |
| Gen X (Age 42-57) | 65.8 |
| Millennials (Age 26-41) | 72.2 |
| Gen Z (Age 10-25) | 68.6 |

**Religion by Generation - 2021**

| Generation | Protestant | Catholic | Other Religions | Atheist/Agnostic | "None" | Other |
|---|---|---|---|---|---|---|
| Silent Gen. | 50% | 22% | 6% | 8% | 10% | |
| Baby Boomers | 41% | 20% | 6% | 9% | 16% | 8% |
| Gen. X | 32% | 18% | 5% | 11% | 24% | 9% |
| Millennials | 24% | 17% | 6% | 15% | 30% | 7% |
| Gen Z | 22% | 14% | 10% | 17% | 31% | 7% |

@ryanburge
Data: CES 2021

**Nealy HALF of Gen. Z'ers and Millennials are Atheist/Agnostic or "none" (no religion).** Prof. Ryan P. Burge, Eastern Illinois University

Millennials (ages 26-41) passed Boomers (ages 58-76) as the largest group in America (over 72 million). Gen Z'ers (ages 10-25) are now at nearly 69 million.

With the voting age is 18, many Gen Z'ers could vote in the 2022 midterms. And they did. Gen Z'ers had a huge turnout, accounting for 12% of all votes!

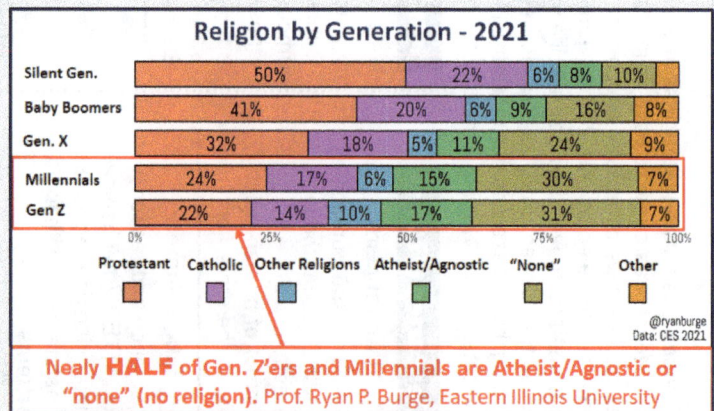

*"Biden goaded young people to vote by canceling half a trillion dollars of student loan debt.*

*He told young women they would die without unlimited abortions.*

*Republicans wrongly assumed young voters cared most about spiking inflation, unaffordable food and fuel, an open border and a disastrous foreign policy."* Victor Davis Hansen, Hoover Institute.

*"Remember your Creator in the days of your youth, before the evil days come."*     Ecclesiastes 12:1

## Consequence #2 of Church's Retreat to "Upper Story" = Allowing "Post-Christian" American Culture to Flourish

| Naturalism | Crayon Christianity | Radical Islam | Race Relations | Sexuality |
|---|---|---|---|---|

*"If Darwinism is true, there are 5 inescapable conclusions:*
*1. There's no evidence for God,*
*2. There's no life after death,*
*3. There's no right and wrong,*
*4. There's no ultimate meaning for life,*
*5. People don't really have free will."*

William Provine, Cornell University Evolutionary Biologist

*"I'm genuinely losing my faith, and it doesn't bother me. What bothers me now is nothing. I am happy now.*
*How many preachers fall? Many. No one talks about it. How many miracles happen? Not many. No one talks about it. Why is the Bible full of contradictions? No one talks about it. How can God be love yet send four billion people to a place, all 'coz they don't believe? It's not for me."*

Marty Sampson, Hillsong

*"Remember all God has promised... the time between you and your marriage in heaven is very short.*
*You are heading for a deed that God loves and will accept. When the hour of reality approaches, wholeheartedly welcome death for the sake of God.*
*Make your last words: 'There is no God but God, and Muhammad is His messenger.'"*
Letter of Mohammed Atta, leader of 9/11 Attacks

*"A consequence of the civil rights victories in mid-60's was WHITE GUILT. America acknowledged that for four centuries it had oppressed black Americans.*
*Anytime you acknowledge a wrong, a price you pay for that is a loss of moral authority. You are then stigmatized as a racist. The pressure on whites due to this stigmatization has had a tremendous impact on culture, politics, public policy in many ways."*
Dr. Shelby Steele

When competing against men in 2018-2019, Lia Thomas ranked 554th in 200 freestyle, 65th in 500 freestyle, and 32nd in 1650 freestyle.

At 2022 NCAA Women's Swim Championship, Thomas beat Riley Gaines by 0.01 seconds.

NCAA officials awarded Thomas the gold, hailing Thomas as first trans athlete named Division I NCAA champion.

## Consequence #3 of Church's Retreat to "Upper Story" = Abandoning Objective Moral Values & Duties

**Columbine HS Littleton, CO**
April 20, 1999

17-year old Dylan Kiebold and 18-year old Eric Harris murdered 12 students & 1 teacher

"Do you believe in God?" Cassie Bernall: "Yes." Kiebold & Harris then shot her dead.

**Virginia Tech Blacksburg, VA**
April 16, 2007

23-year old senior Seung-Hui Cho murdered 27 students & 5 teachers

"Cho sent 27 videos to NBC News where he likened himself to Jesus Christ"

**Sandy Hook Elementary Newton, CT**
December 14, 2012

20-year old Adam Lanza murdered 20 children & 6 adults

"Investigators found Lanza was fascinated with mass shootings, such as Columbine and Virginia Tech."

**Emanuel African Methodist Church Charleston, SC**
June 17, 2015

21-year old Dylann Roof murdered 9 people during Bible Study

"No one is doing anything but talking on the internet. Someone has to have the bravery to take it to the real world; I guess that has to be me."

**Robb Elementary School, Uvalde, TX**
May 24, 2022

18-year old Salvador Ramos murdered 19 children, 2 teachers

"He would livestream himself on Yubo threatening to kidnap and rape girls who used the app and threatening to commit a school shooting."

## Article 145 - America's Culture War: The Myth of Staying Neutral

John 14:6 *"I am the Way, the Truth, and the Life. No one comes to the Father except through Me."*

Two months after the 9/11 terrorist attack, Tom Friedman wrote a New York Times article entitled "The Real War". His suggestion of where the real war in America is waging may surprise you, but as you read excerpts from his 13-year-old article, you may see that the recent deconstruction of traditional, biblical marriage is a direct result from this 'war':

*"If 9/11 was indeed the onset of World War III, we have to understand what this war is about. We're not fighting to eradicate 'terrorism'. We're fighting to defeat an ideology: religious totalitarianism, a view of the world that my faith must reign supreme and be affirmed and held passionately only if all others are negated. All faiths that come out of the biblical tradition - Judaism, Christianity and Islam - have the tendency to believe that they have the exclusive truth.*

*The opposite of religious totalitarianism is an ideology of pluralism - an ideology that embraces religious diversity and the idea that my faith can be nurtured without claiming exclusive truth. America is the Mecca of that ideology."*

As Friedman says, the mecca for pluralism today is America, the nation founded on the objective truths of the Bible. Pluralism says all worldviews are equally valid, so no one can claim to know truth. To be clear, Christianity does not deny that other worldviews may have elements that are true, but this week's verse shows that Jesus Christ claims to be the exclusive truth about God. While most Americans agree that God exists, it is a cultural taboo to claim that God has revealed Himself exclusively in Jesus Christ.

Pluralism is a direct, frontal assault on the Christian worldview. We have just witnessed the destruction of yet another of the exclusive truth claims made by Christ Himself: that marriage is between a man and a woman. Today's culture is at war against any book, code or person claiming to know how we should live. As a follower of Jesus Christ, living in pluralistic America means you can no longer stay neutral.

So how do Christians in America respond to the new definition of marriage? On his 'Reasonable Faith' website, Christian philosopher and theologian Dr. William Lane Craig offers two answers. Below are excerpts from 'Question 429: Supreme Court's Redefinition of Marriage':

*"First, Christians must resolve to be resolutely counter-cultural… With this decision the pressure to conform will become intense in pop culture, the academy, the corporate world, and even in the church. Those who refuse to conform to the new orthodoxy will be vilified and pushed out.*

*My fear is that the next generation of Christians will not have the strength to resist these pressures and will accommodate itself to same-sex marriage. Already, I hear young Christians saying that homosexual activity is not immoral if it is in the confines of marriage, a view that would have been unthinkable to first century Jews like Jesus of Nazareth. Just as early Christians were willing to take a stand against the corrupt pagan culture of the Roman empire, so today Christians must dare to be different and to live counterculturally.*

*That implies Christian activism. Christians must not abandon the political process but see this setback as a call to deeper engagement in the process. In his dissent, Justice Scalia observed that 'Not a single evangelical Christian (a group that comprises about one quarter of Americans), or even a Protestant of any denomination' sits on the Court. That fact is a stinging indictment of the evangelical church.*

*We have not set before our youth the vision of serving God by pursuing a career as a judge. We are reaping the whirlwind of our own passivity and lack of engagement. Now is not the time to withdraw to the sanctuary of our churches and institutions, but to involve ourselves in those public institutions that so shape the culture in which we live.*

*Second, Christians must continue efforts to evangelize the American people. It has been rightly said that America is a nation whose people are as religious as the people of India but whose government is as secular as the government of Sweden. Because of the separation of Church and State in this country - an increasingly precious Constitutional guarantee - we do not need governmental support in order for the Christian church to be dynamic and flourishing. Revival can come to this country even as its governmental institutions go to hell."*

If Christians hold to the truth of John 14:6, our course of action must be to stand firm in the gospel if we wish to remain true to ourselves, to who we are - followers of our Lord and Savior Jesus Christ.

# John 18:38 "What Is Truth?"
# Rome at the time of Jesus Christ

1) Culture of Entitlement: *"The free citizens were idle, their thoughts of the theatre and arena, supported at public cost (200,000 people maintained by the State)".*

2) Spread of Atheism & Self-deification: *"Religion and philosophy based on Stoicism and Epicureanism, leading to atheism and despair - the one, by turning all aspirations self-ward, the other, by indulging every passion and worshipping matter, its ideal."*

3) Rejection of Absolute Truth: *"Among philosophers, all religions were equally false or equally true - the outcome of ignorance. The only religion insisted on by the State was the deification of the Emperor. Absolute right did not exist. Might was right."*

4) End of Marriage and Traditional Family, the Rise of Abortion: *"Sanctity of marriage had ceased. Abortion, and the murder of newly-born children, were common and tolerated."*

5) Culture of Hopelessness: *"Society could not reform itself; philosophy and religion had been tried and found wanting. Seneca, Cicero, Tacitus expressed that the Roman world lay under some terrible curse. All around, despair, conscious need, and unconscious longing."*

> **The Arrival of Jesus Christ**
> *"Can greater contrast be imagined than the proclamation of a coming Kingdom of God, that 'came to seek and to save that which was thus lost'? Upon the ruins of heathenism was the Church of Christ reared."*

Alfred Edersheim, "The Life & Times of Jesus the Messiah"                    Courtesy of Google Images    Fair Use Law 17 U.S. Code § 107

## Exit Ticket #10     <mark>Class 10: Postmodernism</mark>

| 1) On what does Postmodernism place its value? | 2) Why does Postmodernism fail? |
|---|---|
| | |
| **3) According to Nancy Pearcey, how did American Christianity abandon truth?** | **4) Explain the context behind John 18:38?** |
| | |

# Class 11: Christianity

3 Cultural Worldviews in America Today

Christianity: The Foundation of Truth

Why Christianity is *TRUE* = It conforms to *reality*

Comparing Worldviews: Christianity vs. Secular Humanism

If Christianity is true... Why isn't everyone a Christian?

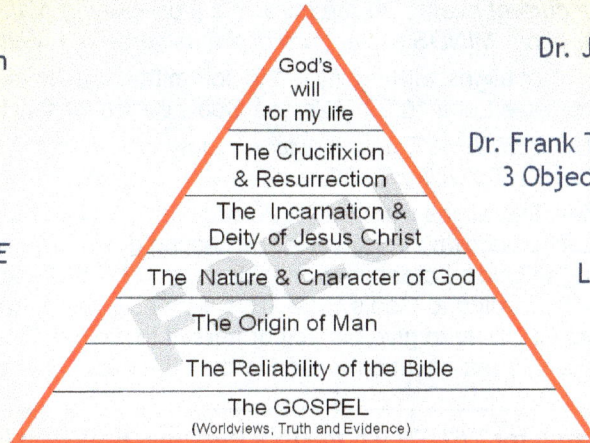

Dr. John Dickson: "Two Reasons Why I Love Jesus" (2:26)

Dr. Frank Turek: "Answering Atheist's 3 Objections to Christianity" (9:05)

'Interview with Dr. William Lane Craig: Handling Doubt' (5:38)

**Pyramid (top to bottom):**
- God's will for my life
- The Crucifixion & Resurrection
- The Incarnation & Deity of Jesus Christ
- The Nature & Character of God
- The Origin of Man
- The Reliability of the Bible
- The GOSPEL (Worldviews, Truth and Evidence)

# HEBREWS 11:1
"Faith = *Substance* of things *hoped for*.... *Evidence* of things *not seen*"

fse.life Lessons 02 - 08

# 3 *Cultural* Worldviews in American Society

## Modern

- truth can be known, but it is based on what I can see, or reason out

- places value on man's ability to **reason** (Rene Descarte: "I think, therefore I am")

- The Enlightenment & Scientific Revolution (late 1600's up to WWII) - truth requires empirical certainty

## Postmodern

- absolute truth doesn't exist, OR.... it may exist, but it cannot be known

- places value on **authenticity** above reason ("I am skeptical of your claim to certainty - how can you be so sure?")

- Post-World War II until today: mans' scientific & technological advances have turned out to fail us: they are not the answers to our society's problems

## Christian

**Truth**

- truth can be known - it is based on the reality as defined by God Himself

- places value on man's capacity to **reason** (God has created man with the capacity to think)

- The Bible: God **transcends** our physical world. He has communicated objective truths to us in a language (God's word) that we can understand

## Worldview #3 in America: *CHRISTIANITY*

"To claim Christianity is the truth about reality means the Bible provides the direction to understand what is real. As Nancy Pearcey explains in 'Total Truth'[3], *"A worldview is like a mental map that tells us how to navigate the world effectively. It is the imprint of God's objective truth on our inner life...it's far more than a mental strategy or a new spring on current events. At the core, it is a deepening of the spiritual character of our lives. It begins with the submission of our MINDS to the Lord of the universe – a willingness to be taught by Him."*

The goal in developing a worldview that aligns with reality is the commitment to 'love the Lord your God with all your heart, soul, strength, and mind" (see Luke 10:27). We see God's desire for this love throughout the Bible:

Proverbs 23:26   *"My son, GIVE ME YOUR HEART, and let your eyes observe My ways."*

Proverbs 3:5     *"Trust in the Lord with ALL YOUR HEART, and lean not on your own understanding."*

If one desires to develop a worldview that aligns with reality, 2Corinthians 10:4-5 explains that to achieve the goal of intellectual growth, where one can 'pull down strongholds and casting down arguments', one must first grow spiritually. That means surrendering to God's Lordship so that God can be your Teacher, where the interpretation of all thoughts and actions is made according to God's Bible. This surrender is not easy. It takes work and discipline because a Christian must be willing to give himself or herself to God as Romans 12:1 describes as a 'living sacrifice'. That requires whole-hearted devotion to God in both the heart and the mind.

---

### Nancy Pearcey[3]:  "My Search for *TRUTH* led me to a Personal Relationship with Jesus Christ"

*"To some people, 'worldview' may be a stuffy academic-sounding term that conjures up images of tweedy professors and dusty lecture halls.... but 'worldview' is not something abstract and academic, but intensely personal. Our worldview is the way we answer the core questions of life that everyone has to struggle with:*
*1)   What are we here for?   2) What is ultimate truth?   3) Is there anything worth living for?*

*I began by asking these question in a serious way myself as a teenager. I had a good background in knowing WHAT Christianity teaches. But I came to realize I didn't know WHY it was true... I had no reason for believing Christianity was true over against the other belief systems I was encountering. When I asked my parents and pastors questions, the typical response was a patronizing pat on the head. One pastor told me, 'Don't worry, we all have doubts sometimes.' No one grasped that I was not merely troubled by 'doubts' but had stepped outside the circle of faith and was questioning the truth of the whole system.*

*Failing to find answers, I took a significant step: I decided the most intellectually honest course would be to reject my faith and then to analyze it objectively alongside all the other major religions and philosophies, in order to decide which one was really true. I'd had a genuine faith, even though it was only a child's faith: I knew God created me, that He loved me, that He had a wonderful purpose for my life. These principles seem very simple – until you reject them. Then suddenly I became acutely aware that I had no answers for the most basic questions – where did I come from? Was life just a chance accident of blind forces? Did it have any purpose? Were there any principles so true and so real that I could build my life on them?*

*Then I stumbled across the ministry of Francis Schaeffer (L'Abri in Switzerland). It was the first time I had ever encountered Christians who actually answered my questions – who gave reasonable arguments for the truth of Christianity instead of simply urging me to have faith. At that time, it was extremely rare to discover Christian ministries capable of crossing the countercultural divide to reach alienated young people, and my curiosity was sparked: Who were these Christians? I had to admit (rather ruefully) that I was already convinced that Christianity was true. Through my discussions at L'Abri and my readings in apologetics, I had come to realize there were good arguments against moral relativism, physical determinism, epistemological subjectivism, and a host of other 'isms' I had been carrying around in my head... The only step that remained was to acknowledge that I had been persuaded - and then give my life to the Lord of Truth.*

*What I hope you take from my experience is that 'worldview' is not an abstract, academic concept. Instead, the term describes our search for answers to those intensely personal questions everyone must wrestle with – the cry of the human heart for purpose, meaning, and a truth big enough to live by. No one can live without a sense of purpose and direction, a sense that his or her life has significance as part of a cosmic story. We may limp along for a while, extracting small installments of meaning from short-term goals like earning a degree, landing a job, getting married, establishing a family. But at some point, these temporal things fail to fulfill the deep hunger for eternity in the human spirit. For we were made by God, and every part of our personality is oriented toward a RELATIONSHIP WITH HIM. 'Our hearts are restless', Augustine said, 'until we find rest in Him.'*

*Once we discover that the Christian worldview is really true, then LIVING IT OUT means offering up to God all our powers – practical, intellectual, emotional, artistic – to live for Him in every area of life. Biblical truth takes hold of our inner being, and we see that it is not only a message of salvation but also the truth about all reality. GOD'S WORD becomes a light to all our paths, providing the foundational principles for bringing every part of our lives under the Lordship of Christ, to glorify Him and to cultivate His creation."*

# Christianity:    The Foundation of Truth

**1TIMOTHY 6:19**
*"...storing up for themselves a GOOD FOUNDATION...*
*that they may lay hold on to eternal life"*

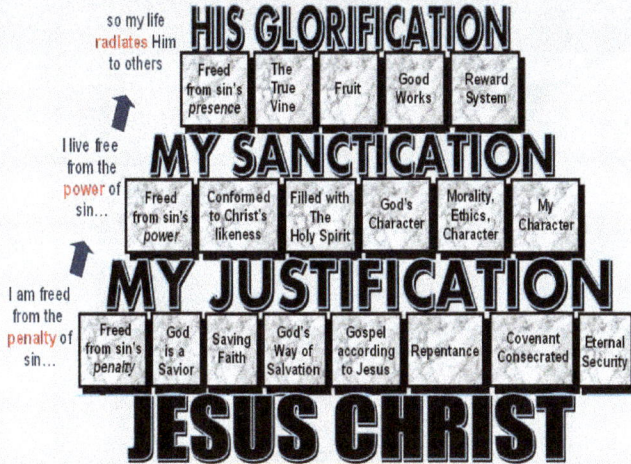

so my life
radiates Him
to others

## HIS GLORIFICATION

| Freed from sin's presence | The True Vine | Fruit | Good Works | Reward System |
|---|---|---|---|---|

I live free
from the
power of
sin...

## MY SANCTICATION

| Freed from sin's power | Conformed to Christ's likeness | Filled with The Holy Spirit | God's Character | Morality, Ethics, Character | My Character |
|---|---|---|---|---|---|

I am freed
from the
penalty of
sin...

## MY JUSTIFICATION

| Freed from sin's penalty | God is a Savior | Saving Faith | God's Way of Salvation | Gospel according to Jesus | Repentance | Covenant Consecrated | Eternal Security |
|---|---|---|---|---|---|---|---|

## JESUS CHRIST

**1CORINTHIANS 3:11**
*"No other FOUNDATION can anyone lay*
*than that which is laid, which is **JESUS CHRIST**"*

**JOHN 18:37**
*"For this cause I was born, and for this cause I came into the world, that I should bear witness to the TRUTH." Pilate said to Him, 'What is truth?'"*

**JOHN 14:5-6**
*"Lord, we do not know where You are going - how can we know the way?' Jesus said to him, 'I am the Way, the TRUTH, and the life...'"*

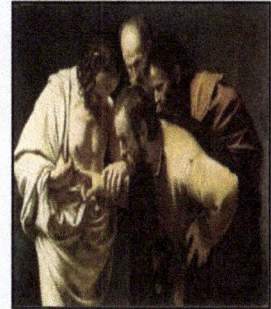

Courtesy of Google Images    Fair Use Law 17 U.S. Code § 107

# Christianity:    The Foundation of Truth is a **PERSON**

Jesus said to him,
"I am the way, the
truth, and the life.
No one comes to
the Father except
through Me.

ONE WAY

**John 14:6**

**Christianity is NOT...**
The intellectual defense of a philosophy...

**Christianity is ...**
The devotion to a *Person*

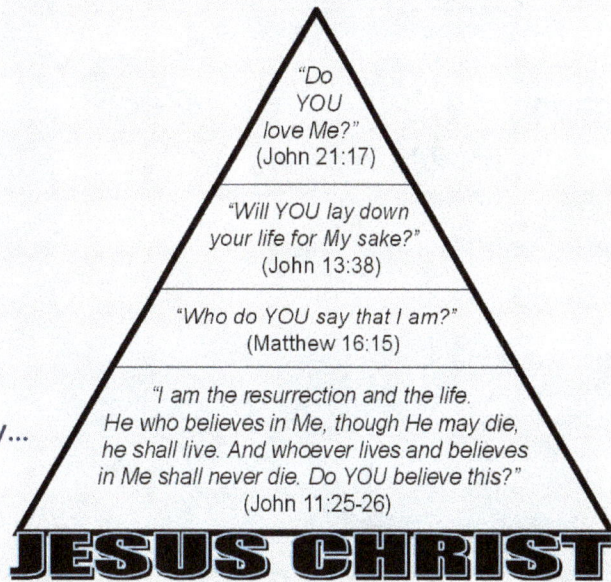

*"Do YOU love Me?"*
(John 21:17)

*"Will YOU lay down your life for My sake?"*
(John 13:38)

*"Who do YOU say that I am?"*
(Matthew 16:15)

*"I am the resurrection and the life. He who believes in Me, though He may die, he shall live. And whoever lives and believes in Me shall never die. Do YOU believe this?"*
(John 11:25-26)

## JESUS CHRIST

**Ever think about the questions Jesus Christ asks *YOU*?**

Dr. John Dickson: 'Two Reasons Why I Love Jesus' (2:26)

Courtesy of Google Images    Fair Use Law 17 U.S. Code § 107

# Christianity: The Foundation of Truth is the Gospel

*"He (the Father) made Him (the Son) who <u>knew no sin</u> to <u>be sin for us</u> ...*

*so that we (you and me) might become the righteousness of God (the Father) in Him (the Son)."*
2Corinthians 5:21

**Are there *Essentials* a person must believe to become the "Righteousness of God in Christ"?**

**The Protestant Reformation – The 5 'Solas':**
1) 'Sola Deo Gloria' = To God Alone be the Glory
2) 'Sola Scriptura' = Understood only in God's Word...
3) 'Sola Fidei' = Salvation is by faith alone
4) 'Sola Christus' = in Jesus Christ alone
5) 'Sola Gratia' = apart from works, by God's grace alone

1) **Existence of God**
Hebrews 11:6; Psalm 14:1

2) **Deity of Christ**
John 1:1,14; John 8:56-58

3) **Atonement (for Sin)**
John 1:29; Mark 10:45

4) **Repentance**
Luke 13:3,5; Acts 11:18

5) **Resurrection**
1Corinthians 15:1-22

6) **'Sola Fidei/Christus/Gratia'**
John 3:16; Romans 1:17; Ephesians 2:8

Paul Washer: 'The Gospel is only Good News to a Needy man' (9:15)

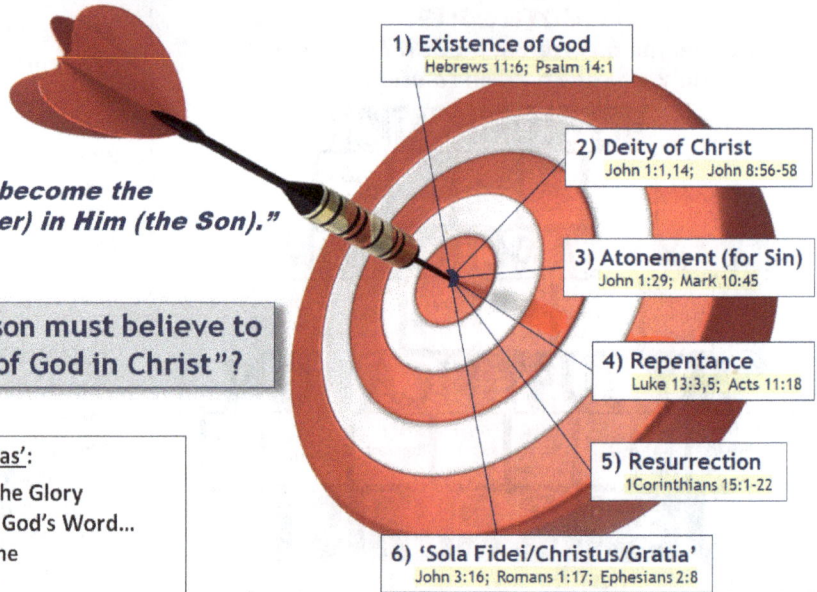

Courtesy of Google Images   Fair Use Law 17 U.S. Code § 107

---

# Why Christianity is *TRUE* = It conforms to *REALITY*

## Natural Theology

**Romans 1:19**     *"known of* God"

'gnōstos' = notable; known by observation or study

- *"things made"* = creation
- *"in them"* = conscience

**No Excuse** if you suppress His evidence

Why?

He has made the evidence *CLEAR TO SEE*
Romans 1:19

## Revealed Theology

**John 17:3**     *"know* God"

'ginōskō' = absolute knowledge; complete understanding

- Old Testament God of creation
- Jesus Christ = God Incarnate

**No Excuse** if you suppress His testimony

Why?

He has made the evidence *CLEAR TO SEE*
John 5:39

Courtesy of Google Images   Fair Use Law 17 U.S. Code § 107

## Christian Worldview:  Engages the *MIND* to discern *TRUTH*

Matthew 22:37 *"You shall love the Lord your God with all your ①HEART, with all your soul and all your ②MIND."*
  ①HEART = Greek *"kardia"* = feelings, thoughts          ②MIND = Greek *"dianoia"* = intellect, understanding

Romans 12:2 *"...do not be conformed to this world, but be transformed by the renewing of your ④MIND"*

Romans 1:28 *"as they did not like to ③RETAIN God in their knowledge, God gave them over to a debased ④MIND..."*
  ③RETAIN = Greek *"echō"* = possess, hold onto          ④MIND = Greek *"nous"* = intellect, understanding

In his book 'Basic Christianity'[2], John Stott explains in the two headings below, "Avoiding Mindless Christianity" and "Why Use My Mind – to discover what is TRUE", why it is so crucial to use your mind, your intellect, to develop a worldview that maps with reality:

**Avoiding Mindless Christianity** ⇨ "What Paul wrote about unbelieving Jews in his day could be said, I fear, of some believing Christians in ours:  Romans 10:2 *'I bear them witness that they have a zeal for God, but not according to knowledge.'* Many have zeal without knowledge, enthusiasm without enlightenment. In more modern jargon, they are keen but clueless. Now I thank God for zeal. Heaven forbid that knowledge without zeal should replace zeal without knowledge! God's purpose is both: zeal directed by knowledge, knowledge fired with zeal.

**Why Use My Mind – to discover what is *TRUE*** ⇨ <u>I was created to *think*</u> = God made man in His own image, and one of the noblest features of the divine likeness in man is his capacity to think. Right from the beginning, God expects man to understand: He expects man to cooperate with Him, consciously and intelligently, in tilling and keeping the garden in which he has placed him, and to discriminate – rationally as well as morally – between what he is permitted to do and the one thing he is prohibited from doing. Scripture bases the regular argument that since man is different from the animals he should *behave* differently (Psalm 32:9 *"Do not be like the horse or like the mule, which have no understanding..."*). While there are many similarities between man and the animals, animals were created to behave by instinct, human beings by intelligent choice. And in spite of the fallenness of man's mind, commands to think, to use his mind, are still addressed to him as a human being.

<u>Christianity is a *revealed* religion (in *words* to *minds*)</u> = If there is a religion in the world which exalts the office of teaching, it is the religion of Jesus Christ. In pagan religions the doctrine is at a minimum. The chief thing is the performance of a *ritual*. But this is precisely where Christianity separates itself from other religions:

  1 - it does contain *DOCTRINE*     2 - it comes to men with definite, positive *teaching*
  3 - it claims to be the *TRUTH*     4 - it bases religion on *knowledge* attainable only under moral conditions

Some people reach the opposite conclusion: since man is finite and fallen, they argue, since he cannot discover God by his intellect and God must reveal Himself, therefore the mind is unimportant. But no. The Christian doctrine of revelation, far from making the human mind unnecessary, actually makes it indispensable and assigns to it its proper place. God has revealed Himself in *words* to *minds*. His revelation is a rational revelation to rational creatures. One of the highest and noblest functions of man's mind is to listen to God's Word, and so to read His mind and think His thoughts after Him.

<u>God will one day judge me on my response to His revelation</u> = Having achieved redemption of mankind through the death and resurrection of His Son, God now announces this redemption through His servants. The proclamation of the gospel – again addressed in *words* to *minds* – is the chief means which God has appointed to bring salvation to sinners. One thing is clear... He will judge me by my knowledge, by my response (or lack of response) to His revelation. This principle of judgment our Lord Himself endorsed in John 12:48 *'He who rejects Me, and does not receive My words, has that which judges him – the word which I have spoken will judge him in the last day.'* God has made us thinking beings; He has treated us as such by communicating with us in words. It is a solemn thought that by our own anti-intellectualism, in which we either refuse or cannot be bothered to listen to God's word, we may be storing up for ourselves the judgment of God."

### The Bible's Emphasis: the goal of Knowledge, Understanding and Wisdom is to *KNOW THE TRUTH*

Proverbs 3:13-14  *"Happy is the man who finds WISDOM, and the man who gains UNDERSTANDING, for her proceeds are better than the profits of silver, and her gain than fine gold."*

Proverbs 4:7  *"WISDOM is the principal thing; therefore get wisdom. And in all your getting, get UNDERSTANDING."*

Ephesians 1:17-18  *"...the God of our Lord Jesus Christ, the Father of glory, may give to you the spirit of WISDOM and revelation in the KNOWLEDGE of Him, the eyes of your UNDERSTANDING being enlightened, that you may KNOW what is the hope of His calling, what are the riches of the glory of His inheritance in the saints..."*

Colossians 1:9-10  *"...(we) do not cease to pray for you, and to ask that you may be filled with the KNOWLEDGE of His will in all WISDOM and spiritual UNDERSTANDING; that you may have a walk worthy of the Lord, fully pleasing Him, being fruitful in every good work and increasing in the KNOWLEDGE of God.."*

Proverbs 23:23  *"BUY THE TRUTH, and don't sell it, also wisdom and instruction and understanding."*

## BOOK REVIEW: "The Normal Christian Life" by Watchman Nee

Watchman Nee (November 4, 1903 – May 30, 1972) was a leader of the original underground church in China, helping to establish local churches in China independent of foreign missionaries that has resulted in one of largest movements of Christianity the world has ever seen.

In 1922, he initiated church meetings in Fuzhou that sparked the beginning of local churches in China. During his 30 years in ministering the gospel of Jesus Christ, he published many books expounding on biblical truth, as well as establishing churches throughout China and leading many conferences to train Bible students and church workers.

Watchman Nee never attended theological schools or Bible institutes. His wealth of knowledge concerning God's purpose, Christ, the Spirit, and the church was acquired through studying the Bible.

The Lord revealed many truths to him, which he taught to others, through his diligent study of the Word, which he explains in his book '*How to Study the Bible*'.

# *The Normal Christian Life*

**Watchman Nee on Romans 3:23**
**(man's thinking vs. God's thinking)**

*"Man's thought is always of the punishment that will come to him if he sins.*

*God's thought is always of the glory man will miss if he sins.*

*The result of sin is that we forfeit God's glory.*

*The result of redemption is that we are qualified again for glory.*

*God's purpose in redemption is glory, glory, glory."*  Page 109

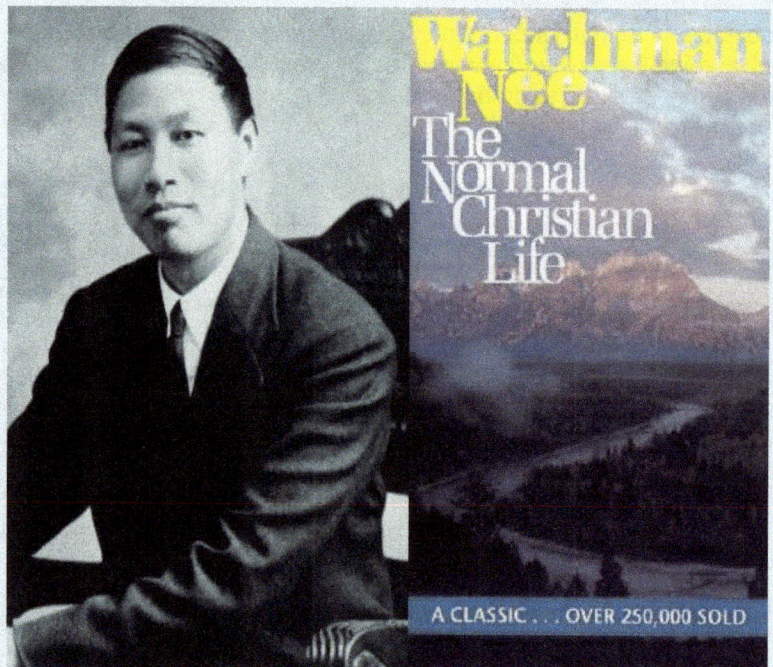

**Watchman Nee**
**The Normal Christian Life**

A CLASSIC . . . OVER 250,000 SOLD

*"I must first have the sense of God's possession of me before I can have the sense of His presence with me. Once His ownership is established, then I dare do nothing in my own interests, for I am His exclusive property."* (page 106)

Nee built a collection of over 3,000 of the best Christian books throughout church history, including nearly all the classical Christian writings from the first century forward.

His incredible ability to grasp and memorize important scriptural truths and spiritual principles from these books, combined with his deep understanding of God's Word, made him one of if not the most impactful church leader during China's Christian explosive growth.

As the Communist Revolution erupted in 1946 (led by the Communist Party of China and its leader, Chairman Mao Zedong), Nee was persecuted and imprisoned for his faith in 1952 at the age of 49, spending the 20 twenty years of his life in prison until his death in 1972.

Throughout the 14 chapters of his book, Watchman provides the following insights into what the "normal" Christian life looks like with their page references. His deep understanding of his own personal knowing and loving Jesus Christ can help all of us in our own personal journeys in our relationship with Jesus.

# Comparing Worldviews:    Detecting the Truth

| Christianity | Modernism, Postmodernism |
|---|---|
| 1. I am a special creation of a good and all-powerful God. | 1. I am a descendant of a tiny cell of protoplasm that showed up 3.5 billion years ago. |
| 2. I am a created in His image, with capacities to think, feel and worship | 2. I am the blind, random product of time, chance and natural forces… a grab bag of atomic particles. |
| 3. I differ from animals not simply in degree but in kind. Not only is my kind unique, but I am unique among your kind. | 3. I am a purely biological entity, different only in degree but not in kind  from a microbe, virus, or amoeba. |
| 4. God loves me so intensely, He desires my companionship and has a plan for my life. | 4. I exist on a tiny planet in a minute solar system in an empty corner of a meaningless universe. |
| 5. God gave the life of His Son so that I might spend eternity with Him. | 5. I have no essence beyond my body, and at death I will cease to exist. |
| 6. If I am willing to **humble myself** to accept His gift of of salvation, I can be His child. | 6. My goal is to **trust, develop and promote myself** in this life. I came from nothing and am going nowhere. |

Dr. Frank Turek: "Answering Atheist's 3 Objections to Christianity" (9:05)

# The Christian Gospel:  It Requires Humility and Brokenness

| The Adulterous Woman | The Prodigal Son | The Pharisee & the Tax Collector | The Ultimate Act of Humility |
|---|---|---|---|
|  |  | 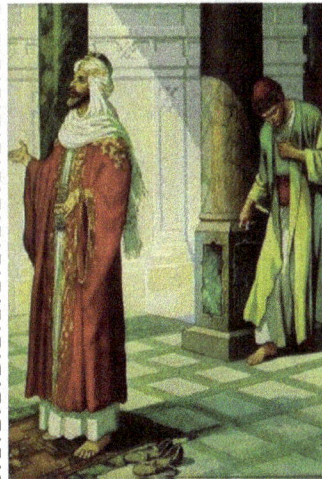 |  |
| *"The Lord sent Me to heal the brokenhearted."* (Isaiah 61:1 – Luke 4:18) | *"The Lord is near to the brokenhearted and saves the crushed in spirit."* (Psalm 34:18) | *"God regards the lowly, but the proud He knows from afar."* (Psalm 138:6) | *"It pleased the Lord to crush Him."* (Isaiah 53:10) |

Jesus of Nazareth: 'Come to Me, all you who are weary…' (3:01)

Courtesy of Google Images    Fair Use Law 17 U.S. Code § 107

## The Christian Gospel: It's Power is in BROKENNESS

What was God's greatest act of His power?

God's power is **RELEASED** at the *CROSS*

God's power is *released* in *MY* brokenness Luke 4:18

to be *EXALTED...*

Philippians 2:9-10

God's power is **REVEALED** at the *CROSS*

God's power is *revealed* in *HIS* brokenness Romans 1:16

God's Act of **REDEMPTION** is greater than His Act of Creation

God's ultimate power is His *breaking of Himself for His creation* Isaiah 53:5,10 Luke 22:41-44

requires being *HUMILIATED...*

Philippians 2:8

What is the Spiritual Law of the Universe in operation at the Cross?

JOHN 3:30 *"He must increase, but I must decrease."*

Courtesy of Google Images    Fair Use Law 17 U.S. Code § 107

## The Christian Gospel: To "See" I Must Admit I am "Blind"

| Isaiah 59:10-12 | Ezekiel 12:2, 7:20 | Revelation 3:16-17 | John 9:39-41 |
|---|---|---|---|
| THE CHURCHES OF REVELATION LAODICEA THE LUKEWARM CHURCH | | | |
| "We grope for the wall like the blind, as if we had no eyes, as dead men in desolate places." | "You dwell in the midst of the rebellious house that have eyes to see and see not.." | "You do not know that that you are wretched, miserable, poor, blind, and naked.." | "I've come into the world that those who don't see may see, and those who see may be made blind." |
| Why? | Why? | Why? | Why? |
| "Our sins testify against us, our transgressions are with us, we know our iniquities." | "They were proud of their of their beautiful jewelry, using it to make detestable idols." | "You are lukewarm... you say 'I am rich, have become wealthy, and have need of nothing...'" | "If you were blind, you would have no sin... But you say 'We see', so your sin remains." |

Who are those who are "Called"?

*"I did not come to CALL the righteous, but sinners to repentance."* (Luke 5:32)

## Ephesians 3:14-19    Christian Worldview: Faith requires Logical Thinking

*"...I bow my knees to the Father of our Lord Jesus Christ, from whom the whole family in heaven and earth is named, that He would grant you, according to the riches of His glory, to be strengthened with might through His Spirit in the inner man, that Christ may dwell in your hearts through ①FAITH; that you, being rooted and grounded in love, may be able to ②COMPREHEND with all the saints what is the width and length and depth and height – to ③KNOW the love of Christ which passes ④KNOWLEDGE; that you may be filled with all the fullness of God."*

① FAITH = Gr. *"pistis"* = moral conviction; persuasive assurance; trust in God based on His character
② COMPREHEND = Gr. *"katalambanô"* = take eagerly or seize; attain; possess; perceive
③ KNOW = Gr. *"ginôskô"* = to be sure of; to be resolved; to fully understand
④ KNOWLEDGE = Gr. *"gnôsis"* = the act of knowing; science (form of *"ginôskô"*)

**John Stott[2]: Faith ≠ credulity**   "H.L. Mencken says 'Faith may be defined briefly as an illogical belief in the occurrence of the improbable'. But Mencken was wrong – faith is not credulity. To be credulous is to be gullible, to be entirely uncritical, undiscerning and even unreasonable in one's beliefs. It is a great mistake to suppose that faith and reason are incompatible. Faith and sight are set in opposition to each other in Scripture (see 2Corin. 5:7), but not faith and reason. On the contrary, true faith is essentially reasonable because it trusts in God's character and promises. A Christian is one whose mind reflects and rests on these certitudes.

**John Stott[2]: Faith ≠ optimism (positive thinking)**
This seems to be the confusion made by Norman Vincent Peale. His fundamental conviction concerns the power of the human mind... Dr. Peale develops his thesis about positive thinking, which he goes on (mistakenly) to equate with faith. In his book 'The Power of Positive Thinking' he says 'According to your faith in yourself, according to your faith in your job, according to your faith in God this far will get you and no farther.' Dr. Peale apparently draws no distinction between faith in God and faith in oneself. Indeed, he does not seem to be at all concerned about faith's object. To Dr. Peale faith is really another word for self-confidence, for a largely ungrounded optimism.

FAITH-BASED CONNECT-THE-DOTS
free inquiry    http://www.secularhumanism.org   20

---

### Matthew 6:28-30    Faith and Evidence belong together (Believing requires Thinking)

*"⑤CONSIDER the lilies of the field.... Now if God so clothes the grass of the field, which today is, and tomorrow is thrown into the oven, will He not much more clothe you, O you of ⑥LITTLE FAITH?"*

⑤ CONSIDER = Gr. *"katalambanô"* = to learn thoroughly; to note carefully; to seize (same as "comprehend")
⑥ LITTLE FAITH = Gr. *"oligopistos"* = lacking confidence or assurance

We must study our Lord's lessons in *observation* and *deduction* from the *evidence*. The bible is full of logic, and we must never think of faith as something purely mystical. Look at the birds about you, and draw your deductions. Look at the grass, look at the lilies of the field, consider them. Faith, can be defined like this: *it is a man insisting upon thinking when everything seems determined to knock him down in an intellectual sense.*

---

**John Stott[2]: Faith = Logically Thinking upon the Trustworthiness of God**   "Christian faith reckons thoughtfully and confidently upon the trustworthiness of God. 1Samuel 30:6 says that *"David strengthened himself in the Lord his God"*. This is true faith. David did not shut his eyes to the facts. Nor did he try to build up his self-confidence or tell himself that he was really feeling fine. No. He remembered the Lord his God, the God of creation and the God of the covenant, the God who had promised to be his God and to set him on the throne of Israel. As David recalled the promises and faithfulness of God, he grew strong in faith. He 'strengthened himself in the Lord his God.' The trouble with the person of little faith is that, instead of controlling his own thought, his thought is being controlled by something else, and as we put it, he goes round and round in circles. That is the essence of WORRY... that is not thought; that is the absence of thought, a FAILURE TO THINK."

**The foundation of my faith = clear and logical *knowledge* of Jesus Christ.**

## Logically Thinking through the Problems of Christianity

1) Problem #1 = there are many **intellectual** reasons to question Christianity

| | |
|---|---|
| a) where did life come from? | The Bible says God created life |
| b) where does evil come from? | The Bible says from man's nature |
| c) how can the Bible have no errors? | The Bible says it is error-free |

2) Problem #2 = there are **emotional** obstacles with Christianity

| | |
|---|---|
| a) aren't there many ways to heaven? | The Bible says Jesus is the only way to eternal life |
| b) how can a loving God create hell? | The Bible says hell is a real place of torment |
| c) why is there so much hypocrisy in Christianity? | The Bible says Christianity is a heart issue |

3) Problem #3 = there are **volitional** reasons to reject Christianity

| | |
|---|---|
| a) why should I have to answer to anyone? | The Bible says to deny yourself and follow Jesus |
| b) why deny myself fun today for promises someday? | The Bible says true rewards are in heaven |
| c) why would I put others ahead of my own desires? | The Bible says esteem others better than yourself |

In their book 'I Don't Have Enough Faith to be an Atheist'[6], Norman Geisler and Frank Turek explain below that the reasonableness of Christianity must withstand the test of evidence in order for faith to make sense:

**Is Christianity reasonable?** "We believe it is. But unless you make a thorough investigation of the *evidence* with an open mind, belief in Christianity may appear to be problematic. Once one looks at the *evidence*, we think it takes more faith to be a non-Christian than it does to be a Christian. The claim that religion is simply a matter of faith is a modern myth - it's just not true. While religion certainly requires faith, religion is not only about faith. Facts are also central to all religions because all religious worldviews - including atheism - make *TRUTH CLAIMS*, and many of those truth claims can be evaluated through *SCIENTIFIC* and *HISTORICAL* investigation."

**Why does every religious worldview require faith?** "As limited human beings, we do not possess the type of knowledge that will provide us with *ABSOLUTE PROOF* of God's existence. Outside of the knowledge of our own existence (I know I exist because I have to exist in order to ponder the question), we deal in *PROBABILITY*. Whatever we've concluded about the existence of God, it's always possible that the opposite conclusion is true. In fact, it is possible that our conclusions in this book ("*I Don't Have Enough Faith to be an Atheist*") are wrong. We don't think they are because we have good *evidence* to support them. Indeed, we think our conclusions are true beyond a REASONABLE DOUBT. This type of certainty, say, 95-plus percent certain, is the best that fallible and finite beings can attain for most questions, and it is more than sufficient for even the biggest decisions in life. Nevertheless, some faith is required to overcome the possibility that we are wrong."

### The Faith of an Atheist[6]

"While some faith is required for our conclusions, it's often forgotten that faith is also required to believe any worldview, including atheism. We were reminded of this recently when we met an atheist named Barry at one of our seminars. Barry was incredulous that a mutual friend, Steve, had become a Christian.

He said, 'I can't figure Steve out. He claims to be an intellectual, but he can't answer all my objections I pose to him about Christianity. He says he doesn't have all the answers because he's new and still learning.'

I (Frank) said, 'Barry, it's virtually impossible to know everything about a particular topic, and it's certainly impossible when that topic is an infinite God. So there has to be a point where you realize you have enough information to come to a conclusion, even if unanswered questions remain."

Barry had decided his view - atheism - was correct even though he did not have exhaustive information to support it. Did he know for sure there is no God? Had he investigated every argument and evidence for the existence of God? Could he answer every objection to atheism? Of course not. It would be impossible to do so. Since Barry, like Steve, is dealing in the realm of probability rather than absolute certainty, he has to have a certain amount of faith to believe that God does not exist.

### "FAITH = what I use to cover any gap in my knowledge"[6]

When thinking through issues of faith, the question is: who has more *evidence* for their conclusion? Which conclusion is more reasonable? The less evidence you have for your position, the more faith you need to believe it (and vice versa).

As we'll see, the empirical, forensic, and philosophical *evidence* strongly supports conclusions consistent with Christianity and inconsistent with any other worldview."

# If Christianity is true... Why isn't Everyone a Christian?

**Problem #1 = there are *intellectual* obstacles with Christianity**

a) where did everything come from?   ← The Bible says God made everything from nothing

b) where does evil come from?        ← The Bible says evil comes from people's nature

c) how can the Bible have no errors?  ← The Bible says it is error-free

**Problem #2 = there are *emotional* obstacles with Christianity**

a) aren't there many ways to heaven? ← The Bible says Jesus is the only way to heaven

b) how can a loving God create hell?  ← The Bible says hell is a real place of torment

c) isn't the Church full of hypocrites? ← The Bible says Christianity is a heart issue

**Problem #3 = there are *volitional* obstacles with Christianity**

a) why should I answer to anyone?    ← The Bible says to deny yourself and follow Jesus

b) why deny myself fun today?        ← The Bible says true rewards are in heaven

c) why put others ahead of me?       ← The Bible says treat others better than yourself

**Is Christianity 'easy believism'?**

**MATTHEW 7:14**
*"Narrow is the gate and difficult is the way which leads to life..."*

'Interview with Dr. William Lane Craig: Handling Doubt' (5:38)

Courtesy of Google Images    Fair Use Law 17 U.S. Code § 107

**Exit Ticket #11**

| | |
|---|---|
| **1) Define what Christianity is NOT and what it IS?** | **2) What Bible verse says God made His evidence for creation "plain for all to see"?** |
| **3) What Bible verse did Jesus say the evidence for Him in the Old Testament is "plain to see"?** | **4) Of the 9 obstacles leading to skepticism of Christianity, which ones resonate with you and why?** |

# Class 12 - America's Founding

Understanding Early America:  Christianity

Understanding America's Pledge of Allegiance: Christianity

Article 301 - The American Experiment:  Guiding Principle #1 = "God is Our Creator"

USS Michael Patrick Murphy: Proudly Flying the Largest American Flag Ever Seen

The Bible's Influence in America's Founding

Article 302 - The American Experiment:  Guiding Principle #2 = "Natural Law"

The Bible's Influence in Forming Our Constitution

Christianity and the Constitution – The Wisdom of Separating Powers

Article 250 - The First Amendment & Myth of "Separation of Church & State"

Christianity and the Constitution – The 2nd Amendment

America's vs. France's Constitution

Article 303 - The American Experiment: Guiding Principle #3 = "The Bible's 'Individual Liberty'"

George Washington: Follower of Jesus Christ

Comparing Early Christianity to Early America: Boldness

The Theme of Biblical, Historical Christianity = Boldness

America and Christmas – Rooted in Jesus Christ

America's Protectors:  Our Christian Roots

Article 200:  Why Police are Targeted - Lies & Deceit have replaced the Truth

Article 244 - Our Military:  America's Defender of Our Many Freedoms

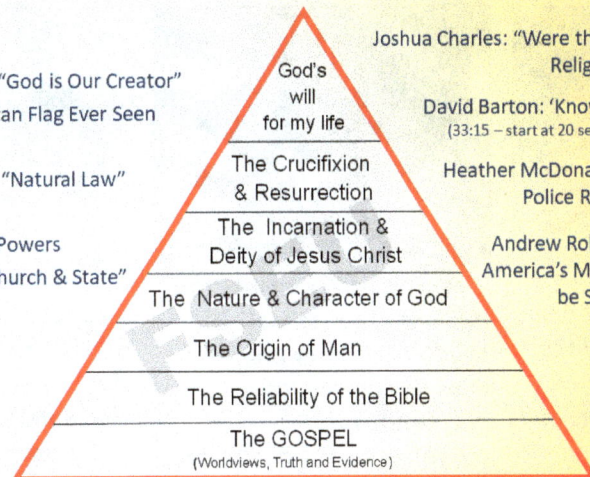

Joshua Charles: "Were the Founders Religious?" (4:55)

David Barton: 'Know the Bible' (33:15 – start at 20 secs, go to 20:13)

Heather McDonald: 'Are the Police Racist?' (5:35)

Andrew Roberts: 'Why America's Military Must be Strong' (5:27)

**Pyramid:**
God's will for my life

The Crucifixion & Resurrection

The Incarnation & Deity of Jesus Christ

The Nature & Character of God

The Origin of Man

The Reliability of the Bible

The GOSPEL (Worldviews, Truth and Evidence)

**HEBREWS 11:1**

"Faith = *Substance* of things *hoped for* …. *Evidence* of things *not seen*"

fse.life Lesson 01

# Understanding Early America:  Christianity

## Declaration of Independence

"We hold these truths to be self-evident, that all men are created equal.

That they are endowed by their Creator with certain unalienable rights,

that among these are life, Liberty and the pursuit of happiness..."

## Constitution

"We the People of the United States, in order to form a more perfect Union, establish Justice, insure domestic Tranquility,

provide for the common defense, promote the general welfare,

and secure the Blessings of Liberty to ourselves and our posterity, do ordain and establish this Constitution for the United States of America."

"Proclaim *Liberty* throughout all the land unto all the inhabitants thereof" (Leviticus 25:10)

Joshua Charles: 'Were the Founders Religious?' (4:55)

# Understanding America's Pledge of Allegiance: Christianity

**Pledge to the Christian Flag**

I pledge allegiance to the Christian flag, and to the Savior for whose kingdom it stands, one brotherhood, uniting all Christians in service and love.

*"I pledge allegiance to the flag of the United States of America, and to the republic for which it stands, one nation UNDER GOD, indivisible, with liberty and justice for all."*

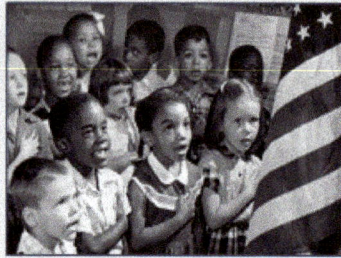

*"From this day forward, the millions of our school children will daily proclaim in every city and town, every village and rural schoolhouse, the dedication of our nation and our people to the Almighty."* (President Eisenhower, 1954, adds "Under God" to Pledge of Allegiance)

*"Every school in Missouri which is supported in whole or in part by public moneys shall ensure that the Pledge of Allegiance to the flag of the United States of America is recited in at least one scheduled class of every pupil enrolled in that school no less than once per week."* (MO Revised Statutes, Sect. 171.021.2)

**Our Pledge of Allegiance is a Christian worldview and eliminates other religious worldviews:**

1) "Under God" eliminates Atheism, Buddhism
2) "indivisible" eliminates Hinduism (Pantheism)
3) "with liberty and justice for all" eliminates Islam

*"Blessed is the nation whose God is the Lord, and the people He has chosen as His own inheritance."* PSALM 33:12

# USS Michael Patrick Murphy entering San Diego Port: Proudly Flying the Largest American Flag Ever Seen

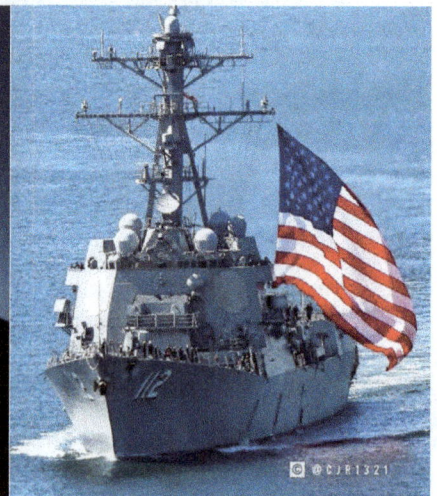

**USS Michael Murphy (DDG 112)**
Yesterday at 12:49 PM · 

Sometimes, just sometimes... you just have to to let them know whos arriving!

MOST LETHAL, BEST DESTROYER of the FLEET!

#LeadTheFight

"I pledge allegiance to the flag of the United States of America, and to the republic for which it stands, one nation UNDER GOD, indivisible, with liberty and justice for all."

# Article 301 - The American Experiment:  Guiding Principle #1 = "God is Our Creator"

Ecclesiastes 5:2   *"God is in heaven, and you are on earth; therefore let your words be few."*

After a narrow 5-4 victory this week in the Supreme Court, President Trump's travel ban on citizens from 7 countries (Syria, Iran, Libya, Somalia, Yemen, North Korea and Venezuela) traveling to the US was upheld. Protestors against the Supreme Court decision are declaring SCOTUS has become partisan, actually violating the Constitution by siding with the President in religious discrimination against Muslims.

This comes on the heels of our ICE (Immigration and Customs Enforcement) officers being advised to not wear any identifying insignias out in public when off duty, for fear of public attack. Those defending our borders against illegal immigration are being targeted as racists, discriminating against Mexicans.

But how did SCOTUS come to their decision? By turning to Constitutional law. The court said the President has, by our Constitution, substantial power to regulate immigration.

In the majority opinion, Chief Justice John Roberts stated: *"The sole prerequisite set forth is that the President find that the entry of the covered aliens would be detrimental to the interests of the United States. The President has undoubtedly fulfilled that requirement here."* By law, the office of the President has been given the power to ban any group of people from entering the US if the President decides their presence would be detrimental to US interests.

In the dissenting statement, Justice Sonia Sotomayor said *"a reasonable observer would conclude that the Proclamation was motivated by anti-Muslim animus."* The fact is that 92% of Muslims in the world are not impacted by the travel ban. Citizens of Saudi Arabia (93% Muslim), Pakistan (96%), Iraq (97%), Turkey (99.5%), Afghanistan (98%), to name just a few, are free to come and go in America as they wish.

We are now accusing Supreme Court Justices, along with anyone supporting our current President, with discriminating against certain people groups (not Mexicans this time, but Muslims).

So now we are seeing attacks on the Constitution itself. The theme of most attacks is that it is outdated and no longer works in a progressive American culture where people are capable of making decisions that are in the best interests of most Americans. In other words, let's allow people to govern people since we are basically good and will mostly do what is best for each other, being accountable for each other's interests. Hence the character attacks now on even our SCOTUS justices, who are upholding Constitutional law.

Thankfully, our Founders knew the danger of implementing a system without checks and balances, where any majority could decide policy. Writing in National Review, Jay Cost's article 'Let's Not Throw Out the Constitution' makes the point of why we need the Constitution – because of the overwhelming tendency of man to turn on one another for each one's own selfish benefits: *"When I look at America in 2018, I see a country where a wide swath of people are uninterested and poorly informed, unaware of even the basics of civics to know how our government works, and unwilling to dedicate the time necessary to learn.*

*I see the special interests that finance politics, employing campaign contributions, lobbying, and other subtle crafts to take advantage of public indolence for their own purposes. I look at the ideological poles, where citizens are more engaged. That is good, but it is also at the extremes where I see intense hatred of their ideological opponents.*

*If granted total power, would one side criminalize the other? Would the broad middle, in its laziness and ignorance, actually let them do it? I still think we require ways to temper and control the rule of the majority, which remains the most fearful power in a republic such as ours."*

As we begin our look at the Founders' 10 guiding principles for the "American Experiment", they form the very basis of our Constitution. And the first one is the foundation of our Declaration of Independence. This most important principle unfortunately no longer guides everyday American life, so you don't hear it discussed much in public. Guiding principle #1 is that there is a God to whom we are accountable.

America is not a theocracy. Our system of government was built on the right of each of us to worship (or not worship) freely. But it is a fact that America was founded with a religious identity. And the #1 principle is that it is a supernatural Creator, not human government, to whom we are accountable for our behavior. Our Founders not only understood there is a God – they also reached that understanding by consensus.

By acknowledging God as our foundational principle, our Founders grounded individual human liberties in our connection as human beings to Him, thus protecting us all from the reaches of government and from the rule of majority opinion. Let us hope our laws remain centered on this Constitutional imperative.

# The Bible's Influence in America's Founding

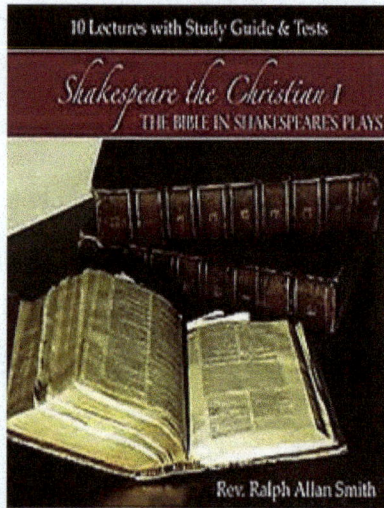

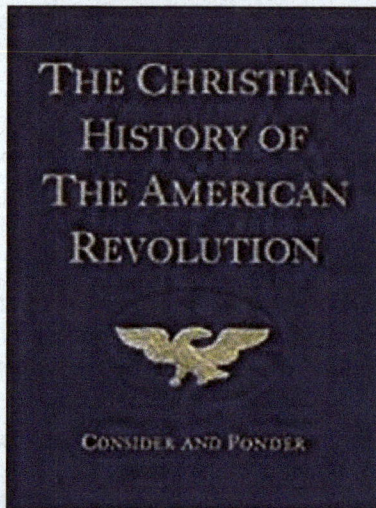

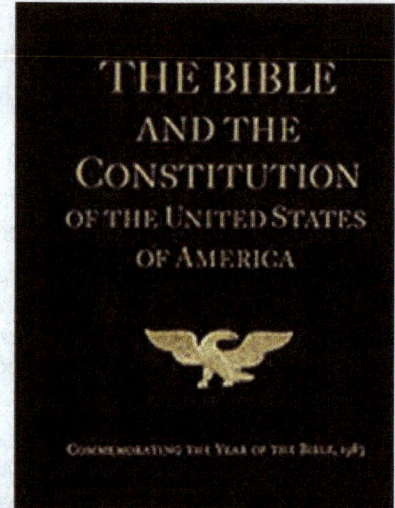

10 Lectures with Study Guide & Tests

Shakespeare the Christian 1
THE BIBLE IN SHAKESPEARES PLAYS

Rev. Ralph Allan Smith

THE CHRISTIAN HISTORY OF THE AMERICAN REVOLUTION

CONSIDER AND PONDER

THE BIBLE AND THE CONSTITUTION OF THE UNITED STATES OF AMERICA

COMMEMORATING THE YEAR OF THE BIBLE, 1983

## *"We shall have no King but Jesus."*

(Battle Cry of the American Revolution, began with 13 Colonies as Committees created their Charters, 1774)

David Barton: 'Know the Bible' (33:15 - start at 20 secs, go to 20:13)     Courtesy of Google Images     Fair Use Law 17 U.S. Code § 107

---

# The Bible's Influence in Forming Our Constitution

| | | |
|---|---|---|
| **The idea for 3 Government Branches?** | • Executive (President)<br>• Legislative (Congress)<br>• Judicial (Supreme Court) | **Isaiah 33:22** *"The Lord is our Judge (Judicial), the Lord is our Lawgiver (Legislative), the Lord is our King (Executive); He will save us."* |
| **The idea for the 1st Amendment (free press, religion, speech)?** | *"Jesus Christ's law was a Law of Liberty. He left human mind and action free."* (John Quincy Adams) | **Mark 2:27** *"The Sabbath was made for man, and not man for the Sabbath."* |
| **The idea for the 2nd Amendment (bear arms)?** | *"Hebrew militia law is part of the background of the 2nd Amendment."* (Prof. David Kopel, 'Ancient Hebrew Militia Law') | **Numbers 26:2** *"Take a census of all the congregation of Israel from 20 years old and above… who are able to go to war."* |
| **The idea for the 5th Amendment (life, liberty, property)?** | *"Nonconformity, dissent, free inquiry, individual conviction, mental independence, are forever consecrated by the religion of the New Testament."* (Stephen Cowell, legal writer for Founders) | **1Corinthians 10:29** *"Why is my liberty judged by another man's conscience?"* |

Courtesy of Google Images     Fair Use Law 17 U.S. Code § 107

## Article 302 - The American Experiment:  Guiding Principle #2 = "Natural Law"

*Acts 5:29   "Peter and the other apostles answered and said: 'We ought to obey God rather than man."*

We continue looking at the guiding principles of our Founding Fathers that has made America so exceptional. As we examine Principle #2, let me take you back to September 2017 and the Senate Judiciary hearing to confirm Amy Coney Barrett as Judge for the US Court of Appeals.

Senator Diane Feinstein claimed Barrett's religious views disqualify her from serving as a judge: *"When you read your speeches, the conclusion one draws is that the dogma lives loudly within you, and that's of concern when you come to big issues that large numbers of people have fought for for years in this country."*

Barrett's answer was clear and concise – no. Neither her personal religious convictions nor the teachings of the Church or the Scriptures would override her responsibilities as a judge: *"Judges cannot, nor should they try to, align our legal system with the Church's moral teaching whenever the two diverge."* Why, although highly qualified, are Barrett's personal religious views being touted as enough to disqualify her?

In his latest book 'Rediscovering Americanism and the Tyranny of Progressivism', Mark Levin provides insight to this question in the first chapter by focusing on the Founding Fathers' Guiding Principle #2 in writing the Declaration of Independence and the ensuing Constitution: Natural Law. As Levin puts it, *"To rediscover Americanism is to rediscover natural law."* So what is 'natural law'? Here's Levin's definition.

*"Natural law provides a moral compass or order—justice, virtue, truth, prudence, etc.—a fundamental, universal, everlasting harmony of mores that transcend human law. Through natural law discovered by right reason, man knows right from wrong and good from bad. Natural law is right law."* Where does natural law originate? Reread last week's article on our Founding Fathers' Guiding Principle #1.

It is Almighty God who is the essence of righteousness and justice. As King David proclaims in Psalm 89:14: *"Righteousness and justice are the foundation of Your throne; mercy and truth go before Your face".*

Natural law originates from the character of God, and therefore transcends man's laws. This is what Levin means when he says that knowing right from wrong, good from evil are innate within every human being. Everyone knows the difference because we have a moral conscience put there by God.

In the New Testament, Romans 2:14-15 backs up Levin's point: *"When the Gentiles, who do not have the law, by nature do the things contained in the law,… they show the work of the law written in their hearts, their conscience also bearing witness… their thoughts accusing or excusing them."*

So with such a universally understood truth, why the backlash against Barrett? Because to be a member of the progressive liberal movement means to reject natural law. To be a secular humanist means to reject a transcendent God who presides over the affairs of men.

You must reject our Founding Fathers' Guiding Principles #1 (God, not government, reigns) and #2 (Natural Law is the moral compass for our legislative system). In addition, you cannot join the progressive liberal party in America today and confess to uphold the words of our Declaration of Independence, because you reject the following two sentences:

*"We hold these truths to be self-evident, that all men are created equal and are endowed by their Creator with certain unalienable rights, that among these are life, liberty and the pursuit of happiness. That to secure these rights, governments are instituted among men, deriving their just powers from the consent of the governed."* In the first sentence, natural law is expressed in 2 terms: self-evident and unalienable.

SELF-EVIDENT means "obvious to everyone, and not needing to be demonstrated or explained". Our Founders use it here in declaring that all of us have been created equal by God, who has endowed each of us with UNALIENABLE rights. And unalienable means sacred. These rights we each possess cannot be taken from you, nor can you give them to someone else. They simply are yours from your Creator.

In the second sentence, we learn why our Founders created our governmental system: to secure (protect) these God-given, unalienable rights. They knew men by their corrupt nature are sinners, and they will, if left unchecked, destroy each other.

But sentence two goes further in asserting that government is to have its power only by the consent of those it is governing. This is the essence of Barrett's answer to Feinstein. While Barrett personally holds to the reality of God ruling over her life, our government's legal system, founded on Abraham Lincoln's famous quote *"Of the people, by the people, for the people"*, is there to administer justice and righteousness across the land.

This is our Constitutionally-mandated natural law, and it is the very basis of the Founders' Guiding Principle #3 for next week – our individual liberty.

# Christianity and the Constitution – The Wisdom of Separating Powers

He will save us." ISAIAH 33:22

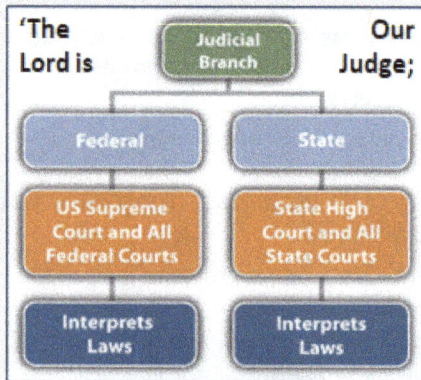

| 'The Lord is | Judicial Branch | Our Judge; |
| --- | --- | --- |
| | Federal | State |
| | US Supreme Court and All Federal Courts | State High Court and All State Courts |
| | Interprets Laws | Interprets Laws |

**Why Judicial Branch?**

To resolve disputes and settle right vs. wrong.

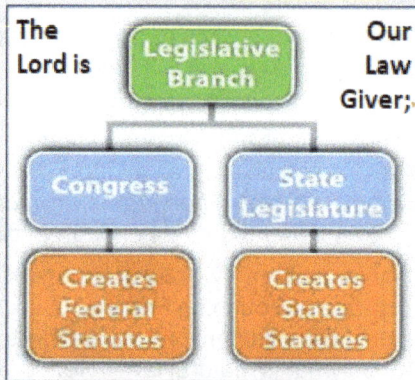

| The Lord is | Legislative Branch | Our Law Giver; |
| --- | --- | --- |
| | Congress | State Legislature |
| | Creates Federal Statutes | Creates State Statutes |

**Why Legislative Branch?**

To establish laws governing a free society (how we treat each other).

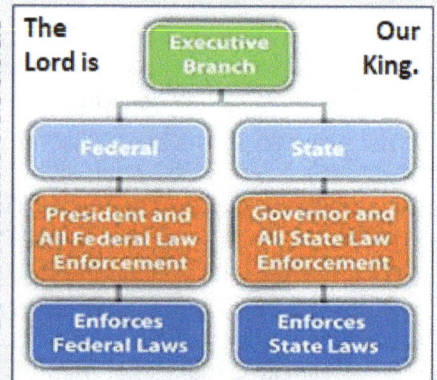

| The Lord is | Executive Branch | Our King. |
| --- | --- | --- |
| | Federal | State |
| | President and All Federal Law Enforcement | Governor and All State Law Enforcement |
| | Enforces Federal Laws | Enforces State Laws |

**Why Executive Branch?**

To protect us (national and homeland security).

*"Our laws and our institutions must necessarily be based upon and embody the teachings of the Redeemer of mankind. It is impossible that it should be otherwise; and in this sense and to this extent our civilization and our institutions are emphatically Christian."* US Supreme Court, 1892

Courtesy of Google Images    Fair Use Law 17 U.S. Code § 107

# Celebrating George Washington:    A Follower of Jesus Christ

*"It was his custom to retire to his library at 9 or 10 pm where he remained an hour before going to bed.*

*He always rose before the sun and remained in his library until called to breakfast.*

*I never witnessed his private devotions. I never inquired about them.*

*I should have thought it the greatest heresy to doubt his firm belief in Christianity. His life, his writings, prove that he was a Christian.*

*He was not one of those who act or pray, 'that they may be seen of me' [Matthew 6:5]. He communed with his God in secret [Matthew 6:6]."*

Nelly Custis-Lewis, his adopted daughter who lived with Washington and his wife 20 years

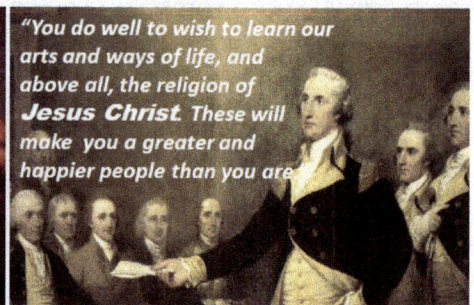

*"You do well to wish to learn our arts and ways of life, and above all, the religion of **Jesus Christ**. These will make you a greater and happier people than you are."*

*"In 1827, Mr. Robert Lewis, a nephew of Washington and his private secretary during the first part of his presidency, lived with him and had the best opportunity for observing his habits.*

*Mr. Lewis said he accidentally witnessed his private devotions in his library both morning and evening; on those occasions he saw him in a kneeling posture with a Bible open before him, and that he believed such to have been his daily practice."*

William White, 'Washington Writings'

*"When you pray, go into your room, and when you have shut your door, pray to your Father who is in the secret place; and your Father who sees in secret will reward you openly."*  Matthew 6:6

## Article 250 - The First Amendment & the Myth of "Separation of Church & State"

Luke 4:18 *"The Lord has sent Me... to set at liberty those who are oppressed."*

About a week ago, the Supreme Court ruled 7-2 in the Trinity Lutheran Church vs State of Missouri that taxpayer-funded grants for playgrounds available to nonprofits under a state program couldn't be denied to a school run by a church. Calling the majority opinion "radical", dissenting Justice Sonia Sotomayor explained how the separation of church and state is now in jeopardy: *"The nation's history guarantees the free exercise of religion without allowing the government to be part of that religious process. The Court today blinds itself to the outcome this history requires and leads us instead to a place where separation of church and state is a constitutional slogan, not a constitutional commitment."*

Mike Whitehead, one of the attorneys for Trinity Lutheran, gave a much different view: *"What's changed for Trinity Lutheran is that they're no longer discriminated against by the State of Missouri"*. The state's case for denying funds to the church was based on the Blaine Amendment. Originating back in 1875, then President Ulysses S. Grant called for a Constitutional Amendment to prohibit the use of public money for religious schools. He declared that "church and state" should be "forever separate." The Constitution was never amended to include Grant's recommendation, but 39 states did adopt this amendment in their laws.

Does our Constitution contain language on separation of church and state? The First Amendment states *"Congress shall make no law respecting an establishment of religion, or prohibiting the free exercise thereof"*. It has two parts: the first is the "establishment clause" (there is to be no government-sanctioned religion for the Unites States) and the second is the "free exercise clause" (government will not prohibit Americans from freedom of worship). These two are foundational to how SCOTUS makes decisions.

So, if our Constitution does not mandate a separation between church and state, why do most Americans think, like Justice Sotomayer, that it does? This concept began from an exchange between newly elected President Thomas Jefferson and the Baptist Association of Danbury, Connecticut.

The Baptists explained that the First Amendment's 'free exercise clause' might be interpreted as government-given rather than God-given, thus allowing government to take away that freedom: *"Religion is at all times and places a matter between God and individuals, that no man ought to suffer in name, person, or effects on account of his religious opinions... But sir, our constitution of government is not specific. . . therefore what religious privileges we enjoy (as a minor part of the State) we enjoy as favors granted, and not as inalienable rights."*

David Barton (WallBuilders) explained Jefferson's answer: *"He had no intention of allowing government to limit, restrict, regulate, or interfere with public religious practices. He believed, along with the other Founders, that the First Amendment had been enacted only to prevent the federal establishment of a national denomination.*

*In his reply on January 1, 1802, Jefferson assured them that they need not fear; that the free exercise of religion would never be interfered with by the federal government: 'Gentlemen, believing with you that religion is a matter which lies solely between man and his God;*

*that he owes account to none other for his faith or his worship; that the legislative powers of government reach actions only and not opinions, I contemplate with sovereign reverence that act of the whole American people which declared that their legislature should "make no law respecting an establishment of religion or prohibiting the free exercise thereof," thus building a wall of separation between Church and State.'"*

So there it is – "separation of church and state" is not a "constitutional commitment" – it's a statement on the God-given right of Americans to worship freely without government intervention, written in a personal, private letter to a specific group of people! As David Barton says, *"There is probably no other instance in America's history where words spoken by a single individual in a private letter... have become the sole authorization for a national policy."*

Jefferson intended that his "wall" to separate church and state was a wall that would limit the government's ability to prohibit or interfere with American's freedom to worship.

Why did the Founders insist on this? It gets at the heart of our verse this week, where Jesus Christ explains, in His first public Scripture reading, part of His mission for coming to earth – that His Father sent Him to proclaim freedom to those under oppression.

The Founders understood His mission was to bring freedom from our sins that have oppressed us, through His sacrificial death on the cross. A freedom that has been paid for by God Himself, that no government provide or take away. A freedom that can be shared openly with no fear of government sanction. Those who know this freedom – are you sharing it with others?

# Christianity and the Constitution – The 2ⁿᵈ Amendment

**July 6, 1775:** Thomas Jefferson's letter to King George III - 'Declaration of the Causes and Necessity for Taking Up Arms'

*"We most solemnly, before God and the world, declare, that, exerting the utmost energy of those powers, which our beneficent Creator hath graciously bestowed upon us,*

*the arms we have been compelled by our enemies to assume, we will, in defiance of every hazard… employ for the preservation of our liberties…*

*Being with one mind resolved to die freemen rather than to live slaves.*

*With a humble confidence in the mercies of the Supreme and impartial God and Ruler of the Universe, we devoutly implore His divine goodness to protect us through this great conflict."*

> *"Plead my cause, O Lord, with those who strive with me; Fight those who fight against me."*
> **PSALM 35:1**

¹ 1791 Bill of Rights (2ⁿᵈ of the first 10 Amendments)

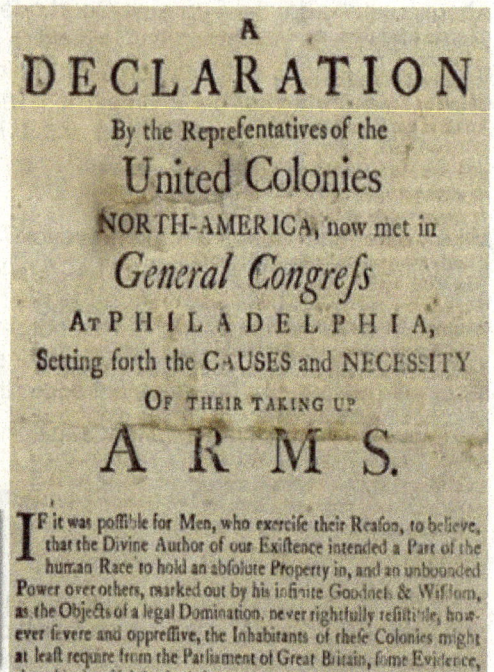

A **DECLARATION** By the Representatives of the **United Colonies** NORTH-AMERICA, now met in **General Congress** AT PHILADELPHIA, Setting forth the CAUSES and NECESSITY OF THEIR TAKING UP **ARMS.**

Courtesy of Google Images    Fair Use Law 17 U.S. Code § 107

## America's Constitution = Republic:   it's about Liberty
## France's Constitution = Socialist:   it's about Equality (Equity)

### American Revolution (1776)

*"Life, Liberty and the pursuit of Happiness…"*

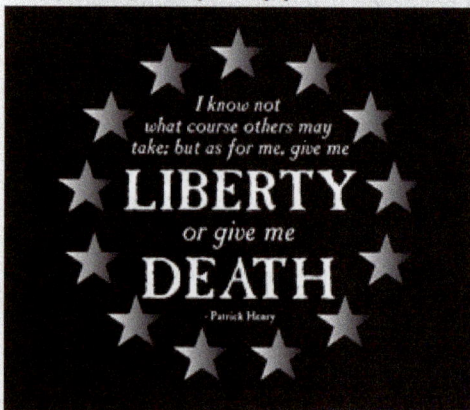

*I know not what course others may take; but as for me, give me* **LIBERTY** *or give me* **DEATH**
- Patrick Henry

*"Why would anyone prefer equality to liberty?*

*I have no problem with someone making more money than me.*

*I just want to be free to make my own life.*

*But the truth is that most people want to be taken care of much more than they want to be free."*
(Dennis Prager)

### French Revolution (1789)

*"Liberty, Fraternity, Equality (of Outcome)"*

Equality **Equality Equality**

> *"If anyone does not provide for his own, and especially for his family, he has denied the faith and is worse than an unbeliever."*   **1 Timothy 5:8**

Courtesy of Google Images    Fair Use Law 17 U.S. Code § 107

## Article 303 - The American Experiment: Guiding Principle #3 = "Bible's Individual Liberty"

Psalm 119:45   *"I will walk in liberty, for I seek Your precepts."*

Nearly 243 years ago on July 6, 1775, the Second Continental Congress published 'The Declaration of the Causes and Necessity of Taking Up Arms' to explain why the 13 Colonies decided to take up arms against Britain in what became the American Revolutionary War. Here are excerpts from this document.

*"A reverence for our Creator, principles of humanity, and the dictates of common sense, must convince all that government was instituted to promote the welfare of mankind, and ought to be administered for the attainment of that end. The legislature of Great-Britain, however, stimulated by an inordinate passion for a power unjustifiable, attempted to affect their cruel purpose of enslaving these colonies by violence, and have thereby rendered it necessary for us to close with their last appeal from reason to arms.*

*Our forefathers, inhabitants of the island of Great-Britain, left their native land, to seek on these shores a residence for civil and religious freedom. At the expense of their blood, at the hazard of their fortunes, and an unconquerable spirit, they effected settlements in the distant and unhospitable wilds of America.*

*In Great Britain, the lords said that 'a rebellion existed by his majesty's subjects in several of the colonies; they besought his majesty to enforce obedience to the laws and authority of the supreme legislature.' Large reinforcements of ships and troops were sent over to General Gage, who in the course of the last year had taken possession of Boston, butchered our countrymen, seized our ships and vessels, intercepted our supplies, and he is exerting his utmost power to spread destruction and devastation around him.*

*We are reduced to the alternative of choosing an unconditional submission to the tyranny of Great Britain or resistance by force. The latter is our choice. We have counted the cost of this contest and find nothing so dreadful as voluntary slavery. Honor, justice, and humanity, forbid us tamely to surrender that freedom which we received from our ancestors. We cannot endure the infamy and guilt of resigning succeeding generations to the wretchedness which inevitably awaits them if we entail hereditary bondage on them.*

*With hearts fortified with these animating reflections, we most solemnly, before God and the world, declare that we will, in defiance of every hazard, with unabating firmness and perseverance, employ arms to preserve our liberties; being with one mind resolved to die freemen rather than to live slaves.*

*With a humble confidence .in the mercies of the supreme and impartial Judge and Ruler of the Universe, we most implore His divine goodness to protect us through this great conflict, to dispose our adversaries to reconciliation on reasonable terms, and thereby to relieve the empire from the calamities of civil war."*

On July 4, 1776, this Second Continental Congress ratified our Declaration of Independence, announcing that these Thirteen Colonies regarded themselves as thirteen independent sovereign states. This was the first step toward forming the United States of America.

The most famous sentence in our Declaration is *"We hold these truths to be self-evident, that all men are created equal, that they are endowed by their Creator with certain unalienable rights, which among these are Life, Liberty and the pursuit of Happiness".*

Our founders were extremely learned men. They drew from many sources in drafting both the Declaration and the Constitution, such as John Locke, Cicero, Aristotle, and most consistently the Bible.

John Locke described individual liberty as *"The natural liberty of man is to be free from any superior power on earth, and not to be under the will or legislative authority of man, but to have only the law of nature for his rule."* By "law of nature" he meant nature's God – man's Creator. The Founders understood liberty is from God.

But the main source for their third guiding principle of individual liberty was the Bible. Daniel Webster, in a speech given in Charleston, South Carolina, on May 10, 1847, explained the biblical concept of liberty: *"Liberty exists in proportion to wholesome restraint."*

As with King David in this week's verse from Psalm 119, Webster understood that while God gives us our liberty, He set limitations on our conduct as defined in the Bible. 'Wholesome restraint' is what comes through the precepts of biblical ethics. The Founders believed that true liberty for each individual isn't doing what you want, but rather doing what you ought.

John Adams, one of the most influential Founders, wrote to Thomas Jefferson how critical biblical ethics are in establishing individual liberty: *"Suppose a nation's every member regulated their conduct by the precepts in the Bible. What a utopia – what a paradise would this region be!"*

## Comparing Early Christianity to Early America:
## Boldness = Spirit-filled speaking about Jesus

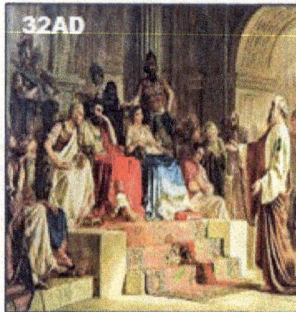

**32AD**

"King Agrippa... To this day I stand, witnessing to small and great, that Christ would suffer, rise from the dead, and proclaim light to Jews and Gentiles.

I am not out of my mind but speak the words of truth and reason; the King knows these things…since they were not done in a corner.'

'Agrippa said, 'You almost persuade me to become a Christian.'" (Acts 26:22-28)

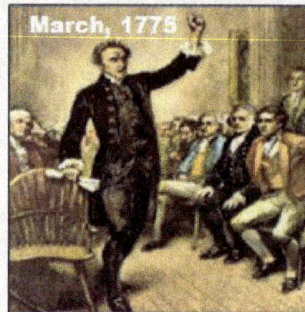

**March, 1775**

"It can't be emphasized too strongly or too often that this great nation was founded, not by religionists, but by Christians: not on religions, but on the Gospel of Jesus Christ.

For this very reason peoples of other faiths have been afforded asylum, prosperity, and freedom of worship here."

April 1956 issue of "The Virginian" magazine

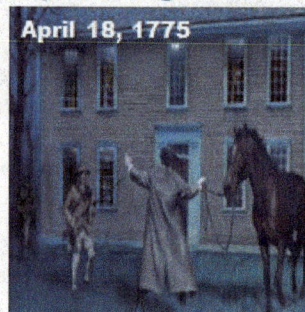

**April 18, 1775**

Arriving at Reverend Jonas Clarke's Lexington home, where Samuel Adams and John Hancock were staying, Paul revere warned them that the Redcoats were approaching.

Earlier that day, British General Gage announced to the colonists that if they would lay down their arms, all would be forgiven, except for Adams and Hancock, who were singled out as the instigators and would be hanged.

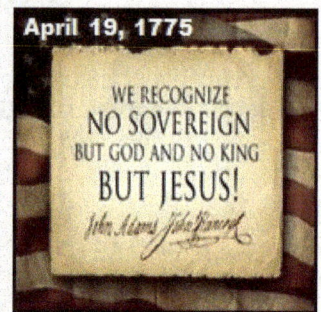

**April 19, 1775**

WE RECOGNIZE NO SOVEREIGN BUT GOD AND NO KING BUT JESUS!

The next morning British Major Pitcairn shouted to an assembled regiment of Minutemen: "Disperse, ye villains, lay down your arms in the name of George the Sovereign King of England."

Reverend Clarke, leader of the Lexington militia, responded with what is known as the Battle Cry of the American Revolution: 'We recognize no Sovereign but God and no King but Jesus."

# The Theme of Biblical, Historical Christianity = BOLDNESS
## (Spirit-filled speaking out for Jesus Christ)

**35AD**

"There is no other name under heaven than Jesus Christ that is given among men by which we must be saved.' Now when they saw the boldness of Peter and John, and perceived that they were uneducated and untrained men, they marveled and realized that they had been with Jesus."
Acts 4:12-13

**April 1521**

"I stand convicted by the Scriptures to which I have appealed; my conscience is taken captive by God's word. I cannot and will not recant anything; to act against our conscience is neither safe for us, nor open to us…

Here I stand. I can do no other. God help me. Amen."
(Martin Luther, Diet of Worms)

**April 2021**

"Boldness is not aggressive, or amplified (whoever shouts loudest wins), or angry.

Boldness is not a feeling – it is a fruit. It is 'Spirit-filled speaking about Jesus Christ'.

Following Jesus Christ is a commitment to be misunderstood by the culture. This is biblical Christianity."
(Pastor Chad Glover, Paradigm)

"The Gospel is like a caged lion. It doesn't need to be defended. It simply needs to be let out of it's cage."
Charles Spurgeon

## America and Christmas – Rooted in Jesus Christ

"'For unto you is born this day in the city of David a Saviour, which is Christ the Lord' ... That's what Christmas is all about. Charlie Brown."

— Linus

*"Bethlehem Ephrathah, though you are little among the thousands of Judah, yet out of you shall come forth to Me the One to be ruler in Israel, whose goings forth are from of old, from the days of eternity."* MICAH 5:2

*"By the way of the sea, beyond the Jordan, in Galilee of the Gentiles. The people who walked in darkness have seen a great light."* ISAIAH 9:1-2

*"As long as I am in the world, I am the light of the world."* JOHN 9:5

tesy of Google Images    Fair Use Law 17 U.S. Code § 107

## America's Protectors: Our Christian Roots

1) 20th Anniversary of 9/11: Our Fire Fighters - Honor & Glory to God through Personal Sacrifice

2) America's Ground Zero Cross – A Symbol of Reconciliation

3) Our Police Force: Godly examples of Servants who Protect Us

4) The Murder of Officer Preston: Only Jesus Christ Can End the War on Our Police

5) Our Veterans: How the Soldier's Oath points to Jesus Christ

6) Veterans Day: Thanking The True Source of Our Liberty

7) Remembering D-Day (June 6, 1944): "The Lord Your God Is With You in Battle"

Courtesy of Google Images    Fair Use Law 17 U.S. Code § 107

# 20ᵗʰ Anniversary of 9/11: Our Fire Fighters
## Honor & Glory to God through Personal Sacrifice

**Jay Jonas**

*"When the tower shook, one firefighter looked at us and said 'We may not make it out of this.' We all turned to each other, shook each others' hands and thanked each other for what we were about to do. I was the only one who made it out."*

*"The Lord God will help Me, therefore I will not be disgraced. I have set My face like a flint, and I know I will not be ashamed."* ISAIAH 50:7

Courtesy of Google Images   Fair Use Law 17 U.S. Code § 107

# America's Ground Zero Cross – A Symbol of Reconciliation

"The shape was oddly identifiable in the blasted wreckage of the World Trade Center. A grief-exhausted excavator found it on Sept. 13, 2001, 2 days after the terrorist attacks.

'Father, you want to see God's House? Look over there.' 'Oh my God,' Father Brian said. 'I see it.' As Father Brian stared, other rescue workers gathered around him.

There was a long moment of silence. Against insuperable odds, a 17-foot-long crossbeam, weighing 2 tons, was thrust in the hellish wasteland. Like a Cross.

Throughout the long recovery effort, the Cross stood at Ground Zero, eventually installed permanently."
Washington Post writer Sally Jenkins, '9/11 Memorials: The Story of the Cross at Ground Zero', Sept. 08, 2011

**Colossians 1:20**
"It pleased the Father that by Jesus Christ all things are reconciled to Himself, having made Peace through the Blood of His Cross."

"Radical repair was needed for God to again show His love for people.

This radical repair came in Christ's death on the Cross.

God was willing to count our trespasses against Christ, rather than against us." RC Sproul

The "Ground Zero Cross" has become a symbol of comfort - peace with God achieved by Jesus Christ for our sakes, at the Cross.

Anyone can come to God based on the merits of Jesus Christ, to be freely forgiven of their sin and welcomed into God's eternal family.

Courtesy of Google Images   Fair Use Law 17 U.S. Code § 107

# Our Police Force:  Godly examples of Servants who Protect Us

**Psalm 46:1**
"God is our refuge and strength, a very present help in time of trouble."

**Police Officer Thomas Jurgens** was trained as a medic in the Army before becoming a police officer.

On September 11, 2001 he was inside the first tower of the World Trade Center when he was warned to get out as fast as he could because the tower's structural integrity was failing.

The last transmission from Jurgens was simple: *"There are people here who need our help."* He died in the tower collapse.

**Psalm 82:4**
"Rescue the weak and the needy; deliver them from the hand of the wicked."

On February 14, 2007, Salt Lake City **Police Officer Kenneth Hammond** was off duty, having Valentine's Day dinner with his wife, when he heard gunshots from the nearby shopping mall.

An 18-year old gunman entered the mall and immediately murdered five people.

Hammond quickly found the gunman and fired on him. The gunman was killed.

If Hammond hadn't sprang into action, many more people would be dead.

**John 15:13**
"Greater love has no one than this, than to lay down one's life for his friends."

On May 1, 1983, heavy rains caused flash flood levels on the Little Blue River, trapping a canoer clinging to a tree after his canoe capsized.

A member of the Underwater Rescue and Recovery unit, Lee's Summit **Police Officer David Hartman** responded to the scene.

As he swam out to the canoer, another officer got stuck in the current. David tried to help him.

A log moving at 20 mph struck him. He lost consciousness and went under water. He was air-lifted to the hospital, where he died. Over 1,000 attended his funeral.

**Isaiah 6:8**
"Whom shall I send, and who will go for us?' Then I said, 'Here am I! Send me.'"

On September 11, 2001, **Police Officer Kenneth Tietjen** arrived at ground zero, rushed into the North tower and rescued many people.

As conditions quickly grew worse, he and his partner realized they only had one respirator left that was now required to be able to breathe in all the smoke.

Officer Tietjen smiled at his partner, said "Seniority rules", took the respirator and rushed back into the tower - just before it collapsed.

Courtesy of Google Images      Fair Use Law 17 U.S. Code § 107

# The Murder of Officer Preston: Only Jesus Christ Can End the War on Our Police

Chicago Police Officer Areanah Preston murdered May 6, 2023

4 black suspects, ages 16-18, out looking for victims in early morning hours, attacked Officer Preston outside her home in Avalon Park as she returned from her shift.

One of them fatally shot her and then stole her gun before all fled in a stolen vehicle. Despite being so young, all have extensive criminal records, including carjacking and robbery.

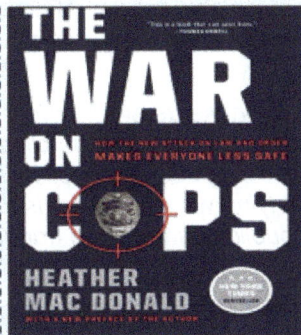

**THE WAR ON COPS**
HOW THE NEW ATTACK ON LAW AND ORDER MAKES EVERYONE LESS SAFE
**HEATHER MAC DONALD**
WITH A NEW PREFACE BY THE AUTHOR

"Heather Mac Donald gives voice to residents of high-crime neighborhoods who want proactive policing.

She warns that race-based attacks on the criminal-justice system erode the authority of law, putting lives at risk." Manhattan Inst.

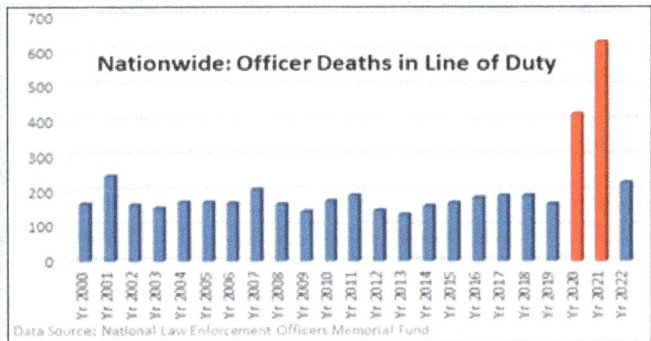

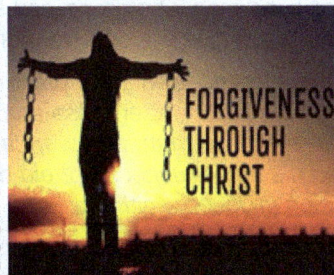

**Nationwide: Officer Deaths in Line of Duty**

Data Source: National Law Enforcement Officers Memorial Fund

FORGIVENESS THROUGH CHRIST

*"He (Jesus Christ) will pour out His soul unto death, He will be numbered with us as transgressors, He will bear our sins, and He will then intercede on our behalf, as the true transgressors."*
**Isaiah 53:12**

*"Behold, their valiant ones cry outside; the ambassadors of peace weep bitterly."* Isaiah 33:7

## Article 200:  Why Police are Targeted - Lies & Deceit have replaced the Truth

*Isaiah 59:13     "In transgressing, and denying the Lord, and turning back from following our God, speaking oppression and revolt, conceiving and uttering from the heart lying words."*

This past Sunday, 3 more police officers were murdered by a lone gunman targeting them. Their names were Montrell Jackson, Brad Garafola and Matthew Gerald. Why? Because they were police officers.

Just 10 days earlier, a lone gunman murdered five police officers in Dallas. Their names were Brent Thompson, Michael Krol, Patrick Zamarripa, Lorne Ahrens, and Michael Smith, Why? Because they were white police officers. In September 2015, Deputy Darren Goforth was ambushed and executed in Texas while pumping gas. Why? For being a law enforcement officer, and no other reason.

Only hours after Goforth's murder, the St. Paul, Minnesota chapter of 'Black Lives Matter' march in unity behind a group of police officers down a highway chanting *"Pigs in a blanket, fry 'em like bacon!"* Why such hatred against our police? The leftist organization 'Black Lives Matter' promotes a revolution against our police force to retaliate against what they claim as a history of police unprovoked racism and use of force towards the black community. But the question all of us should be asking: Is this true?

No, it is not. Black Harvard Professor of economics Richard Fryer Jr. released a very thorough study of thousands of police-related incidents at the ten large police departments in California, Florida and Texas.

He found no evidence of racial bias in police shootings, even though the data shows that police officers are more likely to have physical altercations with non-whites than whites.

His conclusion: *"On the most extreme use of force - officer-involved shootings - we find no racial differences in either the raw data or when contextual factors are taken into account."* Professor Fryer admitted that the finding of this study, that there is no racial discrimination in police shootings, is *"the most surprising result of my career."*

Dennis Prager recently refuted the claim of unprovoked racism by using data: *"In 2015, of the 990 people shot dead by police, 93 were unarmed and 38 of them were black. Of the 505 people shot dead by police thus far in 2016, 37 were unarmed and of them 13 were black.*

*Given that blacks murder and rob more than whites — they committed 62 percent of robberies, 57 percent of murders and 45 percent of assaults in the 75 biggest counties in the country in 2009 (despite comprising about 15 percent of the population in these counties) — an unarmed black is less likely to be killed by police than an unarmed white."*

What has happened in America that has led to such horrific attacks on those we should all be honoring for their courage and service to us? In our verse this week, the prophet Isaiah's proclamation in the streets of Israel over 2700 years ago is all too familiar today to what is happening in the streets of America. Listen to Isaiah's words in chapter 59:

*"Therefore justice is far from us, and righteousness does not overtake us; we hope for light, and behold, darkness, and for brightness, but we walk in gloom. We grope for the wall like the blind; we grope like those who have no eyes;… in transgressing, and denying the Lord, and turning back from following our God, speaking oppression and revolt,  conceiving and uttering from the heart lying words. Justice is turned back, and righteousness stands far away; for truth has stumbled in the public squares, and uprightness cannot enter. Truth is lacking; he who departs from evil makes himself a prey."*

What is God pronouncing through Isaiah? That the root of the problem with the injustice and oppression in the land is we have denied His sovereignty and authority over our lives. And what did Isaiah say was the consequence? We would all be blind men who grope and stumble along a wall, as we lie, deceive, spread revolt and prey on each other in order to achieve our own version of what we think truth is.

But God doesn't end it there. He intervenes with the promise of justice and righteousness that He personally provides. Here are His words as we read further in Isaiah 59: "*The Lord saw it, and it displeased him that there was no justice. He saw that there was no man, and wondered that there was no one to intercede; then his own arm brought him salvation, and his righteousness upheld him. And the Redeemer shall come to Zion, and unto them that turn from transgression in Jacob, saith the Lord."*

Who is this Redeemer who shall come to Jerusalem, whom people will embrace and turn away from their transgressions because He will bring salvation and justice and righteousness to the land?

This is none other than a prophecy of the coming of Jesus Christ, who brought salvation through the death on the Cross. Returning to Jesus Christ is the solution America needs.

## Our Veterans: How the Soldier's Oath points to Jesus Christ

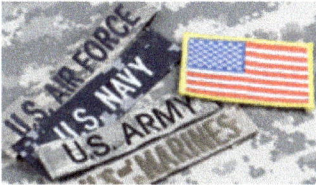

"I, _____, do solemnly swear that I will support and defend the US Constitution against all enemies, foreign and domestic; that I will bear true faith and allegiance to the same; and that I will obey the orders of the President of the United States and the orders of the officers appointed over me, according to regulations and the Uniform Code of Military Justice. So help me God."
Military Oath of Enlistment

**OATH Part 1:**
"I will support and defend the Constitution of the United States against all enemies, foreign and domestic."

<u>Military Core Values:</u>
Air Force = Service before Self
Navy/Marine = Courage
Army = Selfless Service, personal courage, loyalty

<u>Biblical Core Value:</u>
Philippians 2:8 "Being found in appearance as a man, Jesus humbled Himself and was obedient to the point of death, even death of the cross."

**OATH Part 2:**
"I take this obligation freely, without any mental reservation or purpose of evasion."

<u>Military Core Values:</u>
Air Force = Integrity first
Navy/Marines = Honor
Army = Integrity

<u>Biblical Core Value:</u>
Matthew 26:39 "Jesus went a little farther and fell on His face and prayed, saying, 'O My Father, if it is possible, let this cup pass from Me; nevertheless, not as I will, but as You will."

**OATH Part 3:**
"I will well and faithfully discharge the duties of the office upon which I am about to enter."

<u>Military Core Value:</u>
Air Force = Excellence in all we do
Navy/Marines = Commitment
Army = Duty, Respect

<u>Biblical Core Value:</u>
Jesus in the Old Testament
Isaiah 50:7 "I have set My face like a flint, and I know I will not be ashamed."

Jesus in New Testament
John 1:29 "The next day John saw Jesus coming toward him and said, 'Behold, the Lamb of God who takes away the sin of the world!'"

"If a man vows a vow to the Lord, or swears an oath to bind himself to some agreement, he shall not break his word; he shall do according to all that proceeds out of his mouth." Numbers 30:2

Andrew Roberts: 'Why America's Military Must Be Strong' (5:27)

## Veterans Day: Thanking The True Source of Our Liberty

"It is the Soldier, not the minister who gives us freedom of religion.

It is the Soldier, not the reporter who gives us freedom of the press.

It is the Soldier, not the poet who gives us freedom of speech.

It is the Soldier, not the campus organizer who gives us freedom to protest.

It is the Soldier, not the lawyer who gives us the right to a fair trial.

It is the Soldier, not the politician who gives us the right to vote.

It is the Soldier who salutes the flag, who serves beneath the flag, whose coffin is draped by the flag, who allows the protester to burn the flag."
Charles M. Province, US Army, 1970

"Blessed be the Lord my Rock, who trains my hands for war, and my fingers for battle." Psalm 144:1

## Article 244 - Our Military: America's Defender of Our Many Freedoms

Luke 4:18 *"The Lord has sent Me to proclaim liberty to the captives; to liberate those oppressed"*

*"If nothing in life is worth dying for, when did this begin -- just in the face of this enemy? Or should Moses have told the children of Israel to live in slavery under the pharaohs? Should Christ have refused the cross? Should the patriots at Concord Bridge have thrown down their guns and refused to fire the shot heard 'round the world'? The martyrs of history were not fools, and our honored dead who gave their lives to stop the advance of the Nazis didn't die in vain.*

*Where, then, is the road to peace? Well it's a simple answer after all. You and I have the courage to say to our enemies, 'There is a price we will not pay. There is a point beyond which they must not advance."*

Do you recognize these words? As we watched and listened to President Trump condemn radical Islamic terrorism in his speech to the Arab Nations in Riyadh this past week, it almost sounds like the above words came from him. Our President mentioned the words 'extremism', 'terrorism', 'radicalism', 'fanatical violence', 'Islamic extremism', and 'Islamist terror' a total of 38 times throughout his speech, and not from the safety of the Oval Office – but in their very hometown, face to face.

Finally, we have a President who is standing up for the freedom and dignity of all people by demanding the elimination of ISIS, Taliban, all forms of violent Islamic terrorism. But the above quote isn't from President Trump.

This quote is from Ronald Reagan's 1964 speech called "A Time for Choosing." As a young republican he was launched into national prominence, because he resonated with so many Americans who understood (and still understand) that freedom is the most precious gift we have, that must be constantly defended against our enemies.

The road to preserving the precious freedom we enjoy, and the peace that comes with it, isn't preserved through negotiating with those whose mission is to destroy us.

As former President Thomas Jefferson so famously said, *"The price of freedom is eternal vigilance."* And as former President George Washington said, *"To be prepared for war is one of the most effective means of preserving peace."* Vigilance by whom? What resources do we have to defend ourselves against those who attack our freedom?

Again, former President Ronal Reagan says it best: *"There are some who've forgotten why we have a military. It's not to promote war, it's to be prepared for peace."*

As we celebrate this Memorial Weekend, let's be focused on who truly deserves our honor and our respect as our courageous guardians of our freedoms – our men and women of the Military.

As the famous quote reminds us: *"It is the Soldier, not the reporter, who has given us freedom of the press. It is the Soldier, not the poet, who has given us freedom of speech. It is the Soldier, not the campus organizer, who has given us freedom to protest. It is the Soldier, not the lawyer, who has given us the right to a fair trial. It is the Soldier, not the politician, who has given us the right to vote. It is the Soldier who salutes the flag, who serves beneath the flag, and whose coffin is draped by the flag, who allows the protester to burn the flag."*

In our opening quote from Ronald Reagan, he makes a very striking illustration of what courage in the face of an advancing enemy looks like by asking the question *"Should Christ have refused the Cross?"*

This week's verse underscores Reagan's point. Luke 4:18 is part of Christ's first public speech as He began His mission. And what was Christ's mission? To fulfill His Father's plan to not only free people from the enemy but also destroy the enemy which holds people captive their entire lives by their sin.

Hebrews 2:14-15 explains how Christ achieved His Father's plan – by taking on human form and dying on the Cross: *"Inasmuch then as the children have partaken of flesh and blood, Christ likewise shared in the same, that through His death He might destroy him who had the power of death, that is, the devil, and release those who through fear of death were all their lifetime subject to bondage."*

Reagan says Jesus Christ willingly took our sins upon Himself and suffered the just penalty of death for us. Why? So that we might have access to eternal life by trusting in Him as Lord and Savior.

Reagan's calling out of Jesus Christ 's selfless sacrifice of His own life in order to offer true freedom from death is the same message that the apostle Paul announces in his second letter to Timothy, chapter 2 and verse:10: *"Our Savior Jesus Christ, who has abolished death and brought eternal life through the gospel."*

May God bless our military, who embody the very values of courage, commitment, selflessness and personal sacrifice unto death that point to our Savior Jesus Christ. And as we celebrate our military this Memorial Weekend, may we look to Jesus Christ, our ultimate Provider and Defender of true freedom.

# Remembering D-Day (June 6, 1944):
## "The Lord Your God Is With You in Battle"

*"Almighty God: Our sons, pride of our Nation, this day have set upon a mighty endeavor, a struggle to preserve our Republic, our religion, and our civilization, and to set free a suffering humanity... "For these men fight not for the lust of conquest. They fight to end conquest. They fight to liberate. They fight to let justice arise, and tolerance and good will among all Thy people."* FDR's D-Day prayer the evening before the invasion.

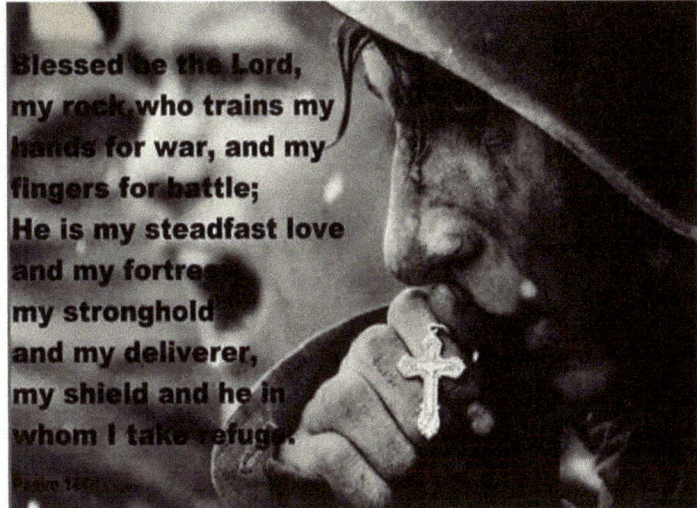

Blessed be the Lord, my rock, who trains my hands for war, and my fingers for battle; He is my steadfast love and my fortress, my stronghold and my deliverer, my shield and he in whom I take refuge.

*"All drank the same spiritual drink, for they drank of that spiritual Rock that followed them; and that Rock was Christ."* 1 CORINTHIANS 10:4

## Exit Ticket #12     Class 12: America's Founding

| | |
|---|---|
| 1) What impresses you about America's early Christianity at it's founding? | 2) How has the Bible influenced our Constitution? |
| 3) What is the difference between America's versus France's government? | 4) Which of the 24 bible verses in this class resonates the most with you on America's founding? |

# Class 13   America Today
# Secularism, Systemic Racism

Comparing Early America to Today's America

Understanding Today's "Post-Christian" America: Assimilating what God Commanded be kept Separate

Today's American Culture: **The Lie of Secularism**
  1) Secularism, 2) Postmodernism, 3) Cancel Culture,
  4) Illegal Immigration, 5) Radical Islam

Today's American Culture: **The Lie of Systemic Racism**

America's Crossroad:  Embracing Equity (Equal Outcome)

Christianity's Stand Against Marxist Systemic Racism -
Speak Out for Biblical Values

The Untold Story of Aaron Judge – Celebrating America's Love, Debunking America as Racist

In Life & Death - Our Heroes Return from Afghanistan: Race Doesn't Seem to Matter

Let's Hear from the Experts: 1) Chris Rufo,
2) Dr. Carol Swain, 3) Dr. Bob Woodson,
4) Dr. Thomas Sowell, 5) Dr. Walt Williams,
6) Dr. Shelby Steele

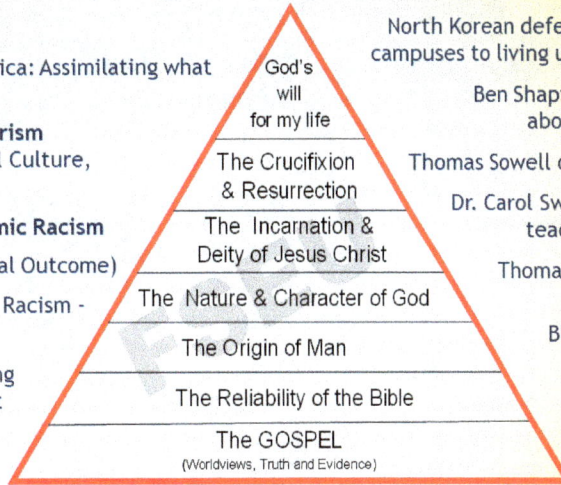

**Pyramid (top to bottom):**
God's will for my life
The Crucifixion & Resurrection
The Incarnation & Deity of Jesus Christ
The Nature & Character of God
The Origin of Man
The Reliability of the Bible
The GOSPEL (Worldviews, Truth and Evidence)

**HEBREWS 11:1**
"Faith = *Substance* of things *hoped for* ... *Evidence* of things *not seen*"

**fse.life Lesson 01**

North Korean defector compares Ivy League campuses to living under the Kim regime (7:02)

Ben Shapiro: 'You are Being Lied to about Israel & Palestine' (8:52)

Thomas Sowell on Black Lives Matter (7:39)

Dr. Carol Swain, PragerU: 'What I can teach you about Racism' (5:47)

Thomas Sowell on current Black Culture' (10:41)

Black Wisdom Matters Part 3: 'State of Racism in America' (7:47)

Black Wisdom Matters Part 2: 'Good Intentions of the Welfare State' (13:37)

The Power of White Guilt (14:10)

# Comparing Early America to Today's America

## Our Founder's Vision: How We are Governed

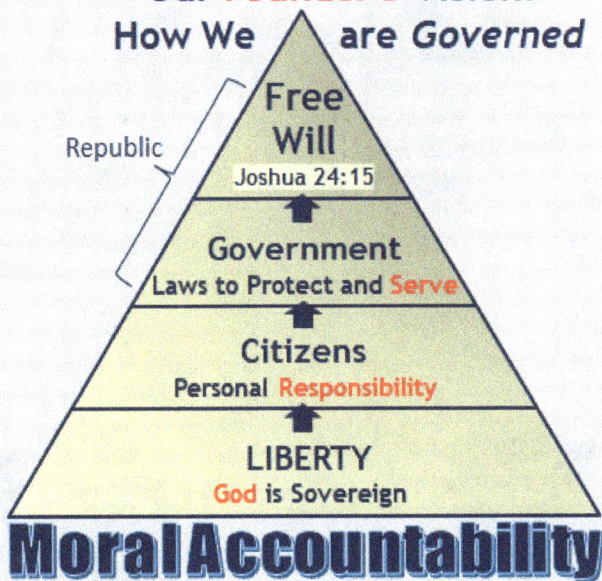

Republic

Free Will
Joshua 24:15

Government
Laws to Protect and Serve

Citizens
Personal Responsibility

LIBERTY
God is Sovereign

**Moral Accountability**

## Our Culture's Movement: How We are to Behave

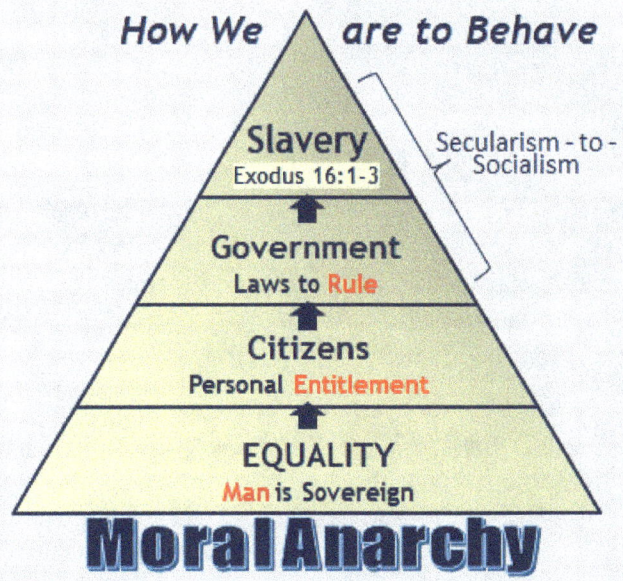

Secularism - to - Socialism

Slavery
Exodus 16:1-3

Government
Laws to Rule

Citizens
Personal Entitlement

EQUALITY
Man is Sovereign

**Moral Anarchy**

## Understanding Today's "Post-Christian" America:
### *Assimilating* what God Commanded be kept *Separate*

### Good vs. Evil
Isaiah 5:20

Objective morality replaced by personal 'feelings'.

### Man vs. God
Psalm 100:3

**AMERICAN HUMANIST ASSOCIATION**
GOOD WITHOUT A GOD

Religion of Secular Humanism

### Man vs. Animal
Genesis 2:7

All animals are our cousins (Common Descent).

### Holy vs. Profane
1Peter 1:15-16

In American culture, profanity is the 'new normal'.

### Man vs. Woman
Genesis 2:22-23

Choose from over 500 gender identities.

## American Culture: Founded Christian, Embracing Secularism

Courtesy of Google Images    Fair Use Law 17 U.S. Code § 107

# Today's American Culture: The Lie of Secularism

**1) SECULARISM**

– How to Renew Your Faith in Jesus Christ: Listen to Today's Secularism

– Today's Secular Universities: The Breeding Ground for Christian Deconstruction

– Antisemitism at Our Universities: The Cowardice of the Secular Left

– Secular Music & Culture: Taylor Swift's Antihero - Sin is an Inside Job

**Secularism**
**America's Religionless Religion**

**2) POSTMODERNISM**

– Book of Jeremiah: How Jesus Christ Defeats Postmodernism

– The Death of "Defund the Police" Movement? Postmodernism is Taking a Hit

**3) CANCEL CULTURE**

– Christians: Stand For Jesus Christ & Against Cancel Culture

– Cancel Culture vs. Jesus Christ: Without Christ, Hurt People Will Hurt People

– Tearing Down Jefferson's Statue - The Worldview Behind Cancel Culture

**4) IMMIGRATION**

– Legal vs. Illegal Immigration = An Oath of Allegiance

– Illegal Immigration & Tribalism: America won't be a Nation of Citizens

– Illegal Immigration & Terrorism: America's Dismantling

**5) RADICAL ISLAM**

– Trump vs. Obama & Biden: Capitulation to the Taliban and Radical Islam

– Christianity vs. Islam Part 20: Anniversary of America's Withdrawal from Afghanistan

Courtesy of Google Images    Fair Use Law 17 U.S. Code § 107

# How to Renew Your Faith in Jesus Christ:  Listen to Today's Secularism

*"MAGA forces are determined to take this country backwards, backwards to an America where there is no right to choose, no right to privacy, no right to contraception, no right to marry who you love...*

***Donald Trump and the MAGA Republicans*** (not China, nor Russia, nor Iran) ***are the threat to America."***

(President Biden, Sept. 01, 2022)

*"If our universities produced wise men and women, curricula of moral clarity, and professors who loved America, liberty, and truth - there is no question that my religious faith would be challenged. I would look at the temple of secularism, the university, and see such goodness and wisdom that I would have to wonder just how important God and religion were.*

*Most people believe in God through the front door of faith. I renew my faith through the back door. I see the confusion and nihilism that godless ideas produce and my faith is restored. The consequences of secularism have been at least as powerful a force for faith in my life as religion."*

(Dennis Prager, 'How I found God at Columbia')

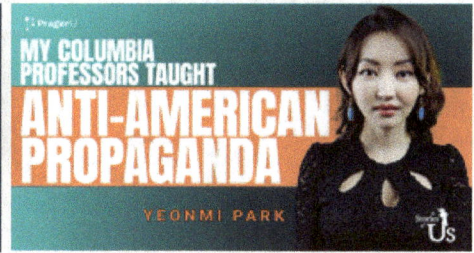

**PSALM 111:10**  *"The fear of the Lord is the beginning of wisdom; all who obey Him have good understanding."*

North Korean defector compares Ivy League campuses to living under the Kim regime (7:02)          Courtesy of Google Images     Fair Use Law 17 U.S. Code § 107

---

# Harvard University:  The Breeding Ground for Christian Deconstruction

**1636**

**"Veritas Christo et Ecclesiae" "Truth for Christ & the Church."** Harvard shield's 3 books: top 2 books face up, bottom faces down: **"There are limits to secular reasoning."**

**1972** "Every child in America entering school at age of 5 is insane because he comes to school with allegiances to our founding fathers, his parents, a belief in God, and the sovereignty of this nation as a separate entity. It is up to you teachers to make all these sick children well by creating the international children of the future." Dr. Chester Pierce, Prof. Education & Psychiatry, Harvard

**1978** "In American democracy at the time of its birth, all individual human rights were granted on the ground that man is God's creature. Man's sense of responsibility to God and society has grown dimmer and dimmer." Why Aleksandr Solzhenitsen was booed at Harvard Commencement Speech "A World Split Apart"

**2011** "We don't look to a god for answers. We are each other's answers." Atheist Greg Epstein, Harvard Chaplains President

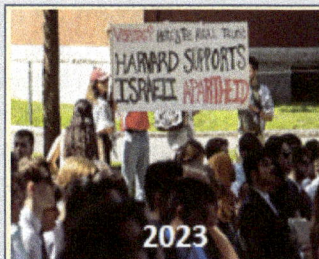

**2023** "We hold the Israeli regime entirely responsible for all unfolding violence in Gaza." 33 Harvard Student Groups protest against Israel after Hamas murdered 1,400 innocent Israel citizens.

"We will walk according to our own plans, and we will obey the dictates of his evil heart." **Jeremiah 18:12**

Courtesy of Google Images

## Antisemitism at Our Universities: The Cowardice of the Secular Left

"We, the undersigned student organizations, hold Israel entirely responsible for all unfolding violence. The Apartheid regime is the only one to blame.

Israeli violence has structured every aspect of Palestinian existence for 75 years.

Palestinians have been forced to live in a state of death, both slow and sudden."
31 Harvard Student Organizations Letter in response to Hamas Terrorism
Ben Shapiro: 'You are Being Lied to about Israel & Palestine' (8:52)

"I have been asked by a number of CEOs if Harvard would release a list of the members of the organizations that issued the letter assigning responsibility for Hamas' heinous acts to Israel, to ensure that none of us inadvertently hire any of them.

These students should not be able to hide behind a corporate shield when issuing statements supporting terrorism."
CEO Bill Ackman

"Everyone practicing evil hates the light and does not come to the light, lest his deeds should be exposed."
Jesus Christ, John 3:20

**Proverbs 28:1**
"The wicked flee though no one pursues, but the righteous are as bold as a lion."

## Secular Music & Culture: Taylor Swift's Antihero - Sin is an Inside Job

"Did you hear my covert narcissism I disguise as altruism - like some kind of congressman? (tale as old as time)." Taylor Swift, 'Antihero'

"If you have been foolish in exalting yourself... put your hand over your mouth."
King Solomon, Proverbs 30:32

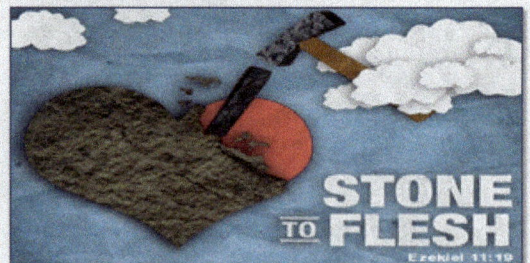

"It's me, hi, I'm the problem, it's me - At teatime, everybody agrees; I'll stare directly at the sun but never in the mirror - it must be exhausting always rooting for the anti-hero." Swift, 'Antihero'

"The heart is deceitful above all things, and desperately sick; who can understand it?"
Jeremiah 17:9

STONE TO FLESH
Ezekiel 11:19

"I will give you a new heart and put a new spirit within you; I will take the heart of stone out of your flesh and give you a heart of flesh." Ezekiel 26:26-28

*"The things that come out of your mouth come from your heart. These defile you."* Matthew 15:18

Courtesy of Google Images    Fair Use Law 17 U.S. Code § 107

## Book of Jeremiah: How Jesus Christ Defeats Postmodernism

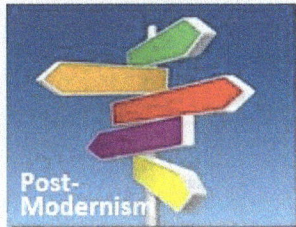

**Post-Modernism**

Objective truth doesn't exist or, if it does, it can't be known.

The key is each person's authenticity over reason (I am skeptical of your claim to truth – how can you be so sure?)

*"Americans should reject the idea that "somehow we alone are in possession of the truth."* (Obama, 2015 National Prayer Breakfast)

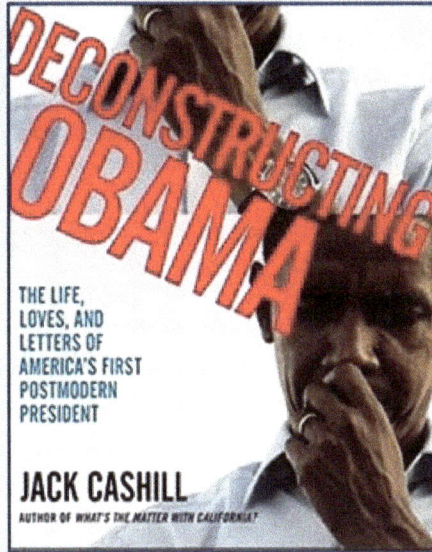

**DECONSTRUCTING OBAMA**

THE LIFE, LOVES, AND LETTERS OF AMERICA'S FIRST POSTMODERN PRESIDENT

**JACK CASHILL**

AUTHOR OF *WHAT'S THE MATTER WITH CALIFORNIA?*

*"The days are coming when I will make a new covenant with the house of Israel and Judah... No more shall every man teach his neighbor, and every man his brother, saying, 'Know the Lord, for <u>they shall all know Me</u>, from the least of them to the greatest of them. For <u>I will forgive their iniquity, and their sin I will remember no more</u>."* Jeremiah 31: 31-34

*"You, child, will be called the prophet of the Highest, for you will go before the face of the Lord to prepare His ways, to give <u>knowledge of salvation</u> to His people by <u>forgiveness of their sins</u>."* Luke 1:76-78

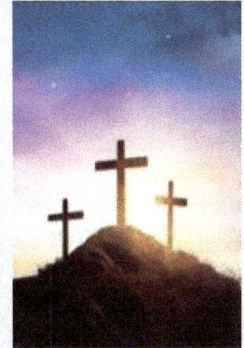

**Jesus Christ:** *"I have come into the world, that I should bear witness to the truth."* JOHN 8:37

Courtesy of Google Images   Fair Use Law 17 U.S. Code § 107

## The Death of "Defund the Police" Movement? Postmodernism is Taking a Hit

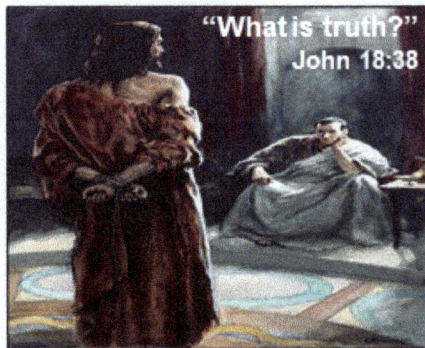

**"What is truth?"**
**John 18:38**

*"Philosophy and religion had been tried and found wanting. The only religion insisted on by the State was the Emperor's deification. Absolute right did not exist. Might was right.*

*Society couldn't reform itself. All around, despair, conscious need, and unconscious longing."*

Rome at the time of Jesus Christ

Thomas Sowell on Black Lives Matter (7:39)

*""This is madness. What is frightening is how many people in responsible positions are caving in to every demand.*

*I was never pessimistic enough to think that things would generate to the point where adult human beings are talking about getting rid of the police, reducing the number of police, reducing the resources put into police work when murder rates are skyrocketing over what they were just a year ago in 2019."*

Dr. Thomas Sowell on Mark Levin Show

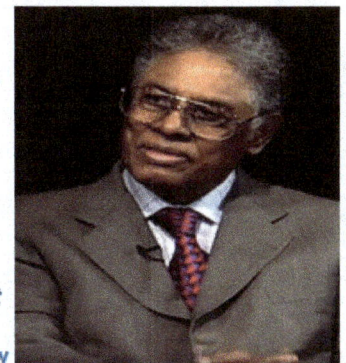

*"Minneapolis crime spike continues as the 'defund the police' philosophy explodes in city's face."*
**Washington Times**

### INCREASE IN MINNEAPOLIS CRIME

| CRIME | 2019 YTD | 2020 YTD | CHANGE |
|-------|----------|----------|--------|
| ARSON | 72 | 127 | +76% |
| ASSAULTS | 2,114 | 2,616 | +24% |
| HOMICIDES | 39 | 73 | +87% |
| ROBBERIES | 1,161 | 1,593 | +37% |

Courtesy of Google Images   Fair Use Law 17 U.S. Code § 107

## Christians: Stand For Jesus Christ & Against Cancel Culture

"What took place last night at the LSR7 school board meeting should sadden, embarrass, and infuriate every family in our school district.

The extremists have organized in Lee's Summit and want to bring the same spirit that resulted in criminals storming our nation's capital on January 6, 2021 to the Lee's Summit R-7 School District."
(Stacy Cronhardt, candidate for Lees Summit Board of Education, accusing parental protest against the book 'All Boys Aren't Blue' as extremism similar to January 6 Capital Riot)

"Do any of you find this book 'All Boys Aren't Blue' that depicts a sexual encounter and rape, acceptable for any minor, regardless of gender or sexual orientation?"
(Vicki Flannery addressing North Penn School Board, Montgomery County, PA, Oct. 2021)

*"So that it spreads no further among the people, let us severely threaten them..."*
**Acts 4:17**

"I'm looking forward to joining thousands of people who will be there to support those unborn babies who don't have a voice."
(Tony Dungy, NFL Commentator & Super Bowl Champion, on speaking at March for Life)

"Done with Tony Dungy and the way the NFL and NBC coddle his right wing extremism.

The NFL's silence is almost as loud as Dungy's hateful blather, almost as loud as the thousands of people descending upon Washington."
(Dave Zirin accusing Dungy as extreme as January 6 rioters)

Courtesy of Google Images
Fair Use Law 17 U.S. Code § 107

## Cancel Culture vs. Jesus Christ: Without Christ, Hurt People Will Hurt People

### The Results from Cancel Culture: No forgiveness, No Grace, No Love

### The Results from the Gospel: Forgiveness, Grace, Love

**"Islamophobia"**

"I said to myself, 'If this guy doesn't look like an Arab terrorist, then no one does.' Then I gave myself a mental slap because in this day and age, it's not nice to say things like this.' I felt kind of embarrassed."
Michael Tuohey, US Airways ticket agent, watched as Mohamed Atta went through the Portland Inter. Jetport on September 11, 2001 on his way to Boston. Atta joined 4 terrorists who hijacked American Flight 11 and flew it into the World Trade Center.

**"Gender phobia"**

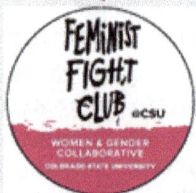

Colorado State Univ - 'Feminist Fight Club': "to aid young women in their struggle for identity and worth in a male-dominated sexist American culture."

**"White Guilt"**

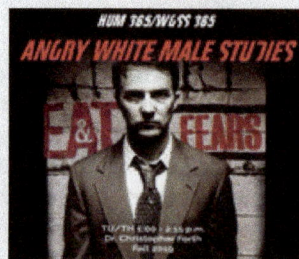

University of Kansas - 'Angry White Male Studies': "Students examine the deeper sources of this emotional state while evaluating manifestations of male anger since 1950s."

**"Free Speech"**
Berkeley students chant "Speech is violence!", claiming Ben Shapiro's disagreeing with them was an attack on their identity.

"This is love, not that we loved God, but that He loved us and sent His Son to be the sacrifice for our sins."
**1John 4:10**

Courtesy of Google Images    Fair Use Law 17 U.S. Code § 107

# Tearing Down Jefferson's Statue - The Worldview Behind Cancel Culture

*"We hold these truths to be self-evident, that all men are created equal and endowed by their Creator with certain unalienable rights, that among these are life, Liberty and the pursuit of happiness..."*

**Thomas Jefferson, Author of Declaration of Independence**

*"Since the origin of the present revolution, the spirit of the master is abating, that of the slave rising from the dust, his condition mollifying, the way I hope preparing, under the auspices of heaven, for a total emancipation."*

**Thomas Jefferson, 1782 letter 'Notes on the State of VA'**

*"We are witnessing a movement to remove statues and monuments to historic figures because something they did or said during their lives now offends someone."*
**Washington Times Nov. 2021**

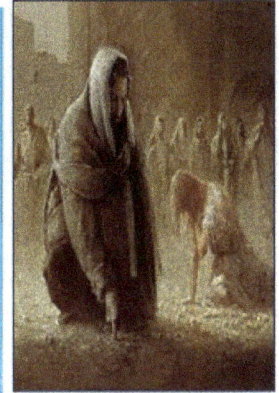

*"He among you who is without sin, let him throw the first stone."*

**Jesus Christ, convicting the "Cancel Culture" who condemned her, then forgiving her past sin John 8:1-11**

Courtesy of Google Images    Fair Use Law 17 U.S. Code § 107

# Legal vs. Illegal Immigration = Biblical Mandate of an Oath of Allegiance

## Naturalization Oath of Allegiance to the USA
(Code of Federal Regulations Section 337.1 of the Immigration and Nationality Act (INA))

*"I hereby declare, on oath, that I entirely renounce and abjure all allegiance and fidelity to any foreign prince, potentate, state, or sovereignty, of whom or which I have heretofore been a subject or citizen...*

- *I will support and defend the Constitution and laws of the USA against all enemies, foreign and domestic*
- *I will bear true faith and allegiance to the same*
- *I will bear arms on behalf of the US when required by the law; that I will perform noncombatant service in the US Armed Forces when required by the law*
- *I will perform work of national importance under civilian direction when required by law;*
- *I take this obligation freely, without any mental reservation or purpose of evasion*
- *So help me God."*

**Legal Immigration = Following INA 337.1**

Swearing in New US Citizens

**Illegal Immigration = Breaking INA 337.1**

Haitian Migrants at TX Border

**Exodus 12:49** *"There shall be one law for the native-born and for the stranger who sojourns among you."*

Courtesy of Google Images    Fair Use Law 17 U.S. Code § 107

## Illegal Immigration & Tribalism:  Why America won't be a Nation of Citizens

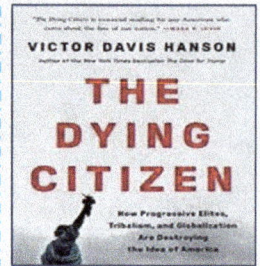

**STILL UNDOCUMENTED STILL UNAFRAID**

**VICTOR DAVIS HANSON**

# THE DYING CITIZEN

How Progressive Elites, Tribalism, and Globalization Are Destroying the Idea of America

Tribalism = exalting one tribe over another; strong 'in-group' loyalty.

Tribe = social group of families, clans, or generations having shared ancestry and language.

Citizen = native or naturalized person owing allegiance to a government and entitled to protection by it.

Naturalized = a foreigner admitted as a citizen to a country.

Immigrant = a foreigner who comes to a new country to take up permanent residence as a citizen to that country.

Legal immigration = process of a foreigner becoming a naturalized citizen.

Swear oath of allegiance to the United States, to live by the laws of the US          CFR Section 337.1

Illegal Immigration = anyone from any tribe settling in our country with no expectation to follow our Constitution, customs or legal system.

*"Western values contradict these of Islam. For Muslims, a full-on citizenship within a Western state is not possible."*
Dr. Mordechai Kedar, Israeli scholar of Arab culture, lecturer at Bar-Ilan Univ., vice president of NEWSRAEL

*"I do not know any Western leader - except Biden and the Obamas - who still advocates open borders and tribal and religious chauvinism in immigrant communities."*
Victor Davis Hanson, Senior Fellow at the Hoover Institution

**Leviticus 24:22**  **"Have the same law for the foreigner and the native-born. I am the LORD your God."**

Courtesy of Google Images    Fair Use Law 17 U.S. Code § 107

## Illegal Immigration & Terrorism: How the Democratic Party is Dismantling Itself

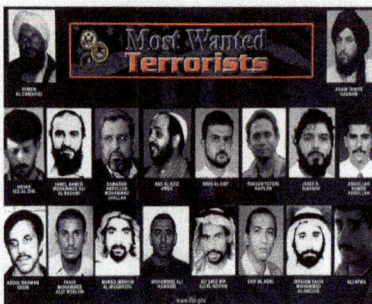

**Most Wanted Terrorists**

www.fbi.gov

*"The FBI's 'Terrorist Screening Center' keeps Americans safe by sharing terrorism-related information across the U.S. government and with law enforcement agencies.*

*We have one Federal Terrorism Watchlist on people suspected to be involved in terrorism (or related activities)."*

**Average Annual Border Apprehensions**

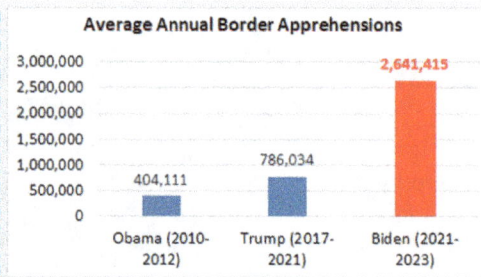

| | |
|---|---|
| Obama (2010-2012) | 404,111 |
| Trump (2017-2021) | 786,034 |
| Biden (2021-2023) | 2,641,415 |

On day one of taking office, President Biden and Secretary Mayorkas intentionally

**Terrorist Apprehensions**

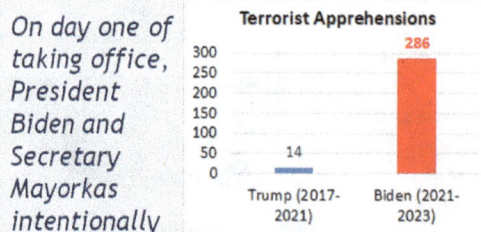

| | |
|---|---|
| Trump (2017-2021) | 14 |
| Biden (2021-2023) | 286 |

dismantled our immigration structure, ignoring federal law and putting Americans' safety in jeopardy."
Florida Attorney General Ashley Moody

**ALERT:**
**Many illegal immigrants look to make new, better lives for themselves, but terrorists look to make new attacks.**

*"If someone on the Terrorist Watchlist executed an attack in the U.S., destroying buildings and/or killing 100's of people...*

*And that person was discovered to have entered during Biden's open-border policies, we would likely see a huge voter backlash in the next election, even if Biden were no longer in office. And rightly so."*
Dr. Merrill Matthews, Institute for Policy Innovation, "Suspected Terrorists are Streaming across Biden's Broken Border," Sept. 26, 2023.

**MICAH 2:1    *"Woe to those who devise wickedness and work evil on their beds!"***

Courtesy of Google Images    Fair Use Law 17 U.S. Code § 107

## Trump vs. Obama & Biden: Capitulation to the Taliban and Radical Islam

**President Donald Trump**
**(Jan 2017 – Jan 2021)**

*"Defeating radical Islamic terror groups is our highest priority. We're up against an enemy that celebrates death and worships destruction. They are determined to strike our homeland as on 9/11, from Boston to Orlando to San Bernardino." (White House plan, Jan. 2017)*

**President Barack Obama**
**(Jan 2009 – Jan 2017)**

*"To prevent people from being susceptible to the false promises of extremism, countries have to invest in skills, education and job training that our extra-ordinary young people need." (Summit on How to End Islamic Terrorism, Feb. 2015)*

**President Joe Biden**
**(Jan 2021 – Present)**

*"We are consulting with the Taliban on every aspect"* (White House plan to rescue 1,000's of Americans from Afghanistan after Taliban seized control of gov't., seized over $20B US military equipment, killed 13 US soldiers by suicide bomber )

**Haibatullah Akhundzada: Taliban supreme leader**

Appointed head of Afghan gov't. after US withdrawal; His son Abdur Rahman died in carrying out a suicide bombing at Afghan military base in Helmand (July 2017)

### Psalm 139:19 (King David)
**"Oh, that you would slay the wicked, O God! Depart from me, you bloodthirsty men."**

## Christianity vs. Islam Part 20
### The Anniversary of America's Withdrawal from Afghanistan

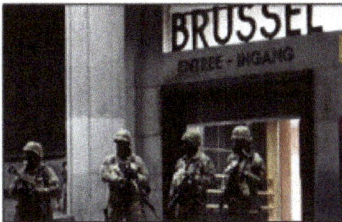

*"It's time we take our blinders off and started openly talking about the connection between ISIS's brutality and Quranic literalism.*

*It has become far too dangerous to be polite and leave religion out of the discussion.*

*It is clear that a significant number of Muslims consider the ideology of ISIS legitimate, honorable and worthy enough to give up their lives for."*

Fathima Imra Nazeer, Assistant Prof. at Mount Ida College, commenting on 2016 Brussels Attack by ISIS

**Taliban Occupying Kabul, August 15, 2021**

*"By March 2022, they closed classrooms from sixth grade and above to all girls.*

*In May 2022, they decreed that all women must wear head-to-toe coverings in public, just like the last time they ruled Afghanistan, and should leave their homes only when necessary."*

Oklahoma Senator Jim Inhole, August 15, 2022

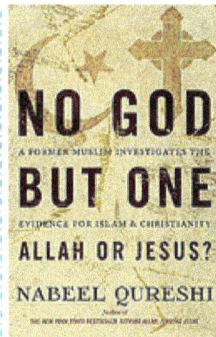

**NO GOD BUT ONE**
*A FORMER MUSLIM INVESTIGATES THE EVIDENCE FOR ISLAM & CHRISTIANITY*
**ALLAH OR JESUS?**
**NABEEL QURESHI**

*"Islam literally means 'submission' through the law.*

*Christianity means freedom through the Person of Jesus Christ.*

*In Islam, the way to paradise is 'sharia,' a code of laws to follow that will please Allah and earn his favor. Sharia is literally translated 'the way.'*

*But in Christianity, 'the way' to eternal life is a Person – Jesus Christ."*
'No God but One,' by Nabeel Qureshi

*"I am the way, the truth, and the life. No one comes to the Father except through Me"* John 14:6

*"The Lord has sent Me to proclaim liberty to the captives"* Luke 4:18b

*"The water I give becomes in him a spring of water welling up to eternal life"* John 4:14b

# Today's American Culture: The Lie of Systemic Racism

1) **America's Crossroad: Embracing Equity (Equality of Outcome)**

2) **Christianity's Stand Against Marxist Systemic Racism - Speak Up for Biblical Values**

3) **The Untold Story of Aaron Judge – Celebrating America's Love, Debunking America as Racist**

4) **In Life & Death - Our Heroes Return from Afghanistan: Race Doesn't Seem to Matter**

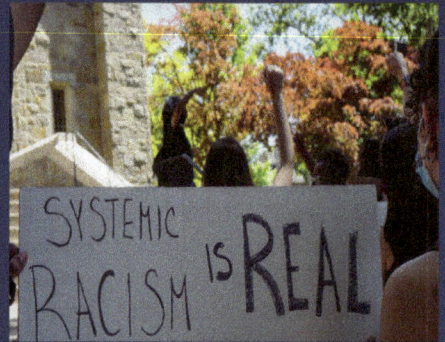

5) **LET'S HEAR FROM OUR EXPERTS**
   - **Chris Rufo & Critical Race Theory; Learn from Children**
   - **Dr. Carol Swain: 1619 Project/CRT vs. Jesus Christ's "Golden Rule"**
   - **Dr. Bob Woodson: Freedom from Slavery is an American Invention**
   - **Dr. Thomas Sowell: Mastering Facts and Evidence to Explain 3 Truths about Slavery**
   - **Dr. Walter Williams: Mastering Evidence & Logic to Advance Black Americans' Cause**
   - **Dr. Shelby Steele: The Solution to Redeeming the Curse of "White Guilt" = Jesus Christ**

SYSTEMIC RACISM IS REAL

# America's Crossroad: Embracing Equity (Equality of Outcome)

" I have a dream that my four little children will one day live in a nation where they will not be judged by the color of their skin but by the content of their character."

Martin Luther King, Jr. "I have a Dream" (28 August 1963)

"A SOCIETY THAT PUTS EQUALITY IN THE SENSE OF EQUALITY OF OUTCOME—AHEAD OF FREEDOM WILL END UP WITH NEITHER EQUALITY NOR FREEDOM. THE USE OF FORCE TO ACHIEVE EQUALITY WILL DESTROY FREEDOM, AND THE FORCE, INTRODUCED FOR GOOD PURPOSES, WILL END UP IN THE HANDS OF PEOPLE WHO USE IT TO PROMOTE THEIR OWN INTERESTS."

DR. THOMAS SOWELL

*"America's center of gravity has shifted away from the colorblind ideal – which is a great mistake."*
(Dr. Glenn Loury)

# Christianity's Stand Against Marxist Systemic Racism - Speak Up for Biblical Values

**MARXISM:**
**Pitting Races Against Each Other to Divide Us**

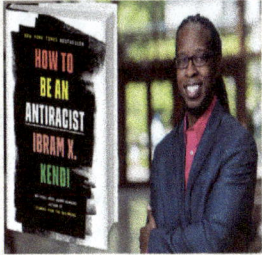

"The only remedy to racist discrimination is present discrimination.

The only remedy to past discrimination is future discrimination."
Ibram X. Kendi, Boston Univ. Ctr for Antiracist Research

**CHRISTIANITY:**
**Born in God's image means we are ALL Equal**

Peter and Cornelius
Acts 10: 28,43,45

*"You know how unlawful it is for a Jewish man to keep company with or go to one of another nation. But God has shown me that <u>I should not call any man common or unclean</u>.*

*Through the name of Jesus Christ, whoever believes on Him will receive forgiveness of sins. The Jews who believed were astonished because the gift of the Holy Spirit had been poured out on <u>the Gentiles also</u>."*

**SPEAKING UP AGAINST MARXISM:**
**Follow God's Biblical Principles**

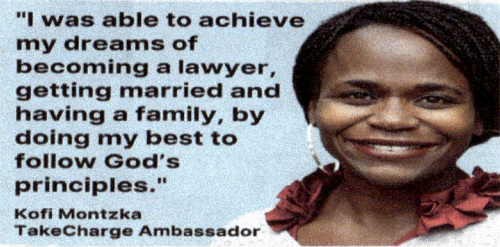

"I was able to achieve my dreams of becoming a lawyer, getting married and having a family, by doing my best to follow God's principles."
**Kofi Montzka**
**TakeCharge Ambassador**

*"I could not believe it when I read the bill's exact language. They talk about institutional racism. They talk about anti-racism and redistributing wealth right in this bill.*

*Although they say it is anti-racist, <u>it is racist at its core</u>. The whole curriculum groups kids by race and pits them against each other, telling kids of color they are stuck in a system based on race. It gives children a reason to stop trying to succeed."*

**"Christians understand that being born in God's image means equality, not pitting races against each other nor making others feel inferior based on race. Christianity is rejected by Marxism and Critical Race Theory."** Carolina Journal writer Ray Nothstine

Courtesy of Google Images     Fair Use Law: 17 U.S. Code § 107

# The Untold Story of Aaron Judge – Celebrating America's Love, Debunking America as Racist

*"I'm a momma's boy. I know I wouldn't be a New York Yankee if it wasn't for my mom. The guidance she gave me as a kid growing up, knowing the difference from right and wrong, how to treat people and how to go the extra mile and put in extra work. She's molded me into the person that I am today."* As for his dad:

*"Growing up, I could tell he was tired. He'd had a long day of work. He never complained, nothing. For me, that's why he's still the hero in my eyes."*

**"When my mother and father forsake me, then the Lord will take care of me."**
**Psalm 27:10**

*"Aaron Judge, and what he accomplished, should be the biggest story in sports and a shining example of America's grace, mercy, and love. Instead, it shows how much we have destroyed America.*

*Aaron is a professing Christian, biracial, and adopted by two white parents. This should be an amazing feel-good story about second chances in America and about how people regardless of race rally around each other. This family took Aaron into their home and raised one of the greatest baseball players of all time.*

*We should be celebrating America and people like the Judges who raise adopted children as if they are their own biological children. Instead, we have ruined the Aaron Judge story."*

Jason Whitlock, host of "Fearless": 'How MLB & the Woke Mob Ruined Aaron Judge's Historic Season'

Courtesy of Google Images     Fair Use Law 17 U.S. Code § 107

# In Life & Death - Our Heroes Return from Afghanistan: Race Doesn't Seem to Matter

Sgt. Johanny Rosario Pichardo   Sgt. Nicole L. Gee   Staff Sgt. Darin T. Hoover

Cpl. Daegan W. Page   Cpl. Humberto A. Sanchez   Lance Cpl. David L. Espinoza

Lance Cpl. Rylee J. McCollum   Lance Cpl. Dylan R. Merola   Lance Cpl. Kareem M. Nikoui   Navy Corpsman Maxton W. Soviak   Staff Sgt. Ryan C. Knauss   Lance Cpl. Jared M. Schmitz   Cpl. Hunter Lopez

*"Greater love has no one than this, than to lay down one's life for his friends."*
(Jesus Christ, John 15:13)

Courtesy of Google Images    Fair Use Law 17 U.S. Code § 107

# Chris Rufo & Critical Race Theory; Learn from Children

*"Critical race theorists reject equality - the principle proclaimed in the Declaration of Independence, defended in the Civil War and codified into law with the 14th and 15th Amendments, the Civil Rights Act of 1964 and the Voting Rights Act of 1965.*

*To them, equality provides camouflage for white supremacy, patriarchy and oppression."* Chris Rufo, Senior Fellow, Manhattan Institute

*"Master, who is greatest in the kingdom of heaven? Jesus called a little child to Him, set him in the midst of them, and said,*

*'Assuredly, I say to you, unless you are converted and become as little children, you will by no means enter the kingdom of heaven.*

*Therefore, whoever humbles himself as this little child is the greatest in the kingdom of heaven.'"* Jesus Christ, Matthew 18:1-3

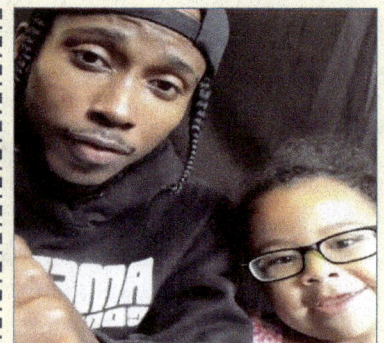

*"Daddy teaches you can be anything in this world that you want to be... right?'* His daughter:

*"And it doesn't matter if you're black or white or if you're any color."* Kory: *"How we treat people is based on who they are."*

His daughter: *"And if they're nice or smart."* Kory Yeshua, Tiktok Video

# Dr. Carol Swain: 1619 Project/CRT  vs.  Jesus Christ's "Golden Rule"

*"The story of my life is a God story. I am a devout Christian whose identity is in Jesus Christ."*

*"I reached my formative years before Critical Race Theory (CRT) and cultural Marxism became dominant in academia.*

*Growing up in Southern poverty during segregation, I was not taught to hate white people or America but* to be proud to live in the greatest country in the world.

*No one told me I was a victim.* I never fixated on being black, poor and female. *Had I done so, I doubt I would have achieved anything."*

*"Within Christian communities, the solution for hatred, bitterness, and distrust can be found in New Testament principles. Rather than wallow in the past and revisionists' efforts to promote reparations, we need to* practice the forgiveness and LOVE OF NEIGHBOR that Jesus espoused *- to transcend racial and ethnic conflicts that keep us from working together and celebrating our victories."*

**It bothers me that blacks are being decieved into supporting programs and policies that are destroying them."**
**Professor Carol M. Swain**

*"You shall love the Lord your God with all your heart, with all your soul, with all your strength, and with all your mind. And you shall LOVE YOUR NEIGHBOR AS YOURSELF."* (Luke 10:27)

# Dr. Bob Woodson:  Freedom from Slavery is an American Invention

Do not talk to me about 'systemic racism' when you have systemic *indifference* to the plight of poor Blacks.

*"A good name (character) is to be chosen rather than great riches."*
Proverbs 22:1

## AMERICA'S LEGACY

"America cannot be defined by its birth defect of slavery... Our Constitution is a document that allows for self-correction.

**And we are the only nation to ever have an emancipation proclamation to end slavery."**

*"The 1776 Unites curriculum offers authentic, inspiring stories from American history that show what is best in our national character and what our freedom makes possible even in the most difficult circumstances."*

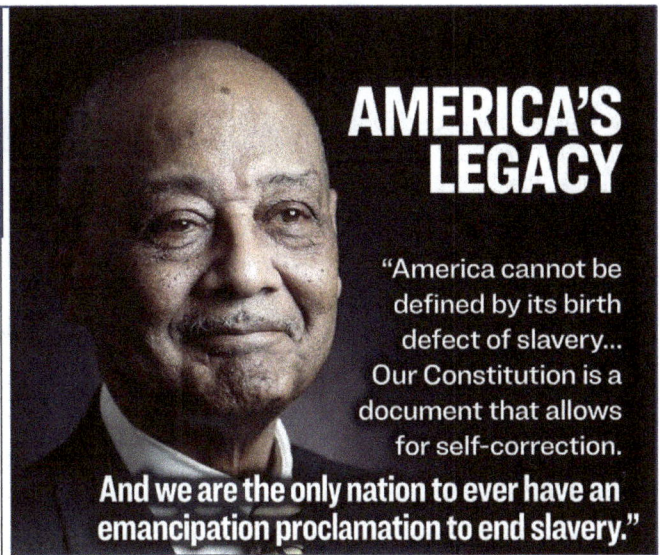

*"Black Reparations is fools' gold.*
*The message to black America is that your destiny is determined by what white people give you and not what you can do for yourself."*

## Article 457 - Black Wisdom Matters: Bob Woodson's 1776unites: It's about Character, not Reparations

Proverbs 22:1 *"A good name is to be chosen rather than great riches."*

*"Black Reparations is fools' gold. It demeans both whites and blacks. The message to black America is you can monetize oppression, that your destiny is determined by what white people give you and not what you are able to do for yourself.*

*Reparations is bandied around by people with 6-figure incomes who live in gated communities with their children in private schools, not black people in the inner cities suffering from violence."* This is the directness of Bob Woodson when interviewed recently on Fox News. He continues.

*"Reparations is virtue signaling for white candidates. For some white guilty people, it's an easy fix, but it's very crippling to the nation. So, hypothetically, if we were to get reparations tomorrow, do you think that there would be fewer shootings in St. Louis or Chicago or Baltimore? No. What problem does it solve?*

*If whites paid blacks money on Monday and we come back 2 weeks later, what would be the impact on black-on-black crime? What would be the impact of drug addiction? The high dropout rate? It's lethal to do virtue signaling on the issue of race and appear to be champions. It is pandering. It is insulting to black America, and as I have said, I have suffered my last rich angry black and guilty white person."*

Bob Woodson, founder of the Bob Woodson Center and 1776 Unites, knows of what he speaks. Deeply ingrained in the Civil Rights movement of the 1960's, his passion is to lift up local neighborhoods with the focus on revitalizing low-income communities. And his method? Transforming people from the inside-out.

As a Christian, Woodson designed 1776 Unites to center on a person's CHARACTER to bring healing and transformation to race relations. As our verse this week says, your character (the Hebrew for 'name' is 'character') – is worth more than riches. Let's hear more about 1776 Unites and the Woodson Center.

*"1776 Unites is a group of voices who uphold our country's authentic founding virtues and challenge those who assert America is forever defined by its past failures, such as slavery. We honor the vision of our nation's Founders who saw beyond their years. Though discrimination and slavery are a tragic part of our history, America has made strides to realize its promise and abide by its founding principles.*

*The 1776 Unites curriculum offers authentic, inspiring stories from American history that show what is best in our national character and what our freedom makes possible even in the most difficult circumstances.*

*1776 Unites maintains a special focus on stories that celebrate black excellence, reject victimhood culture, and showcase black Americans who have prospered by embracing America's founding ideals.*

*For 4 decades, the Woodson Center has brought recognition, training and funding to grassroots leaders and organizations working to confront the problems facing their communities and heal their neighborhoods with proven, sustainable solutions.*

*The Center has aided more than 2,600 leaders of faith-based and community organizations in 39 states and helped them attain more than 10 times the funding expended by the Center."* This is excellent work. But as he explains, the '1619 Project' represents strong opposition.

*"One of the most virulent and volatile areas of division is race, and the purveyors of animosity have fine-tuned their strategy on this issue, creating a villain composed of 'white privilege' and 'institutional racism' that must be countered through a game plan of entitlements and reparations for its victims.*

*The weapon in this warfare is the '1619 Project,' launched by the NY Times in a collection of writings that postulate the 'actual' founding of America occurred in 1619 with the arrival of the first slaves on our nation's shores, and declare that America is essentially and irrevocably rooted in injustice and racism.*

*The weight of the legacy of slavery and Jim Crow laws is said to be the cause of any and all racial disparity that exists today and is declared as the source of the devastation of crime-ridden, predominantly black inner cities and skyrocketing homicides, as well as the dissolution of families and communities."*

Woodson summarizes his mission this way: *"We seek to offer perspectives that celebrate the progress America has made on delivering its promise of equality and opportunity, as well as highlight the resilience of its people. Our focus is on solving problems.*

*We do this in the spirit of 1776, the date of America's true founding."* I encourage you to go to '1776 Unites' website and be encouraged.

## Dr. Thomas Sowell:  Mastering Facts & Evidence to Explain 3 Truths about Slavery

**Truth #1:** Slavery was practiced around the world until western civilization, especially the US, ended it:

*"Everyone hated the idea of being a slave but few had any qualms about enslaving others. Slavery was not an issue, not even among intellectuals and political leaders, until the 18th century. And then it was an issue only in Western civilization."*

**Truth #2:** In the US, slavery was rejected as a moral abomination:

*"It is clear from the private correspondence of Washington, Jefferson, and many others that their moral rejection of slavery was unambiguous, but the practical question of what to do had them baffled. The Civil War answered this, where 1 life was lost (620,000 killed) for every 6 people freed (3.9 million).*

*You could research all of 18th century Africa, Asia or Middle East without finding any comparable rejection of slavery there."*

**Truth #3:** Slavery and its effects are over in US, but is a global crisis:

*"National Geographic's article '21st Century Slaves' claims '27 million men, women, children are enslaved - forced to work, controlled through violence, or treated as property.*

*Where is the moral indignation?*

*There are more slaves today than seized from Africa in 4 centuries of the trans-Atlantic slave trade (11 million, with 450,000, or 4%, brought to the US).*

*Global commerce in humans rivals illegal drug trafficking."*

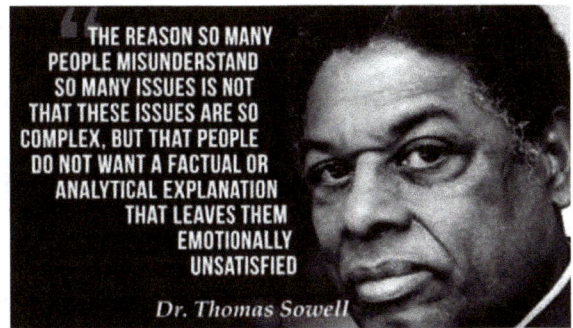

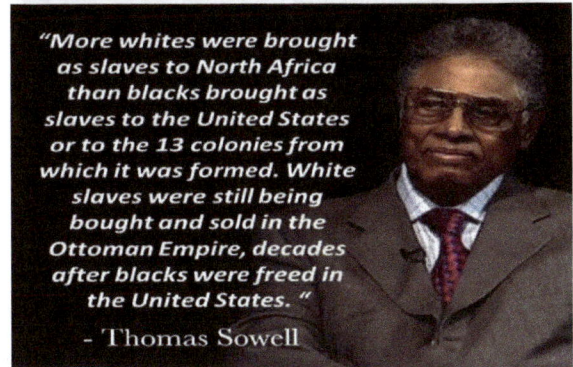

> THE REASON SO MANY PEOPLE MISUNDERSTAND SO MANY ISSUES IS NOT THAT THESE ISSUES ARE SO COMPLEX, BUT THAT PEOPLE DO NOT WANT A FACTUAL OR ANALYTICAL EXPLANATION THAT LEAVES THEM EMOTIONALLY UNSATISFIED
>
> *Dr. Thomas Sowell*

> *"More whites were brought as slaves to North Africa than blacks brought as slaves to the United States or to the 13 colonies from which it was formed. White slaves were still being bought and sold in the Ottoman Empire, decades after blacks were freed in the United States. "*
>
> - Thomas Sowell

**Acts 17:2**   *"Paul, as his custom was, went in to them and reasoned with them from the Scriptures."*

Thomas Sowell on current Black Culture' (10:41)                    Courtesy of Google Images      Fair Use Law 17 U.S. Code § 107

---

## Dr. Walter Williams:  Mastering Evidence & Logic to Advance the Cause of Black Americans

**Logic** = method of reasoning involving thinking through what we hear/observe to then reach conclusions.

**Reasoning** = The expression of your mind's thoughts and convictions.

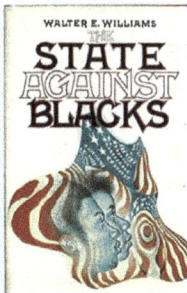

*"It is thought to be self-evident and beyond question that the problems of today's black Americans are a result of a legacy of slavery, racial discrimination and poverty. This is what the civil rights establishment and academics have taught. But as with so much of leftists' claims, there is little evidence to support it."* (Dr. Walter Williams, 2017 article 'The Welfare State's Legacy ')

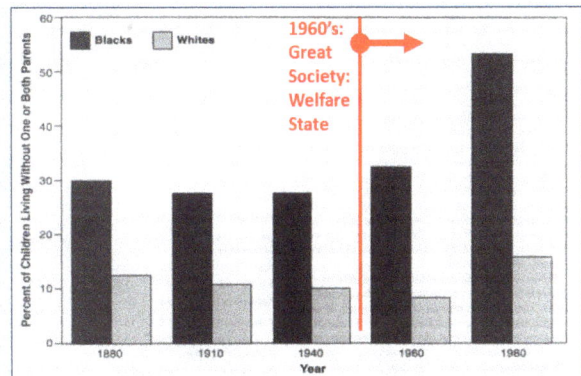

Figure 1. Percentages of Children Ages 0 to 14 With One or Both Parents Absent, by Race: United States, 1880–1980

*"By 1960, just 22% of black children were raised in single-parent families. 50 years later, over 70% of black children were raised in single-family families. The Welfare State has done to black families what slavery couldn't do, what Jim Crow couldn't do, what the harshest racism couldn't do – destroy the black family."* (Dr. Walter Williams, 2017 article 'The Welfare State's Legacy')

*"The most damage done to black Americans is inflicted by those politicians, civil rights leaders and academics who assert that every problem confronting blacks is a result of a legacy of slavery and discrimination. That's a vision that guarantees perpetuity for the problems."*

Black Wisdom Matters Part 2: 'Good Intentions of the Welfare State' (13:37)                    Courtesy of Google Images      Fair Use Law 17 U.S. Code § 107

# Dr. Shelby Steele: "White Guilt" and Jesus Christ

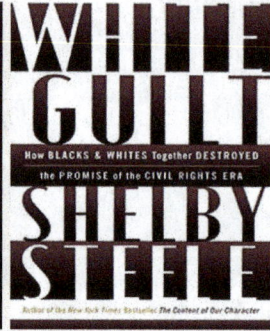

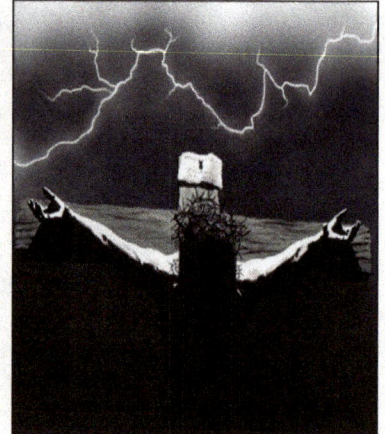

"An unintended consequence of the civil rights victories in the mid-60's was what I call WHITE GUILT. America acknowledged that for four centuries it had oppressed black Americans.

Anytime you acknowledge a wrong, a price you pay for that is a loss of moral authority. You are stigmatized as a racist because you acknowledged your nation practiced racism explicitly for four centuries.

White Americans want to prove that they are not racist. This pressure that comes to whites from this stigmatization has had a tremendous impact on our culture, our politics, our public policy in many, many ways." Dr. Shelby Steele

The Power of White Guilt (14:10)

"Through one man sin entered the world, and death through sin, and thus death spread to all men, because all sinned." Romans 5:12

"Your sins have separated you from your God..." Isaiah 59:2

"All we like sheep have gone astray. We have turned everyone each to his own way. And the Lord has laid on Him the sins of us all." Isaiah 53:4

"Christ has redeemed us from the curse of the law, having become a curse for us." Galatians 3:13

Courtesy of Google Images     Fair Use Law 17 U.S. Code § 107

**Exit Ticket #13    Class 13: Today's American Culture: Secularism, Systemic Racism**

| | |
|---|---|
| 1) How do our secular universities contribute to deconstructing our youth? | 2) How does the failure of the "Defund the Police" movement demonstrate Postmodernism's failure? |
| 3) What 3 facts do Dr. Thomas Sowell present to show America led the charge to end slavery? | 4) Which of the 38 bible verses in this class resonates the most with you when you think of secularism and/or racism in America today? |

# Class 14   America Today
# Sexual Identity, Abortion

Understanding Today's "Post-Christian" America: Assimilating what God Commanded be kept Separate

Leviticus 18  Why God threw Inhabitants out – Sexual Sin, Child Sacrifice

Today's American Culture: **The Lie of Sexual Identity**

- The Bible: Only 2 Genders, Homosexuality and LGBTQ is Sin
- Attacking the Bible
- Corporate Wokeness
- Transgender Sports
- Speak Out for Truth

America Today: **The Lie of Abortion**

- The Bible: God is Pro-Life, Abortion is Sin
- CA Abortion Bill AB 2223
- Washington DC's Arch of Palmyra
- God's Warning to America: Aborting Innocent Babies is Child Sacrifice
- Moses, Jeremiah & Isaiah: The Sin of Child Sacrifice
- America's War on the Unborn
- Science Proves an Unborn Baby is Human
- Deductive Argument Against Abortion
- It's About Objective Morality

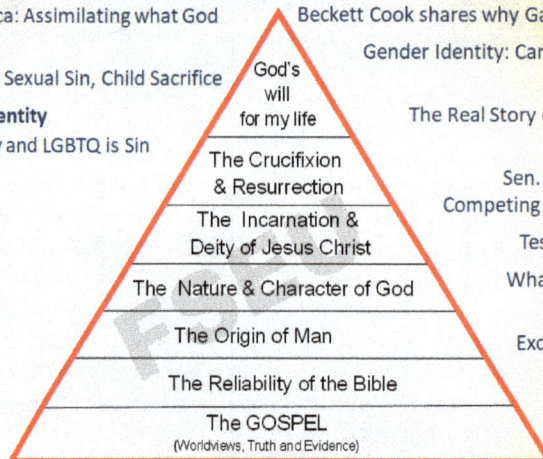

**Pyramid (top to bottom):**

God's will for my life

The Crucifixion & Resurrection

The Incarnation & Deity of Jesus Christ

The Nature & Character of God

The Origin of Man

The Reliability of the Bible

The GOSPEL
(Worldviews, Truth and Evidence)

# H E B R E W S 11:1

"Faith = *Substance* of things hoped for … *Evidence* of things *not seen*"

**fse.life Lesson 01**

Beckett Cook shares why Gay Label falls short of identity' (5:54)

Gender Identity: Can a 5-9 White Guy be a 6-5 Chinese Woman?' (4:13)

The Real Story of John Money – Father of Gender Ideology (6:16)

Sen. Hawley Questions Riley Gaines on Competing Against Transgender Athletes (6:50)

Testimony of Rosario Butterfield (7:58)

What Christians Don't Get About LGBT Folks (3:17)

Excavated Canaanite High Place – the Sin of the Amorites (17:06)

High School Graduate's Speech Abortion (1:14)

Bioethical Argument Against Abortion (3:42)

PragerU: The Most Important Question about Abortion (5:19)

---

# Understanding Today's "Post-Christian" America:
## *Assimilating* what God Commanded be kept *Separate*

**Good vs. Evil**
Isaiah 5:20

Objective morality replaced by personal 'feelings'.

WHO ARE YOU TO JUDGE ME

**Man vs. God**
Psalm 100:3

**AMERICAN HUMANIST ASSOCIATION**
GOOD WITHOUT A GOD

Religion of Secular Humanism

**Man vs. Animal**
Genesis 2:7

All animals are our cousins (Common Descent).

**Holy vs. Profane**
1Peter 1:15-16

In American culture, profanity is the 'new normal'.

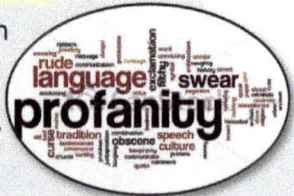

profanity

**Man vs. Woman**
Genesis 2:22-23

Choose from over 500 gender identities.

## American Culture:  Founded Christian,  Embracing Secularism

## Leviticus 18  Why God threw Inhabitants out – Sexual Sin, Child Sacrifice

Leviticus 18:1-3* *"The Lord said to Moses, 'Say to the Israelites: 'I am the Lord your God. You must not do as they do in Egypt, where you used to live. You must not do as they do in the land of Canaan, where I am bringing you. Do not follow their practices.'"*

**I Have A Question**

What are the practices of Egypt and Canaan the Israelites must not do, which are the reasons God vomits them out of the land?

**(1)** Levit. 18:6 Don't have sex with a close relative.

**(2)** Levit. 18:7-8 *Don't have sex with your mother nor your father's wife.*

**(3)** Levit. 18:9 *Don't have sex with your sister.*

**(4)** Levit. 18:10 *Don't have sex with your son's or daughter's daughter.*

**(5)** Levit. 18:11 *Don't have sex with your father's wife's sister.*

**(6)** Levit. 18:12 *Don't have sex with your father's sister.*

**(7)** Levit. 18:13 *Don't have sex with your mother's sister.*

**(8)** Levit. 18:14 *Don't try to have sex with your father's brother's wife.*

**(9)** Levit. 18:15 *Don't have sex with your son's wife.*

**(10)** Levit. 18:16 *Don't have sex with your brother's wife.*

**(11)** Levit. 18:17 *Don't have sex with a woman and her, or her son's, or her daughter's, daughter.*

**(12)** Levit. 18:18 *Don't have sex with your wife's sister as your 2nd wife.*

**(13)** Levit. 18:19 *Don't have sex with a woman during her period.*

**(14)** Levit. 18:20 *Don't have sex with your neighbor's wife.*

**(15)** Levit. 18:21 *Don't sacrifice children to Molech.*

**(16)** Levit. 18:22 *Don't have sex, as a man, with another man.*

**(17)** Levit. 18:22 *Don't have sex with an animal.*

**Leviticus 18:24-25** *God gives DETAILS on sexual sins and slaughtering children because people were/are DOING both!*

*Also read Deuteronomy 18:9-14

Courtesy of Google Images    Fair Use Law 17 U.S. Code § 107

---

# Today's American Culture:   The Lie of Sexual Identity

1) **THE BIBLE** Only 2 Genders, Homosexuality and LGBTQ is Sin

2) **ATTACKING THE BIBLE**

   – **America's Changing Sexuality:  Christians better know their Bible**

   – **What if We Had Renamed June 'Humility Month'?**

3) **CORPORATE WOKENESS**

   – **Anheuser-Busch, Transgenderism & the Bible: Will You Speak the Truth?**

   – **Target's Rude Awakening:  Promoting Child Abuse Costs More than Money**

4) **TRANSGENDER SPORTS**

   – **Transgender Sports? Why Aren't the Men Speaking Out for the Truth?**

5) **SPEAKING TRUTH**

   – **Speaking Out during Pride Month:  Churches Could Learn Boldness from Believers**

   – **Taking Pride in Speaking Out:  Truth was the Safest Place for HS Girls' Volleyball**

Courtesy of Google Images    Fair Use Law 17 U.S. Code § 107

## The Bible: Only 2 Genders, Homosexuality and LGBTQ is Sin

1) Genesis 1:27 *"God created man in His own image; in the image of God He created him; male and female He created them."*

2) Genesis 2:23 Adam said: *"This is now bone of my bones And flesh of my flesh; She shall be called Woman, because she was taken out of Man."*

3) Mark 10:6-9 *"From the beginning of creation, 'God made them male and female.' 'Therefore a man shall leave his father and mother and hold fast to his wife, and the two shall become one flesh.' So they are no longer two but one flesh. What therefore God has joined together, let not man separate."*

4) Deuteronomy 22:5 *"A woman shall not wear anything that pertains to a man, nor shall a man put on a woman's garment, for all who do so are an abomination to the Lord your God."*

5) Leviticus 18:22 *"You shall not lie with a male as with a woman. It is an abomination."*

6) Leviticus 20:13 *"If a man lies with a male as he lies with a woman, both of them have committed an abomination. They shall surely be put to death. Their blood shall be upon them."*

7) Genesis 19:4-7 *"The men of the city, the men of Sodom, both old and young, all the people from every quarter, surrounded the house. And they called to Lot and said to him, 'Where are the men who came to you tonight? Bring them out to us that we may know them carnally.' So Lot went out to them through the doorway, shut the door behind him, and said, 'Please, my brethren, do not do so wickedly!'"*

8) Judges 19:22-23 *"…suddenly certain men of the city, perverted men, surrounded the house and beat on the door. They spoke to the master of the house, the old man, saying, 'Bring out the man who came to your house, that we may know him carnally!' The master of the house went out to them and said 'No, my brethren! I beg you, do not act so wickedly!'"*

9) Jude 1:7 *"Just as Sodom, Gomorrah and surrounding cities, which likewise indulged in sexual immorality and pursued unnatural desire, serve as an example by undergoing a punishment of eternal fire."*

10) Romans 1:26-27 *"For this reason God gave them up to vile passions. For even their women exchanged the natural use for what is against nature. Likewise also the men, leaving the natural use of the woman, burned in their lust for one another, men with men committing what is shameful, and receiving in themselves the penalty of their error which was due."*

11) 1Corinthians 6:9-11 *"Do you not know that the unrighteous will not inherit the kingdom of God? Do not be deceived. Neither fornicators, nor idolaters, nor adulterers, nor homosexuals, nor sodomites, nor thieves, nor covetous, nor drunkards, nor revilers, nor extortioners will inherit the kingdom of God. And such were some of you. But you were washed, but you were sanctified, but you were justified in the name of the Lord Jesus and by the Spirit of our God."*

# America's Changing Sexuality:  Christians better know their Bible

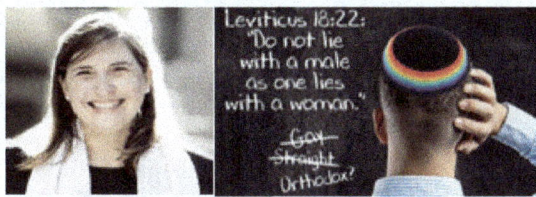

*"Thank God the Torah reminds us that God, in God's own image, created male and female.*

*It is right there in the verse, just two words earlier: 'In the image of God was he created, male and female.'*

*Perhaps those who would otherwise be harmed will find comfort to know that <u>according to Torah, God is not confined to binary genders</u>."*

Rabbi Heather Miller of Beth Chayim Chadashim, an LGBT Reform synagogue in West Los Angeles, explaining how Genesis 1:27 supports transgender.

*"In an attempt to show that the Torah does not seek to preserve male-female identities and the male-female distinction, <u>some distort the verse in the Torah</u> that I cited: 'And God created man in His image; in the image of God He created him; male and female He created them.'*

*They claim that the Torah didn't mean that God created male and female persons.*

*But, the text says, 'male and female He created them;' 'them' (human beings) - not 'him' (Adam). It doesn't say 'he' was created male and female (to support for transgender). It says 'they' were created male and female. A clear distinction between men and women."* Dennis Prager - Genesis 1:27 is clear: it's male and female

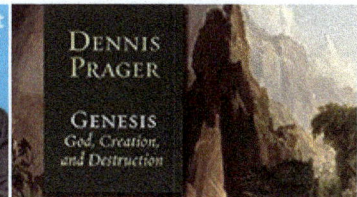

**"God created man in His own image; In the image of God He created him; male and female He created THEM."**
Genesis 1:27

# What if We Had Renamed June's Pride Month 'Humility Month'?

"We gather at the White House to honor the extraordinary courage and contributions of LGBTQI+ Americans.

The People's House sends a clear message to the country and the world.

America is a nation of pride." President Biden, June 10 White House Pride Event

"The behavior was simply unacceptable.

Individuals in the video certainly will not be invited to future events.

This behavior was not a normal thing happening in this administration." White House Press Secretary, on lewd behavior on White House Lawn at Pride Event

"We should include the kink community in Pride Month rallies, as well as exposing children to acts performed by kinks.

This will help children learn about the scope and vitality of the queer life." Washington Post author Lauren Rowello

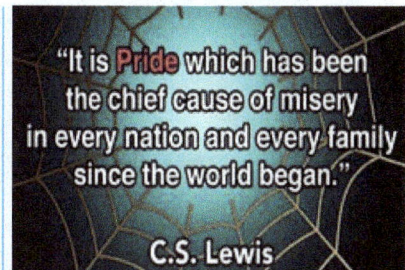

*"It is Pride which has been the chief cause of misery in every nation and every family since the world began."*

C.S. Lewis

"You may remember, when I was talking about sexual immorality, I warned you that the center of Christian morals did not lie there.

Well, now we have come to the center. The essential vice, the utmost evil, is pride. It was through pride that the devil became the devil.

Pride leads to every other vice. It is the complete ANTI-GOD state of mind." CS Lewis, Mere Christianity

**James 4:6 "God opposes the proud but gives grace to the humble."**

## Anheuser-Busch, Transgenderism & the Bible: Will You Speak the Truth?

### How I found God at Columbia - The Dennis Prager Show

"Why do so many people believe the nonsense of Marxism?

Why do so many professors teach the foolishness that men and women are the same?

Why are so many professors morally confused?

A biblical verse from Psalm 111 came to my mind from my childhood days: 'Wisdom begins with fear of God.'"

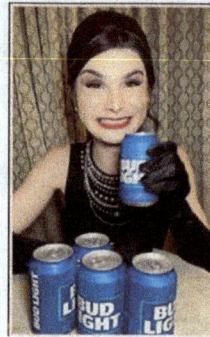

"The Bible is outdated. What could I possibly learn from a book written over 2,000 years ago?" Street Answer when asked why the Bible is not valuable to their lives.

Anheuser Busch lost $5 billion in value when they showcased trans activist Dylan Mulvaney to promote their beer.

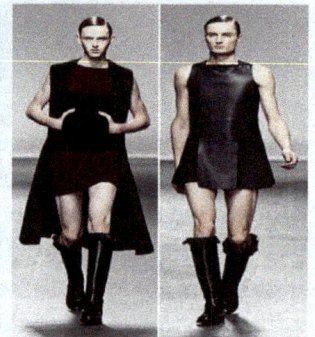

"A woman shall not wear anything that pertains to a man, nor shall a man put on a woman's garment, for all who do so are an abomination to the Lord your God." Deuteronomy 22:5

**"Set them apart by Your Word. Your Word is Truth."   Jesus, John 17:17**

Gender Identity: Can a 5-9 White Guy be a 6-5 Chinese Woman?' (4:13)     Courtesy of Google Images   Fair Use Law 17 U.S. Code § 107

## Target's Rude Awakening:  Promoting Child Abuse Costs More than Money

After losing $10 billion in just 2 days, Target execs held an emergency call across 2,000 stores nationwide:

"You have 36 hours to move all of our Pride stuff from the front to the back of the store."

The Real Story of John Money—Father of Gender Ideology (6:16)

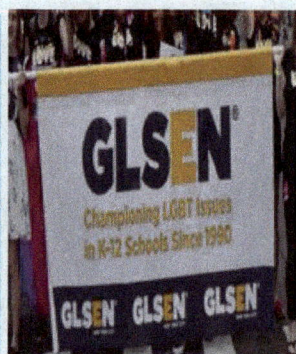

"Do not disclose any information that may reveal a student's gender identity to others, including parents or guardians, unless the student authorizes such disclosure." GLSEN instructions to school staff

"Satan is hope, compassion, equality, and love. Satan respects pronouns. Satan loves all LGBT+ people." Target's Apparel brand Abprallen

"Whoever causes one of these little ones who believe in Me to sin, it would be better for him if a millstone were hung around his neck and he were drowned in the depth of the sea." Jesus, Matthew 18:6.

Courtesy of Google Images   Fair Use Law 17 U.S. Code § 107

# Transgender Sports? Why Aren't the Men Speaking Out for the Truth?

"This is heartbreaking, maddening, and really difficult to watch. I keep thinking I'm going to wake up and be relieved that this was all just a ridiculous, comical, nonsensical dream (#IStandwithRileyGaines)." Sage Steele

"This would take away so many opportunities for biological women and girls in sports. It is a shame in 2023 we must fight for the integrity of Title IX and the reason for it in the first place (#savewomenssports)." Sam Ponder

"Are you really trying to say Lia Thomas would have won a national title against men? Does it not break your heart to see women lose opportunities? Biden's bill denies science, truth, and common sense.

Women of influential are beginning to speak out to the injustice of men competing against women. Sage and Sam have a lot to lose by using their voice yet chose to anyways.

That is what courage is. I am so honored to be able to lean on them as we continue forward with advocating for sex-protected sporting categories." Riley Gaines

Sen. Hawley Questions Female Sports Advocate Riley Gaines On Competing Against Transgender Athletes (6:50)

### Why is it so hard for me to Speak the Truth?

| | | |
|---|---|---|
| I don't **LIKE** the truth | Better to tell 'half-truths', or lie, and avoid the consequences | Jeremiah 17:9 Ecclesiastes 9:3 |
| I don't **TRUST** the truth | Better to try to work things out on my own and with others than trust God's promises to me | Genesis 12:10-20 |

| What I do | Why I do it | What I call it | What God calls it |
|---|---|---|---|
| flatter my boss | he'll like me | 'brown-nosing' | lying to my boss |
| exaggerate things | people will admire me | 'stretching the truth' | lying to people |
| live beyond my means | people will respect me | 'the American way' | lying to myself |
| 'go with the flow' | 'don't make waves' | making a living | living a lie |

*"Say you are my sister, that it might go well with me - that I may live because of you."*
**Genesis 12:13**

---

# Speaking Out during Pride Month: Churches Could Learn Boldness from Believers

**Trevor Williams**

**Brian Treinen**

**'Fearless' Jason Whitlock with Charlie Kirk**

"As a devout Catholic, I am deeply troubled by the Dodgers' decision to honor 'The Sisters of Perpetual Indulgence' at their Pride Night, a group that makes a blatant and deeply offensive mockery of my religion, and the religion of over 4 million people in LA County alone.

We look to Jesus Christ and we realize that any suffering in this world unites us to Him in the next."

Beckett Cook: 'Why Gay Label Falls Short of Identity' (5:54)

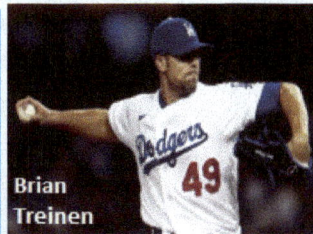

"I am disappointed to see the Sisters of Perpetual Indulgence honored as heroes at Dodger Stadium.

Many of their performances are blasphemous. Their work displays hate and mockery of the Christian faith.

My conviction in Jesus Christ will always come first.

Inviting them to perform promotes hate of Christians and people of faith."

"I don't want to silence people, but I want them to know that their sexual sin does not make them special. I don't have to agree their 'pet sin' is OK with me."

"Believers deserve a lot of credit. We are starting to make decisions based on whether a company shares our values.

The pushback isn't coming from the Church but from believers. We are seeing a new generation of Christians fulfilling Psalm 97:10 – 'love God and hate evil'.

It is a spiritual battle of good versus evil when the LGBTQ community goes after children. If the churches are not going to stand up, a new generation of believers will fill that void. It's time to rebuke this evil."

**Psalm 97:10** *"You who love the Lord. Hate evil!"*

## Taking Pride in Speaking Out: Truth was the Safest Place for Randolph HS Girls' Volleyball

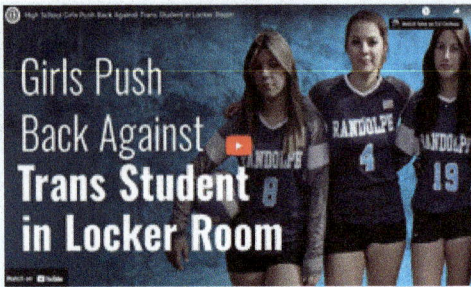

**Girls Push Back Against Trans Student in Locker Room**

*"The trans player on the team came into the girls' volleyball locker room as we were changing. We told him we weren't comfortable and asked him to leave, but instead he looked at girls with their shirts off. It made us very uncomfortable - we felt UNSAFE and violated.*

*When my dad and I contacted school officials, we were punished for speaking out and were told 'the transgender student should be permitted to use the girls' locker room regardless of the discomfort experienced by the girls in the room.'"*

Blake Allen, Randolph High Girls Volleyball Player

Testimony of Rosario Butterfield (7:58)

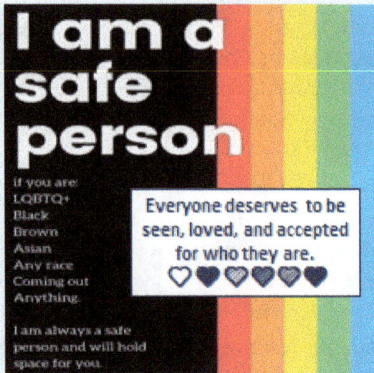

**I am a safe person**

If you are:
LGBTQ+
Black
Brown
Asian
Any race
Coming out
Anything.

I am always a safe person and will hold space for you.

Everyone deserves to be seen, loved, and accepted for who they are.
♡🖤🖤🖤🖤🖤

**REALLY??** Sexuality and ethnicity are not comparable. And it is not loving to make others feel violated by accepting biological males in girls' locker rooms.

Sexual practices in your bedroom is the "safe space", not public locker rooms and bathrooms.

The Randolph Girls Volleyball team spoke out: allowing men in women's locker rooms is UNSAFE.

**Dr. Rosario Butterfield, 'The Secret Thoughts of an Unlikely Convert'**

Former lesbian and LGBTQ+ activist and Professor at Syracuse University explains how she came to give her life to Jesus Christ.

*"This was something a Christian had never done with me before. Ken entered my world and spent time with me.*

*He did not treat me as his 'project'. He didn't even ask me to church. I knew it was SAFE for me to be his friend.*

*I asked my lesbian friend (who was once a pastor): 'What if Christianity is true?' She gave me her theology books and told me she hoped they could help me."*

**"The name of the Lord is a strong tower. The righteous run to it and are SAFE."**
Proverbs 18:10

Courtesy of Google Images - Fair Use Law 17 U.S. Code § 107

---

# Today's American Culture:   The Lie of Abortion

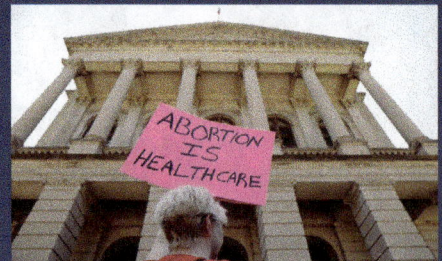

1) **The Bible: God is Pro-Life, Abortion is Sin**

2) **New CA Abortion Bill AB 2223:   One Church Standing Up for Righteousness**

3) **Washington DC's Arch of Palmyra: The Obsession over Abortion**

4) **God's Warning to America:  Aborting Innocent Babies is Child Sacrifice**

5) **Moses, Jeremiah & Isaiah: The Sin of Child Sacrifice**

6) **Abortion:   America's War on the Unborn**

7) **From Darwin (1870) to Roe vs Wade (1973) to Today (2022): Science Proves the Baby is Human at Conception**

8) **The Deductive Argument: How Abortion Violates American Law**

9) **Abortion: It's Not about Legality…. It's about Objective Morality**

Courtesy of Google Images - Fair Use Law 17 U.S. Code § 107

## The Bible: God is Pro-Life, Abortion is Sin

1) Psalm 139:13-16 *"For You formed my inward parts; You covered me in my mother's womb. I will praise You, for I am fearfully and wonderfully made; Marvelous are Your works, And that my soul knows very well."*

2) Psalm 127:3 *"Behold, children are a heritage from the Lord. The fruit of the womb is a reward."*

3) Psalm 22:10 *"I was cast upon You from birth. From My mother's womb You have been My God."*

4) Psalm 51:5 *"Behold, I was brought forth in iniquity, and in sin my mother conceived me."*

5) Jeremiah 1:5 *"Before I formed you in the womb I knew you; Before you were born I sanctified you..."*

6) Isaiah 49:1 *"Listen, O coastlands, to Me, and take heed, you peoples from afar! The Lord has called Me from the womb; from the matrix of My mother He has made mention of My name."*

7) Job 3:3 *"May the day perish on which I was born, and the night in which it was said, 'A male child is conceived.'"*

8) Genesis 25:22 *"The children struggled together within her; and she said, 'If all is well, why am I like this?' So she went to inquire of the Lord."*

9) Proverbs 6:16-19 *"There are 6 things that the Lord hates, 7 that are an abomination to him: haughty eyes, a lying tongue, and hands that shed innocent blood, a heart that devises wicked plans, feet that make haste to run to evil, a false witness who breathes out lies, one who sows discord among brothers."*

10) Exodus 21:21-25 *"If men fight, and hurt a woman with child, so that she gives birth prematurely, yet no harm follows, he shall surely be punished accordingly as the woman's husband imposes on him; and he shall pay as the judges determine. But if any harm follows, then you shall give life for life, eye for eye, tooth for tooth, hand for hand, foot for foot, burn for burn, wound for wound, stripe for stripe."*

11) Amos 1:13 (2Kings 8:12) *"Thus says the Lord: 'For 3 transgressions of the people of Ammon, and for 4, I will not turn away its punishment, because they ripped open the women with child in Gilead, that they might enlarge their territory.'"*

12) Luke 1:15 *"He will be great in the sight of the Lord and shall drink neither wine nor strong drink. He will also be filled with the Holy Spirit, even from his mother's womb."*

13) Luke 1:41 *"It happened, when Elizabeth heard the greeting of Mary, that the babe leaped in her womb; and Elizabeth was filled with the Holy Spirit."*

14) Galatians 1:15 *"But when it pleased God, who separated me from my mother's womb and called me through His grace,..."*

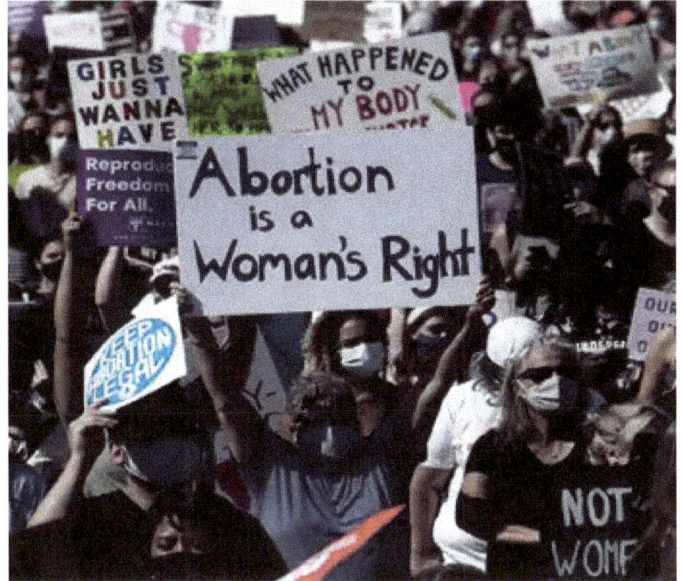

# New CA Abortion Bill AB 2223:  One Church Standing Up for Righteousness

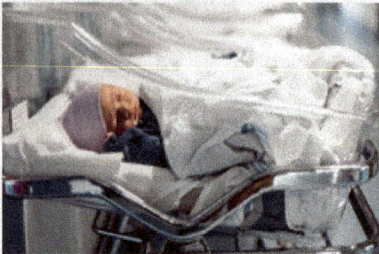

"A person shall not be subject to civil or criminal liability or penalty, or otherwise deprived of their rights under this article, based on their actions or omissions with respect to their pregnancy or actual, potential, or alleged pregnancy outcome, including miscarriage, stillbirth, or abortion, or **PERINATAL (time just before and just after birth) death** due to causes that occurred in utero." CA Bill AB 2223, Section 123467

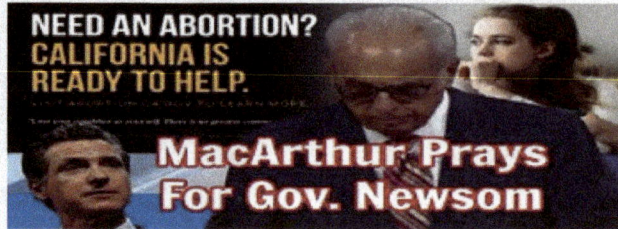

**NEED AN ABORTION? CALIFORNIA IS READY TO HELP.**

**MacArthur Prays For Gov. Newsom**

"Sir, Scripture teaches that it is the chief duty of any civic leader to reward those who do well and to punish evildoers (Romans 13:1–7).  The Word of God pronounces judgment on those who call evil good and good evil (Isaiah 5:20).

My goal in writing is not to contend with your politics, but to plead with you to hear and heed what the Word of God says to men in your position.

You revealed how thoroughly rebellious against God you are when you promoted the slaughter of children, whom He creates in the womb (Psalm 139:13–16;  Isaiah 45:9–12).

You cannot love God as He commands while aiding in the murder of His image-bearers." Pastor John MacArthur

"CA lawmakers crossed a red line by seeking to legitimize the killing of hours-old and even week-old infants.

This is not about expanding abortion rights; this is a degree of evil the over-whelming majority of Americans, regardless of how they identify politically, cannot stomach.

We are working to defeat this insane and diabolical bill." Attorney Matt McReynolds,  Pacific Justice Institute

**Proverbs 16:12**
*"It is an abomination for kings to commit wicked acts, for a throne is established on righteousness."*

# Washington DC's Arch of Palmyra: The Obsession over Abortion

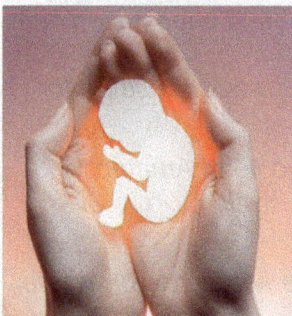

Women cite "social reasons," not mother's health or rape/incest, as their motivation in over 93% of abortions (National Right to Life).

The Arch of Palmyra, entrance to the Temple of Ba'al, installed in Washington, DC.

**Pagan Abortions: Child Sacrifice to Ba'al**

The temple had a blazing furnace below a bronze statue which represented the god Ba'al. Temple priests would place children and babies into its outstretched arms, allowing the children to then roll into the blazing fire as human sacrifices.

**Deuteronomy 12:31**
*"Even their sons and their daughters they have burnt in the fire to their gods."*

# God's Warning to America:  Aborting Innocent Babies is Child Sacrifice

Cuneiform clay tablets (2,500BC) from Amorite King Mari

Sacred Stones (Exodus 23:23-24)

Amorite Altar of Child Sacrifice (Leviticus 18:23)

*"There were multiple sacred stones, standing up to 18 feet tall. A flat stone with a basin in the middle was identified as the altar. The purpose of the carved-out basin was to catch the blood of sacrifices. All around the standing stones were found the mutilated, burnt bodies of little children in jars."* Stewart Macalister's discovery of Amorite child sacrifice to Molek

Gezer: The most critical city on the Via Maris – controlled by the Amorites in 2,500 BC

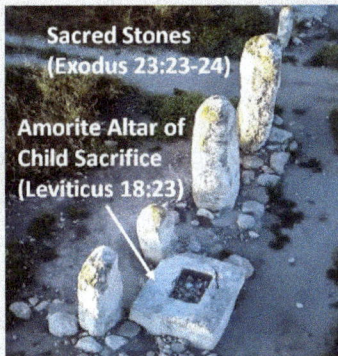

Remains of little children in jars at bases of sacred stones

Leviticus 18:24-26 Why God destroyed the Amorites
*"Do not defile yourselves in any of these ways, because this is how the nations that I am going to drive out before you became defiled. Even the land was defiled. I punished it for its sin, and the land vomited them out."*

**Leviticus 18:23**  *"Do not give any of your children to be sacrificed to Molek. You must not profane the name of your God. I am the Lord."*

Excavated Canaanite High Place – Sin of the Amorites (17:06)

## Moses: The Sin of Child Sacrifice

Leviticus 18:21 *"You shall not let any of your descendants pass through the fire to Molech, nor shall you profane the name of your God: I am the Lord."*

Leviticus 20:1-5 *"You shall say to the children of Israel: 'Whoever of the children of Israel, or of the strangers who dwell in Israel, who gives any of his descendants to Molech, he shall surely be put to death. The people of the land shall stone him with stones. I will set My face against that man, and will cut him off from his people, because he has given some of his descendants to Molech, to defile My sanctuary and profane My holy name. If the people of the land should in any way hide their eyes from the man, when he gives some of his descendants to Molech, and they do not kill him, then I will set My face against that man and against his family; and I will cut him off from his people, and all who prostitute themselves with him to commit harlotry with Molech."*

Leviticus 20:22-24 *"You shall keep all My statutes and all My judgments, that the land where I am bringing you to dwell may not vomit you out. You shall not walk in the statutes of the nation which I am casting out before you; for they commit all these things, and I abhor them. But I have said to you, 'You shall inherit their land, and I will give it to you to possess, a land flowing with milk and honey.' I am the Lord your God, who has separated you from the peoples."*

## 2Kings (Jeremiah): The Sin of Child Sacrifice

2Kings 2-3 *"Ahaz was twenty years old when he became king, and he reigned 16 years in Jerusalem; and he did not do what was right in the sight of the Lord his God, as his father David had done. But he walked in the way of the kings of Israel; Ahaz made his son pass through the fire, according to the abominations of the nations whom the Lord had cast out from before the children of Israel."*

2Kings 17:16-17 *"They left all the commandments of the Lord their God, made for themselves a molded image and 2 calves, made a wooden image, worshiped host of heaven, and served Baal. They caused their sons and daughters to pass through the fire, practiced witchcraft and soothsaying, and sold themselves to do evil in the sight of the Lord, provoking Him to anger."*

2Kings 21:6 *"Manasseh made his son pass through the fire, practiced soothsaying, used witchcraft, and consulted spiritists and mediums. He did much evil in the sight of the Lord, to provoke Him to anger."*

2Kings 23:10,25 *"Josiah defiled Topheth, which is in the Valley of the Son of Hinnom, that no man might make his son or his daughter pass through the fire to Molech. Before him there was no king like him, who turned to the Lord with all his heart, with all his soul, and with all his might, according to all the Law of Moses; nor after him did any arise like him."*

## Jeremiah & Isaiah: The Sin of Child Sacrifice

Isaiah 57:4-5 *"Whom are you mocking? At whom do you sneer and stick out the tongue? Are you not a brood of rebels, the offspring of liars? You burn with lust among the oaks and under every spreading tree. You sacrifice your children in the ravines and under the overhanging crags."*

Jeremiah 3:24 *"From our youth shameful gods have devoured the labor of our fathers… their sons and their daughters."*

Jeremiah 7:30-31 *"'The children of Judah have done evil in My sight,' says the Lord. 'They have set their abominations in the house which is called by My name, to pollute it. They have built the high places of Topheth, which is in the Valley of the Son of Hinnom, to burn their sons and their daughters in the fire, which I did not command, nor did it come into My heart.'"*

Jeremiah 19:4-6 *"'They have forsaken Me and made this an alien place; they have burned incense in it to other gods whom neither they, their fathers, nor the kings of Judah have known, and have filled this place with the blood of the innocents (they have also built the high places of Baal, to burn their sons with fire for burnt offerings to Baal, which I did not command or speak, nor did it come into My mind), therefore behold, the days are coming,' says the Lord, 'that this place shall no more be called Tophet or the Valley of the Son of Hinnom, but the Valley of Slaughter.'"*

Jeremiah 32:35 *"They built the high places of Baal which are in the Valley of the Son of Hinnom, to cause their sons and their daughters to pass through the fire to Molech, which I did not command them, nor did it come into My mind that they should do this abomination, to cause Judah to sin."*

# Abortion: America's War on the Unborn

8 weeks · 12 weeks · 16 weeks · 20 weeks · 24 weeks · 39 weeks

### 27 European Countries LIMIT Elective Abortion to 12 Weeks

| | | |
|---|---|---|
| Albaina | Estonia | Montenegro |
| Armenia | France | Moldovia |
| Azerbaijan | Georgia | Moldovia |
| Belarus | Greece | N. Ireland |
| Bosnia | Hungary | N. Macedonia |
| Bulgaria | Ireland | Norway |
| Cyprus | Kyrgyzstan | Norway |
| Czech Republic | Latvia | Russia |
| Denmark | Lithuania | Slovakia |
| Switzerland | Ukraine | |

STOP ABORTION NOW | PROTECTING THE UNBORN

*"Many of us have been willing to look the other way"*

### 3 Countries ALLOW Elective Abortions at 39 Weeks

**UNITED STATES**
North Korea
China

## Jeremiah 31:33
*"I will put My law in their minds and write it on their hearts. I will be their God, and they shall be My people."*

Courtesy of Google Images    Fair Use Law 17 U.S. Code § 107

## From Darwin (1870) to Roe vs Wade (1973) to Today (2022): Science Proves the Baby is Human at Conception

**The Deductive Argument: How Abortion Kills a Human Being**

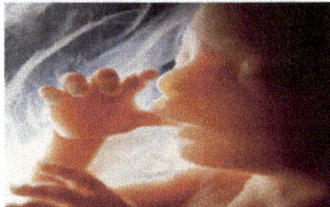

*"The judiciary, at this point in the development of man's knowledge, is in no position to resolve the difficult question of* when life begins*... since those trained in the respective disciplines of medicine, philosophy, and theology are unable to arrive at any consensus."* (Justice Harry Blackmun, 1973 Roe vs. Wade decision)

Darwin (1871): Aren't all animals alike during development? You can't distinguish humans from fish or turtles or rabbits??

**Premise 1:**
It is wrong to intentionally kill an innocent human being.

**Premise 2:**
Abortion kills an innocent human being.

**Conclusion:**
Therefore, Abortion is wrong.

*"I was pleased with Justice Blackmun's conclusions. I could not plumb the ethical or medical reasoning that had produced the conclusions. Our victory had been propped up on a* misreading of obstetrics, gynecology, and embryology*... that's a dangerous way to win."* Dr. Bernard Nathanson, 1973, former founder of NARAL (Nat. Assoc. for Repeal of Abortion Laws) and Director of NY's largest abortion clinic

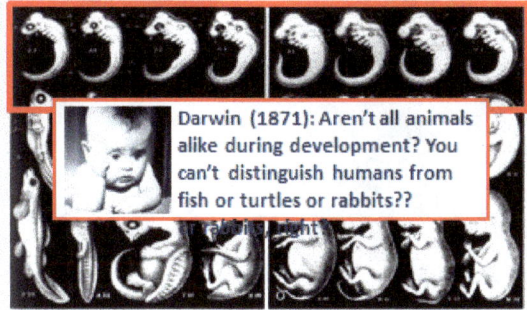

*"A favorite pro-abortion tactic is to insist that the definition of when life begins is a theological one, not a scientific one. But fetology (the science of the fetus in the uterus) makes it undeniably evident that* life begins at conception and requires all the protection and safeguards that any of us enjoy.*"* Dr. Nathanson, after watching an abortion on ultrasound, left atheism and became a Catholic and a staunch Pro-Life activist, creating the famous video "The Silent Scream" in 1984.

**Isaiah 41:21** *"'Present your case,' says the Lord. 'Bring forth your strong reasons,' says the King of Jacob."*

Bioethical Argument Against Abortion (3:42)        Courtesy of Google Images    Fair Use Law 17 U.S. Code § 107

## Article 179 - The Bible & Abortion: The Power of the Cross is in Transforming Lives

Psalm 130:3-4   "There is Forgiveness with You, that You may be feared."

Five years ago this week, Dr. Bernard Nathanson's death was celebrated in St. Patrick's Cathedral in New York City. A giant in the pro-life movement, he is the narrator of one of the most impactful movies ever made – 'The Silent Scream', an actual film of an abortion of a 12-week old baby. In the film, Dr. Nathanson guides us through the visual images as the baby struggles to avoid the oncoming surgical instruments and then the baby's scream as the tools begin to tear him into pieces.

There have been many famous pro-life champions since the infamous 1973 Roe vs. Wade Supreme Court decision. What makes Dr. Nathanson's story so amazing? The fact is, he was at one time the most famous abortionist in America. At the time of the Roe vs. Wade decision, Dr. Nathanson had already personally performed over 5,000 abortions. As the Director of the world's largest abortion clinic in New York City, he was responsible for over 75,000 abortions (by his own estimate). While he was in charge of the New York abortion clinic, he actually performed the abortion of his own child on a woman he had gotten pregnant. And in 1968, he had cofounded NARAL (The National Abortion Rights Action League).

What changed America's most prolific abortionist into the most vocal defender of an unborn baby's right to life? The first step was technology - the invention of the ultrasound machine: *"I am often asked what made me change from prominent abortionist to pro-life advocate? In 1973, I became director of obstetrics of a large hospital in New York City and had to set up a prenatal research unit, just at the start of a great new technology which we now use every day to study the fetus in the womb."*

The next step was his moral conscience when confronted with truth. While doing his normal routine of 15-20 abortions a day, he and a colleague recorded an abortion using ultrasound. After watching the video, his colleague never did another abortion. Nathanson confessed, "I ... was shaken to the very roots of my soul by what I saw... It is clear that permissive abortion is purposeful destruction of what is undeniably human life. It is an impermissible act of deadly violence."

He felt the weight of guilt for what he had been doing all those years, but he did not know where to go to find forgiveness: *"I felt the burden of sin growing heavier and more insistent. I have such heavy moral baggage to drag into the next world that failing to believe would condemn me to an eternity perhaps more terrifying than anything Dante envisioned... I am afraid."*

# The Deductive Argument: How Abortion Violates American Law

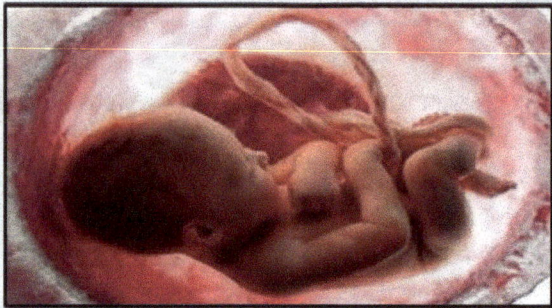

The Bible: *"Before I formed you in the womb, I knew you."* Jeremiah 1:5

**SCIENCE**

**Premise 1:** All human babies in the womb are human life.

**Premise 2:** The right to human life is protected by the Declaration of Independence.

**Premise 3:** Abortions kill innocent, defenseless human life in the womb.

**Conclusion:** Abortion violates American Law.

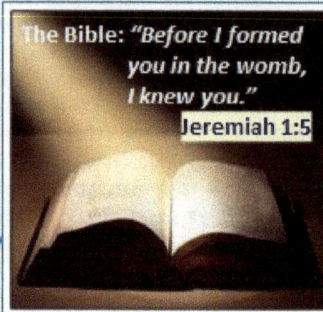

Bioethical Argument Against Abortion (3:42)

### Declaration of Independence

*"We hold these truths to be self-evident, that all men are created equal.*

*That they are <u>endowed by their Creator</u> with certain unalienable rights, that among these are Life, Liberty and the pursuit of happiness..."*

Courtesy of Google Images    Fair Use Law 17 U.S. Code § 107

# Abortion:
# It's Not about Legality.... It's about Objective Morality

**False Abortion Argument #1**: Because a human fetus is not a person, it can be aborted.

**False Abortion Argument #2:** The mother has the moral right to end her fetus's life under any circumstance, for any reason, and at any time in her pregnancy.

**False Abortion Argument #3:** The mother gets to decide whether the fetus has any right to live because she has the right to control her body.

**False Abortion Argument #4:** People agree that the moment the baby exits the womb, killing the baby is murder. But deliberately killing it a few months before birth is considered no more morally problematic than extracting a tooth.

**False Abortion Argument #5:** Abortions are not moral decisions.

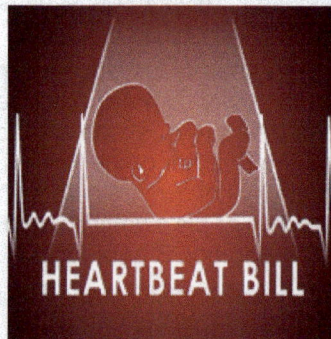

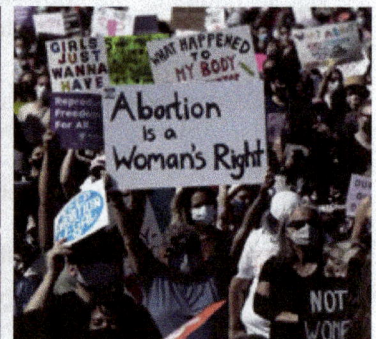

PragerU: The Most Important Question about Abortion (5:19)

**HEARTBEAT BILL**

*Good societies can survive people doing immoral things. But a good society cannot survive if it calls immoral things moral*

### Isaiah 5:20
*"Woe to those who call evil good and good evil."*

Courtesy of Google Images    Fair Use Law 17 U.S. Code § 107

## Article 469 - Abortion: It's Not About Legality... It's About Objective Morality

Isaiah 5:20  *"Woe to those who call evil good and good evil."*

Columnist Dennis Prager once said that "Good societies can survive people doing immoral things. But a good society cannot survive if it calls immoral things moral." This is exactly the point the Prophet Isaiah was making in the Old Testament book that bears his name. Israel had become so debauched in 700BC that God warned them that those who perverted His standards for objective morality would be punished.

"Objective" means that something is moral "regardless of anyone's opinion." The opposite, "subjective" means something is moral "based on your personal opinion."

If objective morality exists, then there will be circumstances where we will be obligated or forbidden to do various actions, regardless of what we think.

When it comes to the issue of abortion, we can all be tricked into treating the issue as one centered on whether it should be legal or illegal. But that is not the issue. With today's technology, we now know that the right question to ask is whether ending the life of the unborn baby is objectively moral or immoral.

At Washington DC's Women's March, Planned Parenthood's President said *"Abortion is health care, basic health care, essential health care, health care that cannot wait."* To the pro-abortion advocate, the mother has an objective moral right to decide if the fetus (the unborn baby) in her womb lives or dies.

With the Texas "Heartbeat Law" going into effect in September, Governor Greg Abbott said, "Our creator endowed us with the right to life and yet millions of children lose their right to life every year because of abortion." To the pro-life advocate, the fetus in the womb has an objective moral right to life.

We know a human fetus is a human life. So, the question is this: Does the human fetus have rights? In his article "Is Abortion Right, or Is It Wrong?", Dennis Prager debunks the 5 arguments made by the pro-abortion movement for why abortion is objectively moral.

Abortion Argument #1: Because a human fetus is not a person, it can be aborted.
**Rebuttal:** *"A living being doesn't have to be a person to have intrinsic moral value and rights. Many living beings are not persons and have both value and rights, like dogs."* Conclusion: Abortion Argument #1 is FALSE.

Abortion Argument #2: The mother has the moral right to end her fetus's life under any circumstance, for any reason, and at any time in her pregnancy.
**Rebuttal:** *"Only if we believe that the human fetus has no intrinsic worth. But everyone believes that the human fetus has essentially infinite worth and an almost absolute right to live when a pregnant woman wants to give birth. Then, society - and its laws - regard the fetus as so valuable that if someone were to kill that fetus, that person could be prosecuted for homicide. Only if a pregnant woman doesn't want to give birth, do many people regard the fetus as worthless. Now, does that make sense?"* Conclusion: Abortion Argument #2 is FALSE.

Abortion Argument #3: The mother gets to decide whether the fetus has any right to live because she has the right to control her body.
**Rebuttal:** *"The fetus is not 'her body;' it is in her body. It is a separate body. No one ever asks a pregnant woman, 'How's your body?' when asking about the fetus. People ask, 'How's the baby?'"* Conclusion: Abortion Argument #3 is FALSE.

Abortion Argument #4: "Everyone agrees that the moment the baby exits the womb, killing the baby is murder. But deliberately killing it a few months before birth is considered no more morally problematic than extracting a tooth."
**Rebuttal:** *"How does that make sense?"* Conclusion: Abortion Argument #4 is FALSE.

Abortion Argument #5: Abortions are not moral decisions.
**Rebuttal:** *"Aren't there instances in which just about everyone - even among those who are pro-choice - would acknowledge that an abortion might be immoral? For example, would it be moral to abort a female fetus solely because the mother prefers boys to girls, as happens millions of times in China?"* Conclusion: Abortion Argument #5 is FALSE.

Prager concludes his article with this point: *"People may differ about when personhood begins; and about the morality of abortion after rape or incest. But regarding the vast majority of abortions - those of healthy women aborting a healthy fetus - let's be clear. Most of these abortions just aren't moral."*

We have used logic to not only debunk all 5 abortion arguments but to also demonstrated that God's moral position - a baby in the womb has a right to life - is objectively true. God help those subject to Isaiah 5:20.

**Exit Ticket #14**    <mark>Class 14: Today's American Culture: Sexual Identity, Abortion</mark>

| | |
|---|---|
| 1) Why is Leviticus chapter 18 so explicit on sexual sin and child sacrifice? | 2) What was the athletes' main conviction for why they spoke out against Dodgers 'Pride Night'? |
| 3) What's the evidence to say that America is at war against the unborn? | 4) Of the 84 bible verses in this class, which 2-3 resonate the most with you when you think of sexual identity and/or abortion in America today? |

# Class 15:  Who Am I?  Part 1

GENESIS 1:26-27  My Original Identity

ROMANS 3:23   My Forfeited Identity

JOHN 1:12, 1JOHN 3:2  My Restored Identity

Comedian Norm McDonald:  Why Christianity Makes Sense - Made in God's Image

The Gospel throughout Isaiah - God's 3 Imputations

My Physical Identity: Table of Nations

Was Jesus a good-looking white guy?

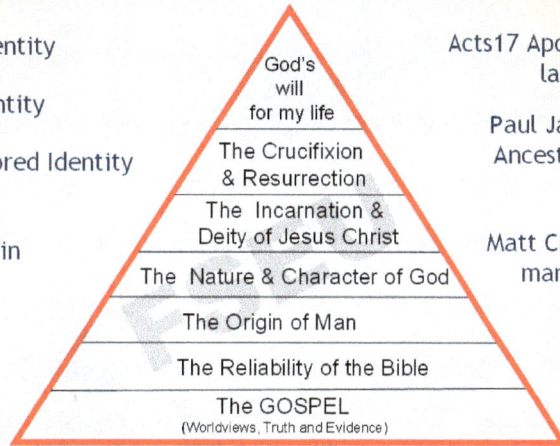

God's
will
for my life

The Crucifixion
& Resurrection

The  Incarnation &
Deity of Jesus Christ

The  Nature & Character of God

The  Origin of Man

The Reliability of the Bible

The GOSPEL
(Worldviews, Truth and Evidence)

**H E B R E W S 11:1**

"Faith = *Substance* of things *hoped for*…. *Evidence* of things *not seen*"

**fse.life Lessons 02 - 08**

Acts17 Apologetics: 'The Comedian who laughed his way to Jesus' (20:45)

Paul James-Griffiths – 'Tracing your Ancestors through History: Table of Nations in Genesis' (1.01.14)

Matt Chandler- 'Jesus is not a white man - Megan Kelly rebuttal' (2.46)

## Genesis 1:26-27     My *Original* Identity

### What does it mean to be a '*person*' made in God's image?

1) I have the power to *reason* — Isaiah 1:18, Acts 17:2

2) I have a *conscience* — Romans 7:18, 22-23

3) I feel a sense of *moral responsibility* — Mark 12:29-31

4) I have a need for *fellowship* — Genesis 2:18

## Romans 3:23   My *Forfeited* Identity

1) Sin became an integral part of my *heritage*     Romans 5:12

2) Sin became a personal experience in my *life*     Romans 3:10

3) Sin has caused *separation* in my *fellowship* with God

Genesis 3:24, Isaiah 59:1-2

What has sin done to the image of God in me?

4) Sin has caused *separation* in my *fellowship* with others

Genesis 3:10-12

Courtesy of Google Images     Fair Use Law 17 U.S. Code § 107

## John 1:12, 1John 3:2   My *Restored* Identity

**How can God's Image in me be restored?**

1) Jesus Christ =   the 'visible Image of the invisible God'     Colossians 1:15,19

2) Jesus Christ =   became the 'likeness' of my sin     Romans 8:3

3) Jesus Christ =   the exact image of God living in me     Colossians 1:27

4) Jesus Christ =   my new heritage through my conformation     Romans 8:29

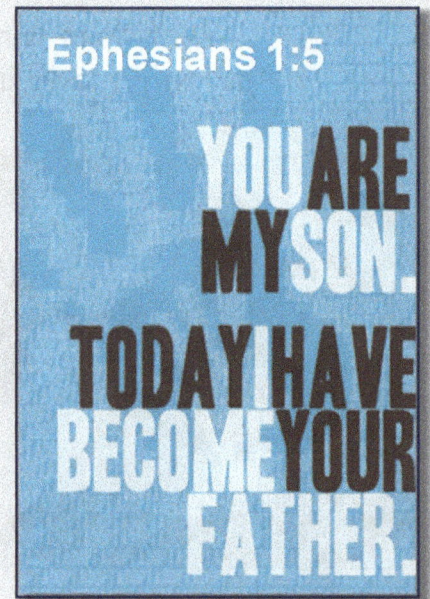

Ephesians 1:5

YOU ARE MY SON. TODAY I HAVE BECOME YOUR FATHER.

Courtesy of Google Images     Fair Use Law 17 U.S. Code § 107

## Comedian Norm McDonald:  Why Christianity Makes Sense - Made in God's Image

"I have always had an intuition there is a God, an actual Person.

"Christianity has this compromise, where we are both divine and wretched.

Thinking we are divine and connected with nature seems like nonsense.

The other, that we are simply beasts of the field, also seems like nonsense.

So, I like that Christian idea."

Acts 17 Apologetics: 'The Comedian who laughed his way to Jesus' (20:45)

"In Christianity, there is this middleman, Jesus Christ, who is the Savior.

Through Him, we can become divine even though we are born wretched.

It is a very fascinating idea.

I kinda like that one because it makes sense."

### My Original Identity
"'Let Us make man in Our image, according to our likeness.'" God created male and female in His own image." Genesis 1:26-27

### My Forfeited Identity
"For all have sinned and fallen short of God's image." Romans 3:23

"Your sins separate you from your God." Isaiah 59:2

### My Restored Identity
"Jesus is the exact image of the invisible God." Colossians 1:15

"God saved those to be conformed to the image of His Son." Romans 8:29

Courtesy of Google Images    Fair Use Law 17 U.S. Code § 107

# The Gospel throughout Isaiah - God's 3 Imputations

**#1. God imputes my sin to my account**

"Your sins have separated you from your God..."
Isaiah 59:2

**#2. God imputes my sin to His Son's account**

"The Lord has laid on Him the sins of us all."
Isaiah 53:4

**#3. God imputes His Son's righteousness to my account**

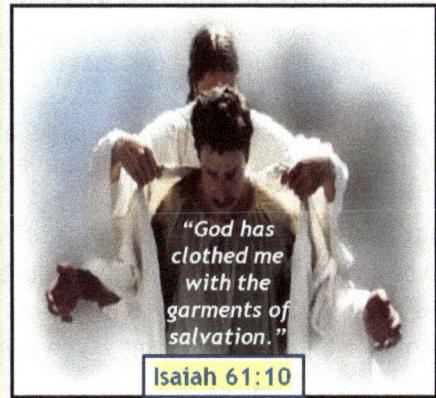

"God has clothed me with the garments of salvation."
Isaiah 61:10

"He made Him who knew no sin to be sin FOR US...
Isaiah 9:6

...that WE might be the righteousness of God IN HIM."

**"And the Scripture was fulfilled which told, 'Abraham believed God, and it was underlined imputed to him for righteousness.'" James 2:23**

2Corinthians 5:21

Courtesy of Google Images    Fair Use Law 17 U.S. Code § 107

## Genesis 1:26   Who I am: made in the "image of God"

*"Let Us make man in Our ①IMAGE, according to Our ①LIKENESS; let them have dominion over the birds of the air, over the cattle, over all the earth and over every creeping thing that creeps on the earth."*

① IMAGE, LIKENESS = Hebrew *"tselem"* = carving, pattern (same word used for graven images in Exodus 20:4); parallel Hebrew terms used for *emphasis*: God Himself is the pattern from which mankind's personhood was carved (directly opposes evolutionary theory of our origins).

• man's spiritual makeup: God is Spirit and not flesh (John 4:24), He is a person, and man is like God: a person.

## What does it mean to be a "person"?

1)   I have the power to <u>reason</u> (Isaiah 1:18)

Acts 17:2 *"Then Paul, as his custom was, went in to them, and for 3 Sabbaths REASONED with them from the Scriptures, explaining and demonstrating that the Christ had to suffer and rise again from the dead..."*

2)   I have a <u>conscience</u>

Romans 7:18,22-23  *"...I know that in me nothing good dwells; for to will is present with me, but how to perform what is good I do not find. For I delight in the law of God according to the inward man, but I see another law in my members, warring against the law of my mind, and bringing me into captivity to the law of sin, which is in my members."*

> <u>Paradox #1</u>:  In the Christian life, as I mature in Christ I become less conscious of self and more conscious of my responsibility to others (Phil. 2:3-4). This forgetfulness of self leads to the highest fulfillment of the self. The fact that I find life by losing my own is a fundamental law of life only discovered in Christ (Matt. 16:24-25).

3)   I feel a sense of <u>moral responsibility</u>

Mark 12:29-31  *"'The first of all the commandments is: "Hear O Israel, the Lord our God, the Lord is one. And you shall love the Lord your God with all your heart, with all your soul, with all your mind, and with all your strength." ... And the second, like it, is "You shall love your neighbor as yourself.' There is no other commandment greater than these."*

> <u>Paradox #2</u>:  My highest self-development is reached when my moral responsibility is first to God and His expectations on me. My highest level of living is reached when my devotion to God and service to people goes from a sense of obligation and duty to a natural result of my inward desire to please Him, not me (John 8:29).

4)   I have a capacity for <u>fellowship and communication</u>

- anything that limits or destroys my fellowship with others will impoverish my personality.
  Genesis 2:18  *"...the Lord God said, 'It is not good for man to be alone; I will make him a helper comparable to him."*
- it is my capacity to commune with God that makes me a being created in God's image.
- God's image within me finds its fulfillment in my fellowship with Him as my Creator, since He is the source of the image and He is the perfect embodiment of that which is so imperfectly expressed by me.

> <u>Paradox #3</u>:  God, who is all-powerful, all-knowing, all-present, limits Himself by my willingness to spend time with Him. I must *respond* to Him for there to be real communication (Isa. 50:2, Jer. 2:5, Matt. 11:28-30)

## What has sin done to the image of God in me?

• I was created in the image of God, but became "recreated" in the image of sin in 2 ways:
1.  Romans 5:12 = sin became an integral part of my heritage
2.  Romans 3:10 =  sin became a very *personal* experience in my life (Jew and Gentile alike: no one is excluded)

• Everyone, regardless of nationality, position or gender, has "de-glorified" God and fallen under condemnation
  Romans 3:23   *"...all have sinned and fallen short of the glory of God."*

## Has sin destroyed God's image in me? marred it? or left it largely untouched?

• Galatians 3:28 = Respect for the human personality is based on the fact that *every single person* was created in God's image.

• If God's image was completely destroyed in man, there would be no reason for universally respecting men (the only people with any real worth and dignity would be those who had the image restored through God's grace).

• But God's image wasn't completely destroyed through sin. Mankind after sin was still sacred in God's eyes.
  Genesis 9:6  *"Whoever sheds man's blood, by man his blood shall be shed; for in the image of God He made man."*

- <u>Why we proclaim the gospel</u>: there is enough of God's image left in every person
  1. while an unsaved person can't communicate with God due to sin, each person has the *potential* because God created each person for that purpose.
  2. Each individual person is still held responsible to God for his or her sin

## So if sin hasn't completely destroyed that image, what has it done?

- While all people have the capacity to reason, and feel a sense self-consciousness and responsibility, sin has definitely marred mankind's' capacity to communicate with each other and with God.
- At its core: SIN IS SEPARATION (first from God, then from each other)

  Genesis 3:24  *"So He DROVE OUT THE MAN; and He placed cherubim at the east end of the garden of Eden, and a flaming sword which turned every way, to GUARD the way to the tree of life."*

  Isaiah 59:1-2  *"... the Lord's hand is not shortened, that it can't save; nor His ear heavy, that it cannot hear. But your iniquities have SEPARATED you from your God, and your sins have hidden His face from you, so that He will not hear."*

  Genesis 4:6-9  *"...the Lord said to Cain, 'why are you angry? Any why has your countenance fallen? If you do well, will you not be accepted? And if you do not do well, sin lies at the door. And its desire is for you, but you should rule over it.'... it came to pass, when they were in the field, that Cain rose against Abel his brother and killed him. Then the Lord said to Cain, 'Where is Abel your brother?' ...he said, "I do not know. AM I MY BROTHER'S KEEPER?"'*

## How does God's image in me become restored?

- Jesus Christ = the "visible image of the invisible God"

  Colossians 1:15,19  *"He is the (EXACT) IMAGE of the invisible God, the firstborn ("preeminent") over all creation. For it pleased the Father that in Him all the FULLNESS should dwell."*

  Hebrews 1:1-3  *"...who being the EXPRESS IMAGE of His person, and upholding all things by the word of His power..."*

- God Almighty, the invisible and unseen, is seen in His Son
  1. Jesus = not only reflects the glory of God, but He is the "exact image" of His person.
  2. Jesus = the "very stamp" of God's nature; the "perfect representation" of God's being
  3. Just as a seal on a document reflects the official seal, so Jesus is the exact reproduction of God the Father

     John 14:9  *"...He who has seen Me has seen the Father. How can you say, 'Show us the Father?'"*

- Jesus Christ = sent into the world in the LIKENESS OF OUR SINFUL FLESH
  1. Jesus came to do what the law couldn't: FREE me from law's penalty for sin (death = separation from God).

     Romans 8:3  *"...what the law could not do in that it was weak through the flesh, GOD DID by sending His own Son in the LIKENESS OF SINFUL FLESH, on account of sin: He condemned sin in the flesh."*
  2. Real Freedom = I am now united with Jesus, living under the guidance of the Spirit  who lives within me

     John 14:26  *"...the Comforter, the Holy Spirit, whom the Father will send in My name, He will teach you all things..."*

     Galatians 5:16  *"...walk in the Spirit, and you shall not fulfill the lust of the flesh."*

- God's purpose in uniting me with Jesus = conform me to His image (who is the exact image of God Himself)
  1. I am freed:  FROM sin and death (negative), IN the Spirit (positive) = God's marred image in me is restored
  2. To be conformed to the image of His Son = "bear the family likeness"

     Romans 8:29  *"...whom He foreknew He also predestined to be CONFORMED TO THE IMAGE OF HIS SON, that He might be the firstborn among many brethren."*
  3. Being conformed to the image of Jesus (God's exact image) = being conformed to the original image of God in man. CHRIST IN ME is the only hope for restoring God's image (and isn't completed until I *see* Him).

     Colossians 1:27  *"To them God willed to make known what are the riches of the glory of this mystery among the Gentiles:  which is CHRIST IN YOU, THE HOPE OF GLORY."*

     Philippians 1:6  *"...He who has begun a good work in you will complete it until the day of Jesus Christ."*

     1John 3:2  *"Beloved, now we are children of God; and it has not yet been revealed what we shall be, but we know that when He is revealed, we shall be like Him, for we shall see Him as He is."*

---

**Am I allowing Christ in me to *mold me* each day towards *His* image?**

**How much of my lifestyle shows Jesus to those around me?**

**HOW MUCH OTHERS *SEE* JESUS IN ME = HOW WELL I *KNOW* HIM PERSONALLY**

## Genesis 10 The "Table of Nations" (Genealogy & Origin of Mankind)

| Darwin's theory on where we came from: | What Darwin's theory implies of our origins: |
|---|---|
| people are modified descendants of an ancestor we shared with other animals (probably apes) | people are nothing but animals (we are not the preordained goal of any directed purpose) |
| our distinctive features form different "races": they are due mostly to natural selection acting randomly on small variations over a long time | J.W. Burrow (evolutionist): *"Nature, according to Darwin, was the product of blind chance and a blind struggle, and man is a lonely, intelligent mutation, scrambling with the brutes for his sustenance."* |

**Darwin (Origin of Species[1]):** *"Man bears in his bodily structure clear traces of his descent from some lower form."*

➜ **What is a "race" of people?** Definition: the dictionary defines race as "a class or kind of individuals with common characteristics, interests, appearances, or habits as if derived from a common ancestor."

1) Race is not based on skin color: biologically, a race is thought of as a subspecies, within a given species.
   (a) we have made the term race to apply to skin color, but race does not apply to skin color alone.
   (b) Skin color is the only biological difference in race. Science can't tell what causes the difference in skin cell pigmentation. This superficial distinction is the basis for how we divide mankind.

2) Genetics determines racial characteristics: Modern genetics shows that when a large, interbreeding group is broken into smaller groups which then breed only among themselves (as the Biblical description of the language dispersion at Babel implies), different racial characteristics will arise very rapidly.
   (a) One pair of middle-brown parents can produce all shades, from very white to very black, in *one* generation.
   (b) The racial characteristics which exist today have not evolved. They are simply different combinations of pre-existing (created) genetic (hereditary) information.

3) Genesis 10 details origin of NATIONS: Biblical viewpoint: there is not a black race, white race, yellow race, etc. Genesis 10 is a historical document of the three distinct families of mankind, indicating how the present population of the world originated and spread after the flood.

➜ **Genesis 9:1 (1:18), 9:19, 10:    I descended from Noah's family**

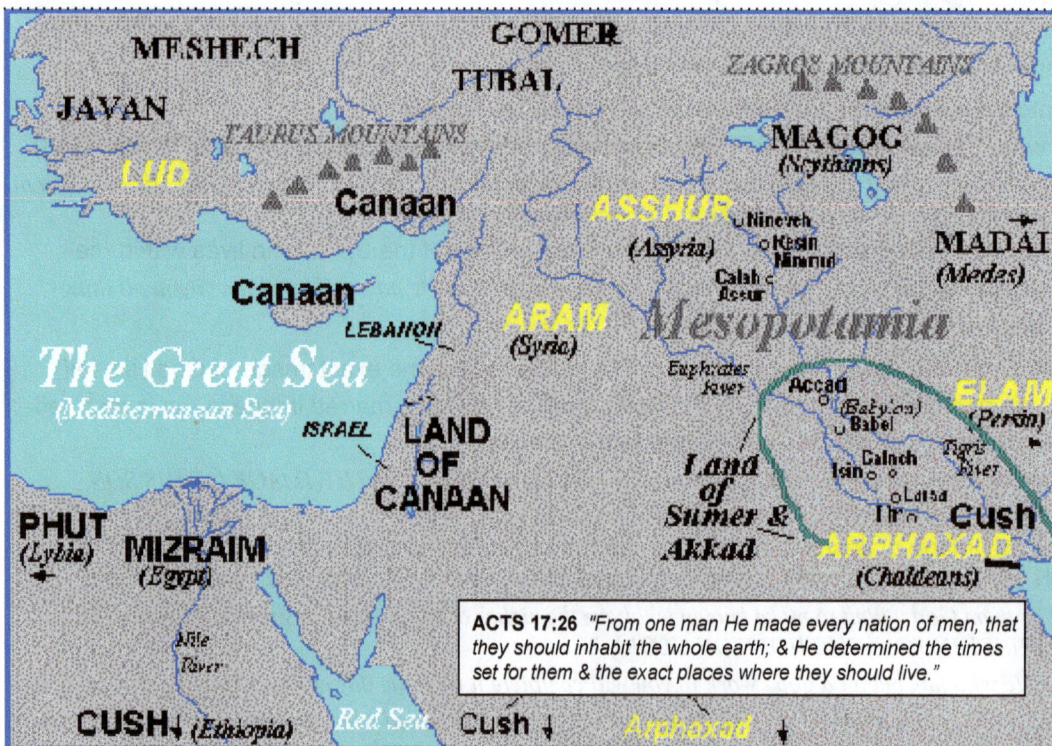

1) Genesis 9:19 we all descended from one of the sons of Noah (Shem, Ham, Japheth), including so-called fossil man, primitive peoples and modern man.

2) Genesis 10:32 Gen. 10 refers to people and nations by genealogies: *persons or families* (ethnology), *then nations or tribes* (ethnography).

3) Genesis 10 Nations settled (geography). They began as hunter-gatherers (live off land as migrated).

ACTS 17:26 *"From one man He made every nation of men, that they should inhabit the whole earth; & He determined the times set for them & the exact places where they should live."*

- The descendants of Japheth (oldest): the Greeks, Romans, Spanish, Celts, Scythians, and Medes ➜ They migrated into Europe and parts of Central Asia. Some people groups merged to form one nation, as did the Persians (Shem) and the Medes (Japheth), which later became the Medo-Persian empire.

- The descendants of Shem: the Hebrews, Persians and Assyrians ➜ They mostly remained in the Middle East.

- The descendants of Ham (youngest): the Egyptians, Ethiopians, Canaanites, Phoenicians and Hittites ➜ His descendants were the 1st to fill the earth (early settlers of Africa, Asia, Australia, South Pacific, and Americas).

## Genesis 10: "Where I came from"

Genesis 9:1 *"...and from these the whole earth was populated."* (Genesis 9:1)

Genesis 9:19 *"These 3 were the sons of Noah,*

**NOAH**

Genesis 10:1-5

### Japheth

**Jawan** — Greeks, Romans, Spartans, Dorians, Britons, Aeolians, Cyprians, Cretans, Basques, Latins, Venetians, Sicanians, Italics, Valentians, Sicilians, Italians, Spaniards, Portugese, Achaeans, Myceneans, Macedonians, Carthaginians
 - Elisha
 - Tarshish
 - Kittim
 - Dodanim

**Magog** — Scots, Irish, Poles, Czechs, Finns, Lapps, Russians, Estonians, Siberians, Croatians, Bosnians, Serbians, Slovenians, Bulgarians, Scythians, Belarusians, Ukranians, Hungarians, Montenegrins, Yugoslavians
 - Elichanaf
 - Lubal
 - Baath
 - Jobhath
 - Fathocta

**Gomer** — Germans, Belgians, Dutch, Austrians, Swiss, Angles, Saxons, Britons, English, Cornish, Irish, Welsh, French, Jutes, Teutons, Franks, Celts, Galatians, Goths, Picts, Alemanni, Armenians, Millesians, Umbrians, Helvetians, Burgundians, Luxembourgens, Liechensteiners, Caledonians, Scandinavians
 - Ashkenaz
 - Riphath
 - Togarmah

**Madai** — Medes, Aryans, Persians, Parsa, Parsees, Achaemenians, Manneans, Caspians, Kassites, Iranians, Kurds, Turks, E. Indians, Pathans, Hazaras, Pakistanis, Afganistanis
 - Achon
 - Zeelo
 - Chazoni
 - Latalso

**Meshech** — Muscovites, Latvians, Lithuanians, Romanians
 - Dedon
 - Zaron
 - Shebashnialso

**Tiras** — Scandinavians, Vikings, Swedes, Norwegians, Danes, Icelandics
 - Lupirion
 - Gera
 - Gilak
 - Benib

**Tubal** — Georgians, Albanians
 - Ariphi
 - Kesed
 - Taari

### Shem

Genesis 10:22-32

**Asshur** — Assyrians, N. Iraqis
 - Mirus
 - Mokil

**Lud** — Ludians, Lydians, Chubs, Asia Minor, N. Africa
 - Pethor
 - Bizayon

**Elam** — Elamites, Persians
 - Shushan
 - Machul
 - Harmon

**Arphaxad** — Chaldeans, S. Iraqis, **Hebrews**, Arabians, Moabites, Jordanians, Palestinians
 - Anar
 - Salah
 - Ashcol

**Aram** — Syrians, Lebanese, Asia, Middle East, N. Africa
 - Uz
 - Hul
 - Gather
 - Mash

**Eber (Heber)** — Genesis 11:10-32
 - Peleg
 - Joktan — Almodad, Sheleph, Hazarmaveth, Abilmael, Uzal, Obal, Diklah, Havilah, Hadoram, Sheba, Jerah, Ophir, Jobab

**Peleg** — Reu — Serug — Nahor — Terah — Abram — Isaac — Jacob

Matthew 1:1-17

Rahab (Hittite) ... Ruth (Moabite) ... Bathsheba (Hittite)

**Terah** — Haran (→ Lot), Nahor, Abram
 - Abram — Isaac — Ishmael (Arabian Muslims), Esau (Edomites)
 - Jacob (Israelites) Genesis 49:1-28

Jacob's sons: Reuben, Simeon, Levi, **Judah**, Issachar, Zebulun, Dan, Gad, Naphtali, Asher, Joseph, Benjamin

**Judah** — Perez (← Zerah), Hezron, Ram, Amminadab, Nahshon
Salmon — Boaz — Obed — Jesse — David — Solomon — Rehoboam — Abijah — Asa — Jehoshaphat — Joram — Uzziah — Jotham — Ahaz — Hezekiah — Manasseh — Amos — Josiah — Jeconiah — Shealtiel — Zerubbabel — Abiud — Eliakim — Azor — Zadok — Achim — Eliud — Eleazar — Matthan — Jacob — Joseph — **JESUS**

### Ham

Genesis 10:6-20

**Put** — Libyans, Cyrenacians, Tunisians, Berbers, Somalians, Sudanese, N. Africans
 - Gebul
 - Hadan
 - Benah
 - Adan

**Mizraim** — Egyptians, Khemets, Philistines, Copts
 - Casluhim
 - Anamim
 - Lehabim
 - Naphtuhim
 - Pathrusim
 - Ludim

**Cush** — Africans, Nubians, Pygmies, Ethiopians, Ghanaians, Bushmen, Aborignies, New Guineans
 - Seba
 - Hawilah
 - Sabtah
 - Sabtechah
 - Raamah — Sheba, Dedan
 - Nimrod

Genesis 10:8-12

**Canaan** — Guamanians, Amer. Indians, Pac. Islanders, Polynesians, Malaysians, Indonesians, Mongols, Chinese, Taiwanese, Vietnamese, Japanese, Asians, Hawaiians, Tahitians, Samoans, Eskimos, Filipinos, Fijians, Tongans
 - Sidon
 - Heth
 - Amori
 - Hivi
 - Arkee
 - Seni
 - Arodi
 - Zimodi
 - Gergashi
 - Chamothi

## The Incredible Historicity of the Bible's Table of Nations

**William F. Albright, PhD John Hopkins Univ., renowned Archaeologist:** *"It stands absolutely alone in ancient literature, without a remote parallel even among the Greeks, where we find the closest approach to a distribution of peoples in genealogical framework. But among the Greeks the framework is mythological. In view of the inextricable confusion of racial and national strains in the ancient near East it would be quite impossible to draw up a simple scheme which would satisfy all scholars; no one system could satisfy all the claims made on the basis of ethnic predominance, ethnographic diffusion, language, physical type, culture, historical tradition. The Table of Nations remains an astonishingly accurate document."*

**Martin Luther on the Table of Nations:** *"Whenever I read these names, I think of the wretched state of the human race. If it were not for Moses, what would you know about the origin of man?...Hence one must consider this chapter of Genesis a mirror in which to discern what we human beings are, namely, creatures so marred by sin that we have no knowledge of our own origin, not even of God Himself, our Creator, unless the Word of God reveals these sparks of divine light to us from afar. Then what is more futile than boasting of one's wisdom, riches, power, and other things that pass away completely? Therefore we have reason to regard the Holy Bible highly and to consider it a most precious treasure. This very chapter, even though it is considered by many to be full of dead words, has in it the thread that is drawn from the first world to the middle and to the end of all things. From Adam the promise concerning Christ is passed on to Seth; from Seth to Noah; from Noah to Shem; and from Shem to this Eber, from whom the Hebrew nation received its name as the heir for whom the promise about the Christ was intended in preference to all other peoples of the whole world. This knowledge the Holy Scriptures reveal to us. Those who are without them live in error, uncertainty, and boundless ungodliness; for they have no knowledge about who they are and whence they came."*
(Martin Luther, Luther's Works, Vol. 2, pp. 2-2.)

## The History of Mankind flows from the *Bible*

Nothing in the archaeological history of the ancient world denies the biblical account of the creation of the world, the entrance of sin and death, the judgment of Noah's flood, and the rise of people groups from their descendants after their dispersal from Babel.

The descendants of Shem, Ham and Japheth are evidenced, not only by Biblical history, but archeological, anthropological, biological, ethnographical, ethnological, etymological, and geological history. The question is not one of worth but of uniqueness of contribution. Though differences exist, one group is not superior or inferior.

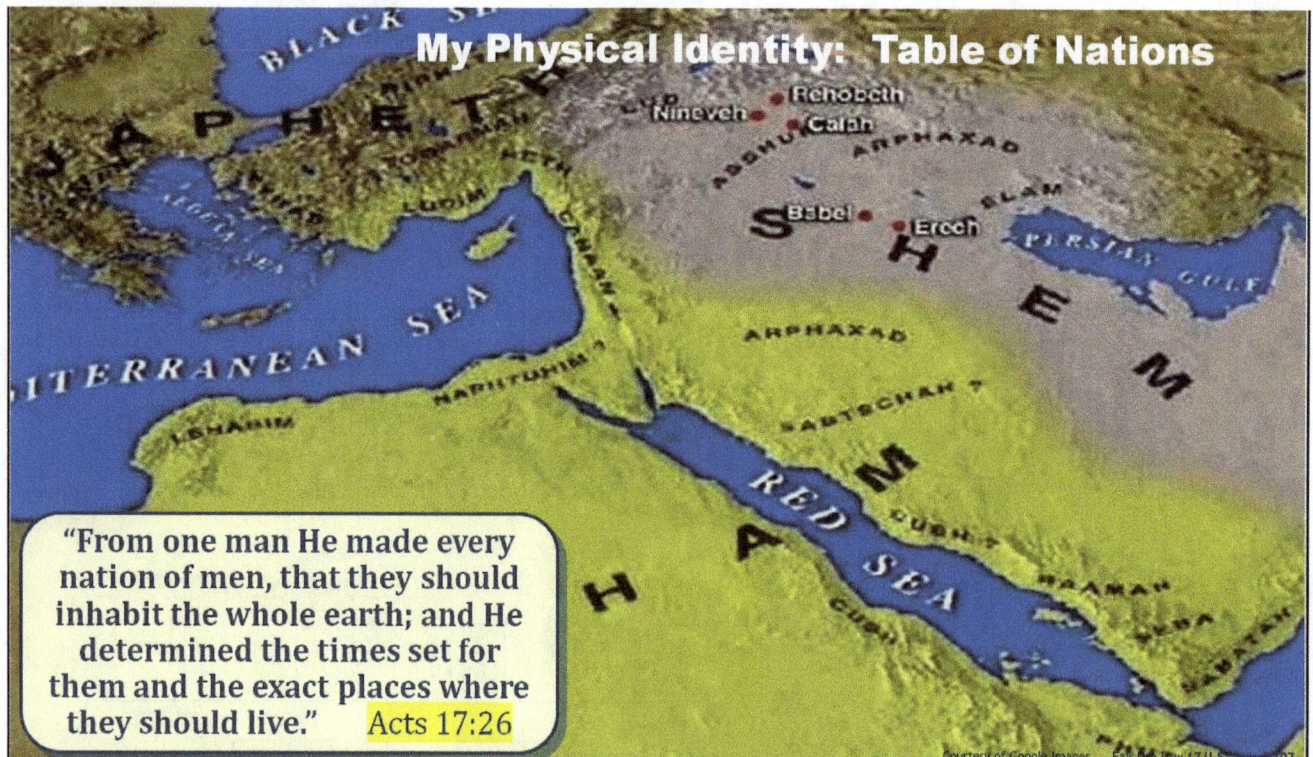

**My Physical Identity: Table of Nations**

"From one man He made every nation of men, that they should inhabit the whole earth; and He determined the times set for them and the exact places where they should live." Acts 17:26

## Genesis 10:22-32 SHEM[27]  or *Sem* - means *named or renown* (father of Semitic races - *Shemites*)

The sons of Shem were:

**(1) Elam** *"eternity"* (sons = Shushan, Machul and Harmon) - Elamites, Persians

**(2) Asshur** *"a step"* or *"strong"* (sons = Mirus and Mokil) - Assyrians/Northern Iraqis

**(3) Arphaxad** *"I shall fail"* (sons = Shelach, Anar and Ashcol) - Chaldeans/Southern Iraqis, Hebrews/ Israelites/ Jews[1], Arabians/Bedouins, Moabites/ Jordanians/ Palestinians

**(4) Lud** *"strife"* (sons = Pethor and Bizayon) - Ludim, Lubim, Ludians, Ludu, Lydians, Chubs, related groups in Asia Minor and North Africa);

**(5) Aram** *"exalted"* (sons = Uz, Chul, Gather and Mash) - Aramaeans/Syrians, Lebanese

• Noah's sons kept together at first, then broke up into small groups and eventually arrived from the east in the southern Mesopotamian Plain (**Genesis 11:2**). The descendants of Elam, the first born son of Shem, were the first people to enter Mesopotamia.

• Susa, the capital city of the Elamites (Shemitic Elamites), gave rise to other early cities like Al-Ubaid (which later gave rise to Hamitic settlements—including the Sumerian civilization) and Jemdet Nasr. Recent excavations have provided very strong evidence of direct cultural links between some of the earliest cities in Babylonia and the lowest layers uncovered at Susa. These people established themselves first in the south and then spread toward the north, but without losing the cultural links. There are no known modern descendants of the Elamites.

• Other excavations have shown that one of the first Hamitic groups, the Sumerians, gave rise to considerable cultural advance and power in that region. Other people groups known very early included the Japhethites, noted especially for their fairness of skin, in the hill country east of the Tigris. Soon the great Babylonian empire arose.

• The descendants of Shem are often called **Semites**, a term first used in the late 18th century for peoples listed in the Bible as descended from Shem. Today the term Semite refers to peoples who speak any of the Semitic languages, including the ancient peoples who inhabited Babylonia. Modern peoples speaking Semitic languages include the Arabs and Jews. Shem's descendants are well documented. Modern day Arabs and Jews trace their lineage to Shem. Many Arabic nomad tribes still claim they descended from Shem.

• Centuries before the Christian Era, many ancient Semitic populations migrated from Arabia to Mesopotamia, the coasts of the Mediterranean Sea, and the Nile River delta. Jews and other Semites settled in Judea (southern Palestine). Today, the Semitic-speaking peoples are concentrated in the Middle East and northern Africa.

## The Hebrews  descended from Eber (Heber), a great-grandsons of Shem.

1) Both Sunnite Arabs and Jews are Semites *and* Hebrews.

2) **Genesis 11:26 =** Abram (Abraham): born 6 generations after Heber– he was both a **Hebrew** and a **Semite**, born of the line of Heber and Shem (people interchange "Jew" and Israelite, though Abraham was not an Israelite or a Jew. The word "Jew" is not used in the Bible until nearly 1,000 years after Abraham).

3) **Genesis 12-15** = God forms His covenant promises with Abram through His grace as Abram exercises his faith in God's promises (Romans 4:1-4).

4) **Genesis 16, 21:9-21**= Sunnite Arabs (specifically Arabian Muslims): consider themselves to be descendants of Ishmael, calling themselves Ishmaelites, and thus are both Semitic and Hebrews (Ishmael born 1st of Abraham).

5) **Genesis 17:18-21, 21:1-8** = Isaac born of Abraham after Ishmael, but God forms His covenant with Isaac.

6) **Genesis 25:21-34** = Isaac had twin sons named Esau and Jacob. Esau was firstborn, and so had the right to inheritance (as was custom), but instead sold his birthright to Jacob during a time of hunger. Esau's name was changed to Edom, and Jacob's name was changed to Israel. The descendants of Esau (Edom) were called Edomites, and the descendants of Jacob (Israel) were called **Israelites**. Jacob fathered twelve sons which became the twelve tribes of Israel (Genesis 29:31-35, 30:1-24, 35:22-26)..

7) **Genesis 49:8-12** = JUDAH (Hebrew *"Yehudah"*): one of Jacob's (Israel's) children - His descendants were called Yehudim ("Judahites"). In Greek the name is *Ioudaioi* ("Judeans"). Most all Bible translations use the word ***"Jew"*** (it's a modern, shortened form of the word "Judahite"). A "Jew" in the Old Testament would be a "Judahite;" and a "Jew" in the New Testament would be a "Judean."

8) **Genesis 26:34, 27:1-45, 28:1-9** = A bitter rivalry between the descendants of Esau and Jacob continued throughout history, and as they lived in close proximity for hundreds of years, their hatred worsened.

• The Romans called the *Edomites Idumeans*, separate from Israelites, when they lived in Palestine together.

• The Romans later divided Palestine into districts, with Idumea (land of Edomites) being one of the districts. As the Roman Empire faded, Idumea fell to an Ishmaelite Moslem army led by Caliph Umar in 8 A.D.

• Historians suggest the remaining Edomites embraced Islam at that time and remained in the land, blending with the Arabs, and uniting against the Israelites.

9) Jerusalem soon became a focal point for the Moslems, being the third most holy city of Islam, after the cities of Mecca and Medina (though Jerusalem is never mentioned in the Koran, it is mentioned over 800X in the Bible).

10) By 691 A.D., the Mosque of Omar (also called the "Dome of the Rock") was completed on the Temple Mount, where Moslems/Muslims believe that Mohammed ascended to heaven from. The Arabic term for the holy place is "al-Haram as-Sharif" meaning "The Noble Sanctuary."

11) To Israelites and Jews, Jerusalem was the city of the great prophets and the capital of the Kingdom of Israel and Judah under King David and his son King Solomon. The first and second temples were the center of worship until the destruction of the city by the Romans in 70 A.D. Christians revere the city as the place where Jesus Christ taught in the temple, and was later crucified.

## The Tower of Babel - Genesis 11:1-9

• The rulers of Babylon attempted to avert dispersal of the people by proposing the building of a monument as a visible rallying point on the flat plain of Mesopotamia.

• Scripture and historical texts note that the tower of Babel, the building of which Nimrod (a Sumerian) supervised, was to have two great significances:
1) The city of Babel would be the metropolis of the world and unite its inhabitants under the rule of Nimrod.
2) The tower was to be a monument to man to stand as a symbol of Babel.

• Given the present knowledge of Babylonian history, **Genesis 11** has a solid historical foundation in early Mesopotamia. Nimrod hoped to prevent the people from scattering abroad into colonies as God intended, thus bringing upon themselves a judgment which led to confusion of the languages and rapid scattering throughout the earth. Babel means *confusion*.

• Urbanization did not occur until after the dispersal of languages. The history of linguistic development and settlement patterns in Mesopotamia support this. There are many unclassified and isolated languages throughout the world, such as Basque, Ainu and Ticuna, testifying to the widespread language distribution at Babel.

• From here the three families of man populate the earth.

## Genesis 10:6-20 HAM[27] Also *Cham or Kham.* Literal meanings are *passionate, hot, burnt or dark*

(father of the Mongoloid and Negroid races - *Hamites*). His four sons were:

**(1) Canaan** "down low" (sons were Zidon, Heth, Amori, Gergashi, Hivi, Arkee, Seni, Arodi, Zimodi and Chamothi) - also *Canaanites, Cana, Chna, Chanani, Chanana, Canaana, Kana, Kenaanah, Kena'ani, Kena'an, Kn'nw, Kyn'nw, Kinnahu, Kinahhi, Kinahni, Kinahna, Kinahne* (Mongols, Chinese, Taiwanese, Thais, Vietnamese, Japanese, Asians, Eskimos, American Indians, Malaysians, Indonesians, Filipinos, Hawaiians, Polynesians, Tahitians, Guamanians, Samoans, Fijians, Tongans, Pacific Islanders and related groups);

**(2) Cush** "black" (sons were Seba, Havilah, Sabta, Raama and Satecha) - also *Chus, Kush, Kosh* (Nubians, Ethiopians, Ghanaians, Africans, Bushmen, Pygmies, Australian Aborigines, New Guineans);

**(3) Mizraim** "double straits" (sons were Lud, Anom, Pathros, Chasloth and Chaphtor) - also *Misraim, Mitzraim, Mizraite, Mitsrayim* (Egyptians, Khemets, Copts, other related groups);

**(4) Phut** "a bow" (sons were Gebul, Hadan, Benah and Adan) - also *Punt, Puta, Put, Puni, Phoud, Pul, Fula, Putaya, Putiya, Libia, Libya* (Libyans, Cyrenacians, Tunisians, Berbers, Somalians, Sudanese, North Africans).

• Tribes in other parts of Africa, Arabia and Asia, aboriginal groups in Australia, native Pacific Islanders, American Indians and Eskimos were birthed from descendants of Canaan, Cush, Mizraim and Phut.

• Looking at history, whichever region is considered, Africa, Europe, Australia, or America, the major migrations have always been from Asia. In every area of the world where Japhethites have subsequently settled, they have always been preceded by Hamites. This pattern applies in every continent.

• In early historic times the circumstance seems always to be true, the earliest fossil remains of man being Mongoloid or Negroid in character and in head shape, whereas those that came last belong to the family of Japheth (Caucasoid). If you study ancient history and technological achievements, which were in many ways the equal of, or superior of, much that we have today, were founded and carried to a high technological proficiency by Hamitic people, showing an amazing adaptability to the world in which they live.

• Their achievements were exploited by Japhetic and Semitic peoples, who became great scientific discoverers. The Hamitic migrations indicate they sought a way of life, not an understanding or a control of nature beyond what was immediately useful.

• **Canaanites:**

a) Ham's first born son was Canaan. **Genesis 10:15-19** identifies a distinctive characteristic of the sons of Canaan: they liked to spread out. The Canaanites are specifically mentioned as migrating far and wide, and afterward the families of the Canaanites were spread abroad.

The territory of the Canaanites extended from Sidon as you go toward Gerar, as far as Gaza; as you go toward Sodom and Gomorrah and Admah and Zeboiim, as far as Lasha." History indicates they did have a propensity for sprawl. The descendants of Canaan would later make up the vast populations of Asia, Africa and the Western Hemisphere.

b) **Zidon (or Sidon)** = he and his descendants settled on the Mediterranean coast of present-day Lebanon, then known as the land of Canaan. The Sidonians called themselves Kena'ani, or **Canaanites**.

c) The Canaanites spoke a Semitic language, probably adopted from a large migration of Semites who came from land and sea, and introduced their language and a sophisticated maritime technology about 1800 B.C.

d) Historians suggest these Canaanites succumbed to racial and linguistic intermixture with the invading Semites, which led to the loss of their own ethnic predominance, as evidenced by modern excavations.

e) They eventually moved westward and occupied a very narrow coastal strip of the east Mediterranean, building new cities, and establishing significant trade with neighboring nations.

f) The Israelite name for **"Canaan"** came to mean "traders," though some suggest the name Canaan is from the Hebrew name *Hurrian*, meaning "land of red purple." The Canaanites were known for their red and purple cloth (a purple dye was extracted from murex snails found near the shores of Palestine, a method now lost).

g) The Greeks called the land of Canaan **"Phoenicia"** which meant "purple." The Phoenicians became a nation of great trade, language, and culture. Phoenician, Hebrew and Moabite were a group of west Semitic languages, all dialects from Canaan, as referred to in **Isaiah 19:18**.

h) The writing system of the Phoenicians is the source of the writing systems of nearly all of Europe, including Greek, Russian, Hebrew, Arabic and the Roman alphabet.

i) The Phoenician empire fell under Hellenistic rule after being conquered by Alexander the Great about 332BC. In 64BC the name of Phoenicia disappeared entirely, becoming a part of the Roman providence of Syria.

j) At the beginning of the Christian era, remaining Phoenicians were the first to accept the Christian faith after the Jews. Zidon's name is still perpetuated in the modern-day city of Sidon (Saidoon is the Phoenician name, Saida in Arabic) in southern Lebanon.

- **Native American Indians:**

a) Evidence for migrations into the Americas comes from research on living **American Indian** populations, which includes data from Mitochondrial DNA (DNA that is passed down from a mother to her children from one generation to the next intact). DNA haplogroups (haplogroups are used in DNA tests for markers that give a broad or regional picture; haplotypes are one person's results on various DNA tests). These studies have consistently shown similarities (deep ancestry) between American Indians and recent populations in Asia, Siberia and northern Scandinavia. These groups include the Lapps in northern Europe/Scandinavia, the Chukchi and Yukaghir in Siberia, plus Indians and Eskimos/Aleuts throughout Canada and America.

b) There is genetic relationship between early Taiwanese populations and southeast Asian, Oceanic (South Pacific) and Native American descendants. Ancient American Indian skeletal remains show a range of physical attributes (round-headed) suggesting separate migrations of different populations from Asia *and* the South Pacific, representing 95 percent of all modern American Indian populations. What of the other five percent?

c) There are exceptions. For example, the Siouan family of tribes (**Sioux Indians**), the popular red-skinned tribes having a long-head shape similar to that of early Italic peoples in Europe. They are thought to be descendants of Canaanites who intermarried with Indo-Europeans while migrating across Europe, and subsequently sailing to America. Settling along the eastern shores of America, and according to tradition, they populated the Carolinas, then migrated to the regions of Louisiana, Mississippi, Missouri, and eventually Minnesota and the Dakotas.

d) Many tribes had fortified villages similar to ancient Canaanites (who lived along the Mediterranean coast, including parts of Egypt and the Jordan Valley). Archeological evidence shows they constructed towns and cities with pyramids and vast road systems throughout the Mississippi Valley. With them came a tradition that is thought to be a reference to the wives of Noah and his three sons. Four women are identified as "mothers of origin" whose names (possibly Canaanite) have been preserved down through the generations.

e) Additionally, there are striking similarities between the languages of ancient Egypt and those of the Native Americans that inhabited the areas around Louisiana about the time of Christ. Epigraphy experts have stated that the languages of the Attakapa, Tunica and Chitimacha tribes have affinities with Nile Valley (Egyptian) languages involving certain words associated with Egyptian trading communities of 2,000 years ago.

- **Aztecs:**

a) Many American Indian people groups migrated southwest into Oklahoma, Texas, New Mexico and eventually Mexico, establishing the powerful **Aztec** tribes with their beautiful fortified cities, integrating with the **Mayas** (who had been there hundreds of years before, and thought of the Aztecs as barbarians).

b) Likely there was a mixing of cultures as they migrated, as there was no conquest of the Maya world by the Aztecs; that title would be given to the Spaniards in the late 17th century.

c) The Aztec's traditions and legends are largely ignored by modern scholars as myths and fables. The Aztecs, according to their own legends, departed from a region in the north called Chicomoztoc, a region that is today the areas of Texas, Oklahoma and New Mexico. Later establishing a city known as Aztlan, somewhere in north or northwest Mexico (now lost), their tribal name *Aztec* was born. Being nomadic, they eventually reached the valley of Mexico in the 12th century A.D.

d) They were known as fearless warriors and pragmatic builders who raised an enormous city called Tenochtitlan, their capital city (now Mexico City).

e) They later called themselves "Mexica" (where Mexico is derived). Their language, Nahuatl, was linguistically related to other native language groups throughout the U.S. southwest and northern Mexico. Linguists note, for instance, the Shoshoni language in the Utah-Nevada region was understood by all the tribes from Mexico, without difficulty. Other related tribes included the Paiute, Hopi, Pima, Yaqui/Apache, Tepehuan, Kiowas and Mayos.

f) Catholic missionaries in the 1850's established that all of those peoples were of one language family. While there are other examples of language similarities, studies of the native languages of the Americas show them to be extremely diverse, representing nearly 200 distinct families, some consisting of a single isolated language.

- **Pacific Islanders:**

a) They have a diverse and unique history. These oceanic peoples of the South Pacific, whom we know as Polynesians, Tahitians, Samoans, Fijians, Tongans and others, have their roots in southern China.

b) Prior to the Mongols establishing themselves in southern China, there were migrations of Negroid peoples from east Africa and the Sahara. Many African cultures kept documents and ancient texts, as well as strong oral history and legends, of migrations to ancient China from Africa.

c) Mongol groups later migrated into southern China, resulting in a mixing of cultures. Southern China is thought to have first come into being out of the mixture of Mongoloids and Negroids. These peoples were likely driven out by other aggressive Mongoloids. Being master seafarers, they sailed into Polynesia and the surrounding region, populating the islands of the South Pacific.

- **Hittites:**

a) Most of the peoples who are classified as **Mongoloid**, who settled the Far East, have been difficult to fit into the Table of Nations. Evidence shows they are Hamitic, although some have reasoned that the Chinese were of Japhetic stock, and the Japanese were either Japhetic or Semitic. There are two names which provide clues.

b) Two of Canaan's sons, *Heth* (Hittites) and *Sin* (Sinites), are presumed to be the progenitors of Chinese and Mongoloid stock. The **Hittites** were known as the *Hatti* or *Chatti*.

c) In Egyptian monuments the Hittite peoples were depicted with prominent noses, full lips, high check-bones, hairless faces, varying skin color from brown to yellowish and reddish, straight black hair and dark brown eyes.

d) The term *Hittite* in Cuneiform (the earliest form of writing invented by the Sumerians) appears as *Khittae* representing a once powerful nation from the Far East known as the *Khitai*, and has been preserved through the centuries in the more familiar term, *Cathay*. The Cathay were Mongoloids, a part of early Chinese stock.

e) There are links between the Hittites and Cathay, for example, their modes of dress, their shoes with turned-up toes, their manner of doing their hair in a pigtail, and so forth. Representations show them to have possessed high cheekbones, and craniologists have observed that they had common characteristics of Mongoloids.

- **Chinese = Sin (or Seni)**, a brother of Heth, has many occurrences in variant forms in the Far East.

a) There is one significant feature concerning the likely mode of origin of Chinese civilization. The place most closely associated by the Chinese themselves with the origin of their civilization is the capital of Shensi, namely, *Siang-fu* (Father Sin). Siang-fu appears in Assyrian records as *Sianu*. Today, Siang-fu can be loosely translated, "Peace to the Western Capital of China."

b) The Chinese have a tradition that their *first* king, Fu-hi or Fohi (Chinese Noah), made his appearance on the Mountains of Chin, was surrounded by a rainbow after the world had been covered with water, and sacrificed animals to God (corresponding to the Genesis record).

c) Sin himself was the third generation from Noah, a circumstance which would provide the right time interval for the formation of early Chinese culture. In addition, the Miao tribe of southwest China had a tradition similar to the Genesis account, even before they met Christian missionaries.

d) According to their tradition, God destroyed the whole world by a flood because of the wickedness of man, and Nuah (Noah) the righteous man and his wife, their three sons, Lo Han (Ham), Lo Shen (Shem), and Jah-hu (Japheth) survived by building a very broad ship and taking on it pairs of animals.

e) Those who came from the Far East to trade were called Sinæ (Sin) by the Scythians. Ptolemy, a Greek astronomer, called China the land of *Sinim or Sinæ*. Reference to the *Sinim* in **Isaiah 49:12** notes they came "from afar," specifically *not* from the north and *not* from the west. Arabs called China *Sin, Chin, Mahachin, Machin*. The Sinæ were spoken of as a people in the remotest parts of Asia.

f) For the Sinæ, the most important town was Thinæ, a great trading emporium in western China. The city Thinæ is now known as Thsin or Tin, and it lies in the province of Shensi. Much of China was ruled by the *Sino-Khitan* Empire (960-1126A.D.), which Beijing became the southern capital. The Sinæ became independent in western China, their princes reigning there for some 650 years before they finally gained dominion over the whole land.

g) In 3rd century B.C., the dynasty of Tsin became supreme. The word Tsin itself came to have the meaning of purebred. This word was assumed as a title by the Manchu Emperors and was changed into the form Tchina. From there the term was brought into Europe as *China,* from the Ch'in or Qin dynasty (255-206B.C.).

h) The Greek word for China is Kina (Latin is Sina). As well, Chinese and surrounding languages are part of the *Sino-Tibetan* language family. Years ago, American newspapers regularly carried headlines with reference to the conflict between the Chinese and Japanese in which the ancient name reappeared in its original form, the *Sino-Japanese* war. *Sinology* refers to the study of Chinese history.

i) With respect to the Cathay people, it would make sense to suppose that the remnants of the Hittites, after the destruction of their empire, traveled towards the east and settled among the Sinites who were relatives, contributing to their civilization, and thus becoming the ancestors of the Asian people groups. Still others migrated throughout the region and beyond, making up present-day Mongoloid races in Asia and the Americas.

j) The evidence strongly suggests that Ham's grandsons, Heth (Hittites/Cathay) and Sin (Sinites/China), are the ancestors of the Mongoloid peoples.

• **Africans =** There are many native African tribes which trace themselves back traditionally to Ham.

a) The Yoruba, who are black skinned, for example, claim to be descendants of Nimrod, son of Cush, whereas the Libyans, who are much lighter skinned, are traced back to Phut (Phut is the Hebrew name for Libya). Ethiopians still trace their ancestry back to Cush.

b) The Egyptians were descendants of Mizraim (the Hebrew name for Egypt). Ancient Egyptians are considered the greatest technicians in all human history. Other African groups trace their roots back to Ham or one of his descendants, so it is suggested that all of Africa was initially settled by members of this one Hamitic family.

c) In the course of time, some of these people groups had migrations to Australia, Melanesia, New Guinea and the surrounding region. For example, there is evidence of similarities in the form of horticulture found in the Sahara and in Papua New Guinea. Recent studies from archaeology have discovered there was once extensive trade between east Africa and New Guinea.

d) The evidence appears to point consistently in the same direction, supporting that not only Africa with its black races, but the Far East, the Americas, Australia and the Oceanic nations with their colored races were all descendants of Ham.

e) The Hamitic people were the first to reach the distant lands of the world, preparing the way for the future. Their inventions and discoveries made a significant impact on the world, and provided inspiration for those to follow.

## Genesis 10:1-8  JAPHETH[27] or *Diphath*. Means *opened, enlarged, light* (father of the Caucasoid/ Indo-Europoid, Indo-European, Indo-Germanic, or Indo-Aryan races - *Japhethites*). His seven sons were:

**(1) Gomer** "complete" (sons were Ashkenaz, Riphath and Togarmah) - Caledonians, Picts, Milesians, Umbrians, Helvetians, Celts, Galatians, Ostrogoths, Visigoths, Goths, Vandals, Scandinavians, Jutes, Teutons, Franks, Burgundians, Alemanni, Armenians, Germans, Belgians, Dutch, Luxembourgers, Liechensteiners, Austrians, Swiss, Angles, Saxons, Britons, English, Cornish, Irish, Welsh, French.

**(2) Magog** "land of God" (sons were Elichanaf, Lubal, Baath, Jobhath and Fathochta) - Scythians, Scots, Irish, Russians, Belarusians, Ukrainians, Hungarians, Finns, Lapps, Estonians, Siberians, Yugoslavians, Croatians, Bosnians, Montenegrins, Serbians, Slovenians, Slovakians, Bulgarians, Poles, Czechs.

**(3) Madai** "middle land" (sons were Achon, Zeelo, Chazoni and Lotalso) - Medes, Aryans, Persians, Parsa, Parsees, Achaemenians, Manneans, Caspians, Kassites, Iranians, Kurds, Turks, East Indians, Pathans, Hazaras, Afghanistan, Pakistan, Azerbaijan, Khazachstan, Turkmenistan, Uzbekistan, Tajikstan and Kyrgyzstan.

**(4) Javan** "miry" (sons were Elisha, Tarshish, Kittim and Dodanim) - Grecians, Greeks, Elysians, Spartans, Dorians, Britons, Aeolians, Achaeans, Myceneans, Macedonians, Carthaginians, Cyprians, Cretans, Basques, Latins, Venetians, Sicanians, Italics, Romans, Valentians, Sicilians, Italians, Spaniards, Portugese.

**(5) Tubal** "brought" (sons were Ariphi, Kesed and Taari) - Georgians, Albanians, others.

**(6) Meshech** "drawing out" (sons were Dedon, Zaron and Shebashnialso) - Muscovites, Latvians, Lithuanians, Romanians.

**(7) Tiras** "desire" (sons were Benib, Gera, Lupirion and Gilak) - Pelasgians, Scandinavians, Varangians, Vikings, Swedes, Norwegians, Danes, Icelandics.

• The Japhetic people are, in general, the peoples of India and Europe (Indo-European stock), with which any demographer is familiar.

- **Celts:**

a) Celtic race descended from Gomer, though history suggests modern Celts descended from Gomer and Magog. Archaeologists and ethnologists agree that the first Indo-European group to spread across Europe were Celts.

b) The Irish Celts claim to be to the descendants of Magog, while the Welsh Celts claim to be to the descendants of Gomer. Irish chronicles, genealogies, plus an extensive number of manuscripts which have survived from ancient times, reveal their roots.

c) The **Irish** were descendants of **Scythians**, also known as Magogians. Archaeological evidence shows that both the Celts (from Gomer) and Scythians (from Magog) mingled cultures at their earliest stages. Russian and eastern European excavations plainly reveal the blending of these two groups. Their geographical locations (what is now eastern Europe, southern Russia and Asia Minor) were referred to by the Greeks under the name of Celto-Scythae, which was populated by the Celts to the south and west, and the Scythians to the north.

d) The ancient Greeks first called the northern peoples by the general name of Scythae; but when they became acquainted with the nations in the west, they began to call them by the different names of Celts, including the Celto-Scythae. Celts and **Scythians** were considered essentially the same peoples, based on geography, though many independent tribes of Celts and Scythians existed.

e) The Latins called them "Galli," and the Romans referred to them as "**Gauls**." Later names used by Greeks were the Galatai or Galatae, Getae, Celtae and Keltoi. In the third century before Christ (about 280 B.C.), the Gauls invaded Rome and were ultimately repelled into Greece, where they migrated into the north-central part of Asia Minor (Anatolia). Known as fiercely independent peoples, they conquered the indigenous peoples of that region and established their own independent kingdom. The land became known as **Galatia**. The Apostle Paul wrote his famous epistle to their descendants, the Galatians. Jewish historian Flavius Josephus wrote that the Galatians or Gauls of his day ( 93A.D.) were previously called Gomerites.

f) Early Celtic tribes (from Gomer) settled in Europe, prior to contact with Scythians. France was called Gaul, after the Celtic descendants of Gomer, whom ceded the territory to Romans and Germanic/Teutonic Franks (whence *France*) in the 4th century A.D. Northwest Spain is called Galicia to this day.

g) Some of the Gomerites migrated further to what is now called **Wales**. The Welsh claim their ancestors "first landed on the Isle of Britain from France, about three hundred years after the flood." The Celtic language survives today mainly in the two variants of Welsh and Irish/Scottish Gaelic. The Welsh call their language Gomeraeg (after Gomer). The Celts of today are descendants of Gomer, and of the blended tribes of Magog and Gomer.

- **Germans:**

a) Present-day Germanic people groups are descendants of both Japheth and Shem, and there are several references from recent and ancient history. Recent history records the descendants of Gomer migrated and settled in the region that is now northern Europe (Germany and Scandinavia).

b) These tribes became the Goths, Ostrogoths, Visigoths, Teutons and Burgundians, descendants of some of the first peoples to migrate to northern Europe from ancient times—the Askaeni. The Askaeni were descendants of Ashkenaz, son of Gomer, son of Japheth. When the Askaeni arrived in northern Europe, they named the land Ascania after themselves, which later translated Scandia, then **Scandinavia**.

c) Later in history, we find the Askaeni being referred to as Sakasenoi, which became Sachsen, and finally Saxon. The **Saxons** played an large part in European and English history. Ashkenaz has been one of the most well preserved names throughout European history.

d) Semitic peoples also migrated to central Europe (southern Germany, Austria and Switzerland). These people were the descendants of Asshur, son of Shem, where Germans originated. Asshur is well known in history as the father of the **Assyrians**.

e) The land of the Assyrians was called "Athur," which became "Tyr" or "Teiw" by early Germanic peoples. Later, the name changes to "Ziu." Germans likely derived their identity and language from these ancestral names.

f) The earliest known name of the German language was called "*Diu*tisc," which later becomes Deutsch (which Germans call themselves today). Deutschland (land of the Deutsch) could be called Asshurland. The Romans referred to the *Deu*tschen as *Teu*tons.

g) The term "German" comes from Latin (Roman) sources. The Assyrians occupied a Mesopotamian city on the lower Tigris River called "Kir" and placed captive slaves there (also referenced in **2 Kings 16:9**). The city was populated by the Assyrians for years, and the inhabitants were known as "Kir-man." The Assyrians (Kerman) were driven from their land shortly after their fall about 610B.C. They migrated into central Europe where they were called "German" or "Germanni," a general name used by the Romans to represent all Assyrian tribes.

h) The known Assyrian tribes were the Khatti (also Hatti, Hessians)—Chatti is still the Hebrew term for German, and Khatti was also used by the Romans to represent Germanic tribes; the Akkadians (Latins called them Quadians); the Kassites (or Cossaei); and the Almani (or Halmani, Allemani was the Latin name).

- **Russians:**

a) Ancient peoples known as the Sarmatians (not to be confused with the Samaritans) and Alans lived in the area around the Caspian Sea from about 900B.C. Sarmatian and Alani tribes were later called **Scythians** (Slavs of today), who were also known as the Rukhs-As, Rashu, Rasapu, Rosh, Ros, and Rus.

b) There is no debate that they were the inhabitants of southern Russia, and the existence of the names of rivers, such as the "Ros," refer to Rus populations.

c) About 739 A.D., the word Rus appears again in eastern Europe, from a different source. Finnish peoples referred to Swedes as "Ruotsi," "Rotsi" or "Rus" in contrast with Slavic peoples, which was derived from the name of the Swedish maritime district in Uppland, "Roslagen," and its inhabitants, called "Rodskarlar."

d) Rodskarlar or Rothskarlar meant "rowers" or "seamen." Those Swedish conquerors (called *Varangians* [**Vikings**] by the Slavs), settled in eastern Europe, adopted the names of local tribes, integrated with the Slavs, and eventually the word "Rusi," "Rhos" or "Rus" came to refer to the inhabitants.

e) Russia means "land of the Rus." Scholars continue to debate the origin of the word Rus, which has derived from two sources: the *Ruotsi* or *Rhos*, the Finnish names for the Swedes, and earlier from the Scythians called the *Rashu* or *Rosh* in southern Russia.

- **Medes and Persians:**

a) The Aryans first come into historical view about a thousand years before Christ, invading India and threatening Babylonia. Historians of old reference an Aryan chief called Cyaxeres, king of the Medes and Persians.

b) The Medes and Persians seem to have been tribes of one nation, more or less united under the rule of Cyaxeres. Elam (son of Shem) is the ancient name for Persia. Elamites are synonymous with Persians. The Persians are thus descended from both Elam, the son of Shem, and from Madai, the son of Japheth.

c) The Medes and Persians had settled in what is now modern Persia, the Medes in the north, the Persians in the south. The most notable Persians of today are the **Iranians**. Interestingly, the word *Iran* is a derivative of *Aryan*.

d) The Medo-Persian people groups are divided into hundreds of clans, all speaking Indo-European languages. Some groups have pronounced Mongoloid characteristics and cultural traits, derived from Mongolian invasions and cultural integration. An example today would be the Uzbeks of Uzbekistan.

- **England =** The history of Great Britain can be traced back to the sons of Japheth.

a) Historical evidence strongly suggests the first inhabitants of the British isles were the descendants of Java (from his sons Elisha and Tar shish), and of Gomer and Magog.

b) Geometries are today's modern **Welsh**. Traditional Welsh belief is that the descendants of Gomer arrived about three hundred years after the flood, and the Welsh language was once called Gomeraeg. The Welsh (Celts) are thought to have created **Stonehenge**.

c) Additionally, the descendants of Tar shish (Elisha's brother) appear to have settled on the British Isles in various migrations about the same time. **Genesis 10:4** refers to Tar shish as those of "the isles of the Gentiles."

d) The Phoenicians traded silver, iron, tin and lead with them (**Ezekiel 27:12**), and even mention the incredible stone monuments at Stonehenge. Around 450B.C., ancient historian Herodotus wrote about shipments of tin coming from the "Tin Isles" far to the north and west. There is no question that the British isles, including the northern coast of Spain, were the seat of the tin trade. King Solomon acquired precious metals from Tar shish (**1 Kings 10:22**). English historians assert that British mines mainly supplied the glorious adornment of Solomon's Temple, and in those days the mines of southwestern Britain were the source of the world's supply of tin.

e) The name Briton came from *Brutus* (a descendant of **Elisha**), the first king on Britain's mainland, in 1100B.C. Brutus had two sons, *Kamber* and *Albanactus*. From Kamber came Cambaria and the *Cambrians* (who integrated with the Geometries [mostly Celts] and became the present-day **Welsh**).

f) The descendants of Albanactus were known as the *Albans* (or the *Albanach* whom the Irish commonly called them). Geographers would later call the land *Albion*. The Britons, Cambrians and Albans populated the British Isles, which later endured multiple invasions, beginning with successive waves of Celts about 700 B.C.

g) The Celts (or *Gaels*) called the land *Prydain*, their name for *Briton*. Those Celts (descendants of Gomer) integrated with the descendants of Elisha and Tar shish (sons of Java), creating what some scholars called "a Celticized aboriginal population" in the British Isles.

h) Some of the invading people groups were Scythians, descended from Magog, who became known as the Skoths or Scots. The name for the Celts or Cymru was "Weahlas," from Anglo-Saxon origins, meaning "land of foreigners"- **Wales**. The Welsh still call themselves Cymru, pronounced "Coomry."

i) Later the Romans called the land *Britannia*, invading it about fifty years before the birth of Christ. By the 3rd century A.D., Jutes, Franks, Picts, Moors, Angles, Saxons and others were invading from surrounding Europe.

j) In the 6th century A.D., Saxons called the land Kemr (Cymru), and the language *Brithenig* (Breton). The Angles eventually conquered Britannia, renaming the territory *Angleland*, which became **England**.

k) Vikings invaded in the ninth century, and the Normans (or Northmen—former Danish Vikings) conquered England in 1066A.D. Today, the British isles are settled by the ancestors of those people groups, which included Gomer and Java (first inhabitants), plus Magog (later invasions by various people groups).

- **Romans:**

a) Migrating nomadic peoples came from across the Alps and across the Adriatic Sea to the east of the Italian peninsula. They were primarily herdsmen, and were technologically advanced. They worked bronze, used horses, and had wheeled carts.

b) They were a war-like people and began to settle the mountainous areas of the Italian peninsula. Historians called these people *Italic*, and they include several ethnic groups: the Sabines, the Umbrians and the Latins, amongst others. Rome was, in part, founded by these agrarian Italic peoples living south of the Tiber river. They were a tribal people, and thus tribal organization dominated Roman society in both its early and late histories.

c) The date of the founding of Rome is uncertain, but archaeologists estimate its founding to around 7 B.C., although it existed as a village or group of villages long before then. As the Romans steadily developed their city, government and culture, they imitated the neighboring civilization to the north, the Etruscans (former Trojans).

d) Romans are sometimes referred to as "Etruscanized Latins." Roman legend states that Aeneas, the founder of the Roman race, was a prince of Troy who was forced to flee that city at the close of the Trojan war against Greece. Rome's founder, Romulus, had a latinized Etruscan name.

e) The Etruscans dominated central Italy, and had already founded many cities, having arrived some 500 years earlier after leaving the city of Troy around 0 B.C. The Etruscans were greatly influenced by the Greeks, and the Etruscans brought that influence to the city of Rome.

f) The Romans called Etruscans the *Tusci*. **Tuscany** still bears the name. The first two centuries of Rome's growth was dominated by the Etruscans. After many battles with the Etruscans, the city of Rome identified itself as Latin, eventually integrating the Estruscans in the region. Rome became a kingdom, then an empire.

- **Scandinavians:**

a) Scandinavians (Danes, Norwegians, Swedes) came from early Germanic people groups, including the Goths, Ostrogoths, Visigoths, Teutons and Burgundians (descendants of Gomer). Ashkenaz, son of Gomer, is ancestor of Germanic peoples. Known as the Askaeni, they were some of the first peoples to migrate to northern Europe, naming the land Ascania. Greeks called the land Scandza or Scandia (now Scandinavia).

b) Roman records describe a large city on the southern shore of the Caspian Sea (about 350 A.D.) where a chain of mountains runs eastward along the shore. Those mountains were called the *Ascanimians*, the region was called *Sakasene* (a form of Ashkenaz), and the people were the *Saki*. The Saki tribes had been migrating north to Europe for some time. The Saki called themselves the *Sakasenoi*, which we know as the *Sachsens* or **Saxons**.

c) Around 280 A.D. the Romans tell of the employment of Saxons to guard the eastern British coasts against barbarians. About 565 A.D., the Saxons battled over territory in the Baltic region with another powerful people, the *Svear*. Historical records indicate that descendants of Tiras also settled in Scandinavia, a people called the Svear.

d) The Svear are descendants of the first inhabitants of Troy, a people known as the Tiracians (also Thracians, Trajans or **Trojans**). They were described as a "ruddy and blue-eyed people." Troy was destroyed around 1260B.C. after several wars with the Greeks. Many Trojans resettled abroad, including Trojan warriors who sailed across the Black Sea to the Caucasus region in southern Russia. One of the most documented Trojan settlement is along the mouth of the River Don on the Black Sea. The locals (Scythians) named those Trojan settlers the "Aes," meaning "Iron" for their superior weapons. Later, the inner part of the Black Sea was named after them, called the "Iron Sea" or "Sea of Aesov" in the local tongue. Today, the name continues as the "Sea of Azov."

e) The Aes or *Aesir*, traveled from the Caucasus region to the Baltic Sea in Scandinavia around 90B.C., which is supported by scholars and modern archaeological evidence. A tribe that migrated with them were the Vanir.

f) The Aesirs traded with local Germanic tribes, including the Gutar. Romans called the Gutar "Goths," the Aesir "Svear"—**Swedes**, and the Vanir "Danir/Daner"—**Danes**. The Svear and Daners were taller and fairer (blonde) than other people in the Baltic region. The Svears flourished, and with the Goths they formed a powerful military alliance of seafarers. The Romans noted that Svear people and the Goths were, from the 3rd century A.D., ravaging the Black Sea, Asia Minor and the Mediterranean, using the same weapons as their Trojan ancestors.

g) The Svear and Goths dominated the Russian waterways, and by 739A.D. together they were called *Varyagans* or *Varangians* (from the Swedish *Vaeringar*), according to written records of the Slavs near the Sea of Azov.

h) Like their ancestors, Scandinavians lived in large communities where their chieftains would send out maritime warriors to trade and plunder. Those fierce warriors were called the *Vaeringar*, which literally meant "men who offer their service to another master." We later know them by their popularized name, the **Vikings**.

i) Further evidence of Aesir (Asir) settlements in the Baltic region came from their Thracian language, which not only influenced, but is very close to the Baltic and Slavic (Balto-Slavic) languages of today.

j) By the 9th century A.D., the Svear state was the major power in Scandinavia. The Svear, Daner and Goths, along with other Germanic tribes, settled in what is now present-day Sweden, Norway, Denmark and other parts of the Baltic region. They were forefathers of the Scandinavians—the descendants of both Gomer and Tiras.

- **Indo-Europeans:**

a) Early history shows the Japhethites split into two groups. One group settled in the region of present-day India and Central Asia, and the other group in the European theater.

b) Indo-European languages originate from people groups who migrated throughout western Eurasia (Europe, the Near East, Anatolia, and the Caucasus). Together they form the "Indo-European" family of nations.

c) Both of these divisions trace their ancestry back to Japheth. For example, early Aryans knew him as *Djapatischta (chief of the race)*, Greeks referred to Japheth as *Iapetos* or *Japetos,* East Indians called him *Jyapeti* or *Pra-Japati*, Romans used *Ju-Pater* or *Jupiter*, the Saxons perpetuated his name as *Iafeth*, subsequently transliterated as *Sceaf* (pronounced "sheef" or "shaif"—and recorded his name in their early genealogies as the son of Noah, the forebear of their various peoples), and the variant *Seskef* was used by early Scandinavians.

d) All of these peoples were pagans whose knowledge or even awareness of the book of Genesis had been lost, or was non-existent.

# Was Jesus a good-looking white guy?

Most popular portrait

#2 most popular

Maybe this?

Jesus Christ superstar

Man from Galilee during Jesus's time

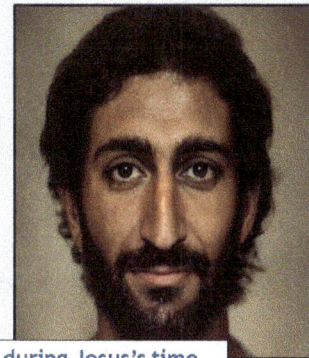

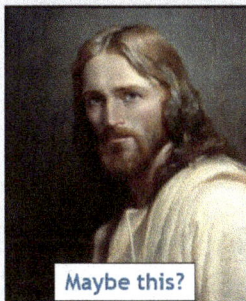

**ISAIAH 53:2**

*"He has no form or comeliness, and when we see Him, there is no beauty that we should desire Him."*

Matt Chandler- Jesus is not a white man - Megan Kelly rebuttal (2.46)          Courtesy of Google Images    Fair Use Law 17 U.S. Code S 107

## Exit Ticket #15        Class 15: Who Am I?  Part 1

| | |
|---|---|
| **1) What does it mean to be a "person"?** | **2) What are the Three "Identities" described about mankind in the Bible?** |
| **3) Where in the Bible is mankind's "Physical Identity" explained?** | **4) Of the 31 Scriptures in this lesson, which 2-3 scriptures resonate with you the most and why?** |

# Class 16:  Who Am I?  Part 2

My Spiritual Identity: from Israel-to-Abraham-to-Christ

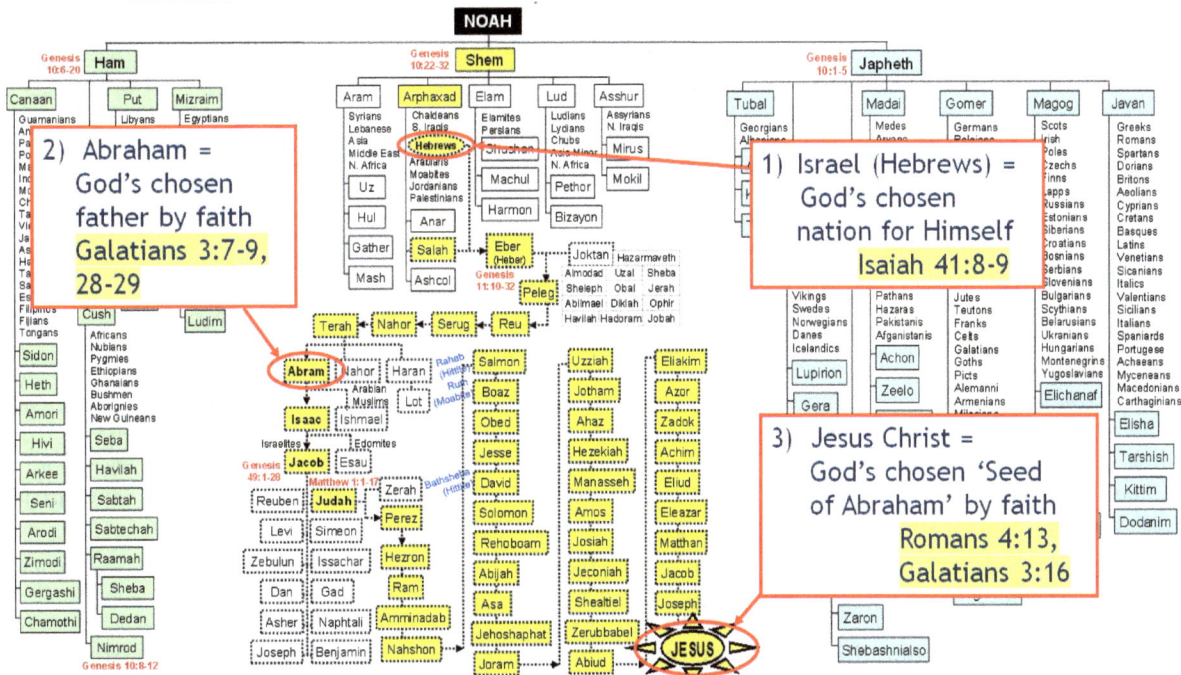

The Book of Isaiah: Answers to the Big 3 Questions

Jesus Christ: The True Vine

Darryl Bock: 'Scholars understanding of Micah 5:2' (2:21)

Francis Chan: 'I am the True Vine - just stay connected' (4:15)

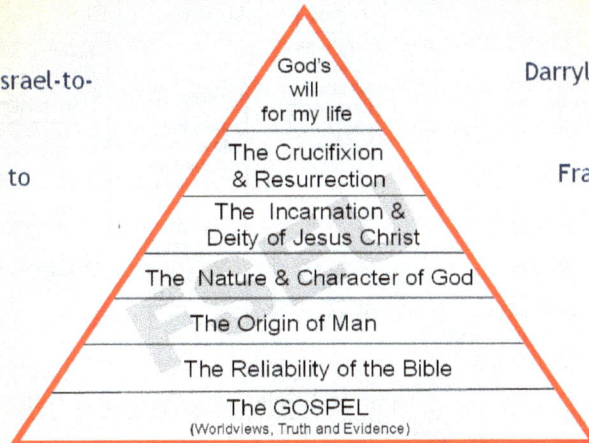

God's will for my life

The Crucifixion & Resurrection

The Incarnation & Deity of Jesus Christ

The Nature & Character of God

The Origin of Man

The Reliability of the Bible

The GOSPEL
(Worldviews, Truth and Evidence)

# HEBREWS 11:1
"Faith = *Substance* of things hoped for.... *Evidence* of things *not seen*"

fse.life Lessons 02 - 08

## My Spiritual Identity:  Israel – to – Abraham – to – Christ

2) Abraham = God's chosen father by faith Galatians 3:7-9, 28-29

1) Israel (Hebrews) = God's chosen nation for Himself Isaiah 41:8-9

3) Jesus Christ = God's chosen 'Seed of Abraham' by faith Romans 4:13, Galatians 3:16

Courtesy of Google Images    Fair Use Law 17 U.S. Code § 107

# Matthew 1: My Christian Roots
## Israel ➜ Abraham ➜ Christ

- **Where did I come from?:**
  1) Why God chose Israel
  2) Why God chose Abraham
  3) Why God chose Joseph and Mary

## 3 Reasons God chose Israel

- The existence of Israel , no bigger than Rhode Island, defies logic. Their survival contradicts all we see in any other nation..

- <u>Mark Twain (Harper's Magazine, 1897)</u>: *"..the Jews are but ¼ of 1% of the human race. It suggests a nebulous dim puff of star dust lost in the blaze of the Milky Way... The Jew ought hardly be heard of; but he has always been heard of. His contributions to the world's list of great names in literature, science, art, music, finance, medicine and learning are way out of proportion to the weakness of his numbers. The Egyptians, Babylonians, and Persians rose, filled the planet with sound and splendor, then passed away; the Greek and Roman followed, made a vast noise, and they were gone. The Jew saw and survived them all. All things are mortal but the Jew; all other forces pass, but he remains. What is the secret of the Jews' immortality?"*

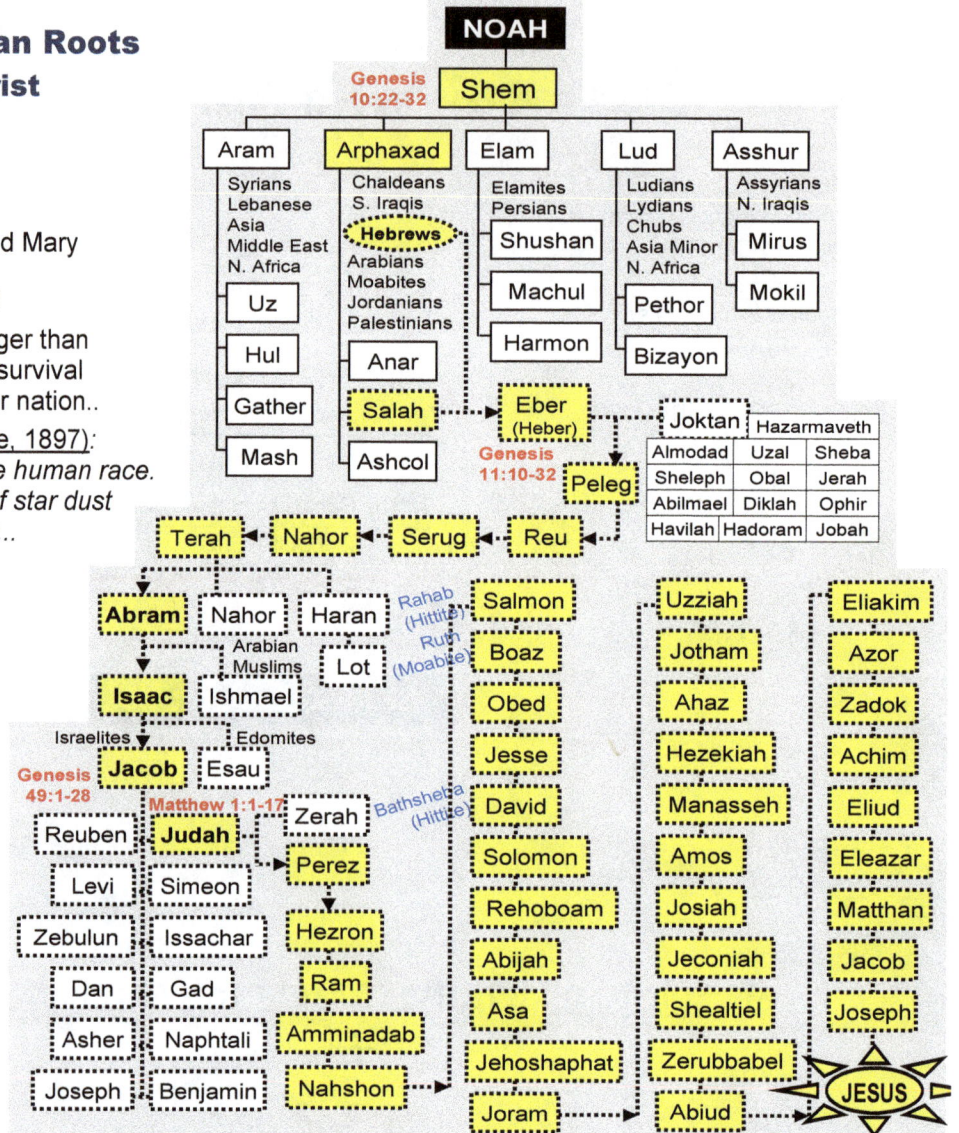

The genealogy chart from Noah through Shem to Jesus, including: Shem (Genesis 10:22-32); sons Aram, Arphaxad, Elam, Lud, Asshur; Aram → Syrians, Lebanese, Asia, Middle East, N. Africa (Uz, Hul, Gather, Mash); Arphaxad → Chaldeans, S. Iraqis, Hebrews, Arabians, Moabites, Jordanians, Palestinians (Anar, Salah, Ashcol); Elam → Elamites, Persians (Shushan, Machul, Harmon); Lud → Ludians, Lydians, Chubs, Asia Minor, N. Africa (Pethor, Bizayon); Asshur → Assyrians, N. Iraqis (Mirus, Mokil); Salah → Eber (Heber) (Genesis 11:10-32) → Peleg, Joktan (Hazarmaveth, Almodad, Uzal, Sheba, Sheleph, Obal, Jerah, Abilmael, Diklah, Ophir, Havilah, Hadoram, Jobab); Peleg → Reu → Serug → Nahor → Terah → Abram, Nahor, Haran; Haran → Lot; Abram → Isaac, Ishmael (Arabian Muslims); Isaac → Jacob (Israelites), Esau (Edomites) (Genesis 49:1-28); Jacob's sons: Reuben, Judah, Levi, Simeon, Zebulun, Issachar, Dan, Gad, Asher, Naphtali, Joseph, Benjamin (Matthew 1:1-17); Judah → Zerah, Perez → Hezron → Ram → Amminadab → Nahshon → Salmon (Rahab, Hittite) → Boaz (Ruth, Moabite) → Obed → Jesse → David (Bathsheba, Hittite) → Solomon → Rehoboam → Abijah → Asa → Jehoshaphat → Joram → Uzziah → Jotham → Ahaz → Hezekiah → Manasseh → Amos → Josiah → Jeconiah → Shealtiel → Zerubbabel → Abiud → Eliakim → Azor → Zadok → Achim → Eliud → Eleazar → Matthan → Jacob → Joseph → JESUS.

- God's plan for mankind centers on one nation: Israel. Here's their lineage: ① Shem, Arphaxad, Salah = *Semites;* ② Eber, Abram = *Hebrews;* ③ Jacob = *Israelite;* ④ Judah = *Judahite* (OT), *Judean* (Greek), *Jew* (NT)

**Isaiah 41: 8-9**   *"But you, Israel, are My servant. Jacob, whom I have CHOSEN, the descendants of Abraham My friend. You whom I have taken from the ends of the earth, and called from its farthest regions, and said to you, 'You are My servant, I HAVE CHOSEN YOU, and have not cast you away."*

- **Reason #1 = God desired that Israel bring His Word to the world**

Joshua 1:7-9 *"Be strong and very courageous, that you may observe to do according to all the law which Moses My servant commanded you; do not turn from it to the right hand or to the left, that you may prosper wherever you go. This BOOK OF THE LAW shall not depart from your mouth, but you shall meditate in it day and night, that you may observe to do according to all that is written in it. For then you will make your way prosperous, and you will have good success. Have I not commanded you? Be strong and of good courage; do not be afraid, nor be dismayed, for the Lord your God is with you wherever you go."*

Romans 3:1-2   *"What advantage then has the Jew, or what is the profit of circumcision? Much in every way! Chiefly because to them were given the ORACLES OF GOD."*

- **Reason #2 = God intended the nation of Israel to be His witness to the world of the one true God**

Isaiah 43:21 *"This people I have formed for Myself; they shall declare MY PRAISE."*

- **Reason #3 = God chose the nation of Israel as His vehicle to bring the Messiah into the world**

Micah 5:2 *"But you, Bethlehem Eprathah, though you are little among the thousands of Judah, yet out of you shall come forth to Me the One to be ruler in Israel, whose goings forth have been from of old, from the days of ETERNITY."*

## Genesis 15:5 / Romans 4:18 — Abraham: Father of Many Nations by *FAITH*

*"... who, contrary to hope, in hope believed, so that he became the FATHER OF MANY NATIONS, according to what was spoken, 'So shall your descendants be'".* Genesis 15:5

*"Now the sons of Noah who went out of the ark were Shem, Ham and Japheth. And Ham was the father of Canaan. These 3 were the sons of Noah, and from these the whole earth was populated."* Genesis 9:18-19

*"You are the Lord God, who chose Abram, and brought Him out of Ur of the Chaldees, and gave him the name Abraham; You found his heart faithful before You, and made a COVENANT with him."* Nehemiah 9:7-8

*"In your seed all the nations of the earth shall be blessed, because you have obeyed My voice."* Genesis 22:18

*"Now to Abraham and his Seed were the promises made. He does not say, 'And to seeds', as of many, but as One, 'and to your Seed', who is Christ."* Galatians 3:16... Genesis 3:15... Genesis 12:3

*"It is of FAITH that it might be according to GRACE, so that the promise might be sure to all the SEED, not only to those who are of the law, but also to those who are of the faith of ABRAHAM, who is the father of us all..."* Romans 4:16

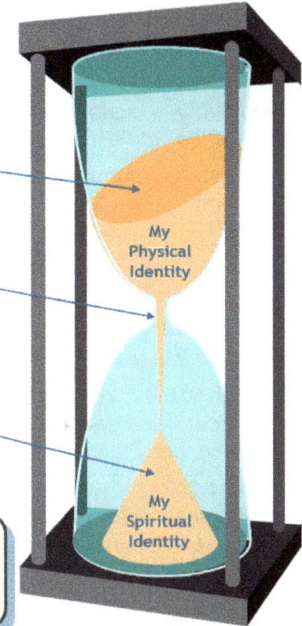

My Physical Identity

My Spiritual Identity

Courtesy of Google Images     Fair Use Law 17 U.S. Code § 107

# The Significance of Abraham:   It's Not Physical Descendancy

*"They said to Him, 'Abraham is our father.' Jesus said to them, 'If you were Abraham's children, you would do the works of Abraham.'"* John 8:39

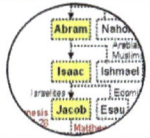

Abram / Nahor / Arabia / Muslim
Isaac / Ishmael
Israelites / Edom
Jacob / Esau
Matthew

*"Jesus said to them, 'If God were your Father, you would love Me, for I proceeded forth and came from God; nor have I come of Myself, but He sent Me.'"* (John 8:42)     John 5:22-23

*"Do not think to say to yourselves, 'We have Abraham as our father.' For I say to you that God is able to raise up children to Abraham from these stones."* Matthew 3:9

**Galatians 3:16**
*"Now to Abraham and HIS SEED were the promises made. He does not say, 'And to seeds', as of many, but as One, 'and to YOUR SEED', who is CHRIST."*

**Galatians 3:17**
*"The law, which was 430 years later, cannot annul the COVENANT that was confirmed before God IN CHRIST, that it should make the promise of no effect."*

**Galatians 3:18**
*"For if the inheritance is of the law, it is no longer of promise; but GOD GAVE IT TO ABRAHAM BY PROMISE."*

**Isaiah 53:10**
*"It pleased the Lord to crush Him; He has put Him to grief. When You make His soul an offering for sin, He shall see HIS SEED, He shall prolong His days, and the pleasure of the Lord shall prosper in His hand."*

Courtesy of Google Images     Fair Use Law 17 U.S. Code § 107

## "The Hourglass" ➔ God narrows His covenant to Abraham

- God personally acted in working out His plan for man with His unique promise to Abraham (Genesis 15:5).
- God promised him Messiah would come through his bloodline (Nehem. 9:7-8, Genesis 22:18, Galatians 3:16).
- Abraham obeyed God by not just trusting in what He said – he trusted in Him (Romans 4:20-22, Romans 4:18).

### Who I am in Christ = a child of Abraham

**Genesis 9:18-19** " Now the sons of Noah who went out of the ark were  Shem, Ham and Japheth. And Ham was the father of Canaan. These 3 were the sons of Noah, and from these the whole earth was populated.

**Genesis 10:32** " These were the families of the sons of Noah, according to their generations, in their nations, & from these the nations were divided on the earth after the flood."

**Genesis 15:5** "Then He brought him outside and said,'  Look now toward heaven, and count the stars if  you are able to number them.'  And He said to him, ' So shall your descendants be.  And he BELIEVED IN THE LORD, and He accounted it to him for righteousness."

**Nehemiah 9:7-8** " You are the Lord God, who chose Abram, and brought him out of Ur  of the Chaldees,  and gave him the name  Abraham; YOU FOUND HIS HEART FAITHFUL  before You, and made a covenant with him."

**Romans 4:20-22**  " He did not waiver at the promises of God through unbelief, but was strengthened in faith, giving glory to God, and being fully convinced  that what He had promised He was also able to perform. And therefore 'it was accounted to him for righteousness.'"

**Genesis 22:18** " In your seed all the nations of the earth shall be blessed,  because you have OBEYED My voice. "

**Galatians 3:16** "Now to Abraham & His Seed were the promises made. He does not say, 'And to seeds,'  as of many, but as One,  'And to your Seed, who is Christ."

**Romans 4:13** "… the promise that he would be the HEIR OF THE WORLD was not to Abraham or to his seed through the law, but through the  righteousness  of faith."

**Romans 4:18** "… who, contrary to hope, in hope believed, so that he became the FATHER OF MANY NATIONS, according to what was spoken,  So shall your descendants be.'"

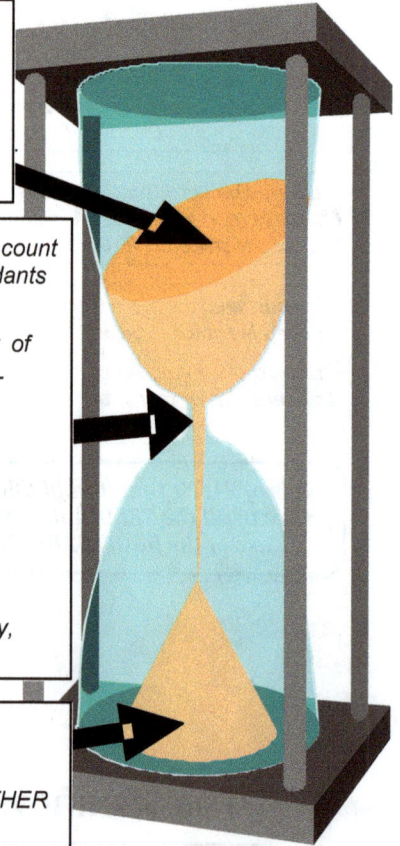

- **John 8:32-41 (Matt.3:9)**  The Jews think they are saved because they descend from Abraham. But God does not promise anything based on the flesh. Salvation is based on FAITH IN CHRIST, who is the Seed of Abraham: Gal. 3:7-9, 28-29   *"…only those who are of FAITH are sons of Abraham. The Scripture, foreseeing that God would justify the nations by faith, preached the gospel to Abraham beforehand, saying, 'In you all the nations shall be blessed.' So then those who are of faith are blessed with believing Abraham…There is neither Jew nor Greek, there is neither slave nor free, there is neither male nor female; for you are all one in Christ Jesus. If you are Christ's, then you are Abraham's seed, and heirs according to the promise."* (see Romans 9:6-8)

### God's *precision* (Romans 11:33) ➔ *The VIRGIN BIRTH*

Matthew ch 1: Jesus's *Deity* ("Son of God") by fulfilling OT requirement of descending from the house of David, since JOSEPH is in David's line. God made a covenant with David that His house would bring Messiah:

Matthew 1:1 *"The book of the genealogy of Jesus Christ, the Son of David, the Son of Abraham."*

2Samuel 7:16  *"…your house and your kingdom shall be established forever before Me…."*

Luke ch 3: Jesus' *humanity* ("Son of Man"), thus belonging not only to Israel but to the world, by tracing Jesus through MARY ➔ see Luke 2:1-5: she returned to Bethlehem because she descended from David).

1) Matt. 1:16 = Gr. relative pronoun "of whom" is *feminine singular*; Matthew shows the **virgin birth** thru Mary.

2) Luke 3:23 = only Joseph's name has no definite article ("as was supposed"); Luke shows the **virgin birth**.

3) Jeremiah 22:30 = King Jeconiah, an ancestor of Joseph (Matt. 1:11-12), was DISQUALIFIED from the throne. if Jesus was the physical son of Joseph, He would have inherited Jeconiah's curse.

4) But He was the physical son of David through MARY, not Joseph's seed – He inherited the throne of David without coming under the curse of Joseph's bloodline!

# Why ISAIAH is so Important for Understanding My Spiritual Identity:
## The Dead Sea Scrolls & Our Messiah Jesus Christ

IQIsaiah[a] =
oldest manuscript of a complete
Old Testament book, dating
**125 years before Christ**

The Isaiah A & B Scrolls
match word-for-word with
our standard Hebrew Bible
in **> 95% of the text**

**The IQIsaiah[a] Scroll:
One of the Greatest
Archaeological Discoveries**

**Isaiah details at least *79 Prophecies* describing God's
Future Messiah in just chapters 52-53 alone!**

*The Great Isaiah Scroll* (1:50)    *The God Who Speaks – The Dead Sea Scrolls* (3:54)    Courtesy of Google Images   Fair Use Law 17 U.S. Code § 107

# Why ISAIAH is so Important for Understanding My Spiritual Identity:
## The Dead Sea Scrolls & Our Messiah Jesus Christ

| | | |
|---|---|---|
| **God = Creator** | God created the earth and everything in it, and all of mankind, to be inhabited. | Isaiah 45:12,18 John 1:1-3 |
| **God = Sustainer** | God not only created all things, but He now holds everything in place. | Isaiah 40:25-26; Hebrews 1:3; Colossians 1:16-18 |
| **God = Sin-Bearer** | God is holy and cannot dwell with sin. So He takes my sin debt upon Himself. | Isaiah 53:5-6; John 1:29; Romans 6:23 |
| **God = Savior** | God delivers me from my sin that condemns me, which I can't fix by myself. | Isaiah 12:2-3, 45:22-23 Matthew 1:21 |
| **God = Shepherd** | God feeds and protects me like a shepherd; He knows I can't care for and defend myself. | Isaiah 40:10-11; John 10:11-15 |
| **God = Jesus Christ** | The Creator became a man, miraculously healed the sick, blind and lame, saved me from my sins, reconciled me to Himself, by His death in my place. | Isaiah 7:14, 9:6-7, 35:4-6, 50:4-7, 55:1-3; Romans 5:1; Luke 7:21-23; John 1:3,14,45; Matthew 11:28-30; John 4:13-14,7:37 |

Courtesy of Google Images    Fair Use Law 17 U.S. Code § 107    173

## The Book of Isaiah:  Who I am, Where I came from, Why I'm here

1) "Isaiah" (740-680 BC) means "The Lord is salvation"; he ministered in southern kingdom of Judah.

2) Isaiah is quoted in the NT > 65X (far more than any other OT prophet), mentioned by name in the NT > 20X.

3) Heb. 11:37… history records that he was martyred: cut in half with a wooden saw by King Manasseh in 680BC.

4) Isaiah's Warnings, Judgments and Future Hope:

- Chap. 1-35:  Judah and Jerusalem (their heartless, empty ritualism and deep Idolatry would result in captivity), and the surrounding pagan nations (rebellion against the Lord would be punished)
- Chap. 36-39:  History of Assyria and Babylon
- Chap. 40-48:  God's promise of future deliverance from Babylonian captivity
- Chap.49-57:  God's promise of the future "Suffering Servant", the Messiah
- Chap. 58-66:  God's promise of the future glory of His people:
  - God's plea to His people to forsake their sinful ways
  - God's conditional promise of salvation
  - God's conditional promise to answer their prayers

5) He is called the "Evangelistic prophet": God's salvation through His grace (>19 prophetic pictures of Christ).

6) **The Historical Accuracy and Reliability of Isaiah: The Dead Sea Scrolls and Isaiah "Great Scrolls"**

- The skeptics' charge: Since the oldest copies of Hebrew OT we have are 895A.D., how can we be sure of their accurate transmission since the time of Christ ( 32A.D.)? Didn't the disciples just add prophecies of Jesus into the book of Isaiah after His death, so there would be irrefutable evidence that He was the OT Messiah?

- THE INCREDIBLE EXACTNESS OF THE  2 ISAIAH SCROLLS (Isaiah "A", the Great Scroll, and "B"):

a) They are the oldest manuscripts of a complete book of the OT, dating before the time of Christ (125 B.C.). Isaiah "B" was found in Cave 1 at Qumran: 17 pieces of leather, sewn together to form a roll > 24 feet long.

b) The Isaiah Scrolls match word-for-word with our standard Bible in > 95% of the text (with the 5% being minor variations due to spelling changes over time).This not only demonstrates the incredible accuracy of the copyists of the Scriptures over this 1,000 year period, but the trustworthiness of the book of Isaiah!

**Qumran Cave #4**

**clay jar**

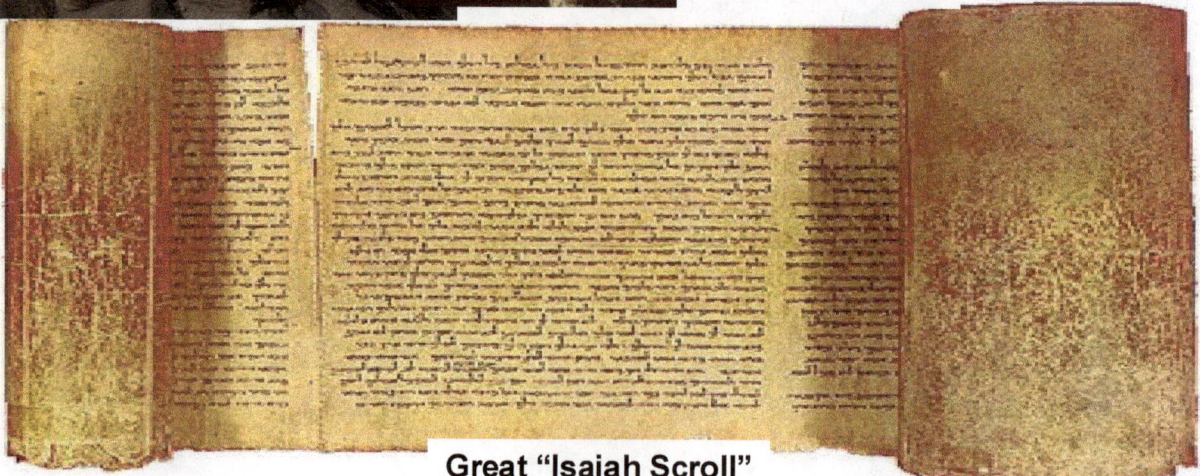

**Great "Isaiah Scroll"**

## Biblical Answers from ISAIAH:   Who am I?   Why am I here?   Where did I come from?

| | Subject | Description | ch., verse(s) |
|---|---|---|---|
| **WHO GOD IS — Where I came from —** | God = Creator | God inserts reminders of creation in His prophecies. He created the earth and everything in it, and all of mankind, to be inhabited | 45:8,12,18 48:12-13 |
| | God = Light | God created (*bara*) darkness (Psalm 104:20); since He is light (1John 1:5), He merely let light "be" (Gen. 1:3); God creates physical calamities on the earth when He deems it is needed (the Flood, earthquakes) | 45:7 |
| | God = Sustainer | God not only created all things, but after His creative work He continues to hold everything in place (Hebrews 1:1-3, Colossians 1:16-18) | 40:25-26 |
| | God = Sin-Bearer | God is holy (Lev. 19:2) and cannot dwell with sin (Ps. 5:4, Hab. 1:13). So He takes my sin upon Himself to pay my sin debt for me (Rom. 6:23) | 6:1-7  53:1-12 52:13-15 |
| | God = Healer and Redeemer | The God who created the universe, formed me in my mother's womb, became my Redeemer, ransomed me from my captivity in sin, and restored me to Him… to bring glory to His name (Exo. 15:26, Matt. 9:35) | 44:21-24 59:14-20  61:1-3 *YHWH RAPHA* |
| | God = Savior | God takes it upon Himself to deliver me from my sin that condemns me, which I can't fix (Exodus 15:2; Psalm 118:14,21; Matthew 1:21) | 12:2-3  45:22-23 *YHWH SHUA* |
| | God = Peace | When I surrender my life to Him. God goes from my enemy to my Father who deeply loves me (Judges 6:24, John 14:27, Romans 5:1) | 54:10 *YHWH SHALOM* |
| | God = Shepherd | Genesis 48:15 = He feeds and protects me (like a shepherd for his sheep); He knows I can't care for and defend myself. (John 10:11-15) | 40:10-11 *YHWH RAAH* |
| | God = Jesus Christ | The Creator (Prov. 8:27-30, John 1:3) became a man (John 1:14), saved me from my sins, reconciling me to Himself. By His love He pours out His mercy on me. He "despised mens' shame and endured the agony of the cross" (Heb. 12:2) – He set His face to humiliation for my sake. | 7:14    9:6-7 11:1-2    12:2 35:4-7    42:1-9 50:4-7    55:1-3 |
| | God = Recreator and Restorer | Although God cursed the physical earth (Genesis 3:17-19) with decay because of mankind's sin (Romans 8:19-22)…He will create a "new heaven and earth", where only righteousness dwells (Revelation 21:1-5) | 51:6 65:17-18 |
| | God = Judge | The "Day of Vengeance", a "Day of the Lord": God's wrath is poured out on an unrepentant world (1Thes. 5:8-9; 2Thes. 1:7-8; Rev. 15:1, 16:1) | 61:2  2:12,17 13:6-13 26:20-21 |
| **Why I'm here** | God = demands glory | God created (*bara*) me to glorify Him: I'm not here to be successful at work, sports, raising my kids…I'm here to glorify God (Matthew 5:16) | 43:1,7,21 |
| | God = Eternal and Sovereign | I think I am a "god", but I'm merely vapor and here on earth for a short time (Eccle. 1:1-4)…it is God who is eternal, and His ways are beyond my understanding – I am merely a "sheep of His pasture" (Psalm 100:3) | 40:6-8, 15-17 40:21-23 55:8-9 |
| | God = wants to be known | Not only is God a Faithful Witness, who gives me fulfilled prophecies that prove He is the true God, but He tells me how beautiful are those people who witness to others about His Lordship over all the earth | 52:7 41:26-27 43:8-13 44:6-8 42:9, 46:10, 48:3-8 |
| **Who I really am** | Satan = the 1st evolutionist | God created (*bara*) him to glorify Him. Satan rebelled against God as Creator by wanting to eliminate Him from creation and become like Him. He knows he'll lose (Ezek. 28:11-19, Gen. 3:15), and he hates God. He trembles at the implications of his refusal to trust in God (James 2:19) | 14:12-15 |
| | I am = rebel | Like Satan, I rebel against God and reject His rightful authority over my life; my sin separated me from Him who is holy and pure | 59:1-2,10-12 1:1-5 64:6-7 66:4 |
| | I am = lost | Without Christ to "open my spiritual eyes", I am blind and helpless – I am described as walking dead (Ephesians 2:1), already condemned at birth for my sins against God (Ps 51:5) | 59:9-10 6:8-10 44:18-20 |
| | I am = forgiven by God's grace through faith | God saves those who, by *humility*, confess their hopelessness in their sin, fear Him as their only hope, and *trust* in Him to redeem them: "wait" = OT for NT "trust" = continue steadfast in God's promises (Gen. 49:18, Prov. 20:22; Ps 27:14, 37:7-9, 130:5-6, 147:10-11; Micah 7:7) | 66:1-2 57:12-15 25:9  26:8-9 30:18  40:28-31 |

# Jesus Christ = The True Vine and Chief Cornerstone

### Isaiah 5:1-7    Israel = "God's Disappointing Vineyard"

*"Now let me sing to my Well-beloved a song of my Beloved regarding HIS VINEYARD: My Well-beloved has a vineyard on a very fruitful hill. He dug it up and cleared out its stones. And planted it with the choicest vine. He built a tower in its midst, and also made a winepress in it; so He expected it to bring forth good grapes, but it brought forth wild grapes. And now, O inhabitants of Jerusalem and men of Judah, judge, please, between Me and My vineyard. What more could have been done in it? Why then, when I expected it to bring forth good grapes, did it bring forth wild grapes?*

*And now, please let Me tell you what I will do to My vineyard: I will take away its hedges, and it shall be burned; and break down its wall, and it shall be trampled down. I will lay it waste; IT SHALL NOT BE PRUNED or dug, but there shall come up briers and thorns. I will also command the clouds that they rain no rain on it.*

*For THE VINEYARD OF THE LORD OF HOSTS IS THE HOUSE OF ISRAEL, and the men of Judah are His pleasant plant. He looked for justice, but behold, oppression; for righteousness, but behold, wailing."*

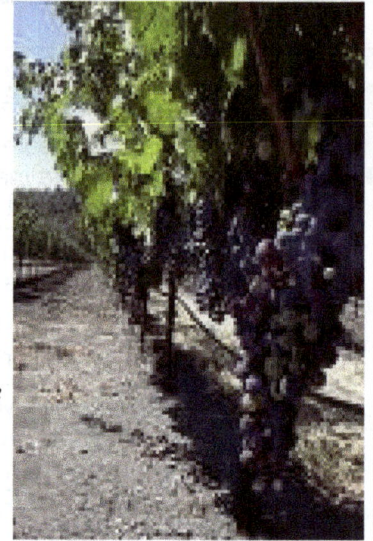

## Growing a Jewish vineyard:

1) The stones are removed and used to build a protecting wall and the bases of watchtowers (Isa 5:2; Mt 21:33).

2) The wine press is cut in a rock at the surface.

3) The vinestocks lie along the ground, many of the fruit-bearing branches falling over the terraces (Gen. 49:22) and sometimes supported on poles to form a bower (1 Kings 4:25).

4) The vineyard requires constant care or the fruit will very soon wither. The ground must be plowed and cleared of weeds- contrast with this the vineyard of the sluggard (Proverbs 24:30-31).

5) In early spring the vines must be pruned by cutting off dead and fruitless branches (Leviticus 25:3,4; Isaiah 5:6), which are gathered and burned (John 15:6).

6) As the grapes ripen, the watchman is stationed in one of the towers overlooking the vineyard, to keep off jackals and foxes (Song of Solomon 2:15), and wild boars (Psalm 80:13).

7) Harvest time: owner's family lives in a booth built on one of the towers. It is a happy time (compare Isaiah 16:10).

8) Gleanings are left for the poor (Levit. 19:10; Deut. 24:21; Judges 8:2; Isaiah 17:6; 24:13; Jerem. 49:9; Micah 7:1).

9) In late summer the vineyards are a beautiful mass of green, as contrasted with the dried-up parched land around, but in the autumn the leaves are dried up and yellow (Isaiah 34:4), and the place desolate.

## God's Old Testament use of the *"VINE"* :

1) "Choicest, noble vine" = Hebr. "*soreq*" (Isaiah 5:2, Gen. 49:11, Jerem. 2:21) = dark, sweet, stoneless grapes.

2) A fruitful wife is compared to a vine (Psalm 128:3).

3) Men rejoiced in wine as one of God's best gifts (Judges 9:13; Psalm 104:15).

4) Israel is a vine brought out of Egypt (Psalm 80:8; Jerem. 2:21; Jerem.12:10; compare Ezek. 15:2,6; Ezek.17:6).

5) Jacob's blessing on Judah spoke of the land he was to inherit as suitable to grow the vine (Genesis 49:11).

6) Joseph "is a fruitful bough; his branches run over the wall" (Genesis 49:22).

7) The land God promised to Israel was one of "vines and fig trees and pomegranates" (Deuteronomy 8:8).

8) Israel inherited vineyards from God as gifts, which they had not planted (Deut. 6:11; Josh. 24:13; Nehem. 9:25).

9) A successful and prolonged vintage signified God's blessing (Leviticus 26:5).

10) Every man "under his vine and his fig-tree" (1 Kings 4:25; Micah 4:4; Zech. 3:10) signified peace and prosperity.

11) To plant vineyards and eat its fruit meant long and settled habitation (2 Kings 19:29; Psalm 107:37; Isaiah 37:30; Isaiah 65:21; Jeremiah 31:5; Ezekiel 28:26; Amos 9:14).

12) To plant and not eat the fruit was a misfortune (Deuteronomy 20:6; compare 1 Corinthians 9:7) and a sign of God's displeasure (Deuteronomy 28:30; Zephaniah 1:13; Amos 5:11).

13) Not to plant vines was a sign of deliberate avoidance of permanent habitation (Jerem. 35:7).

14) A failed vine meant God's wrath (Psalm 78:47; Jeremiah 8:13; Joel 1:7); or a test of faith in Him (Habak. 3:17).

15) "Wild grapes" = be'ushim (Isaiah 5:2,4) = worthless fruit from the vine, of no value.

16) "Vine of Sodom" (Deuteronomy 32:32) = "an unhealthy vine, tainted by corruption like Sodom".

## Isaiah 5:1-7 (Psalm 80)

• In Hebrew: God came to the vineyard looking for *mishpat* (justice), but found *mispach* (bloodshed); for *tsedaqah* (righteousness), but heard *tse'aqah* (cries of distress).

• Isaiah 5 was designed to explain why God could no longer withhold judgment from his own people; they were greedy and proud, experts in food and drink but ignorant of God and his ways. So the vineyard would be left to go wild, to reap the results of its own chosen way.

• God graciously chose Israel as His vineyard and provided for the vine's productivity and protection, so He was justified in expecting a good yield from His investment. But the vine's produce was "sour", inedible and useless. As punishment for her unfruitfulness, Israel became desolate and open to any nation wanting to invade her. First, Babylon invaded in 6BC, and this will happen repeatedly until her national repentance at the 2nd coming of Christ.

## Why is God so harsh with His chosen people?

• **Ezekiel 16:14-15** *"Your fame went out among the nations because of your beauty, for it was perfect through My splendor which I had bestowed upon you," says the Lord God. "But you trusted in your own beauty, played the harlot because of your fame, and poured out your harlotry on everyone passing by who would have it."*

• **Ezekiel 36:20-23** *"When they came to the nations, wherever they went, they profaned My holy name – when they said of them, 'These are the people of the Lord, and yet they have gone out of His land.' But I had concern for My holy name, which the house of Israel has profaned among the nations wherever they went. Therefore say to the house of Israel, 'Thus says the Lord God: I do not do this for your sake, O House of Israel, but for My holy name's sake, which you have profaned among the Gentiles wherever you went. I will sanctify My great name, which has been profaned among the nations, which you profaned in their midst; and the nations shall know that I am the Lord', says the Lord God, 'when I am hallowed in you before their eyes."*

> God protects HIS NAME: He won't allow His character to be slandered by those claiming to belong to Him.
> God is a SAVIOR: nations watching Israel reject Him because of how His people portray Him (**Ezekiel 16:27**).

## Matthew 21:33-46  What makes this parable different from the others He tells?

"vineyard" = Israel      "vinedressers" = religious leaders      "servants" = the OT prophets      "son" = Jesus Christ

• In many parables, Jesus leaves them to puzzle things out, giving extra insight to His followers (Matt.13:10-13).

• But in this parable, everybody knows what he's saying.
  - The chief priests and Pharisees want to kill Him all the more, because they understand that Jesus has cast them as the wicked tenant farmers, and Himself as the son.
  - Like most of Jesus' parables, the story doesn't just convey information; it causes the situation it describes.

• Jesus develops Isaiah 5 to explain why it is that God can no longer withhold judgment from the Israel of his day. This time, there is a new twist to the story. It isn't just that God comes to the vineyard looking for grapes.
  - He has sent messengers to get them, and they've been ignored, ill-treated, stoned and even killed.
  - Jesus is telling the story of Israel and showing that it has come to its true climax, in Him and his work: He is the Prophet as well as the owner's Son, the heir to the estate, coming to the vineyard on the owner's behalf.
  - God as the owner now sends his son, supposing that they will respect Him. They throw him out and kill him.

• **Matthew 21:40-41** Jesus ends his story with a question: what will the vineyard owner do?
  - They give Him the answer: He will come and take the vineyard away from the tenants, and give it to others.
  - The Jewish leaders pronounce judgment on themselves. *Their verdict* against the "evil vinedressers" in the parable is *Christ's verdict* against them.

## Matthew 21:42   Jesus = "Rejected Stone" (His death) = "Chief Cornerstone" (His resurrection)

• The "rejected stone" refers to Christ's crucifixion, and the "chief cornerstone" refers to His resurrection.

• Jesus connects **Psalm 118:22-23** with **Isaiah 28:16** to tell them the Son who was killed and thrown out of the vineyard was also the "chief cornerstone" in God's redemptive plan.

• God's judgment on Israel comes later in the form of the Roman Empire: it is the direct result of what the Jews had chosen. They will not have the vineyard owner as their king, so they end up with the princes of this world.

• **Matthew 21:43** The kingdom and all spiritual advantages are given to "other vinedressers" = the CHURCH.
  Romans 11:11 *"...have they stumbled that they should fall? Certainly not! But through their fall, to provoke them to jealously, SALVATION HAS COME TO THE GENTILES."*
  1Peter 2:9-10 *"...you are a CHOSEN GENERATION, a royal priesthood, a holy nation, His own SPECIAL PEOPLE, that you may proclaim the praises of Him who called you out of darkness into His marvelous light; who once were not a people but are now the people of God, who had not obtained mercy but now have obtained mercy."*

## JESUS =    The "True Vine"                                    John 15:1-5

*"I am the TRUE VINE, & My Father is the vinedresser. Every branch in Me that does not bear fruit He takes away; & every branch that bears fruit HE PRUNES, that it may bear more fruit. You are already clean because of the word which I have spoken to you. Abide in Me, & I in you. As the branch cannot bear fruit of itself, unless it abides in the vine, neither can you, unless you abide in Me. I am the vine, you are the branches. He who abides in Me, & I in him, bears much fruit; for without Me you can do nothing."*

What we see in a vineyard is the vine & its fruit. But it is the vine's intricate & deep ROOTS that no one sees which sustain it through good & bad times. The longer the grapes abide on the vine, and the riper they become, the longer they have time to absorb essential nutrients from the ground

3"

8"

This layer contains permanent humus & is the zone where the vine draws water & mineral s. There are a lot of vine roots here.

2'

Only loose, weathered stony material. Fewer vine roots (ones here are for water absorption).

3.5'

Mostly solid rock. Very few roots penetrate - these supply the vines with water in the driest years. Vine roots can grow to a depth of 15 feet in their search for water.

5'

### Does my life reflect that I am fruit on The Vine?

**Eph. 2:10** *"...we are His workmanship, created IN CHRIST JESUS for good works, which God prepared beforehand that we should walk in them."*

**Eph. 1:12** *"...we who have first trusted IN CHRIST should be to the praise of His glory."*

**Matt. 5:16** *"Let your light so shine before men that they may see your good works & glorify your Father in heaven."*

**Isaiah 61:3** *"...that they may be called TREES OF RIGHTEOUSNESS, the planting of the Lord, that He may be glorified."*

### Do I draw my strength from the Vine?

**Prov. 24:10** *"If you faint in the day of adversity, then your strength is small.."*

**Phil. 4:13** *"I can do all things through CHRIST who STRENGTHENS me."*

**Prov. 8:14** *"Counsel is Mine, & sound wisdom: I (Christ) am understanding - I have STRENGTH."*

**1Sam. 30:6** *"...David was greatly distressed, for the people spoke of stoning him, because the soul of all the people was grieved, every man for his sons & his daughters. But David strengthened himself IN THE LORD HIS GOD."*

**Eph. 3:16-17** *"...He would grant you, according to the riches of His glory, to be STRENGTHENED with might through His Spirit in the inner man, that Christ may dwell in your hearts through faith; that you, being ROOTED & grounded in love, may be able to comprehend with all the saints what is the width & length & depth & height - to know the love of Christ which passes knowledge; that you may be filled with all the fullness of God. Now to Him who is able to do exceedingly abundantly above all that we ask or think, according to the POWER that WORKS IN US..."*

**Col. 2:6-10** *"As you have therefore received Christ Jesus the Lord, so walk IN HIM, rooted & built up IN HIM & established IN THE FAITH, as you have been taught, abounding IN IT with thanksgiving. Beware lest any one cheat you through philosophy & empty deceit, according to the tradition of men, according to the basic principles of the world, & not according to Christ. For IN HIM dwells the fullness of the Godhead bodily, & you are complete IN HIM, who is the head of all rule & authority."*

---

**The "PRUNING" Process**      "PRUNE" = *kathairo* = to cleanse, as in purging; similar to *katharos* ("purify").

**John 15:2** God works in His children's lives to "prune", or "purge" anything hindering fruit-bearing: *"Every branch in Me that does not bear fruit He takes away; and every branch that bears fruit* **He prunes**, *that it may bear more fruit.'*

- God chastises His children to cut away sin that drain spiritual life, just as the farmer removes anything on the branches that keep them from bearing maximum fruit.
- But with whom God does not have a personal relationship, He does not discipline or prune.
- This is what happened to Israel in **Isaiah 5:6** when they rejected Him – He stopped Fatherly discipline, and left them to themselves: *"I will lay it waste;* ***it shall not be pruned*** *or dug, but there shall come up briers and thorns."*

**Hebrews 12:5-11    God's message to me:  His goal for my life is my HOLINESS, not my happiness**

*"My son, do not despise the chastening of the Lord, nor be discouraged when you are rebuked by Him; for WHOM THE LORD LOVES HE CHASTENS, and scourges every SON whom He receives. If you endure chastening, God deals with you as with sons; for what son is there whom the father does not chasten? But if you are WITHOUT CHASTENING, of which all have become partakers, then you are ILLEGITIMATE and NOT SONS. Furthermore, we have had human fathers who corrected us, and we paid them respect. Shall we not much more readily be in subjection to the Father of spirits and live? For they indeed for a few days chastened us as seemed best to them, but He for our profit, that WE MAY BE PARTAKERS OF HIS HOLINESS. Now no chastening seems to be joyful for the present, but painful; nevertheless, afterward it yields the PEACEFUL FRUIT OF RIGHTEOUSNESS to those who have been trained by it."*

# Jesus Christ = My Spiritual Identify = My True Vine

## Isaiah 5:1-7 = God's 'Disappointing Vineyard'

- what God wanted = 'good grapes'          ⇦ Justice, Righteousness
- what God got = 'wild grapes'          ⇦ Bloodshed, wailing
- what God does = 'no more pruning'

## Matthew 21:33-46 = Jesus retells Isaiah 5

- The Vineyard =                    The nation of Israel
- The Vinedressers =                Religious Leaders
- Owner's servants He sends =       The OT prophets
- Owner's son He sends =            Jesus Christ

## John 15:1-5 = God's 'Chosen Vine'

- The Vine          ⇦ Jesus Christ
- The Branches      ⇦ Those attached to the Vine
- Abiding           ⇦ Stop working!.... Be rooted, resting
- Pruning           ⇦ Only if attached (Romans 11)

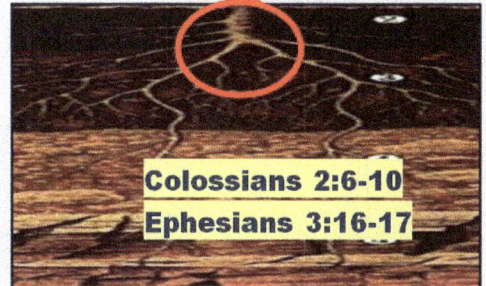

Colossians 2:6-10
Ephesians 3:16-17

Francis Chan: 'I am the True Vine - just stay connected' (4:15)

## Exit Ticket #16        Class 16: Who Am I?  Part 2

| | |
|---|---|
| 1) What are 3 reasons God chose Israel? | 2) Explain the "Hourglass" as a picture of God's Spiritual Identity for mankind? |
| 3) Why are the Dead Sea Scrolls critical to Christians understanding their spiritual identify? | 4) Of the 27 Scriptures in this lesson, which 2-3 scriptures resonate with you the most and why? |

# Class 17:  The Gospel, Part 1

What is the Gospel?

What Beliefs are Essential to be a Christian?

The Gospel: 8 Studies on God's Truth

The Gospel: A Christ-Centered Worldview

The Gospel: Faith-Based

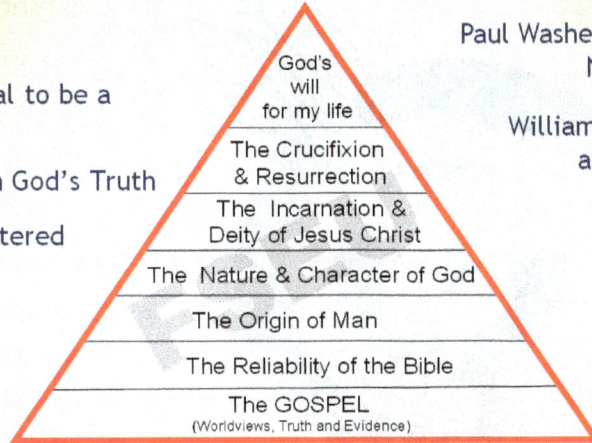

Paul Washer: 'The Gospel is only Good News to a Needy man' (9:15)

William Lane Craig: 'What good is apologetics in a postmodern culture?' (4:55)

God's will for my life

The Crucifixion & Resurrection

The Incarnation & Deity of Jesus Christ

The Nature & Character of God

The Origin of Man

The Reliability of the Bible

The GOSPEL
(Worldviews, Truth and Evidence)

## HEBREWS 11:1

"Faith = *Substance* of things hoped for.... *Evidence* of things *not seen*"

fse.life Lessons 02 - 08

---

## What was it that *drew you* to the Gospel?

## For me, the most important thing about the Gospel is that it is TRUE.

# The Essence of the Christian Worldview = The GOSPEL

## What *essential beliefs* must a person hold, to become a Christian?

The "centermost circle" of the target contains the six core **ESSENTIALS** as defined in the Bible that any person must confess to belief in, in order to be saved and call themselves by the name "Christian".

1) Existence of God
2) Deity of Jesus Christ
3) The Atonement
4) Repentance from my sin
5) The Death, Burial & Resurrection of Jesus Christ
6) "Sola Fidei" = Salvation is by God's Grace alone, through my faith in the Lord Jesus Christ alone.

**The Gospel by John MacArthur:** *"He [the Father] made Him [the Son] to be sin who knew no sin, so that in Him we might become the righteousness of God"* (2 Cor. 5:21).

*"Jesus was guilty of nothing. Yet on the cross, the Father treated Him as if He had committed personally every sin ever committed by every individual who would ever believe.*

*Though He was blameless, He faced the full fury of God's wrath, enduring the penalty of sin on behalf of those He came to save. In this way, the sinless Son of God became the perfect substitute for the sinful sons of men.*

*As a result of Christ's sacrifice, the elect become the righteousness of God in Him. In the same way that the Father treated the Son as a sinner, even though the Son was sinless, the Father now treats believers as righteous, even though they were unrighteous.*

*Jesus exchanged His life for sinners in order to fulfill the elective plan of God. And He did it so that, in the end, He might give back to the Father the love gift that the Father gave to Him."*

1) **The Existence of God (Hebrews 11:6, Psalm 14:1)** –    BOOKS 1 & 4
   I must believe that God exists (I cannot be an atheist and call myself a Christian).

2) **The Deity of Christ – The Incarnation (John 1:1,14, John 8:56-59)** –    BOOK 3
   I must believe Jesus Christ is God who revealed Himself to mankind (as promised in Scripture).

3) **The Atonement (John 1:29, Mark 10:45, 1Corin. 15:3, 2Corinthians 5:21)** –    BOOK 4
   I must believe Jesus atoned for my sins by dying *for* me, thus paying the ransom owed to God the Father (to satisfy His standard for holiness).

4) **Repentance (Luke 13:3,5; Acts 11:18, 2Corinthians 7:9-10)** –    BOOK 4
   I must admit I am a sinner and be willing to repent (turn from my sin and turn to Jesus Christ as my only means to be forgiven by God).

5) **The Death, Burial and Resurrection of Jesus Christ (1Corinthians 15:1-22)** –    BOOK 3
   I must believe Jesus Christ died for my sins and was buried, then rose physically from the dead, to not only affirm my faith in a risen Savior but to make Him my "first fruits" (vs. 20) of my new life ("born again": only by His resurrection can I now be resurrected to new life *in Him*).

6) **"Sola Fidei" = Salvation is by God's grace alone through my faith in the Lord Jesus Christ alone (John 3:16, Romans 1:17, Ephesians 2:8)** –    BOOK 4
   I must actively trust *in* Him (who He is = God the Son) and *in* what He accomplished *for* me (dying for my sins and rising from the dead), by willingly surrendering the control of my life into His hands.

# What is the Gospel?

*"He (the Father) made Him (the Son) who <u>knew no sin</u> to <u>be sin for us</u> ...*

*so that we (you and me) might become the righteousness of God (the Father) in Him (the Son)."*
2Corinthians 5:21

Are there *Essentials* a person must believe to become the "Righteousness of God in Christ"?

**The Protestant Reformation – The 5 'Solas':**

1) 'Sola Deo Gloria' = To God Alone be the Glory
2) 'Sola Scriptura' = Understood only in God's Word...
3) 'Sola Fidei' = Salvation is by faith alone
4) 'Sola Christus' = in Jesus Christ alone
5) 'Sola Gratia' = apart from works, by God's grace alone

Paul Washer: 'The Gospel is only Good News to a Needy man' (9:15)

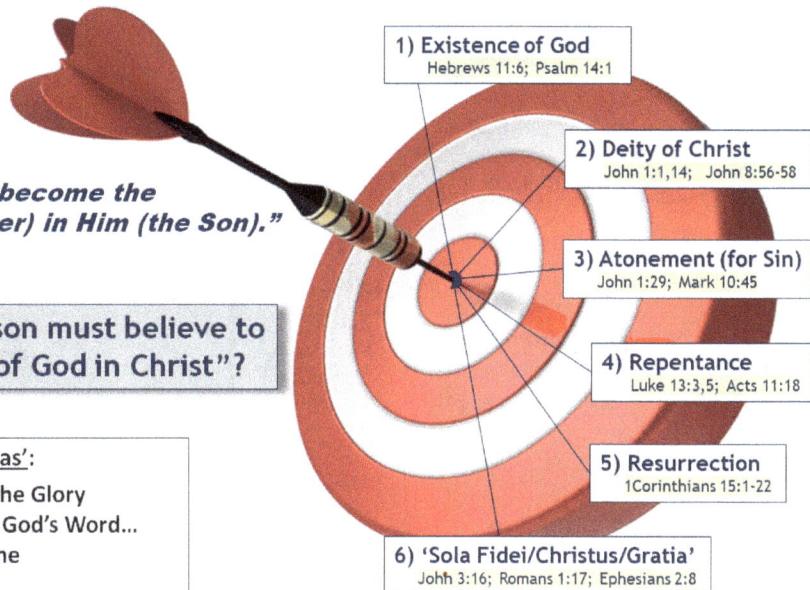

**1) Existence of God**
Hebrews 11:6; Psalm 14:1

**2) Deity of Christ**
John 1:1,14; John 8:56-58

**3) Atonement (for Sin)**
John 1:29; Mark 10:45

**4) Repentance**
Luke 13:3,5; Acts 11:18

**5) Resurrection**
1Corinthians 15:1-22

**6) 'Sola Fidei/Christus/Gratia'**
Johh 3:16; Romans 1:17; Ephesians 2:8

Courtesy of Google Images    Fair Use Law **17 U.S. Code § 107**

## The Christian mandate = Emphasizing the Essentials

In his article 'Representing Christ to a Postmodern World'[17], Michael Patton explains how to distinguish between what are the essential tenets of the Christian faith versus those things that may be interesting but not essential:

"What beliefs are the ***'sine qua non'*** (without which, not) of the true Christian? What are the essentials of the Christian faith versus the non-essentials? Concerning salvation, we need to be able to state exactly what the Bible says is essential for salvation — *what exactly is the content of what a person needs to believe to be saved.* Does one simply have to "believe in the Lord Jesus" (Acts 16:31)? If so what does that entail? What does one have to know about Christ? Does he have to know that He is God? Does he have to believe that Christ vicariously took his place on the cross? Does he have to believe *and* turn from his sin? Or does he just have to believe, as the thief on the cross did, that Christ was the messianic King going to His Kingdom? Do you have to believe in the Trinity, the virgin birth, the inspiration of Scripture, the Second Coming of Christ, or the existence of Hell? Are these all doctrines (the "list") that the unbeliever must accept *before* he or she is considered a believer? It is extremely important that we categorize just exactly what the Bible says about salvation.

The "4-Block" Chart: Help me define what I consider Relative vs. Objective, Essential vs. Non-Essential

This chart (below) has two broad categories, each divided into two sections. Following are the category definitions. Observe the patterns on the chart as you read.

1. **True Relativity**: Everything that exists on the left side of the quadrant is truly relative. It is either completely independent of right or wrong, or the right or wrong is determined by the situation.

  a. *Situational Relativity*: The right and the wrong of those in this category are dependent upon the culture, time, situation, or some other variable. Its sinfulness was dependent upon the cultural expression. The same sin may be expressed in our culture but in a different way.

  b. *Autonomous Relativity*: This category contains those that are truly relative. There is no right or wrong. This category is filled with opinions and customs that are not right nor wrong. One's opinion on the best song is an example of something that is autonomously relative. There is no one correct answer — it's always relative.

2. **True Objectivity**: Everything on the right side has a definite right or wrong. There is always an objective truth that is true no matter whether one believes it. It is not dependent upon time, culture, or any situation. It exists as true or false in and of itself. All biblical principles and doctrines belong on this side.

  a. *Essential Objectivity*: This category contains only those that are essential for salvation. This should contain only those truths which you believe a person must accept to be considered a true Christian.

  b. *Non-Essential Objectivity*: This category contains doctrinal and non-doctrinal issues which are not necessary for one's salvation. An example is the gift of tongues. Tongues either did or didn't cease. The truth is objective. But it is non-essential because it is not necessary to believe one way or the other to be saved.

## "4-Block" Chart

**Situational Relativity**
- Wearing a head covering
- Home Schooling
- Eating meat sacrificed to idols
- Drinking a glass of wine/ beer
- Going to the movies

**Essential Objectivity**
- Deity of Christ
- The Existence of God
- Repentance
- The Atonement
- Death, Burial and Resurrection of Christ
- Faith Alone in Christ as Lord & Savior

**True Relativity** ◄──────► **True Objectivity**

**Autonomous Relativity**
- Best type of church music (traditional, contemporary, rock, etc.)
- Favorite place to eat out
- Best Song
- Best book of the Bible
- Temperature of a room (hot, cold, warm)

**Non-Essential Objectivity**
- Views on Predestination (Calvinism, Arminianism)
- The Date of Christ's return
- Author of Hebrews
- Young - vs - Old Earth
- O.T. Canon
- Cessation of Sign Gifts (tongues, healing, etc.)

---

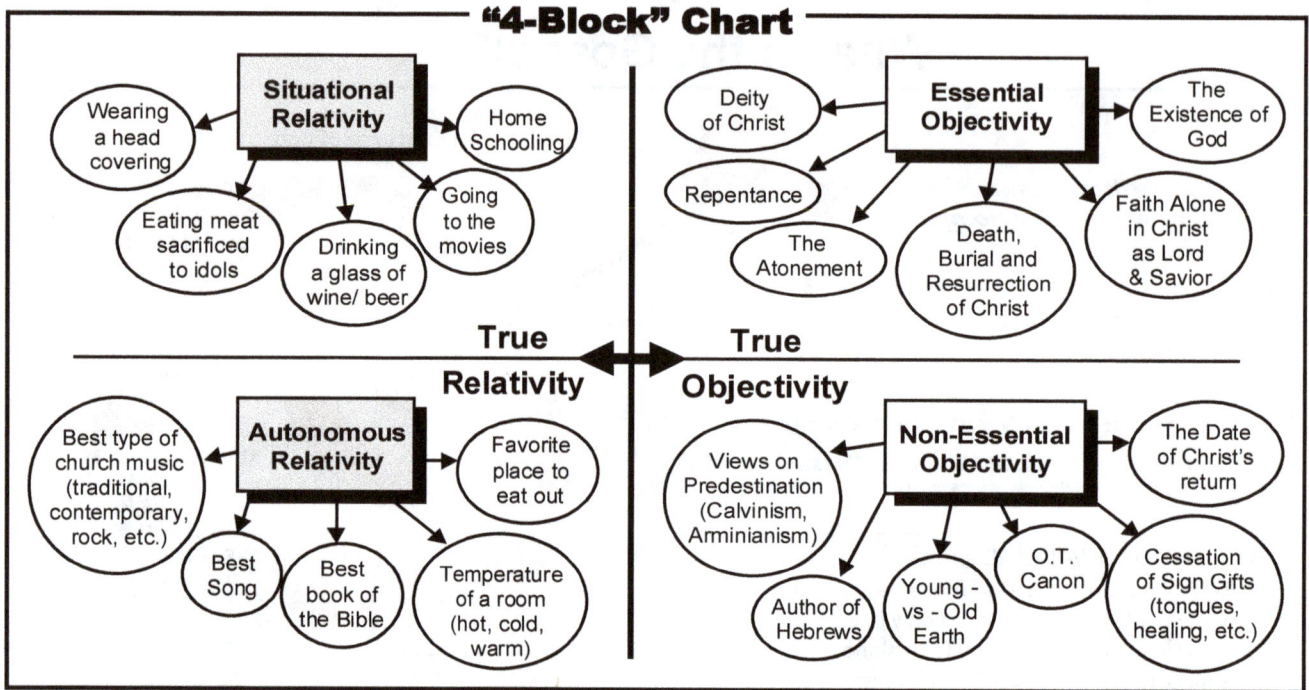

**Construct my own chart:** When issues arise, decide the category in which they belong. BE CRITICAL OF MYSELF. This chart is extremely valuable in understanding that these categories exist. It is not an ironclad never-fail chart that I can use in all situations. My chart will probably look different from the one shown.

**The value of my chart:** It shows the necessity of THINKING ABOUT THESE THINGS MORE DEEPLY. I live in a postmodern culture in which people live their lives on the left side of the quadrant (relativism). I have a Church that wants to counter by living on the right side (objectivism). Being familiar with the principles of this chart allows me to express truth in a more RELEVANT fashion.

## A big problem within the Church = we major in the MINORS

Many Christians overly stress their views on certain issues to an unbelieving postmodern, giving them the wrong impression. We express our opinions about having a glass of wine or some other area just as emphatically as we would the resurrection of Christ. We will argue all day long with the unbeliever about the theory of evolution and never tell them about Christ. We never even give them a chance to believe what is most important.

Let me make this clear: There is nothing wrong with discussing or even debating the non-essentials, but we must keep in mind that the non-essentials do not save. They can be used as primers or springboards for the Gospel, but they cannot replace it. We must get to the Gospel in every witnessing opportunity we have.

Eleven of the twelve sermons in Acts contain the death, burial, and resurrection of Christ. The only one that did not was Stephen's, and if it were not cut short, he surely would have presented the risen Christ to the Sanhedrin. It is imperative that we emphasize the Gospel; it is the only message that contains eternal life. We must understand that convincing someone of any area outside of the objective essential will not save them.

Another Value of the "4-Block" chart = place emphasis where emphasis is due: We have to continually ask ourselves what things we have placed as ESSENTIALS in our lives. If too much emphasis is placed on the non-essentials, it makes the essentials less important. We destroy the "object of our enthusiasm"- the Gospel.

Most people's lives are filled with opinions, pet peeves and disputes. When the unbelieving postmodern looks at you, what would he say that you have in italics in your life? We should have very few things that we greatly emphasize in order to save our stress for the things that really matter. We can give no greater honor to Christ than to emphasize the things that He emphasized."

---

**The list of the 6 Essentials of the Gospel is NOT intended to be dogmatic.**

**The intention of the "List" = to make you THINK**

**As John Stott said, can I clearly and accurately share the GOSPEL?**

**Do I focus on the "majors"... or do I focus on the "minors"?**

## Essential #1 has become a Contradiction in Terms ➜ "CHRISTIAN ATHEISM"

Are there people out there today who would describe themselves as "Christian Atheists"? Believe it or not, the answer is yes. For most of us, this sounds like a contradiction in terms. So what is a Christian Atheist?

Thomas Ogletree (Assistant Professor of Constructive Theology, Chicago Theological Seminary), explains the four common beliefs of a "Christian Atheist":

1) the UNREALITY OF GOD for our age, including traditional Christian theology's understandings of God

2) the need to RESHAPE the Christian message to fit in contemporary culture

3) varying degrees and forms of SEPARATION from today's church

4) the importance of centralizing the person of JESUS in theological reflection

**1) Unreality of God**  Christian atheists believe that there is no God because there is no evidence of Him. In essence, Christian atheists are MODERNISTS – they generally do not believe in things which cannot be proven empirically. To them, God has ceased to be "a 'need fulfiller' and 'problem solver'". Most Christian atheists believe that God never existed, but there are a few (such as Thomas J.J. Altizer) who believe in the death of God literally (not only is God absent, but that His death was an actual historical event). Most Christian atheists do not tend to see God's death literally, though. They see it in the non-literal, atheistic sense. When they say that God is dead, they mean that there is not and never has been such a Being.

**2) Reshaping Christianity to fit the culture**  Christian atheism was created by theologians who attempted to reconcile Christianity and America's increasingly secular culture. Theologians looked at the scientific, empirical culture of today and tried to find religion's place in it. They reject the current state of the Christian message and want to make Christianity more meaningful to people in the modern world. Colin Lyas, a Philosophy lecturer at Lancaster University, stated that "*Christian atheists are united also in the belief that any satisfactory answer to these problems must be an answer that will make life tolerable in this world, here and now and which will direct attention to the social and other problems of this life*". They want something that will help them with life now rather than a religion whose focus is on things of the next life. According to them, people living in today's world are skeptical and can no longer believe in such a Being as God. Instead of looking to the past, they say that Christians must look to the future and reshape theology to fit current culture.

**3) Separation from the church**  Christian atheists believe that the way to true Christianity is through the culture of the world and not the worship of God. They see religions which withdraw from the world as moving away from TRUTH. They say that a belief in God is an escape from the world around us. To a Christian atheist, God is a restrictive and illogical idea; it keeps people from connecting with the world around them. One of the major problems Christian atheists have with Christian beliefs is how ABSOLUTE they are. Christian atheists are RELATIVISTS; they believe that what's true depends on each person's own views and on the cultural circumstances. They criticize Christians for their hypocrisy, by separating themselves from the world. Christian atheists see separating from the world as separating from what a Christian is supposed to be, which is someone who suffers along with everyone else in the world.

THE DESCENT OF THE MODERNISTS

CHRISTIANITY
BIBLE NOT INFALLIBLE
MAN NOT MADE IN GOD'S IMAGE
NO MIRACLES
NO VIRGIN BIRTH
NO DEITY
NO ATONEMENT
NO RESURRECTION
AGNOSTICISM
ATHEISM

**4) The centrality of Jesus** Most Christian atheists think of Jesus as a wise and good man, accepting His moral teachings but rejecting the idea of His divinity. They look to Jesus as an example of what a Christian should be, but they do not see him as a God. Instead of seeing Jesus as the way to heaven, Christian atheists see Him as the way to humanity. To them, following Jesus means being "alongside the neighbor, being for him". So, to follow Jesus means to be human, to help other humans, and to further mankind. In doing this, they see Jesus as an example of a really good human being, nothing more. They want to become the kind of human being Jesus was; they want to be thoroughly human.

**Psalm 14:1   *"The fool has said in his heart, 'There is no God.'"***

# The Gospel: 8 Studies on God's *TRUTH*

**Is Christ-Centered**
John 5:39

**Is Faith-Based**
Genesis 15:5-12,17

**Turns Greeks into Jews**
Acts 2,17

**Is Rational**
Acts 17:2-4

**Uses People to Reach People** 2Peter 2:5

**Is Only for the Weak**
1Corinthians 1:26-29

**Has One Essential**
Colossians 1:26-27

**Must be Scattered**
Matthew 13:3-8

Courtesy of Google Images    Fair Use Law 17 U.S. Code § 107

## John 12:19   The Gospel: A Christ-Centered Worldview

*"The Pharisees.. said among themselves, 'You see that you are accomplishing nothing. Look, the ① WORLD has gone after Him!'"*

① WORLD = Greek *"kosmos"* = mankind and their world system which is alienated from and in opposition to God

### John 12: "A Clash of Worldviews"

| The Religious Elite | Jesus Christ |
|---|---|
| They (and everyone else) believed they were righteous and destined for heaven. | He openly rebuked them as unrighteous and destined for hell Matthew 5:20. |
| They instituted a manmade legal system that everyone must follow to please God. | He preached repentance over personal sin for restoration with God Mark 1:15. |
| They claimed their laws came from God as His requirements for personal righteousness. | He claimed to not only be the Law but that He came to fulfill the Law John 8:51. |
| They claimed God-given authority to judge. | He claimed to be God John 8:56-58. |
| They claimed to know truth concerning God. | He claimed to be Truth John 14:6. |
| They claimed to know the way to eternal life. | He claimed to be Eternal Life John 11:25. |
| They claimed to be God's shepherds. | He claimed to be the Shepherd John 10:11. |

Courtesy of Google Images    Fair Use Law 17 U.S. Code § 107

## John 12:19 The Gospel = Creating a Christ-centered worldview

*"The Pharisees.. said among themselves, 'You see that you are accomplishing nothing.
Look, the ①WORLD HAS GONE AFTER HIM!'"*

① WORLD = Gr. *"kosmos"* = mankind and mans' world system which is alienated from and in opposition to God

John 3:16-17 *"God so loved the ①WORLD that He gave His only begotten Son, that whosoever believes in Him should not perish but have everlasting life. For God did not Send His Son into the ①WORLD to condemn the ①WORLD, but that the ①WORLD through Him might be saved."*

John 7:7 *"The ①WORLD cannot hate you; but it hates Me because I testify of it that its works are evil."*

### The context of John chapter 12: A Clash of Worldviews

"worldview" = the window by which a person views and decides what is real and valuable, unreal and worthless.

1) Jesus confronted the religious elite with who He is by His actions (healing the blind man, raising Lazarus) and His words (the Light of the world, the Door to heaven, the Bread of eternal life) .

2) Jesus turned everyone's worldview upside down: people followed Him because His words and actions fit their worldview; the religious elite felt threatened because the "world" followed Him, not them.

3) Jesus' message = John 12:32 ➔ His sacrificial death on the cross will draw *all people* to Him (John 3:14-15) and fulfill God's requirement for the only way for anyone to be righteous in His eyes.

| John ch. 12: "A Clash of Worldviews" ||
| --- | --- |
| **The Religious Elite** | **Jesus Christ** |
| They (and everyone else) believed they were righteous and destined for heaven | He openly rebuked them as unrighteousness and destined for hell (Matt. 5:20, Matt. 16:12) |
| They instituted a man-made legal system that everyone was required to follow to please God | He preached heartfelt repentance over personal sin for forgiveness and restoration back to God (Mark 1:15) |
| They claimed their laws came from God as His requirements for personal righteousness | He claimed to not only be the Law but that He came to fulfill the law for our sakes (John 8:51, Matt. 5:17) |
| They claimed God-given authority to judge rightly | He claimed to be God (John 8:56-58) |
| They claimed to know truth concerning God | He claimed to be Truth (John 14:6) |
| They claimed to know the way to eternal life | He claimed to be Eternal Life (John 11:25-26) |
| They claimed to be God's shepherds to the people | He claimed to be the Shepherd (John 10:11) |

John chapter 12 shows a worldview system centered around Jewish culture... but it applies to any culture. Now.... jump forward in time 2,000 years to the culture in America today –

| America Today: "A Clash of Worldviews" |||
| --- | --- | --- |
| **Secular Humanism** | ⇆ | **Biblical Christianity** |
| Cosmology: the universe is self-existing and not created | ⇆ | Cosmology: the effect of the universe's existence must have a suitable CAUSE |
| Morality: modern science's universe is self-existing; supernatural guarantees of human values are unacceptable | ⇆ | Morality: man's built-in sense of right and wrong can be accounted for only by an innate awareness of a code of law IMPLANTED by God |
| Rational: man is a part of nature and has emerged as a result of a continuous process | ⇆ | Rational: the operation of the universe, by order and natural law, implies a MIND behind it |
| Ontology: realizing my personality is the end of life; the goal is its development and fulfillment now | ⇆ | Ontology: man's ideas of God imply a God who IMPRINTED such a consciousness |
| Teleology: man is the result of a blind and random process that does not require any kind of meaning | ⇆ | Teleology: the design of the universe implies a PURPOSE behind it |
| Humanism: foundation is in the teaching of Evolution | ⇆ | Christianity: foundation is in teaching the Bible |

**N. Pearcey[3]: A Worldview must fit with Reality** *"If our worldview doesn't fit the larger reality we're trying to explain, then at some point we will find that WE CANNOT FOLLOW IT. C.S. Lewis once wrote, 'The Christian and the Materialist hold different beliefs about the universe. They can't both be right.'"*

**N. Pearcey, 'Total Truth'[3]:  "The Best Way to debunk a false worldview is to offer a Good One"**
*"When the only form of cultural commentary Christians offer is moral condemnation, no wonder we come across to nonbelievers as angry and scolding. The best way to drive out a bad worldview is by offering a good one, and Christians need to move beyond CRITICIZING culture to CREATING culture. Whether we work with our brains or with our hands, whether we are analytical or artistic, whether we work with people or with things, in every calling we are CULTURE-CREATORS, offering up our work as a service to God."*

---

**Christian Worldview: ① God's Creation ➜ ② mans' Fall ➜ ③ mans' Redemption**

- Genesis 1:27-28 =  God originally *created* me to subdue the earth in *His name*
- Romans 3:23 =  My sin short-changed God of *His glory* He would have revealed through me
- Ephesians 4:22-24 =  God is *sanctifying* me to restore *His name*

Effective Evangelism = giving solid answers to the same fundamental questions

Question #1 – CREATION:  "How did it all begin? Where did we come from?"

Question #2 – FALL:  "What went wrong? What is the source of evil and suffering?"

Question #3 – REDEMPTION:  "What has been done about it? How will the world be set right again?"

---

## America Today: 2 Reasons for Creation as the starting point for Evangelism

Today, as we address the biblically illiterate Americans of the 21st century, we need to follow Paul's model (in Acts 17), building a case from Creation before expecting people to understand the message of sin and salvation.

Reason #1:  in our secular culture, starting with the Fall renders the rest of our message incoherent

"In an earlier age, when most Americans were brought up in the church, they were familiar with basic theological concepts. When people said, 'You're a sinner', they had the context to understand what it meant, and many were moved to repentance. But contemporary Americans often have no background in biblical teaching – which means that the concept of sin makes no sense to them. The response is likely to be, *'What right does God have to judge me? How do you even know He exists?'"*

Reason #2:  in our secular culture, starting with the Fall doesn't allow us to explain Redemption

"The goal of Redemption is to restore us to our original created state. If it were true that we are worthless, and that being sinners is our core identity, then in order to have something of value God would have to destroy the human race and start over. But He doesn't do that; instead He restores us to the high dignity originally endowed at Creation – recovering our true identity and renewing the image of God in us."

---

### Today's World: A Battleground for the Souls of People

"Picture the world as God's territory by right of CREATION. Because of the FALL,  it has been invaded and occupied by Satan and his minions, who constantly wage war against God's people. At the central turning point in history, God Himself, the 2nd Person of the Trinity, enters the world in the person of Jesus Christ and deals Satan a deathblow through His resurrection. The enemy has been fatally wounded; the outcome of the war is certain; yet the occupied territory has not actually been liberated.

There is now a period of time where God's people are called to participate in the follow-up battle, pushing the enemy back and reclaiming territory for God. This is the period in which we now live – between Christ's resurrection and the final victory over sin and Satan. Our calling is to apply the finished work of Christ on the cross to OUR LIVES and the world around us, without expecting perfect results until Christ returns."

---

## Today's Evangelism: Fulfilling Psalm 126:1-6  Compassion Towards Those Trapped in our Culture

*"When the Lord brought back the captivity of Zion, we were like those who dream. Then our mouth was filled with laughter, and our tongues with singing. Then THEY SAID AMONG THE NATIONS, 'The Lord has done great things for them.' The Lord has done great things for us, whereof we are glad... Those who SOW IN TEARS shall reap in joy. He who continually goes forth WEEPING, bearing seed for sowing, shall doubtless come again with rejoicing, bringing his sheaves with him."*

"Even when Schaeffer raised serious criticisms in our culture, he expressed a burning compassion for people caught in the trap of false and harmful worldviews. 'These works of art are the expression of men struggling with their lostness. Dare we laugh at such things? Dare we feel superior when we view their tortured expressions in their art? The men and women who produce such things are dying while they live; yet where is our compassion for them?' How many Christians reach out in compassion? How many do the hard work of crafting real answers to their questions? How many cry out to God on behalf of people struggling in the coils of false worldviews?""

---

**Ps 107:2** *"Let the redeemed of the Lord say so,  whom He has redeemed from the hand of the enemy."*

# America Today:   A Clash of Worldviews

| Secular Humanism | Biblical        Christianity |
|---|---|
| Cosmology: the universe is self-existing and not created. | Cosmology: the effect of the universe's existence must have a suitable *CAUSE*. |
| Morality: modern science's universe is self-existing; supernatural guarantees for human values are unacceptable. | Morality: man's built-in sense of right and wrong can be explained only by an innate awareness of a moral code *IMPLANTED* by God. |
| Rationality: man is part of nature and has emerged from a continuous process. | Rationality: the operation of the universe, by order and natural law, implies a *MIND*. |
| Ontology: realizing my personality is the end of life; the goal is its development and fulfillment now. | Ontology: man's ideas of God imply a God who *IMPRINTED* such a consciousness. |
| Teleology: man is the result of a blind, unguided material process that does not require any meaning. | Teleology: the design of the universe implies a *PURPOSE* behind it. |
| Knowledge Transfer: foundation is in the teaching of evolution. | Knowledge Transfer: foundation is in the teaching of the *BIBLE*. |

**Why are these 2 so polarizing?**

*'The Christian and the Humanist hold different beliefs about the universe. They can't both be right'* C.S. Lewis

William Lane Craig: 'What good is apologetics in a postmodern culture?' (4:55)

Courtesy of Google Images    Fair Use Law 17 U.S. Code § 107

---

# Genesis 15:5-12,17      God's Gospel is Faith-Based

## Abrahamic Covenant

Covenant = *'diatheke'*

"to divide by a *sacrifice* to *secure* the promise made"

**Verses 5-7**
God makes an UNCONDITIONAL PROMISE to Abraham and secures it by a COVENANT that puts His own life as the security; He then credits him as righteous (the Gospel) because he trusts IN Him.

Smoking Oven = God's Presence (Exodus 19:17-18)

Burning Torch = God's Salvation (Isaiah 62:1)

1) It's not a contract.

2) It's not a commitment.

Contracts and commitments are just obligations with limited consequences if broken.

3) It's a Covenant: *'may what happened to these animals happen to Me, if I break My promise'.*

**Verse #12**
God puts Abraham to sleep because the covenant does not involve a vow from Abraham!

**GALATIANS 3:8,14**
*"The Scripture, foreseeing that God would justify the nations by faith, preached the GOSPEL to Abraham beforehand…"*

*The blessing of Abraham might come on the Gentiles in Christ Jesus, to receive the PROMISE of the Spirit through FAITH."*

**Verse #17**
Only God passes between the animals - the Covenant of Justified by *GRACE* through *FAITH*.

Courtesy of Google Images    Fair Use Law 17 U.S. Code § 107

## Genesis 15:5
## Romans 4:18 } Abraham: Father of Many Nations by *FAITH*

*"... who, contrary to hope, in hope believed, so that he became the FATHER OF MANY NATIONS, according to what was spoken, 'So shall your descendants be'". (Genesis 15:5)*

*"Now the sons of Noah who went out of the ark were Shem, Ham and Japheth. And Ham was the father of Canaan. These 3 were the sons of Noah, and from these the whole earth was populated." Genesis 9:18-19*

*"You are the Lord God, who chose Abram, and brought Him out of Ur of the Chaldees, and gave him the name Abraham; You found his heart faithful before You, and made a COVENANT with him." Nehemiah 9:7-8*

*"In your seed all the nations of the earth shall be blessed, because you have obeyed My voice." Genesis 22:18*

*"Now to Abraham and his Seed were the promises made. He does not say, 'And to seeds', as of many, but as One, 'and to your Seed', who is Christ."*
                    Galatians 3:16... Genesis 3:15... Genesis 12:3

*"It is of FAITH that it might be according to GRACE, so that the promise might be sure to all the SEED, not only to those who are of the law, but also to those who are of the faith of ABRAHAM, who is the father of us all..."* **Romans 4:16**

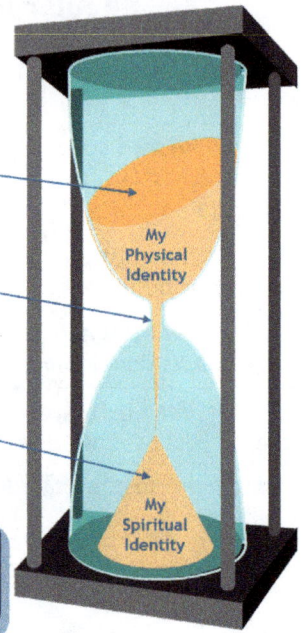

My Physical Identity

My Spiritual Identity

Courtesy of Google Images     Fair Use Law **17** U.S. Code § 107

---

## Exit Ticket #17
## Class 17: The Gospel Part 1

**When it comes to Essential Beliefs to be Christian, In Which Quadrant Should Each of These Go?**

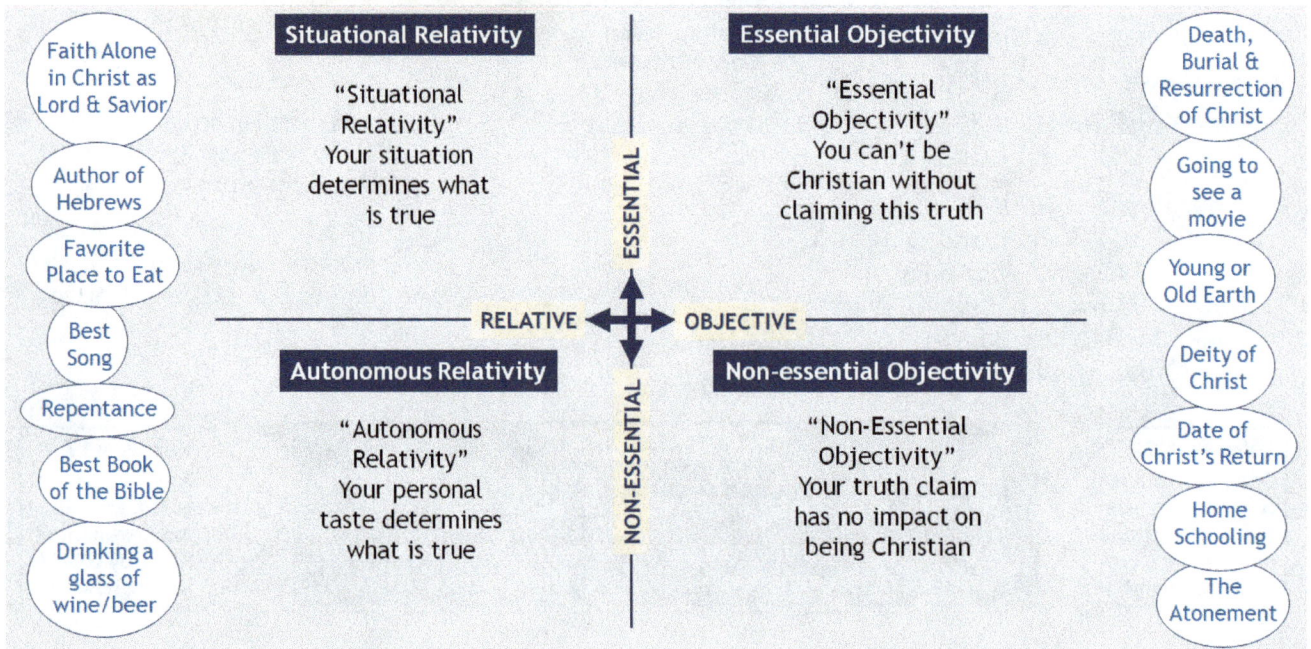

Faith Alone in Christ as Lord & Savior

**Situational Relativity**

"Situational Relativity" Your situation determines what is true

**Essential Objectivity**

"Essential Objectivity" You can't be Christian without claiming this truth

Death, Burial & Resurrection of Christ

Author of Hebrews

Favorite Place to Eat

ESSENTIAL

Going to see a movie

Young or Old Earth

Best Song

RELATIVE ⬌ OBJECTIVE

Repentance

Deity of Christ

**Autonomous Relativity**

"Autonomous Relativity" Your personal taste determines what is true

**Non-essential Objectivity**

"Non-Essential Objectivity" Your truth claim has no impact on being Christian

Date of Christ's Return

Best Book of the Bible

NON-ESSENTIAL

Home Schooling

Drinking a glass of wine/beer

The Atonement

**Exit Ticket #17**          <mark>**Class 17: The Gospel  Part 1**</mark>

| SITUATIONAL RELATIVITY | ESSENTIAL OBJECTIVITY |
|---|---|
| | |
| **AUTONOMOUS RELATIVITY** | **NON-ESSENTIAL OBJECTIVITY** |
| | |

# Class 18:  The Gospel, Part 2

The Gospel: Turning Greeks into Jews

The Gospel: Rational

Jim Warner Wallace: 'Is Christianity Rational?' (3:40)

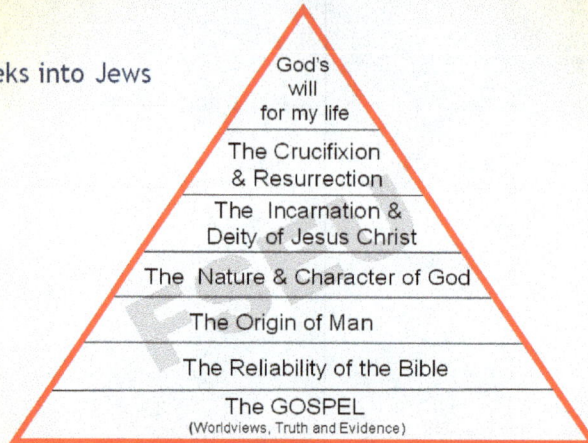

God's will for my life

The Crucifixion & Resurrection

The Incarnation & Deity of Jesus Christ

The Nature & Character of God

The Origin of Man

The Reliability of the Bible

The GOSPEL
(Worldviews, Truth and Evidence)

## HEBREWS 11:1

"Faith = *Substance* of things *hoped for.... Evidence* of things *not seen*"

fse.life Lessons 02 - 08

## The Gospel:  8 Studies on God's *TRUTH*

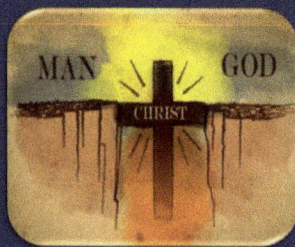

**Is Christ-Centered**
John 5:39

**Is Faith-Based**
Genesis 15:5-12,17

**Turns Greeks into Jews**
Acts 2,17

**Is Rational**
Acts 17:2-4

**Uses People to Reach People** 2Peter 2:5

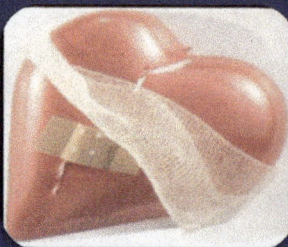

**Is Only for the Weak**
1Corinthians 1:26-29

**Has One Essential**
Colossians 1:26-27

**Must be Scattered**
Matthew 13:3-8

## 1Corinthians 1:22-23   The Gospel: Greeks-to-Jews

*"...①JEWS request a ②SIGN, and ③GREEKS seek after ④WISDOM; but we ⑤PREACH Christ crucified, to the Jews a ⑥STUMBLING BLOCK and to the Greeks ⑦FOOLISHNESS."*

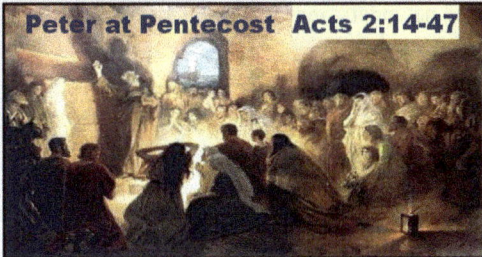
Peter at Pentecost  Acts 2:14-47

Paul at Mars Hill Acts 17:16-32

① JEWS = *"Ioudaios"* = originates from Israel's son Judah Genesis 49:8-12

② SIGN = *"sēmeion"* = a supernatural indication; a miracle Mark 8:11-12

③ GREEKS = *"Hellēn"* = an inhabitant of Hellas; a non-Jew; a Gentile

④ WISDOM = *"sophia"* = human wisdom (earthly, natural)

⑤ PREACH = *"kērussó"* = publicly proclaim

⑥ STUMBLING BLOCK = *"skandalon"* = scandal; snare; thing that offends

⑦ FOOLISHNESS = *"mõria"* = silliness; absurdity (the English word "moron")

Courtesy of Google Images    Fair Use Law 17 U.S. Code § 107

## Acts 2:14-47 vs. Acts 17:16-32   The Gospel: Turning Greeks-to-Jews

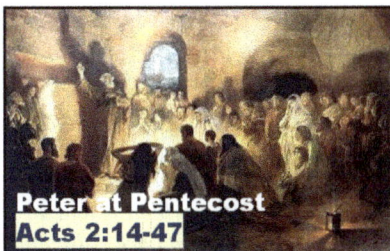
Peter at Pentecost Acts 2:14-47

*"'Let all the house of Israel know assuredly that God has made this Jesus, whom you crucified, both Lord and Christ.'*

*When they heard this, they were cut to the heart, and said to Peter and the rest of the apostles, 'Men and brethren, what shall we do?'*

*Peter said to them, 'Repent, and let every one of you be baptized in the name of Jesus Christ for the remission of sins...'*

*Then those who gladly received his word were baptized, and that day about 3,000 were added to them."* Acts 2:36-38,41

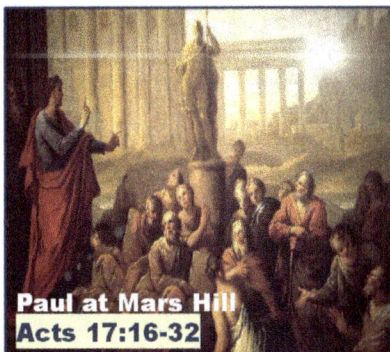
Paul at Mars Hill Acts 17:16-32

*"Paul reasoned with the Gentile worshipers, and in the marketplace daily with those who happened to be there.*

*Certain Epicurean and Stoic philosophers encountered him. Some said, 'What does this babbler want to say?' Others said, 'He seems to be a proclaimer of foreign gods' because he preached to them Jesus and the resurrection.*

*They took him and brought him to Mars Hill, saying, 'May we know what this new doctrine is of which you speak? For you are bringing strange things to our ears... we want to know what these things mean.'*

*When they heard of the resurrection of the dead, some mocked, while others said, 'We will hear you again on this matter.'... some joined him and believed."* Acts 17:17-20,32-34

Courtesy of Google Images    Fair Use Law 17 U.S. Code § 107

## Acts 2:14-47 vs. Acts 17:16-32  The Gospel: Turning Greeks-to-Jews

### Peter & the Jews  Acts 2:14-47

**Cosmology:** the Jews believed the world was created by the Old Testament God.

**Morality:** they understood sin and mankind's fall (they knew what God expected and that they fell short).

**Rationality:** they had the Old Testament Law & the Prophets, which were held sacred as God's Word.

**Ontology:** they believed they needed a sacrifice for their sin to have a right relationship with God.

**Teleology:** man is God's special creation who can know Him and gain eternal life by righteous living.

**The JEWS**
- Already believed both Creation and Sin.
- Convicted that Jesus's death and resurrection solved their Sin Problem.
- 3,000 gave their lives to Christ

### Paul & the Greeks  Acts 17:16-32

**Cosmology:** Greek philosophers knew nothing of the Old Testament God of creation.

**Morality:** they had no understanding of sin being breaking God's standard of moral holiness.

**Rationality:** they used their own reasoning (the Jewish Scriptures held no value).

**Ontology:** they had no understanding of a God who demanded their personal sin be paid for by a perfect sacrifice.

**Teleology:** Epicureanism = man evolved from the dirt and his life has no eternal meaning or purpose.

**The GREEKS**
- No foundation in Creation and Sin.
- Jesus's death and resurrection is just 'babbling'.
- No one responded to Paul's message

Courtesy of Google Images    Fair Use Law **17 U.S. Code § 107**

## 1Corinthians 1:22-23    The Gospel = Turning Greeks into Jews

*"…①JEWS request a ②SIGN, and ③GREEKS seek after ④WISDOM; but we ⑤PREACH Christ crucified, to the Jews a ⑥STUMBLING BLOCK and to the Greeks ⑦FOOLISHNESS."*

① JEWS = Gr. "*Ioudaios*" = originates from JUDAH (Hebrew *"Yehudah"*) in Genesis 49:8-12; Judah was one of Jacob's (Israel's) children - his descendants were called Yehudim ("Judahites"). The word ***"Jew"*** is a shortened form of the word "Judahite"). A "Jew" in the OT would be a "Judahite;" and a "Jew" in the NT would be a "Judean."

② SIGN = Gr. "*sēmeion*" = a supernatural indication; a miracle

Mark 8:11-12  "Jesus rebukes hard-hearted people (they demand a sign in order to believe in Him)"
*"..the Pharisees came out and began to dispute with Him, seeking from Him a SIGN from heaven, testing Him. But He sighed deeply in His spirit, and said, 'Why does this generation seek a sign?'"*

Matthew 11:2-6  "Jesus encourages sincere seekers to pay attention to the OT signs"
*"...when John had heard in prison about the works of Christ, he sent 2 of his disciples and said to Him, 'Are You the Coming One, or do we look for another?' Jesus answered and said to them, 'Go and tell John the things which you hear and see: the blind receive their sight and the lame walk; the lepers are cleansed and the deaf hear; the dead are raised up and the people have the gospel preached to them. And blessed is he who is not OFFENDED because of Me,'"*

Luke 10:13  "Jesus' miracles should have brought repentance and belief (not testing)"
*"Woe to you, Chorazin! Woe to you, Bethsaida! For if the MIGHTY WORKS* (Gr. "*dunamis*" = power; miracles) *which were done in you had been done in Tyre and Sidon, they would have repented long ago, sitting in sackcloth and ashes."*

John 5:39-40 "Use OT Messianic miracles and prophecies as the evidence that Jesus is Messiah"
*"You search the Scriptures, for in them you think you have eternal life, and these are they which TESTIFY OF ME. But you are NOT WILLING to come to Me, that you may have life."*
This is the essence of what Paul means in 1Corinthians 1:22 – the Jews have the OT Scriptures: they were given much detailed evidence by Jesus that He fulfilled the OT requirements for Messiah. But it boils down to a person's *will*, to choose to respond to His offer for eternal life and surrender their life to His control.

③ GREEKS = Gr. "*Hellēn*" = an inhabitant of Hellas; a Greek-speaking person; a non-Jew; a Gentile

④ WISDOM = Gr. "*sophia*" = human wisdom (earthly, natural)

⑤ PREACH = Gr. "*kērussó*" = herald (as in publicly crying out); proclaim; publish

⑥ STUMBLING BLOCK = Gr. "*skandalon*" = snare; cause for displeasure or sin; thing that offends

⑦ FOOLISHNESS = Gr. "*mōria*" = silliness; absurdity (where we get the English word "moron")

Why have western countries continually declined in Christian morality, despite numerous evangelistic campaigns? It comes down to understanding the difference between 'Jews' and 'Greeks'.

**Acts 2:14-47**    "Peter's message to Jews = God's Messianic fulfillment in Christ through His signs and wonders"

- Peter's audience = Jews who believed in the OT God of creation
  a) they knew what God expected of them and knew they fell short (they understood sin and mankind's' fall)
  b) they had the Law of Moses (God's Word was sacred in their eyes)
  c) they understood the need for a sacrifice for sin
  d) they weren't indoctrinated with evolutionary ideas
- Peter's main message = Jesus' death and resurrection and mankind's need for salvation
- Peter's results = 3,000 people responded

> The Jews understood creation and sin: both are necessary to understand the message of salvation (Peter didn't have to convince them that God was Creator or that man had sinned – he concentrated on the cross)

**Acts 17:16-21**    "Paul's message to Greeks = Jesus' death and resurrection are sufficient for salvation"

- Paul's audience = Greek philosophers who knew nothing of the OT God of creation
  a) they believed in many gods
  b) Jewish Scriptures had no value to them
  c) they had no understanding of sin and had no understanding of their need for a sacrifice for sin
  d) their culture was based on evolution (Epicureans, the atheists of their day, believed man evolved from dirt)
- Paul's main message = same as Peter's
- Paul's results = no one responded – they labeled him a 'babbler' (they brought him to Mars Hill)

> The Greeks had no foundational knowledge of God as Creator and mankind' sin; God's Word had no value to them (Paul's preaching was completely foreign to them – they saw it as foolishness)"

### Paul's message to Greeks (Acts 17:22-32) = God created man to seek Him and know Him

➔ vs. 22-23 "Paul focuses them on the one 'unknown God' they worship"

*"...Paul stood in the midst of the Areopagus and said, 'Men of Athens, I perceive that in all things you are very religious; for as I was passing through and considering the objects of your worship, I even found an altar with this inscription: 'To the Unknown God'. Therefore, the One whom YOU WORSHIP WITHOUT KNOWING, Him I proclaim to you: ....*

➔ vs. 24-25 "Paul identifies this 'Unknown God' as the true and only Creator of all"

*"God, who MADE THE WORLD and everything in it, since He is Lord of heaven and earth, does not dwell in temples made with hands. Nor is He worshipped with men's hands, as though He needed anything, since He gives to all life, breath, and all things."*

➔ vs. 26-28 "Paul credits this 'God' with creating all men from one blood, challenging their evolutionary ideas"

*"He has MADE FROM ONE BLOOD every nation of men to dwell on all the face of the earth, and has determined their preappointed times and the boundaries of their habitation, so that THEY SHOULD SEEK THE LORD, in the hope that they might grope for Him and find Him, though He is not far from each one of us; for in Him we live and move and have our being, as also some of your own poets have said, 'For we are also His offspring.'*

➔ vs. 29-32 "Paul calls them to repent (change their worldview), and returns to Christ and His resurrection"

*"Therefore, since we are the offspring of God, we ought not to think that the Divine Nature is like gold or silver or stone, something shaped by art and MAN'S DEVISING. Truly, these times of ignorance God overlooked, but now commands all men everywhere to REPENT, because He has appointed a day on which He will judge the world in righteousness by THE MAN whom He has ordained. He has given us assurance of this to all by RAISING HIM FROM THE DEAD. And when they heard of the resurrection of the dead, some mocked, while others said, 'We will hear you again on this matter.'"*

> ### Paul's challenge is the same today - turning 'Greeks' into 'Jews'
>
> In his article 'On Darwin and Evolution'[20], Ken Ham explains the challenge Christians have today is the same challenge Paul faced in the early days of Christianity: "Unlike Peter, Paul had to take pagan, evolutionist Greeks and change their entire way of thinking about life and the universe, and then get them to think like Jewish people concerning the true foundation of history.
>
> No wonder only a few came to Christ at first. Such a change is dramatic. Imagine trying to get an Australian Aborigine to think like an American. Such a change would be extremely difficult to say the least.

Generations ago: the culture was somewhat like that of the 'JEWS'. People were familiar with their Bible. Most knew the basic concepts of Christianity concerning creation, sin and the message of salvation. When an evangelist preached the message of the cross, it was somewhat like Peter preaching to the Jewish people in Acts 2. Most people had the foundational knowledge to understand the message and respond accordingly.

But most church leaders didn't understand that people who were responding were already 'Greeks' in their thinking about reality. Students were being taught evolutionary ideas in a low-key way that was undermining the credibility of the Bible's history. Consequently, there was no real, lasting impact on western culture, which has become more anti-Christian.

Underneath it all, people had questions about the validity of the Bible.... and evolution is taught as fact throughout the education system. Generations of people now have little or no knowledge of the Bible. They have been thoroughly indoctrinated in an atheistic, evolutionary philosophy.

Western culture today: no longer one of mainly 'JEWS' but is more like 'GREEKS' – genuine, pagan 'Greeks' – increasingly anti-Christian with a predominantly atheistic, evolutionary, secular philosophy.

Children don't automatically go to Sunday School or church programs as they used to. Ministers of religion find it more difficult to conduct programs in schools. And most church leaders tell their congregations its fine to believe in evolutionary ideas, as long as God is somehow involved. After years of subtle indoctrination and an emphasis on rejecting the book of Genesis as literal, generations today doubt the reliability of the entire Bible.

**How can we reach today's 'GREEKS'?**

STEP 1 = their faulty foundation of evolution needs to be rebuilt:  they need to understand and believe that the Bible's account of creation and the fall of man (i.e., that man is a sinner) is true.

STEP 2 = once they have the foundation, they can better understand the message of the Messiah who came to provide forgiveness for them by being the final blood sacrifice for their sin.

### Effectively Evangelizing our American Culture

**#1.  The cross will  not be understood until people can be changed from 'Greeks' into 'Jews'.**

**#2.  Today's culture needs answers from the Bible and science to counter evolutionary teaching.**

**#3.  Teach Genesis 1-11 as literal history, to return the gospel's credibility in our 'Greek' culture.**

# Acts 17:2-4, 18:4  The Gospel is Rational

*"Paul, as his custom was, went in to them, and for 3 Sabbaths ①REASONED with them from the Scriptures, ②EXPLAINING and ③DEMONSTRATING that the Christ had to suffer and rise again from the dead, and saying,*

*'This Jesus whom I ④PREACH to you is the Christ.' And some of them were ⑤PERSUADED... And he reasoned in the synagogue every Sabbath, and persuaded both Jews and Greeks."*

① REASONED = "*dialegomai*" = to bring together different views in open discussion

② EXPLAINING = "*dianoigó*" = to open up completely or expound upon

③ DEMONSTRATING = "*paratithēmi*" = to present; to bring forward

④ PREACH = "*kataggellô*" = to challenge with the facts or evidence

⑤ PERSUADED = "*peithô*" = to convince of the truth with the evidence or by authority

Jim Warner Wallace: 'Is Christianity Reasonable?' (4:58)

## Acts 17:2-4, 18:4   The Gospel = A *Reasoned* Presentation of Jesus Christ

*"Paul, as his custom was, went in to them, and for 3 Sabbaths ①REASONED with them from the Scriptures, ②EXPLAINING and ③DEMONSTRATING that the Christ had to suffer and rise again from the dead, and saying, 'This Jesus whom I ④PREACH to you is the Christ.' And some of them were ⑤PERSUADED... And he reasoned in the synagogue every Sabbath, and persuaded both Jews and Greeks."*

① REASONED = Gr. "*dialegomai*" = to bring together different viewpoints and reckon them up in open discussion

② EXPLAINING = Gr. "*dianoigó*" = to open up completely or expound upon

③ DEMONSTRATING = Gr. "*paratithēmi*" = to place alongside or present; to set before (to bring forward the truth)

④ PREACH = Gr. "*kataggellô*" = declare; proclaim; challenge with facts (different than teach: 'present the facts')

⑤ PERSUADED = Gr. "*peithô*" = to convince by argument or debate; to consent to evidence or authority

---

In his book 'Basic Christianity'[34], John Stott explains how Paul, In Romans 10:14-17, argues for "the necessity of preaching the gospel if people are to become Christians. Sinners are saved, he says, by calling on the name of the Lord Jesus. That much is clear. But...

> Question #1 = How can men call on someone in whom they have no faith?
> Question #2 = And how can they have faith in someone of whom they have never heard?
> Question #3 = And how can they hear of Him unless a preacher tells them?

He concludes his argument: 'So faith comes from what is heard, and hearing comes by preaching Christ.'

His argument implies that there must be a SOLID CONTENT in our evangelistic proclamation of Christ. It is our responsibility to set Jesus Christ forth in the fullness of His divine-human person and saving work so that through this 'preaching of Christ' God may arouse faith in the hearer. Such evangelistic preaching is far removed... from what is all too common today, namely an emotional, anti-intellectual appeal for 'decisions' when the hearers have but the haziest notion what they are to decide about or why."

---

### Two New Testament Reasons for a Rational Proclamation of the Gospel:

Reason #1 = to "persuade men" (Acts 17:2-4, 18:4)

• to "persuade" = to marshal arguments in order to prevail on people to change their mind about something.

• Paul was teaching DOCTRINE and arguing toward a conclusion (he sought to convince in order to convert).

Reason #2 = to "respond to the truth" (Ephesians 1:12-13)

• becoming a Christian is "believing the truth", "obeying the truth", "acknowledging the truth".

• early Christian evangelists, in preaching Christ, were actually teaching DOCTRINE ("truth") about Christ.

### The Gospel is not Academic – its Rational:

• The gospel is for everybody, whatever their education or lack of it... the kind of evangelism for which I am pleading, which sets Jesus Christ forth in His fullness, is relevant to all kinds of people, children as well as adults, the uncultured as well as the cultured...

• This evangelism is not academic (couched in philosophical terms and complicated vocabulary) but RATIONAL. And the uneducated are just as rational as the educated. Their minds may not be trained to think a certain way... but they still think. All human beings think, because God made a human being a thinking creature.

• The teaching of Jesus Himself, although simple, made His listeners THINK. He presented GREAT TRUTHS about God and man, about Himself and the kingdom, about His life and the next. And He often ended His parables with a teasing question to force His hearers to MAKE UP THEIR MINDS on the issue under discussion.

### Our Duty in Evangelism = Present a Gospel that is Understandable:

Again, as John Stott says in Basic Christianity'[34], "Our duty is to avoid distorting or diluting the gospel, and at the same time to MAKE IT PLAIN, to cut the word of truth STRAIGHT so that people can FOLLOW IT, lest *'when any one hears the word of the kingdom and does not ①UNDERSTAND it, the evil one comes and snatches away what is sown in his heart* (Matthew 13:19).'

① UNDERSTAND = Gr. "*suniémi*" = to put together mentally; to consider to level of mentally grasping

I fear that our clumsy explanations can give the devil this very opportunity which he ought never to be allowed."

## Do Doctrine and Arguments negate the work of the Holy Spirit?

• Evangelism is impossible without the Holy Spirit's power, but reasoned evangelism doesn't replace His working.

• <u>Paul's evangelistic approach</u>: to rely on the Holy Spirit but used doctrine, evidence and arguments to appeal to his audience's minds (Acts 17:16-17), then to argue with their mind, plead with their heart, to move their will, trusting in the Holy Spirit (2Cor. 5:17-21).

• John Gresham Machen, former Professor of New Testament at Princeton Theological Seminary, explains the importance of arguments from the evidence and it's alignment with the working of the Holy Spirit: "*There must be the mysterious work of the Spirit of God in the new birth. Without that, all our arguments are quite useless. But because argument is insufficient, it does not follow that it is unnecessary. What the Holy Spirit does in the new birth is not to make a man a Christian regardless of the evidence, but on the contrary to clear away the mists from his eyes and* enable him to attend to the evidence."

---

### 813 Times:  God says He wants people to *KNOW* Him and His great truths

To the atheist, agnostic, 'religious': you are ignorant because you won't respond to the *knowledge* He gives.

To the Christian: I recall the great truths about myself, and I meditate on them until they grip my mind and mold my character. God's way is to remind me who I truly am because He made me that way in Christ.

<u>The Old and New Testament's constant urging to us</u>: "Don't be *ignorant* (don't '*not know*')"

• **"ignorant"** = Hebr. "*lô' lô lôh yâdá*" = not knowing; not understanding nor recognizing

Isaiah 56:10  "*His watchmen are blind, they are all IGNORANT; they are all DUMB DOGS, they cannot bark...*"

• **"ignorant"** or "not know" = Gr. "*agnoeô*" = not understanding due to lack of information or intelligence

1Corinthians 12:1-2  "*...concerning spiritual gifts, brethren, I do not want you to be IGNORANT: you KNOW that you were Gentiles, carried away to these DUMB idols, however you were led.*"

<u>The Old and New Testament's constant urging to us</u>: "*Know* with full understanding"

• **"know"** =          Hebr. "*yâdá*" = to know by recognizing; to be sure; to have understanding
  **"understand"** = Hebr. "*bîyn*" =  to separate out mentally; to regard and discern wisely

Exodus 7:5  "*...the Egyptians shall KNOW that I am the Lord, when I stretch out My hand on Egypt and bring out the children of Israel from among them.*"

Isaiah 43:10  "*'You are My witnesses,' says the Lord, 'and My servant whom I have chosen, that you may KNOW and believe Me, and UNDERSTAND that I am He. Before Me there was no God formed, nor shall there be after Me.'*"

Hosea 14:9  "*Who is wise, Let him UNDERSTAND these things. Who is prudent? Let him KNOW them. For the ways of the Lord are right; the righteous walk in them, but transgressors stumble in them.*"

• **"know"** = Gr. "*ginóskó*" = to know absolutely; to be mentally sure in understanding

John 8:32  "*...you shall KNOW the truth, and the truth shall make you free.*"

John 7:17  "*If anyone wants to do His will, he shall KNOW concerning the doctrine, whether it is from God or whether I speak on My own authority.*"

John 17:3  "*...this is eternal life, that they may KNOW You, the only true God, and Jesus Christ whom You have sent.*"

• **"know"** = Gr. "*eidó*" = to know as in seeing; to be sure of

John 3:2  "*This man came to Jesus by night and said to Him, 'Rabbi, we KNOW that You are a teacher come from God, for no one can do these signs that You do unless God is with him.*"

1John 5:13  "*These things I have written to you who believe in the name of the Son of God, that you may KNOW that you have eternal life, and that you may continue to believe in the name of the Son of God.*"

• **"understand"** = Gr. "*noieô*" = to exercise the mind; to think upon; to consider to the point of understanding

Hebrews 11:3  "*By faith we UNDERSTAND that the worlds were framed by the word of God, so that the things which are seen were not made of things which are visible.*"

John 12:39-40 "*They could not believe, because Isaiah said again, 'He has blinded their eyes and hardened their heart, lest they should see with their eyes and UNDERSTAND with their heart, lest they should turn, so I should heal them.'*"

• **"understand"** = Gr. "*suniémi*" = to put together mentally; to consider to level of mentally grasping

Matthew 15:10  "*...He called the multitude and said to them, "Hear and UNDERSTAND.."*"

Luke 8:9-10  "*...His disciples asked Him, saying, 'What does this parable mean?' And He said, 'To you it has been given to KNOW the mysteries of the kingdom of God, but to the rest it is given in parables, that "Seeing they may not see, and hearing they may not UNDERSTAND."'*"

---

**God regards knowledge, understanding and wisdom as *foundations* of my faith (Psalm 11:3)**

# Discovering Truth:　Learning How to Think

## How can I *know* what is *true*?

> **What's Better?**
> 1) Being taught *what* to think...
> 2) Being taught *how* to think

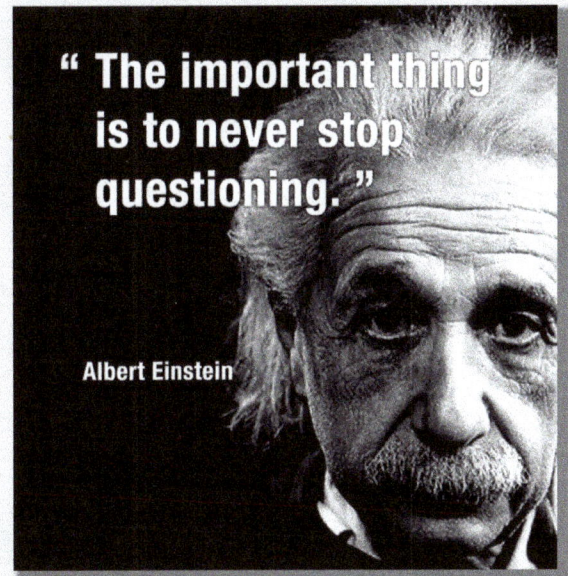

" The important thing is to never stop questioning. "

**Albert Einstein**

## Exit Ticket #18     <mark>Class 18: The Gospel    Part 2</mark>

| | |
|---|---|
| **1) What is the difference between a "Greek" and a "Jew"?** | **2) Why did so many Jews so quickly respond to Peter?** |
| **3) Why did so few Greeks respond to Paul at Mars Hill?** | **4) Of the 21 Scriptures in this lesson, which 2-3 scriptures resonate with you the most and why?** |

# Class 19:  The Gospel, Part 3

The Gospel: God uses People to Reach People

The Gospel: Only for the Weak

The Gospel: Has One Essential

The Gospel: Scattering Seeds

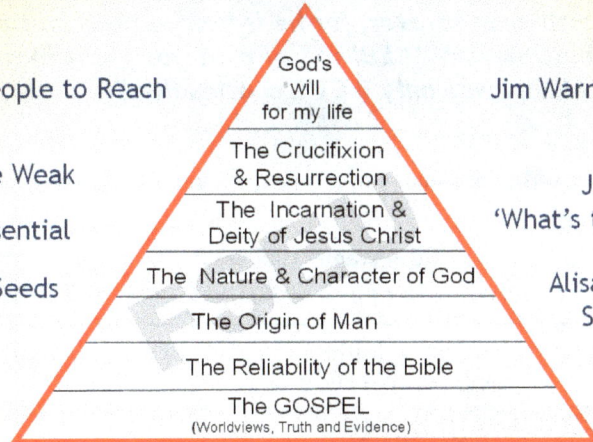

God's will for my life

The Crucifixion & Resurrection

The Incarnation & Deity of Jesus Christ

The Nature & Character of God

The Origin of Man

The Reliability of the Bible

The GOSPEL
(Worldviews, Truth and Evidence)

Jim Warner Wallace: 'Is Christianity Reasonable?' (4:58)

Jim Carry at Golden Globes: 'What's the Meaning to it all?' (1:58)

Alisa Childers/Becket Cook: "A Story of Redemption" (22:30)

# HEBREWS 11:1

"Faith = *Substance* of things hoped for.... *Evidence* of things *not seen*"

fse.life Lessons 02 - 08

# The Gospel:  8 Studies on God's *TRUTH*

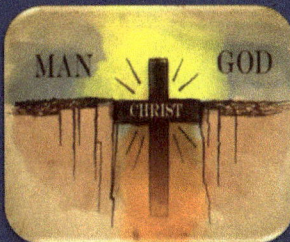

**Is Christ-Centered**
John 5:39

**Is Faith-Based**
Genesis 15:5-12,17

**Turns Greeks into Jews**
Acts 2,17

**Is Rational**
Acts 17:2-4

**Uses People to Reach People** 2Peter 2:5

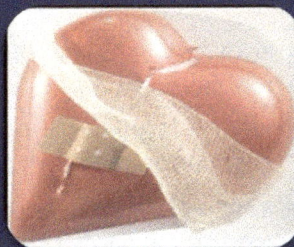

**Is Only for the Weak**
1Corinthians 1:26-29

**Has One Essential**
Colossians 1:26-27

**Must be Scattered**
Matthew 13:3-8

## Genesis 6:3,5  The Gospel: God uses people to reach people

*"'My Spirit shall not strive with man forever, for he is indeed flesh, yet his days shall be 120 years.' Then the Lord saw that the ①WICKEDNESS of man was great in the earth, and that every intent of the thoughts of his heart was only ①EVIL continually."*

① WICKEDNESS, EVIL = *"ra' râ âh"*
It can mean either moral corruption that originates in the heart or physical calamity (earthquakes, etc.); in Genesis 6:3,5, it is clearly moral.

There's another word for WICKEDNESS in the Old Testament:  ②*"resha"* = iniquity (sin)
**Psalm 5:4**  *"...You are not a God who takes pleasure in ②WICKEDNESS, nor shall ①EVIL dwell with You."*

**From the Old Testament to the New**: God uses a 'faithful remnant' to not only warn people about sin but to be a witness that He is the true and only God:

- **NOAH** 2Peter 2:5

- **ENOCH** Jude 1:14-15

- **JESUS CHRIST** John 8:24

- **PAUL** Romans 1:9,14-17

 Noah
 Jesus
 Paul

Jim Warner Wallace: 'Is Christianity Reasonable?' (4:58)          Courtesy of Google Images    Fair Use Law 17 U.S. Code § 107

## 1Corinthians 1:26-29  The Gospel: Is Only for the Weak

*"For you see your calling, brethren, that not many ①WISE according to the flesh, not many ②MIGHTY, not many ③NOBLE, are called.*

*But God has chosen the ④FOOLISH things of the world to put to shame the wise, and God has chosen the ⑤WEAK things of the world to put to shame the things which are mighty, and the ⑥BASE things of the world and the things which are despised God has chosen, and the things which are ⑦NOT, to bring to nothing the things that ⑦ARE, that no flesh should glory in His presence."*

| Where God's power is... | |
|---|---|
| **ABSENT** | **ACTIVE** |
| ① WISE = 'sophos' = naturally learned; 'according to the flesh' | ④ FOOLISH = 'möria' = silly; absurd (English word for 'moron') |
| ② MIGHTY = 'dunatøs' = able or capable by themselves; strong | ⑤ WEAK = 'asthenes' = feeble; unable to do anything on their own power |
| ③ NOBLE = 'eugenés' = well born, as to a family of high society | ⑥ BASE = 'agenes' = despised; of no account by the world's standards |
| ⑦ ARE = 'ousa' = have; seen as something by others. | ⑦ NOT = 'may' = lacking; seen as nothing by others |

Courtesy of Google Images    Fair Use Law 17 U.S. Code § 107

## Genesis 6:3,5   The Gospel = God *uses* people to *reach* people

*"'My Spirit shall not strive with man forever, for he is indeed flesh, yet his days shall be 120 years.' Then the Lord saw that the ①WICKEDNESS of man was great in the earth, and that every intent of the thoughts of his heart was only ①EVIL continually."*

① WICKEDNESS, EVIL = Hebrew "*ra' râ âh*" = can mean either physical calamity (like earthquakes, tsunamis, etc.) or moral corruption that originates from the heart; in this verse, it is clearly moral.

② WICKEDNESS = Hebrew "*resha*" = iniquity (doing what you know is wrong according to God's law)

Habakkuk 1:13  *"...You are of purer eyes than to behold ①EVIL, and cannot look on iniquity."*

Psalm 5:4  *"...You are not a God who takes pleasure in ②WICKEDNESS, nor shall ①EVIL dwell with You."*

- **The Holy Spirit is active in the O.T.:** Genesis 6:3,5 is the second reference to the Holy Spirit. In Genesis 1:2, He energizes and activates the created cosmos. Here, He is STRIVING and LONGSUFFERING with man, calling them to repentance during the 120-year period before the Flood, through the preaching of Noah and Enoch:

1Peter 3:20, 2:5  *"...the longsuffering of God waited patiently in the days of Noah, while the ark was being prepared, in which a few, that is, eight souls, were saved through water...He did not spare the ancient world, but saved Noah, one of eight people,  A PREACHER OF RIGHTEOUSNESS,, bringing in the flood on  the world of the ungodly."*

Jude14-15  *"Now Enoch, the 7th from Adam, PROPHESIED about these men also, saying, 'Behold, the Lord comes with 10,000's of His saints, to execute judgment on all, to convict all who are ungodly among them of all their ungodly deeds which they have committed in an ungodly way, and of all the harsh things which ungodly sinners have spoken against Him."*

- **John 16: 7-11   Jesus confirms the Holy Spirit's continuing ministry of striving with sinful man to repent**

*"...It is to your advantage that I go away; for if I do not go away, the Helper will not come to you; but if I depart, I will send Him to you. And when He has come, He will convict the world of sin, and of righteousness, and of judgment: of sin, because they do not believe Me; of righteousness, because I go to the Father and you see Me no more; of judgment because the ruler of this world is judged."*

**The Holy Spirit doesn't condemn man – He strives WITH man, to CONVICT us of our *need* to be saved.**

- **Romans 1:9, 14-17   God always reserves a FAITHFUL REMNANT to serve Him**

Paul, following in the same footsteps as Enoch and Noah, was *used* by the Holy Spirit to witness to all mankind of God's gift of salvation through His grace. Paul says God has revealed Himself to man through His creation, but man not only refuses God's truth but *suppresses* the truth in their man-made lies, showing themselves to be fools.

*"...God is my witness, whom I SERVE in my spirit in the gospel of His Son, that without ceasing I make mention of you always in my prayers...I AM A DEBTOR both to the Greeks and to barbarians, both to wise and unwise. So much as is in me, I AM READY to preach the gospel to you who are in Rome also. For I AM NOT ASHAMED of the gospel of Christ, for it is the power of God to salvation for everyone who believes, for the Jew first and also for the Greek. For in it the righteousness of God is revealed from faith to faith: as it is written: 'The just shall live by faith.'"*

- **1Corinthians 2:1-5  God demonstrates His power as He works through Paul**

*"...I, brethren, when I came to you, did not come with excellence of speech or of wisdom declaring to you the mystery of God. For I determined not to know anything among you except JESUS CHRIST and HIM CRUCIFIED. I was with you in weakness, in fear, and in much trembling. And my speech and my preaching were not with persuasive words of human wisdom, but in DEMONSTRATION OF THE SPIRIT and of power, that your faith should not be in the wisdom of men but in the power of God."*

This is exactly what God means in **2Chronicles 16:9** – *"...the eyes of the Lord run to and fro throughout the whole earth, to SHOW HIMSELF STRONG on behalf of those whose HEART IS LOYAL TO HIM."*

---

**Isaiah 66:1-2 "God is looking for Humble Hearts to dwell in"**

*"Heaven is My throne, and earth is My footstool. Where is the house that you will build Me? And where is the place of My rest? For all those things My hand has made, and all those things exist," says the Lord. "But on this one I will look: on him who is POOR and of a  CONTRITE SPIRIT, and who TREMBLES AT MY WORD."*

John MacArthur[25]: *"Isaiah reminds us that God is not looking for a temple of stone, since as Creator of all things, the whole universe is His dwelling place... God is looking for a HEART TO DWELL IN, a heart that is tender and broken, not one concerned with the externalities of religion (Matthew 5:3-9). God desires to dwell in the heart of a person who takes HIS WORD seriously by LIVING IT OUT (Isaiah 66:5, John 14:23)."*

- **Philippians 3:3-6** **Paul's achievements, which he saw as required for salvation, before he knew Jesus**

*"We are the circumcision, who worship God in the Spirit, rejoice in Christ Jesus, and have no confidence in the flesh, though I also might have confidence in the flesh. If anyone else thinks he has confidence in the flesh, I more so:*
1) *circumcised the 8ᵗʰ day*   (Genesis 17:12, Leviticus 12:3 – the prescribed day per the law)
2) *of the stock of Israel*   (Paul is a true Jew because he descended directly through Abraham, Isaac and Jacob)
3) *of the tribe of Benjamin*   (Genesis 35:18, 1Kings 12:21 - Benjamin was one of the elite tribes of Israel who, with Judah, stayed loyal to David and formed the southern kingdom)
4) *a Hebrew of the Hebrews* (Acts 26:4-5, 21:40 - Paul was born a Hebrew and kept his Hebrew traditions)
5) *concerning the law, a Pharisee* (Acts 26:5 – Pharisees were the legalists of Judaism, whose zeal to apply the OT Scriptures directly to life led to their complex system of tradition and works righteousness)
6) *concerning zeal, persecuting the church* (Acts 8:1-3 – to a Jew, "zeal" combines love and hate, and is the highest single religious virtue. Paul loved Judaism - he hated the church because it threatened what he loved).
7) *concerning the righteousness which is in the law, blameless*  (Paul outwardly kept the law, so that no one could accuse him of breaking it. He was sinful and self-righteous – not an OT believer, but a proud and lost legalist).

- **Philippians 3:7-11** **Paul contrasts his achievements against personally knowing Jesus Christ**

*"But what things were ①GAIN to me, these things I have counted ②LOSS for Christ. But indeed I also count all things loss for the excellency of the ③KNOWLEDGE of Christ Jesus my Lord, for whom I have suffered the loss of all things, and count them as rubbish, that I may gain Christ, and be found in Him, not having my own righteousness, which is from the law, but that which is through ④FAITH in Christ, the righteousness which is from God by faith; that I may ③KNOW Him and the power of His resurrection, and the fellowship of His sufferings, being conformed to His death. If, by any means, I may arrive at the resurrection from the dead."*

① GAIN = Gr. "*kerdos*" = an accounting term meaning "to make a profit"
② LOSS = Gr. "*zēmia*" = an accounting term meaning "to enter a business loss"
   John MacArthur: *"Paul used the language of business to describe the spiritual transaction that occurred when Christ redeemed him. All his Jewish religious credentials that he thought were in his profit column, were actually worthless and damning….he only put them in his loss column when he saw the glories of Christ."*
③ KNOW = Gr. "*ginōskō*" = moving toward total understanding (compared to Gr. "*oida*", which is having full knowledge) in a personal relation between the one knowing and the object known (what is known is highly important to the one who knows, which cements the relationship). Paul's emphasis is on gaining a deeper knowledge and intimacy with Christ.
   John 17:3  *"…this is eternal life, that they may KNOW You, the one true God, and Jesus Christ whom You have sent."*
④ FAITH IN CHRIST = Gr. "*pistis*" or "*pisteuo*" =
   1) to "cling" to: a firm conviction based upon hearing, resulting in a pledge of fidelity (commitment to promise)
   2) a personal surrender to the invisible God, and the conduct inspired by that surrender (2Corin. 5:7)
   3) its object is a Person: not God's promises (the occasion to exercise faith), but in Him (the object of faith)
   John MacArthur: *"Faith is the confident, continuous confession of total dependence on and trust in Jesus for God's necessary requirement to enter His kingdom…and that requirement He demands is the righteousness of Christ Himself, which God imputes to every believer who places his/ her faith in Him."*

Romans 1:16-17  *"…I am not ashamed of the gospel of Christ, for it is the power of God to salvation for everyone who believes, for the Jew 1ˢᵗ and then the Greek. For in it the righteousness of God is revealed from faith to faith: as it is written, 'The just shall live by faith.'"*

> **People don't impress God – *Psalm 1:10-11, Acts 10:34***
> **He is only impressed with His Son – *Luke 3:21***
> **He gives me 1 way to please Him:  make Him my #1 priority by…**
> 1) **obeying Him and…**
> 2) **using the gifts He has given me to glorify Him on earth as I…**
> 3) **strive to be more like His Son everyday – *John 8:29***

## 1Corinthians 1:26-29   The Gospel = God works through the *Base Things*

*"For you see your calling, brethren, that not many ①WISE according to the flesh, not many ②MIGHTY, not many ③NOBLE, are called. But God has chosen the ④FOOLISH THINGS of the world to put to shame the wise, and God has chosen the ⑤WEAK THINGS of the world to put to shame the things which are mighty, and the ⑥BASE THINGS of the world and the things which are despised God has chosen, and the things which are ⑦NOT, to bring to nothing the things that ⑦ARE, that no flesh should glory in His presence."*

① WISE = Gr. "*sophos*" = naturally learned (often used in context with the world system: "according to the flesh")

② MIGHTY = Gr. "*dunatos*" = able or capable; strong

③ NOBLE = Gr. "*eugenēs*" = well born, as to a family of high society

④ FOOLISH = Gr. "*mŏria*" = silly; absurd (our English word "moron")

⑤ WEAK = Gr. "*asthenēs*" = strengthless; impotent; feeble or sick (unable to do anything on their own power)

⑥ BASE = Gr. "*agenēs*" = despised; of no account or reputation by the world's standards

⑦ NOT = Gr. "*may*" = lack; seen as nothing      ⑦ ARE = Gr. "*ousa*" = have; seen as something

### John MacArthur[25]: "If the world calls you a fool for publicly following Christ, thank God"

• God disdained human wisdom, not only by disallowing it as a means to knowing Him, but also choosing to save the lowly; He doesn't call to salvation many whom the world would call wise, mighty and noble.

• God's wisdom is revealed to the foolish, weak and common (those considered nothing): He gets the glory when the "lowly" come to know Him – saved sinners cannot boast that they have achieved salvation by their intellect

Zechariah 4:6   *"'... Not by might nor by power, but by My Spirit', says the Lord of hosts."*

Matthew 11:25   *"I thank You, Father, Lord of heaven and earth, because You have hidden these things from the wise and prudent and have revealed them to babes."*

Isaiah 40:29-31   *"He gives power to the WEAK, and to those who have NO MIGHT He increases strength. Even the youths shall faint and be weary, and the young men shall utterly fail. But those who WAIT ON THE LORD shall renew their strength; they shall mount up with wings like eagles, they shall run and not be weary, they shall walk and not faint."*

---

### "Entrusted with the Gospel: The Story of Edward Kimball"    (Harvest OnLine.com)

Question #1:     If you were asked today what the main purpose of your life is, what would you say?

Answer:     The Bible teaches that we were put on this earth to bring glory to God.

Question #1:     How am I personally taking care of this responsibility to get the gospel out?

Answer:     Not every Christian is called as an evangelist, every Christian is called to evangelize.

Edward Kimball was a faithful Christian who wanted to be used by God. He was not a pastor or a missionary, but he knew that he should go and share the gospel. Kimball felt especially burdened for a young man named Dwight, who worked in a Chicago shoe store. He mustered up the courage to go and tell Dwight about Jesus. Much to Kimball's delight, he responded and gave his life to Christ. Dwight later began a preaching ministry. He became known as **D.L. Moody**, one of the greatest evangelists in church history.

When Moody was out preaching one day, a man named Frederick Meyer was listening. Meyer was already a Christian, but Moody's preaching motivated him to enter full-time ministry. We know him as **F.B. Meyer**. Kimball reached Moody, and Moody reached Meyer, but the story doesn't end there.

When Meyer was preaching, a young man named **Wilbur Chapman** responded and gave his life to Christ. Chapman became an evangelist. One of the young men he mentored was a former professional baseball player who also wanted to preach the gospel and did so with great success. His name was **Billy Sunday**.

Sunday held a crusade in Charlotte, North Carolina, where many people came to faith. The people there were so thrilled that they wanted to have another crusade. Sunday wasn't available, so an evangelist named **Mordecai Hamm** was invited to speak. While the campaign wasn't considered as successful as the first one, a young, lanky farm boy walked down the aisle on one of the final nights. We know him as **Billy Graham**.

You may not be a Billy Graham, but you are an Edward Kimball - Kimball reached Moody, who touched Meyer, who reached Chapman, who helped Sunday, who reached the businessmen in Charlotte who invited Hamm, who then touched Billy Graham. We all have been entrusted with the gospel. We all have a part to play.

It comes down to this: One day, when you stand before God, He will want to know what you did with His sacred charge of the gospel. You are entrusted with the gospel. He said in Luke 19, "Do business until I come."

### What are you going to do with what God has entrusted to you?

# The Gospel: How God's "Election" Works...

## Are these the people God calls to follow Him?

1) FOOLISH over WISE
2) WEAK over MIGHTY
3) BASE over NOBLE
4) NOTHING (NOT) over SOMETHING (ARE)

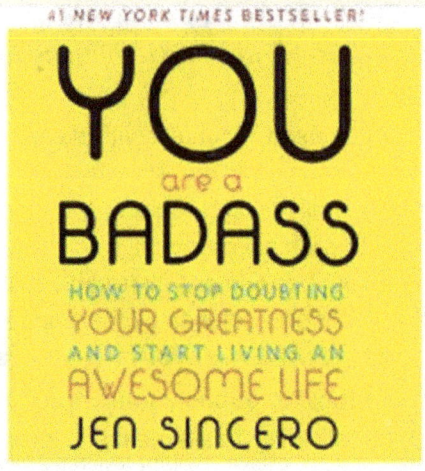

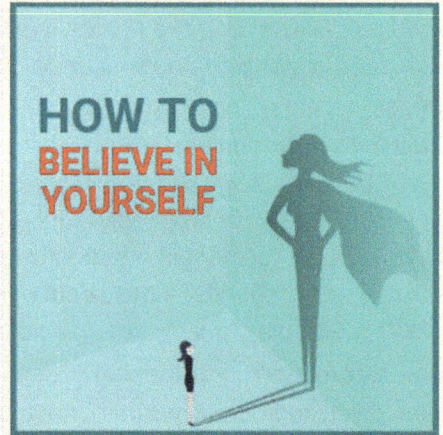

## WHY or WHY NOT?

#1 NEW YORK TIMES BESTSELLER!

**YOU are a BADASS**

HOW TO STOP DOUBTING YOUR GREATNESS AND START LIVING AN AWESOME LIFE

JEN SINCERO

**HOW TO BELIEVE IN YOURSELF**

"...no flesh should glory in My presence"
1Corinthians 1:29

Jim Carry at Golden Globes: 'What's the Meaning to it all?' (1:58)

---

# So... What is the 1 Essential of the Gospel?

**DEUTERONOMY 29:29** (1,450 BC)

"The secret things belong to the Lord our God, but those things which are REVEALED belong to us and our children forever, that we may do all the words of this law."

**COLOSSIANS 1:26** (60 AD)

"The mystery (hidden truth) which has been hidden from ages and from generations, but now has been REVEALED to HIS SAINTS."

**COLOSSIANS 1:27** (60 AD)

"To them God willed to MAKE KNOWN what are the riches of the GLORY of this mystery (hidden truth) among the Gentiles: which is **CHRIST IN YOU**, the hope of GLORY."

## Allowing Jesus Christ to Reign in *ME*

**JOHN 15:5,8** (32 AD)

"I am the Vine, you are the branches. He who abides in Me, and I IN HIM, bears much fruit; for without Me you can do nothing. By this My Father is GLORIFIED, that you bear much fruit, so you will be My disciples."

## Matthew 13:3-8  The Gospel = Scattering the Seed

*"Behold, a sower went out to sow. And as he sowed, some seed fell by the ①WAYSIDE; and the birds came and devoured them. Some fell on ②STONY PLACES, where they did not have much earth; and they immediately sprang up because they had no depth of earth. But when the sun was up they were scorched, and because they had no root they withered away. And some fell among ③THORNS, and the thorns sprang up and choked them. But others fell on ④GOOD GROUND and yielded a crop: some a hundredfold, some sixty, some thirty."*

① **"Wayside Soil"** = hard-packed dirt of the travelers' paths, bordering the farmers' fields (no fences separated fields from dirt roads). Because of the continual foot traffic, the dry hot climate, and the fact this soil was never loosened and turned over as the field soil, the ground became as hard as pavement. As the sower broadcast the seed, some fell directly on the hard-packed earth of these paths. This seed never gets a chance to germinate – it gets eaten by the birds (Satan – Luke 8:12).

② **"Shallow Soil"** = the "stony places" doesn't mean soil with stones in it. Farmers removed stones from any soil. Because Israel has natural limestone beds in many places just beneath topsoil, any seed falling in this type of soil germinates quickly but its roots can't penetrate the limestone. At first, these plants look spectacular – until the hot sun comes up. These plants were the first to die, never bearing fruit. Their roots cannot reach the moisture.

③ **"Thorny Soil"** = this soil looks good –it is deep, tilled and fertile. At sowing time the seed would germinate, but hidden with the seed were weeds. The weeds have the advantage because they are native to the soil, while the seed was a foreigner. The weeds need no care, but the foreign seed requires care from the farmer to survive. If the weeds gain a foothold, they dominate and steal the moisture and sun. They choke out the good plants.

④ **"Good Soil"** = this soil is soft (unlike "wayside soil"), it is deep (unlike "shallow soil"), and it is clean (unlike "thorny soil"). This seed, under the farmer's care, bursts into life and yields a huge harvest – hundredfold, sixtyfold, thirtyfold.

### A simple parable with a DEEPER MEANING that many miss:

Jesus exhorts people to heed its message (vs. 9), but only those who have Him to teach them can understand it, and only those who truly want to know even bother to ask (Mark 4:10).

• **"SEED"** = the Gospel (vs. 19); Luke 8:11 says it is the "word of God." Seed, like the message of the gospel, is not created but reproduced. God doesn't call us to create our own seed – the only seed to spread is His Gospel.

• **"SOWER"** = anyone who "spreads" the gospel in hearts by sharing God's word (Jesus = the ultimate Sower).

• **"SOIL"**  = the human heart (vs. 19). The heart of the hearer = the soil receiving the sower's seed.

• **THE MORALE** = nothing is wrong with the sower, or the seed, or the way the sower spreads the seed, or the soil composition. The problem is the condition of the soil (the *HEART*): whether hard-packed, shallow, weedy or deep, it's the same soil. All soil can receive the seed if it is prepared. Soil not prepared will never bear a crop.

### The Hardened, Unresponsive Heart = the poorly-conditioned soil = the UNSAVED (NO CROP)

• **"Wayside Heart"** (verse 19)  = REJECTOR
Hearts so hardened by sin, they are indifferent to the gospel - never broken up by sorrow for offending God, and they hate anyone trying to share what the Bible says. They are unregenerate – they don't even pretend to believe.

• **"Shallow Heart"** (verse 20-21)  = PRETENDER #1
Superficial response with no commitment. It receives the promises (joy, fellowship), but rejects the command to "deny yourself, take your cross, follow Me." Under the thin veneer of "good soil" is an unrepentant heart.

• **"Thorny Heart"** (verse )  = PRETENDER #2
People who live for the things of this world (career, possessions, looks, hobbies), but not for Him. They say they are Christians, but they care nothing about the things of God. This "weedy soil", which at first looked so good, gets overwhelmed with thorns of worldliness (eventually, you can't tell if there ever was good soil).

> **Truth #1 =  God doesn't hold the sower responsible for where the seed lands**
>
> **Truth #2 =  God doesn't hold the sower responsible for whether or not there is a harvest**
>
> **Truth #3 =  God only holds the sower responsible for *scattering* the seed**

# Matthew 13:3-8   The Gospel: Scattering Seed

*"Behold, a sower went out to sow. And as he sowed, some seed fell by the ① WAYSIDE: and the birds came and devoured them.*
*Some fell on ② STONY places, where they did not have much earth; and they immediately sprang up because they had no depth of earth. But when the sun was up they were scorched, and because they had no root they withered away. And some fell among ③ THORNS, and the thorns sprang up and choked them. But others fell on ④ GOOD ground and yielded a crop: some a 100-fold, some 60, some 30."*

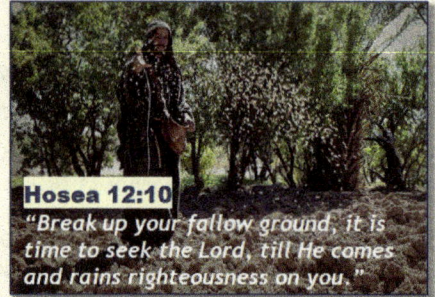

**Hosea 12:10**
*"Break up your fallow ground, it is time to seek the Lord, till He comes and rains righteousness on you."*

| ① WAYSIDE = concrete-like (seed bounces off, birds eat it) | ④ GOOD = soft, deep, no weeds (receives the seed) | ③ THORNS = weed-filled (choke out the seed) | ② STONY = shallow (roots can't get to water) |
|---|---|---|---|

What about the SOIL determines if the SEED brings a crop?

**SOIL  CONDITION**

**HEART Condition**

④ GOOD (vs. 23) =          *broken-up* (ready to receive seed)

③ THORNS (vs. 22) =          *worldly* (seed is choked out)

② STONY (vs. 20-21) =          *shallow* (never made a commitment)

① WAYSIDE (vs.19) =   *sin-hardened* (seed bounces right off)

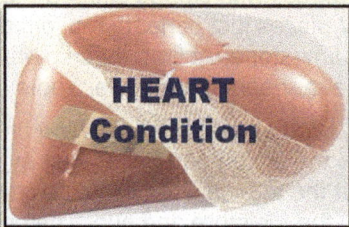

Alisa Childers/Becket Cook: "A Story of Redemption" (22:30)

**Exit Ticket #19    Class 18: The Gospel    Part 3**

| | |
|---|---|
| 1) Explain 2 examples from history of God's "faithful remnant" to share the Gospel? | 2) Where is the power of the Gospel absent vs. active? |
| 3) What is the 1 Essential to sharing the Gospel? | 4) Of the 15 Scriptures in this lesson, which 2-3 scriptures resonate with you the most and why? |

## Class 20: How the Gospel Removes Guilt, Part 1

Formal (Deductive) Logic: Premises-to-Certainty

Informal (Inductive) Logic: Evidence-to-Probability

Which Statements fit Deductive vs Inductive Logic?

8 Evidences: The Argument for the Gospel

The Gospel: Love that can Satisfy Justice

The Gospel: Exposes Your Heart

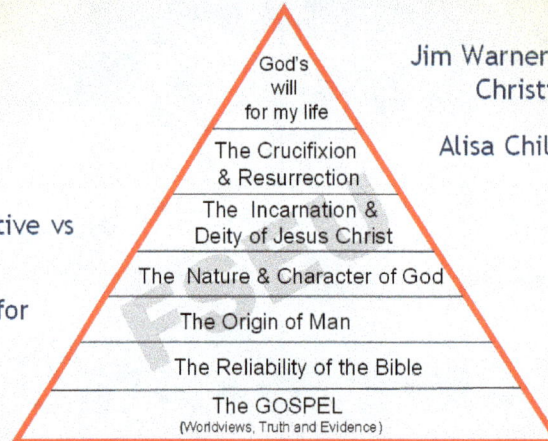

Jim Warner Wallace Testimony: "I'm a Christian because it's True" (5:05)

Alisa Childers/Becket Cook: "A Story of Redemption" (22:30)

**Pyramid (top to bottom):**
- God's will for my life
- The Crucifixion & Resurrection
- The Incarnation & Deity of Jesus Christ
- The Nature & Character of God
- The Origin of Man
- The Reliability of the Bible
- The GOSPEL (Worldviews, Truth and Evidence)

**H E B R E W S 11:1**
"Faith = *Substance* of things hoped for.... *Evidence* of things *not seen*"

fse.life Lessons 02 - 08

## Formal (Deductive) Logic:   Premises-to-Certainty

- We evaluate someone's deductive argument by determining if their REASONING is correct.

- Reasoning = has the person structured their argument so that they can logically move from "truth to truth" (i.e., premise-to-premise).

- Another way of saying it: Does their conclusion logically FOLLOW from their premises?

- We use the process of deduction to discover new truths (conclusions) based on accepted truths (premises).

Acts 17:2

The Conclusion in a Deductive Argument MUST be true IF...
The *Premises* supporting the Conclusion are true!

# Informal (Inductive) Logic:   Evidence-to-Probability

- Also known as <u>Inductive</u> Logic.

- Evaluate an argument's <u>content</u>, presented in a group of evidences, to support a conclusion.

- <u>Evidence</u> = available information or facts to help determine if the conclusion is TRUE.

- The conclusion is probable, but not certain.

- We evaluate the weight and relevance of the evidence presented to reach a conclusion.

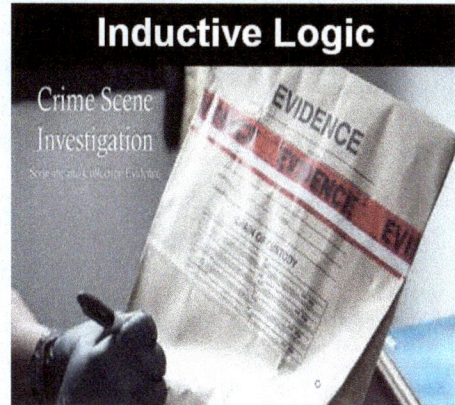

**Inductive Logic**

Crime Scene Investigation

EVIDENCE

The Conclusion does not follow with certainty (as in deductive arguments) but rather PROBABILITY!

**While Deductive Logic argues from STRUCTURE...
Inductive Logic argues from EVIDENCE!**

Courtesy of Google Images    Fair Use Law 17 U.S. Code § 107

# Which Statements fit Deductive vs Inductive Logic?

## 5 Statements on How Guilt Ruins Lives

My moral code defines how I see right vs. wrong.

Most people feel guilt (moral failure) when they violate their moral code.

But... once I fail morally, I can't undo it, so I can't completely remove my guilt.

**DEDUCTIVE**

I will say or do almost anything to remove my guilt.

guilt

I hope to have my guilt removed.

## 2 Statements on How the Gospel Gives New Life

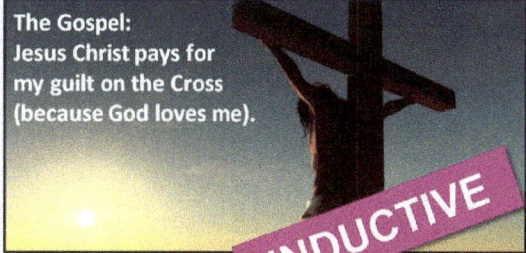

The Gospel: Jesus Christ pays for my guilt on the Cross (because God loves me).

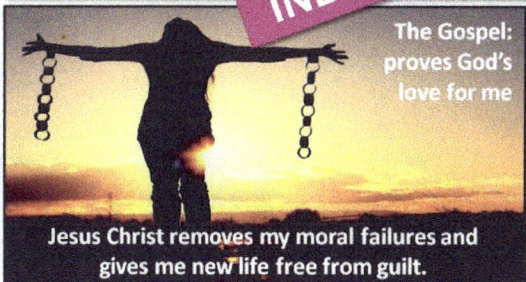

**INDUCTIVE**

The Gospel: proves God's love for me

Jesus Christ removes my moral failures and gives me new life free from guilt.

Courtesy of Google Images    Fair Use Law 17 U.S. Code § 107

# 8 Evidences:  The Argument for the Gospel

**Reasonable**
The Bible explains why Christ's suffering and resurrection were needed Acts 17:2-4.

**Exposes the Heart**
Good soil isn't it's composition - but it's condition Matthew 13:3-8.

**Demands Response**
Christ crucified - a stumbling block (Jews) or foolish (Gentiles) 1Corin. 1:22-23.

**Christ-centered**
"I thought I arrived at a place, but I discovered it is a Person" (CS Lewis) John 12:19.

Premise 1 = People's moral code defines right vs. wrong.

Premise 2 = Most people feel guilt (moral failure) when they violate their moral code.

Premise 3 = People who have failed morally often hope to have their guilt removed.

Premise 4 = People who have failed morally often will do, say or pay almost anything to remove their guilt.

Premise 5 = Once people fail morally, they can't undo their failure, so they can't remove their guilt.

Premise 6 = In the Gospel, Jesus Christ pays for people's guilt on the Cross (because of God's love).

Premise 7 = The Gospel proves God's love: He removes our moral failures and gives us new life free from guilt.

Conclusion = ☑ The Gospel is the Solution for Our Moral Failure and the Revelation of God's Love.

**Love that can satisfy Justice**
Death = sin's payment; Eternal Life = God's free gift Romans 3:23.

God's Justice     God's Love

**A "Calling"**
It's never ability, but it's always availability 1Corin. 1:26-29.

HERE AM I SEND ME

**A Covenant**
"Blessing for the Gentiles in Christ, by the promise through faith." Gal. 3:14.

**A Consecration**
"Not even the 1st covenant was consecrated without blood" Hebrews 9:16-18.

---

## 1John 4:10     The Gospel: Love that can Satisfy Justice

### What is God's 'AGAPE' LOVE?

| | |
|---|---|
| 1) Supernatural (from God). | 1John 4:8,12 |
| 2) Doesn't require a relationship. | Galatians 2:20 |
| 3) A choice of the will, not of feelings. | Romans 13:8-10 |
| 4) Based on action, not reaction. | Galatians 5:13-14 |
| 5) It gives based on the needs of the one loved. | John 3:16 |
| 6) It doesn't matter how loveable the one loved is. | Romans 5:8 |
| 7) It asks for nothing in return. | Ephesians 5:2 |

*"In this is love, not that we loved God, but that He loved us and sent His Son to be the propitiation for our sins."*

Courtesy of Google Images     Fair Use Law 17 U.S. Code § 107

# Matthew 13:3-8   The Gospel: Exposes Your Heart

*"Behold, a sower went out to sow. And as he sowed, some seed fell by the ① WAYSIDE; and the birds came and devoured them.*

*Some fell on ② STONY places, where they did not have much earth; and they immediately sprang up because they had no depth of earth. But when the sun was up they were scorched, and because they had no root they withered away. And some fell among ③ THORNS, and the thorns sprang up and choked them.*

*But others fell on ④ GOOD ground and yielded a crop: some a 100-fold, some 60, some 30."*

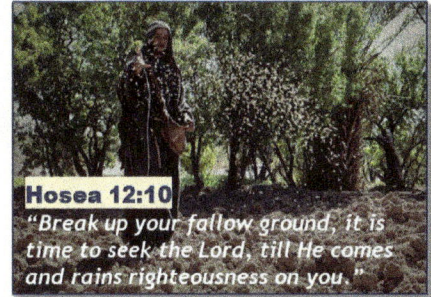

**Hosea 12:10**
*"Break up your fallow ground, it is time to seek the Lord, till He comes and rains righteousness on you."*

| ① WAYSIDE = concrete-like (seed bounces off, birds eat it) | ④ GOOD = soft, deep, no weeds (receives the seed) | ③ THORNS = weed-filled (choke out the seed) | ② STONY = shallow (roots can't get to water) |
|---|---|---|---|

What about the SOIL determines if the SEED brings a crop?

**SOIL CONDITION**

**HEART Condition**

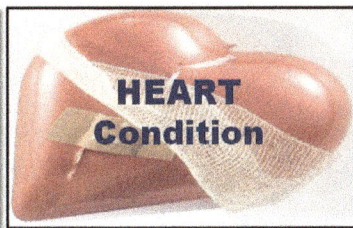

| ④ GOOD (vs. 23) = broken-up (ready to receive seed) |
|---|
| ③ THORNS (vs. 22) = worldly (seed is choked out) |
| ② STONY (vs. 20-21) = shallow (never made a commitment) |
| ① WAYSIDE (vs. 19) = sin-hardened (seed bounces right off) |

Alisa Childers/Becket Cook: "A Story of Redemption" (22:30)

**Exit Ticket #20**     <mark>**Class 20: How the Gospel Removes Guilt   Part 1**</mark>

| | |
|---|---|
| **1) Explain the difference between a Deductive versus an Inductive argument?** | **2) Explain at least 3 of the attributes of Agape Love?** |
| **3) How does the Parable of the Sower expose someone's heart?** | **4) Of the 19 Scriptures in this lesson, which 2-3 scriptures resonate with you the most and why?** |

# Class 21: How the Gospel Removes Guilt, Part 2

The Logical Argument: How the Gospel Removes Guilt

Understanding the Gospel = Understanding God as a Person

Sharing the Gospel: How to Get Your Friends to Open Up

Sharing the Gospel: The COLUMBO Tactic

Memorization Tool (to help you share): The Gospel in Romans

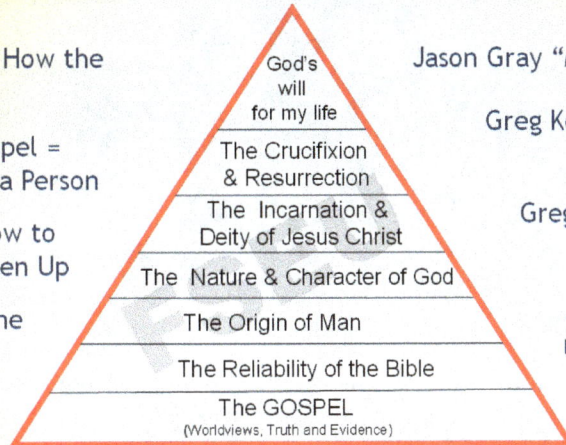

**Pyramid (top to bottom):**
- God's will for my life
- The Crucifixion & Resurrection
- The Incarnation & Deity of Jesus Christ
- The Nature & Character of God
- The Origin of Man
- The Reliability of the Bible
- The GOSPEL (Worldviews, Truth and Evidence)

**H E B R E W S 11:1**
"Faith = *Substance* of things hoped for.... *Evidence* of things *not seen*"

**fse.life Lessons 02 - 08**

Jason Gray "More Like Falling in Love" (3:44)

Greg Kohkl: 'You do not have to be an expert in Apologetics' (4:34)

Greg Kohkl: 'The Columbo Tactic in Apologetics' (4:06)

JW Wallace: "Why I rarely share my personal testimony and why you shouldn't be quick to share yours" (10:41)

# The Logical Argument: How the Gospel Removes Guilt

## Formal (Deductive) Logic: The Gospel

**Premise 1** = People's moral code defines right vs. wrong.

**Premise 2** = Most people feel guilt (moral failure) when they violate their moral code.

**Premise 3** = People who have failed morally often hope to have their guilt removed.

**Premise 4** = People who have failed morally often will do, say or pay almost anything to remove their guilt.

**Premise 5** = Once people fail morally, they can't undo their failure, so they can't completely remove their guilt.

**Premise 6** = In the Gospel, Jesus Christ pays for people's guilt on the Cross (because of God's love for people).

**Premise 7** = The Gospel proves God's love: He removes our moral failures and gives us new life free from guilt.

**Conclusion** = Therefore, the Gospel is the Solution for Our Moral Failure and the Revelation of God's Love.

By common sense (it's a *self-evident* truth): we all feel guilty when we fail morally!

Everyone agree Premises 1-5 are true?

How do you know?

Everyone agree Premises 6-7 are true?

How do you know?

Where's the evidence? We need an Inductive Argument to support Premises 6-7

## Understanding the Gospel = Understanding God as a Person

### God is *JUST*

| | |
|---|---|
| God's Character | He is Holy, Righteous , Just |
| God's Law | He credits the penalty of my sin to me |
| God's Law | He declares me *Guilty* and *Wicked* because of <u>my works</u> |

### God is *LOVE*

| | |
|---|---|
| God's Character | He is Kind & Merciful |
| God's Grace | He credits the penalty of my sin to Christ |
| God's Grace | He declares me *Not Guilty* and *Righteous* because of <u>Christ's works</u> |

"God so LOVED the world, that He gave His only begotten Son, that whosoever believes in Him will not perish but have eternal life" John 3:16

**ROMANS 3:23a**
*"The WAGES of my sin is my death"*

**Courtroom**

**BUT**

**ROMANS 3:23b**
*"God's FREE GIFT to me is ETERNAL LIFE in Christ Jesus our Lord."*

**Not Guilty!**

Jason Gray "More Like Falling in Love" (3:45)    Courtesy of Google Images    Fair Use Law 17 U.S. Code § 107

## Sharing the Gospel:    How to Get Your Friends to Open Up

The most effective way to respond to someone's claim is to understand <u>their point of view</u> (i.e., worldview).

The most effective way to understand their worldview is to *ASK THEM*.

We think our job in sharing the Gospel is to defend our beliefs.

We think we are the ones being backed in a corner, being put on the defensive – DON'T FALL FOR THE TRICK.

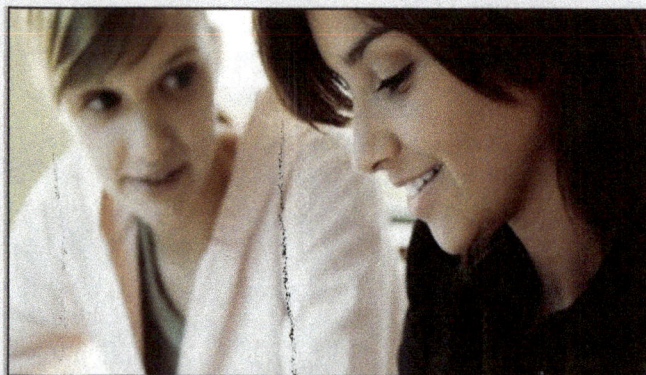

Remember:
Who bears the burden of proof in any conversation?

The person who is making the claim!

Greg Kohkl: 'You do not have to be an expert in Apologetics' (4:34)    Introduction to Logic, Mr. Croteau    Courtesy of Google Images    Fair Use Law 17 U.S. Code § 107

# Sharing the Gospel: The COLUMBO Tactic

**Greg Kohkl:** M.A. in Philosophy of Religion & Ethics, Talbot School of Theology; M.A. in Christian Apologetics, Simon Greenleaf School of Law; Founding Director of 'Stand to Reason' and CPA (Center for Public Christianity).

<u>Question #1</u> = **"What do you mean by that?"**

The Goal: I want to <u>understand</u> what the person means.

<u>Question #2</u> = **"How did you reach that conclusion?"**

The Goal: I want to know on what <u>evidence</u> is their view based?

<u>Question #3</u> = **"May I ask you a question?"**

The Goal: I want them to now defend <u>their claim</u>.

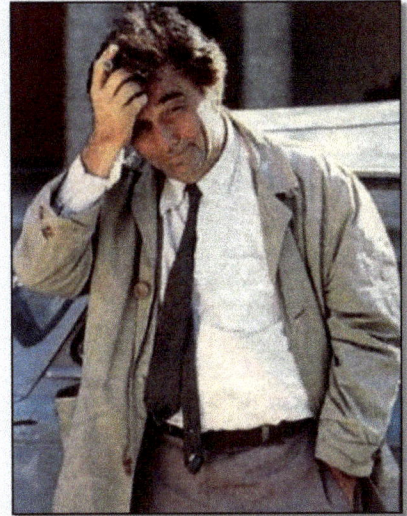

> **Most people associate sharing the Gospel with conflict – it's not!**
> **The Goal is to guide someone from their faulty thinking toward TRUTH**

Greg Kohkl: 'The Columbo Tactic in Apologetics' (4:06)     Introduction to Logic_ Mr. Croteau     Courtesy of Google Images     Fair Use Law 17 U.S. Code § 107

# Memorization Tool (to help you share): The Gospel in Romans

| | |
|---|---|
| **1) Who is Good?** | *"As it is written, 'There is none righteous, no, not one"* Romans 3:10 |
| **2) Who has Sinned?** | *"All have sinned and fallen short of the glory of God"* Romans 3:23 |
| **3) Where does sin come from?** | *"Whereby, as through one man sin entered the world, and death through sin, and so death spread to all men, because all sinned"* Romans 5:12 |
| **4) How can I escape death?** | *"God demonstrated His love toward us, in that while we were still sinners, Christ died for us"* Romans 5:8 |
| | *"The wages of sin is death, but the free gift of God is eternal life in Christ Jesus our Lord"* Romans 6:23 |
| | *"If you confess with your mouth the Lord Jesus Christ and believe in your heart God raised Him from the dead, you will be saved. For with the heart man believes unto righteousness, and with the mouth confession is made unto salvation"* Romans 10:9-10 |
| | *"Whosoever shall call upon the name of the Lord shall be saved"* Romans 10:13 |

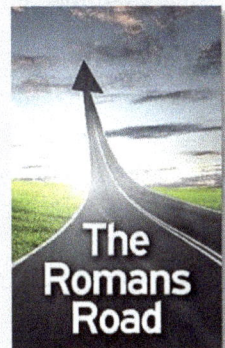

> <u>**With just these 7 verses memorized, you can lead anyone in a prayer for their salvation:**</u>
> *"Take God at His word and claim His promise for your salvation. If you are willing to bow your head in humility and sincerely ask Jesus Christ to forgive your sins and be your Lord and Savior, He will."*

JW Wallace: "Why I rarely share my personal testimony and why you shouldn't be quick to share yours" (10:41)     Introduction to Logic_ Mr. Croteau     Courtesy of Google Images     Fair Use Law 17 U.S. Code § 107

**Exit Ticket #21**　　<mark>**Class 21: How the Gospel Removes Guilt　Part 2**</mark>

1) Give a full explanation of what Premise 1 ("People's moral code defines right vs. wrong") means?

2) Do you think Premise 3 ("People who have failed morally often hope to have their guilt removed") is true? Explain why or why not.

3) Explain your understanding of Agape Love and how it ties to Premise 7 ("The Gospel proves God's love: He removes our moral failures and gives us new life free from guilt")?

4) When trying to share the Gospel with someone, what is the most effective way to respond to their claim?

# Class 22: Understanding the Gospel Part 1

What Would Help You to Be More Excited to Share the Gospel More Often?"

The Logic of the Gospel

How to be Righteous before God

Jesus Christ: "YHWH Tsidkenu"

The 4 Keys to the Gospel

Key #1: Understanding Holiness

Why Moses Couldn't Lead Israel into the Promised Land

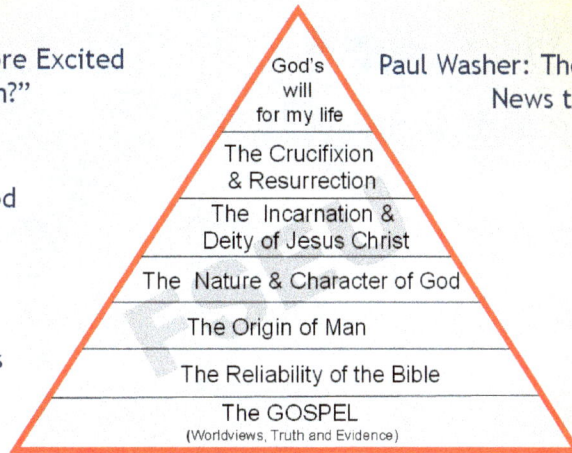

Paul Washer: The Gospel is only Good News to a Needy Man" (9:36)

**Triangle (top to bottom):**
- God's will for my life
- The Crucifixion & Resurrection
- The Incarnation & Deity of Jesus Christ
- The Nature & Character of God
- The Origin of Man
- The Reliability of the Bible
- The GOSPEL (Worldviews, Truth and Evidence)

# HEBREWS 11:1

"Faith = *Substance* of things *hoped for*.... *Evidence* of things *not seen*"

fse.life Lessons 02 - 08

---

# High School Logic Class: "What Would Help You to be more Excited to Share the Gospel more Often?"

## Top Answers from Our Class:

1) I need the Gospel put in terms I can understand.

2) I need more information on how to share the Gospel.

3) I need more evidence that God is real.

4) It would help if I had someone with me to keep me going and not give up.

5) I would if I wasn't so afraid.

6) I would if people reacted better to it.

7) I would if I saw more people my age sharing it.

**In-Class Homework #13 Class 26**   Name _____   Date _____

1) What are the 4 Goals of this "Introduction to Logic" Class?

2) What would help you be more excited to share the gospel more often?

3) On the slide called "The Challenge in America Today", which (if any) of the four boxes do you have trouble understanding, and why?

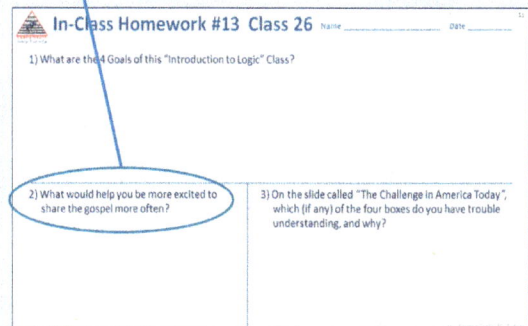

**Romans 1:18** *"I am not ashamed of the Gospel of Jesus Christ, for it is the POWER OF GOD to salvation for everyone who believes..."*

# The LOGIC of the Gospel

## What is "Logic"?

LOGIC = The art and science of ***reasoning*** to discover truth.

Method of ***reasoning*** involving thinking through what we hear/observe to then reach conclusions.

## Is the Gospel logical?

a living sacrifice, holy, acceptable unto God, which is your reasonable service
ROMANS 12:1

*"'Come now, and let us <u>reason</u> together', says the Lord. Though your sins are like scarlet, they shall be white as snow; though they are red like crimson, they shall be as wool."* Isaiah 1:18

Courtesy of Google Images   Fair Use Law 17 U.S. Code § 107

# How to be "Righteous" before God: It's Not a Secret

Abraham Believed Jehovah, and He accounted it to him as Righteousness Gen. 15:6

1500 BC

Foretold 1,570 years beforehand

Abraham believed God and it was counted unto him for righteousness.
ROMANS 4:3

70 AD

Now this is His name by which He will be called:

The LORD Our Righteousness

Jeremiah 23:6

580 BC

Foretold 650 years beforehand

GOD DID THIS TO DEMONSTRATE HIS **RIGHTEOUSNESS**, FOR HE HIMSELF IS **FAIR** AND **JUST**, AND HE MAKES SINNERS RIGHT IN HIS SIGHT WHEN THEY **BELIEVE IN JESUS.**

ROMANS 3:26

70 AD

## 2 Corinthians 5:21

*"He (the Father) made Him (Jesus Christ) who knew no sin to be sin for us... so that we might be the <u>RIGHTEOUSNESS</u> OF GOD (the Father) IN HIM (Jesus)."*

## Romans 1:17

*"In the Gospel the <u>RIGHTEOUSNESS</u> OF GOD is revealed from faith to faith; as it is written, 'The just shall live by faith.'"*

Courtesy of Google Images   Fair Use Law 17 U.S. Code § 107

## Jesus Christ  =  God the Father's Righteousness

Old Test. "ṣə·ḏā·qāh", New Test. "dikaiosunē" = God's character as right and just; meeting God's demands to be right with Him

"Abraham believed in the LORD, and He accounted it to him for righteousness." Genesis 15:6

"For what does the Scripture say? 'Abraham believed God, and it was counted to him as righteousness.'" Romans 4:3

"For in it the righteousness of God is revealed from faith for faith, as it is written, 'The righteous shall live by faith.'" Romans 1:17

"He put on righteousness as a breastplate and a helmet of salvation on His head..." Isaiah 59:17

JESUS CHRIST
Our Righteousness

"And to the one who does not work but believes in Him who justifies the ungodly, his faith is counted as righteousness." Romans 4:5

"But for you who fear My name, the Sun of Righteousness shall rise with healing in His wings." Malachi 4:2

"In those days and at that time I will cause to grow up to David a Branch of righteousness; He shall execute judgment and righteousness in the earth." Jeremiah 33:15

"God made Him who knew no sin to be sin for us, so that we might become the righteousness of God in Him." 2 Corinthians 5:21

"God set Him forth as a propitiation by His blood, through faith, to demonstrate His righteousness, because in His forbearance God had passed over the sins that were previously committed, to demonstrate at the present time His righteousness, that He might be just and the justifier of the one who has faith in Him." Romans 3:25-26

# 4 Keys to the Gospel

**#1. Understanding Holiness**

What it means to say God is "Holy"

**#2. Understanding Sin**

What is Sin, and How does it Work?

**#3. Understanding How the Gospel Works**

The Gospel's 3 "Credits"

**#4. Understanding the Gospel's Power**

The Lordship of Jesus Christ

## Gospel Key #1:

### Understanding HOLINESS

1) Holy = *"hagios"*
2) Pure = *"hagnos"*

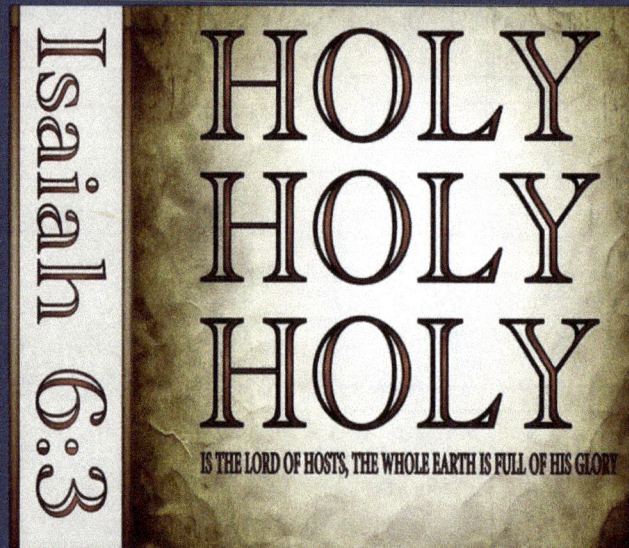

Isaiah 6:3

**HOLY HOLY HOLY**

IS THE LORD OF HOSTS, THE WHOLE EARTH IS FULL OF HIS GLORY

Courtesy of Google Images    Fair Use Law 17 U.S. Code § 107

## What it means to say God is "Holy"

**Holy = *"hagios"***
   - **moral perfection in character and conduct**
   - **separated from sin (no moral blemish)**

Exodus 15:11 *"Who is like You, O Lord, among the gods? Who is like you, glorious in HOLINESS?"*

Leviticus 19:2 *"You shall be HOLY; for I, the Lord your God, am HOLY."*

**Pure = *"hagnos"***
   - **undefiled**
   - **not contaminated with anything immoral**

Habakkuk 1:17 *"You are of PURER eyes than to behold evil, and You cannot look on wickedness."*

James 3:17 *"The wisdom that is from God is first PURE."*

Holiness to the Lord

Courtesy of Google Images    Fair Use Law 17 U.S. Code § 107

# Why Moses Couldn't Lead Israel into the Promised Land

**Deuteronomy 32:51-52**   *"...because you did not hallow Me in the midst of the children of Israel, yet you shall see the land before you, though you shall not go there, into the land which I am giving to the children of Israel."*

### Was Moses faithful?

*"If there is a prophet among you, I make Myself known to him in a vision and speak to him in a dream. Not with My servant Moses. He is faithful in all My house."* Numbers 12:7

### Was Moses humble?

*"Moses was very humble, more than all men on the face of the earth."* Numbers 12:3

### Did God know Moses?

*"The Lord spoke to Moses face to face, as a man speaks to his friend... you have found grace in My sight – I know you by name."* Exodus 33:11

**Numbers 20:7-12**

*"The Lord said to Moses, 'Take the rod; you and Aaron gather the assembly together. Speak to the rock before their eyes, and it will yield its water; you shall bring water for them out of the rock and give drink to the congregation and their animals.'*

*So, Moses and Aaron gathered the congregation together before the rock; and he said to them, 'Hear now, you rebels! Must **WE** bring water for you out of this rock?'*

*Then Moses lifted his hand and struck the rock twice with his rod; water came out abundantly, and the congregation and their animals drank.*

*Then the Lord spoke to Moses and Aaron, 'Because **YOU DID NOT BELIEVE ME, TO HALLOW ME** in the eyes of the children of Israel, you shall not bring this congregation into the land which I have given them.'"*

**"By those who come near Me I must be regarded as HOLY; Before all the people I must be glorified."** Leviticus 10:3

Courtesy of Google Images     Fair Use Law 17 U.S. Code § 107

## Exit Ticket #22      Class 22: Understanding the Gospel Part 1

| | |
|---|---|
| 1) What would help you to be more excited to share the Gospel? | 2) What makes the Gospel logical/reasonable? |
| 3) What is the secret to being called righteous by God? | 4) Of the 28 Scriptures in this lesson, which 2-3 scriptures resonate with you the most and why? |

## Classes 23:  Understanding the Gospel   Part 2

4 Keys to the Gospel

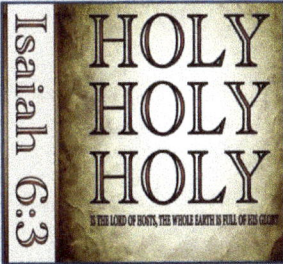

Key #2: Understanding Sin

Sin's 7 Definitions in the Bible

Sin's 5 Operations in the Bible

Three Ways to Grasp Sin's Power

Sin's Vicious Cycle

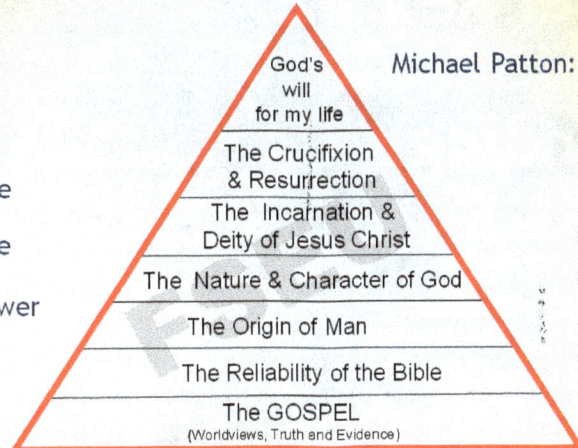

Michael Patton: 'What is the Gospel?"
(3:27)

God's will for my life

The Crucifixion & Resurrection

The Incarnation & Deity of Jesus Christ

The Nature & Character of God

The Origin of Man

The Reliability of the Bible

The GOSPEL
(Worldviews, Truth and Evidence)

# HEBREWS 11:1

"Faith = *Substance* of things *hoped for*.... *Evidence* of things *not seen*"

fse.life Lessons 02 - 08

# 4 Keys to the Gospel

**Isaiah 6:3**

**HOLY HOLY HOLY**
IS THE LORD OF HOSTS, THE WHOLE EARTH IS FULL OF HIS GLORY

**#1. Understanding Holiness**

What it means to say God is "Holy"

**#2. Understanding Sin**

What is Sin, and How does it Work?

**#3. Understanding How the Gospel Works**

The Gospel's 3 "Credits"

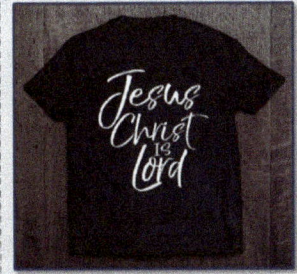

*Jesus Christ is Lord*

**#4. Understanding the Gospel's Power**

The Lordship of Jesus Christ

# Gospel Key #2:

## Understanding SIN

1) What is it?

2) How does it work?

3) Three ways to grasp it's power

4) Sin's Vicious Cycle

Courtesy of Google Images     Fair Use Law 17 U.S. Code S 107

## What *IS* Sin?

### Sin's 7 Definitions in the Bible

**He who is without sin is no fun at all**

**1) TRANSGRESSION** = an overstepping of the law; the Divine boundary between good and evil

Psalm 51:1 *"... According to the multitude of Your tender mercies, blot out my transgressions."*

Romans 2:23 *"You who make your boast in the law, do you dishonor God through breaking the law?"*

**2) INIQUITY** = an act that is inherently wrong, whether expressly forbidden or not

Romans 1:21 *"Although they knew God, they did not glorify Him as God, nor were they thankful, but became futile in their thoughts, and their foolish hearts were darkened."*

**3) ERROR** = a departure from what is right

Romans 1:18 *"The wrath of God is revealed from heaven against all ungodliness and unrighteousness of men, who suppress the truth in unrighteousness."*

**4) TRESPASS** = the intrusion of self-will into the sphere of divine authority

Ephesians 2:1 *"You He made alive, who were dead in trespasses and sins..."*

**5) MISS THE MARK** = *a failure to meet the Divine standard*

Romans 3:23 *"All have sinned and fallen short of the glory of God."*

**6) LAWLESSNESS** = spiritual anarchy

1Timothy 1:9-10 *"... the law was not made for a righteous person, but for the lawless and insubordinate, for the ungodly and for sinners, for the unholy and profane, for murderers of mothers, for manslayers, for fornicators, for sodomites, for kidnappers, for liars, for perjurers, and any other thing that opposes sound doctrine."*

**7) UNBELIEF** = an insult to Divine Truth

John 16:8-9 *"When He has come, He will convict the world of sin, and of righteousness, and of judgment. Of sin, because they do not believe Me..."*

Michael Patton: 'What is the Gospel?' (3:27)

Courtesy of Google Images     Fair Use Law 17 U.S. Code S 107

# How does Sin *WORK*?

## Sin's 5 Operations in the Bible

**I believe most people are essentially good. I know that I am. It's you I'm not entirely sure of.**

Stephen King

### 1) Sin originated with Satan

Isaiah 14:12-14 *"How have you fallen from heaven, O Lucifer son of the morning! How you are cut down to the ground, you who weakened the nations! For you have said in your heart: 'I will ascend into heaven, I will exalt my throne above the stars of God, I will also sit on the mount of the congregation, on the farthest sides of the north. I will ascend above the heights of the clouds. I will be like the Most High.'"*

### 2) Sin entered the world through Adam

Romans 5:12 *"Just as through one man sin entered the world, and death through sin, and thus death spread to all men, because all sinned."*

### 3) Sin was, and is, universal (Christ alone the exception)

Romans 3:23 *"All have sinned and fallen short of the glory of God."*

1Peter 2:21-22 *"...Christ also suffered for us, leaving us an example that you should follow His steps: 'Who committed no sin, nor was guile found in His mouth.'"*

### 4) Sin incurs the penalties of spiritual and physical DEATH

Genesis 2:17 *"Of the tree of the knowledge of good and evil you shall not eat, for in the day that you eat of it you shall surely die."*

Ezekiel 18:4 *"All souls are Mine; the soul of the father as well as the soul of the son is Mine; the soul who sins shall die."*

Romans 6:23 *"The wages of sin is death..."*

### 5) Sin's ONLY remedy = the sacrificial death of Jesus Christ available by the gift of faith

Acts 4:12 *"... there is no other name under heaven given among men by which we must be saved."*

Hebrews 9:26 *"... now, once at the end of the ages, He has appeared to put away sin by the sacrifice of Himself."*

Acts 13:38-39 *"Let it be known to you, brethren, that through this Man is preached to you the forgiveness of sins, and by Him everyone who believes is justified from all things from which you could not be justified by the law of Moses."*

Courtesy of Google Images     Fair Use Law 17 U.S. Code § 107

# Three Ways to Grasp Sin's Power

## #1. Sin is an ACT

= violating or disobeying God's revealed will
**James 2:10**

## #2. Sin is a STATE

**How We Rationalize Our Sin**
I exercised poor judgment. I made a mistake. It was the result of poor communication. I couldn't help it. It was an accident. We all fall short. Nobody's perfect. We're all growing. I did something stupid. I was born this way. I just can't help myself. If I've offended someone, I'm sorry. I'm a victim of some bad circumstances. It wasn't that bad.

= the absence of righteousness
**Romans 3:9-10**

## #3. Sin is a NATURE

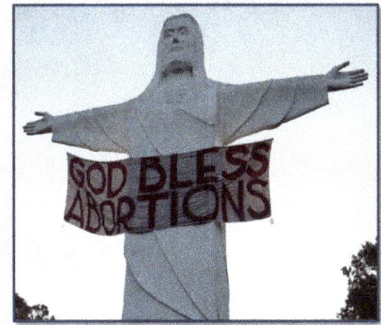

= enmity (hostility) towards God
**Romans 8:7**

**"Sin, when it is full-grown, brings forth death"** James 1:15
**"The wages of sin is death"** Romans 6:23a

Courtesy of Google Images     Fair Use Law 17 U.S. Code § 107

# Sin's Vicious Cycle

**LOT:**
"...that righteous man, dwelling among them, tormented his righteous soul from day to day by <u>SEEING AND HEARING</u> their lawless deeds." 2Peter 2:8; Gen.19

**DAVID:**
"Then it happened one evening that David arose from his bed and walked on the roof of the king's house. And from the roof he saw a woman bathing, and the woman was very beautiful to behold. So <u>DAVID SENT AND INQUIRED ABOUT THE WOMAN</u>. And someone said, 'Is this not Bathsheba, the daughter of Eliam, the wife of Uriah the Hittite?' David sent messengers, and took her; and she came to him, and he lay with her." 2Samuel 11:2-4

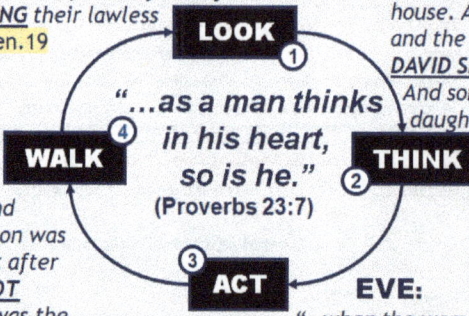

**SOLOMON:**
"...Solomon loved many foreign women, as well as the daughter of Pharaoh; women of the Moabites, Ammonites, Edomites, Sidonians and Hittites. For so it was, when Solomon was old, that his wives turned his heart after other gods, and <u>HIS HEART WAS NOT LOYAL TO THE LORD HIS GOD</u>, as was the heart of his father David. Solomon did evil in the sight of the Lord, and did not fully follow the Lord, as did his father David." 1Kings 11:1,4,6

LOOK ①
THINK ②
ACT ③
WALK ④

" *...as a man thinks in his heart, so is he.*" (Proverbs 23:7)

**EVE:**
"...when the woman saw that the tree was good for food, that it was pleasant to the eyes and a tree desirable to make one wise, <u>SHE TOOK OF IT'S FRUIT AND ATE</u>." Genesis 3:6

**"All that is in the world – the lust of the flesh, the lust of the eyes, and the pride of life – is not of the Father but is of the world"** 1John 2:16

## Exit Ticket #23    Class 23: Understanding the Gospel Part 2

| | |
|---|---|
| **1) Of the 8 descriptions of sin, which 2-3 resonate with you and why?** | **2) Of the 5 ways sin operates, which 2-3 resonate with you and why?** |
| **3) Looking at Sin's Vicious Cycle in a person's life, which resonates with you and why?** | **4) Of the 20 Scriptures in this lesson, which 2-3 scriptures resonate with you the most and why?** |

# Class 24: Understanding the Gospel, Part 3

4 Keys to the Gospel

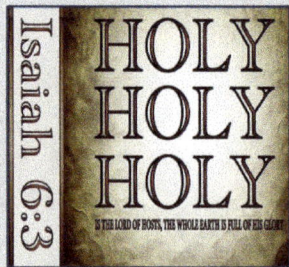

Key #3: Understanding How the Gospel Works

Understanding the Gospel = Understanding God as a Person

How God Applies the Gospel to My Life

The Gospel's 3 "Credits"

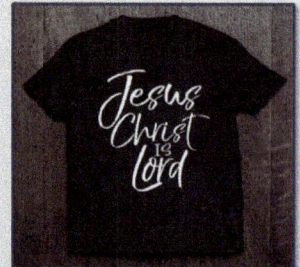

Key #4: Understanding the Gospel's Power
The #1 Essential to Sharing the Gospel = Knowing Jesus Christ as Lord & Savior

Being Righteous in God's Eyes = Trusting in Jesus Christ

The Lordship of Jesus Christ

Voddie Baucham 'How Ordinary Christians do Apologetics' (44:17)

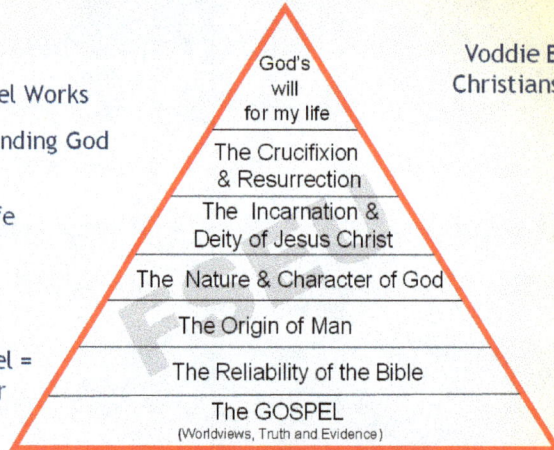

God's will for my life

The Crucifixion & Resurrection

The Incarnation & Deity of Jesus Christ

The Nature & Character of God

The Origin of Man

The Reliability of the Bible

The GOSPEL
(Worldviews, Truth and Evidence)

## HEBREWS 11:1

"Faith = *Substance* of things *hoped for*.... *Evidence* of things *not seen*"

fse.life Lessons 02 - 08

# 4 Keys to the Gospel

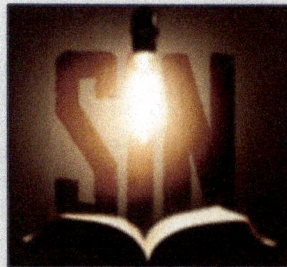

| #1. Understanding Holiness | #2. Understanding Sin | #3. Understanding How the Gospel Works | #4. Understanding the Gospel's Power |
|---|---|---|---|
| What it means to say God is "Holy" | What is Sin, and How does it Work? | The Gospel's 3 "Credits" | The Lordship of Jesus Christ |

Isaiah 6:3 — HOLY HOLY HOLY — IS THE LORD OF HOSTS, THE WHOLE EARTH IS FULL OF HIS GLORY

Jesus Christ is Lord

Voddie Baucham 'How Ordinary Christians do Apologetics Effectively' (44:17)　　Courtesy of Google Images　Fair Use Law 17 U.S. Code § 107

# Gospel Key #3:

## Understanding How the Gospel Works

1) Understanding God as a Person
2) How God Applies the Gospel in My Life
3) The Gospel's 3 "Account Credits"

Courtesy of Google Images   Fair Use Law 17 U.S. Code § 107

## Understanding the Gospel = Understanding God as a Person

### God is *JUST*

| | |
|---|---|
| God's Character | The Judge is Holy, Righteous & Just |
| God's Law | The Judge credits the penalty of my sin to me |
| God's Law | The Judge declares me *Guilty* and *Wicked* because of <u>my works</u> |

PSALM 89:14

### God is *LOVE*

| | |
|---|---|
| God's Character | The Judge is Kind & Merciful |
| God's Grace | The Judge credits the penalty of my sin to Christ |
| God's Grace | The Judge declares me *Not Guilty* and *Righteous* because of <u>Christ's works</u> |

**ROMANS 3:23a**
*"The WAGES of <u>my sin</u> is <u>my DEATH</u>..."*

**BUT**

**ROMANS 3:23b**
*"God's FREE GIFT <u>to me</u> is ETERNAL LIFE in Christ Jesus our Lord."*

Courtesy of Google Images   Fair Use Law 17 U.S. Code § 107

## How God Applies the Gospel to My Life

Salvation = A legal verdict taking place *in God's Courtroom...*    not *in a sinner's heart*.

An *instantaneous change* in one's standing before God...    not a *gradual change* in the one being justified.

Salvation = God performs a *SWAP...*

- my sin credited to Christ.
- Christ's righteousness credited to me.

God's 3 options in His Courtroom:

1) condemn me for my sinfulness
2) accept me in my sinfulness
3) change my sinfulness to righteousness

**If God can exercise the 3rd option:** He can declare me righteous in His Courtroom based on the righteousness of Christ.

**How does the Bible depict the situation in God's courtroom?**

**HEBREWS 9:24**
*"Christ has not entered the holy places made with hands which are copies of the true, but into heaven itself, now to appear in the presence of God FOR ME."*

Courtesy of Google Images   Fair Use Law 17 U.S. Code § 107

## The Gospel's 3 "Credits"

**#1. God's HOLINESS**
He **credits** my sin to my account.

**#2. God's PROVISION**
He **credits** my sin to His Son's account.

**#3. God's GRACE**
God **credits** His Son's righteousness to my account.

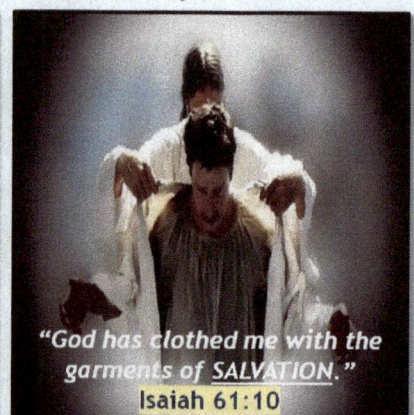

*"Your SINS have separated you from your God..."*
Isaiah 59:2

*"The Lord has laid on Him the SINS of us all."*
Isaiah 53:6

*"God has clothed me with the garments of SALVATION."*
Isaiah 61:10

**2Corinthians 5:21** *"He made Him who knew no sin to be sin for us, so that we might become the righteousness of God in Him."*

Courtesy of Google Images   Fair Use Law 17 U.S. Code § 107

# Gospel Key #4:

## Understanding the Gospel's Power

1) **#1 Essential for Sharing the Gospel**

2) **Being Righteous in God's Eyes**

3) **The Lordship of Jesus Christ**

*Jesus Christ IS Lord*

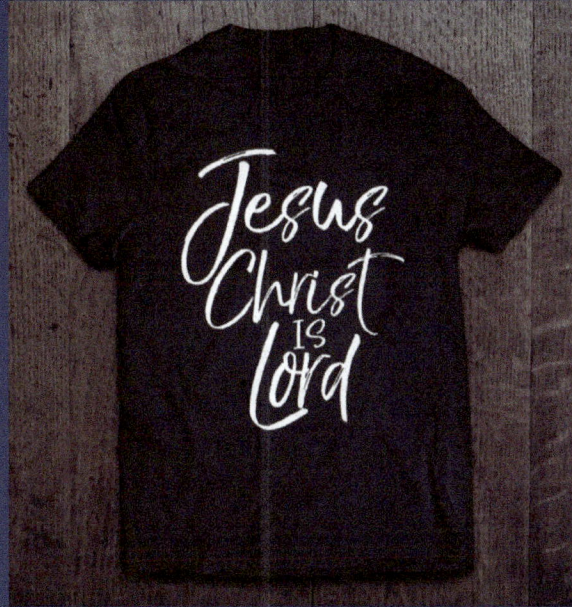

Courtesy of Google Images    Fair Use Law 17 U.S. Code § 107

---

## The #1 Essential to Sharing the Gospel = Knowing Jesus Christ as Your Lord & Savior

**DEUTERONOMY 29:29**
(1,450 BC)

*"The secret things belong to the Lord our God, but those things which are REVEALED belong to us and our children forever, that we may do all the words of this law."*

**COLOSSIANS 1:26**
(60 AD)

*"The mystery (hidden truth) which has been hidden from ages and from generations, but now has been REVEALED to HIS SAINTS."*

**COLOSSIANS 1:27**
(60 AD)

*"To them God willed to MAKE KNOWN what are the riches of the GLORY of this mystery (hidden truth) among the Gentiles:*
*which is **CHRIST IN YOU**, the hope of GLORY ."*

**Allowing Jesus Christ to Reign in *ME***

**JOHN 15:5,8** (32 AD)

*"I am the Vine, you are the branches. He who abides in Me, and I IN HIM, bears much fruit; for without Me you can do nothing. By this My Father is GLORIFIED, that you bear much fruit, so you will be My disciples."*

Courtesy of Google Images    Fair Use Law 17 U.S. Code § 107

## Being Righteous in God's Eyes = Trusting in Jesus Christ

| | |
|---|---|
| John 3:16 | *'whosoever believes IN Me has everlasting life'* |
| John 3:36 | *'whoever believes IN the Son has everlasting life'* |
| John 5:24 | *'He who believes IN Him who sent Me has everlasting life'* |
| John 6:40 | *'Everyone who believes IN Me may have everlasting life'* |
| John 6:47 | *'He who believes IN Me has everlasting life'* |
| John 8:24 | *'If you do not believe that I am He, you will die in your sins'* |
| John 8:51 | *'If anyone keeps My word, he shall never see death'* |
| John 10:9 | *'If anyone enters BY Me, he will be saved'* |
| John 10:28 | *'I give them eternal life, and they shall never perish'* |
| John 11:26 | *'Whoever believes IN Me shall never die'* |
| John 17:3 | *'This is eternal life… knowing the Father and the Son'* |

**What challenge does Jesus make to me?**

**JOHN 11:27**
*"Do you believe this?"*

Courtesy of Google Images    Fair Use Law 17 U.S. Code § 107

---

# The Lordship of Jesus Christ

"The terrible thing,
the almost impossible thing,
is to hand over your whole self
— all your wishes and precautions —
to Christ."

*C. S. Lewis.*

Courtesy of Google Images    Fair Use Law 17 U.S. Code § 107

## Exit Ticket #24     Class 24: Understanding the Gospel Part 3

| | |
|---|---|
| **1) How can God be both just and loving?** | **2) How does God apply the Gospel to me?** |
| **3) Explain God's 3 "Credits"?** | **4) Of the 24 Scriptures in this lesson, which 2-3 scriptures resonate with you the most and why?** |

# Class 25: Where Did I Come From? Part 1

Genesis 1:1  Battle for the Beginning

What do people mean by "Evolution"?

What does the Scientific Community say?

What do Government Lobbyists say?

What do High Schools say?

If Evolution is true, what's the logical conclusion?

Has Evolution devalued the meaning of life?

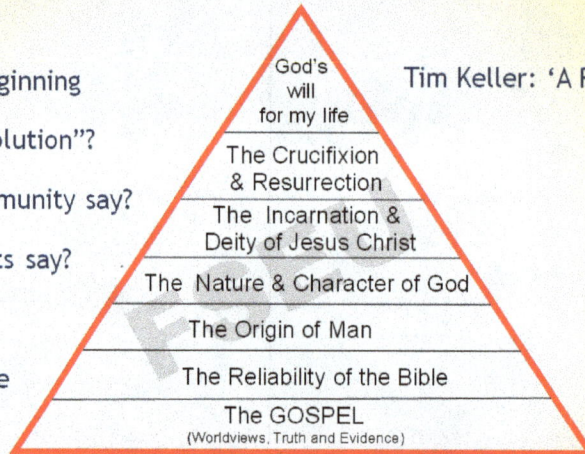

God's will for my life

The Crucifixion & Resurrection

The Incarnation & Deity of Jesus Christ

The Nature & Character of God

The Origin of Man

The Reliability of the Bible

The GOSPEL
(Worldviews, Truth and Evidence)

Tim Keller: 'A Reason for Living' (32:43)

**HEBREWS 11:1**

"Faith = *Substance* of things *hoped for.... Evidence* of things *not seen*"

fse.life Lessons 02 - 08

# Genesis 1:1  The Battle for the Beginning

*"In the beginning God ①CREATED the heavens and the earth."*

① CREATED = *"bara"* = only God can call into existence what never has existed ("something out of nothing")

### CREATION THEORY

Design (purpose, information, mind)

Finely-Tuned Universe from nothing

Irreducible Complexity

Information Machines (DNA, Cell)

Design in the Animal Kingdom

### EVOLUTION THEORY

Chance (purposeless, unguided, nature)

Spontaneous Generation ("Abiogenesis")

Common Descent with Modification

Natural Selection  ("survival of the fittest")

Transitional Forms  ("missing links")

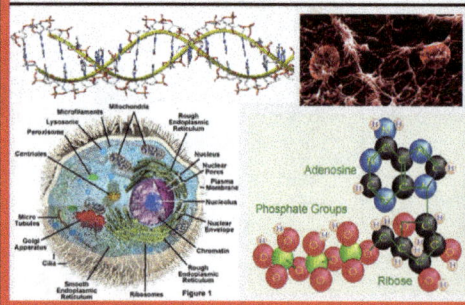

## Genesis 1:1   The Battle for the Beginning

*"In the beginning God ①CREATED the heavens and the earth."*

① CREATED = Hebr. *"bara"* = only God can call into existence what never existed ("something out of nothing")

### What is "Creationism"?                    G.S. McLean, "The Evidence for Creation"[8]

"A creationist is a person willing to accept that the biblical account of origins and the history of the earth are accurate and reliable. A creationist also believes that the statements made in God's Word should be able to be backed up and supported by *physical evidence* from the world that God has created. A creationist apologizes to no one that Scriptures are used as a key for understanding the principle of origins and the history of the earth."

### What is "Darwinian Evolution"?            Henry M. Morris, PhD "Scientific Creationism"[18]

"Evolution attempts to explain the origin, development, and meaning of all things by natural laws and processes which operate today as they have in the past. No extraneous processes, requiring the special activity of an external agent, or Creator, are permitted. The universe, in all its aspects, evolves itself into higher levels of order ("particles to people") by means of its innate properties. Evolution is a process occurring in time, which in its course gives rise to an increase of variety and an increasingly high level of organization. Particles evolve into elements, elements into complex chemicals, complex chemicals into simple living systems, simple life forms into complex life, complex animal life into man."

### Michael Denton, "Evolution: A Theory in Crisis"[19]

"Evolution has as its core idea that living things have originated gradually as a result of the interplay of chance and selection. According to Darwin, all the design, order and complexity of life and the eerie purposefulness of living systems were the result of a simple blind random process – natural selection. He believed that life was all related by common descent from an original ancestral species (i.e, that new species had arisen from pre-existing species in nature) and that, therefore, species were not the fixed immutable entities most biologists supposed."

---

### Who was Charles Darwin?[20]

Charles Darwin was born February 12, **1809** in Shrewsbury, England. His grandfather, Erasmus Darwin, was a naturalist and philosopher. His father, Robert, was a successful and wealthy doctor. His mother died when he was eight.

As a youngster, Charles was very interested in science and nature. At his father's urging, he studied medicine at the University of Edinburgh. But after 2 years he found he didn't like it and transferred to Christ's College in Cambridge for a major in theology, where he seriously was considering entering the clergy of the Church of England. He later wrote, *"I did not then in the least doubt the strict and literal truth of every word in the Bible."*

After graduating in **1831**, he served on a 5-year British science expedition as a naturalist aboard the *HMS Beagle.* In South America, Darwin found fossils of extinct animals that were similar to modern species. On the Galapagos Islands he recorded many variations among plants and animals of the same general type as he observed in South America. It was at this time that he read Charles Lyell's work, *Principles of Geology*, and his religious beliefs came into direct conflict with his expanding knowledge of science.

By **1836**, at the close of the expedition, he confessed in his writings that he wrestled over 2 theological issues:
1. the presence of evil in a world created by God: *"There seems to me too much misery in the world. I cannot persuade myself that a beneficent and omnipotent God would have designedly created the Ichneumonidae with the express intention of feeding within the living bodies of caterpillars, or that a cat should play with mice."*
2. the inerrancy of Scripture: *"I had gradually come by this time (1836– 1839) to see that the Old Testament as no more to be trusted than the sacred books of the Hindus or the beliefs of any barbarian."*

In 1838, he began writing up his notes from the *Beagle* expedition. A 230-page paper was published in 1844, and in **1859** he published *The Origin of Species by Means of Natural Selection.* He laid out his view that all life came not from the hand of a creator but from the process of 'survival of the fittest'. In a letter to a friend he said *"my deity is Natural Selection."* In **1871** Darwin published his 2nd book, *The Descent of Man.* In it he argued that humans are no different from other forms of life and that we, too, evolved through natural selection.

Darwin's son, Francis, quotes him as saying *"I never gave up Christianity until I was 40 years of age"*. The death of his eldest daughter Annie from fever at this same time in his life hammered the final nail in the coffin of his Christianity. In a letter written in **1880** Darwin stated, *"I am sorry to have to inform you that I do not believe in the Bible as a divine revelation and therefore not in Jesus Christ as the Son of God. Thus disbelief crept over me at a very slow rate, but was at last complete. The rate was so slow that I felt no distress."* He proclaimed himself an agnostic.

As an old man in failing health, Darwin wrote *"Science has nothing to do with Christ, except in so far as the habit of scientific research makes a man cautious in admitting evidence. For myself, I do not believe that there has ever been any revelation. As for a future life, every man must judge for himself between CONFLICTING VAGUE PROBABILITIES."*

# What do people mean by 'Evolution'?

**Do you mean...**

**1) Change over time?**

I can 'evolve' into a better baseball player or more responsible person.

**2) All life (including me) descended from a common ancestor?**

> This is referred to as '*microevolution*' (variation *within* a species), but the cause of the change is not defined ('Intelligent Design').

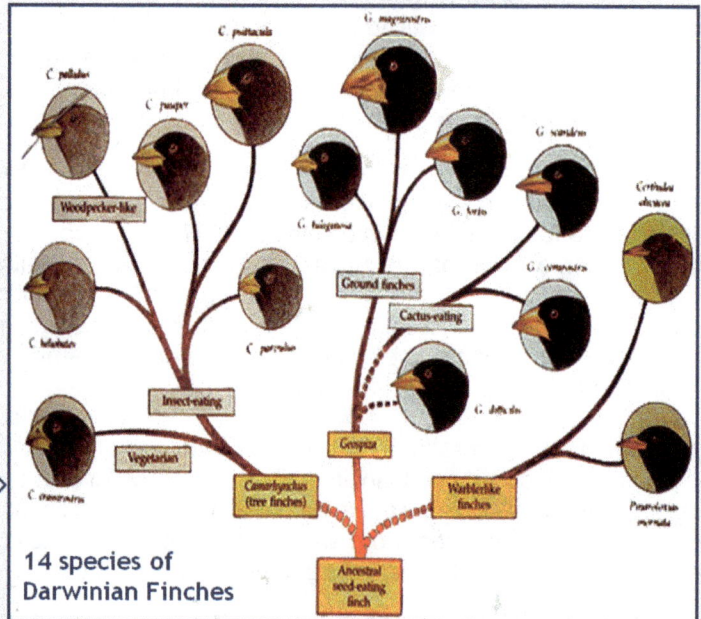

14 species of Darwinian Finches

Courtesy of Google Images     Fair Use Law 17 U.S. Code § 107

# What do people mean by 'Evolution'?

**Or do you mean...**

**3) All ordered, complex living creatures (including me) are the product of billions of years of *unguided* events which worked together to produce design and order from a starting point of *simplicity* and *randomness*.**

> This is DARWIN's, and today's scientific community's, definition: '*macroevolution*' = change *between* unique species.

from a single-celled organism that came from somewhere (???)

to a fully-formed human being

THE MODERN THEORY OF THE DESCENT OF MA

Courtesy of Google Images     Fair Use Law 17 U.S. Code § 107

## More Definitions: What is "Darwinian Evolution"?

**Michael J. Behe, PhD[16]** "Evolution is a flexible word. It can be used by one person to mean something as simple as change over time, or by another person to mean the descent of all life forms from a common ancestor, leaving the mechanism of change unspecified. In its full-throated, biological sense, however, evolution means a process whereby life arose from nonliving matter and subsequently developed by entirely natural means. This is the sense that Darwin gave to the word, and the meaning that it holds in the scientific community."

**John Ankerberg and John Weldon[8]** "The general theory that all life on earth has evolved from non-living matter and progressed to more complex forms with time; hence, it refers to *macroevolution* and not *microevolution* (minor changes within species illustrated in crossbreeding, such as varieties of dogs or varieties of corn)."

**Richard A. Swenson, MD[15]** "The theory of first things goes something like this: first you start with nothing, which then becomes something. The something then becomes a prebiotic soup with hydrogen, carbon, nitrogen, and water vapor (free oxygen arrives later). The soup bubbles into compounds like methane and ammonia. Lightning strikes periodically, stirring the pot. This frightens various molecules into each other's arms. Eventually, after this happens enough, you get an AMINO ACID. Then several. These get frightened into each other's arms (they don't like lightning either), and you get a PROTEIN. Then larger and larger proteins. Then more and more of them. And pretty soon (well, actually, not so soon) you have an ORGANISM with 100,000 proteins made by DNA that has 3,000,000,000 base pairs – all because of random benefit mutations. When the pot stops bubbling and the smoke clears, out of the cave steps Arnold Schwarzenegger: tens of trillions of cells with 100,000,000,000 neurons, 60,000 miles of blood vessels, and a retina that in a fraction of a second solves nonlinear differential equations that would take a Cray-2 supercomputer 100 years to solve."

**Jonathan Wells, PhD[21]** "Biological evolution is the theory that all living things are modified descendants of a common ancestor that lived in the distant past. It claims that you and I are descendants of ape-like ancestors, and that they in turn came from still more primitive animals. This is the primary meaning of "evolution" among biologists. 'Biological evolution', according to the National Academy, explains that living things share common ancestors. Over time, evolutionary change gives rise to new species. Darwin called the process 'descent with modification,' and it remains a good definition of biological evolution today. For Charles Darwin, descent with modification was the origin of all living things after the first organisms. He wrote in *The Origin of Species*, 'I view all beings not as special creations, but as the lineal descendants of some few beings' that lived in the distant past'. The reason living things are now so different from each other, Darwin believed, is that they have been modified by natural selection, or survival of the fittest: 'I am convinced that Natural Selection has been the most important, but not exclusive, means of modification.'"

**Lee Strobel[22]** "…you don't need a Creator if life can emerge unassisted from the primordial slime of the primitive earth, and you don't need God to create human beings in his image if we are merely the product of the impersonal forces of natural selection. In short, you don't need the Bible if you've got The Origin of Species."

**Hugh Ross, PhD[14]** "Evolution is the belief that inorganic material evolves into simple cells and later into advanced life without any input from a divine being."

**G.S. McLean[23]** "The foundation of evolution is the belief that the origin of all ordered, complex systems including living creatures can be explained by the operation of natural laws without the initiation or the intervention of God. According to evolution, all living creatures including man are the product of billions of years of random chance events which have worked together to produce design and order out of randomness."

**A.E. Wilder Smith, PhD[24]** "The development of life from nonliving matter took place spontaneously by stages, the first stage being that simple organic compounds (such as hydrocarbons) arose spontaneously under the influence of various radiations on a lifeless earth (in other words, spontaneous chemical evolution up to simple organic compounds occurred). In the second stage of evolution, very complicated molecules (protein-like substances, nucleic acids, etc.) arose. The lithosphere, atmosphere and hydrosphere were the 'theatre of operation', with the general laws of chemistry and physics as known today, combined with chance events over long time spans. The third stage in the spontaneous evolutionary process up to life was reached when the complex molecules formed during the second stage were acted upon and changed under the influence of the external medium and which then underwent selection. Thus arose the most primitive primary organisms under the influence of nothing but chance, time, a suitable environment and simple chemicals."

# How Strong is the *Belief* in Evolution in the Scientific Community?[8]

- Associated Press, "Biology Textbooks OK'd" (Nov. 8, 2003): *"The State of Texas Board of Education voted overwhelmingly to approve biology textbooks that drew criticism from the religious academia who say the books fail to present the anti-evolution point of view. Most of the scientists and educators argued that the theory of evolution is widely believed and is a cornerstone of modern scientific research. Texas, California and Florida account for more than 30% of the nation's $4 billion public school book market."*

- Carl Sagan (Cornell Univ. Astronomer, Pulitzer Prize winner): *"Evolution is a fact, not a theory."*

- Julian Huxley ("Evolution and Genetics"): *"Evolution can be defined as a directional and essentially irreversible process occurring in time, which in its course gives rise to an increase in variety and an increasingly high level of organization in its products. Our present knowledge indeed forces us to the view that the whole of reality is evolution – a single process of self-transformation."*

- Francisco Ayala ("Biology as an Autonomous Science") *"Biological evolution can be explained without recourse to a Creator or a planning agent external to the organisms themselves. There is no evidence of any vital force directing the evolutionary process toward the production of specified kinds of organisms."*

- George Gaylord Simpson (Prof. of vertebrate paleontology at Harvard's Museum of Comparative Zoology): *"Ample proof has been repeatedly presented and is available to anyone who really wants to know the truth. In the present study the factual truth of organic evolution is taken as established."*

- Ashley Montagu (Prof. Princeton University): *"The attack on evolution, the most thoroughly authenticated fact in the history of science, is an attack on science itself."*

- American Association for the Advancement of Science: *"The evidences in favor of evolution of man are sufficient to convince every scientist of note in the world."*

- Rene Dubos ("Humanistic Biology") *"Most enlightened persons now accept as a fact that everything in the cosmos – from heavenly bodies to human beings – has developed and continues to develop through evolutionary processes."*

- American Institute of Biological Sciences: *"The theory of evolution is the only scientifically defensible explanation for the origin of life and development of species. As a community, biologists agree that evolution occurred and that the forces driving the evolutionary process are still active today. This consensus is based on more than a century of scientific data gathering and analysis."*

- American Society of Parasitologists: *"Evolution is believed by nearly all professional life scientists. Virtually all scientists accept the evolution of current species from fewer, simpler ancestral ones as undisputed."*

- American Geological Institute: *"Scientific evidence indicates beyond any doubt that life has existed on Earth for billions of years. This life evolved through time producing vast numbers of species of plants and animals."*

- Geological Society of America: *"We geologists find incontrovertible evidence in the rocks that life has existed here on earth for several billions of years and that it has evolved through time."*

- Society of Vertebrate Paleontology: *"Scientists do not argue about whether evolution took place: that is a fact."*

## The 7 Assumptions of Evolution  (G.A. Kerkut, evolutionist and author, "Implications of Evolution"[8])

| **"The evidence we have at present is insufficient to allow us to decide the answer to these problems. Evolution has to be taken on pure faith. *The evidence is circumstantial and can be argued either way*."** | |
| --- | --- |
| Assumption | Comment |
| #1. non-living things gave rise to living material ("abiogenesis") | There is little if any evidence for abiogenesis; we have no indication it can be performed. It s a matter of faith by the biologist that it occurred. |
| #2. non-living things gave rise to living material ("abiogenesis") only once | This is again purely a matter of belief rather than proof. |
| #3. viruses, bacteria, protozoa and higher animals were all interrelated | We have as yet no definite evidence about the way in which viruses, bacteria or protozoa are interrelated |
| #4. protozoa gave rise to the metazoa | Here again, nothing definite is known. |
| #5. various invertebrate phyla are interrelated | Evidence for the affinities of the invertebrates is circumstantial; not the type of evidence needed to form a verdict of definite relationships. |
| #6. invertebrates led to vertebrates | In a sense, this account is science fiction. |
| #7. fish, amphibia, reptiles, birds and mammals are interrelated | many of the key transitional forms are not well documented and we have as yet to obtain a satisfactory objective method of dating fossils. |

# What does the Scientific Community say?

**American Association for the Advancement of Science:**

*"The evidences in favor of evolution of man are sufficient to convince every scientist of note in the world."*

**American Institute of Biological Sciences:**

*"The theory of evolution is the only scientifically defensible explanation for the origin of life and development of species. As a community, biologists agree that evolution occurred and that the forces driving the evolutionary process are still active today. This consensus is based on more than a century of scientific data gathering and analysis."*

**American Geological Institute:**

*"Scientific evidence indicates beyond any doubt that life has existed on Earth for billions of years. This life evolved through time producing vast numbers of species of plants and animals."*

**Society of Vertebrate Paleontology:**

*"Scientists do not argue about whether evolution took place: that is a fact."*

**American Society of Parasitologists:**

*"Evolution is believed by nearly all professional life scientists. Virtually all scientists accept the evolution of current species from fewer, simpler ancestral ones as undisputed."*

**What message is being communicated?**

**The message from the Scientific Community: Evolution is not theory - it's *FACT***

Courtesy of Google Images    Fair Use Law 17 U.S. Code § 107

# What do our High Schools teach?

**"Modern Biology" (Holt, Rinehart, Winston) - Advanced Biology class, LSHS, Lees Summit, MO...**

"To understand the story of human evolution, we must understand both our ancestry and our relationship to our closest living kin. Humans are members of the ancient mammalian order **Primates**. Many of our behaviors and characteristics are *similar to* other primates, and some are uniquely human.

Anthropoid Primates = marmosets, monkeys, apes, **HUMANS**
Prosimian Primates = lemurs, lorises, tarsiers

Of the anthropoid species, the chimpanzees may be the most closely related to humans. Comparisons of chimpanzee and human DNA *have shown* a high degree of similarity.

This similarity *suggests* that humans and chimpanzees *may have* shared an ancestor less than 6 million years ago.

It is important to understand, however, that humans are not descended from chimpanzees or from any other modern ape. Rather, modern apes and humans are *probably* descended from a more primitive apelike ancestor."

**What message is being communicated?**

**The message from Public High Schools: Evolution is not theory – It's *FACT***

Courtesy of Google Images    Fair Use Law 17 U.S. Code § 107

## If Evolution is Fact... What's the Logical Conclusion?

THERE'S PROBABLY NO GOD. NOW STOP WORRYING AND ENJOY YOUR LIFE.

Richard Dawkins, Oxford University Evolutionary Biologist ('Out of Eden')

*"In a universe of blind physical forces and genetic replication, some people are going to get hurt, and other people are going to get lucky;*

*you won't find any rhyme or reason to it, nor any justice.*

*The universe we observe has precisely the properties we should expect if there is at the bottom...*
*1) no design,*
*2) no purpose,*
*3) no evil and no good.*

*Nothing but blind pitiless indifference. DNA neither knows nor cares. DNA just is, and we dance to its music."*

Courtesy of Google Images    Fair Use Law 17 U.S. Code § 107

## If Evolution is Fact... What's the Logical Conclusion?

**Professor William Provine, Cornell University Evolutionary Biologist**

*"If Darwinism is true, then there are 5 inescapable conclusions:*

① *there's...  no evidence for God,*

② *there's...  no life after death,*

③ *there's...  no absolute foundation for right and wrong,*

④ *there's...  no ultimate meaning for life,*

⑤ *people...  don't really have free will."*

### Dr. William Provine

Professor of Biological Sciences at Cornell University

"Let me summarize my views on what modern evolutionary biology tells us loud and clear ... There are no gods, no purposes, no goal-directed forces of any kind. There is no life after death. When I die, I am absolutely certain that I am going to be dead. That's the end for me. There is no ultimate foundation for ethics, no ultimate meaning to life, and no free will for humans, either."

Science cannot address intent, purpose, value or ultimate meaning

Courtesy of Google Images    Fair Use Law 17 U.S. Code § 107

## What difference does it make whether I believe in Darwinian Evolution or Creation?

**1. Man is an advanced animal and has no unique relevance other than what he chooses to give himself**

- George Gaylord Simpson (evolutionist)[8]: *"man has no special status other than his definition as a distinct species of animal. He is in the fullest sense a part of nature and not apart from it. He is literally kin to every living thing, be it an amoeba, a tapeworm, a seaweed, an oak tree, or a monkey…"*

**2. If man is just an animal and an accident of nature, where does he get ultimate meaning, dignity, or absolute values?**

- William Provine (Prof., Cornell University)[8]: *"The implications of modern science are clearly inconsistent with most religious traditions. No inherent moral or ethical laws exist, nor are there absolute guiding principles for human society. The universe cares nothing for us and we have no ultimate meaning in life."*

- Leslie Paul ("The Annihilation of Man")[8]: *"No one knows what time this lonely planet will cool, all life will die, all minds will cease, and it will all be as if it had never happened. That is the goal to which evolution is traveling… life is no more than a match struck in the dark and blown out again. The end is to deprive life of meaning."*

**3. If the universe is meaningless, why bother with morals? Isn't it "survival of the fittest"?**

**HITLER and NAZISM**[8]    Nazi General Friedrich von Bernhardi: *"…from an evolutionary viewpoint, it is biologically right to crush the weaker peoples of the earth. War is not only a biological law, but a moral obligation."*

Sir Arthur Keith (evolutionist): *"It was often said in 1914 that Darwin's doctrine of evolution had bred war in Europe, particularly in Germany. There is no question that evolution was basic in all Nazi thought, from beginning to end. Yet, it is a remarkable phenomenon how few are aware of this fact today."*

Adolf Hitler: *"I regard Christianity as the most fatal, seductive lie that ever existed. He who would live must fight; he who does not wish to fight in this world where permanent struggle is the law of life, has no right to exist. I do not see why man should not be as cruel as nature; all that is not of pure race in this world is trash."*

John Koster (historical philosopher): *"Many names have been cited beside that of Hitler to explain the Holocaust. Oddly enough, Charles Darwin's is almost never among them. Yet, Darwin's picture of man's place in the universe prepared the way for the Holocaust…the term neo-Darwinism was openly used to describe Nazi racial theories. The expression 'natural selection', as applied to human beings, turns up at the Western Conference in the prime document of the Holocaust. "*

**STALIN and COMMUNISM**[8]    G. Gludjidze, "Landmarks in the Life of Stalin": *"At a very early age, the young Stalin was a seminary student, studying to become a priest in the Russian Orthodox Church. We were discussing religion: Joseph heard me out, and then said: 'You know, they are fooling us, there is no God.' I was astonished at these words. I had never heard anything like it before. 'I'll lend you a book to read; it will show you that the world and all living things are quite different from what you imagine, and all this talk about God is sheer nonsense,' Joseph said. 'What book is that?' I inquired. 'Darwin. You must read it.' Having become an atheist, Stalin murdered millions of his own people in his attempt to construct an official atheistic state."*

**MAO TSE TUNG and COMMUNISM**[8]    *"Being a Marxist and an atheist and a firm believer in evolutionism himself, Mao mandated that the reading material used in this early day "Great Leap Forward" in literacy would be the writings of Charles Darwin and other materials supportive of the evolution paradigm."*

| Secular Humanism's 10 Lies to promote Darwinian Evolution |
| --- |
| From his book 'And God created Darwin'[30], we can learn from Duane Schmidt ten lies that evolutionists who hold to a worldview of secular humanism use, as Schmidt says, to "ease me on in" to the *theory* of evolution, in an effort to make evolution tolerable for me to accept as a *proven fact*… |

| # | Lie | Description | Example | The Truth |
| --- | --- | --- | --- | --- |
| 1 | "I'm really on your side" | Evolutionists quote or mention a Scripture reference, in an attempt to pacify Creationists that they share some "common ground" | Stephen Gould (Harvard Prof. Geology) refers to Biblical stories in his essays, and Darwin himself quotes Bible passages without referencing the verses | 1)  Gallup polls: while only 9% of Americans believe in evolution, 87% believe God created the universe all at once or used evolution. But 84% of American scientists interviewed don't believe God created the universe, 96% don't believe in hell, and only 8% believe in heaven. <br> 2)  Creation claims there is a reason for being - humans have a specific God-based purpose; evolution claims there is no reason for being (you can't get more apart than that). |

## Secular Humanism's 10 Lies to promote Darwinian Evolution

Evolutionists who hold to a worldview of secular humanism use a variety of outright lies to "ease me on in" to the *theory* of evolution in an effort to make evolution tolerable for me to accept as a *proven fact*…

| # | Lie | Description | Example | The Truth |
|---|-----|-------------|---------|-----------|
| 2 | "discredit the messenger" | Anti-evolutionists are derogatorily called creationists, religious freaks, the "Religious Right", "Bible Thumpers", "Genesis Freaks", who "believe in such nonsense as Noah and the Flood, etc. | Dawkins: *"anti-evolutionist propagandists try to buy credibility by concealing fact; an opponent of evolution is a person who is ignorant, stupid or insane (or wicked, but I'd rather not consider that); opposition to evolution is 'redneck creationism'; those who find no merit in the evolution argument are 'backwoodsmen', pretending scientific credentials."* | There is an enormous body of scientists with credentials equal to or greater than Dawkins, who strongly oppose evolution. There is also a rich history of Christian creationists, who *invented* many fields of science. Evolutionists use an old tactic: by charging his antagonist with religious bias, he puts the questioner on the defensive, removing his need to defend his position (an evolutionist offense is far easier than mounting a good defense of evolution). |
| 3 | "the flat-out statement" | School textbooks flatly state that evolution "has been proven", or "is a scientific fact", or "can be seen in nature", without a single fact to support their statement | American Association for the Advancement of Science: *"The evidences in favor of evolution of man are sufficient to convince every scientist of note in the world."* | Einstein published his theories for the scientific community to test. They tested them, found them credible, and used them as keystones of science. But there is no published proof on evolution that scientists have tested and found credible. |
| 4 | "drop names" | Prestigious university names and titles and positions can cause people, especially students, to take their statements as truth | National Geographic and Nature magazines, Smithsonian museum, Harvard/ Yale/ Cambridge universities: all install a sense of respect in people – when these institutions publish evolutionary information, most take it as unquestionable truth. | (a) Jan. 2000: Nature and National Geographic magazines published the hoaxes "archaeoraptor" and "bambiraptor" as true intermediary species between birds and dinosaurs, only to be embarrassed when found to be deceptions by Chinese peasant farmers. (b) Michael Behe researched past issues of the Journal of Molecular Evolution and didn't find even *ONE* article in over 10,000 published that offered a scenario for the evolution of complex biological systems! |
| 5 | "invent a vocabulary" | Evolutionists invent words that attach "evolution" to them, so people grow comfortable with developing an evolutionary mindset. It was Russian ento-mologist Iuri Philip-chenko, a secular scientist, who, in 1927, first introduced the terms "micro" vs. "macro" evolution… Christians have bought it ever since. | The word *"microevolution"* never existed until evolutionists made it up. No one disputes dogs or roses come in many varieties. But evolutionists reclassify varieties as microevolution, suggesting that there is some sort of analogy to be made between variation within a species and creating a new species gradually over time (which is true evolution, disguised by the word, you guessed it, *"macroevolution"*). But "a rose is still a rose", as is a dog or a cat or anything else. | 1) Variation is no proof for evolution, just as conformity is worlds apart from adaptation (another clever word game played by evolutionists). Just because a species fits its environment doesn't mean it adapted to get there. These words are meaningless and contribute nothing to science literature. 2) The word *"evolve"* is now being used to describe everything, from governments to language and art. Yet "evolve" as originally used in biology means accidental change that is gradual, over time….not by plan or design or intentional (as used so often today). |

## Secular Humanism's 10 Lies to promote Darwinian Evolution

Evolutionists who hold to a worldview of secular humanism use a variety of outright lies to "ease me on in" to the *theory* of evolution in an effort to make evolution tolerable for me to accept as a *proven fact*...

| # | Lie | Description | Example | The Truth |
|---|-----|-------------|---------|-----------|
| 6 | "semantic browbeating" | The language of science originates mainly from Greek and Latin - many scientists arguing evolution slip back into this language (everyday folks get lost in their meaning) | Steven Gould: "*...contemporary science has massively substituted notions of indeterminacy, historical contingency, chaos and punctuation for previous convictions about graduated, progressive, predictable determinism.*" (what he really meant: "the reason you don't see fossils of in-between species is we now agree that's not how evolution works"). | 1) Science is not that complicated that it can't be explained. US District Judge James Graham (May 2000): "*Science is not an inscrutable priesthood. Any person of reasonable intelligence should, with some diligence, be able to understand and critically evaluate a scientific theory.*" 2) remove the invalidated, unverified, irrelevant, unproven statements: you'll be amazed at how little is left of evolution literature. |
| 7 | " circular reasoning (tautology)" | Giving the answer that only restates the problem | Q: "What species survive?" A: "The fittest." Q: "Which are the fittest?" A: "Those that survive." "Survival of the Fittest" is one of those Darwinian phrases that means nothing. After hearing it defined, you know absolutely nothing about survivors. | Darwin saw right through circular reasoning in other scientists: "*Authors sometimes argue in a circle when they state that important organs never vary; for these same authors rank these parts as important because they do not vary.*" Since he nailed circular reasoning in others, it's amazing he failed to see it in his own answers. |
| 8 | The " Just So" Explanation | Evolutionists give answers to explain something after it has happened - not to try to be right, but to avoid ever being wrong. Their answer need not be correct, since it can't be disproved; but it must sound like it could or should be a suitable answer. | Evolutionists point to marmots, which cling together in tight family communities, as an example of how evolution favors closeness and cooperation. They will then point to bears, which live solitary lives of hermits, as an example of evolution favoring animals that spread themselves far and wide to forage for nourishment. | There is no evidence for each individual case that can link directly back to the subject of evolutionary development in an organism. Rather than pursuing the truth through the use of the scientific method, evolutionists spend a lot of energy deflecting questions that lead to exposing the lie. "*A lie, repeated often enough and loud enough, remains a lie. What thinking people really want are proofs beyond nimble argument.*" |
| 9 | "drown the argument with extraneous data" | Evolutionists lull people into belief by constant repetition of irrelevant technical details that make the theory appear scientific | High school science books publish detailed technical data on the Galapagos Islands "Darwin" finch population's migratory patterns, food types, and interbreeding patterns, without publishing exact data to support their claim for evolutionary origins. | Reviewing the scientific literature shows that almost no direct research is going on in evolution. |
| 10 | present " favorable mutations" as if a fact | Since the theory of evolution requires favorable mutations, they "must" be there. The fact that we can't point to any is just a stupid inconvenience. | How can an eye, just beginning to be an eye, and yet can't see, benefit the organism over no eye at all? If the eye developed such complexity, and evolution occurs in tiny steps of favorable mutations, each of the millions of mutations it would take to reach the present form of the eye had to be *favorable*. | The exact opposite is true: no favorable mutation has ever been observed – Michael Denton: "*Most mutations damage function.*" "*What is very remarkable about this whole issue is that, as is typical of any 'unquestioned article of faith,' evidence for the doctrine of spontaneous mutation is hardly ever presented.*" |

# Evolution: Devaluing Life's Ultimate Meaning

There *must* be a reason

1) Why do I get up in the morning?    2) Have I ever thought about what's my purpose – my 'end game'?

**Leo Tolstoy (1828-1910):**
*"My deeds, whatever they may be, will be forgotten sooner or later, and I myself will be no more. Why then do anything?*

*I then could not attach a rational meaning to a single act of my entire life. The only thing that amazed me was how I had failed to realize this from the very beginning.*

*How could anyone fail to see this? That's what is amazing!"*

Don't I hope there is an *ultimate* meaning for *why* I do what I do?

**Bertrand Russell (1872-1970):**
*"We are the product of causes that had no provision of the end they were achieving.*

*That is the origin of our growth, our hopes and fears, our loves and beliefs are all but the outcomes of the accidental collocation of atoms, all of our labors all of our devotion, all of our geniuses are destined to the extinction in the vast death of the solar system.*

*Only within the scaffolding of these truths, only within the firm foundation of unyielding despair can the soul's habitation be safely built"*

Tim Keller: 'A Reason for Living' (32:43)

## Exit Ticket #25        Class 25: Where did I Come From? Part 1

| 1) Explain the difference between microevolution versus macroevolution? | 2) How do major scientific organizations regard the Theory of Evolution? |
|---|---|
| 3) How do Materialist Evolutionary Biologists teaching at our Universities see life's ultimate meaning? | 4) How did Tolstoy and Russell view meaning for living? |

# Class 26:  Where Did I Come From?  Part 2

Genesis 1:1  Battle for the Beginning

Comparing Views on Origins:   Detecting the Truth

Romans 1:18-20   Science, Truth & Faith

Using Science to Search for Truth

Applying 'Historical' Science to past, unobservable events

The History of Scientific Discovery: You can thank Christianity

Science & Religion: A Worldview Battle

There is a God – How the World's Most Notorious Atheist Changed His Mind

"There is a God": Prof. Flew's Turning Points

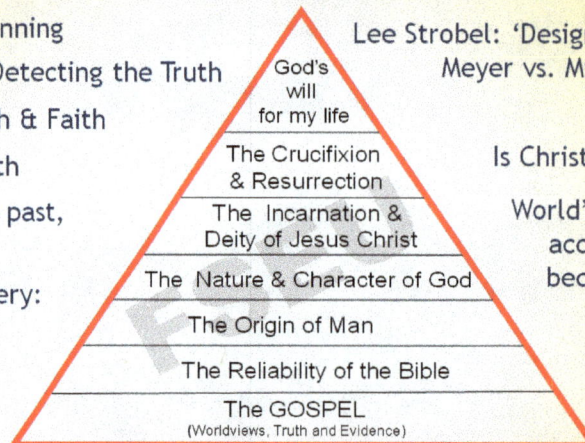

God's will for my life

The Crucifixion & Resurrection

The  Incarnation & Deity of Jesus Christ

The  Nature & Character of God

The Origin of Man

The Reliability of the Bible

The GOSPEL
(Worldviews, Truth and Evidence)

**H E B R E W S 11:1**

"Faith = *Substance* of things hoped for.... *Evidence* of things *not seen*"

**fse.life Lessons 02 - 08**

Lee Strobel: 'Design vs. Darwin_ Stephen Meyer vs. Michael Shermer' (10:51)

'J. Warner Wallace, Is Christianity Rational?' (3:40)

World's most famous atheist accepts existence of God because of Science' (5:05)

# Genesis 1:1   The Battle for the Beginning

*"In the beginning God* ①*CREATED the heavens and the earth."*

① CREATED = *"bara"* = only God can call into existence what never has existed ("something out of nothing")

| CREATION THEORY | EVOLUTION THEORY |
|---|---|
| Design (purpose, information, mind) | Chance (purposeless, unguided, nature) |
| Finely-Tuned Universe from nothing | Spontaneous Generation ("Abiogenesis") |
| Irreducible Complexity | Common Descent with Modification |
| Information Machines (DNA, Cell) | Natural Selection  ("survival of the fittest") |
| Design in the Animal Kingdom | Transitional Forms  ("missing links") |

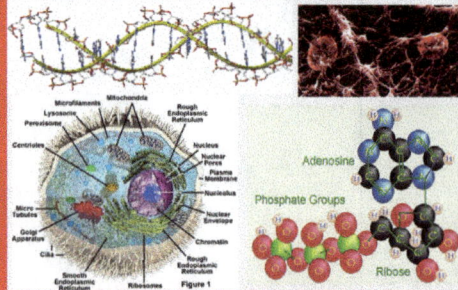

Lee Strobel: 'Design vs. Darwin_ Stephen Meyer vs. Michael Shermer' (10:51)

## Comparing Views on Origins:    Detecting the Truth

| Creation | Evolution |
|---|---|
| 1. I am a special creation of a good and all-powerful God. | 1. I am a descendant of a tiny cell of protoplasm that showed up 3.5 billion years ago. |
| 2. I am a created in His image, with capacities to think, feel and worship | 2. I am the blind, random product of time, chance and natural forces… a grab bag of atomic particles. |
| 3. I differ from animals not simply in degree but in kind. Not only is my kind unique, but I am unique among your kind. | 3. I am a purely biological entity, different only in degree but not in kind from a microbe, virus, or amoeba. |
| 4. God loves me so intensely, He desires my companionship and has a plan for my life. | 4. I exist on a tiny planet in a minute solar system in an empty corner of a meaningless universe. |
| 5. God gave the life of His Son so that I might spend eternity with Him. | 5. I have no essence beyond my body, and at death I will cease to exist. |
| 6. If I am willing to humble myself to accept His gift of of salvation, I can be His child. | 6. My goal is to trust, develop and promote myself in this life. I came from nothing and am going nowhere. |

## Romans 1:18-20   Science, Truth & Faith

*"The wrath of God is revealed from heaven against all ①UNGODLINESS and ②UNRIGHTEOUSNESS of men, who ③SUPPRESS the truth in unrighteousness, because what may be known of God is ④MANIFEST in them, for God has shown it to them.*

*For since the creation of the world His invisible attributes are clearly seen, being understood by the ⑤THINGS THAT ARE MADE, even His eternal power and Godhead, so they are ⑥WITHOUT EXCUSE."*

① UNGODLINESS = *"asebeia"* = lack of reverence to God

② UNRIGHTEOUSNESS = *"adikia"* = result of ungodliness = moral wrongfulness

③ SUPPRESS = *"katechō"* = to hold down, oppose

④ MANIFEST = *"phaneros"* = made public

⑤ THINGS MADE = *"poiēma"* = workmanship

⑥ WITHOUT EXCUSE = *"anapologētos"* = you can't give your own personal defense

# Romans 1:18-20        "Science, Truth and Faith"

*"The wrath of God is revealed from heaven against all ①UNGODLINESS and UNRIGHTEOUSNESS of men, who ②SUPPRESS the truth in unrighteousness, because what may be known of God is ③MANIFEST in them, for God has shown it to them. For since the creation of the world His invisible attributes are clearly seen, being understood by the ④THINGS THAT ARE MADE, even His eternal power and Godhead, so they are ⑤WITHOUT EXCUSE."*

① UNGODLINESS =  Gr. ""*asebeia*" = lack of reverence to, and worship of, God (no relationship with Him)
   UNRIGHTEOUSNESS = Gr. ""*adikia*" = result of ungodliness = moral wrongfulness (of character)

② SUPPRESS = Gr. ""*katechō*" = although God has provided the *evidence* from conscience (1:19, 2:14) and creation (1:20), as well as His Word (2Tim. 3:16), men choose to "hold down" and oppose His truth.

③ MANIFEST = Gr. ""*phaneros*" = shine, make public;  intelligence, conscience = *evidence*  (1:20,21,28,32, 2:15).

④ THINGS MADE = Gr. ""*poiēma*" = products,  workmanship (Ps 19:1-8, Ps 94:9, Acts 14:15-17, Acts 17:23-28).

⑤ WITHOUT EXCUSE = Gr. ""*anapologētos*" = indefensible; but when anyone who responds to God's revelation, even if only nature, God provides for that person to hear the gospel (Acts 17:24-31).

## Are Scientists interested in finding Truth about Origins, whether Creation or Evolution?

Linus Pauling (2X Nobel Prize winner)[21]: *"Science is the search for TRUTH"*

Bruce Alberts (president, US National Academy of Sciences)[21]: *"Science and lies cannot coexist."*

## How can distinguished scientists get such opposing views from the same information?

Philip Johnson (Berkeley Law Prof., "Reason in the Balance: The Case Against Naturalism in Science, Law and Education"):

• What is reasonable" is not based on searching for truth but on pre-conceived definition of what is reasonable.

• The accepted definition today of "science" = MATTER is the final absolute and only cause for all existence.

• Any supernatural or nonphysical explanation for reality is unacceptable and unreasonable in the field of science.

• Sir Julian Huxley[8]: *"the idea of God is entirely removed from the sphere of rational discussion."*

## I'm not a scientist – how can I be expected to determine *TRUTH* from lies?

• Jonathan Wells[21]: *"In a surprising number of instances, the average person is as competent to make a judgment as the most highly trained scientist. If a theory of gravity predicts heavy objects will fall upwards, it doesn't take an astrophysicist to see the theory is wrong. And if a picture of an embryo doesn't look like the real thing, it doesn't take an embryologist to see that the picture is false. So an average person with access to the evidence should be able to understand and evaluate many scientific claims."*

• Dr. L.R. Wysong[8], "The Creation/ Evolution Controversy": *"Evolution is not a form of true scientific method… evolution means the initial formation of unknown organisms from unknown chemicals produced in an unknown atmosphere or ocean of unknown composition under unknown conditions, which organisms have then climbed an unknown evolutionary ladder by an unknown process leaving unknown evidence."*

• US District Judge James Graham[21]: *"Science is not an inscrutable priesthood. Any person of reasonable intelligence should, with some diligence, be able to understand and critically evaluate a scientific theory."*

---

**Jonathan Wells** (1979  -  ) - two Ph.D's: 1) Molecular and Cell Biology , Univ. of California at Berkeley, 2) Religious Studies, Yale University; former Research biologist at the Univ. of California at Berkeley; former Prof. Biology at California State University in Hayward; currently, Senior Fellow at Discovery Institute's Center for Science and Culture, where he is a proponent of the Intelligent Design movement and critic of evolution. The quote below is from his book "Icons of Evolution"[21]:

*"Truth must tie to evidence: If science wasn't the search for TRUTH, our bridges wouldn't support the weight we put on them, our lives wouldn't be as long as they are, and modern technological civilization wouldn't exist. Storytelling is a valuable enterprise, too. Without stories, we would have no culture. But we do not call on storytellers to build bridges or perform surgery. For such tasks, we prefer people who have disciplined themselves to understand the realities of steel or flesh.*

*Any theory that purports to be scientific must somehow, at some point, be compared with observations or experiments. Theories that survive repeated testing may be tentatively regarded as true statements. But if there is persistent conflict between a theory and evidence, the former must yield to the latter. When science fails to obey nature, bridges collapse and patients die on the operating table."*

**Deuteronomy 4:32**        *"… ask now concerning the days that are past, which were before you, since the day that God created man on the earth…."*

## "Mind & Cosmos" by Dr. Thomas Nagel[7]

Dr. Thomas Nagel, Professor of Philosophy and the School of Law at New York University, is one of the most influential atheist philosophers in America.

Winner of the 2008 Rolf Schock Prize in Logic and Philosophy, he is known for his expertise in the philosophy of the mind, political philosophy and ethics. He is also well known for his critique of material reductionism and especially Darwinian evolution, focusing on the failure of evolution to account for consciousness, cognition, reasoning and moral value judgments.

### Mind and Cosmos – Why the Materialist Neo-Darwinian Conception of Nature is almost certainly False

*"My guiding conviction is that mind is not an afterthought or an accident or an add-on, but a basic aspect of nature.*

*The intelligibility of the world is no accident."*

**Thomas Nagel**
**Page 16,17**

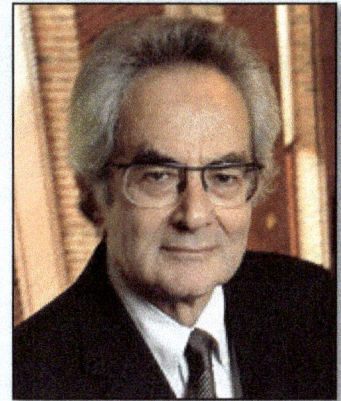

*"A theistic account has the advantage over a reductive naturalistic one in that it admits the reality of more of what is so evidently the case."* (page 25)

He further takes evolutionary biology to task on its inability to even stand up to the common sense of anyone, regardless of whether they are trained in the biological sciences: *"It is prima facie highly implausible that life as we know it is the result of a sequence of physical accidents together with the mechanism of natural selection. My skepticism is not based on religious belief, or on a belief in any definite alternative. It is just a belief that the available scientific evidence, in spite of the consensus of scientific opinion, does not in this matter rationally require us to subordinate the incredulity of common sense."*

He also explains why people find this position outrageous – because the scientific community continues to brow-beat anyone who raised the same doubts as he is in this book: *"I realize that such doubts will strike many people as outrageous, but that is because almost everyone in our secular culture has been browbeaten into regarding the reductive research program as sacrosanct, on the ground that anything else would not be science."*

He further explains why current evolutionary theory is in serious need of repair – because of discoveries in science!: *"Doubts about the reductionist account of life go against the dominant scientific consensus, but that consensus faces problems of probability that I believe are not taken seriously enough, both with respect to the evolution of life forms through accidental mutation and natural selection and with respect to the formation from dead matter of physical systems capable of such evolution. The more we learn about the intricacy of the genetic code and its control of the chemical processes of life, the harder those problems seem."*

He goes deeper in his critique of evolution: *"With regard to evolution, the process of natural selection cannot account for the actual history without an adequate supply of viable mutations, and I believe it remains an open question whether this could have been provided in geological time merely as a result of chemical accident, without the operation of some other factors determining and restricting the forms of genetic variation. It is no longer legitimate simply to imagine a sequence of gradually evolving phenotypes, as if their appearance through mutations in the DNA were unproblematic – as Richard Dawkins does for the evolution of the eye.".*

Then he goes to the origin of life, explaining how our discovery of the DNA molecule eliminates materialistic naturalism as a sufficient explanation for life's origins: *"With regard to the origin of life, the problem is much harder, since the option of natural selection as an explanation is not available. And the coming into existence of the genetic code – an arbitrary mapping of nucleotide sequences into amino acids, together with mechanisms that can read the code and carry out its instructions – seems particularly resistant to being revealed as probable given physical law alone."*

In his book, Dr. Nagel asks 36 questions to proponents of evolution. These questions are not new – but they are coming from one of the most respected analytical atheist philosophical minds today – and they are meant to be a challenge to evolutionists to examine the evidence, because it will lead open-minded seekers away from evolution.

# Are Science and Faith compatible in the search for *TRUTH*?
## 22 World-renown Scientists say *YES*

**1** Michael Faraday (1791-1867) – British Physicist, founder of electromagnetism: *"…his religious belief in a single Creator encouraged his scientific belief in the "unity of forces", the idea that magnetism, electricity and the other forces have a common origin."* (B. Bowers, Michael Faraday and Electricity, 1974).

**2** Sir George Gabriel Stokes (1819-1903) – Irish Mathematician and Physicist; Lucasian Prof. of Mathematics, Cambridge Univ.: *"A deeply religious man and a renowned physicist and mathematician, Stokes tries to combine his religiosity with his determined belief in the existence of natural laws."* (J. Petrunic, Abstract of Stoke's Gifford Lectures, 'Natural Theology', delivered before the Univ. of Edinburgh, 1891-1893).

**3** Lord William Kelvin (1824-1907) – Scottish Mathematical Physicist: *"Do not be afraid of being free thinkers. If you think strongly enough you will be forced by science to the belief in God, which is the foundation of all Religion. You will find science not antagonistic, but helpful to Religion."* (The Times, May 2, 1903, Lord Kelvin speaking at Univ. College of London, on Religion and Science).

**4** James Clerk Maxwell (1831-1879) – Scottish Mathematician and Theoretical Physicist: *"I think men of science as well as other men need to learn from Christ, and I think Christians whose minds are scientific are bound to study science that their view of the glory of God may be as extensive as their being is capable of."* (Campbell and Garnet, 'The Life of James Clerk Maxwell', London 1882).

**5** Lord Rayleigh (1842-1919) – 1904 Nobel Prize in Physics: *"…I may say that in my opinion true Science and true Religion neither are nor could be opposed."* (Religion and Health, James John Walsh, 1920).

**6** Max Planck (1858-1947) – 1918 Nobel Prize in Physics: *"Anybody who has been seriously engaged in scientific work of any kind realizes that over the entrance to the gates of the temple of science are written the words: Ye must have faith. It is a quality which the scientist cannot dispense with… There can never be any real opposition between religion and science; for one is the complement of the other. Every serious and reflective person realizes, I think, that the religious element in his nature must be recognized and cultivated if all the powers of the human soul are to act together in perfect balance and harmony. And indeed it was not by accident that the greatest thinkers of all ages were deeply religious souls."* ('Where Is Science Going?', 1932).

**7** Robert Millikan (1868-1953) – PhD Physics; 1923 Nobel Prize in Physics *"…the combination of science and religion provides today the sole basis for rational intelligent living… religion and science are the two great sister forces which have pulled, and are still pulling, mankind onward and upward."* ('The Autobiography of Robert A. Millikan', Prentice-Hall, New York, 1950).

**8** Albert Einstein (1879-1955) – PhD Theoretical Physics; 1921 Nobel Prize in Physics; Time Person of the Century, *"…everyone who is seriously involved in the pursuit of science becomes convinced that a spirit is manifest in the laws of the Universe - a spirit vastly superior to that of man, and one in the face of which we with our modest powers must feel humble."* (Letter, Jan. 24, 1936, quoted in Helen Dukas and Banesh Hoffman, 'Albert Einstein: The Human Side',1981).

**9** Erwin Schrödinger (1887-1961) – PhD Physics; 1933 Nobel Prize in Physics: *"In the presentation of a scientific problem, the other player is the good Lord. He has not only set the problem but also has devised the rules of the game--but they are not completely known, half of them are left for you to discover or deduce…"* ('Schrödinger: Life and Thought', Walter Moore, Cambridge: Cambridge Univ. Press, 1990).

**10** Arthur Compton (1892-1962) – PhD Theoretical Physics; 1927 Nobel Prize in Physics: *"Science has created a world in which Christianity is a necessity… I believe that its insistence on the inherent value of individual men and women Christianity has the key to survival and the good life in the modern world… In their essence there can be no conflict between science and religion. Science is a reliable method of finding truth. Religion is the search for a satisfying basis for life."* ('The Human Meaning of Science', 1940).

**11** William Henry Bragg (1890–1971) – MA Theoretical Physics, Cambridge Univ.; 1915 Nobel Prize in Physics: "In 1940 Bragg identified 'two sad mistakes' current in science-religion debates: *'The one is to suppose that science, that is to say, the study of Nature, leads to materialism. The other that the worship of God can be carried on without the equipment which science provides."…"From religion comes a man's purpose; from science, his power to achieve it. Sometimes people ask if religion and science are not opposed to one another. They are: in the sense that the thumb and fingers of my hand are opposed to one another. It is an opposition by means of which anything can be grasped."* ('The Scientific God Journal', April 2010, ISSN 2153-831X).

**12** Werner Heisenberg (1901-1976) – PhD Physics; 1932 Nobel Prize in Physics: *"In the history of science, ever since the famous trial of Galileo, it has repeatedly been claimed that scientific truth cannot be reconciled with the religious interpretation of the world. Although I am now convinced that scientific truth is unassailable in its own field, I have never found it possible to dismiss the content of religious thinking as simply part of an outmoded phase in the consciousness of mankind, a part we shall have to give up from now on, Thus in the course of my life I have repeatedly been compelled to ponder on the relationship of these two regions of thought, for I have never been able to doubt the reality of that to which they point."* ('Das Universum – Hinweis auf Gott?', 1988).

**13** Wernher von Braun (1912-1977) – PhD Physics; NASA Director of Marshall Space Flight Center and chief architect of the Saturn V launch vehicle: *"I find it as difficult to understand a scientist who does not acknowledge the presence of a superior rationality behind the existence of the universe as it is to comprehend a theologian who would deny the advances of science."* (*'The Skeptical Inquirer'*, 10:258-276).

**14** Charles Townes (1915 - ) – PhD Physics, CalTech; 1964 Nobel Prize in Physics: "Townes' answer to interview question 'If science and religion share a common purpose, why have their proponents tended to be at loggerheads throughout history?' = *"Science and religion have had a long interaction: some of it has been good and some of it hasn't. As Western science grew, Newtonian mechanics had scientists thinking that everything is predictable, meaning there's no room for God - so-called determinism. Religious people didn't want to agree with that. Then Darwin came along, and they really didn't want to agree with what he was saying, because it seemed to negate the idea of a creator. So there was a real clash for a while between science and religions. But science has been digging deeper and deeper, and as it has done so, particularly in the basic sciences like physics and astronomy, we have begun to understand more. We have found that the world is not deterministic: quantum mechanics has revolutionized physics by showing that things are not completely predictable. That doesn't mean that we've found just where God comes in, but we know now that things are not as predictable as we thought and that there are things we don't understand. So as science encounters mysteries, it is starting to recognize its limitations and become somewhat more open. There are still scientists who differ strongly with religion and vice versa. But I think people are being more open-minded about recognizing the limitations in our frame of understanding."* (2005 interview for *Berkeley News* by Bonnie Powell).

**15** Richard Feynman (1918-1988) – PhD Quantum Physics);1965 Nobel Prize in Physics: "*I also agree that a belief in science and religion is consistent… science cannot produce 'the meaning of life' nor can it tell us 'the right moral values'. These must come from somewhere else."* (*'The Meaning of It All'*, 1998, p. 36).

**16** Robert Jastrow (1925-2008) – PhD Theoretical Physics; 1961 Director of NASA's Goddard Institute for Space Studies; *"For the scientist who has lived by faith in the power of reason, the story ends like a bad dream. He has scaled the mountains of ignorance; he is about to conquer the highest peak; as he pulls himself over the final rock, he is greeted by a band of theologians who have been sitting there for centuries."* (*'God and the Astronomers'*, 2nd edition, New York and London: W.W. Norton & Company, 199).

**17** Arthur L. Schawlow (1921-1999) – PhD Physics; 1981 Nobel Prize in Physics: *"The context of religion is a great background for doing science. In the words of Psalm 19, 'The heavens declare the glory of God and the firmament showeth his handiwork'. Thus scientific research is a worshipful act, in that it reveals more of the wonders of God's creation."* (quoted by Margenau & Varghese,1997).

**18** Arno Penzias (1933 - ) – PhD Physics; 1978 Nobel prize in Physics: *"The best data we have are exactly what I would have predicted, had I had nothing to go on but the five books of Moses, the Psalms, the Bible as a whole."* (*New York Times* on March 12, 1978).

**19** Henry "Fritz" Schaefer (1944 - ) – PhD Chemical Physics; Director of the Center for Computational Quantum Chemistry, Univ. of Georgia: *"Why are there so few atheists among physicists? Many scientists are considering the facts before them.* They say things like: 'The present arrangement of matter indicates a very special choice of initial conditions.' (Paul Davies). 'In fact, if one considers the possible constants and laws that could have emerged, the odds against a universe that produced life like ours are immense.' (Stephen Hawking), 'A common sense interpretation of the facts suggests that a superintellect has monkeyed with physics, as well as with chemistry and biology, and that there are no blind forces worth speaking about in nature.' (Fred Hoyle). As the Apostle Paul said in his epistle to the Romans: 'Since the creation of the world, God's invisible qualities—His eternal power and divine nature—have been clearly seen, being understood from what has been made.'" (*'Scientists and their Gods: Science and Christianity, Conflict or Coherence?'*,1999).

**20** George Smoot (1945 - ) – PhD Particle Physics; 2006 Nobel Prize in Physics: "George Smoot commenting on the discovery by the COBE Science Working Group of the expected "ripples" in the microwave background radiation. He called these fluctuations *"the fingerprints from the Maker."* Smoot draws attention not only to the fact that his team had provided more *evidence* for the creation event, but for a 'finely orchestrated' creation event."

**21** Frank Tipler (1947 - ) – PhD Physics; Prof. of Mathematics and Physics, Tulane Univ.: *"From the perspective of the latest physical theories, Christianity is not a mere religion, but an experimentally testable science."* (*'The Physics Of Immortality'*, New York, Doubleday, 2007).

**22** William Philips (1948 - ) – PhD Physics; 1997 Nobel Prize in Physics: *"Many scientists are also people with quite conventional religious faith. I, a physicist, am one example. I believe in God as both creator and friend. That is, I believe that God is personal and interacts with us."* (Lecture "Ordinary Faith, Ordinary Science", delivered at the conference "Science and the Spiritual Quest", April 2002); *"There are probably more Nobel Laureates who are people of faith than is generally believed. Most people in most professions don't make a special point to make their religious views known, since these are very personal."* ("Letter to the compiler T. Dimitrov", May 19, 2002).

## Dinesh D'Souza[13]:  The History of Scientific Inquiry is rooted in Christianity

*"We often hear that science was founded in the 17th century in revolt against religious dogma. In reality, science was founded between the 13th and 14th centuries through a dispute between two kinds of religious dogma. The first kind held that scholastic debate, operating according to the strict principles of DEDUCTIVE REASON, was the best way to discover God's hand in the universe. The other held that INDUCTIVE EXPERIENCE, including the use of experiments to 'interrogate nature,' was the preferred approach. Science benefited from both methods, using experiments to test propositions and then rigorous criticism and arguments to establish their significance.*

*In the 16th century the Reformation introduced a new idea. This was the notion that knowledge is not simply the province of ecclesiastical institutions but that, especially when it comes to matters of conscience, each man should decide for himself. The 'priesthood of the individual believer' was an immensely powerful notion because it rejected the papal hierarchy, and by implication all institutional hierarchy as well... it was a charter of independent thought, carried out not by institutions but by individuals. The early Protestants didn't know it, but they were introducing new theological concepts that would give new vitality to the emerging scientific culture of Europe."*

*"It is widely accepted on all sides that, far from undermining it, science is deeply indebted to Christianity and has been so from at least the scientific revolution. Recent historical research has uncovered many unexpected links between scientific enterprise and Biblical theology."* (Russell, 1984, 777).

The following 20 Scientists were not only Christians, but are credited with discovery of their science discipline:

**Johannes Kepler (1571-1630) - Celestial Mechanics**   He was a German mathematician and astronomer who postulated that the Earth and planets travel about the sun in elliptical orbits. He is chiefly remembered for discovering the 3 laws of planetary motion that bear his name. He did important work in optics (1604, 1611), gave the first proof of how logarithms worked (1624), and contributed to the development of calculus (1615, 1616). He calculated the most exact astronomical tables known today, whose continued accuracy established the truth of heliocentric astronomy.

**Blaise Pascal (1623-1662) - Hydrostatics, Probability Science**   French mathematician, physicist and religious philosopher. He was a child prodigy, educated by his father. His earliest work was in the natural and applied sciences, where he made important contributions to the construction of mechanical calculators, the study of fluids, and clarified the concepts of pressure and the vacuum. Pascal wrote powerfully to defend the scientific method. Pascal helped create 2 major new areas of research. He wrote a significant treatise on the subject of projective geometry at the age of 16 and later on probability theory, strongly influencing the development of modern economics.

**Robert Boyle (1627-1691) - Chemistry and Gas Dynamics**   He is regarded as the first modern chemist. Among his works, *The Sceptical Chymist*  is seen as a cornerstone book in the field of chemistry. Boyle was also a major apologist for the new science, reflecting at length on the mutual relations between science and religion. He made important contributions to physics and chemistry and is best known for Boyle's law, describing an ideal gas. Boyle's great merit as a scientific investigator is that he carried out the principles of scientific investigation. On several occasions he mentions that in order to keep his judgment as unbiased as possible with any of the modern theories of philosophy, he "provided with experiments" to help him judge of them. Nothing was more alien to his mental temperament than the spinning of hypotheses.

**Sir Isaac Newton (1643-1727) - Calculus and Dynamics**   He was the greatest English mathematician of his generation. He laid the foundation for differential and integral calculus. His work on optics and gravitation make him one of the greatest scientists the world has known. Newton is regarded as the founding exemplar of modern physical science, his achievements in experimental investigation being as innovative as those in mathematical research. With equal, if not greater, energy and originality he also plunged into chemistry, the early history of Western civilization, and theology; among his special studies was an investigation of the form and dimensions, as described in the Bible, of Solomon's Temple in Jerusalem.

**Sir William Herschel (1738-1822) - Galactic Astronomy**   Probably the most famous astronomer of the 18th century, Sir William Herschel discovered, in addition to the planet Uranus, many new nebulae, clusters of stars and binary stars. He was the first person to correctly describe the form of our Galaxy, The Milky Way. During the course of his career, he constructed more than 400 telescopes. The largest and most famous of these was a reflecting telescope with a 40 ft focal length. Herschel discovered that unfilled telescope apertures can be used to obtain high angular resolution, something which became the essential basis for interferometric imaging in astronomy.

**Sir David Brewster (1781-1868) - Optical Mineralogy**    Brewster was a Scottish scientist, inventor and writer. His most important scientific work falls under 5 headings: (1) The laws of polarization by reflection and refraction; (2) The discovery of the polarizing structure induced by heat and pressure; (3) The discovery of crystals with 2 axes of double refraction, and many of the laws of their phenomena, including the connection between optical structure and crystalline forms; (4) The laws of metallic reflection; (5) Experiments on the absorption of light.

**Michael Faraday (1791-1867) - Electromagnetics and Field Theory**    He was one of the greatest experimenters ever. He formulated the second law of electrolysis: "the amounts of bodies which are equivalent to each other in their ordinary chemical action have equal quantities of electricity naturally associated with them." He published many of his results in the three-volume *Experimental Researches in Electricity* (1839-1855). One of his most important contributions to physics was his development of the concept of a field to describe magnetic and electric forces in 1845.

**Charles Babbage (1791-1871) - Computer Science**    Known as the "Father of Computing" for his contributions to the basic design of the computer through his Analytical machine. He is widely regarded as the first computer pioneer and the great ancestral figure in the history of computing. Babbage's present-day reputation rests largely on the invention and design of his vast mechanical calculating engines. His Analytical Engine conceived in 1834 is one of the startling intellectual feats of the nineteenth century. The design of this machine has all the essential logical features of the modern general purpose computer.

**Matthew Maury (1806-1873) - Oceanography, Hydrology**    He was nicknamed *Pathfinder of the Seas* and *Father of modern Oceanography* and later, *Scientist of the Seas*, due to the publication of his extensive works. He charted winds and ocean currents, including pathways for ships at sea. He published his *Wind and Current Chart of the North Atlantic* which showed sailors how to use the ocean's currents and winds to their advantage, drastically reducing the length of ocean voyages. Maury's uniform system of recording synoptic oceanographic data was adopted by navies and merchant marines around the world and was used to develop charts for all the major trade routes.

**Louis Agassiz (1807-1873) - Glacial Geology, Ichthyology**    One of the "founding fathers" of modern American science. A renowned teacher and promoter of science in America, he was also a lifelong opponent of Darwin's theory of evolution. He worked in paleontology, systematics, and glaciology. In 1848 he accepted a professorship at Harvard, where he acquired funding for a great museum of natural history, and founded the Museum of Comparative Zoology in 1860. He was a founding member of the National Academy of Sciences in 1863, and was appointed a regent of the Smithsonian Institution.

**Sir George Gabriel Stokes (1819-1903) - Fluid Mechanics, Mathematics**    Stokes was an Irish mathematician and physicist, who at Cambridge made important contributions to fluid dynamics, optics and mathematical physics (including Stokes' theorem). His work on fluid motion and viscosity led to his calculating the terminal velocity for a sphere falling in a viscous medium. This became known as Stokes' Law. His best-known research dealt with the wave theory of light. In 1852, in his famous paper on the change of wavelength of light, he described the phenomenon of fluorescence. The Stokes' shift, which describes this conversion, is named in Stokes' honor.

**Louis Pasteur (1822-1895) - Bacteriology**    He solved the mysteries of rabies, anthrax, chicken cholera, and silkworm diseases, and helped develop the first vaccines. He debunked the widely accepted myth of spontaneous generation, setting the stage for modern biology and biochemistry. Pasteur's work gave birth to many branches of science. He is revered for possessing the most important qualities of a scientist: the ability to survey all the known data and link the data for all possible hypotheses, the patience and drive to conduct experiments under controlled conditions, and the brilliance to uncover the road to the solution from the results. On the discipline of rigid and strict experimental tests he said, "Imagination should give wings to our thoughts but we always need decisive experimental proof. When the moment comes to draw conclusions and to interpret the observations, imagination must be checked and documented by the factual results of the experiment."

**Gregor Mendel (1822-1884) - Genetics**    His work became the foundation for modern genetics. His work in heredity was so brilliant and unprecedented that it took 34 years for the rest of the scientific community to catch up to it. In his *Experiments with Plant Hybrids*, Mendel described how traits were inherited. It has become one of the most influential publications in the history of science. He was the first person to trace the characteristics of successive generations of a living thing, He was an Augustinian monk who taught natural science to high school students. The practical result of Mendel's research is that it not only changed the way we perceive the world, but also the way we live in it.

**Lord William Thomson Kelvin (1824-1907) - Energetics**   Scottish mathematician and physicist who contributed to many branches of physics. He calculated the age of the earth from its cooling rate and concluded that it was too short to fit with Lyell's theory of gradual geological change or Darwin's theory of the evolution of animals though natural selection. He used the field concept to explain electromagnetic interactions. He speculated that electromagnetic forces were propagated as linear and rotational strains in an elastic solid, producing "vortex atoms" which generated the field. He proposed that these atoms consisted of tiny knotted strings, and the type of knot determined the type of atom. With Tait, Kelvin published *Treatise on Natural Philosophy* (1867), which was important for establishing energy within the structure of the theory of mechanics.

**Bernhard Riemann (1826-1866) - Non-Euclidean Geometry**   He was the most influential mathematician of the mid-19th century. He was a German mathematician who made important contributions to analysis and differential geometry, some paving the way for the later development of general relativity. These would subsequently be major parts of the theories of Riemannian geometry, algebraic geometry and complex manifold theory. The theory of Riemann surfaces became an area of mathematics that was foundational in topology, and in the 21st century is still being applied to mathematical physics.

**Joseph Lister (1827-1912) - Antiseptic Surgery**   He is known as the 'Father of Antiseptic Surgery'. He discovered the link between lack of cleanliness in hospitals and deaths after operations. Lister believed that it was microbes carried in the air that caused diseases to be spread in wards. People who had been operated on were especially vulnerable: their bodies were weak and their skin had been cut open, so germs could enter the body easily. Lister covered the wound with a piece of lint covered in carbolic acid. His success rate for survival was very high. Lister then developed his idea further by devising a machine that pumped out a fine mist of carbolic acid into the air around an operation.

**James Clerk Maxwell (1831-1879) - Electrodynamics, Magnetics**   Maxwell, a Scottish mathematical physicist, had one of the finest mathematical minds of any theoretical physicist of any time. Maxwell is widely regarded as the 19th century scientist who had the greatest influence on 20th century physics, making contributions to the fundamental models of nature. In 1931, on the centennial anniversary of Maxwell's birthday, Einstein described Maxwell's work as the "*most profound and the most fruitful that physics has experienced since the time of Newton.*" Maxwell demonstrated that electric and magnetic fields travel through space, in the form of waves, at a constant velocity of $3.0 \times 10^8$ m/s.

**Lord Rayleigh (1842-1919) - Dimensional and Model Analysis**   His real name was John Strutt. He was an English physicist and winner of the Nobel Prize in Physics in 1904 "for his investigations of the densities of the most important gases and for his discovery of argon in connection with these studies". He also discovered the phenomenon now called "Rayleigh scattering" and predicted the existence of the surface waves now known as "Rayleigh waves". Lord Rayleigh's first researches were mainly mathematical, concerning optics and vibrating systems, but his later work ranged over almost the whole field of physics. His patient and delicate experiments led to the establishment of the standards of resistance, current, and electromotive force. His later work was concentrated on electric and magnetic problems.

**John Ambrose Fleming (1849-1945) - Electronics**   He was an English electrical engineer and physicist. He was the first professor of Electrical Engineering, where he lectured at the Univ. of Cambridge, Univ. of Nottingham and Univ. College of London. In 1904, he invented and patented the 2-electrode vacuum-tube rectifier, which he called the oscillation valve. It was also called the Fleming valve. This invention is often considered to have been the beginning of electronics, for this was the first vacuum tube. Fleming's contributions to electronic communications and radar were of vital importance in winning World War II. He was awarded the IRE Medal of Honor in 1933 for "the conspicuous part he played in introducing physical and engineering principles into the radio art."

**Sir William Ramsay (1852-1916) - Inorganic Chemistry**   He was a Scottish chemist who discovered the noble gases and received the Nobel Prize in Physics along with Lord Rayleigh in1904 (without working together, he and Lord Rayleigh proved there must exist a previously unknown gas in the atmosphere- argon). In 1887 he held the prestigious chair of Chemistry at the University College of London, where his most celebrated discoveries were made. He published several notable papers on the oxides of nitrogen. His most notable discoveries included the elements of argon, helium, neon, krypton, and xenon.

# The History of Science & Religion ⇦ The Great Scientists

Timeline: 1600's   1800's   1900's   2000's   Today

**Johannes Kepler** (1571-1630) German Astronomer, Mathematician; Founder: Laws of Planetary Motion

**Blaise Pascal** (1623-1662) French Mathematician, Physicist, Philosopher; Founder: Statistics

**Isaac Newton** (1643-1727) British Mathematician, Physicist; Invented Differential Calculus; Founder: Law of Gravity, Laws of Motion

**William Herschel** (1738-1822) British Astronomer, Founder: Galactic Astronomy; Telescope Designer; Detailed description of Milky Way Galaxy

**Bernard Riemann** (1826-1866) German Mathematician; Founder: Riemannian Geometry; Paved way for Theory of Relativity by proposing how light bends In space

**Michael Faraday** (1791-1867) British Physicist, Mathematician; Greatest Experimenter in History; Founder: 2nd Law of Electrolysis, Science of Electromagnetism

**James Maxwell** (1831-1879) Scottish Physicist; 19th century's greatest scientist; Founder: equations for a unified model of electromagnetism

**George Stokes** (1819-1903) Irish Mathematician, Physicist ; Founder: Stokes Law, Fluid Dynamics, Mathematical Physics

**Lord William Kelvin** (1824-1907) Scottish Mathematician, Physicist; Founder: Absolute Zero; helped derive 1st & 2nd Laws of Thermodynamics

**Lord Rayleigh** (1842-1919) British Physicist; 1904 Nobel Prize; Founder: Argon, "Rayleigh Waves"

**Arthur Eddington** (1882-1944) British Astrophysicist; Director, Cambridge Observatory; helped Einstein with Theory of Relativity

**John Fleming** (1849-1945) English Physicist; 1st Prof. of Electrical Engineering; Founder: "Fleming Valve" (started field of Electronics)

**Max Planck** (1858-1947) German Physicist; 1918 Nobel Prize; Founder: Quantum Theory

**Robert Milliken** (1868-1953) American Physicist; 1923 Nobel Prize; Founder: electron charge

**Albert Einstein** (1879-1955) German Physicist; 1921 Nobel Prize; Founder: Theory of Relativity

**Erwin Schrödinger** (1887-1961) Austrian Physicist; 1933 Nobel Prize; Founder: Wave Mechanics, Schrödinger Equation

**Arthur Compton** (1892-1962) American Physicist; 1927 Nobel Prize; Founder: Compton Effect

**William Bragg** (1890-1971) British Physicist; 1915 Nobel Prize; Founder: Crystal Structures via X-rays

**Werner Heisenberg** (1901-1976); German Physicist; 1932 Nobel Prize; Founder: Quantum Mechanics

**Wernher von Braun** (1912-1977) German Physicist; 1st Rocket Scientist; Director of Marshall Space Center

**Richard Feynman** (1918-1988 ) American Physicist; 1965 Nobel Prize; Founder: Quantum Electrodynamics

**Arthur Schawlow** (1921-1999) American Physicist; 1981 Nobel Prize; Founder: Laser Spectroscopy

**Fred Hoyle** (1915-2001) British Astrophysicist; Founder: Institute of Theoretical Astronomy

**Robert Jastrow** (1925-2008) American Physicist; Director NASA Institute for Space Studies

**Alan Sandage** (1926-2010) American Astronomer; Founder: Observational Cosmology; measured universe size and age

**Charles Townes** (1915 - ) American Physicist; 1964 Nobel Prize; Founder: Maser Technology

**Steven Weinberg** (1933 - ) American Physicist; 1975 Nobel Prize; Founder, Electroweak Unification Theory

**Arno Penzias** (1933 - ) American Physicist; 1978 Nobel Prize; Co-founder: Cosmic Background Radiation

**Robert Wilson** (1936 - ) American Physicist; 1978 Nobel Prize; Co-founder, Cosmic Background Radiation

**George Ellis** (1939 - ) South African Mathematician & Physicist; one of world's leading Theorists in Cosmology

**Paul Davies** (1942 - ) British Physicist; Chair, Post-Detection Science of International Academy of Aeronautics

**Stephen Hawking** (1942 - ) British Physicist & Cosmologist; Director, Cambridge Center for Theoretical Cosmology

**Henry Schaefer** (1944 - ) American Physicist & Chemist; Director, Center Computational Quantum Chemistry

**George Smootz** (1945 - ) American Physicist; 2006 Nobel Prize; Senior Scientist, Berkeley National Lab

**Frank Tipler** (1947 - ) American Mathematician, Physicist, Cosmologist; Prof. Tulane Univ.

**William Phillips** (1948 - ) American Physicist; 1997 Nobel Prize; Founder: Laser Cooling

Legend:
- Christian (yellow)
- Pantheist (blue)
- Deist (gray)
- Agnostic (black)
- Atheist (red/orange)

*"I strongly believe in the existence of God, based on intuition, observations, logic, and scientific knowledge."*
**(Charles Townes, 1964 Nobel Prize in Physics)**

**Johannes Kepler (1571-1630)** ⇨ CHRISTIAN   German Mathematician and Astronomer (University of Tübingen); Chancellor at Tübingen (1590); as assistant to Tycho Brahe (1600), Kepler calculated orbits as ellipses (not circles, as assumed), paving the way for Kepler's discovery of his Three Laws of Planetary Motion for the Solar System; his works credited by Newton as laying the foundation for his Theory of Universal Gravitation; Mathematics teacher at two schools in Graz and Linz, Austria; Imperial mathematician to Emperor Rudolf II; invented an improved version of the refracting telescope (the Keplerian Telescope); Kepler lived in an era when there was distinction between astronomy (a branch of mathematics within the liberal arts) and physics (a branch of natural philosophy); First published manuscript in 1596 = *Mysterium*: heliocentric universe (Copernican system), showing God's geometric plan for the universe; he incorporated religious arguments and reasoning, motivated by his belief that God had created the world according to an intelligible plan that is accessible through the natural light of reason.

• *"Great is God our Lord, great is His power and there is no end to His wisdom. Praise Him you heavens, glorify Him, sun and moon and you planets. For out of Him and through Him, and in Him are all things..... We know, oh, so little. To Him be the praise, the honor and the glory from eternity to eternity."*

• *"The chief aim of all investigations of the external world should be to discover the rational order and harmony which has been imposed on it by God and which He revealed to us in the language of mathematics."*

• Somnium: The Posthumous Work on Lunar Astronomy*: "When things are in order, if the cause of the orderliness cannot be deduced from the motion of the elements or from the composition of matter, it is quite possibly a cause possessing a mind."*

• Letter to Michael Maestlin, Oct. 3, 1595: *"For a long time, I wanted to become a theologian. For a long time, I was unhappy. Now, however, behold, how through my efforts God is being glorified through astronomy."*

• *"Geometry is unique and eternal, a reflection from the mind of God. That mankind shares in it is because man is an image of God."*

• *"The Six-Cornered Snowflake", Prague, 1611: "The cause of the six-sided shape of a snowflake is none other than that of the ordered shapes of plants and of numerical constants; and since in them nothing occurs without supreme reason -- not, to be sure, such as discursive reasoning discovers, but such as existed from the first in the Creator's design and is presented from the origin to the day in the wonderful nature of animal faculties, I do not believe that even in a snowflake this ordered pattern exists at random".*

**Blaise Pascal (1623-1662)** ⇨ CHRISTIAN   French mathematician, physicist and religious philosopher. He was a child prodigy, educated by his father. His earliest work was in the natural and applied sciences, where he invented mechanical calculators, contributed to the study of fluids, and clarified the concepts of pressure and the vacuum. Pascal wrote powerfully to defend the scientific method. He was a mathematician of the first order. Pascal helped create 2 major new areas of research. He wrote a significant treatise on the subject of projective geometry at the age of 16 and later on probability theory, strongly influencing the development of modern economics. In his writings called "*Pensees*", he says: *"If we submit everything to reason our religion will be left with nothing mysterious or supernatural. If we offend the principles of reason our religion will be absurd and ridiculous . . . There are two equally dangerous extremes: to exclude reason, to admit nothing but reason… There is a God shaped vacuum in the heart of every man which cannot be filled by any created thing, but only by God, the Creator, made known through Jesus."*

• "Thoughts on Religion and Other Subjects": *"Faith is different than proof; the latter is human, the former is a gift from God."*

• *"We can only know God well when we know our own sin. And those who have known God without knowing their wretchedness have not glorified Him but have glorified themselves."*

• *"In faith there is enough light for those who want to believe and enough shadow for those who don't."*

• *"Not only do we know God through Jesus Christ, we only know ourselves through Jesus Christ."*

**Isaac Newton (1643-1727)** ⇨ CHRISTIAN  He published his Theory of Universal Gravitation in 1687; one of history's greatest mathematicians, he laid the foundation for differential and integral calculus. Newton is regarded as the founding exemplar of modern physical science. With equal, if not greater, energy and originality he also plunged into chemistry, the early history of Western civilization, and theology; among his special studies was an investigation of the form and dimensions, as described in the Bible, of Solomon's Temple in Jerusalem.

• *"This most beautiful system [The Universe] could only proceed from the dominion of an intelligent and powerful Being."*

• *"Did blind chance know that there was light and what was its refraction and fit the eyes of all creatures after the most curious manner to make use of it? These and such like considerations always have and ever will prevail with mankind to believe that there is a being who made all things and has all things in his power and who is therefore to be feared."*

♦ "*We account the scriptures of God to be the most sublime philosophy. I find more sure marks of authenticity in the Bible than in any profane history whatsoever.*"

♦ "Opticks": "*It seems probable to me that God, in the beginning, formed matter in solid, massy, hard, impenetrable, moveable particles, of such sizes and figures, and with such other properties, and in such proportions to space, as most conduced to the end for which He formed them; and that these primitive particles, being solids, are incomparably harder than any porous bodies compounded of them, even so very hard as never to wear or break in pieces; no ordinary power being able to divide what God had made one in the first creation.*"

♦ "*And for rejecting such a Medium, we have the Authority of those the oldest and most Gravity of Atoms, the first Principles of their Philosophy; tacitly attributing Gravity to some other celebrated Philosophers of Greece and Phoenicia, who made a Vacuum, and Atoms, and the Cause than dense Matter. Later Philosophers banish the Consideration of such a Cause out of natural Philosophy, feigning Hypotheses for explaining all things mechanically, and referring other Causes to Metaphysics. Whereas the main Business of natural Philosophy is to argue from Phenomena without feigning Hypotheses, and to deduce Causes from Effects, till we come to the very first Cause, which certainly is not mechanical; and not only to unfold the Mechanism of the World, but chiefly to resolve these and such like Questions. What is there in places almost empty of Matter, and whence is it that the Sun and Planets gravitate towards one another, without dense Matter between them? Whence is it that Nature doth nothing in vain; and whence arises all that Order and Beauty which we see in the World? ... does it not appear from phenomena that there is a Being incorporeal, living, intelligent, omnipresent, who in infinite space, as it were in his Sensory, sees the things themselves intimately, and thoroughly perceives them, and comprehends them wholly by their immediate presence to himself*".

**William Herschel (1738-1822)** ⇨ CHRISTIAN  Probably the most famous astronomer of the 18th century, Sir William Herschel discovered, in addition to the planet Uranus, many new nebulae, clusters of stars and binary stars. He was the first person to correctly describe the form of our Galaxy, The Milky Way. During the course of his career, he constructed more than 400 telescopes. The largest and most famous of these was a reflecting telescope with a 40 ft focal length. Herschel discovered that unfilled telescope apertures can be used to obtain high angular resolution, something which became the essential basis for interferometric imaging in astronomy. He measured the axial tilt of Mars, discovered that the martian ice caps (first observed by Giovanni Cassini and Christian Huygens ( in the 1670's) changed size with the planet's seasons. From studying the motion of stars, he discovered the movement and direction of our solar system through space. He also discovered the structure of the Milky Way as in the shape of a disk. He coined the word "asteroid" (Greek for *star-like*) in 1802, to describe the star-like appearance of the small moons of the giant planets and of the minor planets ('asteroid' became a standard term for describing certain minor planets in the 1850's). Upon his discovery of Uranus, he showed that the laws that govern our Earth and Moon are the same throughout the heavens.

♦ Ann Lamont, 'Great Creation Scientists: Sir William Herschel – Founder of Modern Stellar Astronomy' 2000: "*Herschel strongly believed that God's universe was characterized by order and planning. His discovery of that order led him to conclude that 'the undevout astronomer must be mad'*".

♦ The Diary of Sir William Herschel: "*The difference was occasioned by an exclamation of the First Consul's, who asked in a tome of exclamation or admiration (when we were speaking of the extent of the sidereal heavens) 'and who is the author of all this'. M. de la Place wished to shew that a chain of natural causes would account for the construction and preservation of the wonderful system; this the First Consul rather opposed. Much may be said on the subject, but joining the arguments of both we shall be led to 'Nature and Nature's God.'*"

♦ *Time! Time! Time! — we must not impugn the Scripture Chronology, but we must interpret it in accordance with whatever shall appear on fair inquiry to be the truth for there cannot be two truths. And really there is scope enough: for the lives of the Patriarchs may as reasonably be extended to 5,000 or 50,000 years apiece as the days of Creation to as many thousand millions of years.*"

**Michael Faraday (1791-1867)** ⇨ CHRISTIAN  Having no formal education, yet he is one of the most influential scientists in history, often called the greatest experimentalist in the history of science; Fullerian Professor of Chemistry at Royal Institute of Great Britain; Einstein kept a portrait of Faraday on his study wall, alongside Isaac Newton and James Maxwell; during his lifetime, Faraday rejected a knighthood and twice refused to become President of the Royal Society; elected a foreign member of the Royal Swedish Academy of Sciences in 1838; one of eight foreign members elected to the French Academy of Sciences in 1844; he formulated the second law of electrolysis: "*the amounts of bodies which are equivalent to each other in their ordinary chemical action have equal quantities of electricity naturally associated with them.*" He published many of his results in the three-volume *Experimental Researches in Electricity* (1839-1855). His most important contributions to physics were: 1) his research on magnetic fields, establishing the basis for electromagnetism in physics, 2) he established that magnetism could affect rays of light and that there was an underlying relationship between the two phenomena; 3) he discovered the principle of electromagnetic induction, diamagnetism, and the laws of electrolysis;

4) he invented electromagnetic rotary devices (the basis of electric motor technology); and 5) his research made electricity practical for use in technology. A devout Christian, he did consider religion and science to be "two distinct things" but not conflicting with one another. As quoted in H. Bence Jones's, *'The Life and Letters of Michael Faraday'*, 1870: "*Yet even in earthly matters I believe that 'the invisible things of Him from the creation of the world are clearly seen, being understood by the things that are made, even His eternal power and Godhead,' and I have never seen anything incompatible between those things of man which can be known by the spirit of man which is within him, and those higher things concerning his future, which he cannot know by that spirit.*"

♦ B. Bowers, *Michael Faraday and Electricity*, 1974: "*It seems likely that his religious belief in a single Creator encouraged his scientific belief in the "unity of forces", the idea that magnetism, electricity and the other forces have a common origin.*"

♦ H. Bence Jones, *'The Life and Letters of Michael Faraday'*, 1870: "*... I cannot doubt that a glorious discovery in natural knowledge, and the wisdom and power of God in the creation, is awaiting our age, and that we may not only hope to see it, but even be honored to help in obtaining the victory over present ignorance and future knowledge.*"

♦ H. Bence Jones, *'The Life and Letters of Michael Faraday'*, 1870: "*To complete this picture, one word more must be said of his religion. His standard of duty was supernatural. It was not founded upon any intuitive ideas of right and wrong; nor was it fashioned upon any outward expediencies of time and place; but it was formed entirely on what he held to be the revelation of the will of God in the written Word, and throughout all his life his faith led him to endeavour to act up to the very letter of it*"

♦ ` *... the Christian who is taught of God ... finds his guide in the Word of God ... and looks for no assurance beyond what the Word can give him ... the Christian religion is a revelation, and that revelation is the Word of God. ... No revival and no temporal teaching comes between it and him. He who is taught of the Holy Spirit needs no crowd and no revival to teach him; if he stand alone he is fully taught ...*"

♦ Letter to his niece, 1859: "*... the saying that separation is the brother of death; I think that it does death an injustice, at least in the mind of the Christian; separation simply implies no reunion; death has to the Christian everything hoped for, contained in the idea of reunion.*"

♦ L.P. Williams, *'Michael Faraday'*, 1971: "*His true humility lay in a profound consciousness of his debt to his Creator. That Michael Faraday, poor uneducated son of a·journeyman blacksmith and a country maid was permitted to glimpse the beauty of the eternal laws of nature was a never-ending source of wonder to him.*"

**Sir George Gabriel Stokes (1819-1903)** ⇨ CHRISTIAN  Irish mathematician and physicist; Lucasian Prof. of Mathematics, Cambridge Univ. 1849-1903; President of Royal Society 1885-1890; made important contributions to fluid dynamics, optics and mathematical physics (including Stokes' theorem); "Stoke's Law": calculated the terminal velocity for a sphere falling in a viscous medium; in 1852, in his famous paper on the change of wavelength of light, he described the phenomenon of fluorescence. The Stokes' shift, which describes this conversion, is named in Stokes' honor; 1886 Vice President of the Evangelical British and Foreign Bible Society and active in the Church Missionary Society; president of the Victoria Institute (created in 1865 to explore the relationship between religion and science) from 1886 to 1903; at Pembroke College, Cambridge, he was introduced to the theological works of William Paley, whose books, *Evidences of Christianity* and *Moral Philosophy*, became themes in Stokes's Gifford Lectures; his 10-Lecture series within the Gifford Lectures (1891-1893) on Natural Theology document his firm Christian theological beliefs as a noted scientist (selected quotes from Lecture 1 contained below)

♦ Abstract (by J. Petrunic) of Stoke's Gifford Lectures, 'Natural Theology', delivered before the Univ. of Edinburgh, 1891-1893: "*In his Gifford lectures, Stokes takes a particular interest in criticizing the materialistic view of life that he thinks is engendered in Darwinian natural selection. He also takes a particular interest in emphasizing the role Christian Revelation plays in limiting the types of knowledge claims that scientists think they can make. A deeply religious man and a renowned physicist and mathematician, Stokes tries to combine his religiosity with his determined belief in the existence of natural laws.*"

♦ **Gifford Lecture #1, 'Natural Theology', 1891 – God's existence by observing nature:** "*The recognition of the existence of God derived from the observation of nature seems to require a further exercise of the reasoning powers… Take, for example, the STRUCTURE OF THE EYE. The more it is examined, anatomically and physically, the more forcibly is one impressed with the conviction that it was really designed to do that which in fact it does accomplish. Our supposed infant, now come to man's estate, being of a reflecting turn of mind, is led to perceive that there must be some power above that of man, directed by will, through the operation of which these results were brought about. The idea of will involves that of personality…. Will, design, implies mind, and mind as we know it is an essentially personal attribute. In this sense we attribute personality to the First Cause.*"

♦ **Gifford Lecture #1, 'Natural Theology',1891 – Design behind the laws of gravity and Planetary Motion:** "*In thus referring the motions of the planets in their orbits to a general property of matter, that of gravitation, we introduce an idea of causation; we speak of the attraction of gravitation as the cause of the retention of the planets in their orbits. Yet from one point of view the two things seem to stand upon the same footing. In the one case, we have a few simple laws which express completely the motions of the planets…;*

*in the other case, we have a still simpler law which not only explains the laws of Kepler but also the planetary perturbations and other phenomena having, at first sight, no connection with the planetary motions. Is there any reason why we should think of causation in the one case more than in the other? The difference seems to me to be this. In the case of gravitation, we believe that we have arrived at a knowledge of a general property of matter, which we are content to regard as in a certain sense self-existent; we do not go behind it. The law of gravitation is so simple that we hardly think of it as requiring to be accounted for. But in the case of Kepler's laws we have merely a succinct expression for observed facts, not connected with anything outside the immediate phenomena which are thus summed up. We cannot in any way regard them as expressing laws of nature; we cannot help feeling that they themselves require explanation…. the study of nature forcibly impresses us with the idea of design lying somewhere. This leads us to the conception of a designing mind lying behind the furthest causes, of the nature of what are called second causes,… that we could even conceivably attain to by purely scientific investigation."*

• **Gifford Lecture #1, 'Natural Theology', 1891 – on miracles:** *"Admit the existence of a God, of a personal God, and the possibility of miracle follows at once. If the laws of nature are carried on in accordance with His will, He who willed them may will their suspension. And if any difficulty should be felt as to their suspension, we are not even obliged to suppose that they have been suspended; it may be that the event which we call a miracle was brought about, not by any suspension of the laws in ordinary operation, but by the super-addition of something not ordinarily in operation, or if in operation, of such a nature that its operation is not perceived."*

• **Gifford Lecture #1, 'Natural Theology',1891 – on evil and free will:** *"The question then arises, If there be no limitation to the power of the Supreme Being, and if He desires the happiness of His creatures, why should not man have been so constituted as always to act rightly? In that case there might still have been some suffering belonging to his animal nature just as there is in the case of the lower animals; but at least those dire evils which arise from wrong-doing would have been avoided. Now it seems that there are only two conceivable alternatives as to what might have been; either man must have been endowed with a free will, capable of acting in accordance with the will of God, but also capable of acting in opposition thereto, or else he must have been made a sort of machine, incapable of acting otherwise than in accordance with the course laid down for hire. On the latter plan he could not arrive at the dignity of a being always doing right, though he had the power of doing wrong; always acting in accordance with the will of God, though he had the power of acting in opposition to it. This is clearly a higher state than that of a mere conscious machine. But the power of doing right from choice involves the power of doing wrong; and we can hardly conceive that millions and millions of rational creatures, each endowed with this power of choice, should each of them and always exercise that power in a right direction. Such a supposition seems almost a contradiction in terms. Even if the probability were very great that an individual taken at random, on an occasion taken at random, would exercise that choice in the right direction, still the chance that that would always be so is utterly infinitesimal. I speak here of chance, as I am obliged to do in endeavoring to express my ideas, but I freely allow that it is only a refuge for our ignorance; there can be no chance to perfect knowledge. Now even without going beyond the bounds of natural theology it is readily conceivable that the superiority of the state of those who act aright, though they have the power of acting wrongly, to that of mere conscious machines, may outweigh the disadvantages of free will arising from the evil consequences of its abuse."*

**Lord William Kelvin (1824-1907)** ⇨ CHRISTIAN  Scottish mathematical physicist best known for determining the correct value of absolute zero as -273.15° Celsius; graduated Cambridge Univ. 1845; Chair of Natural Philosophy, Univ. of Glasgow 1846-1900; at Univ. of Glasgow, did important work in formulating first and second laws of thermodynamics; published over 650 scientific papers and applied for over 70 patents; he calculated the age of the earth from its cooling rate and concluded that it was too short to fit with Lyell's theory of gradual geological change or Darwin's theory of the evolution of animals though natural selection. He used the field concept to explain electromagnetic interactions. He speculated that electromagnetic forces were propagated as linear and rotational strains in an elastic solid, producing "vortex atoms" which generated the field. He proposed that these atoms consisted of tiny knotted strings, and the type of knot determined the type of atom. With Tait, Kelvin published *Treatise on Natural Philosophy* (1867), which was important for establishing energy within the structure of the theory of mechanics; he was a devout Christian, viewing his Christian faith as supporting and informing his scientific work, compelling him to speak out against the idea of atheism as a philosophy: "*Overwhelming strong proofs of intelligent and benevolent design lie around us….I believe that the more thoroughly science is studied, the further does it take us from anything comparable to atheism…The more thoroughly I conduct scientific research, the more I believe that science excludes atheism.*"

• Speech after the Victoria Institute Annual Address of 1899: *"The atheistic idea is so nonsensical that I do not see how I can put it in words."*

• The Times, May 2, 1903, Lord Kelvin speaking at Univ. College of London, on Religion and Science: *"Do not be afraid of being free thinkers. If you think strongly enough you will be forced by science to the belief in God, which is the foundation of all Religion. You will find science not antagonistic, but helpful to Religion."*

• Lord Kelvin following lectures on "Christian Apologetics" at Univ. College, London in May, 1903 by Rev. Prof. Henslow: *"I cannot admit that, with regard to the origin of life, science neither affirms nor denies Creative Power. Science positively affirms Creative Power. It is not in dead matter that we live and move and have our being, but in the creating and directing Power which science compels us to accept as an article of belief."*

• Excerpt from Kelvin's address to Christian Evidence Society, 23 May 1889: *"My primary reason for accepting the invitation to preside was that I wished to show sympathy with this great Society which has been established for the purpose of defending Christianity as a Divine Revelation. I also thought something was due from Science. I have long felt that there was a general impression in the non-scientific world, that the scientific world believes Science has discovered ways of explaining all the facts of Nature without adopting any definite belief in a Creator. I have never doubted that that impression was utterly groundless. It seems to me that when a scientific man says—as it has been said from time to time—that there is no God, he does not express his own ideas clearly. He is, perhaps, struggling with difficulties; but when he says he does not believe in a creative power, I am convinced he does not faithfully express what is in his own mind, He does not fully express his own ideas. He is out of his depth. We are all out of our depth when we approach the subject of life. The scientific man, in looking at a piece of dead matter, thinking over the results of certain combinations which he can impose upon it, is himself a living miracle, proving that there is something beyond that mass of dead matter of which he is thinking. His very thought is in itself a contradiction to the idea that there is nothing in existence but dead matter. Science can do little positively towards the objects of this society. But it can do something, and that something is vital and fundamental. It is to show that what we see in the world of dead matter and of life around us is not a result of the fortuitous concourse of atoms. I may refer to that old, but never uninteresting subject of the miracles of geology. Physical science does something for us here. St. Peter speaks of scoffers who said that 'all things continue as they were from the beginning of the creation;' but the apostle affirms himself that 'all these things shall be dissolved.' It seems to me that even physical science absolutely demonstrates the scientific truth of these words."*

• Excerpt from Presidential Address to British Assoc. for the Advancement of Science; August, 1871: *"I feel profoundly convinced that the argument of design has been greatly too much lost sight of in recent zoological speculations. Reactions against the frivolities of teleology, such as are to be found, not rarely, in the notes of the learned commentators on Paley's 'Natural Theology,' has, I believe, had a temporary effect in turning attention from the solid and irrefragable argument so well put forward in that excellent old book. But overwhelmingly strong proofs of intelligent and benevolent design lie all around us, and if ever perplexities, whether metaphysical or scientific, turn us away from them for a time, they come back upon us with irresistible force, showing to us through nature the influence of a free will, and teaching us that all living beings depend on one ever-acting Creator and Ruler."*

• Excerpt from 'Good Words', 1862: *"Thus we have the sober scientific certainty that the heavens and earth shall 'wax old as doth a garment,' and that this slow progress must gradually, by natural agencies which we see going on under fixed laws, bring about circumstances in which 'the elements shall melt with fervent heat.' With such views forced upon us by the contemplation of dynamical energy and its laws of transformation of dead matter, dark indeed would be the prospects of the human race if unillumined by that light which reveals 'new heavens and a new earth'".*

• *"Science positively affirms Creative Power. It is not in dead matter that we live and move and have our being, but in the creating and directing Power which science compels us to accept as an article of belief."*

**Bernhard Riemann (1826-1866)** ⇨ CHRISTIAN   PhD Mathematics, Univ. of Gottingen, 1849; head of Mathematics Dept. Univ. of Gottingen, 1859; he was the most influential mathematician of the mid-19th century. He made important contributions to analysis and differential geometry, some paving the way for the later development of Einstein's general relativity; first to propose greater than 3 or 4 dimensions to describe physical reality, which was later validated by Einstein (he proposed introducing a collection of numbers at every point in space which would describe how much space was bending - in four spatial dimensions, he said that you need a collection of ten numbers at each point to describe the properties of a manifold, no matter how distorted it is. This is the famous construction central to his geometry, known today as a Riemannian metric); founder of the theories of Riemannian geometry, algebraic geometry and complex manifold theory. The theory of Riemann surfaces became an area of mathematics that was foundational in topology, and in the 21st century is still being applied to mathematical physics. He also studied the Bible intensively, and at one point even tried to prove mathematically the correctness of the Book of Genesis.

• Bell, E.T., 'Men of Mathematics', 1965: *"Bernhard Riemann had poor health throughout much of his life. He contracted pleurisy at the age of 35 and passed away four years later. During his life, he held closely to his Christian faith and considered it to be the most important aspect of his life. At the time of his death, he was reciting the Lord's Prayer with his wife and passed away before they finished saying the prayer. He left her with one child. Sometimes people's lives are short, but they make great contributions while they are here. Bernhard Riemann's life was of this type."*

• 'Monuments of Mathematicians', 2011: *"His tombstone has the inscription of Romans 8:28, 'All things work together for good to them that love God."*

**James Clerk Maxwell (1831-1879)** ⇨ CHRISTIAN 1850 honors graduate mathematics Cambridge Univ.; 1860, Prof. of Physics and Astronomy at King's College in London; 1876, Honorary member, NY Academy of Sciences; Scottish mathematical theoretical physicist, widely regarded as the 19th century scientist who had the greatest influence on 20th century physics, making contributions to the fundamental models of nature. In 1931, on the centennial anniversary of Maxwell's birthday, Einstein described Maxwell's work as the "most profound and the most fruitful that physics has experienced since the time of Newton." Einstein kept a portrait of Maxwell on his study wall, alongside Isaac Newton and Faraday. His achievements in electromagnetism have also been called the "second great unification in physics", after the first one realized by Isaac Newton. His equations demonstrate that electricity, magnetism and light are all manifestations of the electromagnetic field. He demonstrated that electric and magnetic fields travel through space in the form of waves and at the constant speed of light (3.0 × 108 m/s). In 1865, Maxwell published *A Dynamical Theory of the Electromagnetic Field*, in which he proposed that light was in fact undulations in the same medium that is the cause of electric and magnetic phenomena. His work in producing a unified model of electromagnetism is one of the greatest advances in physics; at Cambridge. Albert Einstein, referring to Maxwell's unparalled contributions to physics: *"One scientific epoch ended and another began with James Clerk Maxwell. This change in the conception of reality is the most profound and the most fruitful that physics has experienced since the time of Newton"*. The great physicist Richard Feynman said of him, *" From a long view of the history of mankind the most significant event of the 19th century will be judged as Maxwell's discovery of the laws of electrodynamics."* Carl Sagan said of Maxwell, *"Maxwell's Equations have had a greater impact on human history than any 10 presidents"*. He was a member of the "Apostles", an exclusive debating society of the intellectual elite on religion and Christianity. Maxwell strongly opposed Darwin's theory of evolution, which was becoming popular at that time. He believed that the speculations involved in evolutionary thinking contradicted scientific evidence. Using mathematics, Maxwell disproved French atheist LaPlace's 1796 *nebular hypothesis* (LaPlace hypothesized that because the solar system began as a cloud of gas which contracted over millions of years to produce planets, etc. there was thus no need for a Creator). With his mathematical proof that LaPlace's proposed process could not occur, Laplace's theory was subsequently discarded.

♦ E.L. Williams and G. Mulfinger, *'Physical Science for Christian Schools'*, Bob Jones Univ. Press, Greenville, SC, 1974: *"Maxwell was convinced that scientific investigation and the teachings of the Bible were not only compatible but should be linked together. This was reflected in a prayer found among his notes: 'Almighty God, Who hast created man in Thine own image, and made him a living soul that he might seek after Thee, and have dominion over Thy creatures, teach us to study the works of Thy hands, that we may subdue the earth to our use, and strengthen the reason for Thy service; so to receive Thy blessed Word, that we may believe on Him Whom Thou hast sent, to give us the knowledge of salvation and the remission of our sins. All of which we ask in the name of the same Jesus Christ, our Lord.'"*

♦ Campbell and Garnet, *'The Life of James Clerk Maxwell'*, London 1882: *"I think men of science as well as other men need to learn from Christ, and I think Christians whose minds are scientific are bound to study science that their view of the glory of God may be as extensive as their being is capable of."*

♦ J.C. Maxwell, *'Discourse on Molecules'*, a paper presented to the British Assoc. For the Advancement of Science, 1873: *"No theory of evolution can be formed to account for the similarity of molecules, for evolution necessarily implies continuous change.. The exact equality of each molecule to all others of the same kind gives it.. the essential character of a manufactured article, and precludes the idea of its being eternal and self-existent."*

♦ Campbell and Garnet, *'The Life of James Clerk Maxwell'*, London 1882, in a letter to his wife (June 23, 1864): *"Think what God has determined to do to all those who submit themselves to His righteousness and are willing to receive His gift. They are to be conformed to the image of His Son, and when that is fulfilled, and God sees that they are conformed to the image of Christ, there can be no more condemnation, for this is the praise which God Himself gives, whose judgment is just."*

♦ L. Campbell and W. Garnett, *'The Life of James Clerk Maxwell'*, London, 1882 (prior to his death of abdominal cancer in Nov. 1879, at age 48): *"One of his close colleagues wrote: 'We his contemporaries at college, have seen in him high powers of mind and great capacity and original views, conjoined with deep humility before his God, reverent submission to His will, and hearty belief in the love and atonement of that Divine Saviour Who was his portion and comforter in trouble and sickness."*

**Lord Rayleigh (John William Strutt) (1842-1919)** ⇨ CHRISTIAN   PhD Physics 1868, Cambridge Univ.; 1879-1884: succeeded James Clerk Maxwell as 2nd Cavendish Prof. of Physics at Univ. of Cambridge; 1887-1905: Prof. of Natural Philosophy at Cambridge. 1904 Nobel Prize in Physics (densities of the most important gases and discovery of argon); member of Royal Swedish Academy of Sciences (1897); he also discovered "Rayleigh scattering" (explains why the sky is blue) and predicted the existence of the surface waves now known as "Rayleigh waves". Lord Rayleigh's first researches were mainly mathematical, concerning optics and vibrating systems, but his later work ranged over almost the whole field of physics. His patient and delicate experiments led to the establishment of the standards of resistance, current, and electromotive force. Asteroid 22740 Rayleigh was named in his honor on 1 June 2007.

♦ quoted in *Religion and Health*, James John Walsh, 1920: *"…I may say that in my opinion true Science and true Religion neither are nor could be opposed."*

♦ Lord Rayleigh prefixed Psalm 111:2 ( *"The works of the Lord are great; sought out of all them that have pleasure therein")* on the cover of each volume of his collected scientific papers (this verse is also carved on the great door of the Cavendish Laboratory in Cambridge, put there at James Clerk Maxwell's request).

**John Fleming (1849-1945)** ⇨ CHRISTIAN   PhD Physics Univ. College of London; the first Professor of Physics and Mathematics at the Univ. of Nottingham; the first Professor of Electrical Engineering, lecturing at the Univ. of Cambridge, Univ. of Nottingham and Univ. College of London; in1882, Fleming took up the advisory post of "Electrician" to the Edison Electrical Light Company, as well as advisor to Marconi Wireless Telegraph Company; in 1897, he was Chair of the Pender Laboratory at Univ. College, London, retiring from the position in 1927 (age 77); in 1904, he invented the 2-electrode vacuum-tube rectifier, which he called the oscillation valve (also called the Fleming valve), considered to have been the beginning of electronics. His contributions to electronic communications and radar were of vital importance in winning World War II. He was awarded the IRE Medal of Honor in 1933 for "the conspicuous part he played in introducing physical and engineering principles into the radio art." A devout Christian, he preached once at St Martin-in-the-Fields in London on the evidence for the resurrection. In 1932, he (along with Douglas Dewar and Captain Bernard Acworth) founded the EPM (Evolution Protest Movement), later named the CSM (Creation Science Movement. The EPM's purpose continues the same today: to protest Darwin's theory of evolution and the subsequent effects of atheistic humanism (they were concerned about the scientific, ethical, and theological repercussions following the acceptance of evolutionary theory). Not only was the EPM the first to organize scientific creationists in England, but it was also the first creationist organization in the world.

♦ *"Busy though he was at scientific affairs, he had another loyalty to the Friend he had found as a young man. He began to be less quiet as a Christian believer and to use his remarkable powers as a lecturer in speaking about the Bible. He loved the Bible and studied it as the Word of God. 'It contains,' he said, 'the record of events quite out of line with normal human experience and predictions - some of which have already been remarkably fulfilled... it is, and always has been, revered as the communication to us from the Creator of the Universe, the Supreme and Everlasting God.'"*

♦ Fleming quoted in 'The Times', February 12, 1935, at first public EPM meeting (over 600 attendees): *"..of late years the Darwinian anthropology had been forced on public attention by numerous books in such a fashion as to create a belief that it was a certainly settled scientific truth. The fact that many eminent naturalists did not agree that Darwin's theory of species production had been sufficiently established as a truth was generally repressed. If there had been no creation, there was no need to assume any Creator; the chief basis for all religion was taken away and morality reduced to mere human expediency. It had seemed to a large number of thoughtful persons that it was of national importance to counteract the effects of reckless and indiscriminate popularization of the theory of the wholly animal origin of mankind, especially among the young, by the diffusion of a truly scientific cause for all those altruistic, aesthetic, intellectual, spiritual and religious faculties in man, of which not the very slightest trace was seen in the animal species... they desired to oppose a one-sided materialistic presentation of human origin which rejected altogether any suggestion of creation. They said that the arguments of the Darwinian anthropologists were defective in logic and did not give the proof they assumed."*

♦ From 1904, under the title *Evidence of Things Not Seen,* he lectured on the unadorned facts about Evolution. He was an outspoken opponent of Evolution theory, and could not bear to look on quietly while an *"unproven and unscientific theory was blatantly taught as fact to the ordinary public."* He was a brilliant speaker, getting popular scientific lectures across to non-scientific audiences; copies of his published works kept in University College fill five volumes.

♦ Fleming, *'Evolution or Creation?'* (1933): `The theory of evolution is totally inadequate to explain the origin and manifestation of the inorganic world.'

♦ Fleming, *'Evolution or Creation?'*, 1933: *"…evolution is essentially atheistic… and is an attempt to dispense with the very idea of God and substitute for an Intelligent Creator an impersonal non-intelligent agency… namely mutations, time, chance, and natural selection".*

**Max Planck (1858-1947)** ⇨ CHRISTIAN  PhD Theoretical Physics, Univ. of Munich (age 21); "Father of Modern Physics"; 1918 Nobel Prize in Physics (founder of quantum theory, the basis of knowledge of atomic and subatomic processes); 1892 Professor Theoretical Physics, Friedich Wilheim Univ. in Berlin; he held a strong religious belief in the existence of God.

♦ 1937 Lecture, Religion and Natural Science: *"Both religion and science require a belief in God. For believers, God is in the beginning, and for physicists He is at the end of all considerations… To the former He is the foundation, to the latter, the crown of the edifice of every generalized world view".*

◆ Planck 1958: *"Religion represents a bond of man to God. It consists in reverent awe before a supernatural Might, to which human life is subordinated and which has in its power our welfare and misery. To remain in permanent contact with this Might and keep it all the time inclined to oneself, is the unending effort and the highest goal of the believing man. Because only in such a way can one feel himself safe before expected and unexpected dangers, which threaten one in his life, and can take part in the highest happiness – inner psychical peace – which can be attained only by means of strong bond to God and unconditional trust to His omnipotence and willingness to help."*

◆ "The Nature of Matter", speech at Florence, Italy (1944): *"As a man who has devoted his whole life to the most clear headed science, to the study of matter, I can tell you as a result of my research about atoms this much: There is no matter as such. All matter originates and exists only by virtue of a force which brings the particle of an atom to vibration and holds this most minute solar system of the atom together. We must assume behind this force the existence of a conscious and intelligent mind. This mind is the matrix of all matter".*

◆ "Where Is Science Going?" (1932): *"Anybody who has been seriously engaged in scientific work of any kind realizes that over the entrance to the gates of the temple of science are written the words: Ye must have faith. It is a quality which the scientist cannot dispense with… There can never be any real opposition between religion and science; for one is the complement of the other. Every serious and reflective person realizes, I think, that the religious element in his nature must be recognized and cultivated if all the powers of the human soul are to act together in perfect balance and harmony. And indeed it was not by accident that the greatest thinkers of all ages were deeply religious souls."*

◆ Planck, 1958: *"… it is no wonder, that the movement of atheists, which declares religion to be just a deliberate illusion, … eagerly makes use of progressive scientific knowledge and in a presumed unity with it, expands in an ever faster pace its disintegrating action on all nations of the earth and on all social levels. I do not need to explain in any more detail that after its victory not only all of the precious treasures of our culture would vanish, but--which is even worse--also any prospects at a better future."*

◆ The Observer (January 25th, 1931), To the question of The Observer, "Do you think that consciousness can be explained in terms of matter?" Max Planck replied: *"No. I regard consciousness as fundamental. I regard matter as derivative from consciousness. We cannot get behind consciousness. Everything that we talk about, everything that we regard as existing, postulates consciousness."*

**Albert Einstein (1879-1955)** ⇨ DEIST  PhD Theoretical Physics; 1921 Nobel Prize in Physics; Time Person of the Century, 1999; from "The Expanded Quotable Einstein", Princeton Univ. Press, 2000: *"The scientist is possessed by the sense of universal causation ... His religious feeling takes the form of a rapturous amazement at the harmony of natural law, which reveals an intelligence of such superiority that, compared with it, all the systematic thinking and acting of human beings is an utterly insignificant reflection... In the view of such harmony in the cosmos which I, with my limited human mind, am able to recognize, there are yet people who say there is no God. But what makes me really angry is that they quote me for support for such views… I see a pattern, but my imagination cannot picture the maker of that pattern. I see a clock, but I cannot envision the clockmaker. The human mind is unable to conceive of the four dimensions, so how can it conceive of a God, before whom a thousand years and a thousand dimensions are as one?... What I see in Nature is a magnificent structure that we can comprehend only very imperfectly, and that must fill a thinking person with a feeling of 'humility'. This is a genuinely religious feeling that has nothing to do with mysticism."*

◆ "The Life of Ernst Chain: Penicillin and Beyond", Ronald Clark, 1973: *"I want to know how God created this world. I am not interested in this or that phenomenon, in the spectrum of this or that element. I want to know his thoughts. The rest are details."*

◆ Memorial speech for Christian Anfinsen at Memorial Garden Dedication, Weizmann Institute. Nov. 16, 1995: *"The most beautiful and most profound emotion we can experience is the sensation of the mystical. It is the sower of all true science. He to whom this emotion is a stranger, who can no longer stand rapt in awe, is as good as dead. That deeply emotional conviction of the presence of a superior Reasoning Power, which is revealed in the incomprehensible Universe, forms my idea of God."*

◆ Letter, Jan. 24, 1936 (quoted in Helen Dukas and Banesh Hoffman, "Albert Einstein: The Human Side (1981)": *"But, on the other hand, everyone who is seriously involved in the pursuit of science becomes convinced that a spirit is manifest in the laws of the Universe—a spirit vastly superior to that of man, and one in the face of which we with our modest powers must feel humble."*

**Robert Millikan (1868-1953)** ⇨ CHRISTIAN  PhD Physics Columbia Univ.; 1923 Nobel Prize in Physics (measured charge of electron, work on photoelectric effect); Prof. of Physics Univ. of Chicago 1896-1921; President CalTech 1921-1945; studied under Max Planck; he opposed to Darwinian evolution and philosophical naturalism; quoted in "*The Autobiography of Robert A. Millikan*", Prentice-Hall, New York, 1950: *"…humans are not animals; one cannot even imagine a mere animal thinking about a future life as do humans.*

*The chasm between humans and animals is so enormous that the "great spiritual forces which are in varying degrees in all mankind … sharply differentiate man from the whole lower animal kingdom…. When asked if life and the creation resulted from 'blind, unintelligent chance', Millikan answered "the fool hath said in his heart, there is no God" and "instead of calling what had happened accident, thank God for creating His creation… the teachings of Jesus created the Christian church, that is unquestionably the greatest social institution in the country…the combination of science and religion provides today the sole basis for rational intelligent living… religion and science are the two great sister forces which have pulled, and are still pulling, mankind onward and upward."*

♦ "Address to the American Chemical Society", The Commentator, June 1937: *"…everyone who reflects believes in God…it is pathetic that many scientists are trying to prove the doctrine of evolution, which no scientist can do."*

♦ *"Evolution in Science and Religion"*, Yale University Press,1927*: "The most amazing thing in all life, the greatest miracle there is, is the fact that a mind has got here at all, 'created out of the dust of the earth.' This is the Bible phrase, and science today can find no better way to describe it—a mind" that thinks… The laws of physics allowed humankind to know a God not of caprice and whim, such as were all the gods of the ancient world, but a God who works through law who revealed a nature of orderliness, and a nature capable of being known; a nature, too, whose functioning might be predicted, a nature which could be relied upon; a nature, also, of possibly unlimited forces, capable of being discovered, and then of being harnessed for the benefit of mankind."*

♦ Millikan's view of Naturalism ("*Evolution in Science and Religion*"): *"…irrational and unscientific because it asserts that there is nothing behind or inherent in all the phenomena of nature except blind force, and that in the face of the fact that he [the atheist] sees evidence of what he is wont himself to call intelligence in the workings of his own mind, and in the myriads of other minds which are a part of nature."*

♦ Millikan's view of Atheism ("*Evolution in Science and Religion*"): *"…so anti-science that I knew of nothing that could possibly be more antagonistic to the whole spirit of science… even Voltaire condemned it as unintelligent when he wrote: 'If God did not exist it would be necessary to invent him.'…if I was confronted with a choice between these two types of dogmatic religion, fundamentalism and atheism … I should choose fundamentalism as the less irrational of the two and the more desirable, for atheism is essentially the philosophy of pessimism, denying, as it does, that there is any purpose or trend in nature, or any reason for our trying to fit into and advance a scheme of development."*

♦ McMurray, E., Notable 20th-Century Scientists, vol.1, Gale Research, New York, 1995*: "At times he used the word "evolution", not with reference to Darwinism, but rather to progress in scientific research and knowledge by intelligent agents (mankind), a point that needs to be stressed when reading his writings."*

♦ Millikan, R., '*Time, Matter, and Values*', The University of North Carolina Press, Chapel Hill, NC, 1932 (his critical view of naturalism): *"the eighteenth-century French philosophers forget that the essence of the scientific method lay in sticking close to the observed facts and not asserting knowledge beyond the range of observation, yielded to the lure of such inclusive generalizations as had rendered Greek philosophy impotent and proceeded to convert Galileo's and Newton's science into a mechanical philosophy in which the whole of the past and future was calculable from the positions and motions of inert material bodies and man became a machine… although materialism was sometimes called scientific, it is in its very method and essence unscientific because it was universally assertive and dogmatic…clear-thinking minds in all countries refused to be stampeded by it, realizing the limitations of the scientific method."*

**Arthur Eddington (1882-1944)** ⇨ CHRISTIAN   British astrophysicist best known for his work with Einstein on his General Theory of Relativity Cambridge Plumian Prof. of Astronomy and Experimental Philosophy; Director of Cambridge Observatory;– quoted from "The End of the World: From the Standpoint of Mathematical Physics", Nature, vol. 127 (1931): *"Philosophically, the notion of a beginning of the present order of Nature is repugnant to me … I should like to find a genuine loophole."*

♦ Heeren, F. 1995. *Show Me God*. Wheeling, IL, Searchlight Publications: *"The idea of a universal mind or Logos would be, I think, a fairly plausible inference from the present state of scientific theory."*

♦ 'The Decline of Determinism' in Robert L. Weber, 'More Random Walks in Science' (1982): *"Science is one thing, wisdom is another. Science is an edged tool, with which men play like children, and cut their own fingers. If you look at the results which science has brought in its train, you will find them to consist almost wholly in elements of mischief. See how much belongs to the word 'Explosion' alone, of which the ancients knew nothing."*

**Erwin Schrödinger (1887-1961)** ⇨ PANTHEIST   Austrian physicist; PhD Univ. of Vienna 1910; 1933 Nobel Prize for the "new productive forms of atomic theory", centered around his *Schrödinger Equation* (creation of wave mechanics - he showed how electrons moved within an atom as a wave. His work was celebrated as one of the most important achievements of the 20th century); 1937 Max Planck Medal; 1927 Prof. of Physics at the Friedrich Wilhelm University in Berlin (succeeding Max Planck); 1933 Fellow at Oxford Univ.; Director of the School for Theoretical Physics, Institute for Advanced Studies, Dublin, Ireland (1940-1955); he rejected the idea of a personal God (no single concept of God,

all souls are eternal and accountable for their actions throughout time); he rejected the idea that science could give answers to life's questions about eternity, God, purpose: "*Whence came I and whither go I? That is the great unfathomable question, the same for every one of us. Science has no answer for it.*"
♦ *Nature and the Greeks*", Cambridge Univ. Press, 1954: "I am very *astonished that the scientific picture of the real world around me is very deficient. It gives a lot of factual information, puts all our experience in a magnificently consistent order, but is ghastly silent about all that is really near to our heart, that really matters to us. It cannot tell us a word about red and blue, bitter and sweet, physical pain and physical delight; it knows nothing of beautiful and ugly, good or bad, God and eternity. Science sometimes pretends to answer questions in these domains, but the answers are very often so silly that we are not inclined to take them seriously.*"
♦ "*Schrödinger: Life and Thought*", Walter Moore, Cambridge: Cambridge Univ. Press, 1990: "*In the presentation of a scientific problem, the other player is the good Lord. He has not only set the problem but also has devised the rules of the game--but they are not completely known, half of them are left for you to discover or deduce…. The grave error in a technically directed cultural drive is that it sees its highest goal in the possibility of achieving an alteration of Nature. It hopes to set itself in the place of God, so that it may force upon the divine will some petty conventions of its dust-born mind.*"

**William Henry Bragg** (**1890–1971**) ⇨ CHRISTIAN  MA Theoretical Physics, Cambridge Univ. 1884; 1915 Nobel Prize in Physics (analysis of crystal structures by means of X-rays); Professor of Physics, Universities of Adelaide, Leeds, and London; President of the Royal Society of London (1935-1940). The following quotes are taken from "The Scientific God Journal", April 2010 (ISSN 2153-831X), published by Scientific God Inc.: In 1940 Bragg identified 'two sad mistakes' current in science-religion debates: *"The one is to suppose that science, that is to say, the study of Nature, leads to materialism. The other that the worship of God can be carried on without the equipment which science provides."…"From religion comes a man's purpose; from science, his power to achieve it. Sometimes people ask if religion and science are not opposed to one another. They are: in the sense that the thumb and fingers of my hand are opposed to one another. It is an opposition by means of which anything can be grasped."*
♦ In his lecture Science and Faith (1941): "*Science is experimental, moving forward step-by-step, making trial and learning through success and failure. Is not this also the way of religion, and especially of the Christian religion? The writings of those who preach the religion have from the very beginning insisted that it is to be proved by experience. If a man is drawn towards honor and courage and endurance, justice, mercy, and charity, let him follow the way of Christ and find out for himself. No findings in science hinder him in that way.*"
♦ "*Conviction of the truth of any faith, so far as a man can measure the truth he finds himself, it may be a small circle, his means may be small also, can try the Christian way, and discover for himself and acquire his own convictions. He tests his faith. As to the actual mode of the experiment, I will say nothing. We all know it well already: it has been enshrined in a thousand testimonies; it has been displayed in countless lives; it is all included in the lovely words of St. Paul, simple though they are: 'And the greatest of these is charity'.*"
♦ Bragg's daughter Gwendolen Mary Caroe wrote about her father's faith: "*Religious faith to W. H. Bragg was the willingness to stake his all on the hypothesis that Christ was right, and test it by a lifetime's experiment in charity.*"
♦ "*Christ's rule and example showed God as our Father and us as His children, a society in which love governs all… For we trust that this life is a preparation: not a final probation.*"

**Arthur Compton (1892-1962)** ⇨ CHRISTIAN   PhD Princeton Univ. 1916; 1927 Nobel Prize for *Compton Effect* (electromagnetic radiation can be explained as the recoil of a high-energy photon with longer wavelength from a free electron, like an elastic collision); Head of Physics Dept., Washington Univ. in St. Louis: Head of Physics Dept. (1920 to 1923), then Chancellor (1946); 1934 visiting Prof. at Oxford; Chairman Univ. of Chicago Physics Dept. and Director of Metallurgical Lab (1940-1945), in charge of the WWII Plutonium Project (the first self-sustaining nuclear reaction took place Dec. 2, 1942); NASA's Compton Gamma Ray Observatory was named in his honor): "*What nobler ambition can one have than to cooperate with his Maker in bringing about a better world in which we can live? Science has created a world in which Christianity is a necessity… I believe that its insistence on the inherent value of individual men and women Christianity has the key to survival and the good life in the modern world.*"
♦ "*In their essence there can be no conflict between science and religion. Science is a reliable method of finding truth. Religion is the search for a satisfying basis for life.*"
♦ quoted in Chicago Daily News on the 1st verse of the Bible, 1936: "*For myself, faith begins with the realization that a supreme intelligence brought the universe into being and created man. It is not difficult for me to have this faith, for it is incontrovertible that where there is a plan there is intelligence. An orderly, unfolding universe testifies to the truth of the most majestic statement ever uttered: 'In the beginning God …'*"
♦ "*The Human Meaning of Science*", 1940: "*The scientist who recognizes God knows only the God of Newton. To him the God imagined by Laplace and Comte is wholly inadequate. He feels that God is in nature, that the orderly ways in which nature works are themselves the manifestations of God's will and purpose. Its laws are his orderly way of working.*"

◆ *"The Cosmos of Arthur Holly Compton"*, Johnston, 1967: *"From earliest childhood I have learned to see in Jesus the supreme example of one who loves his neighbors and expresses that love in actions that count, who knows that people can find their souls by losing themselves in something of great value, who will die rather than deny the truth in favor of the popular view held by his most respected contemporaries. That Jesus lives so vitally in men today makes me hope that by following in his footsteps in my small way I also may live forever."*

**Werner Heisenberg (1901-1976)** ⇨ CHRISTIAN   PhD Physics Univ. of Munich, 1923; 1932 Nobel Prize for Physics (creation of quantum mechanics); 1933 Max Planck Medal; Prof. Theoretical Physics at Univ. of Leipzig, 1927; President of the German Research Council; Director of the Max Planck Institute for Physics; Chairman of the Commission for Atomic Physics; Chairman of the Nuclear Physics Working Group. He spoke of how science and religion work together to point man to God: *"In the history of science, ever since the famous trial of Galileo, it has repeatedly been claimed that scientific truth cannot be reconciled with the religious interpretation of the world. Although I am now convinced that scientific truth is unassailable in its own field, I have never found it possible to dismiss the content of religious thinking as simply part of an outmoded phase in the consciousness of mankind, a part we shall have to give up from now on, Thus in the course of my life I have repeatedly been compelled to ponder on the relationship of these two regions of thought, for I have never been able to doubt the reality of that to which they point."*

◆ "Das Universum – Hinweis auf Gott?", 1988:  *"The first gulp from the glass of natural sciences will turn you into an atheist, but at the bottom of the glass God is waiting for you."*

◆ *"Why I Am a Christian"*, 1985 *Truth Magazine*, Henry Margenau (*Professor Emeritus of Physics and Natural Philosophy at Yale University*): *"I have said nothing about the years between 1936 and 1950. There were, however, a few experiences I cannot forget. One was my first meeting with Heisenberg, who came to America soon after the end of the Second World War. …Our conversation was intimate and he impressed me by his deep religious conviction. He was a true Christian in every sense of that word."*

**Sir Fred Hoyle (1915-2001)** ⇨ DEIST   Cambridge Professor of Astrophysics and Natural Philosophy; Founder, Institute of Theoretical Astronomy in Cambridge, President Royal Astronomical Society,1971; expressed his religious views as "anti-theistic":

◆ *The Intelligent Universe* New York: Holt, Rinehard, and Winston, 1983: *"The big bang theory requires a recent origin of the Universe that openly invites the concept of creation."*

◆ *"The Big Bang in Astronomy"*, New Scientist, Vol. 92, No. 1280 (November 19, 1981), p. 527: *"The notion that not only the biopolymer but the operating program of a living cell could be arrived at by chance in a primordial organic soup here on the Earth is evidently nonsense of a high order."*

◆ The Oxford Dictionary of Quotations (1999) edited by Elizabeth Knowles and Angela Partington: *"There is a coherent plan in the universe, though I don't know what it's a plan for."*

◆ *"A common sense interpretation of the facts suggests that a superintellect has monkeyed with the physics, as well as with chemistry and biology, and that there are no blind forces worth speaking about in nature. The numbers one calculates from the facts seem to me so overwhelming as to put this conclusion almost beyond question."*

◆ Fred Hoyle, *Evolution from Space'* (London: J.M. Dent & Sons, 1981): *"Life cannot have had a random beginning ... The trouble is that there are about two thousand enzymes, and the chance of obtaining them all in a random trial is only one part in $10^{40,000}$, an outrageously small probability that could not be faced even if the whole universe consisted of organic soup.... Once we see, however, that the probability of life originating at random is so utterly miniscule as to make it absurd, it becomes sensible to think that the favorable properties of physics on which life depends are in every respect deliberate ... . It is therefore almost inevitable that our own measure of intelligence must reflect ... higher intelligences ... even to the limit of God ... such a theory is so obvious that one wonders why it is not widely accepted as being self-evident. The reasons are psychological rather than scientific."*

◆ Fred Hoyle, *Hoyle on evolution*, Nature, Vol. 294, No. 5837 (November 12, 1981): *"The chance that higher life forms might have emerged in this way is comparable with the chance that a tornado sweeping through a junkyard might assemble a Boeing 747 from the materials therein."*

**Wernher von Braun (1912-1977)** ⇨ CHRISTIAN   PhD Physics, Univ. of Berlin; 1975 winner, National Medal of Science; German-American rocket scientist, aerospace engineer, space architect, and a leader in the development of rocket technology in Nazi Germany during WW II and then in the US; Under NASA, he served as director of Marshall Space Flight Center and chief architect of the Saturn V launch vehicle (the superbooster that propelled the Apollo spacecraft to the Moon);  considered by NASA sources to be "the greatest rocket scientist in history". Following quotes taken from the article "Profiles in Christianity and Science: Wernher von Braun, The Christian Rocket Scientist", Ray and Gale Lawson, Sept. 2005:

• *"While technology controls the forces of nature around us, ethics try to control the forces of nature within us. I think it is a fair assumption that the Ten Commandments are entirely adequate--without amendments--to cope with all the problems the technological revolution not only has brought up, but will bring up in the future. The real problem is not a lack of ethical legislation, but a lack in day-to-day guidance and control. When science freed itself from the bonds of religious dogma, thus opening the way for technological revolution, the Church also lost much of its influence on the ethical conduct of man."*

• *"They (evolutionists) challenge science to prove the existence of God. But must we really light a candle to see the sun? They say they cannot visualize a Designer. Well, can a physicist visualize an electron? What strange rationale makes some physicists accept the inconceivable electron as real while refusing to accept the reality of a Designer on the grounds that they cannot conceive Him?"*

• *"To be forced to believe only one conclusion--that everything in the universe happened by chance--would violate the very objectivity of science itself. What random process could produce the brains of a man or the system of the human eye?"*

• *"In this age of space flight, when we use the modern tools of science to advance into new regions of human activity, the Bible--this grandiose stirring history of the gradual revelation and unfolding of moral law--remains in every way an up-to-date book."*

• *The Skeptical Inquirer* 10:258-276: *"I find it as difficult to understand a scientist who does not acknowledge the presence of a superior rationality behind the existence of the universe as it is to comprehend a theologian who would deny the advances of science."*

**Charles Townes (1915 - 2015)** ⇨ CHRISTIAN    PhD Physics, CalTech; 1964 Nobel Prize in Physics (invention of 'maser' = 'microwave amplification by stimulated emission of radiation', using microwave spectra for the study of the structure of molecules, atoms, and nuclei); Prof. Astrophysics, Univ. of Berkeley, 1967; Technical Staff Bell Labs (1933-1947): Chairman Physics Dept. Columbia Univ. 1952-1955; Exec. Director of the Columbia Radiation Laboratory 1950-1952; Prof. Physics MIT 1961-1966; teamed with brother-in-law Dr. Arthur Schawlow on optical and infrared 'lasers'; Vice Chairman of the Science Advisory Committee to the US President; 2005 Templeton Prize for "Progress Toward Research or Discoveries about Spiritual Realities." Only Townes, Mother Teresa and the Dalai Lama have won both a Templeton Prize and a Nobel Prize.

• Charles Townes letter to T. Dimitrov, May 2002, in response to the question, "What do you think about the existence of God?' = *"I strongly believe in the existence of God, based on intuition, observations, logic, and also scientific knowledge."*

• Quoted from a 2005 interview for Berkeley *News* by Bonnie Powell: *"I'm a Protestant Christian, I would say a very progressive one. This has different meanings for different people. But I'm quite open minded and willing to consider all kinds of new ideas and to look at new things. At the same time it has a very deep meaning for me: I feel the presence of God. I feel it in my own life as a spirit that is somehow with me all the time."*

• Townes' answer to interview question 'If science and religion share a common purpose, why have their proponents tended to be at loggerheads throughout history?' = *"Science and religion have had a long interaction: some of it has been good and some of it hasn't. As Western science grew, Newtonian mechanics had scientists thinking that everything is predictable, meaning there's no room for God - so-called determinism. Religious people didn't want to agree with that. Then Darwin came along, and they really didn't want to agree with what he was saying, because it seemed to negate the idea of a creator. So there was a real clash for a while between science and religions. But science has been digging deeper and deeper, and as it has done so, particularly in the basic sciences like physics and astronomy, we have begun to understand more. We have found that the world is not deterministic: quantum mechanics has revolutionized physics by showing that things are not completely predictable. That doesn't mean that we've found just where God comes in, but we know now that things are not as predictable as we thought and that there are things we don't understand. For example, we don't know what some 95 percent of the matter in the universe is: we can't see it - it's neither atom nor molecule, apparently. We think we can prove it's there, we see its effect on gravity, but we don't know what and where it is, other than broadly scattered around the universe. And that's very strange. So as science encounters mysteries, it is starting to recognize its limitations and become somewhat more open. There are still scientists who differ strongly with religion and vice versa. But I think people are being more open-minded about recognizing the limitations in our frame of understanding."*

• Townes' answer to interview question 'You've said "I believe there is no long-range question more important than the purpose and meaning of our lives and our universe." How have you attempted to answer that question?' = *"Those aren't easy questions to answer, of course, but they're important and they're what religion is all about. I maintain that science is closely related to that, because science tries to understand how the universe is constructed and why it does what it does, including human life. If one understands the structure of the universe, maybe the purpose of man becomes a little clearer. I think maybe the best answer to that is that somehow, we humans were created somewhat in the likeness of God. We have free will. We have independence, we can do and create things, and that's amazing. And as we learn more and more - why, we become even more that way.*

*What kind of a life will we build? That's what the universe is open about. The purpose of the universe, I think, is to see this develop and to allow humans the freedom to do the things that hopefully will work out well for them and for the rest of the world."*

◆ Townes' answer to interview question 'Should intelligent design be taught alongside Darwinian evolution in schools as religious legislators have decided in Pennsylvania and Kansas?' = *"I think it's very unfortunate that this kind of discussion has come up. People are misusing the term intelligent design to think that everything is frozen by that one act of creation and that there's no evolution, no changes. It's totally illogical in my view. Intelligent design, as one sees it from a scientific point of view, seems to be quite real. This is a very special universe: it's remarkable that it came out just this way. If the laws of physics weren't just the way they are, we couldn't be here at all. The sun couldn't be there, the laws of gravity and nuclear laws and magnetic theory, quantum mechanics, and so on have to be just the way they are for us to be here. Some scientists argue that 'well, there's an enormous number of universes and each one is a little different. This one just happened to turn out right.' Well, that's a postulate, and it's a pretty fantastic postulate - it assumes there really are an enormous number of universes and that the laws could be different for each of them. The other possibility is that ours was planned, and that's why it has come out so specially. Now, that design could include evolution perfectly well. It's very clear that there is evolution, and it's important. Evolution is here, and intelligent design is here, and they're both consistent."*

**Richard Feynman (1918-1988)** ⇨ AGNOSTIC   PhD Princeton Univ. 1942 (Quantum Physics);1965 Nobel Prize (developed quantum electrodynamics); Prof. Theoretical Physics Cornell Univ. (1945-1950); winner 1979 National Medal of Science; winner 1954 Albert Einstein Award; in a 1999 poll of 130 leading physicists worldwide by the British journal Physics World, he was ranked as one of the ten greatest physicists of all time; he was not religious, he believed that Science can't provide answers to life's questions for what is true and not true, only what is more or less likely.

◆ *"The Meaning of It All"*, 1998, p. 36: *"Science cannot disprove the existence of God… I also agree that a belief in science and religion is consistent… science cannot produce 'the meaning of life' nor can it tell us 'the right moral values'. These must come from somewhere else."*

◆ *The Relation of Science and Religion"*, Caltech YMCA Luncheon, 1956: *"I do not believe that science can disprove the existence of God; I think that is impossible. And if it is impossible, is not a belief in science and in a God – an ordinary God of religion — a consistent possibility? Yes, it is consistent. Despite the fact that I said that more than half of the scientists don't believe in God, many scientists do believe in both science and God, in a perfectly consistent way… For the student, when he learns about science, there are two sources of difficulty in trying to weld science and religion together. The first source of difficulty is this – that it is imperative in science to doubt; it is absolutely necessary, for progress in science, to have uncertainty as a fundamental part of your inner nature. To make progress in understanding we must remain modest and allow that we do not know. Nothing is certain or proved beyond all doubt. You investigate for curiosity, because it is unknown, not because you know the answer. And as you develop more information in the sciences, it is not that you are finding out the truth, but that you are finding out that this or that is more or less likely. That is, if we investigate further, we find that the statements of science are not of what is true and what is not true, but statements of what are known to different degrees of certainty."*

◆ Quoted in 'Superstrings: A Theory of Everything?' (1988): *"God was always invented to explain mystery. God is always invented to explain those things that you do not understand. Now when you finally discover how something works, you get some laws which you're taking away from God; you don't need him anymore. But you need him for the other mysteries. So therefore you leave him to create the universe because we haven't figured that out yet; you need him for understanding those things which you don't believe the laws will explain, such as consciousness, or why you only live to a certain length of time—life and death—stuff like that. God is always associated with those things that you do not understand. Therefore, I don't think that the laws can be considered to be like God because they have been figured out."*

**Robert Jastrow (1925-2008)** ⇨ AGNOSTIC   PhD Theoretical Physics; 1961 Director of NASA's Goddard Institute for Space Studies; NASA Medal for Exceptional Scientific Achievement; Dartmouth Univ. Professor Earth Science; Columbia Univ. Professor Geophysics); an agnostic who clearly expressed his views of the existence of God – following quotes from his book "*God and the Astronomers,* 2nd edition, New York and London: W.W. Norton & Company, 1992:

◆ *"For the scientist who has lived by faith in the power of reason, the story ends like a bad dream. He has scaled the mountains of ignorance; he is about to conquer the highest peak; as he pulls himself over the final rock, he is greeted by a band of theologians who have been sitting there for centuries."*

◆ *"We see how the astronomical evidence supports the biblical view of the origin of the world. The details differ, but the essential elements in the astronomical and biblical accounts of Genesis are the same: the chain of events leading to man commenced suddenly and sharply at a definite moment in time, in a flash of light and energy."*

◆ The Enchanted Loom: Mind in the Universe (1981*): "Scientists have no proof that life was not the result of an act of creation."*

◆ *"There is a strange ring of feeling and emotion in these reactions [of scientists to evidence that the universe had a sudden beginning]. They come from the heart whereas you would expect the judgments to come from the brain. Why? I think part of the answer is that scientists cannot bear the thought of a natural phenomenon which cannot be explained, even with unlimited time and money. There is a kind of religion in science; it is the religion of a person who believes there is order and harmony in the Universe. Every event can be explained in a rational way as the product of some previous event; every effect must have its cause, there is no First Cause. … This religious faith of the scientist is violated by the discovery that the world had a beginning under conditions in which the known laws of physics are not valid, and as a product of forces or circumstances we cannot discover. When that happens, the scientist has lost control. If he really examined the implications, he would be traumatized."*

◆ *"Consider the enormity of the problem. Science has proved that the universe exploded into being at a certain moment. It asks: What cause produced this effect? Who or what put the matter or energy into the universe? And science cannot answer these questions, because, according to the astronomers, in the first moments of its existence the Universe was compressed to an extraordinary degree, and consumed by the heat of a fire beyond human imagination. The shock of that instant must have destroyed every particle of evidence that could have yielded a clue to the cause of the great explosion."*

◆*"The essential element in the astronomical and biblical accounts of Genesis is the same; the chain of events leading to man commenced suddenly and sharply, at a definite moment in time, in a flash of light and energy."*

◆*"The Hubble Law is one of the great discoveries in science; it is one of the main supports of the scientific story of Genesis."*

◆ Christianity Today, Aug. 6, 1982*: "Astronomers now find they have painted themselves into a corner because they have proven, by their own methods, that the world began abruptly in an act of creation to which you can trace the seeds of every star, every planet, every living thing in this cosmos and on the earth. And they have found that all this happened as a product of forces they cannot hope to discover. That there are what I or anyone would call supernatural forces at work is now, I think, a scientifically proven fact."*

**Arthur L. Schawlow (1921-1999)** ⇨ CHRISTIAN   PhD Physics, Univ. of Toronto; 1981 Nobel Prize in physics, laser spectroscopy; Professor of Physics at both Columbia & Stanford Universities; openly expressed his Christianity – quoted by Margenau & Varghese,1997:
◆ *"But the context of religion is a great background for doing science. In the words of Psalm 19, 'The heavens declare the glory of God and the firmament showeth his handiwork'. Thus scientific research is a worshipful act, in that it reveals more of the wonders of God's creation."*
◆ *"We are fortunate to have the Bible, and especially the New Testament, which tells us so much about God in widely accessible human terms."*
◆ *"Cosmos, Bios, Theos: Scientists Reflect on Science, God, and the Origins of the Universe, Life, and Homo Sapiens* (Open Court Pub. Co., La Salle, IL, 1992): *It seems to me that when confronted with the marvels of life and the universe, one must ask why and not just how. The only possible answers are religious. . . . I find a need for God in the universe and in my own life."*

**Alan Sandage (1926-2010)** ⇨ CHRISTIAN   PhD Astronomy, CalTech; Winner of the Crawford prize in astronomy, National Medal of Science; the most influential astronomer of the last half-century, credited with founding the discipline of observational cosmology; he began his career in the late 1940s as observing assistant to Edwin Hubble, the astronomer who discovered the expansion of the universe. When Hubble died of a heart attack in 1953, Sandage took on his grand project: measuring the size and age of the universe. He became a born-again Christian later in his career, reasoning that *"I could not live a life full of cynicism. I chose to believe, and a peace of mind came over me."*
◆ quoted from "Sizing up the Cosmos: An Astronomer's Quest", NY Times, 1991: *"I find it quite improbable that such order came out of chaos. There has to be some organizing principle. God to me is a mystery but is the explanation for the miracle of existence, why there is something instead of nothing."*

**Arno Penzias (1933 - )** ⇨ CHRISTIAN   PhD Physics Columbia Univ.; 1978 Nobel prize in Physics (discovery of Cosmic Background Radiation, confirming Big Bang); 1977 co-winner (with Wilson) of the Henry Draper Medal of the National Academy of Sciences; Fellow of the American Academy of Arts and Sciences in 1975); in connection with the "Big Bang" theory and the issue of the origin of our highly ordered universe, Dr. Penzias stated to the *New York Times* on March 12, 1978: *"The best data we have are exactly what I would have predicted, had I had nothing to go on but the five books of Moses, the Psalms, the Bible as a whole."*
◆ *"Cosmos, Bios, and Theos"* by Margenau, H and R.A. Varghese, 1992: *"Astronomy leads us to a unique event, a universe which was created out of nothing, one with the very delicate balance needed to provide exactly the conditions required to permit life, and one which has an underlying (one might say 'supernatural') plan."*

◆ *'The God I Believe in'* (New York, Maxwell Macmillan International, 1994): *"…by looking at the order in the world, we can infer purpose and from purpose we begin to get some knowledge of the Creator, the Planner of all this. This is, then, how I look at God. I look at God through the works of God's hands and from those works imply intentions. From these intentions, I receive an impression of the Almighty."*

◆ *"'When Science and Religion Collide' or 'Why Einstein Wasn't an Atheist': Scientists Talk about Why They Believe in God"*, Gordy Slack 1997 quote of Dr. Penzias: *"If God created the universe, he would have done it elegantly. The absence of any imprint of intervention upon creation is what we would expect from a truly all-powerful Creator. You don't need somebody diddling around like Frank Morgan in The Wizard of Oz to keep the universe going. Instead, what you have is half a page of mathematics that describes everything. In some sense, the power of the creation lies in its underlying simplicity."*

◆ Penzias 1983 quote on the Big Bang theory and the observational evidence that the universe was created: *"How could the everyday person take sides in this dispute between giants? One held that the universe was created out of nothing, while the other proclaimed the evident eternity of matter. The 'dogma' of creation was thwarted by the 'fact' of the eternal nature of matter. Well, today's dogma holds that matter is eternal. The dogma comes from the intuitive belief of people (including the majority of physicists) who don't want to accept the observational evidence that the universe was created – despite the fact that the creation of the universe is supported by all the observable data astronomy has produced so far. As a result, the people who reject the data can arguably be described as having a 'religious' belief that matter must be eternal. These people regard themselves as objective scientists."*

**Steven Weinberg (1933 - )** ⇨ ATHEIST   PhD Physics Princeton Univ.; 1979 Nobel prize in Physics (discovery of the electroweak unification theory - unification of electromagnetism and of nuclear weak forces); former Professor of Physics at MIT and Harvard University;  Prof. Physics at Univ. Texas, Austin; His two textbooks, The Quantum Theory of Fields and Gravitation and Cosmology, are among the most influential texts in the scientific community in their subjects; one of the most sought-after public spokesmen for science.

◆ The New York Times, "Physicist Ponders God, Truth and 'a Final Theory'" by James Glanz, January 25, 2000: *"The more the universe seems comprehensible, the more it also seems pointless."*

◆ Natalie Angier, 'Confessions of a Lonely Atheist,' *New York Times Magazine*, January 14, 2001: *"It's a consequence of the experience of science. As you learn more and more about the universe, you find you can understand more and more without any reference to supernatural intervention, so you lose interest in that possibility. Most scientists I know don't care enough about religion even to call themselves atheists. And that, I think, is one of the great things about science -- that it has made it possible for people not to be religious."*

◆ 'Dreams of a Final Theory': *"Religious people have grappled for millennia with the theodicy, the problem posed by the existence of suffering in a world that is supposed to be ruled by a good God. They have found ingenious solutions in terms of various supposed divine plans. I will not try to argue with these solutions, much less to add one of my own. Remembrance of the Holocaust leaves me unsympathetic to attempts to justify the ways of God to man. If there is a God that has special plans for humans, then He has taken very great pains to hide His concern for us. To me it would seem impolite if not impious to bother such a God with our prayers… Premature as the question may be, it is hardly possible not to wonder whether we will find any answer to our deepest questions, any signs of the workings of an interested God, in a final theory. I think that we will not."*

◆ 'A Designer Universe?': *"I don't need to argue here that the evil in the world proves that the universe is not designed, but only that there are no signs of benevolence that might have shown the hand of a designer. But in fact the perception that God cannot be benevolent is very old. Plays by Aeschylus and Euripides make a quite explicit statement that the gods are selfish and cruel, though they expect better behavior from humans. God in the Old Testament tells us to bash the heads of infidels and demands of us that we be willing to sacrifice our children's lives at His orders, and the God of traditional Christianity and Islam damns us for eternity if we do not worship him in the right manner. Is this a nice way to behave? I know, I know, we are not supposed to judge God according to human standards, but you see the problem here: If we are not yet convinced of His existence, and are looking for signs of His benevolence, then what other standards can we use?"*

◆ 'Freethought Today', April 2000: *"Science should be taught not in order to support religion and not in order to destroy religion. Science should be taught simply ignoring religion… Religion is an insult to human dignity. With or without it you would have good people doing good things and evil people doing evil things. But for good people to do evil things, that takes religion… I can hope that this long sad story, this progression of priests and ministers and rabbis and ulamas and imams and bonzes and bodhisattvas, will come to an end. I hope this is something to which science can contribute ... it may be the most important contribution that we can make."*

◆ Quoted from Michael King, "In Search of Intelligent Life at the SBOE (State Board of Education)" (*Austin*, [Texas], *Chronicle*: September 19, 2003: *"Their [the proponents of Christian "intelligent design"] discussion of the supposed weakness of evolution rests on a fallacy about the way science works. Scientific theory is never regarded as certain; it's continually confronted with testing, asking if it can explain what we can see in nature.*

*That work is never finished. There are always some things left that haven't yet been explained. That's true of physics as well as biology.... This work goes on and on -- it's not a weakness of the theory. I don't regard it as a weakness of my own work that it hasn't explained everything in elementary particle physics."*

**Robert W. Wilson (1936 - )** ⇨ AGNOSTIC   PhD Physics, California Institute of Technology; 1978 Nobel Prize in Physics (co-discovery of CMB); 1977 Henry Draper Medal of the National Academy of Sciences; Adjunct Professor of Physics, State Univ. of New York.
♦ An interview with Fred Heeren, *Show Me God: What the Message from Space Is Telling Us About God,* Day Star Publications, 2000, p. 157: *"Certainly there was something that set it all off. Certainly, if you are religious, I can't think of a better theory of the origin of the universe to match with Genesis."*

**George Ellis (1939 - )** ⇨ DEIST   PhD. in applied Mathematics and Theoretical Physics, Cambridge Univ.; Prof. of Complex Systems in Dept. of Applied Mathematics, Univ. of Cape Town, South Africa; co-authored *The Large Scale Structure of Space-Time* with Stephen Hawking; one of the world's leading theorists in cosmology; 1989-1992, past President of International Society on General Relativity and Gravitation; past President of International Society for Science and Religion.
♦ "*Before the Beginning – Cosmology Explained,* London and New York, Boyars/ Bowerdean, 1993, 1994, p. 97: *"To make sense of this view (design as opposed to accident), one must accept the idea of transcendence: that the Designer exists in a totally different order of reality or being, not restrained within the bounds of the Universe itself."*
♦ Ellis, G.F.R. 1993. The Anthropic Principle: Laws and Environments. *The Anthropic Principle,* F. Bertola and U.Curi, ed. New York, Cambridge University Press: *"Amazing fine tuning occurs in the laws that make this [complexity] possible. Realization of the complexity of what is accomplished makes it very difficult not to use the word 'miraculous' without taking a stand as to the ontological status of the word."*

**Paul Davies (1942 - )** ⇨ DEIST   PhD Theoretical Physics, Univ. College of London; Prof. of Physics. at Arizona State Univ.; Chair of Post-Detection Science of the International Academy of Astronautics; studied under Fred Hoyle; quoted from "*Superforce: The Search for a Grand Unified Theory of Nature*" (New York: Simon & Schuster, 1984), p. 243: *"The laws [of physics] ... seem to be the product of exceedingly ingenious design... The universe must have a purpose".*
♦ "*The Cosmic Blueprint: New Discoveries in Nature's Creative Ability To Order the Universe.* New York: Simon and Schuster, p.203: *"There is for me powerful evidence that there is something going on behind it all....It seems as though somebody has fine-tuned nature's numbers to make the Universe....The impression of design is overwhelming".*
♦ Interview, "The Creative Cosmos", 1995: *"The mechanism of the coming-into-being of the universe, as discussed in modern science, is actually much more profound than the biblical version because it does not merely involve order emerging out of chaos. It's not just a matter of imposing some sort of organization or structure upon a previous incoherent state, but literally the coming-into-being of all physical things from nothing."*

**Stephen Hawking (1942 - )** ⇨ ATHEIST   PhD Cosmology & Theoretical Physics, Cambridge Univ. 1966; Cambridge Prof. of Mathematics (1979-2009); recipient of the Presidential Medal of Freedom (highest civilian award in the United States (2009); Research Director at Cambridge Univ. Centre for Theoretical Cosmology; *"It would be very difficult to explain why the universe should have begun in just this way, except as an act of a God who intended to create beings like us."*
♦ "*You cannot understand the glories of the universe without believing there is some Supreme Power behind it."*
♦ "*A Brief History of Time*", p. 175: *"Then we shall…be able to take part in the discussion of the question of why it is that we and the universe exist. If we find the answer to that, it would be the ultimate triumph of human reason - then we would know the mind of God."*
♦ "*A Brief History of Time*": *"It would be very difficult to explain why the universe should have begun in just this way, except as an act of a God who intended to create beings like us."*
♦ *A Brief History of Time—From the Big Bang to Black Holes,* New York: Bantam Books, 1988, p. 125: *"The laws of science, as we know them at present, contain many fundamental numbers, like the size of the electric charge of the electron and the ratio of the masses of the proton and the electron …. The remarkable fact is that the values of these numbers seem to have been finely adjusted to make possible the development of life."*
♦ "*The whole history of science has been the gradual realization that events do not happen in an arbitrary manner, but that they reflect a certain underlying order, which may or may not be divinely inspired."*
♦ "*What I have done is to show that it is possible for the way the universe began to be determined by the laws of science. In that case, it would not be necessary to appeal to God to decide how the universe began. This doesn't prove that there is no God, only that God is not necessary."*

♦ "A Brief History of Time: From the Big Bang to Black Holes" (1998): *Even if there is only one possible unified theory, it is just a set of rules and equations. What is it that breathes fire into the equations and makes a universe for them to describe? The usual approach of science of constructing a mathematical model cannot answer the questions of why there should be a universe for the model to describe. Why does the universe go to all the bother of existing?"*

♦ Website for PBS program, "Stephen Hawking's Universe" (1997): *"All of my life, I have been fascinated by the big questions that face us, and have tried to find scientific answers to them. If, like me, you have looked at the stars, and tried to make sense of what you see, you too have started to wonder what makes the universe exist."*

♦ "A Brief History of Time: From the Big Bang to Black Holes" (1998): *"Hubble's observations suggested that there was a time, called the big bang, when the universe was infinitesimally small and infinitely dense. Under such conditions all the laws of science, and therefore all ability to predict the future, would break down. If there were events earlier than this time, then they could not affect what happens at the present time. Their existence can be ignored because it would have no observational consequences. One may say that time had a beginning at the big bang, in the sense that earlier times simply would not be defined. It should be emphasized that this beginning in time is very different from those that had been considered previously. In an unchanging universe a beginning in time is something that has to be imposed by some being outside the universe; there is no physical necessity for a beginning. One can imagine that God created the universe at literally any time in the past. On the other hand, if the universe is expanding, there may be physical reasons why there had to be a beginning. One could still imagine that God created the universe at the instant of the big bang, or even afterwards in just such a way as to make it look as though there had been a big bang, but it would be meaningless to suppose that it was created before the big bang. An expanding universe does not preclude a creator, but it does place limits on when he might have carried out his job!"*

**Henry "Fritz" Schaefer (1944 - )** ⇨ CHRISTIAN   PhD Chemical Physics, Stanford Univ.; Prof. of Chemistry, UC Berkeley (1969-1987); Graham Perdue Professor of Chemistry and Director of the Center for Computational Quantum Chemistry, Univ. of Georgia; member of International Academy of Quantum Molecular Science and former chairman of WATOC (World Assoc. of Theoretical and Computational Chemists); Fellow of the Discovery Institute's Center for Science and Culture, and a signer of the Discovery Institute's anti-evolution letter, A Scientific Dissent From Darwinism.

♦ Sheler, J. L. and J.M. Schrof, *"The Creation"*, U.S. News & World Report, Dec. 23, 1991): *"The significance and joy in my science comes in those occasional moments of discovering something new and saying to myself, 'So that's how God did it.' My goal is to understand a little corner of God's plan."*

♦ "Scientists and their Gods (Science and Christianity, Conflict or Coherence?"), 1999: *Why do so many people still think that there is an ongoing battle between science and Christianity? I don't deny that there is an ongoing discussion. But I think the facts are that, what you think about God doesn't depend on whether you have a Ph.D. in the sciences. Why would some people like to think that this supposed battle rages on? At least in part, I honestly feel it is a misrepresentation."*

♦ "Scientists and their Gods (Science and Christianity, Conflict or Coherence?"), 1999: *"Why Are There So Few Atheists Among Physicists? Many scientists are considering the facts before them. They say things like: 'The present arrangement of matter indicates a very special choice of initial conditions.' (Paul Davies). 'In fact, if one considers the possible constants and laws that could have emerged, the odds against a universe that produced life like ours are immense.' (Stephen Hawking), 'A common sense interpretation of the facts suggests that a superintellect has monkeyed with physics, as well as with chemistry and biology, and that there are no blind forces worth speaking about in nature.' (Fred Hoyle). As the Apostle Paul said in his epistle to the Romans: Since the creation of the world, God's invisible qualities—His eternal power and divine nature—have been clearly seen, being understood from what has been made."*

**George Smoot (1945 - )** ⇨ AGNOSTIC   PhD Particle Physics; 2006 Nobel Prize in Physics; Prof. of Physics at Univ. California Berkeley & Paris Diderot Univ.; Senior Scientist at Lawrence Berkeley National Laboratory – following quotes from his book *"Wrinkles in Time"*, New York: William Morrow and Company, 1993: *"There is no doubt that a parallel exists between the big bang as an event and the Christian notion of creation from nothing…. In order to make a universe as big and wonderful as it is, lasting as long as it is—we're talking fifteen billion years and we're talking huge distances here—in order for it to be that big, you have to make it perfectly. Otherwise, imperfections would mount up and the universe would either collapse on itself or fly apart, and so it's actually quite a precise job. And I don't know if you've had discussions with people about how critical it is that the density of the universe come out so close to the density that decides whether it's going to keep expanding forever or collapse back, but we know it's within one percent."*

♦ *"The question of 'the beginning' is as inescapable for cosmologists as it is for theologians."*

♦ *"Until the late 1910's humans were as ignorant of cosmic origins as they had ever been. Those who didn't take Genesis literally had no reason to believe there had been a beginning."*

◆ Interviewed by Fred Heeren, *Show Me God: What the Message from Space Is Telling Us About God*, Day Star Publications, 2000: *"The big bang, the most cataclysmic event we can imagine, on closer inspection appears finely orchestrated."*

◆ *"George Smoot commenting on the discovery by the COBE Science Working Group of the expected "ripples" in the microwave background radiation. He called these fluctuations "the fingerprints from the Maker." Smoot draws attention not only to the fact that his team had provided more evidence for the creation event, but for a "finely orchestrated" creation event. Stephen Hawking was so impressed with this finding that he called it "the most important discovery of the century, if not of all time."*

**Frank Tipler (1947 - )** ⇨ CHRISTIAN   PhD Physics, Univ. of Maryland; Prof. of Mathematics and Physics, Tulane Univ., quoted in his book "*The Physics Of Immortality*", New York, Doubleday, 1994 Preface: *"When I began my career as a cosmologist some twenty years ago, I was a convinced atheist. I never in my wildest dreams imagined that one day I would be writing a book purporting to show that the central claims of Judeo-Christian theology are in fact true, that these claims are straightforward deductions of the laws of physics as we now understand them. I have been forced into these conclusions by the inexorable logic of my own special branch of physics."*

◆ "*The Physics Of Immortality*", New York, Doubleday, 2007: *"From the perspective of the latest physical theories, Christianity is not a mere religion, but an experimentally testable science."*

**William Philips (1948 - )** ⇨ CHRISTIAN   PhD Physics, MIT, 1976; 1997 Nobel Prize in Physics (laser cooling); Prof. of Physics at Univ. of Maryland; he is one of three well-known scientists engaged in the religion and science dialogue (along with chemist Charles Coulson and 1981 Nobel laureate Arthur Schawlow); *"Being an ordinary scientist and an ordinary Christian seems perfectly natural to me. It is also perfectly natural for the many scientists I know who are also people of deep religious faith."*

◆ Phillips, William D., "Letter to the compiler T. Dimitrov", May 19, 2002: *"I believe in God. In fact, I believe in a personal God who acts in and interacts with the creation. I believe the observations about the orderliness of the physical universe, and the apparently exceptional fine-tuning of the conditions of the universe for the development of life suggest that an intelligent Creator is responsible. I believe in God because of a personal faith, a faith consistent with what I know about science."*

◆ Lecture "Ordinary Faith, Ordinary Science", delivered at the conference "Science and the Spiritual Quest", April 2002: *"Many scientists are also people with quite conventional religious faith. I, a physicist, am one example. I believe in God as both creator and friend. That is, I believe that God is personal and interacts with us."*

◆ Phillips, William D., "Letter to the compiler T. Dimitrov", May 19, 2002: *"There are probably more Nobel Laureates who are people of faith than is generally believed. Most people in most professions don't make a special point to make their religious views known, since these are very personal."*

| Weighing the Evidence on Origins  =  A combination of *SCIENCE* and *FAITH* | |
| --- | --- |
| **Creation cannot be proven 100%** | **Evolution cannot be proven 100%** |
| 1. Creation is not taking place now (so far as we can observe): it was accomplished sometime in the past, so it is inaccessible to the scientific method. | 1. If evolution happens today, it operates too slowly to measure (to change from one kind of organism to a higher kind is presumed to take millions of years – no team of scientists can measure such an experiment). |
| 2. It is impossible to devise a scientific experiment to describe the creation process (or even tell if such a process can take place). The Creator doesn't create at the whim of a scientist. | 2. Small variations in organisms we observe today can't be proven to lead to different, higher kinds of life. These small variations are expected in the creation model just as much as in the evolution model. |
| Job 38:3-5 *"...prepare yourself like a man; I will question you, and you shall answer Me. Where were you when I laid the foundations of the earth? Tell Me, if you have understanding. Who determined its measurements? Surely you know!"* | 3. If scientists create life from non-life, or higher forms from lower, in the lab, this wouldn't *prove* that such changes could have taken place in the past by natural processes (they *designed in* these events in the lab). |
| Henry Morris[5]:  *"It must be emphasized that it is impossible to prove scientifically any particular concept of origins to be true. This is obvious from the fact that the essence of the scientific method is experimental observation and repeatability. A scientific investigator, be he ever so resourceful and brilliant, can neither observe nor repeat origins. This means that, though it is important to have a philosophy of origins, it can only be achieved by FAITH, not by sight. One must believe with respect to ultimate origins. However, for optimally beneficial application of that belief, his faith should be a REASONED faith."* | |

# Science & Religion: A Worldview Battle

### Arthur Compton (1892-1962)

American Physicist;
1927 Nobel Prize;
Founder: Compton Effect

**"Science has created a world in which Christianity is a necessity."**

### BILL PHILLIPS (1948 - )

PhD Physics, MIT; 1997 Nobel Prize in Physics (laser cooling); Prof. of Physics at Univ. of Maryland

Christian

*"So many of my colleagues are Christians that I can't walk across my church's fellowship hall without tripping over a dozen physicists."*

### STEVEN WEINBERG (1933-2021)

PhD Physics Princeton Univ.; 1979 Nobel Prize in Physics (electroweak unification theory); Prof. Physics at Univ. of Texas, Austin

Atheist

*"As you learn more and more about the universe, you can understand more and more without any reference to the supernatural, so you lose interest in that possibility."*

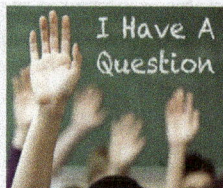

I Have A Question

How do 2 distinguished scientists, with such similar professional backgrounds, see things so differently?

It's not their science... it's their *WORLDVIEW*.

Courtesy of Google Images   Fair Use Law 17 U.S. Code § 107

# *There is a God – How the World's Most Notorious Atheist Changed His Mind*

**"My discovery of the Divine has been a pilgrimage of reason and not faith."**

Prof. Antony Flew
Page 93

THERE IS A NO GOD

How the world's most notorious atheist changed his mind

**ANTONY FLEW**
WITH ROY ABRAHAM VARGHESE

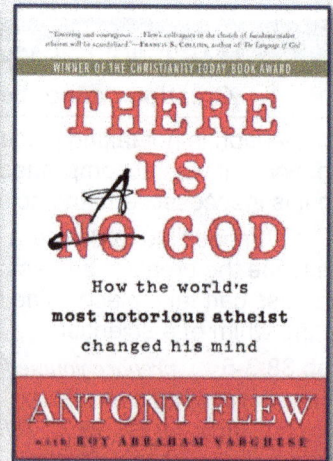

*"It speaks very well of Professor Flew's honesty. After all these years of opposing the idea of a Creator, he reverses his position based on the evidence."* Alvin Plantinga

World's most famous atheist accepts existence of God because of Science' (5:05)

Courtesy of Google Images   Fair Use Law 17 U.S. Code § 107

# "There is a God": Prof. Flew's Turning Points

| Chapter 5: Who Wrote the Laws of Nature? | Chapter 6: Did the Universe know We were coming? | Chapter 7: How did Life go live? | Chapter 8: How did something come from nothing? |
|---|---|---|---|
| "There must be an unchanging rational ground in which the logical, orderly nature of the universe is rooted." (Professor Paul Davies). "A personal God with the traditional properties best explains the operation of the laws of nature." (Flew on Professor Richard Swinburne). | "The anthropic principle is sometimes countered with 'multiverse' approaches, but we are still left with the question of how those 'deeper' laws originated. No matter how far you push back the properties of the universe as somehow 'emergent', their very emergence has to follow certain prior laws." (Professor Paul Davies). | "George Wald argued 'we choose to believe the impossible: that life arose by chance.' But later he concludes 'mind, rather than emerging as a late outgrowth in the evolution of life, has existed always.'" | "There is quite a chance that, if there is a God, He will make something of the finitude and complexity of a universe. It is very unlikely that a universe would exist uncaused. Hence the argument from the existence of the universe to the existence of God." (Professor Richard Swinburne). |

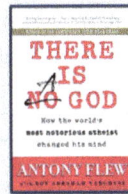

THERE IS ~~NO~~ GOD
How the world's most notorious atheist changed his mind
ANTONY FLEW

## *Science* and *Reason*: The Evidence for Christianity

In today's debates over the origin of the universe, the origin of life, the reliability of the Bible, and the Person of Jesus Christ, we may not appreciate the fundamental problem people have in trying to apply the discipline of science to uncover solid evidences for *events that occurred in the past and can't be repeated today.*

We would all agree that in its most basic definition, science is the disciplined approach to finding the *CAUSE* for the effects we *observe* in the world. But is there a difference in the *type* of science we use when trying to find the cause for non-repeatable events of the past that we cannot observe today (like creation, or the Resurrection)?

In his book 'When Skeptics Ask'[12], Dr. Norman Geisler explains there are really two kinds of 'science' we are dealing with when investigating any event, depending on whether the event we wish to study is observable in the present or occurred in the past and thus cannot be repeated (so it could be observed):

1) The first type of science he calls 'Operation Science' = it deals with how observable events work.

2) The second type he calls 'Origins Science" = it deals with how nonobservable events happened in the past.

**Operation Science** = It looks at how things presently WORK, and follows the classical scientific method (see below). It seeks answers that are TESTABLE by repeating the experiment over and over, and falsifiable if the cause does not always yield the same effect.

Its conclusions should allow one to project what will happen in future experiments. Operation science likes things to be very regular and predictable. No changes; no surprises. So the idea of a supernatural being coming around to stir things up occasionally is strongly resisted.

**The classical Scientific Method = observation, demonstration, confirmation**

① defining a problem → **natural phenomenon observed**

② gathering & observing the relevant data → **observations compiled, data studied**

③ formulating a hypothesis → ***Scientific Hypothesis*[1] presented**

④ Interpreting one's results → **do the observations *confirm* or *conflict* with the hypothesis?**

CONFIRM 👍

CONFLICT 👎

⑤ reaching a logical conclusion → ***Theory*[2] is presented**

**observations confirm the theory**

⑥ peer review[3] to reach consensus → **Theory is accepted as Fact[4]**

**1) Hypothesis** = a well-supported speculation for the probable cause of an event, based on observed data.

**2) Theory** = an explanation based on observation, experimentation and testing, that helps explain and predict natural phenomenon. A theory must be verifiable, and is grounded upon observed facts. If *evidence* is found that contradicts the stated theory, the theory must be modified or discarded.

**3) Peer Review** = *public scrutiny* of theories, to test them objectively and so they don't become subjective myths. Peer Reviews work to eliminate individual bias and subjectivity, because others must also be able to determine whether a proposed explanation is consistent with the available *evidence*.

**4) Fact (law)** = a statement of something that is always observed to be true in certain conditions. Scientific theories don't become laws or facts - they explain them (example: the law of gravity states all airborne objects left to themselves fall to the ground - the theory of gravity explains why).

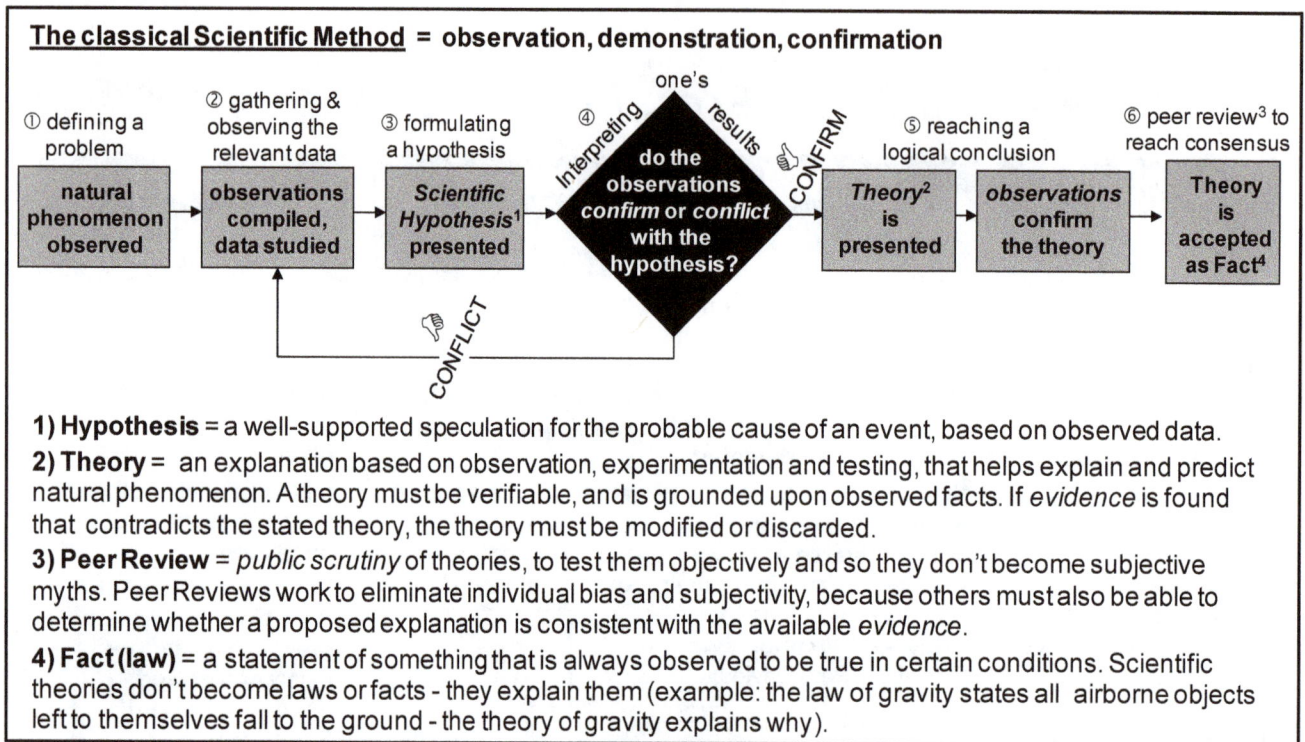

**Origin Science** = It looks at how things BEGAN, not how they work. It studies things that happened ONCE and don't happen again. Rather than being an empirical science like physics or biology, it is more like a *FORENSIC SCIENCE*. Origin Science works on different principles than Operation Science. Since the past events that it studies cannot be repeated today, … it does not claim to give definitive answers but only plausible ones. We did not observe the events of origins, and we cannot repeat them. So the remaining EVIDENCE must be STUDIED and interpretations of it MEASURED by what seems MOST LIKELY (*i.e., PROBABILITY SCIENCE – my italics added, and explained on next page*) to explain the evidence.

**What is Forensic Science?** *'Forensic'* is a synonym for "legal" or "related to courts". *Forensics* is related to the notion of AUTHENTICATION, where the goal is to determine, through accepted scholarly or scientific methods of investigation, if the FACTS regarding an event, an artifact, or some other physical item (such as a corpse) can be verified beyond a reasonable doubt as being the case.

The word *forensic* comes from the Latin adjective *forensis*, meaning *'of or before the forum.'* In Roman times, a criminal charge meant presenting the case before public individuals in the forum. Both the person accused of the crime and the accuser would give speeches based on their side of the story. The individual with the best argument and delivery determines the outcome of the case. This origin is the source of the two modern usages of the word *forensic* – as a form of legal evidence and as a category of public presentation.

**Columbia College, MO: Requirements for a Bachelor of Science in FORENSIC SCIENCE**

The major in *Forensic Science* draws from the biological sciences, physics and chemistry as well as from the fields of criminal justice and the law. The degree is generated from a cross-disciplinary perspective, blending expertise from both the criminal justice and science program areas. The program focus is on professions in the criminal justice and science areas, which require specific coursework as shown below:

| Criminalist I - Physical Evidence | Coursework: ≥ 2 natural science classes, algebra, and trigonometry (coursework in calculus can be substituted for the algebra and trigonometry). |
|---|---|
| Criminalist I - DNA | Coursework: 20 semester hours in genetics, biochemistry, molecular biology to provide a basic understanding of forensic DNA analysis |
| Criminalist I – Trace Evidence | Coursework: ≥ 20 hours of chemistry (organic and inorganic) |
| Criminalist I - Toxicology | Coursework: 20 hours of chemistry (2 semesters of general chemistry, 2 semesters of organic chemistry, and 1 semester of quantitative analysis) |
| Criminalist I - Latent Prints | Coursework should include ≥ 2 natural science classes |

> **The Goal** = Become skilled in uncovering *evidence* for an event that occurred in the past, to make conclusions that can be upheld in a court of law with a reasonably high degree (≥ 95%) of certainty

**What is Probability Science?** It is the discipline used to calculate the CHANCE of a future event occurring, to a certain degree of accuracy. It first came into use when situations presented themselves that had potential for great GAINS, but also had RISKS that the desired outcomes might not happen, so people wanted a way to use facts (data) to PREDICT the gains and the chance of the risks happening. The "Fathers of Probability Science" were Pascal (1623-1662), Pier de Fermat (1601-1665).It was the initial work of Pascal, Fermat, Graunt, Bernoulli, DeMoivre, and Laplace that set probability theory on its way to being the valuable inferential science it is today.

• Accomplishment #1 (1600's) = one could predict to a certain degree of accuracy events which were yet to come.

• Accomplishment #2 (1800's) = probability and statistics could converge to form a well defined, firmly grounded science, with limitless applications and possibilities.

Question: "When I roll dice, what's the chance of getting a pair of 6's?"

Answer = 36 ➜ since there are 6 sides to each dice, and each possible combination of numbers has an equal likelihood of occurring when the dice are randomly rolled, multiply the number of possible "events" to get the chance of the desired event.

So…. what are the odds of rolling a pair of 6's when you pick up a pair of dice?

  - 1 chance in 36 rolls = 1: 36, or 1 divided by 36 (1/ 36) = 2.8% chance of rolling 6's

  - or…. there's a 97.2% chance of not rolling 6's (high risk of failure)

**Dice #1**: if it rolls a "6"… it could just as likely roll 1-5

**Dice #2**: if it rolls a "1"… it could just as likely roll 2-6

• Back to the Dice Example: You've got a 2.8% chance of rolling a pair of 6's. You're offered $100,000 if, on your one and only chance, you roll a pair of 6's. But you have to wager $10 to have the chance of playing for the $100,000…. would you take the risk of losing $10 for the chance to gain $100,000? What if you had to wager $10,000 (not $10) to gain $100,000 – would you? WHY or WHY NOT?

• Examples: Odds of an Event:    1: 6,357 to die in auto accident    1: 600,000 to be struck by lightning    1: 19,000 to contract AIDS    1: 11,000,000 to be in a plane crash

| Summarizing: 'Operation' Science vs. 'Origin' Science | |
| --- | --- |
| **Operation Science** | **Origin Science** |
| Studies how present events work | Studies how past events happened |
| Studies testable, repeatable, observable events | Studies untestable, unrepeatable, unobservable events |
| Can recreate and retest events, so any conclusion can be *proven* false | Cannot recreate events, so any conclusion cannot be *proven* false (only *inferences* can be made) |
| Data collected during event (direct evidence) | Data collected after event (circumstantial evidence) |

### The *TYPES* of Evidence available when evaluating a Hypothesis

1) **Direct evidence** = Supports the truth of a hypothesis *directly* (if repeatable, it's Operational Science; if not, it's Origin Science); an example would be if credible eyewitnesses *observed* the event from start to finish.

2) **Circumstantial Evidence** = Evidence after an unobserved, nonrepeatable, nontestable event that can *infer* towards a hypothesis, but does not directly support it (example: fingerprints at a crime scene). A hypothesis based on circumstantial evidence becomes more valid when any alternative explanations can be ruled out.

3) **Corroborating Evidence** = Circumstantial evidence becomes stronger when there are *multiple pieces* that all point to the same hypothesis (together, the pieces give weight to one hypothesis over another).

4) **Forensic Evidence** = Type of circumstantial evidence that is supplied by an *expert witness*.

  • A forensic scientist who testifies that ballistics *proves* the defendant's gun was used to shoot the victim gives circumstantial evidence from which the defendant's guilt may be *inferred*, but this inference of guilt could be incorrect if it was someone else who actually pulled the trigger.

  • But if there was additional circumstantial evidence of the defendant's fingerprint on the trigger, it would strengthen the conclusion by the corroborating evidence.

**Whenever no one is there to *see* the event, we have no direct evidence to support any hypothesis, so *circumstantial evidence* is the most important evidence available.**

# Using Science to Search for Truth

## 'Observable Science'

1. Studies how present events happen
2. Studies testable, repeatable, observable events
3. Data collected *during* the event, so *direct* evidence
4. Can recreate and retest events, so conclusions **CAN** be proven false

## 'Historical Science'

1. Studies how past events happened
2. Studies untestable, non-repeatable, unobservable events
3. Data collected *after* the event, so *circumstantial* evidence
4. Can't recreate events, so conclusions **CAN'T** be proven false (only inferences made)

CSI (Crime Scene Investigation)
Legal System (Jury Duty)
Business (Analytics)
Sports (Moneyball)
Stock Market

Origin of Universe & Life
Design of Universe & Life
Reliability of the Bible
The Person of Jesus Christ

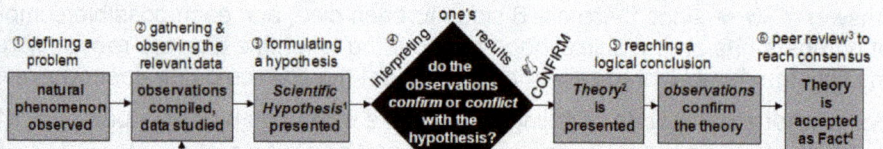

① defining a problem — natural phenomenon observed
② gathering & observing the relevant data — observations compiled, data studied
③ formulating a hypothesis — Scientific Hypothesis[1] presented
④ Interpreting one's results — do the observations *confirm* or *conflict* with the hypothesis?
CONFIRM
CONFLICT
⑤ reaching a logical conclusion — Theory[2] is presented — observations confirm the theory
⑥ peer review[3] to reach consensus — Theory is accepted as Fact[4]

**When, and how, is Historical Science used today?**

Courtesy of Google Images    Fair Use Law 17 U.S. Code § 107

# Applying 'Historical Science' to past, unobserved events

**The Tribune, Oct. 23, 2012:** "The shark that fatally attacked a man has been identified as a 15 to 16-foot great white shark, according to the Santa Barbara County Sheriff's Office."

**How could they know, if no one observed the event?**

1) <u>Forensics</u> = Expert Testimony (Shark Research Committee):
   a) victim's body (injuries infer a shark, vs. other possibilities?)
   b) teeth pattern and size on the surf board (infer a Great White?)

2) <u>Circumstantial</u> = Historical Data and Probability Science
   a) What is the chance of a shark attack off the coast of northern CA?
   b) What is the chance of a Great White Shark in these waters?

3) <u>Corroborating</u> = Taking all the circumstantial evidence together, is it convincing enough to reach a conclusion?
   a) Injuries on the victim
   b) Teeth pattern, size left behind by the 'Cause'
   c) History of the suspected 'Cause' in the vicinity

**Do you think local authorities REASONABLY knew what happened (even though no one, including the victim, saw the shark)?**

'J. Warner Wallace, Is Christianity Rational?' (3:40)          Courtesy of Google Images    Fair Use Law 17 U.S. Code § 107

# Applying Origin Science to the *Bible* and the *Person of Jesus Christ*

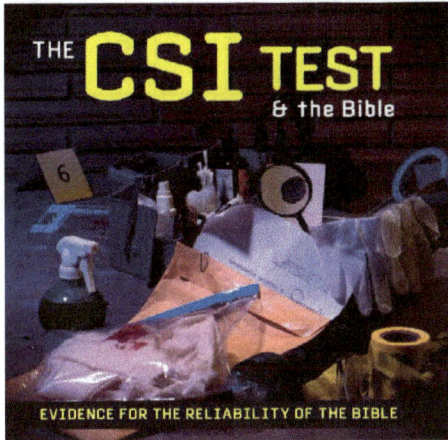

I start with the questions I am trying to solve.... How can I **trust** the content and events recorded in the Bible?

➔ Can I have a high level of certainty that the Bible is God's revelation to me about Himself, and His instructions for how to live my life?

➔ How do I gather *evidence* so I can test the certainty of my faith?

➔ Using Dr. Geisler's method of 'Origin Science', can I collect facts to measure how reliable the Bible is as a truth source (especially when checked against all the other ancient writings that people have trusted)?

In his book *Evidence that Demands a Verdict*[11], Josh McDowell uses three tests taken from the book *Introduction to Research in English Literary History* by military historian **Dr. Chauncey Sanders** (a non-Christian). These three tests are used in this series as the method of Forensic Science to validate historicity and reliability of the Bible.

## TEST #1: Bibliographical Test

This test exams the textual transmission of the manuscripts through time. Since I don't have the hand-written originals, how reliable are the copies I do have in terms of their *number* and the *time interval* between the original writing and the earliest existing copy?

I'll apply this test not only to the most famous secular literature taught today in our schools and universities, but also to both the New Testament and Old Testament.

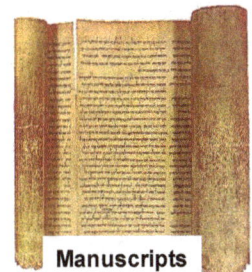

**Manuscripts**

## TEST #2: Internal Evidence Test

This test asks the question "Does the internal evidence of the document itself contain any inaccuracies or contradictions that would bring to question its reliability and trustworthiness?

It is based on Aristotle's dictum: *"The benefit of the doubt is given to the document itself; don't assume fraud or error unless I can prove contradictions by the author within the text or known factual inaccuracies."* I'll again apply this test to both the New and Old Testaments, examining the *Eyewitness Accounts* of Jesus Christ and Old Testament *Fulfilled Prophecies*.

**Prophecy**

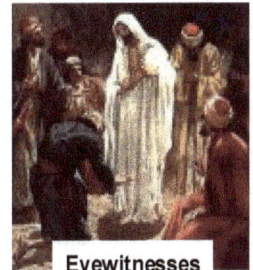

**Eyewitnesses**

## TEST #3: External Evidence Test

This test evaluates sources outside the document: "do other historical documents confirm or deny the internal testimony provided by the documents themselves?

What sources exist apart from the literature under examination that confirm its accuracy, reliability and authenticity?" I'll once again apply this test to both the New Testament and Old Testaments, using the evidence of *Non-biblical sources* (writings outside the Bible) and the findings of *Archaeology*.

**Historians**

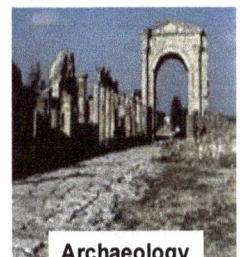

**Archaeology**

| # | **Is the Bible Reliable? (Book 3)**<br>***Corroborating Evidence: 53 Measurable Data Points***<br>(applying Dr. Chauncey Saunders Tests) | Manuscript Test | Internal Test | External Test |
|---|---|---|---|---|
| 1 | Bible's continuity | ✓ | | |
| 2 | Bible's circulation and transmission | ✓ | | |
| 3 | Bible's survival | ✓ | | |
| 4 | Bible's influence | ✓ | | |
| 5 | Bibliographic Test: New Testament manuscripts | ✓ | | |
| 6 | Bibliographic Test: Old Testament manuscripts | ✓ | | |
| 7 | Bibliographic Test: Dead Sea Scrolls | ✓ | | |
| 8 | Eyewitness Testimony: The Incarnation of Jesus Christ | | ✓ | |
| 9 | Eyewitness Testimony: The Death, Burial and Resurrection of Jesus Christ | | ✓ | |
| 10 | Prophecy: Destruction of Tyre | | ✓ | |
| 11 | Prophecy: Destruction of Nineveh | | ✓ | |
| 12 | Prophecy: Destruction of Memphis and Thebes | | ✓ | |
| 13 | Prophecy: Destruction of Babylon | | ✓ | |
| 14 | Prophecy: Destruction of Moab and Ammon | | ✓ | |
| 15 | Prophecy: Destruction of Petra and Edom | | ✓ | |
| 16 | Prophecy: Destruction of Samaria | | ✓ | |
| 17 | Prophecy: Gaza-Ashkelon | | ✓ | |
| 18 | Prophecy: Palestine | | ✓ | |
| 19 | Archaeology: The walls of Jericho | | | ✓ |
| 20 | Archaeology: The Ebla Tablets and Kings of Mesopotamia | | | ✓ |
| 21 | Archaeology: The Roman Census | | | ✓ |
| 22 | Archaeology: The Hittite Empire | | | ✓ |
| 23 | Archaeology: The Assyrian Empire and The Library of King Assurbanipal | | | ✓ |
| 24 | Archaeology: The Black Obelisk of King Shalmaneser III | | | ✓ |
| 25 | Archaeology: King Shalmaneser III attacking Hamath | | | ✓ |
| 26 | Archaeology: King Tiglath-pileser conquering cities | | | ✓ |
| 27 | Archaeology: King Sargon II capturing and deporting Israel | | | ✓ |
| 28 | Archaeology: King Sennacherib exiling Lachish of Judah | | | ✓ |
| 29 | Archaeology: Nabonidus Stele: King Sennacherib murdered by his sons | | | ✓ |
| 30 | Archaeology: Siloam Inscription: King Sennacherib attacks King Hezekiah | | | ✓ |
| 31 | Archaeology: King Esarhaddon restoring Babylon | | | ✓ |
| 32 | Archaeology: King Assurbanipal royal bodyguards | | | ✓ |
| 33 | Archaeology: King Assurbanipal conquering Hamanu in Elam | | | ✓ |
| 34 | Archaeology: Mesha Stele: King of Moab war on Omri (King of Israel) | | | ✓ |
| 35 | Archaeology: Canaanite gods Molech, Chemosh | | | ✓ |
| 36 | Archaeology: Canaanite god Ba'al | | | ✓ |
| 37 | Archaeology: Philistine god Dagon (sanctuary of Tell Qasileh) | | | ✓ |
| 38 | Archaeology: Philistine warrior carvings (Thebes) | | | ✓ |

| # | **Is the Bible Reliable?   (Book 3)**<br>*Corroborating Evidence:  53 Measurable  Data Points*<br>(applying Dr. Chauncey Saunders Tests) | Manuscript Test | Internal Test | External Test |
|----|----|----|----|----|
| 39 | Archaeology: Ruins of Petra | | | ✓ |
| 40 | Archaeology: Ruins of Tyre | | | ✓ |
| 41 | Archaeology: Ruins of Nineveh | | | ✓ |
| 42 | Archaeology: Ruins of Babylon | | | ✓ |
| 43 | Archaeology: Ruins of Samaria | | | ✓ |
| 44 | Archaeology: Amaran Letters (King Yidya of Ashkelon) | | | ✓ |
| 45 | Archaeology: Merneptah Stele (King Merneptah conquers Israel, others) | | | ✓ |
| 46 | Archaeology: The Practice of Crucifixion | | | ✓ |
| 47 | Early Church manuscripts: Irenaeus "Against Heresies III" | | | ✓ |
| 48 | Secular Historians: Eusebius "Ecclesiastical History III" | | | ✓ |
| 49 | Secular Historians: Plinius Secundus "Writings to Emperor Trajan" | | | ✓ |
| 50 | Secular Historians: Cornelius Tacitus "Nero blames Christians for 64AD Fire" | | | ✓ |
| 51 | Secular Historians: Flavius Josephus "Antiquities XVIII, 63" | | | ✓ |
| 52 | Secular Historians: Flavius Josephus "Antiquities XX, 197" | | | ✓ |
| 53 | Secular Historians: Flavius Josephus "Antiquities XVIII, 106" | | | ✓ |

**After weighing these 53 pieces of circumstantial evidence as a whole…**
**Does the *evidence* favor the Bible as historically accurate and reliably transmitted?**

**Archaeology:**
"Archaeological work has unquestionably strengthened confidence in the reliability of the Scriptural record." Millar Burrows (Yale Univ.)

**Prophecy:** Foretold events in the Bible have been verified historically.

**Nonbiblical Authors:** 14 writers outside the Bible verify the contents of the Bible.

**Eyewitnesses:** People don't willingly die horrible deaths for what they know is a lie.

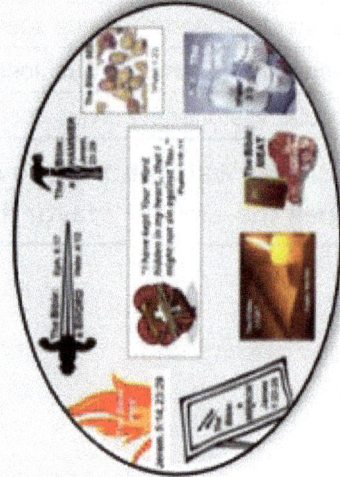

There are 9 Facts about the Bible to which majority of scholars agree...

Together these 9 Facts make a strong case *for the truth of the Bible*

**Life-changing Impact:** The Bible teaches, convicts, inspires.

**History - Assyrian Empire:** Discovery of city of Nineveh and King Ashurbanipal's 10,000-tablets validate biblical records.

**Dead Sea Scrolls:** Old Testament books, with prophecies pointing to Jesus Christ, date to 125BC.

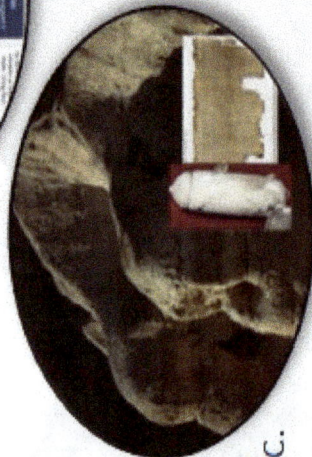

**Manuscripts & Text Criticism:** > 24,000 New Testament copies: no Christian doctrine rests on a disputed reading.

**Uniqueness:** Written by 40 authors on 3 continents over 1,500 years, with complete harmony.

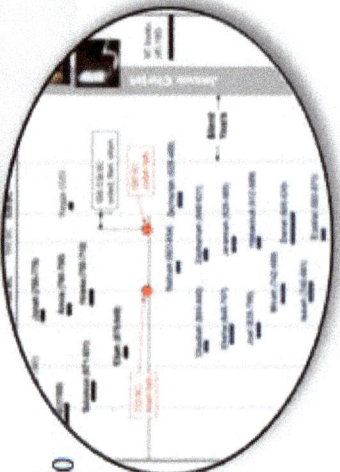

| # | Require-ment | Is Jesus Christ the Messiah?   (Book 3)<br>*Corroborating Evidence: 87 Measurable Data Points*<br>(confirm Old Testament Prophecies by New Testament facts) | New Testament<br>Evidence Test |
|---|---|---|---|
| 1 | | Genesis 22:18 ➜ Jesus is a Hebrew | Matt. 1:1; Luke 3:34; Gal.3:16 |
| 2 | | Genesis 21:12 ➜ Jesus descended from Isaac | Matt. 1:2; Luke 3:34 |
| 3 | Messiah's Lineage | Genesis 35:10-12 ➜ Jesus descended from Jacob | Matt. 1:2; Luke 1:33, 3:34 |
| 4 | | Genesis 49:10; Jeremiah33:14 ➜ Jesus descended from Judah | Matt. 1:2,2:6; Luke 3:33 |
| 5 | | Isaiah 11:1,10 ➜ Jesus descended from Jesse | Matt. 1:5; Luke 3:32 |
| 6 | | Isaiah 9:7; Jerem. 23:5,33:15-17 ➜ Jesus descended from David | Matt. 1:6; Luke 1:32, 3:30 |
| 7 | | Genesis 3:15 ➜ Jesus is our Victor over Satan | John 8:41-44; 1John 3:8; Rom. 16:20; Hebr. 2:14-15 |
| 8 | | Genesis 22:7-14 ➜ Jesus is our Sin Offering | John 1:29; Hebr. 7:27, 9:26 |
| 9 | | Genesis 49:10 ➜ Jesus is the 'One who brings Peace' (Shiloh) | Rom. 5:1; Eph. 1:2, 2:14-16 |
| 10 | | Exodus 3:13-15 ➜ Jesus is the 'I AM' | John 8:24, 56-59 |
| 11 | | Exodus 12:21-27 ➜ Jesus is the Passover Lamb | 1Cor. 5:7; Rom. 3:21-26 |
| 12 | | Exodus 16:32 ➜ Jesus is the Bread of Life | John 6:31-35,48-51,63 |
| 13 | | Exodus 25:17-22 ➜ Jesus is the Way to meet with God | Matt. 27:51; Heb. 10:19-20 |
| 14 | | Exodus 33:18-23 ➜ Jesus is the Rock through which we see God | John 1:14, 14:7-9; 1Cor. 10:4 |
| 15 | | Leviticus 9:15-18 ➜ Jesus is our High Priest | Hebr. 2:17, 4:14-15, 10:11-12 |
| 16 | | Leviticus 14:1-7 ➜ Jesus is our Cleansing from Sin | 1John 1:7-9; Matt. 8:2-4 |
| 17 | | Leviticus 16:8-9,15-19 ➜ Jesus is our Sin Atonement | 1John 3:5, 1Peter 1:18-19 |
| 18 | | Leviticus 16:10,20-22 ➜ Jesus is our Sin Scapegoat | Mark 15:33-34, Gal. 3:13 |
| 19 | | Leviticus 16:14-17 ➜ Jesus is our Propitiation for our sin | Romans 3:21-26 |
| 20 | | Leviticus 17:11 ➜ Jesus is the Blood of the Covenant | Luke 22:20, Hebr. 9:14-15 |
| 21 | Messiah's Titles | Numbers 20:7-13 ➜ Jesus is the Water of Life | John 4:10-14, 7:37-38 |
| 22 | | Numbers 21:7-9 ➜ Jesus is the Bronze Serpent | John 3:14-17 |
| 23 | | Numbers 24:8 ➜ Jesus is God's Son out of Egypt | Matthew 2:13-15 |
| 24 | | Deuteronomy 18:18-19 ➜ Jesus is the Prophet | John 6:14, 12:49-50, 17:8 |
| 25 | | Job 19:25-27 ➜ Jesus is the Redeemer who lives forever | Gal. 4:4-5, Col. 1:14, Rev. 5:9 |
| 26 | | Psalm 16:10 ➜ Jesus is the Resurrection | John 11:25-26, 14:19 |
| 27 | | Psalm 118:22-23, Isaiah 28:16 ➜ Jesus is the Cornerstone | Matthew 21:33-46 |
| 28 | | Proverbs 8:14-31 ➜ Jesus is the Creative 'Logos' | John 1:1-3,14, 1Corin. 1:24,30 |
| 29 | | Isaiah 5:1-7 (Psalm 80:8-16, Jeremiah 2:21) ➜ Jesus is the True Vine | Matt. 21:33-45, Luke 20:9-19, John 15:1-7 |
| 30 | | Isaiah 7:14 ➜ Jesus is 'God with us' | Matthew 1:22-23, Luke 7:16 |
| 31 | | Isaiah 9:6 ➜ Jesus is the God-Child | Luke 2:10-21,25-35,40 |
| 32 | | Isaiah 9:6 ➜ Jesus is God's Son given to man | John 3:16, Galatians 2:20 |
| 33 | | Isaiah 9:6 ➜ Jesus is El Gibbor ('Mighty God') | John 1:1, 8:58, Hebr. 1:8 |
| 34 | | Isaiah 9:6 ➜ Jesus is equal to the Father | John 10:30, 14:7-9 |
| 35 | | Isaiah 9:6 ➜ Jesus is the Prince of Peace | John 14:27, 16:33, Rom. 5:1 |
| 36 | | Isaiah 11:1-2 ➜ Jesus is anointed with the Holy Spirit | John 1:32-34, Matt. 3:13-17 |
| 37 | | Isaiah 12:2 ➜ Jesus is our Savior | Matt. 1:21, 18:11, Acts 4:12 |

| # | Require-ment | Is Jesus Christ the Messiah?   (Book 3)  *Corroborating Evidence: 87 Measurable Data Points* (confirm Old Testament Prophecies by New Testament facts) | New Testament Evidence Test |
|---|---|---|---|
| 38 | | Isaiah 28:16 ➜ Jesus is our Foundation Stone | Luke 20:17-18, Rom. 9:31-33 |
| 39 | | Isaiah 40:10-11 ➜ Jesus is the Great Shepherd | John 10:11-16 |
| 40 | | Isaiah 42:6-7, 49:6 ➜ Jesus is the Light of Salvation to Gentiles | Luke 2:28-32, Acts 13:46-48 |
| 41 | | Isaiah 52:10 ➜ Jesus is the Arm of Salvation | John 14:6, Rom. 1:16, Phil. 2:9 |
| 42 | | Isaiah 53:5-6,8 ➜ Jesus is our Sin-Bearer | John 1:29, 2Corin. 5:21 |
| 43 | Messiah's Titles | Isaiah 53:10-11 = Jesus is God's Pleasing Sacrifice for our sins | Matt. 3:17, Mark 10:45 |
| 44 | | Isaiah 59:16-17 ➜ Jesus is the Armor of Salvation | Rom. 13:14, Eph. 6:10 |
| 45 | | Jeremiah 23:5-6, 33:15-17 ➜ Jesus is our Righteousness | Rom. 1:17, 3:22, 2Corin. 5:21 |
| 46 | | Daniel 3:24-25 ➜ Jesus is the 4th Man in the Furnace Fire | John 11:43-44, Hebr. 13:5-6 |
| 47 | | Daniel 7:13 ➜ Jesus is the "Son of Man" | Mark 14:61-64 |
| 48 | | Daniel 9:24-26 ➜ Jesus is the Coming Messiah Prince | Luke 19:41-44, Hebr. 10:5-7 |
| 49 | | Zechariah 13:1 ➜ Jesus is our Fountain of Water | John 4:10, Rev. 21:6 |
| 50 | | Malachi 4:2, Psalm 19:4-6 ➜ Jesus is the Sun of Righteousness | Matt. 4:16, Luke 1:78-79 |
| 51 | Messiah's Beginnings | Isaiah 7:14 (Isaiah 53:9) ➜ Jesus is virgin-born (without sin) | John 8:45-46, 1Peter 1:19 |
| 52 | | Isaiah 40:3-5 ➜ Jesus' forerunner (prepares for His arrival) | Luke 1:76-77,  John 1:22-29 |
| 53 | | Isaiah 53:1-2 ➜ Jesus' poor, humble upbringing | Luke 1:27, 2:22-24, John 6:42 |
| 54 | | Micah 5:2 ➜ Jesus is born in Bethlehem Ephrathah | Matt. 2:6, Luke 2:4, John 7:42 |
| 55 | Messiah's Public Displays & Pronouncements | Psalm 69:9 ➜ Jesus is zealous for God | John 2:14-17 |
| 56 | | Psalm 78:2 ➜ Jesus teaches in Parables | Matt. 13:34-35, Mark 4:33-34 |
| 57 | | Isaiah 9:1-2 ➜ Jesus starts His ministry in Galilee | Matt. 4:12-17, John 2:11 |
| 58 | | Isaiah 35:4-6 ➜ Jesus performs miracles of physical healing | Mark 7:37, Luke 7:20-23 |
| 59 | | Isaiah 42:1-4 ➜ Jesus is meek but resolute | Matt. 11:28-30, 12:15-21 |
| 60 | | Isaiah 50:4-9 ➜ Jesus 'sets His face' to do His Father's will | Matt. 26:39, Luke 9:51, John 8:29 |
| 61 | | Isaiah 55:1-3 ➜ Jesus invites everyone to come to Him | Matt. 11:28-30, John 7:37-38 |
| 62 | | Isaiah 61:1-2 ➜ Jesus came to bring salvation from sin | Luke 4:17-21, John 8:32-36 |
| 63 | | Isaiah 61:2-3 ➜ Jesus came to console, comfort and  bring joy | Matt. 22:9-12, Luke 15:22-24 |
| 64 | | Zechariah 9:9 ➜ Jesus enters Jerusalem on a donkey | Matt. 21:1-5, John 12:14-15 |
| 65 | | Malachi 3:1 ➜ Jesus comes before Temple destroyed | Matt. 24:1-2, Mark 11:11 |

| # | Require-ment | Is Jesus Christ the Messiah?   (Book 3)<br>*Corroborating Evidence:  87 Measurable Data Points*<br>(confirm Old Testament Prophecies by New Testament facts) | New Testament<br>Evidence Test |
|---|---|---|---|
| 66 | Events leading up to Messiah's Death | Psalm 27:12, 35:11 ➔ Jesus is falsely accused | Matt. 26:59-62, Mark 14:55-60 |
| 67 | | Psalm 41:9 ➔ Jesus is betrayed by a close friend | John 13:11,18-30,  Luke 22:48 |
| 68 | | Psalm 35:19, 69:4, 109:3-5 ➔ Jesus is hated for no reason | John 15:18-25 |
| 69 | | Isaiah 50:6, 52:13-15 (Matt. 20:17-19, Mark 10:32-34) ➔ Jesus is publicly mocked, spit on, beaten, scourged, physically mutilated | Matt 26:67, 27:26-30, Mark 14:65, 15:15-20, John 19:1-3 |
| 70 | | Isaiah 53:3-4 ➔ Jesus is rejected by the people | Luke 4:28-29, John 19:14-16 |
| 71 | | Isaiah 53:7 (Psalm 38:13-14)  ➔ Jesus is silent during accusations | Matt 26:63, 27:12-14 |
| 72 | | Jeremiah 20:8-11, Psalm 38:12 (Nehemiah 6:10-13) ➔ Jesus is persecuted throughout His ministry | Matt 9:23-24, 12:10-14, 22-24, 13:54-58, 21:23-46,  22:34-46, Mark 6:2-3, Luke 20:20-26 |
| 73 | | Zechariah 11:12 ➔ Jesus is betrayed for 30 pieces of silver | Matt 26:14-16, Luke 22:3-6 |
| 74 | | Zechariah 11:13 ➔ 30pcs silver thrown in God's house, buys Field | Matt 27:3-10, Acts 1:18-19 |
| 75 | | Zechariah 13:7 (Matt 26:31, Mark 14:27) ➔ Disciples forsake Jesus | Matt 26:56, Mark 14:50 |
| 76 | Events during and after Messiah's Death | Psalm 22:1 ➔ Jesus is forsaken by God on the cross | Matt 27:46, Mark 15:34 |
| 77 | | Psalm 22:7-8 ➔ Jesus is publicly ridiculed on the cross | Matt. 27:39-44, Mark 15:32 |
| 78 | | Psalm 22:15, 69:21 ➔ Jesus thirsts on the cross (gall/ vinegar mix) | Matt 27:48, John 19:28-30 |
| 79 | | Psalm 22:14-16 ➔ Jesus is crucified | Matt 27:35, John 19:17-22 |
| 80 | | Psalm 22:18 ➔ Jesus' clothing gambled for while He dies | Matt 27:35, John 19:23-24 |
| 81 | | Psalm 31:5 ➔ Jesus commits His soul to God as He dies | Luke 23:46 |
| 82 | | Psalm 34:20 (Exo.12:46) ➔ Jesus' bones not broken on the cross | John 19:33,36 |
| 83 | | Psalm 38:11 ➔ Jesus' friends watch Him die on the cross | Matt 27:55, Mark 15:40, Luke 23:49 (2:35), John 19:25-27 |
| 84 | | Isaiah 53:9 ➔ Jesus is buried in rich man's tomb | Matt 27:57-60, John 19:38-42 |
| 85 | | Isaiah 53:9,12 (Luke 22:37) ➔ Jesus is crucified with criminals | Mark 15:27-28, Luke 23:33-43 |
| 86 | | Isaiah 53:12 ➔ Jesus intercedes for sinners | Luke 23:34, Heb. 7:25, 9:15,24 |
| 87 | | Zechariah 12:10 ➔ Jesus' side pierced on the cross | John 19:34-37, 20:24-27 |

**After weighing these 87 pieces of circumstantial evidence as a whole…**

**Does the *evidence* point to Jesus Christ as the Messiah predicted in the Old Testament?**

**Messiah's First Coming:** Jesus fulfills Daniel 9:24-26 (and He says so in Luke 19:41-44).

**Suffering Servant:** Dead Sea Scroll of Isaiah dates to 125BC and records the suffering of a Person for our sins (Isaiah 53).

**Crucifixion:** Scholars agree Jesus was tried, scourged and crucified as foretold about Messiah in Old Testament (Isaiah 50, Psalm 22).

**Resurrections:** 4 historical facts that are best explained by Jesus's resurrection.

**Son of Man:** Jesus's favorite name for Himself points to Daniel 7:13.

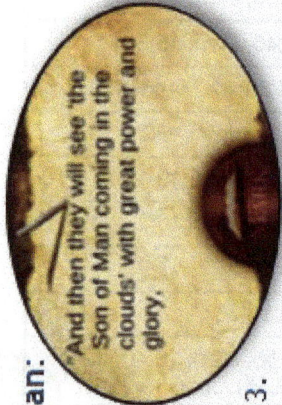

"And then they will see 'the Son of Man coming in the clouds' with great power and glory,"

There are 10 Claims about Jesus Christ to which majority of scholars agree...

Together these 10 Claims make a strong case for *the Deity of Jesus Christ* (John 8:58)

**Creator, Life, Light:** Jesus constantly refers to Himself as the Creator, Light and the Source of Life in Old Testament.

**God in Flesh:** Dead Sea Scroll of Isaiah dates to 125BC and records birth of a child who is Mighty God (Isaiah 9:6).

**Immanuel:** Jesus claimed to fulfill Old Testament promise that God would personally be with us (Isaiah 41:10).

**Incarnation:** Dead Sea Scroll of Isaiah dates to 125BC and records virgin birth (Isaiah 7:14) - which only Jesus fulfilled.

**Lineage:** 8 requirements for anyone claims to be Messiah only fulfilled in history by Jesus Christ.

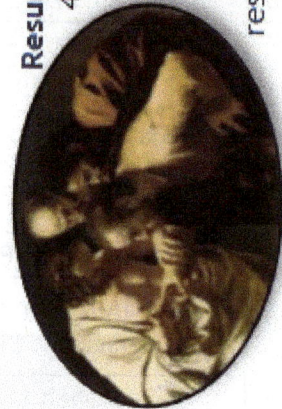

## Applying Origin Science to *Origins*

I start with the questions I am trying to solve.... Does the Bible provide greater PROBABILITY that I was created by God, or is there more convincing evidence that Natural Laws and/ or Evolution is more PROBABLE to be the basis for my origin? ➔ **Who am I?** ➔ **Where did I come from?** ➔ **Why am I here?**

Using Dr. Geisler's method of 'Origin Science', can I gather *circumstantial evidence* (data, facts) to help me answer these questions?

---

**Albert Einstein**   November 28, 1919 "The Times" magazine article "Time, Space and Gravitation":

**Analytics (measurable data) = circumstantial evidence to reach sound conclusions**

*"The theory of relativity belongs to the class of 'principle-theories'. As such it employs an Analytic method.*
1. *The elements which comprise this theory are not based on hypothesis but on empirical discovery.*
2. *The empirical discovery leads to understanding the general characteristics of natural processes.*
3. *Mathematical models are used to separate natural processes into theoretical-mathematical descriptions.*
4. *Therefore, by analytical means the necessary conditions that have to be satisfied are deduced.*
5. *Separate events must satisfy these conditions.*
6. *Experience should then match these conclusions."*

| # | **Universe & Life: specially created? (Book 2)** *Corroborating Evidence: 60 Measurable Data Points* (Bible explanations match Scientific Findings) | **Biblical Reference(s)** |
|---|---|---|
| 1 | Kepler's 3rd Law of Planetary Motion | Isaiah 40:26, Rom. 1:19-20 |
| 2 | Newton's 2nd & 3rd Laws of the Universe | Gen. 1:1, Ps 90:2, Heb 1:8-11 |
| 3 | 1st Law of Thermodynamics (Conservation of Mass/Energy: $E = mc^2$) | John 1:3, Gen. 2:2, Heb 1:3 |
| 4 | 2nd Law of Thermodynamics (Disintegration of Energy) | 1Ki. 2:1-2, Ps 102:26, Rom. 8:21 |
| 5 | Einstein's General Theory of Relativity | Psalm 8:3, 89:11-12, 124:8 |
| 6 | Hubble Constant | Ps 104:1-2, Isa. 42:5, Jer 10:12 |
| 7 | Doppler Red Shifts, Cosmic Microwave Background Radiation | Gen. 1:1,3 |
| 8 | Corotation Circle | Psalm 8:3-4, Isaiah 45:8, Hebrews 11:3 |
| 9 | Circumstellar Habitable Zone | |
| 10 | Precision of the Expansion Rate of the Universe | Job 38:4-6, Isaiah 40:21-22 |
| 11 | Precision of Gravitational Exponent | Genesis 1:1-26, Job 38:4-6, Psalm 8:3-4, Psalm 19:1-4a, Romans 1:19-20, Colossians 1:15-17, 2Peter 3:10, Hebrews 1:1-5, Hebrews 11:1-3 |
| 12 | Precision of Electromagnetic Force | |
| 13 | Precision of Ratio of Electromagnetic Force – to – Gravitational Force | |
| 14 | Precision of Atomic Strong Nuclear Force | |
| 15 | Precision of Atomic Weak Nuclear Force | |
| 16 | Precision of # Protons – to – # Neutrons in the Universe | |
| 17 | Precision of Electron – to – Proton Mass in Atomic Nucleus | |
| 18 | Precision of Neutron – to – Proton Mass in Atomic Nucleus | |
| 19 | Precision of nuclear ground state energies of He, BE, C, $O_2$ | |
| 20 | Precision of mass density of the Universe | |
| 21 | Precision of velocity of light | |
| 22 | Precision of Fine Structure Constant (splitting of spectral lines) | |
| 23 | Precision of decay rate of a proton | |
| 24 | Precision of Carbon – to – Oxygen Energy Level in the Universe | |

| # | **Universe & Life: specially created? (Book 2)** <br> *Corroborating Evidence: 60 Measurable Data Points* <br> (Bible explanations match Scientific Findings) | **Biblical Reference(s)** |
|---|---|---|
| 25 | Precision of decay rate of Beryllium | Gen 1:1-26, Ps 8:3-4, 19:1-4a, Rom 1:19-20, Coloss 1:15-17, 2Peter 3:10, Heb 1:1-5, 11:1-3 |
| 26 | Ratio of exotic – to – ordinary matter in the Universe | |
| 27 | Earth's location and position in the *spiral* Milky Way Galaxy | Psalm 8:3-4, <br> Psalm 115:14-16, <br> Job 12:8-9, <br> Isaiah 45:18 |
| 28 | Earth's protection from asteroid hits | |
| 29 | Earth's distance from the Sun | |
| 30 | Earth's Water and Carbon | |
| 31 | Precision of Earth's Rotational Axial Tilt | |
| 32 | Precision of size of Earth's Moon | |
| 33 | Earth's suspension in space, as a sphere | Job 40:22, Isaiah 40:22 |
| 34 | Earth's Hydrologic Cycle | Ecclesiastes 1:7 |
| 35 | Sun's Uniqueness as Earth's Energy Source | Ps 19:4b-6, John 1:4-5, 8:12 |
| 36 | Stability of Sun's energy output | Mal 3:6, Heb 1:12, 13:8 |
| 37 | Fact that our Sun is only star in Solar System | Matt 17:2-3,6,8, John 14:6 |
| 38 | Sun's mass (dwarfs the Earth) and metal composition | Exo 33:20, Isa 40:22, Heb 12:29 |
| 39 | Bat's echolocation system | Genesis 1:24-25, <br> Job 12:7,9, <br> Job 39:26, <br> Jeremiah 8:7 |
| 40 | Godwit's migratory flight patterns | |
| 41 | Giraffe's rete mirabile caroticum (blood control valves) | |
| 42 | Camel's oval-shaped red blood cells | |
| 43 | Bombadier Beetle's inhibitor chemical reservoir | |
| 44 | Precision/ complexity of Human Eye (light to electrical impulse) | Psalm 139:1-18, <br> Psalm 66:3, 94:8-9, 103:11-14, 119:73 <br> Genesis 9:3-4, 16:13, <br> Deuteronomy 12:15-16, 23-25, <br> Ezekiel 18:4, 48:35, <br> Matt 28:20, Luke 15:31, <br> Revelation 21:3, <br> Daniel 5:23, <br> Isaiah 43:7, <br> Jeremiah 1:5 |
| 45 | Precision/ complexity of Human Ear (sound to electrical impulse) | |
| 46 | Precision/ complexity of Human Brain (control center) | |
| 47 | Precision/ complexity of Human Heart (auto-rhythmic pumping of blood) | |
| 48 | Precision/ complexity of DNA (specific instructions for each organism) | |
| 49 | Precision/ complexity of ATP to create energy packets for life | |
| 50 | Precision/ complexity of Blood Clotting (auto-catalytic cascade) | |
| 51 | Precision/ complexity of Eukaryote Cell to regulate its own health | |
| 52 | Precision/ complexity of Human Body to regulate its own health | |
| 53 | Human intelligence (example: vocabulary of > 20,000 words) | Ps 139:23-24, 4:4-5, 23:2, 46:10, <br> Matt 10:28, 22:37, Luke 2:19, <br> John 8:7-9, Acts 24:16, Gen. 2:7, <br> 1Ki 18:21, 1Thes 5:23, Heb 4:12 |
| 54 | Human consciousness (example: capacity for self-awareness) | |
| 55 | Human Soul (example: people have a free will – we can make choices) | |
| 56 | Homologous Structures (unique creations at earliest stages) | Genesis 1:11-12, <br> Genesis 1: 20-22, 24-27, <br> Ecclesiastes 1:9-10, <br> Psalm 102:26, <br> John 1:1-3, <br> Colossians 1:16-17, <br> Romans 8:20-21 |
| 57 | Embryology (unique creations at earliest stages) | |
| 58 | Natural Selection (operates within range of a species' DNA) | |
| 59 | The Cambrian Explosion (abrupt appearance in fossil record) | |
| 60 | Foramen Magnum (unique only to humans – allows for bipedalism) | |

**After weighing these 60 pieces of circumstantial evidence as a whole…**
**Does the *evidence* point to the Universe and Life as originating by an Intelligent Designer?**

## There are 9 Facts about the Universe to which all scientists agree...

## Together these 9 Facts make a strong case for a Universe that is *FINITE, CREATED*
(Genesis 1:1)

### Newton's Law of Causality

$$\Sigma F_{a,b} = -\Sigma F_{b,a}$$

Every action (*cause*) has an equal and opposite reaction (*effect*).

### Newton's Law of Motion

$$F = (m)(dv/dt) = ma$$

Applied Force

An external force acting on an object causes it to accelerate or decelerate, depending on it's mass.

### Newton's Law of Inertia

$$\Sigma F = 0$$
$$(dv/dt = 0)$$

Objects at rest stay at rest, or objects in motion stay in motion, unless acted upon by an external force.

### 1st Law of Thermodynamics

$$\Delta E = E_{in} - E_{out}$$

Nothing is created nor destroyed; systems using energy don't use it up - they convert it to other energy forms.

### 2nd Law of Thermodynamics

$$\Delta S = \Delta Q/T$$

Energy available for an isolated system to do useful work is *always* decreasing.

### Cosmic Microwave Background Radiation

The universe erupted from an explosion that accounts for 99.97% of the radiant energy in the universe.

### General Theory of Relativity

$$G\mu v = 8\pi GT\mu v$$

In a vacuum, space and time change based on the velocity of a moving object relative to the frame of reference of the observer.

### Doppler Red Shift

Light waves moving away from point of reference emit red wavelength.

### Hubble Law of Universal Expansion

$$Ho = V/d$$

There is a linear relationship between the *radial velocities* of galaxies and their *distance* from each other.

Without the **finely tuned values of > 50 variables** (accurate and precise), life in the Universe is impossible.

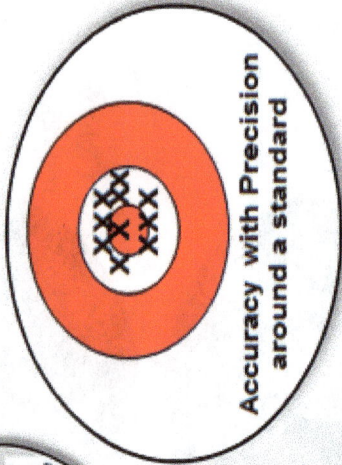

**Accuracy with Precision around a standard**

Without it's many **precise physical properties**, life in the Milky Way Galaxy is impossible.

Without it's many **precise physical properties**, life in the Solar System is impossible.

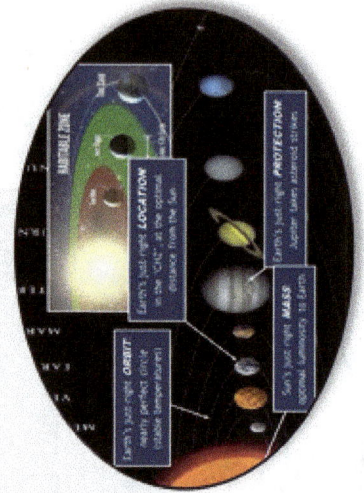

Physical laws of the Universe can be written in **math equations** on one side of one sheet of paper!

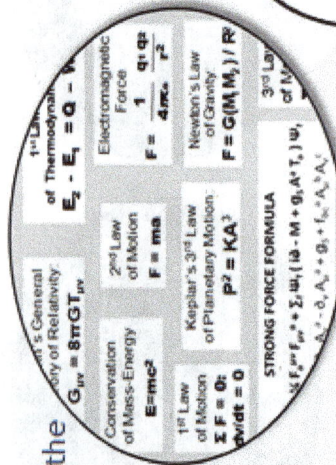

Here are 8 Facts about the Universe to which all scientists agree...

Together these 8 Facts make a strong case for a Universe that is **_DESIGNED, CREATED_** (Psalm 19:1-3)

Without it's many **precise physical properties**, life on Earth is impossible.

Without the **precise four forces** to govern the behavior of matter, life in the Universe is impossible.

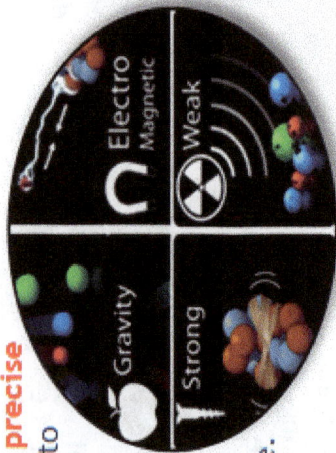

Material objects are made of minute particles with **precise chemical properties** or life in the Universe is impossible.

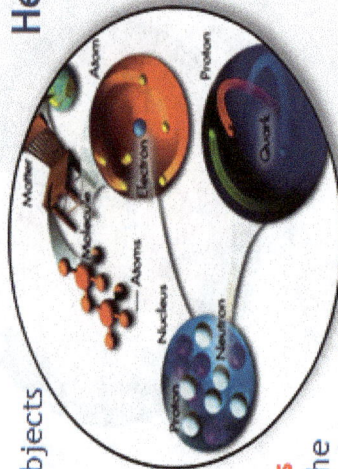

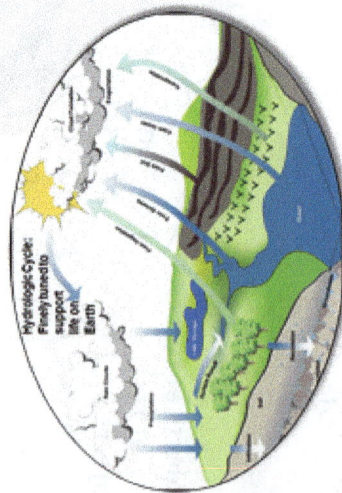

Without it's **precise, continuous water circulation**, life on Earth is impossible.

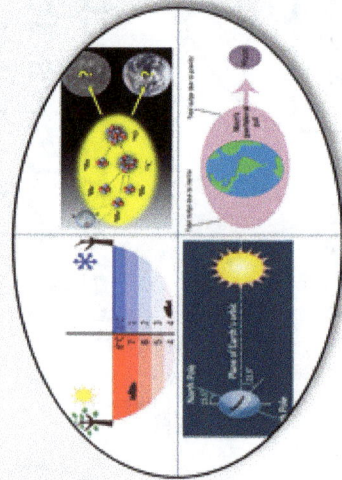

Brain's highly organized network of 10,000,000,000 nerve cells processes billions of signals in billionths of seconds.

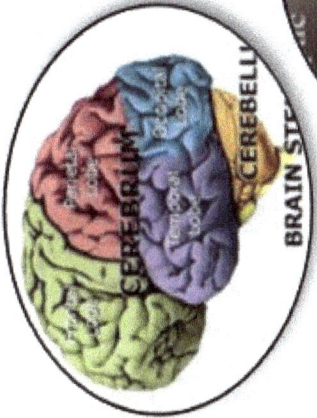

Eye's irreducible complexity transforms light photons to electricity so I can see.

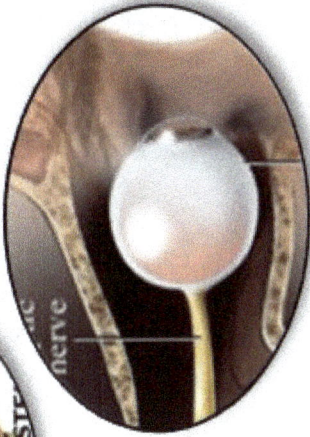

Ear's irreducible complexity transforms sound waves to mechanical vibrations to electricity so I can hear.

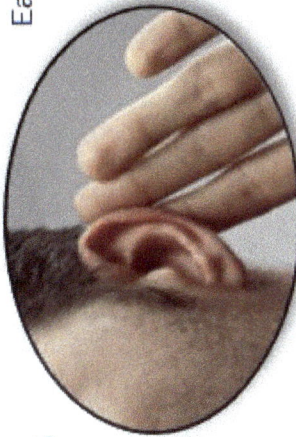

Blood's irreducibly complex clotting system runs on autopilot so I don't bleed to Death.

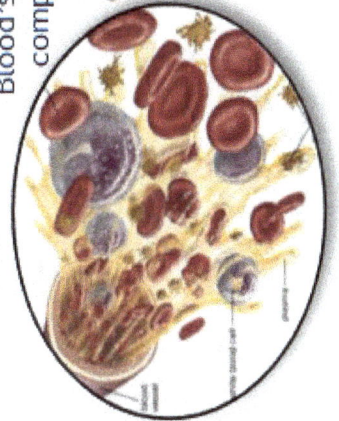

## There are 9 selected Facts about Animals and Humans...

## Together these 9 Facts make a strong case for Living Things being *DESIGNED*
(Job 12:7,9... Psalm 139)

DNA in my cells has all the detailed Info. to create me!

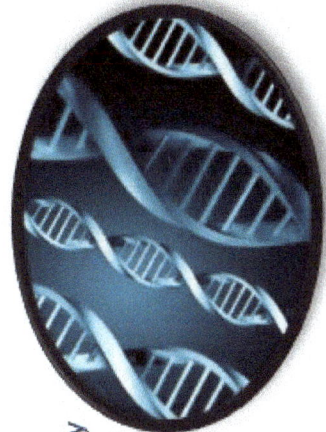

Bombadier beetles' irreducibly complex defense system allows them to fire explosive chemicals without blowing themselves up.

Giraffes' irreducibly complex pressure-regulating valve system prevents their 25-pound heart from blowing their brains out when they take a drink..

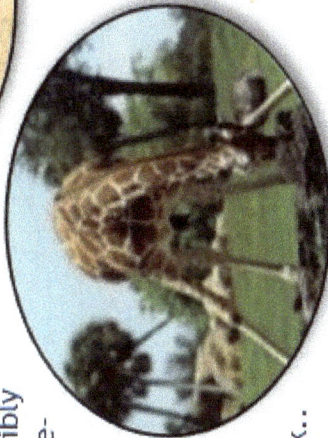

The 1-pound godwit flies the exact same 7,145-mile migratory route year after year in 9 days without stopping for food, water or rest.

Bat echolocation is millions of times more efficient than any man-made radar or sonar.

## There are 9 Facts about Evolution to which all scientists agree...

## Together these 9 Facts make a strong case *against Darwinian Evolution*

**Natural Selection:**
Galapagos finch beak sizes oscillate, but they have always stayed finches.

**Fossil Record:**
"It offers no support for gradual change; there is precious little in the way of intermediate forms."
Stephen J. Gould

**Cambrian Explosion:**
40 phyla of complex animals suddenly appear without transitions; fish suddenly appear without transitions.

**Transitional Forms:**
Archaeopteryx is not a dinosaur-to-bird; it's a feathered dinosaur.

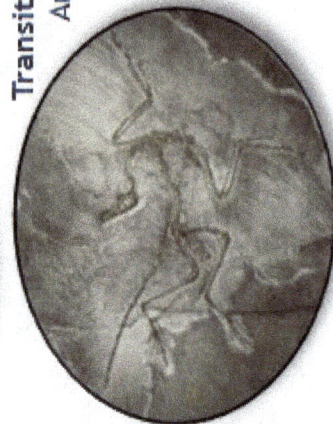

**Homology:**
Similar structures have independent origins at genetic level (evidence for creation, not evolution).

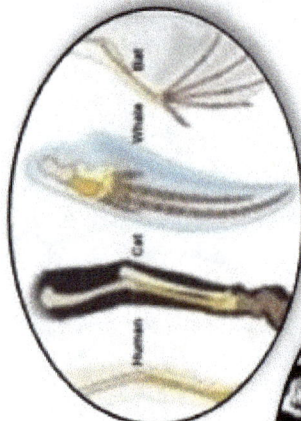

**Embryology:**
Haeckel's embryos were a deliberate distortion to promote evolution.

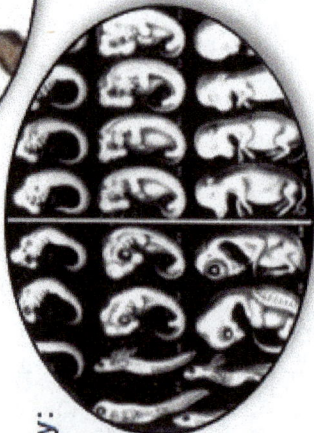

**Common Ancestry:**
Darwin's Tree of Life a man-made invention (no evidence).

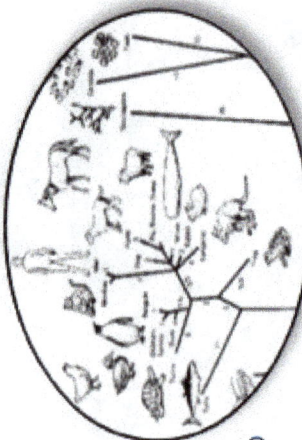

**Human Evolution:**
The Missing Link (ape-to-man) doesn't exist - it's a fairy tale.

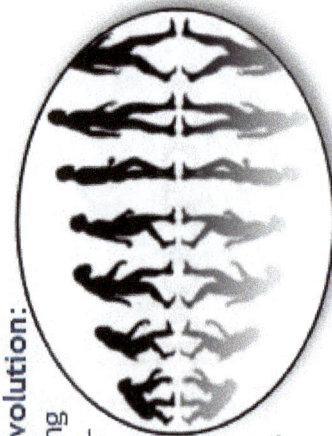

**Miller-Urey Experiment:**
Proving life can arise from non-life (abiogenesis) failed.

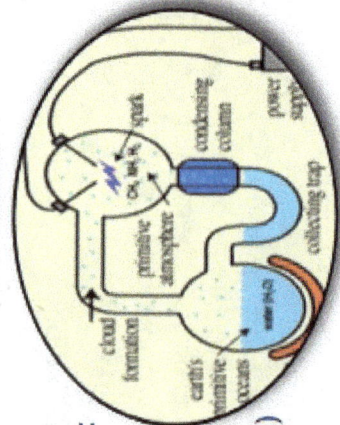

**Exit Ticket #26**     <mark>**Class 26: Where did I Come From? Part 2**</mark>

| | |
|---|---|
| 1) What makes Romans 1:18-20 a powerful statement about why one has no excuse when they face God? | 2) Why does the history of scientific discovery dating back 10 the 1600's have Christianity to thank? |
| 3) What causes Bill Phillips and Steven Weinberg to view the same evidence completely differently? | 4) Of the 3 Scriptures in this lesson, which one scripture resonates with you the most and why? |

# Class 27: Statistics of Christianity, Part 1

Using Statistics to Search for Truth

What do we mean by 'Statistics'?

What do we mean by '6 Sigma'?

Descriptive Statistics & Process Capability

What's the Difference between Precision vs. Fine Tuning

Process Capability: "Finely Tuning" a Process's Performance

Fine Tuning: Connecting Deductive to Inductive Arguments

The Statistics of Christianity: Deductive Argument for God's Existence

Article 548 - The Statistics of Christianity Part 1: How Fine Tuning Demonstrates God Exists

Finely-Tuned Earth Rotation: Process Description & Capability

Probability Science: Precision plus Fine Tuning is everywhere

Article 293 - The Statistics of Christianity: A Designed Universe and Jet Engines

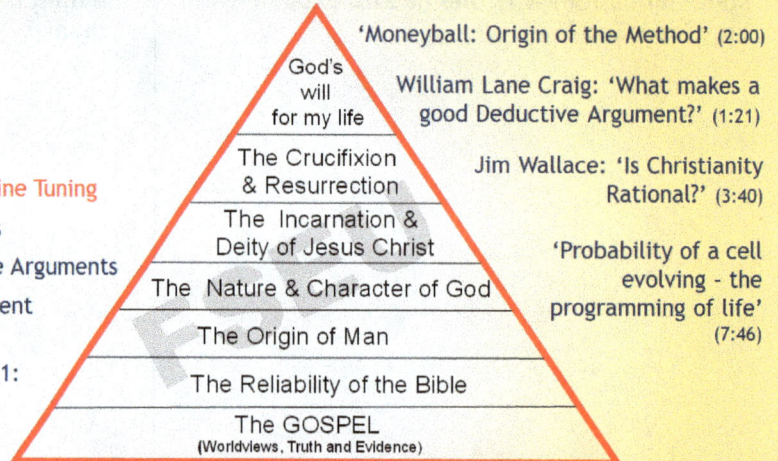

'Moneyball: Origin of the Method' (2:00)

William Lane Craig: 'What makes a good Deductive Argument?' (1:21)

Jim Wallace: 'Is Christianity Rational?' (3:40)

'Probability of a cell evolving - the programming of life' (7:46)

**Pyramid (top to bottom):**
- God's will for my life
- The Crucifixion & Resurrection
- The Incarnation & Deity of Jesus Christ
- The Nature & Character of God
- The Origin of Man
- The Reliability of the Bible
- The GOSPEL (Worldviews, Truth and Evidence)

FSEU

# HEBREWS 11:1

"Faith = *Substance* of things *hoped for.... Evidence* of things *not seen*"

**fse.life Lessons 02 - 08**

# Using Statistics to Search for Truth

## 9 Techniques

1. "6 Sigma"
2. Descriptive Statistics
3. Precision vs. Fine Tuning     Universal Expansion
4. Process Capability     Earth Axial Tilt
5. Linear Regression     Hubble Law
6. Stability Factor     Fine Tuned Constants
7. Probability Plot
8. System Design (Top Down)     Human Eye, Cell
9. Throughput Yield     Fulfilled Prophecy

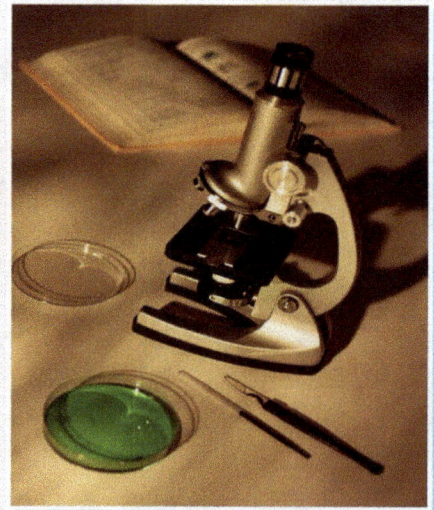

# The Science of Statistical Analysis = Very useful in strengthening your faith in God's existence!

# What do we mean by 'Statistics'?

A Science focused on two things:
1) calculating the probability of a future event occurring, to a certain degree of accuracy.
2) collecting, organizing, analyzing, interpreting, and presenting data.

**"Fathers of Probability Science"**
1) Blaise Pascal (1623-1662)
2) Pier de Fermat (1601-1665)

Statistics was first used for situations with potential for great GAINS, but also RISKS that not only those gains might not happen but might result in huge LOSSES.

People wanted a way to use facts (data) to PREDICT the gains and the probability of the risks happening.

- *Descriptive Statistics* – organizing and summarizing the data for population behavior.
- *Inferential Statistics* – drawing inferences about the larger population's behavior.

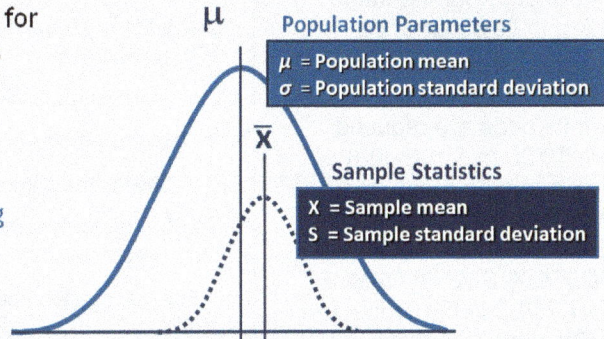

**Population Parameters**
$\mu$ = Population mean
$\sigma$ = Population standard deviation

**Sample Statistics**
X = Sample mean
S = Sample standard deviation

**Sample Statistics = used to *represent* the overall population**

'Moneyball: Origins of the Method' (3:09)          Courtesy of Google Images     Fair Use Law 17 U.S. Code § 107

# What do we mean by '6 Sigma'?

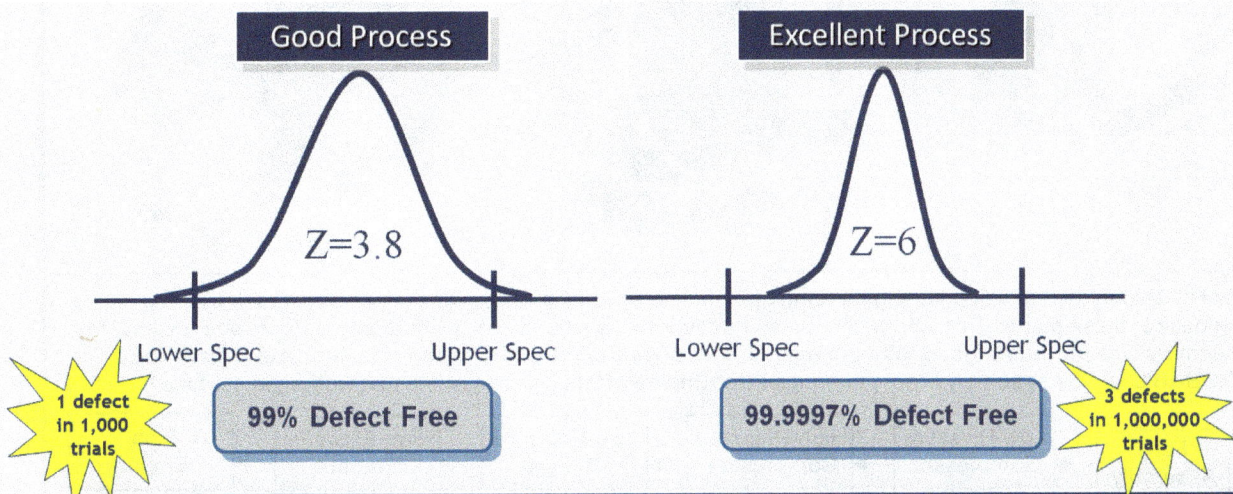

**Good Process**

$Z=3.8$

Lower Spec          Upper Spec

1 defect in 1,000 trials

**99% Defect Free**

**Excellent Process**

$Z=6$

Lower Spec          Upper Spec

3 defects in 1,000,000 trials

**99.9997% Defect Free**

**The Science of Statistical Analysis =
Apply mathematics to evaluate any process's operating capability within specifications-
INCLUDING THE UNIVERSE AND LIFE!**

Technique = Capability Analysis          Courtesy of Google Images     Fair Use Law 17 U.S. Code § 107

## Applying Probability Science to *Origins, The Bible & Deity of Christ*

There are three methods commonly used in Probability Science to determine the chance that someone is right or wrong when they make a statement about an event that happened in the past, that cannot be repeated.

### Method #1:  use historical data to calculate the odds of an event occurring

We can use statistics to calculate the odds that any historical event happened by chance, as well as the odds of its reoccurrence in the future, if we have historical data for its occurrence or for the steps leading to its occurrence.

The table gives examples of how often an event will occur when its odds are reduced (from 1:100 to 1:100,000). In order to reduce these odds (since these are undesirable events), we must implement *ORDERLY, SUSTAINABLE CONTROLS* in the processes by which the events occur.

| An Event's chance of occurrence when "as-is" process is '99% Good' (1:100 chance for a defect) | Same Event's chance of occurrence if we could improve it's process to '99.99999% Good' (1:100,000 chance for a defect) |
|---|---|
| • Unsafe drinking water 15 minutes each day | • Unsafe drinking water 1 minute every seven months |
| • 2 short or long landings at most major airports each day | • One short or long landing at most major airports every five years |
| • No electricity for 7 hours each month | • No electricity for 1 hour every 34 years |
| • 20,000 lost articles of mail each hour | • 7 lost articles of mail each hour |
| • 300,000 incorrect invoices each year | • 102 incorrect invoices each year |
| • 2,500 improperly handled cargo claims each year | • 1 improperly handled cargo claim each year |
| • 1,500 inaccurate expense reports each year | • 1 inaccurate expense report every 2 years |

Another example is the chance of building a defect-free Jet Engine. Say a company wants to hire me to build jet engines for them, and they ask me to prove I can build them defect-free. I can use historical data to answer that question. As shown below, there are six main assemblies that must be built separately, then come together, in a final assembly of a jet engine. The historical data shows each assembly's chance of being built without defects. Unfortunately for me, history shows I only have a 28% chance of building a defect-free engine (a 72% chance that my engines won't work). I doubt the company would hire me, based on my history of building engines.

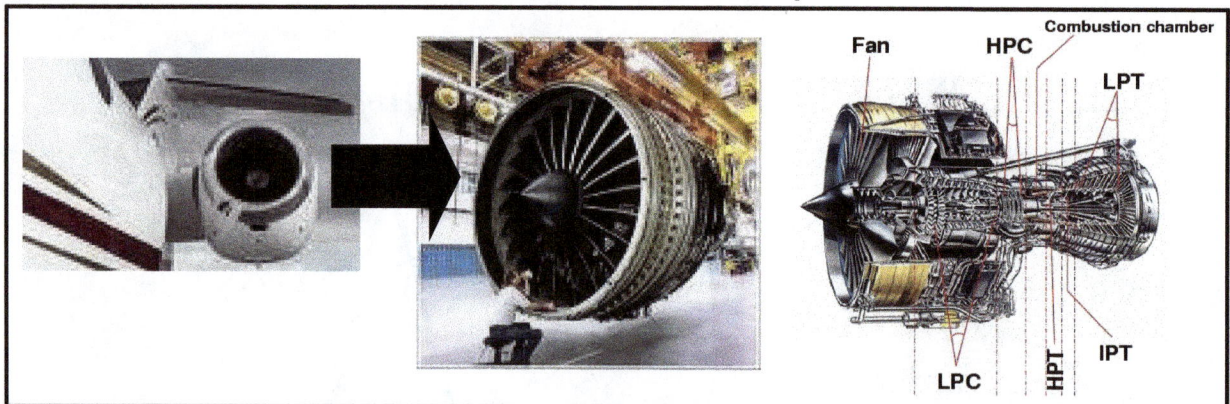

The US Military needs 1,000 jet engine fighter planes, so I submit a bid to win their contract to deliver the jet engines for these planes. The contract requires I deliver these jet engines without any defects and on time. My Assembly Line produces "good" components of a Jet Engine at the percentages shown below. What's the PROBABILITY my Assembly Plant producies a Jet Engine off the assembly line that works the 1st time?

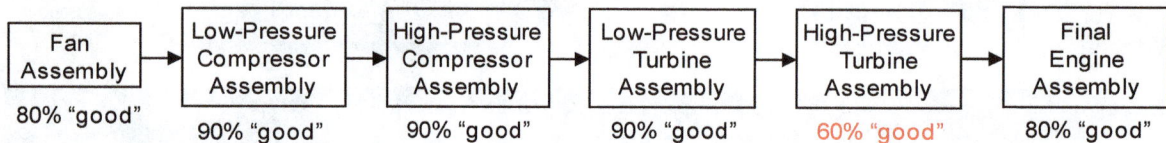

| Fan Assembly | Low-Pressure Compressor Assembly | High-Pressure Compressor Assembly | Low-Pressure Turbine Assembly | High-Pressure Turbine Assembly | Final Engine Assembly |
|---|---|---|---|---|---|
| 80% "good" | 90% "good" | 90% "good" | 90% "good" | 60% "good" | 80% "good" |

"1st Time" = (.80) x (.90) x (.90) x (.90) x (.60) x (.80) = $.28$ ← I have a *28% chance* of making a working Jet Engine (a 72% chance of one that fails)!

We'll use this method when pondering these questions: ① "What are the odds that the Old Testament prophecies against nations could have been fulfilled by chance?", ② "What are the odds that any one person could fulfill the Old Testament prophecies on the Messiah by chance?", ③ "What are the odds that life could have arisen by chance?" ④ "What are the odds that life processes (blood clotting, eyesight) occurred randomly?"

## Method #2:  use historical data to prove causal relationships

This is commonly used in sports, where statistics measure the performance of an athlete or team to try and predict future results. For example, if we have data on how many points a basketball team scores per game, and we have data on how many practice hours they spent in preparing for the games, we can use statistics to see if there is a relationship between these two factors.

The graph to the right shows there is greater than *74% certainty* that the amount of practice time the team puts in each month directly affects how many points they score each week in their games.

We'll use this method when pondering the question:
① "Does the data support that the universe was CAUSED (and not a random occurrence)?"

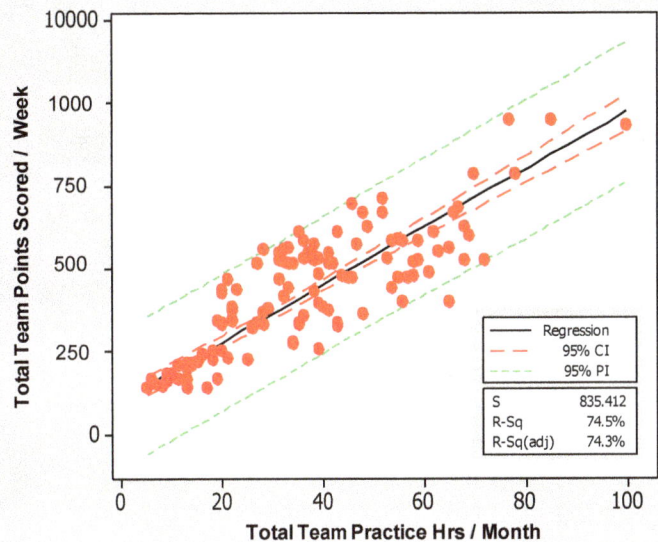

Scatter plot: Total Team Points Scored / Week (y-axis, 0 to 10000) versus Total Team Practice Hrs / Month (x-axis, 0 to 100). Legend: Regression, 95% CI, 95% PI. S = 835.412, R-Sq = 74.5%, R-Sq(adj) = 74.3%.

## Method #3:  use historical data to prove the precision and order in a system

By analyzing the historical data from the operation of an event, process or system, we can determine whether that event operates by *random chance* or it is *designed.* How do we do this? We are looking for evidence of: Simplicity and Randomness versus Complexity, Order, and / or Precision.

1) **Simple** = plain; lacks intelligence
2) **Complex** = intricate assembly of parts, units
3) **Order** = correctness according to a set of rules or laws; the state of effectively controlled operation
4) **Precise** = being minutely accurate, rigidly strict (i.e., "tuned" to its standard)
5) **Tuned** = the act of adjusting for proper functioning; to be precise to a known standard (ex: the correct pitch of a musical instrument to achieve its intended function)
6) **Design** = an intended outline or plan; to plan or fashion skillfully, especially for a definite purpose
7) **Random or Unguided** = without plan or order

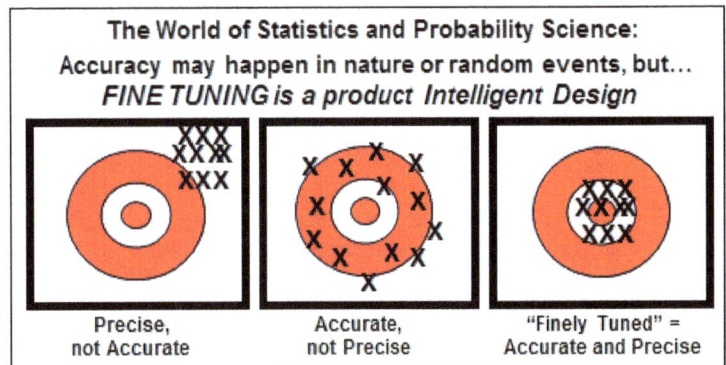

The World of Statistics and Probability Science: Accuracy may happen in nature or random events, but... *FINE TUNING is a product Intelligent Design*. Precise, not Accurate | Accurate, not Precise | "Finely Tuned" = Accurate and Precise

An example of how statistics is used to assess a system or process for whether it behaves *randomly* or is under *intentional control* is by evaluating the precision or stability in its output data with a tool called the "Precision" or "Stability" Factor.

- The "Stability" or "Precision" Factor is simply the ratio of $Q_1$ to $Q_3$: $SF = Q_1 / Q_3$

- It is often used in statistics to get an idea of how repeatable or "stable" a process is over time ("over time" means "the data being observed includes all sources of long-term variation that it should be exposed to)"

- $Q_3$, or the 3rd Quartile, also contains within its population the $Q_1$, or 1st Quartile, data.

- When SF is close to "1": The closer the $Q_1$ value is to the $Q_3$ value, the closer the SF is to a value of "1". The closer SF is to "1", the *TIGHTER* (or more "spiked") the histogram is. And the tighter it is, the more *REPEATABLE* or *PRECISE* the process variation is over time. This type of process is what you see in intelligent, intentional design.

- When SF is far from "1": $Q_1$ is a smaller number than $Q_3$, so the histogram isn't tight but instead very "flat" or "spread out", which represents a process with a lot of variation. This type of process is what you see with unguided, naturally-occurring systems or processes, and are much harder to control).

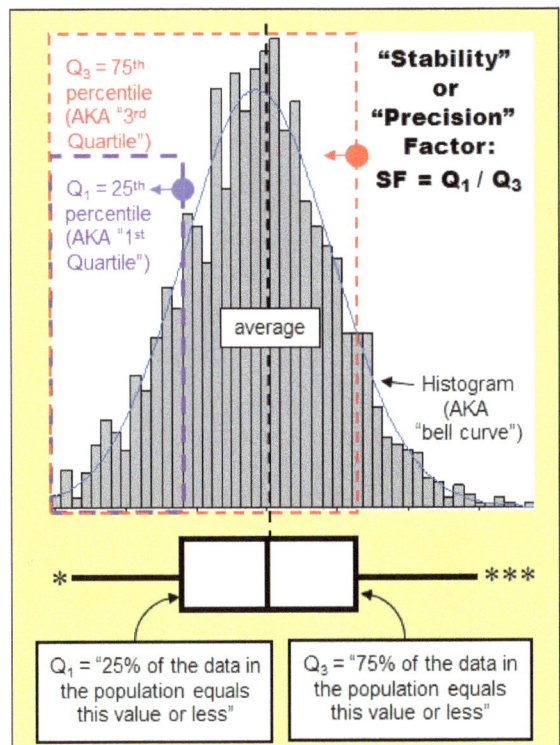

"Stability" or "Precision" Factor: $SF = Q_1 / Q_3$. $Q_3 = 75$th percentile (AKA "3rd Quartile"). $Q_1 = 25$th percentile (AKA "1st Quartile"). Histogram (AKA "bell curve") with average marked. $Q_1$ = "25% of the data in the population equals this value or less". $Q_3$ = "75% of the data in the population equals this value or less".

An example of using Stability Factors to assess a system's or process's precision is shown to the right, where two different Telecommunication Call Centers "A" and "B" are being compared over the same period of time for their capability to resolve the same customer issue.

There is nothing different about the "inputs" into the process or system of customer resolution at these two call centers:

1) Both centers have the same customer issues being communicated to their agents manning the phones and taking these customer calls.

2) The time period when this analysis was performed was the same for both call centers.

3) Both centers are located within the same geographic region of the country (same state).

But as the data shows, both visually (looking at each histogram) and analytically (looking at each center's resulting Stability Factor), the capability of these two Call Centers is very different:

Call Center "A": As a collective group, the agents at this center are not only accurate in resolving the customer issues (they average a 95.3% resolution rate, close to the 95% target), they are also precise (SF = .99). Call Center "A" resolves customer issues at a very stable rate and on target.

Call Center "B": As a collective group, the agents at this center are way off the target of 95%, averaging only 80.1% (they are not very accurate). Plus, these agents as a collective group are very imprecise and unstable in resolving the customers' issues, with a SF = .79 and a histogram that is very spread out.

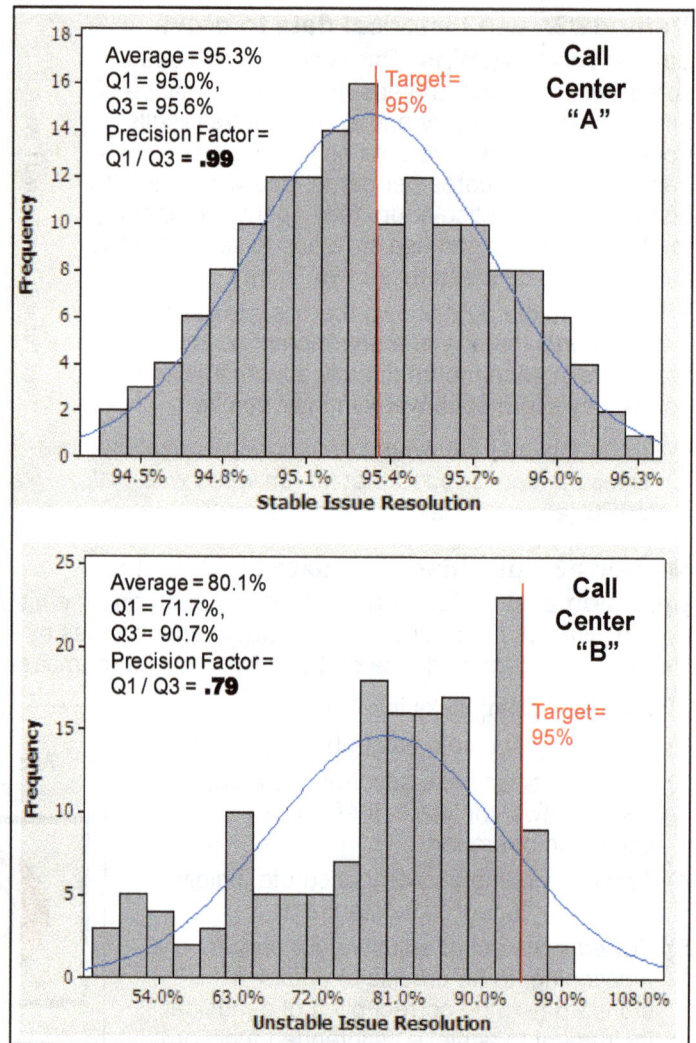

**Call Center "A"**

Average = 95.3%
Q1 = 95.0%,
Q3 = 95.6%
Precision Factor = Q1 / Q3 = **.99**

Target = 95%

*Stable Issue Resolution*

**Call Center "B"**

Average = 80.1%
Q1 = 71.7%,
Q3 = 90.7%
Precision Factor = Q1 / Q3 = **.79**

Target = 95%

*Unstable Issue Resolution*

What did we find when we investigated the *CAUSE* for the huge difference between these centers (notice how we used the Law of Causality... more later)?

Center "A" implemented *DESIGN CONTROLS*, where each agent follows standard operating procedures for how to resolve customer issues, with weekly follow-up supports from their supervisors when they run into problems.

Center "B" allowed the agents to operate base on each agent's own experience and skill level, with no external controls in place. Solution: implement Center "A" external controls at Center "B".

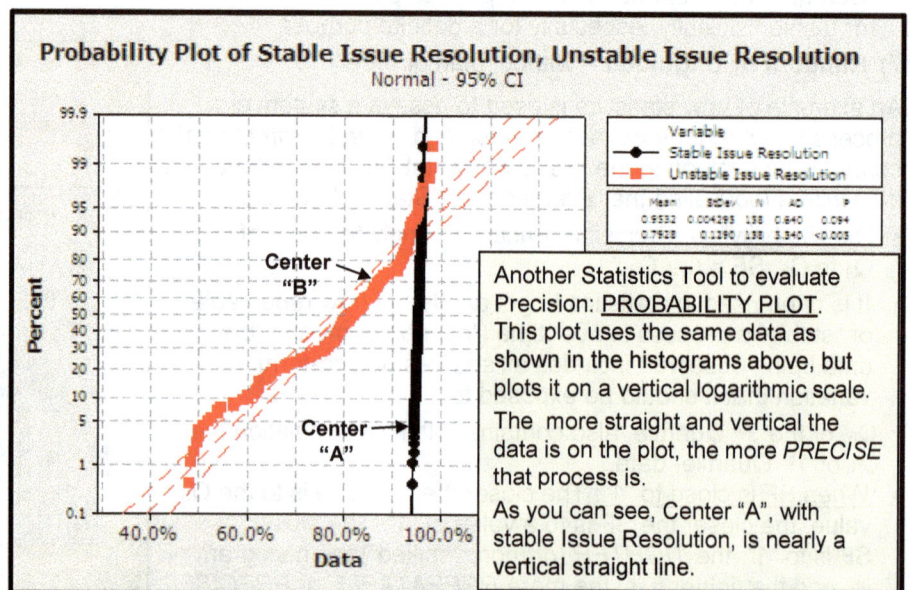

**Probability Plot of Stable Issue Resolution, Unstable Issue Resolution**
Normal - 95% CI

Center "B"

Center "A"

Another Statistics Tool to evaluate Precision: PROBABILITY PLOT. This plot uses the same data as shown in the histograms above, but plots it on a vertical logarithmic scale.

The more straight and vertical the data is on the plot, the more *PRECISE* that process is.

As you can see, Center "A", with stable Issue Resolution, is nearly a vertical straight line.

We'll use this method when pondering these questions: ① "What's the explanation for the incredible precision of the constants in the universe, which scientists have proven are responsible for sustaining life on earth today?", ②"What's the explanation for the incredible precision in the bat's echolocation system? The giraffe's rete mirabile caroticum?" ③ "What's the explanation for the incredible precision in the cell's functioning as a mini metropolitan 'city'?" ④ "What's the explanation for the incredible precision in the DNA protein (not to mention ATP, and others), which scientists have proven is responsible for the information that defines each living organism?"

# ORIGIN OF LIFE: Probability & Precision point to an Intelligent Designer!

**UNIVERSE**
Expansion
Electromagnetic force
Gravitational force

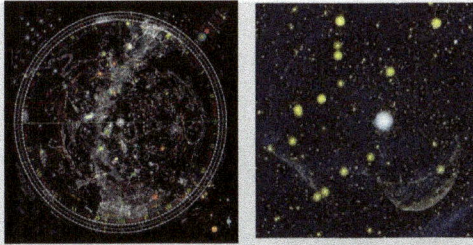

- Electromagnetic-to-Gravitational force = *precise* to $1 \times 10^{40}$ [14]
- Gravitational Constant = *precise* to 5 decimals (2.00000) [14]
- Universe Expansion rate = *precise* to $1 \times 10^{55}$ [14]

**MILKY WAY, SOLAR SYSTEM**

Milky Way Galaxy

Solar System

- Stars: *odds* - only .001% have the right location and have host star properties that could support life [14]
- Milky Way is spiral galaxy = req'd for life to exist (*odds* - only 5% of all galaxies are spiral) [14]

**SUN, EARTH**

Angle of tilt

sunlight

23.5° ± 1.2°

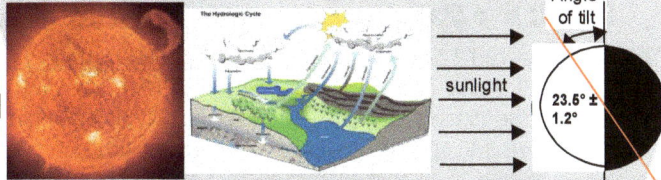

- Earth *precise* tilt = 23.5° ± 1.2° [14]
- Sun's *precise* energy output = constant to 0.1% [14]

**BODY, MIND, BRAIN**

Human brain: A, cerebrum; B, cerebellum.

- my brain's *precision:* 1,000x storage capacity of a supercomputer; holds and sorts $10^{14}$ bits of information [15]
- *odds* that a human being formed by *chance* = $1 \times 10^{2,000,000,000}$ [15]

**HEART, EYE, EAR**

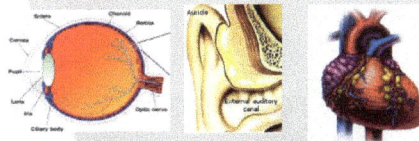

- 100 yrs of supercomputer processing to simulate the *precision* of what occurs in my eye many times every second [15]

**BLOOD CELL**

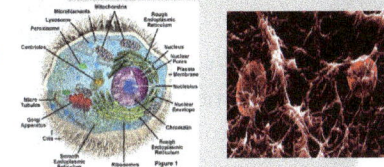

- Blood Clotting: *odds* of getting just the one factor TPA and its activator to work = $1 \times 10^{31}$ (there are at least 32 others) [16]

**DNA, ATP**

Adenine

Phosphate Groups

Ribose

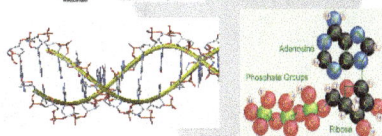

- DNA code formation = 1 in $10^{600}$ by *chance* [15]
- *odds* of all proteins needed for life might form in one place by *random events* = $1 \times 10^{40,000}$ [15]

**Matter**
Atoms, Molecules

**Nuclear Forces**
Strong nuclear force
Weak nuclear force

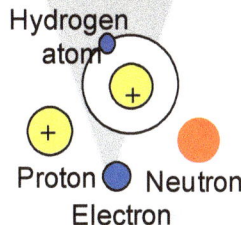

Hydrogen atom

Proton   Neutron
Electron

- Strong nuclear force = *precise* to 2% [14]
- neutron-to-proton mass = *precise* to 0.1% [14]
- #electrons-to-protons = *precise* to $1 \times 10^{37}$ [14]

> "...the probability of life originating at random is so utterly miniscule as to make it absurd... the favorable properties of physics on which life depends are in every respect deliberate... It is therefore almost inevitable that our own measure of intelligence must reflect ... higher intelligences ... even to the limit of God ... such a theory is so obvious that one wonders why it is not widely accepted as being self-evident. The reasons are psychological rather than scientific."
> (Fred Hoyle, Cambridge Professor of Astrophysics and Natural Philosophy, 1981)

# Descriptive Statistics & Process Capability

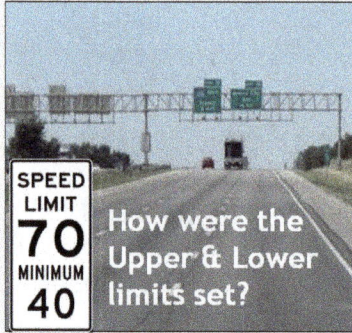

**Process Limits Known**

Drivers can go as fast or slow as they want (free will), but they are warned <u>there are upper and lower limits</u>

**Descriptive Statistics**

Trooper collected 2,500 readings on Hwy 29 in MO - now we can describe drivers' speed (average and spread)

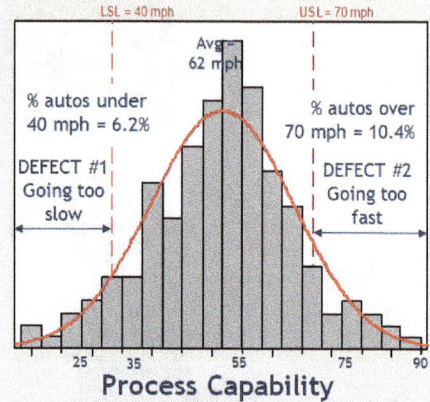

LSL = 40 mph          USL = 70 mph
Avg = 62 mph
% autos under 40 mph = 6.2%
% autos over 70 mph = 10.4%
DEFECT #1 Going too slow
DEFECT #2 Going too fast

**Process Capability**

<u>Apply the Limits to Descriptive Stats:</u>
Total Defect Rate = 10.4 + 6.2 = 16.6%
(for every 6 autos the trooper reads, 1 is either going too slow or too fast!)

> **The Science of Statistical Analysis** = We can DESCRIBE the behavior of a process, and assess a process's CAPABILITY, with mathematics!

Technique = Process Capability

# What's the Difference between "Precision" vs. "Fine Tuning"?

**Precision**

Degree to which a process/system's measurements <u>repeat themselves</u> in unchanging conditions.

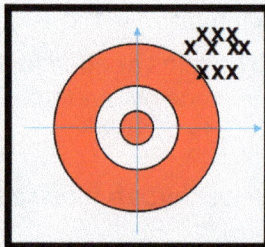

Is this "Fine Tuning"?

❌ Process is NOT Finely Tuned
(precise behavior, but OUTSIDE the target)

**Fine Tuning**

Precision of a process/system's measurements <u>within set target(s)</u> to achieve it's purpose.

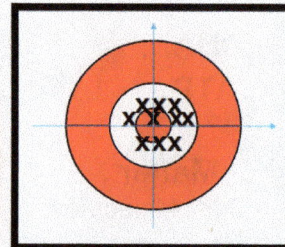

How about this??

☑ Process is Finely Tuned
(precise behavior WITHIN the target)

> **FINE TUNING** =
> Very high level of **Precision** (describing the <u>process</u>)
> within the **Target** (describing the <u>capability</u>)

* Example of fine tuning = setting the pitch of a musical instrument to within the designer's target value, to achieve the designer's intended sound.

## Process *Capability*:  "Finely Tuning" a Process's *Performance*

| Activity | 99%  Defect Free (3.8 Sigma) | 99.9997% Defect Free (6 Sigma) |
|----------|------------------------------|--------------------------------|
| Mail Delivery | 20,000 lost articles of mail per hour. | 7 lost articles of mail per hour. |
| Drinking Water | Unsafe drinking water for 15 minutes each day. | Unsafe drinking water for 2 minutes per year. |
| Hospital Surgery | 5,000 incorrect procedures each week. | 2 incorrect procedures each week. |
| Air Travel | 2 abnormal landings at most airports each day. | 1 abnormal landing at most airports every 5 years. |
| Drug Prescription | 200,000 wrong drug prescriptions each year. | 68 wrong drug prescriptions each year. |

Do you think improvements to these processes happened by chance?

OR... would an Intelligent Agent be a better explanation?

**Process Capability (not behavior)**

**Where we can use this approach to examine if God might exist:**
**1) Universal Fine Tuning,     2) Mathematical Precision in the Universe & Life**

Technique = Descriptive Statistics & Capability Analysis

Courtesy of Google Images     Fair Use Law 17 U.S. Code § 107

## Fine Tuning: Connecting Deductive to Inductive Arguments

**Deduction:**
**The Fine Tuning Argument**

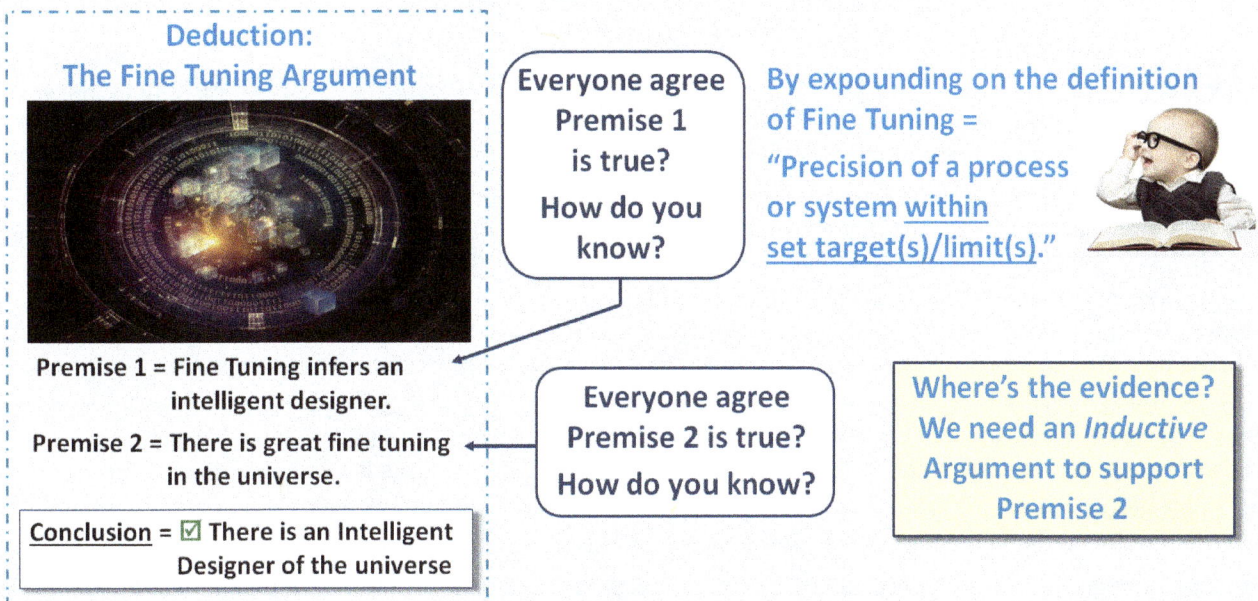

Premise 1 = Fine Tuning infers an intelligent designer.

Premise 2 = There is great fine tuning in the universe.

Conclusion = ☑ There is an Intelligent Designer of the universe

Everyone agree Premise 1 is true? How do you know?

Everyone agree Premise 2 is true? How do you know?

By expounding on the definition of Fine Tuning = "Precision of a process or system within set target(s)/limit(s)."

Where's the evidence? We need an *Inductive* Argument to support Premise 2

William Lane Craig: 'What makes a good Deductive Argument?' (1:21)          Courtesy of Google Images     Fair Use Law 17 U.S. Code § 107

## Article 548 - The Statistics of Christianity Part 1: How Fine Tuning Demonstrates God Exists

Job 38:8,10 *"Who shut in the sea with doors; I fixed My limit for it and set bars and doors."*

My wife recently sent me to pick up a table from someone on Facebook Marketplace, where I had the pleasure of meeting Trevor, a young man who just graduated from University of Kansas with a PhD in Statistics.

Trevor was moving to Colorado for his first job as Director of "Big Data." As a system engineer and statistician, I told him that statistics, especially fine tuning, demonstrates God's existence. Trevor, who knew what I meant by fine tuning as it applies to statistics, said he is spiritually minded but considered himself an atheist.

He was immediately interested in my challenge. We spent an hour together in his garage as I went through the logical argument for God's existence using statistics. It is an easy, and powerful, argument to grasp. Here it is.

Premise 1: Fine tuning requires an intelligent designer.

Premise 2: There is great fine tuning in the universe.

Conclusion: There is an Intelligent Designer of the Universe.

## The Statistics of Christianity: Deductive Argument for God's Existence

| ① Understanding **Precision** | ② Understanding **Fine Tuning** | ③ Fine Tuning needs a **DESIGNER** | ④ Finely-Tuned Design: **Universe Expansion** |
|---|---|---|---|
| • describes process <u>behavior</u><br>• "High" = process under set conditions yield very similar results (low variation)<br>• "Low" = process under set conditions yield different results (high variation) | • calculates process <u>capability</u> = probability of a defect against established limits<br>• "High" = process generates very few defects outside the limits<br>• "Low" = process generates high #defects outside the limits | • Left to themselves, processes only behave - they do not perform<br>• To measure capability, a source *outside* the process - a Designer - sets the process limits | Universal Expansion Rate =<br>• average = 71 km/sec/mpc Limits: Lower 70, Upper 72<br>• 1 defect in $10^{55}$ opportunities<br>• 99.99999999999999999999 99999999999999999999 9999999999% defect free |

| **Premise 1** | **Premise 2** | **Conclusion** |
|---|---|---|
| Fine Tuning requires an intelligent designer. | There is great fine tuning in the universe. | ☑ There is an Intelligent Designer of the Universe |

Courtesy of Google Images     Fair Use Law 17 U.S. Code § 107

To understand this, we need to understand fine tuning and precision. Precision is a term used in statistics to describe a process's behavior. It refers to a process that yields very similar, repeatable results. Fine tuning goes further by placing limits on the process and then checking how well it performs against those limits.

Notice something significant. Limits on a process never originate from the process itself. To measure process performance, someone or something outside the process must impose limits on that process so it can then be assessed for how capable it is to operate within those limits. So, from where do the limits originate?

There are statistical tools to describe the behavior of any process. Engineers use these tools to describe that process's level of precision, which is a behavior. But an engineer still can't tell if that process is capable of meeting the needs of the customer. A highly precise process might still fail. This is where fine tuning comes in.

Until an external source applies limits to that process, we cannot tell how capable that process is to perform to customer requirements. In process and system design, limits always come from intelligent engineers.

Once an engineer (intelligent agent) sets the limits for that process to deliver to the customer's results, that engineer can now determine the level of performance of that process to operate within those limits.

We do this all the time in normal everyday life. For example, when a young adult like Trevor graduates from college and gets their first job, suddenly they are responsible for lots of bills such as insurance, car payment, student loans, rent or mortgage, and it goes on and on (I miss those easy, carefree college days).

Each month money comes in from their first job (earnings) and money goes out (bills, spending). Do you think a young adult should pay attention to the behavior of the budget process of "Money In – Money Out"?

While that young adult's budget precision matters, every month they could be precise at $300 in the red (overspending). Overspending creates defects (bounced checks is one example). So, precision is not enough.

To have a high-performing budgeting process, young adults must finely tune their budget. That means they set a limit for their spending so it does not exceed their earnings. Then, if they are wise, they monitor their spending throughout each month to ensure they never exceed their limit. This limit is imposed from the outside by that young adult. Without a limit, no one knows the budget's capability (even when knowing its behavior).

In the same way, this week's verse shows how God applied limits in His creation. He reveals His omnipotence to Job by explaining it is His limits set on the seas that prevent them from overrunning the land, so life can exist (we know what happened to life when He removed those limits in Genesis and water covered the earth!).

God tells us He is the Earth's Intelligent Designer who set limits to the sea, metaphorical "bars and doors." God finely tuned the seas' operations so He can get the expected results - life on earth.

A more amazing example of fine tuning is our universe's expansion rate. In 1929, astronomer Edwin Hubble discovered our universe expands at roughly 71 km/sec/mpc. But the amazing finding is the rate is precise to 71 such that only one time in 10,000,000,000,000,000,000,000,000,000,000,000,000,000,000,000,000 occurrences will it differ. That's precise. But it must stay at this precision or life cannot exist. That's fine tuning.

There is an intelligent designer outside the universe who finely tuned universal expansion by setting limits to its behavior so the designer gets the needed results - life. The best candidate for this intelligent designer is God.

# Finely-Tuned Earth Rotation: Process Description & Capability

Earth's orbital, rotational *axial tilt* = **23.5° ± 1.2°**

Descriptive Statistics:

Average = 23.5°

Lower Limit = 22.3°
Upper Limit = 24.7°

Process Capability:
If earth ever rotates outside these limits, life on earth would be impossible.

**How were these limits set, since they are independent of the process?**

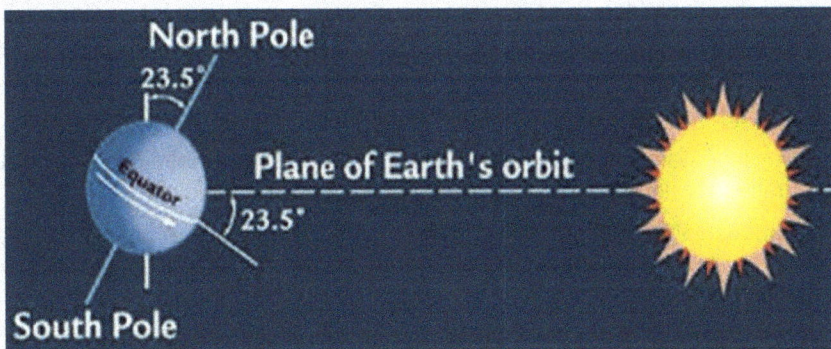

Earth is tilted at a stable 23.5° angle that stays within 1.2°, thanks mainly to our **moon**. Without our moon, Earth would experience catastrophic climate changes.

Planets that have no moons or a relatively small moon have a rotation axis that tilts very chaotically.

This tilt gives Earth predictable, pleasant seasonal changes that provide variety and facilitate Earth's annual food production.

## Article 293 - The Statistics of Christianity: A Designed Universe and Jet Engines

Ephesians 3:9 *"God who created all things through Jesus Christ."*

Last Tuesday, one of Southwest Airline flight 1380's engines exploded in midflight, tragically killing a passenger (the first airline passenger fatality since 2009). Experts think one of its 18 fan blades broke due to metal fatigue. The pilot was able to land the plane with one engine, even with such devastating damage. At the time, I was in the Kansas City terminal, boarding a flight for a business trip to Detroit.

As people in the terminal watched the events unfold on the airport monitors, the mood was not panic nor fear. Passengers continued boarding their flights. Wouldn't you think people would be terrified after seeing an engine blow up with 250 passengers 10,000 feet in the air going nearly 300 miles per hour?

When the media interviewed technical experts for their explanation of what happened to SW flight 1380, the unanimous opinion was that the CFM56-7B engine failure was a "fluke", issuing the following statement:

*"You can't completely rule out a manufacturing error. You can't rule out external damage. You can't rule out isolated wear and tear. But given the amazing run this CFM56-7B engine has had, you can rule out a design flaw."* How can the experts so quickly dismiss design as the cause for the failure?

In my professional career, I have run a jet engine service shop, where companies like UPS, Boeing, Southwest, United Airlines and the military have sent their engines to be completely disassembled, their over 9,000 parts sent all over the world for refurbishment or repair, and then returned, the engine reassembled, tested and shipped to the airline to be remounted on the airplane. I am well versed on the depth of design, manufacturing and service control necessary to ensure proper engine function.

I have also spent over 30 years leading teams in statistical process control, responsible for implementing improvements in products and processes as well as teaching statistics techniques and tools to employees.

One of my favorite teaching methods is to go through examples of jet engine failure modes to explain how statistics is used to tell the difference between a system or process that is designed versus one based on unguided, random events. It isn't that difficult to recognize design vs. random when you see it.

And that is why no one panics at an airport when another flight somewhere in the world fails. They know jet engines are reliably designed, even without ever working in a jet engine facility. How do they know this?

About 100,000 airplanes take off every day from airports around the world. That equates to 37,000,000 flights every year. The engine that exploded on the Southwest flight is the single most-used engine ever, powering over 6,700 aircraft worldwide since being introduced in 1997 (over 20 years ago).

In the world of statistics, that means jet engines (and especially this one) have about 1 chance in 10,000,000 opportunities (or, in scientific notation, $1 \times 10^7$ chance), of failure.

With about 37,000,000 flights around the world, that means you can expect about 3 failures somewhere in the world every year. That means any open-minded person can see how improbable it is that jet engines would fail during flight.

Our verse this week, from the New Testament book of Ephesians, is one over nearly 200 unique verses throughout the Bible where God is called out as the Designer of the Universe, all life, and us. And even more so than the jet engine, the level of design throughout the universe is staggering.

For example, if the number of electrons in the universe doesn't equal the number of protons to a precision of $1 \times 10^{37}$, electromagnetic forces would overwhelm gravitational forces and galaxies, stars and planets could not form... so life would not exist. And when it comes to life, the probability that the DNA code found in each cell occurred by unguided, random processes is $1 \times 10^{600}$!

In both these examples, the levels of precision ($1 \times 10^{37}$ and $1 \times 10^{600}$) are much greater than the precision required to convince people jet engines are safely designed ($1 \times 10^7$). So why isn't the obvious conclusion taught in our schools as possible explanations for the origin of our universe and of life: that it was created by a Great Designer? Just as with the jet engine, any open-minded person knows design when they see it.

As the noted Cambridge Professor of Astrophysics Sir Frederick Hoyle once said, *"The probability of life originating at random is so miniscule as to make it absurd. The favorable properties of physics on which life depends are in every respect deliberate.*

*It is therefore inevitable that our own measure of intelligence must reflect higher intelligences, even to the limit of God. Such a theory is so obvious that one wonders why it is not widely accepted as being self-evident. The reasons are psychological rather than scientific."*

# THE STATISTICS OF CHRISTIANITY:
## Probability & Precision point to an Intelligent Designer!

**UNIVERSE**
Expansion Rate
Electromagnetic Force
Gravitational Force

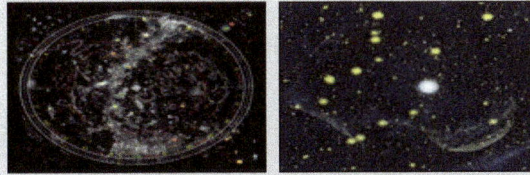

- Electromagnetic-to-Gravitational force = *precise* to $1 \times 10^{40}$ [18]
- Gravitational Constant = *precise* to 5 decimals $(2.00000)$ [18]
- Universe Expansion rate = *precise* to $1 \times 10^{55}$ [18]

**MILKY WAY, SOLAR SYSTEM**

Earth — Milky Way Galaxy

Solar System

- Stars: *odds*- only .001% have the right location and have host star properties that could support life [18]
- Milky Way is spiral galaxy = req'd for life to exist (*odds* are only 5% of all galaxies are spiral) [18]

**SUN, EARTH**

- Earth *precise* tilt = $23.5° \pm 1.2°$ [18]
- Sun's *precise* energy output = constant to 0.1% [18]

**BODY, MIND, BRAIN**

Human brain: A. cerebrum; B. cerebellum.

- my brain's *precision*: 1,000x storage capacity of a supercomputer; holds and sorts $10^{14}$ bits of information [15]
- *odds* that a human being formed by *chance* = $1 \times 10^{2,000,000,000}$ [15]

**HEART, EYE, EAR**

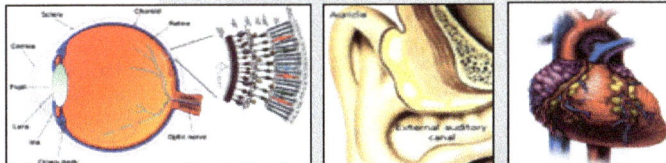

- 100 years of supercomputer processing to simulate the *precision* of what occurs in my eye millions of times every second [15,16]
- no one knows what causes my heart's *precise* "auto-rhythmic" beat 100,000X/day, so I can have life [15]

**BLOOD CELL**

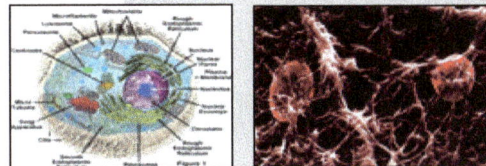

- Blood Clotting: *odds* of getting just the one factor TPA and its activator to work = $1 \times 10^{31}$ (there are at least 32 others) [16]
- Each cell has an all-powerful city hall (nucleus) surrounded by communication centers, factories, power plants, with the complete DNA for my unique design [15]

**DNA, ATP**

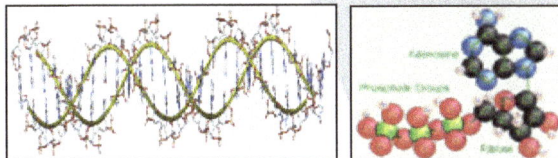

- DNA code formation = 1 in $10^{600}$ by *chance* [15]
- ATP = mini "motors" 200,000X smaller than a pinhead spinning at 6,000 rpm (faster than any made-made engines) [15]
- *odds* of all proteins needed for life might be formed in one place by random events = $1 \times 10^{40,000}$ [15]

**Matter**
Atoms, Molecules

**Nuclear Forces**
Strong nuclear force
Weak nuclear force

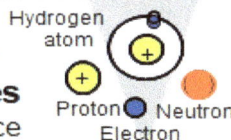

Hydrogen atom
Proton   Neutron
Electron

- Strong nuclear force = *precise* to 2% [18]
- neutron-to-proton mass = *precise* to 0.1% [18]
- #electrons-to-protons = *precise* to $1 \times 10^{37}$ [18]

---

*"The probability of life originating at random is so utterly miniscule as to make it absurd...*
*The favorable properties of physics on which life depends are in every respect deliberate...*
*It is therefore almost inevitable that our own measure of intelligence must reflect higher intelligences...*
*Even to the limit of God ... such a theory is so obvious that one wonders why it is not widely accepted*
*as being self-evident. The reasons are psychological rather than scientific."*

(Fred Hoyle, Cambridge Professor of Astrophysics and Natural Philosophy, 1981)

**Exit Ticket #27     Class 27: Statistics of Christianity  Part 1**

| | |
|---|---|
| **1) What is the difference between Precision and Fine Tuning?** | **2) Explain the deductive argument for God's Existence by comparing precision to fine tuning?** |
| **3) When it comes to the Earth's finely-tuned axial rotation, what is the best explanation for its upper and lower limits?** | **4) What is Professor Fred Hoyle's conclusion from the fine tuning in the universe?** |

# Class 28: Statistics of Christianity, Part 2

Linear Regression: Relating Cause to Effect

Linear Regression: Hubble Law

Probability Science: Accuracy plus Precision

Stability Factor: Quantifying Precision

Fine-Tuning: Where Average = Target with High Stability Factor

Probability Plotting: Detecting Precision

Fine-Tuning of Constants

Information Processing

The Cell: City of Information Processing Machines

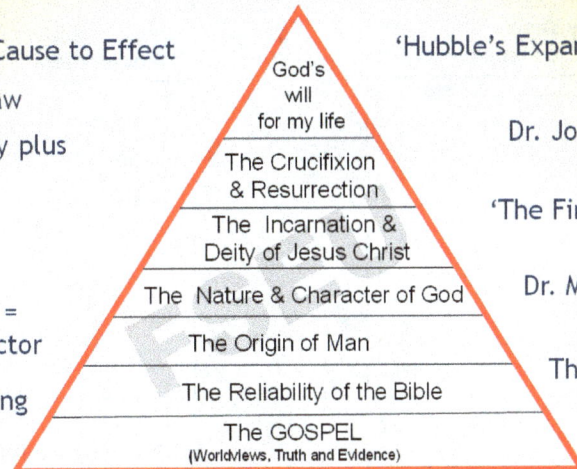

God's will for my life

The Crucifixion & Resurrection

The Incarnation & Deity of Jesus Christ

The Nature & Character of God

The Origin of Man

The Reliability of the Bible

The GOSPEL
(Worldviews, Truth and Evidence)

## HEBREWS 11:1

"Faith = *Substance* of things *hoped for*.... *Evidence* of things *not seen*"

**fse.life Lessons 02 - 08**

'Hubble's Expanding Universe Red Shifts, The Big Bang' (4:14)

Dr. John Lennox: 'Design of the Universe' (1:43)

'The Fine Tuning of the Universe' (6:26)

Dr. Mark Eastman: 'Something from Nothing' (8:30)

The Workhouse of the Cell - Kinesin (3:32)

Science Uprising - DNA (6:35)

# Applying Statistics to Search for Truth

## 9 Techniques

1. "6 Sigma"
2. Descriptive Statistics
3. Precision vs. Fine Tuning    Universal Expansion
4. Process Capability    Earth Axial Tilt
5. Linear Regression    Hubble Law
6. Stability Factor    Fine Tuned Constants
7. Probability Plot
8. System Design (Top Down)    Human Eye, Cell
9. Throughput Yield    Fulfilled Prophecy

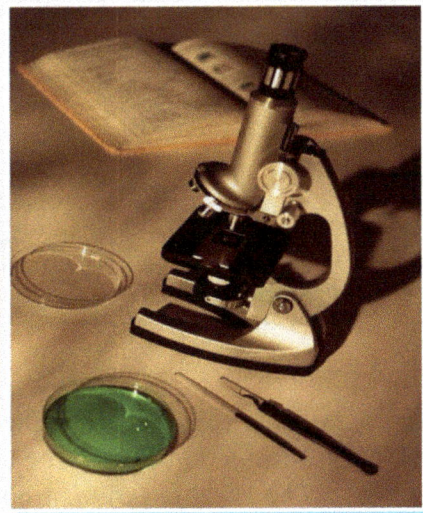

## The Science of Statistical Analysis = Very useful in strengthening your faith in God's existence!

Courtesy of Google Images    Fair Use Law 17 U.S. Code § 107

# Linear Regression: Relating the Cause to an Effect

### Trend Graph by Year:
### Government Spending vs. Unemployment

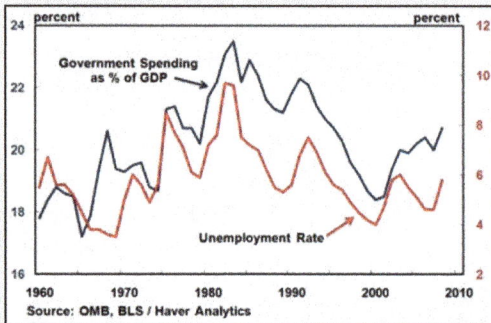

Government Spending as % of GDP

Unemployment Rate

Source: OMB, BLS / Haver Analytics

### Linear Regression Model:
### Government Spending vs. Unemployment

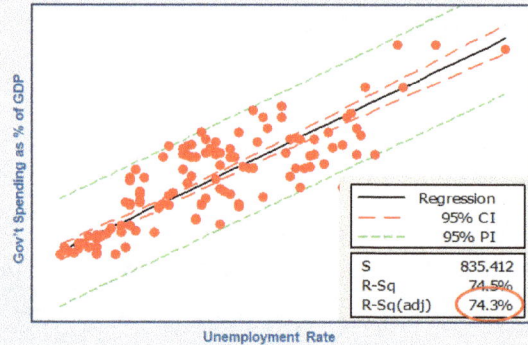

Gov't Spending as % of GDP

Unemployment Rate

| | Regression |
| | 95% CI |
| | 95% PI |

| S | 835.412 |
| R-Sq | 74.5% |
| R-Sq(adj) | 74.3% |

When people *see* a *pattern* of relationship in the data between two variables, they intuitively *think* there is a relationship between them (i.e., 'Cause & Effect')

Linear Regression can calculate a *numeric value* for the level of *probability* that there is a causal relationship  (i.e., 'Cause & Effect')

**Use this approach to examine if God exists:
1) The Expansion Rate of the Universe, 2) The Laws of Causality**

Technique = Simple Linear Regression

Courtesy of Google Images     Fair Use Law 17 U.S. Code § 107

# Linear Regression: The Hubble Law of Expansion

Astronomer Edwin Hubble used linear regression to show the relationship between

1) *radial velocities* of galaxies and
2) their *distance* from each other.

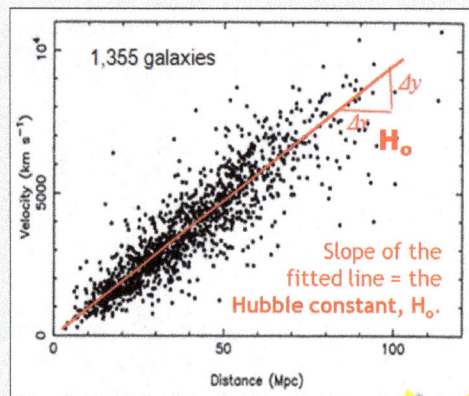

1,355 galaxies

Velocity (km s⁻¹)

Distance (Mpc)

$\Delta y$
$\Delta x$
$H_o$

Slope of the fitted line = the **Hubble constant, $H_o$.**

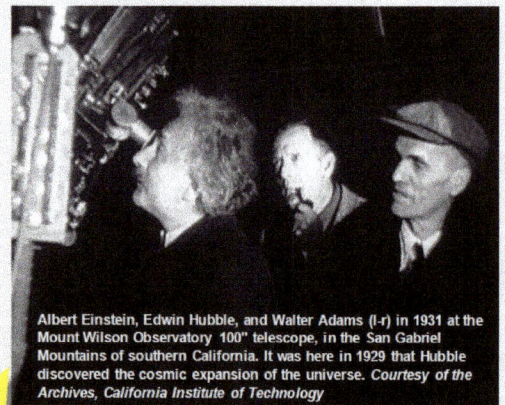

Albert Einstein, Edwin Hubble, and Walter Adams (l-r) in 1931 at the Mount Wilson Observatory 100" telescope, in the San Gabriel Mountains of southern California. It was here in 1929 that Hubble discovered the cosmic expansion of the universe. *Courtesy of the Archives, California Institute of Technology*

**Robert Jastrow (1925-2008), Director of NASA's Goddard Institute for Space Studies:** *"The Hubble Law is one of the great discoveries in science; it is one of the main supports of the scientific story of Genesis."*

'Hubble's Expanding Universe Red Shifts, The Big Bang' (4:14)

Why did Hubble's Law move Einstein's worldview from Atheism to Deism?

**The evidence for Expansion convinced Einstein that there was a 'First Cause' for the Universe!**

Technique = Simple Linear Regression

Courtesy of Google Images     Fair Use Law 17 U.S. Code § 107

# Probability Science:   Accuracy plus Precision

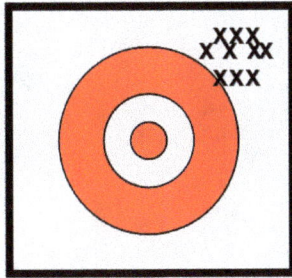

**Precise but not Accurate**          **Accurate but not Precise**          **Accurate and Precise**

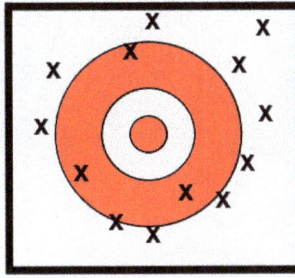

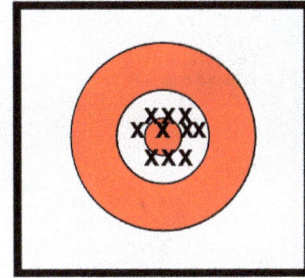

### The World of Statistics and Probability Science:
**Accuracy may happen in nature or random events, but...**
*Accuracy plus Precision is a product of Intelligence*

## Where we can use this approach in examining the Existence of God:
### 1) The Cell,     2) DNA,     3) Animal systems,
### 4) Precision in the universe (motions and forces)

Technique = Descriptive Statistics

Courtesy of Google Images    Fair Use Law 17 U.S. Code § 107

---

# Stability Factor:   Quantifying Precision

## What's the "Precision" or "Stability" Factor in Statistics?

- The "Stability" or "Precision" Factor is simply the ratio of $Q_1$ to $Q_3$:  **$SF = Q_1 / Q_3$**

- It is used in statistics to get an idea of how precise or stable a process performs.

- $Q_1$ = the 1st Quartile (25% of data)

- $Q_3$ = the 3rd Quartile (75% of data) - it also contains the $Q_1$ data.

- Here's what's cool:

The closer the $Q_1$ value is to the $Q_3$ value, the closer SF is to a value of "1".

The closer SF is to "1.0", the *TIGHTER* the bell curve.

The tighter the bell curve, the more repeatable or *PRECISE* the process behaves over time.

## The Fine-Tuned 'Constants' in the Universe: 'SF = .999999999' !!

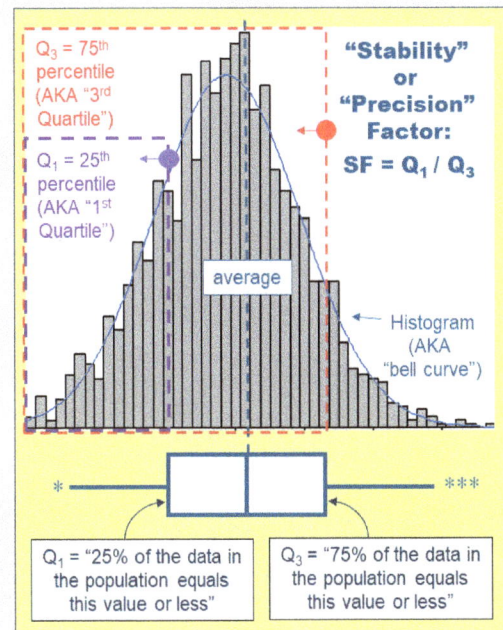

$Q_3$ = 75th percentile (AKA "3rd Quartile")

$Q_1$ = 25th percentile (AKA "1st Quartile")

**"Stability" or "Precision" Factor:** $SF = Q_1 / Q_3$

average

Histogram (AKA "bell curve")

| $Q_1$ = "25% of the data in the population equals this value or less" | $Q_3$ = "75% of the data in the population equals this value or less" |
|---|---|

Dr. John Lennox: 'Design of the Universe' (1:43)          Technique = Precision or Stability Factor          Courtesy of Google Images    Fair Use Law 17 U.S. Code § 107

# Fine-Tuning:  Where Average = Target with High Stability Factor

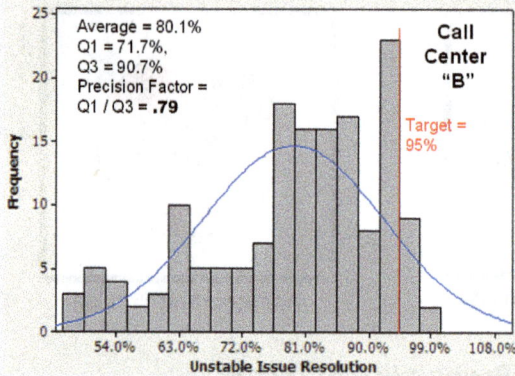

Average = 80.1%
Q1 = 71.7%,
Q3 = 90.7%
Precision Factor =
Q1 / Q3 = **.79**

Call Center "B"

Target = 95%

**Unstable Issue Resolution**

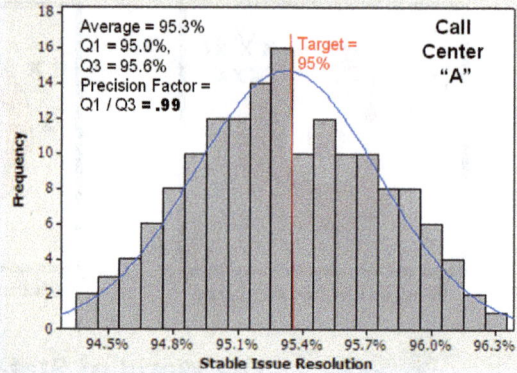

Average = 95.3%
Q1 = 95.0%,
Q3 = 95.6%
Precision Factor =
Q1 / Q3 = **.99**

Call Center "A"

Target = 95%

**Stable Issue Resolution**

Any measurable process whose average misses it's required target and it's 'spread' has a <u>low precision factor</u> is '<u>out of control</u>' to the target. Our intuition tells us that process is *UNGUIDED*.

Any measurable process whose average hits it's required target *AND* it's 'spread' has a <u>high precision factor</u>, that process is '<u>in control</u>'. Our intuition tells us there is *DESIGN* to that process.

**Where we can use this approach to examine if God might exist:**
**1) Finely-Tuned Universal Constants**

Technique = Stability Factor

Courtesy of Google Images     Fair Use Law 17 U.S. Code § 107

# Probability Plotting:  Detecting Precision

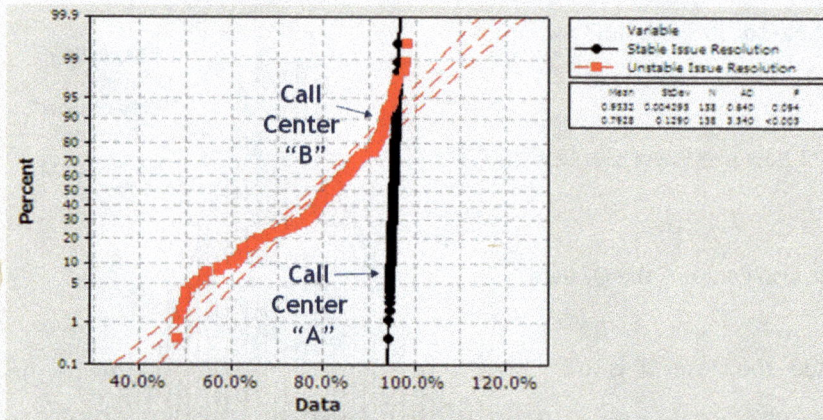

Call Center "B"

Call Center "A"

**Data**

Variable
— Stable Issue Resolution
— Unstable Issue Resolution

| Mean | StDev | N | AD | P |
|------|-------|---|----|---|
| 0.9532 | 0.004595 | 138 | 0.640 | 0.094 |
| 0.7928 | 0.1390 | 138 | 3.340 | <0.005 |

Center "A": Avg =    0.95
(Stable)      StDev = 0.004
$Q_1 = 0.95$, $Q_3 = 0.96$
$SF = Q_1 / Q_3 = $ **99%**

Center "B": Avg =    0.79
(Unstable)   StDev = 0.13
$Q_1 = 0.71$, $Q_3 = 0.91$
$SF = Q_1 / Q_3 = $ **79%**

- Probability plots are used to measure a process's <u>level of stability or precision</u>.
- Here, the same data used to create the histograms for Call Centers "A" and "B" are plotted on a vertical logarithmic scale.
- The more *straight* and *vertical* the data, the more *PRECISE* that process is.
- Call Center "A", with Stable Issue Resolution, is nearly a <u>vertical straight line</u>.

Technique = Probability Plot

Courtesy of Google Images     Fair Use Law 17 U.S. Code § 107

# 9 Finely Tuned *Universal Constants*

| VARIABLE | REQ'd TUNING | OTHERWISE... | LIFE IS... |
|---|---|---|---|
| Cosmological Constant<br>$\Lambda = (2.3 \times 10^{-3} \text{ eV})^{-4}$ | If increase by $1:10^{120}$ | Larger stars and galaxies cannot form | impossible |
| Gravitational Constant<br>$G = 6.674 \times 10^{-11} \text{ m3} \cdot \text{kg}^{-1} \cdot \text{s}^{-2}$ | If increase by $1:10^{34}$<br>If decrease by $1:10^{60}$ | Universe expands too rapidly – no stars<br>Universe collapses on itself – no stars | impossible |
| Mass Density of Universe<br>$\Omega = 9.9 \times 10^{-30} \text{ g/cm}^3$ (5.9 protons/m³) | If increase by $1:10^{34}$<br>If decrease by $1:10^{59}$ | If too much De: Stars burn too rapidly<br>If too little He: Too few heavy elements | impossible |
| Universal Expansion Rate<br>$H_o = 71 \pm 1$ km/sec/mpc | If increase by $1:10^{55}$<br>If decrease by $1:10^{55}$ | Matter can't clump – no galaxies<br>Matter clumps – universe collapses | impossible |
| #Electrons = #Protons  $N \approx 1.57 \times 10^{79}$<br>(universe has neutral charge) | If increase by $1:10^{37}$<br>If decrease by $1:10^{37}$ | Galaxies, stars, planets cannot form | impossible |
| Mass Ratio: Neutron (939.565 MeV)<br>to Proton (938.272 MeV) = .138% | If neutron 0.1%<br>less massive... | Universe collapses into either<br>neutron stars or black holes | impossible |
| Stable Decay Rate of a Proton<br>(half-life of $10^{32}$ years) | If greater...<br>If smaller... | Life exterminated by radiation<br>Not enough matter for life | impossible |
| Ground state energies<br>of He, Be, C, $O_2$ | If higher by 4%<br>If lower by 4% | Universe with too little oxygen<br>Universe with too little carbon | impossible |
| Initial Uniformity of Cosmic Back-<br>ground Radiation (balanced to 1x10⁵) | If smoother...<br>If coarser... | Stars and galaxies wouldn't form<br>Universe = black holes, emptiness | impossible |

Mass Density determines how efficiently nuclear fusion operates in universe        Cosmological Constant: "Dark Energy"; energy density of empty space; could account for accelerating universe

## Exit Ticket #28    <mark>Class 28: Statistics of Christianity  Part 2</mark>

| | |
|---|---|
| **1) Why did Hubble's Law move Einstein's worldview from Atheism to Deism?** | **2) What is the difference between accuracy and precision?** |
| **3) How does the Stability Factor Quantify Precision?** | **4) Of the 9 finely tuned constants in this lesson, which 1-2 resonate the most with you and why?** |

# Class 29:  Statistics of Christianity, Part 3

System Design (Top Down, not Bottom Up)

Information Processing and the Design Argument

The Cell: A City of Information-Processing MACHINES

Throughput Yield: Jet Engine Manufacturing

Throughput Yield: Fulfilled Prophecy

20 Evidences: Messianic Prophecies Fulfilled in Jesus Christ

Fulfilled Prophecy: Putting Things in Perspective

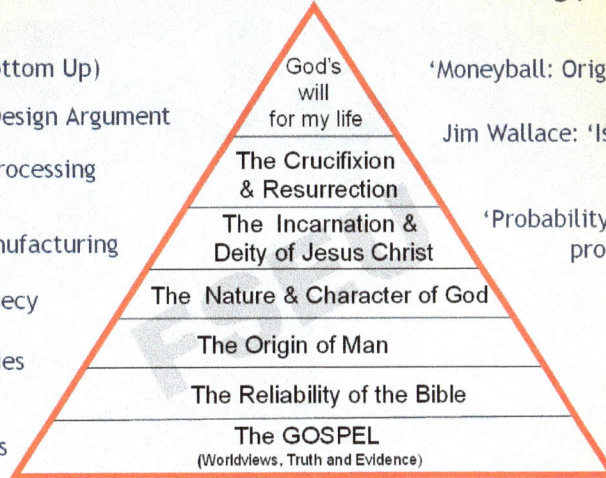

'Moneyball: Origin of the Method' (2:00)

Jim Wallace: 'Is Christianity Rational?' (3:40)

'Probability of a cell evolving – the programming of life' (7:46)

God's will for my life

The Crucifixion & Resurrection

The Incarnation & Deity of Jesus Christ

The Nature & Character of God

The Origin of Man

The Reliability of the Bible

The GOSPEL
(Worldviews, Truth and Evidence)

# H E B R E W S 11:1

"Faith = *Substance* of things *hoped for.... Evidence* of things *not seen*"

fse.life Lessons 02 - 08

# Applying Statistics to Search for Truth

## 9 Techniques

1. "6 Sigma"
2. Descriptive Statistics
3. Precision vs. Fine Tuning        Universal Expansion
4. Process Capability        Earth Axial Tilt
5. Linear Regression        Hubble Law
6. Stability Factor        Fine Tuned Constants
7. Probability Plot
8. System Design (Top Down)        Human Eye, Cell
9. Throughput Yield        Fulfilled Prophecy

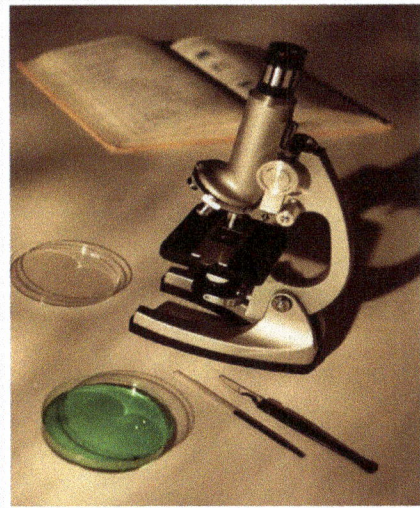

## The Science of Statistical Analysis =
## Very useful in strengthening your faith in God's existence!

# Information Processing and the Design Argument

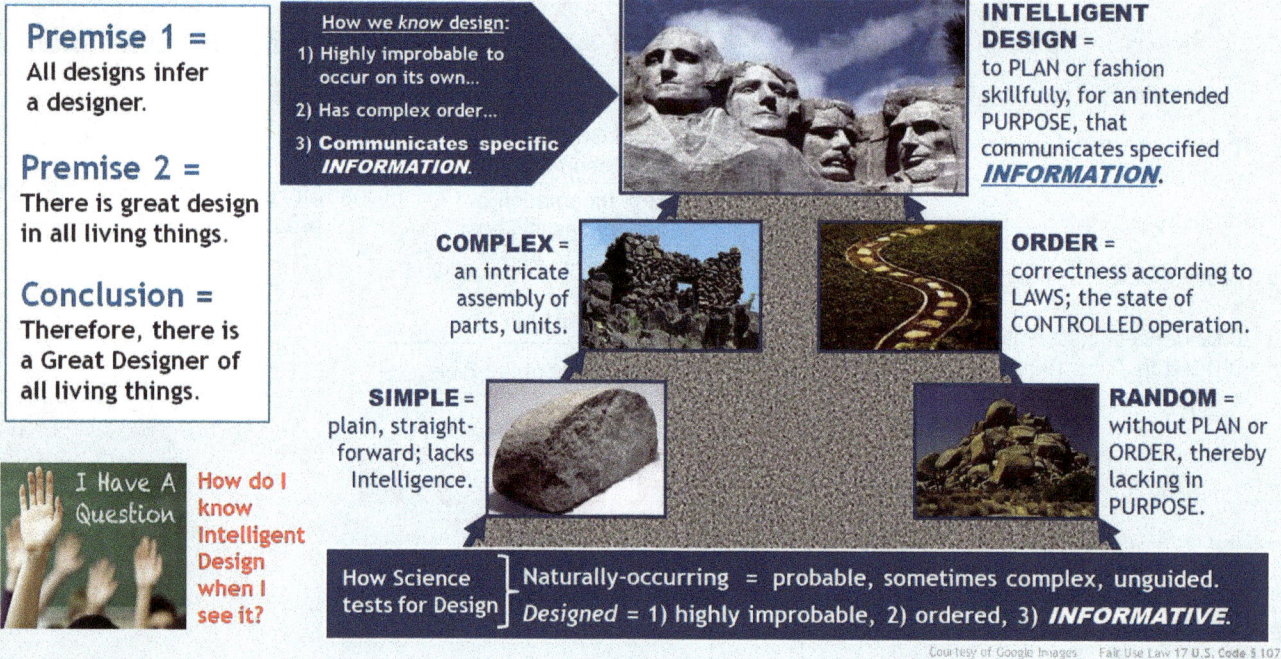

**Premise 1 =**
All designs infer a designer.

**Premise 2 =**
There is great design in all living things.

**Conclusion =**
Therefore, there is a Great Designer of all living things.

*I Have A Question*
**How do I know Intelligent Design when I see it?**

**How we *know* design:**
1) Highly improbable to occur on its own...
2) Has complex order...
3) **Communicates specific *INFORMATION*.**

**INTELLIGENT DESIGN =**
to PLAN or fashion skillfully, for an intended PURPOSE, that communicates specified *INFORMATION*.

**COMPLEX =**
an intricate assembly of parts, units.

**ORDER =**
correctness according to LAWS; the state of CONTROLLED operation.

**SIMPLE =**
plain, straight-forward; lacks Intelligence.

**RANDOM =**
without PLAN or ORDER, thereby lacking in PURPOSE.

**How Science tests for Design**
Naturally-occurring = probable, sometimes complex, unguided.
Designed = 1) highly improbable, 2) ordered, 3) *INFORMATIVE*.

# The Cell: *CITY* of Information-Processing *MACHINES*

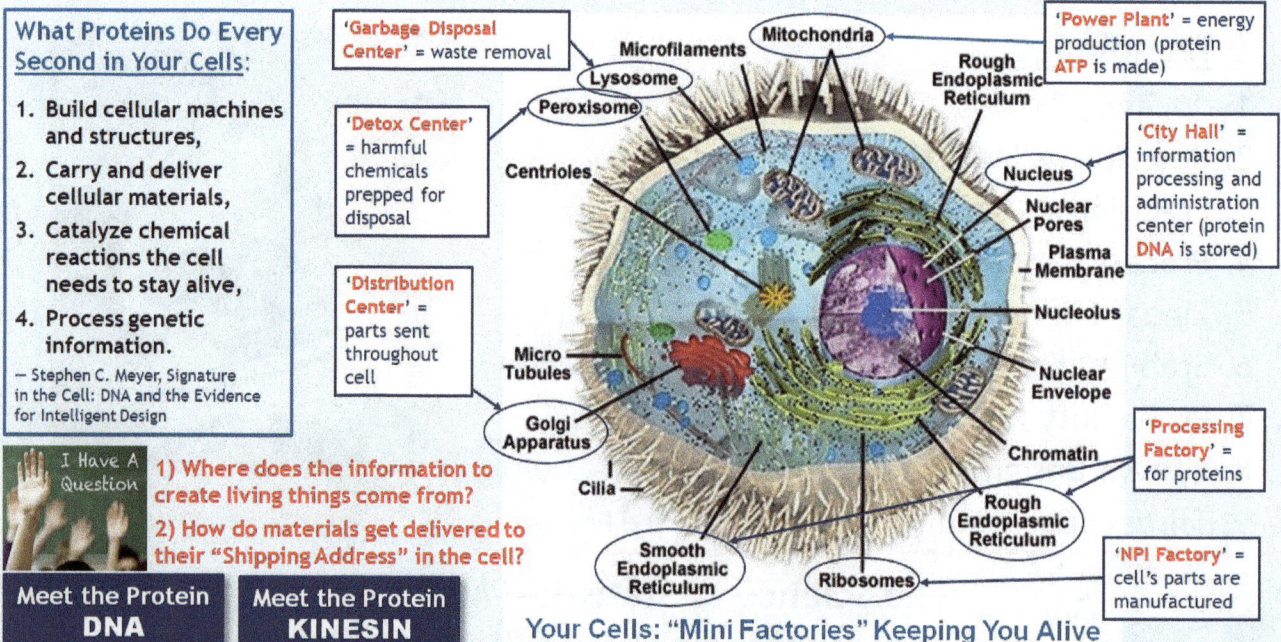

**What Proteins Do Every Second in Your Cells:**

1. **Build cellular machines and structures,**
2. **Carry and deliver cellular materials,**
3. **Catalyze chemical reactions the cell needs to stay alive,**
4. **Process genetic information.**

— Stephen C. Meyer, Signature in the Cell: DNA and the Evidence for Intelligent Design

*I Have A Question*
1) **Where does the information to create living things come from?**
2) **How do materials get delivered to their "Shipping Address" in the cell?**

**Meet the Protein DNA**        **Meet the Protein KINESIN**

**'Garbage Disposal Center'** = waste removal

**'Detox Center'** = harmful chemicals prepped for disposal

**'Distribution Center'** = parts sent throughout cell

**'Power Plant'** = energy production (protein ATP is made)

**'City Hall'** = information processing and administration center (protein DNA is stored)

**'Processing Factory'** = for proteins

**'NPI Factory'** = cell's parts are manufactured

Microfilaments — Mitochondria — Rough Endoplasmic Reticulum

Lysosome — Peroxisome — Centrioles — Nucleus — Nuclear Pores — Plasma Membrane — Nucleolus — Nuclear Envelope — Chromatin — Rough Endoplasmic Reticulum — Micro Tubules — Golgi Apparatus — Cilia — Smooth Endoplasmic Reticulum — Ribosomes

**Your Cells: "Mini Factories" Keeping You Alive**

# Throughput Yield : Jet Engine Manufacturing

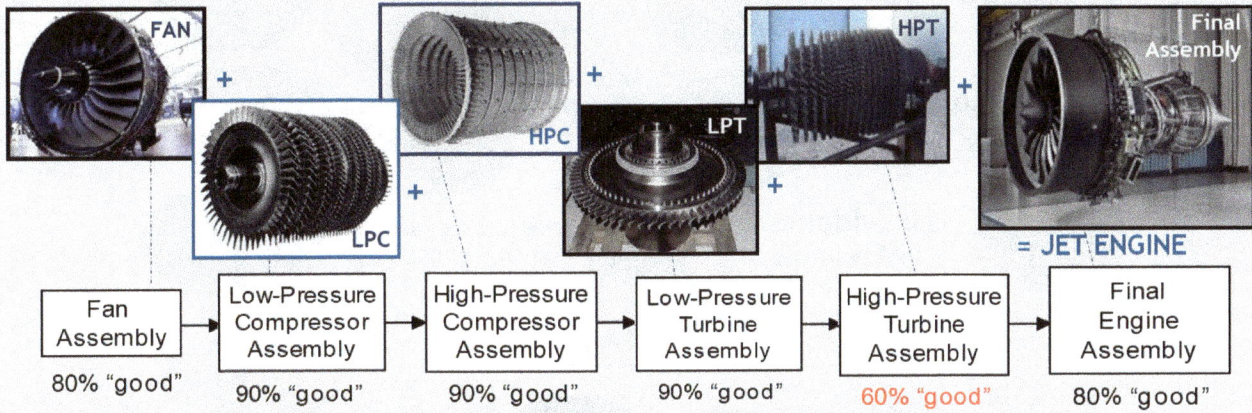

| Fan Assembly | Low-Pressure Compressor Assembly | High-Pressure Compressor Assembly | Low-Pressure Turbine Assembly | High-Pressure Turbine Assembly | Final Engine Assembly |
|---|---|---|---|---|---|
| 80% "good" | 90% "good" | 90% "good" | 90% "good" | 60% "good" | 80% "good" |

"1st Time" = (.80) x (.90) x (.90) x (.90) x (.60) x (.80) = **.28** ← I have a *28% chance* of making a working Jet Engine (a 72% chance of one that fails)!

**Where "Throughout Yield" is used to measure CONTROL/DESIGN in data sets:**
1) Jet Engine Manufacturing   2) Biochemical Irreducible Complexity
3) Jesus Christ fulfilling Messianic Prophecies

**"THROUGHPUT YIELD"**
An event's overall probability of occurring is calculated by MULTIPLYING the individual probabilities of each event together!

Probability of a cell evolving - the programming of life (7:46)          Technique = Throughput Yield          Courtesy of Google Images    Fair Use Law 17 U.S. Code § 107

# Throughput Yield: Fulfilled Prophecy

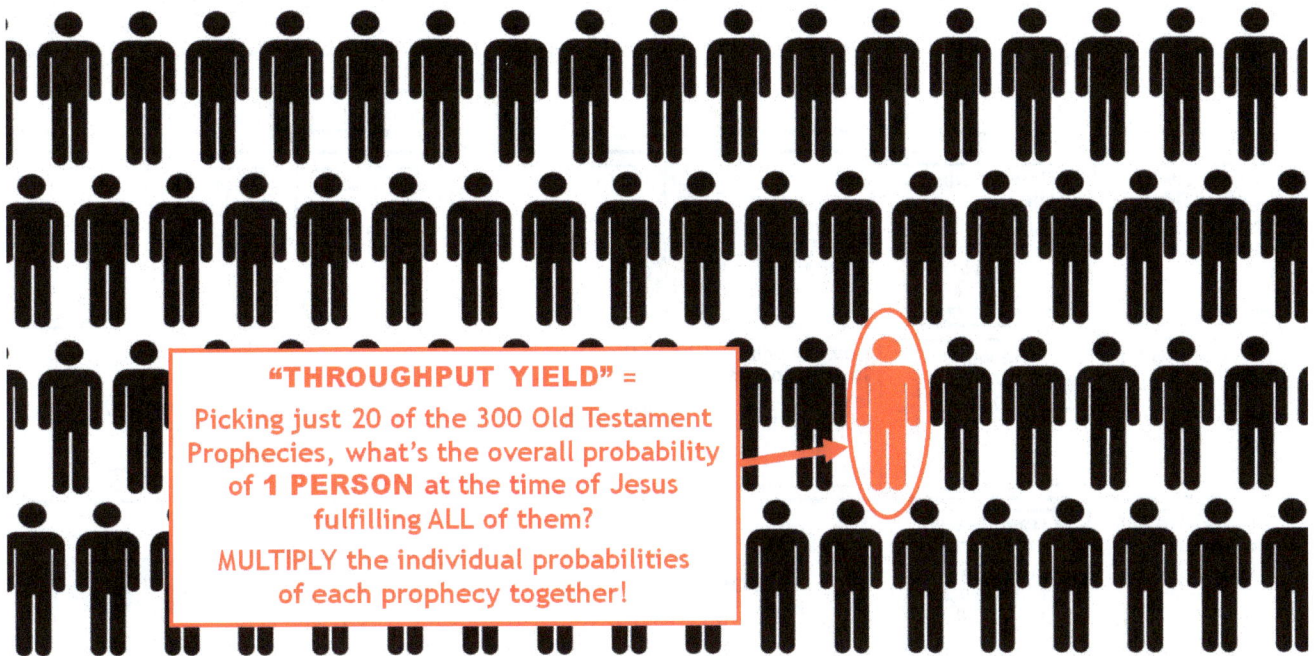

**"THROUGHPUT YIELD"** =

Picking just 20 of the 300 Old Testament Prophecies, what's the overall probability of **1 PERSON** at the time of Jesus fulfilling ALL of them?

MULTIPLY the individual probabilities of each prophecy together!

**#6. How He will Forgive Sin[3]** Scapegoat
Leviticus 16:7-22
Isaiah 53:6 Mark 15:34

**#7. How He will Speak for God**
Prophet
Deuter. 18:18-19,
John 12: 49- 50

**#8. How He will Defeat Death[2]**
Bronze Serpent
Numbers 21:4-9
John 3:14

**#11. How He will Come to Earth**
Virgin Birth
Isaiah 7:14
Matthew 1:18-25

**#5. How He will Forgive Sin[2]**
Wash in Blood
Leviticus 14:1-7 Isaiah
61:1-3 John 8:36, 11:44

**#9. How He will Give Life**
Living Water from the Rock
Numbers 20:7-11
John 4:13-14

**#10. How He will Redeem Us**
God's Curse
Deuter. 21:23,
Galatians 3:13

**#12. From where He will Appear**
Light of Galilee
Isaiah 9:1-2
Matt. 4:12-16
John 1:28,7:52

**#4. How He will Forgive Sin**
Mercy Seat
Exodus 25:16-22
Romans 3:23-26

**20 Evidences: Messianic Prophecies Fulfilled in Jesus Christ**

I Have A Question

What's the Chance that ONE PERSON could have fulfilled all 20 of these Prophecies?

**#13. Who He will Be**
Son of God
Isaiah 9:6-7
John 14:7-9

**#3. How He will Defeat Death**
Passover Lamb
Exodus 12:3-13
John 1:29

**#18. How He will Justify Sinners[2]**
Suffering Servant
Isaiah 53 2Corin.
5:21 1Peter 3:18

JEHOVAH TSIDKENU

**#17. How He will Justify Sinners**
Righteousness of God Jerem. 31:3, 33: 14-18, Luke 1: 76-77, Romans 3:23-26

**#14. How He will be Announced**
Forerunner
Isaiah 40:3-5
John 1:6-9,19-23

**#2. His Ancestry**
Abraham thru David
Genesis, Isaiah, Jeremiah Matthew, Luke

**#15. Who He will Be[2]**
Son of Man
Daniel 7:13-14
Mark 14:61-64

**#1. How He will Die** Crucifixion
Genesis 3:15 Psalm 22
Zechariah 12:10
Mark 15:25

**#20. How He will enter Jerusalem**
King on a Donkey
Zech. 9:9
Matthew 21:1-9

**#19. Where He will Be Born**
Bethlehem Ephrathah
Micah 5:2
Matthew 2:3-6

**#16. When He will Show Up**
First Coming
Daniel 9:24-26,
Luke 19:41-44

Courtesy of Google Images      Fair Use Law 17 U.S. Code § 107

# Throughput Yield:  Fulfilled Prophecy

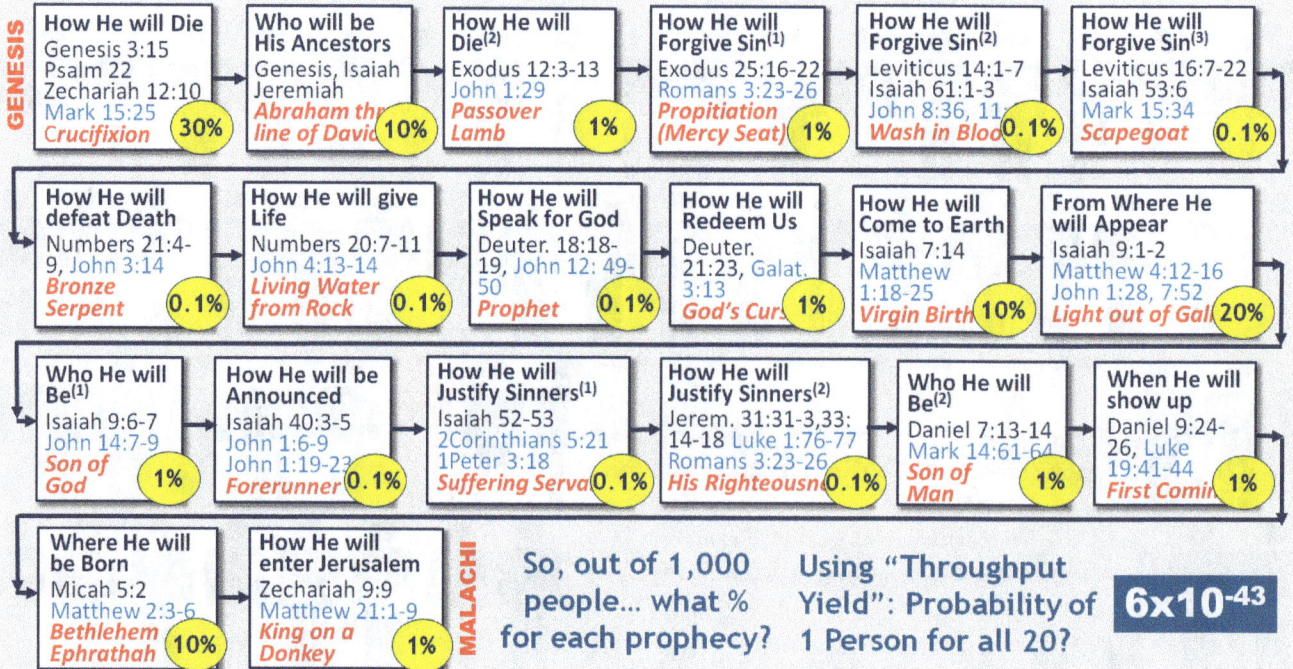

**GENESIS**

| How He will Die | Who will be His Ancestors | How He will Die[2] | How He will Forgive Sin[1] | How He will Forgive Sin[2] | How He will Forgive Sin[3] |
|---|---|---|---|---|---|
| Genesis 3:15 Psalm 22 Zechariah 12:10 Mark 15:25 *Crucifixion* **30%** | Genesis, Isaiah Jeremiah *Abraham thru line of David* **10%** | Exodus 12:3-13 John 1:29 *Passover Lamb* **1%** | Exodus 25:16-22 Romans 3:23-26 *Propitiation (Mercy Seat)* **1%** | Leviticus 14:1-7 Isaiah 61:1-3 John 8:36, 11:44 *Wash in Blood* **0.1%** | Leviticus 16:7-22 Isaiah 53:6 Mark 15:34 *Scapegoat* **0.1%** |

| How He will defeat Death | How He will give Life | How He will Speak for God | How He will Redeem Us | How He will Come to Earth | From Where He will Appear |
|---|---|---|---|---|---|
| Numbers 21:4-9, John 3:14 *Bronze Serpent* **0.1%** | Numbers 20:7-11 John 4:13-14 *Living Water from Rock* **0.1%** | Deuter. 18:18-19, John 12: 49-50 *Prophet* **0.1%** | Deuter. 21:23, Galat. 3:13 *God's Curse* **1%** | Isaiah 7:14 Matthew 1:18-25 *Virgin Birth* **10%** | Isaiah 9:1-2 Matthew 4:12-16 John 1:28, 7:52 *Light out of Galilee* **20%** |

| Who He will Be[1] | How He will be Announced | How He will Justify Sinners[1] | How He will Justify Sinners[2] | Who He will Be[2] | When He will show up |
|---|---|---|---|---|---|
| Isaiah 9:6-7 John 14:7-9 *Son of God* **1%** | Isaiah 40:3-5 John 1:6-9 John 1:19-23 *Forerunner* **0.1%** | Isaiah 52-53 2Corinthians 5:21 1Peter 3:18 *Suffering Servant* **0.1%** | Jerem. 31:31-3,33: 14-18 Luke 1:76-77 Romans 3:23-26 *His Righteousness* **0.1%** | Daniel 7:13-14 Mark 14:61-64 *Son of Man* **1%** | Daniel 9:24-26, Luke 19:41-44 *First Coming* **1%** |

**MALACHI**

| Where He will be Born | How He will enter Jerusalem | | |
|---|---|---|---|
| Micah 5:2 Matthew 2:3-6 *Bethlehem Ephrathah* **10%** | Zechariah 9:9 Matthew 21:1-9 *King on a Donkey* **1%** | **So, out of 1,000 people… what % for each prophecy?** | **Using "Throughput Yield": Probability of 1 Person for all 20?**  $6 \times 10^{-43}$ |

Courtesy of Google Images      Fair Use Law 17 U.S. Code § 107

# Fulfilled Prophecy: Putting Things in Perspective

## With Jet Engines...

**What does *"28% chance to make a working jet engine"* mean?**

**Out of every 3 engines we build, 1 works.**

Wow... that sucks

## With Old Testament Prophecies...

**What does *"6x10⁻⁴³ chance to find 1 person who fulfilled all 20 prophecies"* mean?**

0.000000000000000000000000000000000000000006

SO YOU'RE TELLING ME

THERE'S A CHANCE

| | |
|---|---|
| # people in the world = | $8 \times 10^9$ = 8,000,000,000 |
| # grains of sand in the world = | $7.5 \times 10^{18}$ = 1,000,000,000,000,000,000 |
| # insects in the world = | $1.0 \times 10^{19}$ = 10,000,000,000,000,000,000 |

Out of 1,000,000,000,000,000,000,000,000,000,000,000,000,000,000 (**$1.0 \times 10^{42}$**) people, **ONE** will be found to fulfill all 20 prophecies.

Courtesy of Google Images     Fair Use Law 17 U.S. Code § 107

## Exit Ticket #29    Class 29: Statistics of Christianity Part 3

| | |
|---|---|
| **1) How is an event's overall probability of occurring calculated with Throughput Yield?** | **2) Of the 20 Messianic Prophecies listed, which 1-2 prophecies resonate the most with you and why?** |
| **3) In Throughput Yield calculation for fulfilled prophecy, are any probabilities on individual prophecies skeptical to you?** | **4) Why is Throughput Yield a powerful argument for Jesus Christ as the only Person to fulfill prophecy?** |

# REFERENCES

1. Charles Darwin — "The Origin of the Species" — Bantam Books — 1859
2. John Stott — "Your Mind Matters" — Inter-Varsity Press Books — 1972
3. Nancy Pearcey — "Total Truth" — Crossway Books — 2004
4. Greg Koukl — "Tactics" — Zondervan Publishers — 2009
5. Antony Flew — "There is A God" — Harper One Publishers — 2007
6. F. Turek, N. Geisler — "I Don't have…Faith to be an Atheist" — Crossway Books — 2004
7. Thomas Nagel — "Mind & Cosmos" — Oxford University Press — 2012
8. John Ankerberg — "Darwin's Leap of Faith" — Harvest House Publishers — 1998
9. Philip Johnson — "Darwin on Trial" — Inter-Varsity Press Books — 1991
10. M.R. DeHann, MD — "Portraits of Christ in Genesis" — Zondervan Publishers — 2002
11. Josh McDowell — "Evidence that Demands A Verdict" — Here's Life Publishing — 1986
12. Norman Geisler — "When Skeptics Ask" — Baker Book Publishers — 2008
13. Dinesh D'Souza — "What's So Great About Christianity" — Tyndale House Publishers — 2007
14. Hugh Ross, PhD — "The Creator and the Cosmos" — Navpress Publishers — 1993
15. Richard A. Swenson, M.D. — "More than meets the Eye" — Navpress Publishers — 2000
16. Michael J. Behe, PhD — "Darwin's Black Box" — Touchstone Books — 1996
17. Michael Patton — "Representing Christ to Postmodern" — www.Bible.org — 2004
18. Henry M. Morris, PhD — "Scientific Creationism" — Creation-Life Publishers — 1974
19. Michael Denton, PhD — "Evolution: A Theory in Crisis" — Adler and Adler Publishers — 1986
20. Steve Herzig/ Ken Ham — "On Darwin and Evolution" — Israel My Glory, July/ August — 2005
21. Jonathan Wells, PhD — "Icons of Evolution" — Regnery Publishing, Inc. — 2000
22. Lee Strobel — "The Case for a Creator" — Zondervan Publishers — 2004
23. G.S. McLean — "The Evidence for Creation" — Understand the Times Publisher — 1995
24. A.E. Wilder Smith, PhD — "Man's Origin, Man's Destiny" — Bethany House Publishers — 1968
25. John MacArthur — "The Gospel According to Jesus" — Zondervan Publishers — 1994
26. John MacArthur — "The Battle for the Beginning" — Word Publishing Group — 2001
27. Tim Osterholm — "The Table of Nations" — www.soundchristian.com — 2005
28. Mark Robinson — "Israel: God's Answer to Skeptics" — Israel My Glory, June/ July — 2006
29. Norman Geisler — "Christian Apologetics" — Baker Book Publishers — 1989
30. Duane Arthur Schmidt — "And God Created Darwin" — Allegiance Press — 2001
31. Bertrand Russell — "Why I am not a Christian" — Simon & Schuster — 1957
32. Ergun & Emir Caner — "Unveiling Islam" — Kregel Publications — 2002
33. Walter Martin — "The Kingdom of the Cults" — Bethany House Publishers — 1985
34. John Stott — "Basic Christianity" — Eerdsman Publishing — 1971

## Book 1  Additional Reading

1. F.F. Bruce — "The Canon of Scripture" — Intervarsity Press — 1988
2. Timothy Keller — "The Reason for God" — Riverhead Books — 2008
3. Henry M. Morris, PhD — "Many Infallible Proofs" — Master Books — 1974
4. Henry M. Morris, PhD — "The Genesis Record" — Baker Book Publishers — 1976
5. A.E. Wilder Smith, PhD — "He who Thinks has to Believe" — TWFT Publishing — 1981
6. Hugh Ross, PhD — "The Fingerprint of God" — Navpress Publishers — 1993
7. William Lane Craig, PhD — "On Guard" — David C Cook Distributors — 2010
8. Jay W. Richards, PhD — "The Privileged Planet" — Regnery Publishing, Inc. — 2004
9. J. Warner Wallace — "God's Crime Scene" — David C Cook Distributors — 2015
10. Josh McDowell — "Beyond Belief to Convictions" — Tyndale House Publishers — 2002
11. Chuck Colson, N. Pearcey — "How Now Shall We Live?" — Tyndale House Publishers — 1999
12. John C. Lennox — "God and Stephen Hawking" — Lion Books — 2011
13. Henry M. Morris, PhD — "Biblical Creationism" — Baker Book Publishers — 1993
14. Robert Jastrow — "God and the Astronomers" — W.W. Norton & Co, Inc. — 1978
15. Charles Darwin — "The Descent of Man" — Bantam Books — 1871
16. Nabeel Qureshi — "No God But One – Allah or Jesus?" — Zondervan Publishers — 2016

## Glossary of Terms ➔ CULTURE, TRUTH & LOGIC

**1. Philosophy** = The study of the truths and principles of being, knowledge or conduct.

**2. Metaphysics** = The branch of philosophy focusing on the ultimate source of existence, reality, and experience, that exists outside the realm of the physical laws of the universe (it literally means "that which is after or beyond physics").

**3. Ontology** = The branch of metaphysics that studies the nature of existence.

**4. Teleology** = (from the Greek word "*telos*", meaning "end or purpose") The philosophical study of design, purpose, directive principle, or finality in nature or human creations. It is traditionally contrasted with metaphysical naturalism, which views nature as lacking design or purpose. In opposition to      this, teleology holds there is a final cause or purpose inherent in all beings.

**5. Epistemology** = The Study of "How We Know" (how people determine what is TRUE for them)

**6. Correspondence Test for Truth** = Truth claim must conform to objective features of the world (i.e. reality, or facts). Truth about reality is what corresponds to the way things really are. Truth is "telling it like it is." There is a reality, and truth accurately expresses it. Falsehood tells or claims things like they are not, misrepresenting the facts or the way things are.

**7. Coherence Test for Truth** = Truth claim must make sense when measured against competing claims on the same belief or topic. Truth is rational or logical when it is self-consistent within some set of propositions or beliefs. It allows the evidence for competing claims to be weighed against each other. But, by itself it is inadequate for testing truth. For example, to say "All bachelors are unmarried men" is by itself consistent, but it does not tell us anything about reality. The statement would be true, even if there were no bachelors.

**8. Logic** = The art and science of reasoning to discover truth. Method of reasoning involving thinking through what we hear/observe to then reach conclusions.

**9. Formal Logic** = Also known as Deductive Logic. First developed by Aristotle as the basis behind Western philosophy, it is the evaluation of an argument's <u>structure</u>, presented in a set of premises that lead to a conclusion. Each premise must stand on its own (i.e., be true) in a logical sequence of premises in order to move from "truth-to-truth" towards the conclusion. The Conclusion will always follow with certainty (valid or invalid) from the premises.

**10. Premise** = A statement or proposition that can be demonstrated to be true.

**11. Informal Logic** = Also known as Inductive Logic. The evaluation of an argument's <u>content</u>, presented in a group of evidences, to support a conclusion. We evaluate the weight and relevance of the evidence presented to reach a conclusion. The Conclusion does not follow with certainty (as in deductive argument being valid versus invalid) but rather probability (weak versus strong). While Deductive Logic argues from structure, Inductive Logic argues from evidence.

**12. Evidence** = Available information or facts to help determine if the conclusion is true.

**13. Rhetoric** = Art form of argument used to persuade an audience. 3 types of Rhetorical Argument:
(1) Logos = Evidence-based, (2) Ethos = Expert's knowledge Speaker's charisma, (3) Pathos = Emotion-based (my feelings)

**14. Properly Basic Beliefs** = beliefs that do not need an argument to be true – they are reasonable to hold on their own (experience of sadness or joy).
While you would be wrong to argue God exists because you've had a religious experience (example: Mormons argue God exists because of the "warming of the bosom"), it is properly basic since through the internal witness of the Holy Spirit, Christians have an objective knowledge of Jesus Christ as their personal Lord & Savior (John 3:3).

**15. Preceding Beliefs** = beliefs that must be validated to be true (religious experiences, your belief on abortion).

**16. Knowledge** = Facts and information gained about a subject. The theoretical or practical understanding of a subject.

**17. A Priori Knowledge** = Means "from that which comes before", it is knowledge existing in your mind before experiencing or observing the physical world. It is knowledge that is gained based on "self-evident" truths that everyone agrees with (it's a "given").

**18. A Posteriori Knowledge** = Means "from that which comes later", it is knowledge coming from experiencing/observing the physical world. It is knowledge that is gained by reasoning the "most probable" explanation (it is not a "given").

**19. Acquired Knowledge** = Information/understanding about something a person has gained through study, observation or experience (reality of physical objects, learning to ride a bike).

**20. Acquainted Knowledge** = information/understanding about something a person has gained by direct or non-inferential access (feeling physical pain, dreams).

**21. Propositional Knowledge** = information/understanding about something a person has gained through a coded or formal language (learning Spanish, logic, mathematics, human genome).

**22. Worldview** = A translation of the German word 'Weltanschauung', which means 'a way of looking at the world ('welt' = world; 'schauen' = to look). German Romanticism developed the idea that cultures are complex wholes, where a certain outlook on life, or spirit of the age, is expressed across the board – in art, literature, and social institutions as well as formal philosophy. The best way to understand the products of any culture is to grasp the underlying worldview being expressed.
 Our worldview is not something abstract and academic, but intensely personal. Our worldview is the way we answer the core questions of life that everyone must struggle with: For what are we here? What is ultimate truth? Is there anything worth living for? The purpose of a worldview is to explain the world – and if it fails to explain some part of the world, then there is something wrong with that worldview.

**23. Biblical Worldview** = An outlook on life that gives rise to distinctively Christian forms of culture, with the important qualification that it is not merely the relativistic belief of a particular culture but is based on the very Word of God, true for all times and places (see more details in Nancy Pearcey's answer to the question "What is a Biblical Worldview?").

**24. Secular Humanism** = A world view with the following six main principles:
a) a conviction that dogmas, ideologies, and Humanism traditions, whether religious, political, or social, must be weighed and tested by each individual and not simply accepted on faith.
b) a commitment to the use of critical reason, facts, and scientific methods of inquiry, rather than faith and mysticism, in seeking solutions to human problems and answers to important human questions.
c) a concern for only this life.
d) a commitment to making this life meaningful through better understanding of themselves, their history, their intellectual and artistic achievements, and the outlooks of those who differ from us.
e) a search for viable individual, social and political principles of ethical conduct, judging them on their ability to enhance human well-being and individual responsibility.
f) a conviction that with reason, an open marketplace of ideas, good will, and tolerance, progress can be made in building a better world for themselves and their children.
 Secular humanists accept a world view called naturalism and typically describes themselves as nonreligious. They do not rely upon any supernatural forces to solve their problems or provide guidance for their conduct. They rely upon applying reason, the lessons of history, and personal experience to form an ethical/moral foundation and to create meaning in life.
 Secular humanists look to science as the most reliable source of information for the truth about the universe, acknowledging that new discoveries will alter and expand their understanding of it and even change their approach to ethical issues.

**25. Logical Positivism** = A philosophy holding that only science, mathematics and logic are meaningful for ascertaining facts, and religion, ethics and metaphysics are meaningless.

**26. Darwinism** = A philosophy that designates a distinctive form of evolutionary explanation for the history and diversity of life on earth. Darwinism is used within the scientific community to distinguish modern evolutionary theories from those first proposed by Darwin.
 Historians use Darwiniam to differentiate it from other evolutionary theories from around the same period. Its original form is provided in 1859 publication of *On the Origin of Species*, and is summarized in four main points:
1) probability and chance,
2) common ancestry,
3) natural selection ("survival of the fittest") and
4) transitional forms between distinctly different species.

**27. Naturalism** = A philosophy based on the principle that the physical laws of the universe are not superseded by non-material or supernatural entities outside the realm of the natural universe. Supernatural events such as miracles (in which physical laws are defied) and psi phenomena, such as ESP, telekinesis, etc., are not dismissed out of hand, but are viewed with a high degree of skepticism.

**28. Modernism** = Term that describes a series of reforming cultural movements in Western society in art, music, literature which emerged roughly in the period of 1884-1914. It is a trend of thought that affirms the power of human beings to create, improve, and reshape their environment, with the aid of scientific knowledge, technology, and practical experimentation.
 Modern (quantum and relativistic) physics, modern (analytical and continental) philosophy and modern number theory in mathematics also date from this period.

Modernism encompasses the works of thinkers who rebelled against 19th century academic and historicist traditions, believing the "traditional" forms of art, architecture, literature, religious faith, social organization, and daily life were becoming outdated.

They directly confronted the new economic, social, and political aspects of an emerging fully industrialized world. Some divide the 20th Century into movements designated Modernism and Postmodernism, whereas others see them as two aspects of the same movement.

**29. Post-Modernism** = A general and wide-ranging term applied to literature, art, philosophy, architecture, fiction, and cultural and modernist literary criticism, among others. Postmodernism is largely a reaction to the assumed certainty of scientific, or objective, efforts to explain reality. Postmodernism is highly skeptical of explanations which claim to be valid for all groups, cultures, traditions, or races, and instead focuses on the *relative truths of each person*.

For the postmodern, *interpretation is everything*; reality comes into being through our interpretations of what *the world means to us individually*. Postmodernism is "post" because *it denies the existence of any ultimate principles*, and it lacks the optimism of there being a scientific, philosophical, or religious truth which will explain everything for everybody - a characteristic of the so-called "modern" mind.

The paradox of the postmodern position is that, in placing all principles under the scrutiny of its skepticism, it must realize that even its own principles are not beyond questioning. As the philosopher Richard Tarnas states, postmodernism "cannot on its own principles ultimately justify itself any more than can the various metaphysical overviews against which the postmodern mind has defined itself."

# Religious Worldviews

1. Atheism
2. Secular Humanism
3. Taoism
4. Confucianism
5. Islam
6. Buddhism
7. Hinduism

I often don't see my worldview

But I see      everything else by looking through it.

David Marshall holds a B.A. in "the Russian and Chinese Languages and Marxism," an M.A. in Chinese Religions, and a Ph.D. in Christian Thought and Chinese Tradition. He's now living in Washington state.
He is the founder and director of the Kuai Mu Institute for Christianity and World Cultures and the author of four books, including The Truth About Jesus and the "Lost Gospels," as well as Why the Jesus Seminar Can't Find Jesus and Grandma Marshall Could.

## Is Atheism a Religion (or part of one)?

If one asks if A is a member of class B, the first thing one must do is define A and B clearly. In one of the pinned articles above, I began answering this question by trying to define the word "religion."

After discussing substantive and functional definitions of "religion," (Peter Berger) and whether one should focus on a faith's founder, scriptures, or developed tradition, I offered the following working definition of religion: "A system of belief and action held sometimes by an individual, but more often by a practicing community, that is held or experienced as ultimate in their lives."

From which it follows that whichever definition of "atheism" we choose, by itself it probably is NOT a religion for many people. Most atheists have some other ultimate concern: family, or nation, or pleasure, or art, or (saints preserve us) the Boston Red Sox or Alabama Crimson Tide . . .

But then, theism is not a religion either. Belief in God is an element in some religions. So, atheism may be an element in other religions, including those mentioned above, or Marxism, Communism, Objectivism, Environmentalism, Critical Race Theory, and so forth.

One needs more than bare belief in or against God to constitute an ultimate commitment around which one orients one's values, spending, activities, and thought life. But denial of God often opens the door for some other ultimate source of truth and meaning -- if only the ego, or some guru and his or her teachings, life example, and social cache.

So that is an easy question to answer, if you accept my premises. No, atheism is not usually a religion -- and neither, by itself, is theism. Both are often elements in developed religions.

But what is "atheism?" People have been batting this question around quite a bit lately, too. (Dancing around the word, in fact, as if trying to gain the advantage of a rhetorical high spot from which to lob shells at enemy positions.) Is atheism:
a. Denial that God exists?
b. Lack of belief that God exists?
c. Living as if God did not exist?
d. Or the same state of mind or life, in relation to all supernatural beings (the gods)?

The advantage of (b) is that one can position oneself as more rational and objective than one's opponents. "You religious people believe in gods. We Brights simply demand evidence before we accept an extraordinary proposition like that. We will hang out at the pool sipping drinks -- come back to us when you have evidence worthy of the name, and of course we will evaluate it fairly. "

No, no, read Pascal. You will do no such thing. All of us have a stake in life and must gamble. You are already gambling -- and your arguments prove how committed you are to your real religion.

Like everyone else, your feet are firmly planted upon an implicit religious position, and you are gambling that it is true. The gods you have chosen are evidenced by your life.

The advantage of (d) is that this definition of "atheism" allows one to conflate "God" and "the gods." I wonder if anyone can do that, after reading G. K. Chesterton's The Everlasting Man? Of course, to deny the Creator of the Universe, is not the same as to deny the proto-Marvel comic book characters we call "gods."

That there are beings more powerful than humans somewhere in the universe. Believing or disbelieving in them is of little religious consequence.

A famous work of anthropology in Chinese folk religion is called Gods, Ghosts, and Ancestors. These three categories are not really that distinct, in Chinese or many other nations' thinking: 神, they are called in Chinese: spirits, one can translate. How you die, what sort of person you are, what impact you have on those around you, determine your status after death, and into which category you will fall.

As in Journey to the West, the monsters and demons and monkeys and dragons and pigs and humans and gods change from one to the other, depending on their actions and how the Jade Emperor judges them. One does not "believe" such stories, one enjoys them, or shudders as the door slams in a winter storm and thinks one may have seen a ghost . . .

So, I prefer definition (a), and find (c) also useful. Atheism is not lack of belief in God: trees lack belief, so do babies and, presumably, many who have been raised in communist countries, and have not really thought about the question yet.

Atheism is most usefully defined as positive denial of God.

It is not in itself a religion. But just as one deposes a king, usually, to set a new king in place, or a president, party chairman or generalissimo, so denial of God is usually prefaced to worshipping some other entity. And that entity, even if only a football team or a bank statement, is the atheist's true effectual religion."

Response from Atheist - Atheism is at minimum a lack of belief in any version of gods or God. But most people have heard of several.

If you met group of people with zero concept of a metaphysical reality or personality like a god or God. You could call them atheistic. I am not sure such a group exists though.

Is it a religion? Probably. We live in a society mixed with Christian culture and beliefs and anti- culture and beliefs. A post Christian society. Some of these new atheist groups could probably be defined as religious or a religion in certain contexts.

I do not like using semantics to win debates outright though. Or to slyly shift the burden of proof. Or letting others act similarly. And based on your words and tone, it seems like you do not either.

But I *think* that is what you are edging towards. And it is not worth your or my time. Though I understand it is frustrating.

In debates, the burden of proof lies on the one making the claim. Atheist or Christian. In debates, as the affirmative you get to make the definitions of key words/concepts in your arguments.

I am not certain, but I believe the negative team usually must accept the definition and provide a defense that fits it. That is what I remember from high school anyway. And the best negative strategies usually involve catching the affirmative in changing the definition mid argument. That is, breaking their own rules.

I am rambling, but that is usually how I handle such conflicts. If you make a claim, you must defend it. No Matter who you are. And if you define something I will usually accept it tentatively and look for holes elsewhere.

I deny the God of the Christianity Bible exists. So, I make arguments in the affirmative of this position. The burden of proof is on me. But if a Christian also make a claim, they also must make an argument. Or I mean, I guess they could just say stuff. But it should not be as convincing. Not to me anyway.

<u>Response from David Marshall</u> - I am not debating, I am analyzing. But you can debate about the analysis if you think it is flawed.

You are right that when making an argument, one has the duty to define key terms, and that responses to that argument need to keep those definitions in mind (though may challenge them, if the critic finds them confusing.)

But at present I am not making an argument for or against atheism, I am just trying to understand what it is, or is not.

## Is Secular Humanism a Religion?

"Secular Humanism is a 'religion,' in the sense defined here earlier, which posits four truths:

(1) There is no God, or not knowing that there is a God, we should live as if there were none.

(2) Human beings are mortal and do not survive death (at least not yet).

(3) We should, nonetheless, care for ourselves. We should not give in to despair, nihilism, or mere individualistic hedonism.

(4) We should also care for humanity, or for other humans. (Whether or to what degree we should care for animals, or for inanimate objects like Planet Earth or The Rain Forest, may be debated. One might also extend this duty to what C. S. Lewis called other hnau, sentient beings with human-like rationality, on other planets or, perhaps, higher animals.)

Secular Humanism is thus distinguished from forms of humanism that recognize God or an afterlife, including Christian humanism, some forms of Buddhism, some forms of Confucianism, the Stoicism of Epictetus or Cleanthes, etc.

Other forms of Buddhism, Stoicism, Cynicism, Confucianism, or neo-Confucianism do not recognize God, but do recognize a duty to humanity. "All within the four seas are brothers." They should also be called forms of Secular Humanism. One could debate whether belief in non-transcendent super-human beings disqualifies one from being a "secular" humanist or not: perhaps it depends on how one sees one's relation to them.

What about communism? I would maintain that in practice, most communists do fulfill the criteria for Secular Humanist faith. In theory, Marx and Engels may have claimed to "abolish" all morality, but as I argue in Jesus and the Religions of Man, in practice they brought back not one but three moral systems: to criticize capitalists, to justify their own actions, and by which citizens of their dictatorships should live.

Indeed, the Chinese history text I reviewed for First Things recognizes that Chinese Marxism and Greek Humanism were related.

Of course, Secular Humanism evolves, as popular notions of the human being change. Critical Theory is one shape it has adopted in recent years, which is influenced by Christianity, in its emphasis on the marginalized, and by Marxism, in its focus on power politics.

## Is Taoism a Religion?

Taoism is both a philosophy and a religion. The two differ dramatically. The goal of one can be said to "go with the flow" of Nature or the Power beyond Nature. The goal of the other is to counteract Nature to attain long life or magical powers, or perhaps to get good at kungfu. Founders and chief texts: Taoist philosophy and religion both trace back to the same two texts, the Dao De Jing, by "Lao Zi," and the Zhuang Zi, by a master of that name.

DDJ takes about two hours to read and is full of paradoxical epigrams: "The Dao that is spoken ('daoed') is not the true Dao. The Name you can name, is not the true Name." "The greater Virtue is like water." "Act without action (or striving), and all will be attained." It mentions Heaven -- or God -- a few times.

But following Yuan Zhiming, I argue in Fulfillment: A Christian Model of Religion, that Dao is not pantheistic or naturalistic, but can itself be seen as a name for God, modeled on early Chinese theism. This is a highly contentious claim, so I spend some time making the case.

DDJ was written for an official, arguing that the best style of rule is, one is tempted to say, laissez-faire, or libertarian. The two chief concepts in the book are Dao (Tao), the Way, Logos, "God," but a God who works subtly and perhaps slowly through Nature. ("Dao gave birth to One, One gave birth to Two, Two gave birth to Three, and Three gave birth to all things.")

Here one sees something that seldom showed up in Greco-Roman thinking outside the New Testament, I think: the power of humility. In DDJ one even finds the idea of redemptive sacrifice, in one later chapter. But it is a highly enigmatic book, which has been interpreted many ways, and been joined to alchemy, Yin-Yang, Chinese medicine, the search for eternal life, and all sorts of things which are not in the original.

The Zhuang Zi is a much longer book.  ZZ's forte is the parable. Lin Yutang argues that he is the greatest prose writer in Chinese history. His book is fun to read, whimsical, humorous, also paradoxical. One early chapter talks much of the Creator, a concept that is not always discussed among ancient Chinese theists. See my article on Epictetus and Zhuang Zi in Touchstone Magazine, and Lin Yutang's beautiful work, From Pagan to Christian. (He also translated both DDJ and ZZ.)

As a philosophy, Taoism is somewhat like the Cynic school in the West. The story goes that Alexander the Great came to visit Diogenes the Cynic, found him lying on the ground, and asked if he wanted anything.

"Yeah, move out of my light!"  Diogenes reportedly replied. That is much the spirit of Taoist philosophy, which also reports such rebukes to the powerful. "You return and be silent! I do not need the world!"

Taoist philosophers liked fishing, if they could sit on the boat and let the river take them where it would. Indeed, the Christian philosopher Lin Yutang, who was fond of the Taoists, designed his house overlooking Taipei with a fishpond in it. He sat there and pretended to fish.

The Taoist religion made use of Nature to overcome Nature, of Force to overcome Force -- as in kungfu. A Taoist "immortal" gained power through self-cultivation, often in a cave on a holy mountain, through drugs, meditation, and rituals.

Some of these can seem bizarre and even harmful, as I describe in True Son of Heaven. Yet I also argue that the religious Taoist's search for life is, in some ways, more understandable than the philosophical Taoist's quietism.

A Taoist who lived on a mountain in Guangdong (which I have climbed) once visited James Legge in Hong Kong. Legge reports their conversation in one of his books. He found that man, who had long meditated on the DDJ, almost uniquely prepared for the Gospel of Jesus Christ.

So, Taoism can be defined as either a philosophy or a religion based in some sense on the teachings of Lao Zi and Zhuang Zi. Religious Taoism often also adds older elements from other Chinese beliefs: Yin and Yang, the Five Elements, magic, deities and immortals, and various forms of self-cultivation -- not to mention martial arts, or even black arts.

But the term "Tao" or "Dao,' meaning "the Way," is used by nearly all Chinese schools of thought, including Confucius, and including Christians.

Indeed, the Gospel of John reads in Chinese: "In the beginning was the Tao, and the Tao was with God, and the Tao was God . . . and the Tao became flesh, and dwelt among us, full of grace and truth."
I regard this as an excellent translation.

### Is Confucianism a Religion?

"The question is especially worth asking today, because the "Confucian" world (as Samuel Huntington defined it) has now produced a superpower rival to the United States. Officially, China is run by the Chinese Communist Party. But even their high school history texts (see my article on this in First Things) describes Confucianism as the "mainstream" of the Chinese tradition.

Mao attacked Confucius, at which time the Republic of China on Taiwan emphasized the moral virtues of Confucianism, including his "eagerness to learn."

Korea is, in some ways, perhaps more Confucian than Mainland China, while Japan was deeply influenced by this philosophy or religion. Including the Samurai warriors we all know and love.
Some, indeed, converted to Christianity because they perceived (truly, I have argued) that the Gospel fulfills the deepest truths of the Confucian tradition. For the popular version of that argument, see True Son of Heaven: How Jesus Fulfills the Chinese Culture; for the academic version, see Fulfillment: A Christian Model of Religions.

So, what is Confucianism?

In Chinese, there are two words, neither of which mentions Confucius: "rujia," and "rujiao." The first refers to "the school of the scholars / elders," the other to "the teaching / religion of the scholars / elders." So Confucian thought and lifestyle can be read as either a philosophy or a religion.

More than anything, Confucius emphasized the "Way" (Dao, yes, the same word as in Taoism), how one lives, that is. While there is a strong idea of the Supreme God in early Confucianism, and of other spirits, and Confucius himself was a theist, Confucianism stresses function over substance, to revert to Berger's terminology and Durkheim's sociology.

What matters is forming a certain kind of society. That society stresses hierarchy, kindness, consideration, appropriate courtesy, and faithfulness. Everyone is in their place, and within that place can find meaning and significance.

History and texts: Confucius himself most often cited two ancient anthologies: the Book of Poetry (most) and the Book of History. Along with the core parts of the Book of Changes (Yi Jing), these are the earliest Chinese texts, probably from the early Zhou, mostly. They are highly theistic, speaking frequently of God by the names "Shang Di," "Tian" and related terms, often combining them into one name. These books constitute the "Old Testament" of Confucianism, you could say, and were studied by Confucian scholars for state exams up until the early 20th Century.

The "New Testament" of Confucianism consists mainly of the Analects of Confucius and the Mencius, written by a disciple of Confucius 150 years later.

Along with some other books, or parts of books, but I do not want to make things too complicated. The Analects was put together by Confucius' disciples in the centuries following his death, some of it early enough that it carries strong historical markings (as I argue in TSOH -- but not so strong as the gospels.)

Together, the texts that became the basis for Confucian exams are the Five Scriptures and the Four Books, including BOP, BOH, and YiJing among the former, the Analects and Mencius among the latter.

While the Chinese word for "Confucianism" does not contain the name of Confucius, he is in some ways its Jesus Christ, its "first teacher," if not its savior. The Analects are comparable to the gospels in form (written by disciples, words, and acts, early), and in some teachings (kindness, reverence for God).

Confucius is not presented as a worker of miracles, nor as a threat to the Powers That Be, however. While his teachings are profound, they do not startle and shock quite as the teachings of Jesus.

Confucianism is a social and political philosophy. In later generations, especially from the neo-Confucianism of the Song a thousand years ago, God became much more abstract, or was denied in a pantheistic view of "Heaven-Earth-man" joined together. At the same time, Confucian hierarchy became more oppressive to women. (Coincidence? I touch on this subject in TSOH, I will not steal my own thunder here!)

Confucianism arose when the Zhou had become falling apart into feudal states. The idea of the "Son of Heaven," a "sage" who would represent the "Will of Heaven" on earth, had become extremely important, though.

Confucian philosophy and religion are more closely linked than the "schools" and the "teachings" of Taoism. But in modern times, Confucian reformism has tended to fade into Christianity or Communism.

That is to say, the CCP has adapted Confucian ideas of the secular order and of hierarchy for its own purposes. Many great East Asian (not just Chinese) reformers have been Christians who saw their faith as a fulfillment of Confucian ideals.

On a religious level, Confucianism is tied to "worship" or obeisance to ancestors. This word worship, or bai, is tricky to translate. Even in the Bible, some forms of obeisance to respected human beings are translated as "worship" in English -- reflected in that term, "your worship."

The Jesuits after Matteo Ricci sometimes recognized that ceremonies in memory or honor of ancestors might be just as spiritually innocuous as, say, setting flowers by the grave of one's grandparents.
But Chinese also tended to believe fervently in "gods, ghosts, and ancestors," with no clear line between these categories.

So Confucian popular religion without God could degenerate into fear of spirits, sacrifice to keep them from bothering you, and the like. And morally, it could degenerate into sucking up to power, whether of a parent, a husband, or the emperor. This was probably not Confucius' fault.

Something like the notion of the prophet was also part of the portfolio of Confucian scholars at times. And I believe Confucius WAS a prophet, in the sense of looking forwards to the coming of Jesus. (As was Mencius, more specifically.) Nor am I the only Christian to come to that conclusion.

So, Confucianism, as either a religion or philosophy, is a way of life and death in agreement with the teachings and life of Confucius, and of the sages who preceded him and whom he was thought to have edited.

One can find its essence in the Five Classics and Four Books. But this tradition evolved over time, and over the past millennia became, for the scholarly elite, often more skeptical.

For the masses, it remains closely tied to family and rites of death and the importance of obedience up and kindness down, and of education.

For the elite, it describes how society works as a hierarchical whole. While some Confucian scholars criticized or attacked Buddhism, and then Christianity, Confucian philosophy in some senses easily combines with more full-fledged religions. This is why, as Christianity spread in Korea, Confucianism did not lose its influence either.

## Is Islam a Religion?

The world's second-largest religion? A community of those devoted to serving God in obedience to the words of the Prophet Mohammed? A "religion of peace?" All those who affirm Allah and his prophet, pray, give to the poor, fast during Ramadan, and attempt the pilgrimage to Mecca?

A gang of theocratic thugs who conquered by the sword from Iberia to Indonesia, and threatened world peace until China, Russia, and AI pushed their religion out of the headlines?

According to Berger's typology of religious definitions mentioned in the article pinned above, we might use the word to refer to the substance of Islamic teaching, which is Quranic beliefs, or to its functions in society or family, to how Muslims are required to act. Or should we look instead at how self-identifying Muslims believe and act, across the vast spectrum of Islamic societies, down through the centuries?

My definition of "religion" is pinned at the top of the page. Now I am trying to define religions both "substantively" and "functionally," as explained in that article. I began with Hinduism. In some ways, Islam is much easier to understand.

Commonly, Islam is defined by The Five Pillars. The first is the Shahada, the affirmation that "Allah is One, and Mohammed is his prophet." (Meaning, the final true prophet, after a long line of previous prophets.) Muslims also practice Salah, or ritual prayer five times a day, beginning with ablutions, Zakat, or giving 2.5% of their income to the needy or to Islamic charities, Sawm or fasting at Ramadan, and the Hajj or pilgrimage to Mecca, if possible.

But theological "conservatives" and "liberals" tend to define religion in different ways. Putting it crudely, Islam seems easier to define for conservatives, while Hinduism is easier to define from a liberal perspective.

Aside from the question of whether a religion is defined by the substance of a belief or its social function, any religion can be described in relation to three potential sources of authority:
1. By the character, teachings, and actions of its founder or founders.
2. By its sacred scriptures or bodies of oral / online knowledge.
3. By its developed tradition.

"Conservatives" tend to emphasize founder and scriptures. "Liberals" tend to look more at developed traditions. So, you might encounter an argument like this:
L: "Islam is a religion of peace! Look at the Sufis! Look at how the Caliphate accommodated multi-ethnic, multi-religious empires!"
C: "But Mohammed started numerous wars with his neighbors – that is where the Caliphate came from! And look at these Quranic verses, which seem to justify fighting with unbelievers until they submit!"

Historians often take the "liberal" approach and tell us how "richly diverse" the religious traditions they study are. Of course, they have a professional interest in the complexity of their field: who needs an historian, if the phenomena they describe are simple?

Also, "diversity" is an academic cliché, treasured for its own sake, a value no doubt rooted in post-modernism. But to be fair, all things being equal, social movements really do evolve, diversify, and fill ecological niches in a society.

And as they spread to other cultures, they take on the colorings of those cultures, borrow myths, holidays, and sacred places (or steal them, a big controversy in India!) And a few people are naturally inclined to play Gandhi, while more have the temperament for the role of Atilla the Hun.

To be effective, however, both Atilla and Gandhi must appeal to "myths" (Jacques Ellul) that predominate under a given "sacred canopy" (Peter Berger). So, religion as defined by the character of a founder and its holy texts constrains developed tradition, even as that tradition seeks to evolve and expand like melted plastic into every mold.

If a religion has a hard dogmatic shell, restraining that movement, if heretics are despised and persecuted and clearly defined by a body of orthodox law, then that religion may not easily evolve beyond set limits.

A "Muslim" who does not believe in God, or who thinks Mohammed was a scoundrel, may take part in Islamic rituals and thus be counted a faithful believer – so long as she keeps watch over her mouth and dress.

Bernard Lewis says Islam never developed reform movements on behalf of the slave, the unbeliever, or women. That is because within Islam, there is no developed tradition without Mohammed or the Quran, and attitudes towards these three hardened into theological stone.

Regardless of what evolutionary pressure is put on Islam, by human nature, cultural traditions, or by the Gospels in early Sufism, change is ultimately constrained by the power of orthodoxy, set in written texts which endure, and are often enforced legally or by the community.

Which is not to deny that Islam is fluid. Sufism does exist, and it often is quite different from the obvious meaning of the Quran.

Many Muslims do try to placate jinn or the evil eye. Numerous Muslim or pseudo-Muslim sects have arisen. One can watch theology creep and flow under the tidal forces of:

(a) Personal desire. Did Mohammed really say that a man can only have four wives? And yet he married many more, and so did powerful Muslim kings – or else call them concubines or slaves.

(b) Hadiths, a larger mass of sayings ascribed to the prophet, also have great defining force in Islam.

The Five Pillars, for instance, is from the Hadith of Gabriel, collected by Al Bukhari in the following form:

"Narrated Abu Huraira: One day while the Prophet (ﷺ ['God bless him and grant him salvation']) was sitting in the company of some people, (The angel) Gabriel came and asked, "What is faith?" Allah's Messenger (ﷺ) replied, 'Faith is to believe in Allah, His angels, (the) meeting with Him, His Apostles, and to believe in Resurrection."

Then he further asked, "What is Islam?" Allah's Messenger (ﷺ) replied, "To worship Allah Alone and no one else, to offer prayers perfectly to pay the compulsory charity (Zakat) and to observe fasts during the month of Ramadan." Then he further asked, "What is Ihsan (perfection)?" Allah's Messenger (ﷺ) replied, "To worship Allah as if you see Him, and if you cannot achieve this state of devotion then you must consider that He is looking at you."

Then he further asked, "When will the Hour be established?" Allah's Messenger (ﷺ) replied, "The answerer has no better knowledge than the questioner. But I will inform you about its portents.

"1. When a slave (lady) gives birth to her master.

"2. When the shepherds of black camels start boasting and competing with others in the construction of higher buildings . . . "

(c) Cultural traditions differ enormously across North Africa, from Chad to Nigeria, in the Middle East, the subcontinent, and Southeast Asia.
In Beyond Belief, a bitter VS Naipaul describes how, as young people become more literate, Mohammed and the Quran and the orthodoxy that derives from them have overcome "developed tradition" and the cultures in which they are imbedded, at different rates in Indonesia, Iran, Pakistan, and Malaysia. Islam has become stricture, more uniform, and more "orthodox."

(d) Schizmogenesis. This term refers to how people often develop cultures in conscious opposition to neighboring cultures. For example, David Graeber and David Wengrow argue that the slave-owning native peoples of the Pacific Northwest and the freer peoples of northern California developed their radically different cultures in opposition to one another. Think also of Scots and English and Irish, Poles and Russians, followers of the Nation of Islam and Baptists.

This is probably one reason Persians became Shiite: they adopted a brand of Islam different from the majority faith among Arabs, their neighbors and often enemies. (One Iranian told me how distraught he was when he went on pilgrimage to Mecca and was told that because he could not pronounce the required formulae in clear Arabic, he should divorce his wife! He ultimately became a Christian.)

Likewise, Kurds and Persians, Bengalis and Punjabis, Berbers and Arabs, and no doubt herding Fulani and urban Muslims in Africa, tend to define themselves against "the Other" in religion as in much else.

Hinduism is intellectually more "diverse" and flexible than Islam, being founded by no one in particular, having had thousands of years to develop, and allowing believers to choose from a panoply of gods, divas, gurus, and Scriptures.

It is constrained socially, however, by caste traditionally, and now by the ideology of Hindutva. In any case, both faiths are easy to understand as instruments of social cohesion and the form of functionalism described by Emile Durkheim.

One of the functions of religion is to define a community, in contrast to neighboring communities. So, in that sense, a Muslim who disbelieves in God, or drinks alcohol, need be contradiction in terms: he may see himself as part of a religious community and participate sincerely in its rituals.

But unlike Hinduism, Islam carries the advantage and disadvantages of a hard doctrinal skeleton. (Even an exoskeleton, like an oyster or an armadillo.) It endures over centuries because it is founded on the fixed written teachings and person of Mohammed.

Even his act of marrying a child has an enduring effect, still more the concept and practice of jihad, which he modeled. Islam does diversify and adapt to new situations, but within tighter bounds – which may be why Islamic nations have often found it difficult to develop the civil institutions that allow for democracy and technological inventiveness.

So, then, to define Islam, we should not overlook 1500 years of social evolution. But most Muslims will rightly insist that we begin with Mohammed and with the text which he claimed to be inspired by Allah.

The Quran is the more important of the two for dual reasons:

(a) It is our earliest and most-trusted source for Mohammed. Of course, hadiths flesh that picture out, and Islamic tradition has developed methods of determining which hadiths should be trusted.

(b) The Quran is considered the Word of God in a stronger sense, even, than the Bible. The Quran was, it is believed, written word-for-word in heaven. It is to Muslims as Jesus Christ is to Christians: the ultimate manifestation of God's will to humanity.

The Five Pillars of Islam combine function and substantive faith. Muslims act certain ways in society, gaining Durkheimian solidarity by mass prayer, fasting, feasting, and pilgrimage. Beggars play their role by lining up outside the mosque on Friday to receive their due.

The main "substantive" belief – God and Mohammed – is fleshed out first in the Quran, secondly in certain hadith, and thirdly by a vast body of Islamic Law, in competing schools. And that is how I have come to understand Islam, so far."

## Is Buddhism a Religion?

Like a Babylon Bee joke about Matt Walsh's book What is a Woman, I am tempted to confess I am only asking because I do not know the answer! Yet I have taken classes in Buddhism, visited countless Buddhist temples, read numerous books on the religion, wrote one of my MA papers on the True Buddha Movement . . . Better keep it simple as possible, then add notes as needed later.

One can, as I said, define a religion by (a) the character and acts of its founder (s); (b) its holy Scriptures; or (c) by developed tradition. Also, either substantively or functionally.

(a) The Buddha "myth" is well-known. Siddhartha Gautama was a prince of a state in northern India. It having been foretold that he would be either a great religious or political leader, his father shut him up in the palace to keep him from encountering the "bad things in life" and getting into religion. He married his beautiful cousin and they had a baby, whom he called "Obstacle." (Lucky kid.)

Then Sid snuck out of the palace and encountered the "four sights:" a sick man, an old man, a corpse, and a mendicant. He asked his servant: "What are these?" And was shocked by the answers. "Do sickness, old age, and death happen even to princes?" So, he left wife and son and went into the world to seek a solution to the problem of suffering.

After years of extreme tapis, or self-deprivation, Sid meditated under a tree for many weeks. He experienced temptation, then became enlightened. Enlightenment consisted of realizing the "Four Noble Truths:"

(1) Life is, or contains, suffering.
(2) The cause of suffering is desire (or, perhaps, lust, attached striving, etc.).
(3) The solution to suffering is to end such illicit desire.
(4) Which one can do by the "8-fold path:" right view, resolve, speech, conduct, livelihood, effort, action, mindfulness, and meditative awareness.

That is how Buddhism is often defined in the West, in terms of the "Buddha myth." Did any of this happen? That is not a question Buddhists often answer. The texts are rather late, and do not contain the kinds of internal evidences which I find in the gospels or even (less powerfully) in the Analects of Confucius. My guess is, Sid did live, but what kind of person he was, is uncertain.

(b) One can also define Buddhism by a library of Buddhist Scriptures. This is harder to do, because as Buddhism evolved and spread east into SE Asia and northwest then east into Afghanistan, Central, then East Asia, also south into Sri Lanka, all kinds of books gained scriptural authority within various Buddhist communities.

The simplest division of schools and canons is into Hinayana or Theraveda (Burma, Thailand, etc.); Mahayana (East Asia); and Vajrayana (Tibet, Mongolia, here and there in East Asia). But while I have read some famous Buddhist sutras, and skimmed many others, I cannot claim expertise to summarize Buddhist scriptures. One of them, the Diamond Sutra, is the oldest extant printed book in the world, from the 9th Century.

(c) Neither will I describe the many schools of Buddhism. The school I wrote my MA anthropology paper on was founded by a Taiwanese Buddhist who blended folk religion, Tibetan (Vajrayana), and Mahayana Buddhism, with a talent for storytelling and painting. He was, it seemed to me, a likeable scoundrel, who may or may not have kept a few devils in his temples. He didn't seem able to read my mind, though I suspect he tried, during our one, rather odd encounter.

A few mistakes people make about Buddhism:

Whereas liberal westerners tend to define Islam by "developed tradition," they tend to define Buddhism by the life and acts of Siddhartha Gautama. I guess because Buddha is more attractive than Mohammed! But most Asians who call themselves "Buddhists" care, or even know, little about formal Buddhist teachings. Partly this is because Buddhism emphasizes the need to pragmatically adjust teachings to the capacity of the hearer.

More typical, perhaps, was the Dalai Lama's mother. For her, Buddhism seemed to mean finding a way of dealing with the evil spirits that had killed some of her children.

I often enjoyed vegetarian Buddhist restaurants in Taiwan and China. But the Buddhists I knew did not seem so strict about their vegetarian diets.
Or they might pretend to be, until they had a hankering for certain dishes . . . A Zen nun in downtown Seattle complained about True Buddhists eating meat (which I did with them once). Their excuse was that Tibetans do, too.

Like every tradition, Buddhists also have a militant wing. Temples would often fight. Christians in Japan and Tibet were persecuted by Buddhists. This may not fit the western image of Buddhism, but again, that comes of confusing Buddhism in senses (1) and (3).

What is the function of Buddhism? It is part of how Thai and Burmese and Tibetans self-identify. I have been told that most Thais do not actually know much about Buddhism, though. It tends to evolve into a syncretistic blend of custom, ritual, temples, political power, fear of spirits, foods, and stories.

Note that Buddhism in SE Asia was mostly the religion of the lowland elite. This was also the elite that enslaved hill tribes for centuries. But the hill peoples retained their spiritual independence, to a large extent, either by refusing to convert to Buddhism, or by borrowing just what they wanted, and leaving the rest.

One of the best ways of understanding Chinese Buddhism in its evolved form, is to read the kung fu classic, Journey to the West.

So, if someone tells you they are a Buddhist, do not assume you know what that means. You need to ask more questions! Buddhism is probably the most protean of major world religions."

## Is Hinduism a Religion?

Background and difficulties: Hinduism is, among other things, the majority religion of what now has officially become the largest country in the world, by population. India remains much poorer than its neighbor over the fence to the north, but is now making rapid economic progress, and is figuring ever more deeply in the geopolitical concerns of other nations. But is "Hindu" more than a geographical or cultural designation, or a rallying cry for Prime Minister Narendra Modi's ruling party?

"Hindu" is an exonym, like "Christian" and "Bolshevik:" coined from the outside, not a term "Hindus" invented for themselves. It is related to the name of the Indus River, and to its country of origin, India. So, in origin, it is in fact a geographical designation.

But it is difficult to define "Hinduism" as merely "the religion of India," or even "the dominant religion of the cultural circles pulsing out from the civilizations that grew up along the Indus River," for several reasons.

For one thing, India is also the world's second or third largest Muslim country, with about 200 million Muslims, about tied with Pakistan which was also originally a part of "India. "

Bangladesh, the home of Bengalis who are also "Indian" in the broad sense, are also mostly Muslim. So greater "India" contains more than a half-billion Muslims. India is also home to many Christians, Buddhists, Sikhs, and people of other faiths. And some "outcastes" or "lower castes" may not identify much with the Brahmin belief system. So, it is hard to define "Hinduism" as "the religion of India.

Before Islam arrived, Indian civilization was never completely unified (though two great empires briefly ruled much of the subcontinent - one of them temporarily Buddhist!).

Even earlier than that, several large families of ethnicities with differing cultures shared the subcontinent.
The religions of the forest tribes, who may be the true Indian aboriginals, of the Indus River Civilization, and then of the later Vedic peoples spoke Indo-European, are all very different from what we call "Hinduism" today. Yet geographically, their faiths were as Indian as modern Hinduism.

The Rig Veda is still recognized as a sacred text, though the gods worshiped in it are largely neglected now, and its core beliefs were very different from what "Hinduism" has become today. For instance, there is almost nothing about caste or reincarnation in the Rig Veda. Indra, Agni, and Soma are the most-named deities, not Vishnu, Kali or Shiva or Krishna, and sacrifice is those texts' chief theme.

Brahmanism, which evolved into modern Hinduism, seems roughly to have consisted of the beliefs and practices of India's upper castes or varnas. Some "lower caste" or "outcaste" / Dalit Indians reject that religion, seeing it as an instrument for their subjugation. Yet they may also be considered "Hindus." "

Aside from the four major castes, Indian communities are also divided into communities called jatis, by occupation, location, or tribe. What "Hinduism" means to these communities, is more than I can say.

Some indigenous peoples do not seem to identify much with "Hinduism" in the developed sense. Some have converted to Islam, Christianity, or Buddhism, while others are probably counted as Hindus for political reasons. Since Hindutva defines itself in opposition to Islam and Christianity, and India in opposition to Pakistan and, increasingly, China, it is in the interests of the ruling party to "circle the wagons" and include groups that were formerly discriminated against by Brahmins.

How should Hinduism be defined? One can try to define Hinduism by etymology, class, history, or traits, or by opposition to what it is not. As we have seen, the etymology of "Hinduism" is linked to the geography of India. And indeed, Hinduism is the most geographically-fixed major religion, even more than Judaism. An American who holds to most Hindu beliefs can barely be described as a Hindu.

She might identify with the New Age movement, instead, or with one guru like Sai Baba or Muktananda.

What is Hinduism not? Hinduism is a religion with no founder, that has evolved over thousands of years in the subcontinent. It is not Buddhism, Islam, Sikhism, Jainism, or Christianity. But some atheists may consider themselves Hindus. And some Hindus may see themselves as followers of Christ.

Class: Hinduism belongs to the class "religions," which I defined functionally along the lines of "an ultimate concern held by a community." How a group of people see the world, seek salvation, and feel obliged to act. But Emile Durkheim was correct, religion also serves the function of uniting a community.

Doctrines: Hindus tend to believe in such doctrines as karma and reincarnation (40% say this now), while taking different views of God or the gods, or expressing devotion (bhakti) towards a particular deity. (There is even something called Christ bhakti.)

Most would say God is one but has many manifestations. Guruism has become an important part of Hindu practice - following a human teacher as a guide to or incarnation of the divine. (Vishal Mangalwadi's World of the Gurus is one of several interesting introductions to how guruism works.)

Most Hindus in India practice puja, prayer and offering to deities, usually at home, sometimes in temples.

History: The history of "Hinduism," and how the word came to be used, is complex: recommend the works of J. N. Farquhar on this topic, also perhaps The Invention of Religions.

Traditionally, Hindu beliefs and practices relate to one's community, and worship of ancestors by sons within the family was once important. (Which Farquhar believes is one way the status of women in India grew much worse after the time of Christ.)

Sacred texts: among the most influential texts in modern Hinduism are Ramayana, Mahabharata (esp. the Bhagavad Gita), Upanishads and Law of Manu, which sets out the duties and taboos of the major castes and of males and females.

The Rig Veda represents an older stage of Hinduism and does not say much of modern "Hindu" doctrines. (There is one mention of caste from a later portion of the text. And after death, one ascends to heaven: I do not recall any mention of reincarnation.)

So, finally, what is Hinduism? Is it the world's oldest major religion, or its youngest?

In a practical sense, Hinduism might be recognized as a "sacred canopy" (Peter Berger) forming over modern India. It is an attempt to create one "big tent" within which the peoples of India who do not belong to some other "religion" can create a common culture, to unite the country against its enemies and competitors, and give it pride.

Almost all Hindus believe in God, though most would say "He has many manifestations." Caste is less important than it used to be in the growing cities. Certain deities are in vogue, but also in flux, but set to some extent by popular stories like the Ramayana.

But unlike Christianity and Islam, Hinduism has no single definitive sacred text. As India has evolved, and is taking its place as a rising superpower, one can therefore expect Hindus to continue showing great flexibility in how they define what they believe.

Sociologists like Durkheim and Stark would recognize, I think, that the ruling Bharatiya Janata Party (BJP perceives that modern Hinduism must define itself not, as traditionally, from the perspective of competing communities within India, but as a nation-state competing with other nations on the world stage.

Yet in such a competition, as during the Crusades in Europe, or the Cold War, it is often useful to have a domestic "other" against which to define oneself. In its panoply of domestic heretics and outcastes, India is richly blessed."

| | TOPIC | Christian Position | Secular Position | Location | Date |
|---|---|---|---|---|---|
| **YouTube Discussions and Debates** | | | | | |
| **The Existence of God** | Does God Exist? | Dr. John Lennox (PhD Philosophy of Science) | Dr. Michael Shermer (PhD Philosophy) | Wesley Ctr., Australia | Oct. 29, 2008 |
| | Does God Exist? | Dr. William Lane Craig (PhD Philosophy) | Christopher Hitchins (writer) | Biola University | Apr. 4, 2009 |
| | Poison or Cure: Religious Belief | Dr. Alistar McGrath (PhD Molecular Biology, Theology) | Christopher Hitchins (writer) | Georgetown University | Oct. 11, 2007 |
| | Is God a Human Invention? | Dinesh D'Souza (MA History) | Dr. Daniel Dennett (PhD Philosophy) | Tufts University | Nov. 30, 2007 |
| | The God Debate | Dinesh D'Souza (MA History) | Christopher Hitchins (writer) | Notre Dame University | April 22, 2010 |
| | The God Debate | Dr. William Lane Craig (PhD Philosophy) | Dr. Sam Harris (PhD Neuroscience) | Notre Dame University | April 12, 2011 |
| | What Best Explains Reality? | Dr. Frank Turek (PhD Apologetics) | Christopher Hitchins (writer) | College of New Jersey | May 23, 2011 |
| **Science vs. Religion** | The Veritas Forum: Language of God | Dr. Francis Collins (PhD Molecular Biology) | n/a | Univ. CA, Berkeley | Feb. 4, 2008 |
| | Atheism vs Theism: Scientific Evidence | Dr. Jay Richards (PhD Philosophy, Theology) | Christopher Hitchins (writer) | Stanford University | July 23, 2009 |
| | Evolution vs. Intelligent Design | Dr. Jonathan Wells (PhD Microbiology, Theology) | Dr. Michael Shermer (PhD Philosophy) | CATO Institute | Aug. 28, 2009 |
| | Has Science buried God? | Dr. John Lennox (PhD Philosophy of Science) | Dr. Richard Dawkins (PhD Zoology) | University of Alabama | June 29, 2010 |
| | Has Science buried God? | Dr. John Lennox (PhD Philosophy of Science) | Dr. Richard Dawkins (PhD Zoology) | Oxford University | Nov. 20, 2012 |
| | God and Cosmology | Dr. William Lane Craig (PhD Philosophy) | Dr. Sean Carroll (PhD Theoretical Physics) | 2014 Greer Heard Forum | March 14, 2014 |
| **Christianity** | Is Christianity good for America? | Dinesh D'Souza (MA History) | David Silverman (Pres., American Atheists) | Kings College | Oct. 29, 2011 |
| | Is Christianity good for the World? | Dinesh D'Souza (MA History) | Dr. Michael Shermer (PhD Philosophy) | Oregon St. University | July 1, 2011 |
| | God, Theodicy and Suffering | Dinesh D'Souza (MA History) | Dr. Bart Ehrmann (PhD Biblical Studies) | Gordon College | Nov. 11, 2010 |
| | Did Jesus rise from the dead bodily? | Dr. Gary Habermas (PhD Philosophy) | Dr. Arif Ahmed (PhD Philosophy) | Cambridge University | Oct. 21, 2011 |
| | Historical Evidence for Resurrection? | Dr. William Lane Craig (PhD Philosophy) | Dr. Bart Ehrmann (PhD Biblical Studies) | Holy Cross University | Mar. 28, 2006 |
| | Is New Testament Reliable? | Dr. Dan Wallace (PhD New Testament Studies) | Dr. Bart Ehrmann (PhD Biblical Studies) | SMU (CSNTM.org) | Oct. 1, 2011 |
| | New Testament misquote Jesus? | Dr. Craig Evans (PhD New Testament Studies) | Dr. Bart Ehrmann (PhD Biblical Studies) | First Family Church, KS | Mar. 31, 2010 |

www.ingramcontent.com/pod-product-compliance
Lightning Source LLC
Chambersburg PA
CBHW062023090426

42811CB00005B/933